Sicily

THIS EDITION WRITTEN AND RESEARCHED BY

Gregor Clark, Cristian Bonetto

PLAN YOUR TRIP

SABINE LUBENOW/LOOK-FOTO/GETTY IMAGES ©

PANAREA P146

BILDAGENTUR ZOONAR GMBH/SHUTTERSTOCK ©

NOTO P197

ON THE ROAD

Contents

Welcome to Sicily

Eternal crossroads of the Mediterranean, the gorgeous island of Sicily continues to seduce travellers with its dazzling diversity of landscapes and cultural treasures.

Classical Crossroads

Seductively beautiful and perfectly placed in the Mediterranean, Sicily has been luring passersby since the time of legends. The land of the Cyclops has been praised by poets from Homer to Virgil and prized by the many ancient cultures – Phoenicians, Carthaginians, Elymians, Romans and Greeks – whose bones lie buried here. Whether in the classical perfection of Agrigento's Concordia temple, the monumental rubble of Selinunte's columns or the rare grace of a dancing satyr statue rescued from Mazara del Vallo's watery depths, reminders of bygone civilisations are everywhere.

Mediterranean Flavours

A delectable layer-cake of culinary influences, Sicily's ancient cuisine continues to rely on a few key island-grown ingredients: shellfish and citrus, tuna and swordfish, pistachios, almonds and ricotta. Talk to the septuagenarian chef at a Catania restaurant and she'll confide that she still uses her grandmother's recipe for *pasta alla Norma*, joyfully sharing the poetic imagery that links it to Mt Etna: the tomatoes are lava; the aubergines, cinders; the basil, leafy greenery; the ricotta, snow. Modern chefs may play with the details, but Sicily's timeless recipes – from the simplest *cannolo* to the most exquisite fish couscous – live on.

Sparkling Seas, Restless Mountains

Sicily's varied landscape makes a dramatic first impression. Fly into Catania and the smoking hulk of Etna greets you; arrive in Palermo and it's the sparkling Golfo di Castellammare. This juxtaposition of sea, volcano and mountain scenery makes a stunning backdrop for outdoor activities. Hikers can wind along precipitous coastlines, climb erupting volcanoes and traipse through flowery mountain meadows; birders benefit from the plethora of species on the Africa-Europe migration route; and divers and swimmers enjoy some of the Mediterranean's most pristine waters.

Byzantine to Baroque

As if its classical heritage weren't formidable enough, Sicily is bursting at the seams with later artistic and architectural gems. In a short walk around Palermo you'll see Arab domes and arches, Byzantine mosaics and Norman palace walls. Circle around to southeast Sicily and you'll find a stunning array of baroque architectural masterpieces, from the golden-hued domes and palaces of Noto to the multi-tiered cathedral facades of Ragusa and Modica. This embarrassment of cultural riches remains one of the island's most distinctive attractions.

Why I Love Sicily

By Gregor Clark, Writer

Decades after my first visit, I still find Sicily one of the world's most captivating places. Among the island's innumerable charms, here are a few personal favourites: the ever-present scent of lemon trees, the purity of dawn light on terracotta walls, the colourful decrepitude of Palermo's markets, the drama of Stromboli erupting against a darkening sky, the sense that history lurks always just around the next corner, the reflective marble glow of late-night Ortygia and Marsala streets, the lonely majesty of Segesta, the exotic flavours of Sicilian food and the island's endless cultural complexities.

For more about our writers, see page 320

Above: Ortygia (p185), Syracuse

Sicily

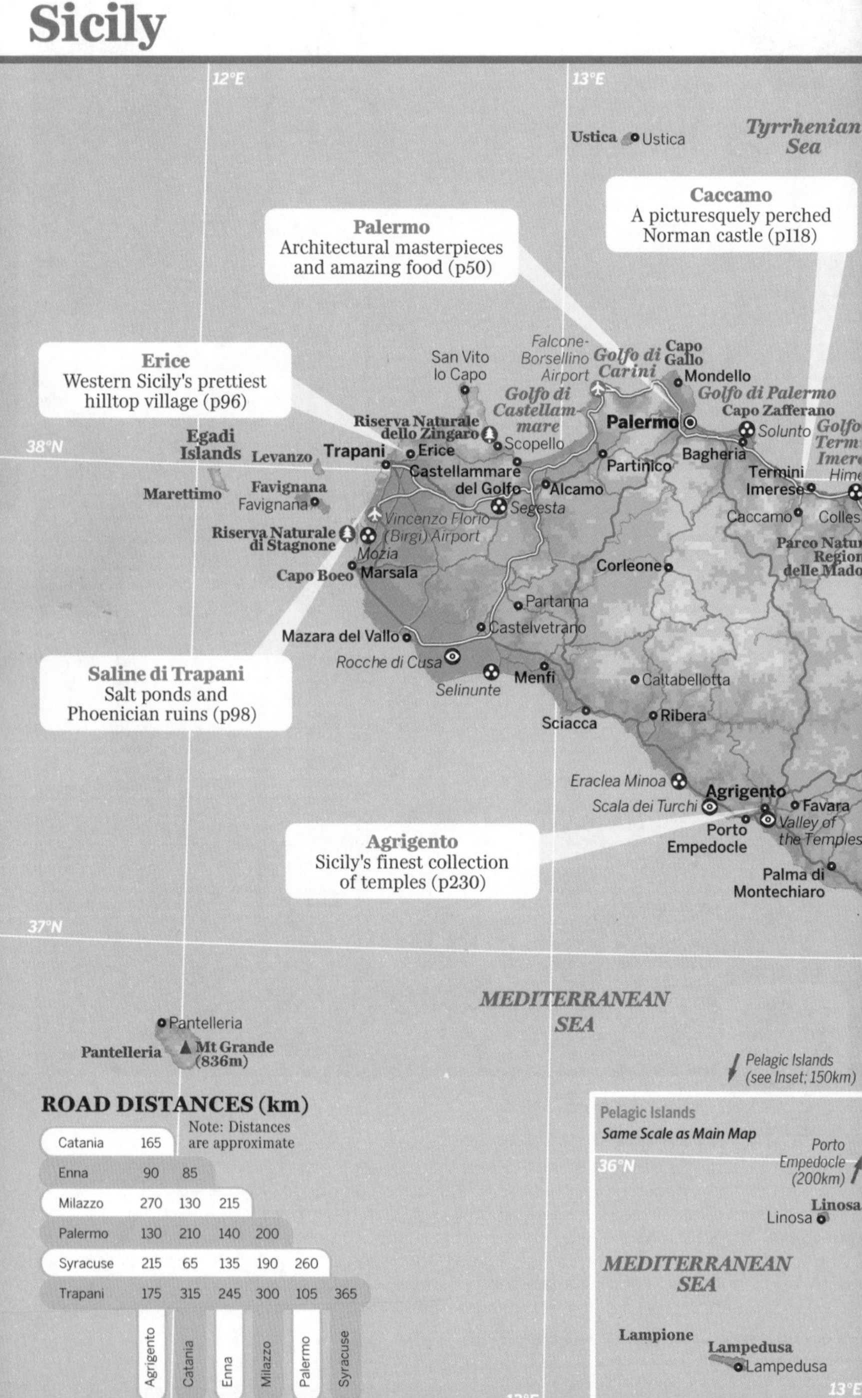

ROAD DISTANCES (km)

Note: Distances are approximate

	Agrigento	Catania	Enna	Milazzo	Palermo	Syracuse
Catania	165					
Enna	90	85				
Milazzo	270	130	215			
Palermo	130	210	140	200		
Syracuse	215	65	135	190	260	
Trapani	175	315	245	300	105	365

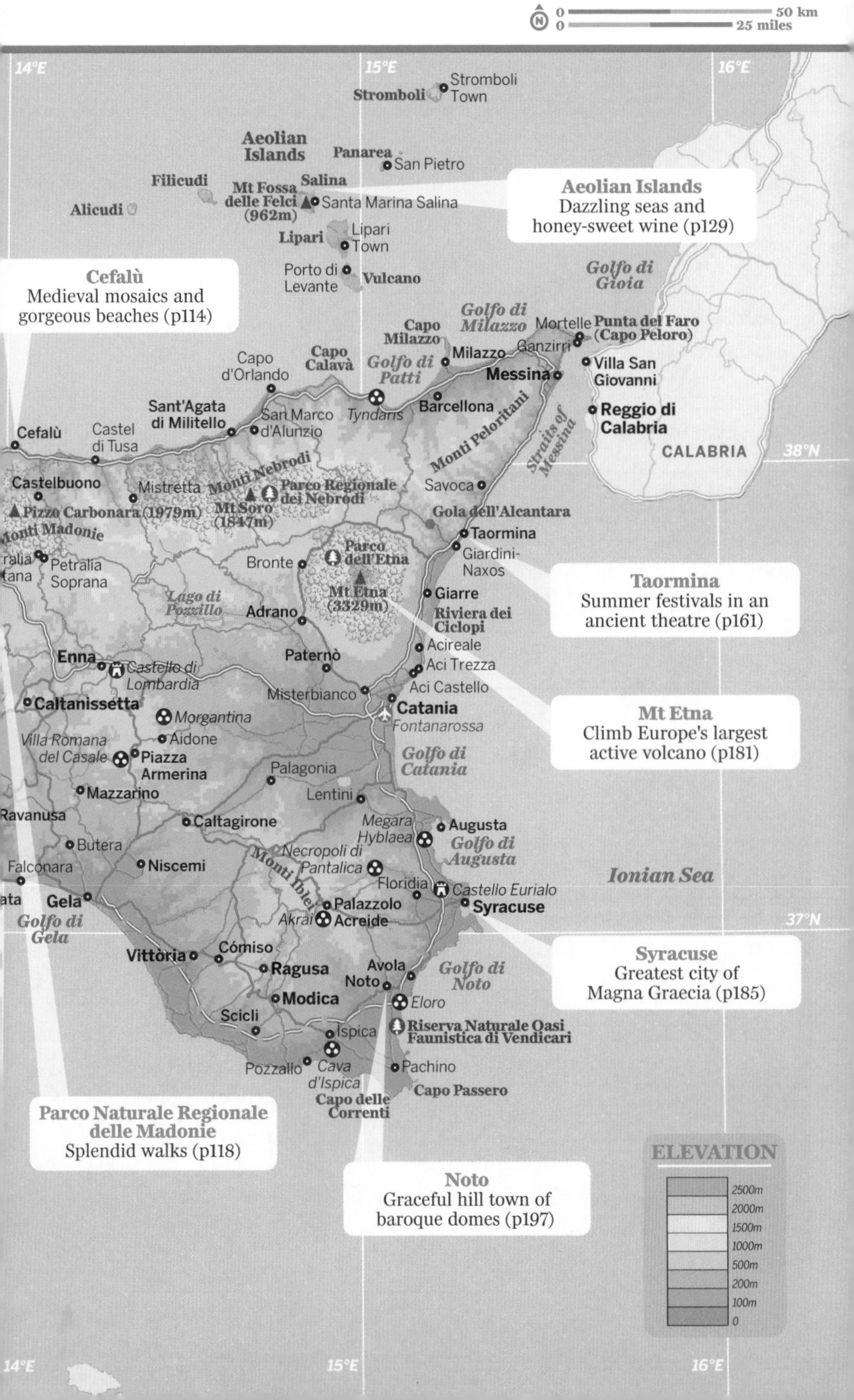

0 — 50 km
0 — 25 miles

Aeolian Islands
Dazzling seas and honey-sweet wine (p129)

Cefalù
Medieval mosaics and gorgeous beaches (p114)

Taormina
Summer festivals in an ancient theatre (p161)

Mt Etna
Climb Europe's largest active volcano (p181)

Syracuse
Greatest city of Magna Graecia (p185)

Parco Naturale Regionale delle Madonie
Splendid walks (p118)

Noto
Graceful hill town of baroque domes (p197)

14°E
15°E
16°E
38°N
37°N

Stromboli
Stromboli Town
Aeolian Islands
Panarea
San Pietro
Filicudi
Salina
Mt Fossa delle Felci (962m)
Santa Marina Salina
Alicudi
Lipari
Lipari Town
Porto di Levante
Vulcano
Golfo di Gioia
Golfo di Milazzo
Capo Milazzo
Mortelle
Punta del Faro (Capo Peloro)
Ganzirri
Capo d'Orlando
Capo Calavà
Golfo di Patti
Milazzo
Villa San Giovanni
Messina
Sant'Agata di Militello
San Marco d'Alunzio
Tyndaris
Barcellona
Reggio di Calabria
Cefalù
Castel di Tusa
Monti Peloritani
Straits of Messina
CALABRIA
Monti Nebrodi
Castelbuono
Mistretta
Parco Regionale dei Nebrodi
Savoca
Pizzo Carbonara (1979m)
Mt Soro (1847m)
Gola dell'Alcantara
Monti Madonie
Taormina
Parco dell'Etna
Giardini-Naxos
Petralia Soprana
Bronte
Mt Etna (3329m)
Giarre
Lago di Pozzillo
Adrano
Riviera dei Ciclopi
Acireale
Enna
Paternò
Aci Trezza
Castello di Lombardia
Aci Castello
Misterbianco
Caltanissetta
Catania
Morgantina
Fontanarossa
Aidone
Villa Romana del Casale
Piazza Armerina
Golfo di Catania
Palagonia
Mazzarino
Lentini
Ravanusa
Caltagirone
Megara Hyblaea
Augusta
Butera
Golfo di Augusta
Necropoli di Pantalica
Niscemi
Monti Iblei
Falconara
Ionian Sea
Floridia
Castello Eurialo
Gela
Palazzolo Acreide
Syracuse
Akrai
Golfo di Gela
Cómiso
Vittòria
Avola
Golfo di Noto
Ragusa
Noto
Modica
Eloro
Scicli
Riserva Naturale Oasi Faunistica di Vendicari
Ispica
Pachino
Pozzallo
Cava d'Ispica
Capo Passero
Capo delle Correnti

ELEVATION
2500m
2000m
1500m
1000m
500m
200m
100m
0

Sicily's Top 14

1

Syracuse

1 Alight from the train or bus station the into the sterile modern centre of Syracuse (p185), and you just might wonder what the fuss is all about. But enter the labyrinthine alleyways of the ancient island of Ortygia, or the vast archaeological park north of town, and layers of history will soon have you swooning. Suddenly you're standing in a vast field of Greek ruins, gazing down over delicate papyrus plants in an ancient pool or wandering through a glimmering marble-paved square where ancient temple columns peek out from under a cathedral's baroque facade.

Below left: Chiesa di Santa Lucia alla Badia (p185)

Sicilian Cuisine

2 Sicilian cuisine will radically alter your concept of Italian food. Ingredients that repeatedly appear in the island's distinctive dishes include citrus, wild fennel and mint, pistachios and almonds, cherry tomatoes, capers and olives, tuna and sardines, swordfish and shrimp. Stroll through Catania (p168) and you'll encounter uniquely Sicilian treats such as *pasta alla Norma*, made with local aubergines and ricotta, or *arancini*, savoury stuffed rice balls. Tuck into saffron-scented couscous in Trapani, or *pasta con le sarde* (pasta with sardines, pine nuts, raisins and wild fennel) in Palermo – but whatever you do, save room for legendary desserts such as *cannoli* and *cassata*!

WESTEND61/GETTY IMAGES ©

NEIL FARRIN/GETTY IMAGES ©

Aeolian Islands

3 Extraordinarily beautiful and surprisingly diverse, the seven volcanic islands of the Aeolian archipelago (p129) are packed with standout attractions – Vulcano's smoking crater, Salina's verdant vineyards, Panarea's whitewashed luxury hotels – yet their greatest appeal may lie in their markedly slower rhythm. With very few cars and zero stress, this place feels a world apart from the Sicilian 'mainland'; indeed, when leaving the islands, locals speak of 'going to Sicily'. You might just want to adopt the same mindset, lingering here your whole vacation and saving 'Sicily' for later. Below: Panarea (p146)

Erice

4 With every hairpin curve on the long climb to Erice (p96) , it seems that the views can't possibly get any better. But they do. Save your camera battery for the top of the hill, where the Norman Castello di Venere affords 360-degree views clear out to San Vito Lo Capo, the Egadi Islands and the salt pools and windmills of the Saline di Trapani. It's small wonder that earlier cultures considered this a sacred site, building a temple to Venus that even earned a mention in Virgil's *Aeneid*. Top right: Castello di Venere (p97)

Open-Air Performances

5 Aeschylus himself would doubtless be pleased to see Greek drama still flourishing in Syracuse's great amphitheatre, two-and-a-half millennia later. Every spring, the Cycle of Classical Plays brings a solid month's worth of live performances to the very venue where the venerable playwright once sat. From June through August, the action moves up the coast to Taormina's Teatro Greco (p161), where you can watch everything from international film premieres to famous rockers, dancers and divas performing under the balmy night air, all with Mt Etna as the scenic backdrop.

Left: Teatro Greco (p161), Taormina

Volcanoes

6 Never content to sit still, Sicily's great volcanoes keep belching sulphurous steam and sending fireworks into the night sky. Three-and-a-half centuries after burying Catania in volcanic ash, Mt Etna (p181) still broods over the city, keeping locals on their toes, while Stromboli continues lighting the way for passing ships as it did in ancient times. Climbing either or both of these fiery beauties is easily done in a day, or you can just admire them from afar. Either way, they're an unforgettable part of the Sicilian experience. Below: Mt Etna (p181)

Cefalù

7 With its long sandy beach hugging the sparkling Tyrrhenian, and its twin cathedral towers juxtaposed against the rugged heights of La Rocca, Cefalù (p114) provokes many a 'love at first sight' reaction. The dazzling Byzantine mosaics of the cathedral's apse and the carved columns of its cloister will keep you busy on a rainy day, but once summer rolls around it's hard to resist the waterfront's allure. You won't find a better blend of beach resort and medieval town centre anywhere in Italy.

6

7

FUTUREGALORE/SHUTTERSTOCK ©

NEIL FARRIN/GETTY IMAGES ©

Hill Towns

8 Sicily's interior is a rugged place, full of rocky outcrops, precipitous hillsides and fields parched by the summer sun. It can sometimes look downright uninhabitable, but scan the horizon and you'll quickly find evidence of the island's long centuries of human settlement. Gorgeous hill towns such as Enna, Petralia Soprana, Gangi, Ragusa, Noto and San Marco d'Alunzio are sprinkled throughout the island, most of them clinging to impossible heights and crowned by crumbling Norman castles or traces of other long-past civilisations.

Above: Noto (p197)

Palermo

9 Unapologetically gritty and endlessly fascinating, Palermo (p48) is a full-on urban adventure. You may find yourself cursing the traffic or the inscrutable garbage collection system, but you'll also find moments of pure grace: gazing up at the exquisite carved ceilings and arches of the Cappella Palatina, listening to the cacophonous singing of fruit vendors at Mercato del Capo or the harmonic perfection of an opera performance at Teatro Massimo, poring through millennia of well-catalogued treasures at the Museo Archeologico Regionale or stumbling across baroque facades on a workaday backstreet.

Top right: Mosaics, Cappella Palatina (p53)

Valley of the Temples

10 The magnificent temples of Agrigento's Valley of the Temples (p234) make an impression like no other ruins in Sicily. Strung out along the long rocky promontory where the ancient Greeks erected them 2500 years ago, their magical aura is enhanced at night, when they're brilliantly floodlit. On summer evenings, don't miss the chance to walk among the temples of the Eastern Zone after dark, an experience unparalleled at any other Sicilian ancient site. A short way up the hill, Agrigento's Museo Archeologico is one of the island's finest museums.

Above: Tempio di Hera (p235)

SABINE LUBENOW/LOOK-FOTO/GETTY IMAGES ©

Parco Naturale Regionale delle Madonie

11 Deluged with so many seaside attractions, many visitors never get around to exploring Sicily's interior. Big mistake! All it takes is a half-hour drive into the lofty reaches of the Madonie regional park (p118) and the world completely changes. Coastal heat gives way to mountain breezes, overcrowded beach resorts yield to tranquil hill towns, and high-country trails offer endless outdoor recreation. Add to this one of Sicily's most unique regional cuisines, and you just might be tempted to alter your beach vacation plans.

Caccamo

12 Formidable Norman strongholds straddle the hilltops throughout the Sicilian countryside, but perhaps nowhere as dramatically as at Caccamo (p118). The castle's spiky crenellations and the underlying crag appear fused into a single impregnable mass, towering above the valley floor. Climb up top and survey the vast domains below, then stop in for lunch downstairs under the atmospheric brick-and-stone arches of the castle's former grain stores. You'll feel transported back to the Middle Ages, yet modern downtown Palermo is only an hour away. Above right: Castello di Caccamo (p118)

Markets

13 A feast for the senses, Palermo's Mercato di Ballarò (p54) is as much akin to a north African bazaar as to a mainland Italian market: fruit vendors raucously hawking their wares in Sicilian dialect, the irresistible perfume of lemons and oranges, and the crackle of chickpea fritters emerging from the deep-fryer. Across the island, Catania's La Pescheria (p168) offers an equally evocative slice of Sicilian life, with a chaotic crush of market stalls where severed swordfish heads cast sidelong glances across heaps of silvery sardines on ice. Top right: Mercato di Ballarò (p54)

Saline di Trapani

14 After so many dramatic mountainous landscapes in the rest of Sicily, the Saline di Trapani (p98) come as a complete revelation. These vast flats between Trapani and Marsala, dotted with windmills and shimmering pools, have been prized since ancient times as a source of salt. Zigzag through the watery landscape under big open skies, then take the ferry across to ancient Mozia, an island whose Phoenician relics are some of Europe's most significant, displayed *in situ* and in the adjoining Whitaker Museum.

Right: Windmill

Need to Know

For more information, see Survival Guide (p295)

Currency
Euro (€)

Language
Italian

Visas
Generally not required for stays of up to three months.

Money
ATMs widely available. Credit cards accepted in most hotels and restaurants.

Mobile Phones
Italian mobile phones operate on the GSM 900/1800 network.

Time
Central European Time (GMT/UTC plus one hour)

When to Go

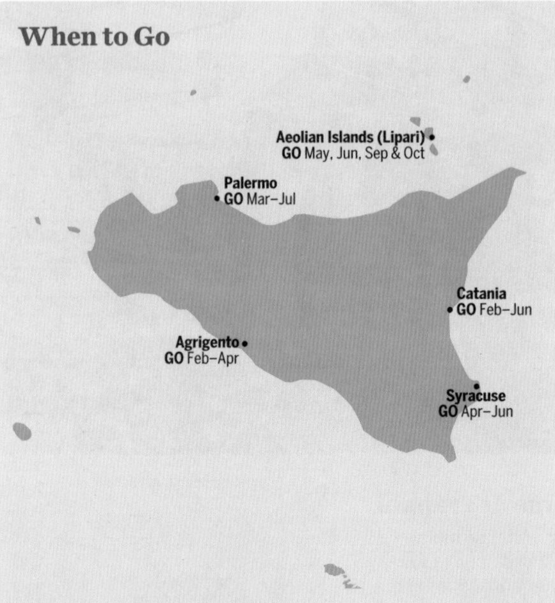

High Season (Jul–Aug)

- Prices skyrocket, especially surrounding Ferragosto (15 August), and roads and beaches are jam-packed.
- Festival season in Taormina, Palermo, Piazza Armerina and elsewhere.
- Good time to hike in the mountains.

Shoulder (Apr–Jun & Sep–Oct)

- Best period for good weather, with reasonable prices.
- Spring is ideal for hiking, wildflowers and local produce.
- June and September are best for diving.
- Easter is marked by colourful religious festivities; book ahead.

Low Season (Nov–Mar)

- Accommodation prices drop by 30% or more.
- Offshore islands and coastal resorts largely shut down.
- Experience local culture without the crowds.

Useful Websites

Sicily for Tourists (www.regione.sicilia.it/turismo) Sicily's official online tourism portal.

Best of Sicily (www.bestofsicily.com) Comprehensive coverage of the island.

Lonely Planet (www.lonelyplanet.com/italy/sicily) Destination information, hotel bookings, traveller forum and more.

Important Numbers

Italy's country code	☎39
Ambulance	☎118
Fire	☎115
Police	☎112
General emergency	☎113

Exchange Rates

Australia	A$1	€0.67
Brazil	R$1	€0.27
Canada	C$1	€0.69
Japan	¥100	€0.87
New Zealand	NZ$1	€0.64
Switzerland	Sfr1	€0.92
UK	UK£1	€1.16
US	US$1	€0.89

For current exchange rates, see www.xe.com.

Daily Costs

Budget: less than €100

➡ Double room in a B&B or budget hotel: €60–80

➡ Pizza or pasta: €15–20

➡ Bus or train tickets: €5–10

Midrange: €100–200

➡ Double room in a hotel: €80–150

➡ Lunch and dinner in local restaurants: €30–60

Top end: more than €200

➡ Double room in a four- or five-star hotel: from €150

➡ Lunch and dinner in top restaurants: €60–120

Opening Hours

Banks 8.30am to 1.30pm and 2.45pm to 3.45pm Monday to Friday.

Restaurants Noon to 2.30pm and 7.30pm to 11pm; many close one day per week.

Cafes 7am to 8pm (or later if offering bar service at night).

Shops 9.30am to 1.30pm and 4pm to 7.30pm Monday to Saturday.

Museums Hours vary, but many close on Monday.

Arriving in Sicily

Falcone-Borsellino Airport (p302; Palermo) Trains (€5.50) and buses (€6.30) run to the city centre every 30 to 60 minutes from 5am to 12.15am. Taxis cost €35 to €45. The journey takes from 30 minutes to an hour.

Fontanarossa airport (p302; Catania) AMT's Alibus (€4, 30 minutes) runs from the airport to the train station every 25 minutes. Taxis cost €18 to €22.

Vincenzo Florio airport (p302; Trapani) Buses (€4.90, 20 minutes) run hourly to Trapani's bus station and port between 8.30am and 12.30am. Taxis cost €30 to €35.

Getting Around

Train Trenitalia service is dependable and frequent along the Palermo–Messina and Messina–Syracuse coastal routes. Other well-served routes include Palermo to Agrigento and Trapani to Marsala to Mazara del Vallo.

Ferry/hydrofoil Efficient ferries and hydrofoils serve Sicily's outer islands. Main ports include Milazzo (Aeolian Islands), Palermo (Ustica), Trapani (Egadi Islands) and Porto Empedocle (Pelagic Islands).

Car The most convenient option for visiting smaller interior towns and remote archaeological sites (Segesta, Selinunte, Piazza Armerina etc). Car hire is readily available at airports and many towns.

Bus The best option for certain intercity routes, including Palermo–Trapani, Palermo–Syracuse and Catania–Agrigento. Also useful for some villages not served by train.

For much more on **getting around**, see p304

First Time Sicily

For more information, see Survival Guide (p295)

Checklist

- Verify validity of your passport
- Organise travel insurance
- Pre-book popular festivals, opera and theatre performances, rental cars and accommodation
- Inform your credit-card company of your travel plans
- Check if you can use your mobile (cell) phone

What to Pack

- Sturdy shoes for walking/hiking, sandals for the beach
- Round two-pin electrical adapter (to fit Italian sockets)
- Picnic-friendly pocket knife with corkscrew
- Sunglasses, sunscreen and a hat
- Driver's licence and map if hiring a car
- Mobile (cell) phone charger

Top Tips for Your Trip

- Late spring and early autumn are ideal times to visit Sicily; temperatures are more moderate, prices are lower and crowds are much smaller than during July and August.
- Most hotels and other accommodation in Sicily include a simple breakfast in the price.
- Sicilians dine late, especially in bigger cities, where restaurants don't typically start filling until after 9pm.
- *Cannoli* are meant to be eaten with your fingers, not a knife and fork!

What to Wear

Appearances matter in Italy. The concept of *la bella figura* (literally 'making a good impression') encapsulates the Italian obsession with beauty, gallantry and looking good. In cities, suitable wear for men is generally trousers and shirts or polo shirts, and for women skirts, trousers or dresses. Shorts, T-shirts and sandals are fine for summer and at the beach. For evening wear, smart casual is the norm. A light sweater or waterproof jacket is useful in spring and autumn, and sturdy shoes are advisable at archaeological sites.

Sleeping

Advance booking is recommended during Easter Week and in the busy summer months, especially along the coast.

Agriturismi Working farms or country houses that offer rooms and often delicious home-cooked meals.

B&Bs Range from the basic to the luxurious. Most have five rooms or fewer, sometimes with a shared bathroom outside the room.

Pensioni Family-run guesthouses – facilities tend to be more basic (and prices lower) than at hotels.

Alberghi (hotels) Ranked on a star system (one to five) based on amenities.

Rifugi Offer simple accommodation for outdoors enthusiasts.

Affittacamere Low-cost rooms rented out by private owners.

Driving

Always carry your driving licence, the vehicle's registration papers and proof of third-party (liability) insurance when driving in Sicily. Driving licences from all EU member states' and the United States are recognised in Sicily, as are licences from most other major countries.

Etiquette

Greetings Shake hands and say '*buongiorno*' (good day) or '*buona sera*' (good evening) to strangers; kiss both cheeks and say '*come stai?*' (how are you?) to friends. Use '*lei*' (formal 'you') in polite company; use '*tu*' (informal 'you') with friends and children. Only use first names if invited.

Asking for help Say '*mi scusi*' (excuse me) to get someone's attention; say '*permesso*' (permission) when you want to pass someone in a crowded space.

Religious etiquette Dress modestly (cover shoulders, torsos and thighs) and be quiet and respectful when visiting religious sites. Never intrude on a church service.

Eating and drinking At restaurants, summon the waiter by saying '*per favore*' (please). When dining in an Italian home, bring a small gift of sweets *(dolci)* or wine, and dress well.

Scheduling Take official opening hours and timetables with a grain of salt.

Avoid Discussing the Mafia can be a touchy subject.

Language

English is not as widely spoken in Sicily as in northern Europe. In the main tourist centres you can get by, but in the countryside it will be helpful to master a few basic phrases. This will improve your experience no end, especially when ordering in restaurants, some of which have no written menu.

1. **What's the local speciality?**
Qual'è la specialità di questa regione?
kwa·*le* la spe·cha·lee·*ta* dee *kwes*·ta re·*jo*·ne

A bit like the rivalry between medieval Italian city-states, these days the country's regions compete in speciality foods and wines.

2. **Which combined tickets do you have?**
Quali biglietti cumulativi avete?
kwa·lee bee·*lye*·tee koo·moo·la·*tee*·vee a·*ve*·te

Make the most of your euro by getting combined tickets to various sights; they are available in all major Italian cities.

3. **Where can I buy discount designer items?**
C'è un outlet in zona? che oon *owt*·let in *zo*·na

Discount fashion outlets are big business in major cities – get bargain-priced seconds, samples and cast-offs for *la bella figura.*

4. **I'm here with my husband/boyfriend.**
Sono qui con il mio marito/ragazzo.
so·no kwee kon eel *mee*·o ma·*ree*·to/ra·*ga*·tso

Solo women travellers may receive unwanted attention in some parts of Italy; if ignoring fails have a polite rejection ready.

5. **Let's meet at 6pm for pre-dinner drinks.**
Ci vediamo alle sei per un aperitivo.
chee ve·*dya*·mo *a*·le say per oon a·pe·ree·*tee*·vo

At dusk, watch the main piazza get crowded with people sipping colourful cocktails and snacking the evening away: join your new friends for this authentic Italian ritual!

Bargaining

Gentle haggling is common in outdoor markets; in all other instances you're expected to pay the stated price.

Tipping

Restaurants Most have a cover charge (*coperto*, around €2), and some also levy a service charge (*servizio*, 10% to 15%). If there is no service charge, consider rounding the bill up.

Bars In cafes people often place a €0.10 or €0.20 coin on the bar when ordering coffee. Consider leaving small change when ordering drinks.

Taxis Optional, but most people round up to the nearest euro.

If You Like...

Ancient Sites

Taormina's Teatro Greco (p161) Divine architecture and a dreamy setting come together at this splendid Greek theatre with a front-row view of Mt Etna.

Segesta (p90) Sitting in moody isolation on a windswept hillside, the Elymians' perfect Doric temple is one of Sicily's most magical spots.

Villa Romana del Casale (p222) This Roman villa's ancient floor mosaics are among the most extensive and best-preserved anywhere.

Valley of the Temples (p234) Splendidly arrayed on Agrigento's craggy heights, five temples and a superb archaeological museum make this the granddaddy of Sicilian ancient sites.

Parco Archeologico della Neapolis (p189) Syracuse's vast complex of amphitheatres and altars is backed by citrus groves and limestone caves.

Ruins of Selinunte (p108) One of western Sicily's top draws, Selinunte blends an idyllic coastal setting and a magnificent diversity of ruins.

Necropoli di Pantalica (p196) This honeycomb of Iron and Bronze Age tombs may have once been the capital of the ancient Sicilian culture.

Coastal Walks

Stromboli Crater (p147) Nothing in Sicily compares to climbing Europe's most active volcano and watching the sunset over the Tyrrhenian Sea.

Riserva Naturale Oasi Faunistica di Vendicari (p201) Flamingos migrate through this peaceful southeastern coastal reserve, a prime birdwatching spot.

Riserva Naturale dello Zingaro (p88) In Sicily's oldest nature reserve, a spectacular coastal trail zigzags past secluded coves and museums of local culture.

Pianoconte to Quattropani (p136) Tracing the bluffs of Lipari's western shore, this walk affords stunning views of the other Aeolian Islands.

Punta Troia (p102) Hugging the coastline from Marettimo's whitewashed main village to a dramatically perched seaside castle, this walk is one of the Egadi Islands' prettiest.

Sentiero del Mezzogiorno (p82) Leading to a lighthouse at Ustica's western edge, this scenic hike can be extended into a full-island loop.

Zucco Grande (p153) An easy day hike leads to this abandoned village on Filicudi's wildflower-strewn coastal bluffs.

Dessert

Pasticceria Cappello (p65) Try *delizia al pistacchio*, possibly the world's tastiest pistachio dessert, with an exquisite mix of creaminess and granular crunch.

Pasticceria Fratelli Magrì (p65) Loosen your belt and succumb to lesser-known sweet treats like *patata*, a spongy, custardy, almondy thrill.

Ti Vitti (p116) *Cannoli* are perfect pastry tubes hand-filled on the spot with homemade ricotta from the nearby Madonie Mountains.

Da Alfredo (p144) *Granita alla mandorla*, a refreshing blend of crushed ice, local almonds and sugar, is the perfect summertime treat.

Caffè Adamo (p203) Using the freshest seasonal ingredients, gelato maestro Antonio Adamo concocts extraordinary flavour combos, including the highly addictive raspberry-pistachio.

Dolceria Bonajuto (p205) At Modica's famous chocolate factory, hot peppers add an Aztec-inspired kick to the *Xocoatl* chocolate.

Maria Grammatico (p96) *Frutta martorana*, marzipan fruit, made by Erice's famous confectioner.

Top: Necropoli di Pantalica (p196)
Bottom: *Frutta martorana* (marzipan fruit)

Performing Arts

Ciclo di Rappresentazioni Classiche (p192) Watch classic Greek dramas in the same Syracusan theatre where Aeschylus once sat.

Teatro Massimo (p62) Palermo's great opera house makes for an elegant night out.

Teatro Massimo Bellini (p175) Classical concerts in classy surrounds are the hallmark of this opera house named for Catania's native son.

Taormina Arte (p164) This popular summer festival brings Taormina's ancient theatre back to life with music, dance, theatre and film.

Teatro dei Pupi di Mimmo Cuticchio (p68) Sword-wielding knights and damsels in distress delight multi-aged crowds at Palermo's outstanding traditional puppet theatre.

Beaches

Cefalù (p114) The Tyrrhenian's prettiest beach town boasts a long stretch of sand backed by medieval streets and a palm-fringed cathedral.

Scala dei Turchi (p237) Just west of Agrigento, this chalky white staircase of natural stone makes a dazzling sunset-watching spot.

Spiaggia dei Faraglioni (p85) Scopello's rough-pebbled beach has shimmering turquoise waters backed by towering rock formations.

Lido Mazzarò (p164) Sparkling far below Taormina, this idyllic cove's crystal-clear waters cradle the islet of Isola Bella.

Spiaggia Valle i Muria (p134) Fabulously far from civilisation, save for its cavelike beachside bar, this cliff-backed beach is one of the Aeolians' finest.

Marianelli (p201) This tranquil sweep of sand and turquoise waves form part of the beautiful Riserva Naturale Oasi Faunistica di Vendicari in Sicily's southeast.

Baroque Architecture

Cattedrale di San Nicolò (p197) Dominating Noto's skyline, this cathedral's golden-hued dome is one of Sicily's baroque masterpieces.

Chiesa di San Giorgio (p202) Gagliardi's three-tiered beauty of a facade is well worth the 250-step climb from lower Modica.

Oratorio di Santa Cita (p61) Search for snakes and cherubs in Giacomo Serpotta's swirling stuccowork at this 17th-century Palermitan chapel.

Cattedrale di San Giorgio (p206) Ragusa's pride and joy is this mid-18th-century cathedral with its magnificent dome and stained-glass windows.

Panoramic Vistas

Castello di Venere (p97) Fairy-tale coastal views extend from Erice's castle to the distant point of San Vito Lo Capo.

Quattrocchi (p134) Arched sea-rocks, precipitous cliffs and a smoking volcano on the horizon make this one of the Aeolians' unmissable viewpoints.

La Rocca (p114) A long-abandoned hilltop castle provides the moody backdrop for perfect views of Cefalù and the Tyrrhenian Sea beyond.

Piazza IX Aprile (p161) On a clear day, Taormina's main square offers mesmerising perspectives of Mt Etna and the Ionian Sea.

Chiesa di Santa Maria delle Scale (p207) Stunning views of Ragusa's lower town from this church astride a panoramic staircase.

Capo Grillo (p139) Spy all six of the other Aeolian Islands from this prime perch on Vulcano's east coast.

Chiaramonte Gulfi (p211) Dubbed Il Balcone della Sicilia (Sicily's Balcony), this hilltop town delivers views stretching from Sicily's southern coast to Mt Etna in the north.

Mosaics

Cappella Palatina (p53) Dazzling gilded wall mosaics contrast with the intricate Arabic-influenced *muqarnas* (honeycomb-style vaulting) ceiling at this multicultural masterpiece.

Cattedrale di Monreale (p80) Widely considered the Normans' greatest Sicilian legacy, Monreale's cathedral shimmers with gorgeously detailed Byzantine mosaics.

Duomo di Cefalù (p114) Gaze into the eyes of a 12th-century Christ in this Arab-Norman cathedral's iconic apse mosaic.

Villa Romana del Casale (p222) Deities and dancing beasts adorn the floors at this amazingly well-preserved Roman hunting villa.

La Martorana (p50) This 12th-century church's splendid mosaics include Sicily's only surviving portrait of Norman king, Roger II.

Outdoor Activities

Area Marina Protetta di Ustica (p83) This fabulous marine reserve off Ustica's western shore is one of the Mediterranean's top dive sites.

San Vito Lo Capo (p85) Backed by a rugged coastal promontory, San Vito Lo Capo is Sicily's rock-climbing capital.

Piscina di Venere (p128) Swimmers couldn't ask for a more idyllic spot than this natural pool at the Mediterranean's edge.

Amici Del Cavallo (p231) Ride horses through the Valley of the Temples with this Agrigento-based outfit.

Markets

La Pescheria (p168) Catania's morning market is alive with noisy banter and swordfish heads casting sidelong glances across silvery heaps of sardines.

Mercato di Ballarò (p54) Vendors croon the merits of artfully stacked artichokes, wild strawberries and lemons at Palermo's liveliest market.

Antico Mercato (p195) Syracuse's top spot for fresh seasonal produce.

Mercatino Antiquariato Piazza Marina (p69) Palermo's Sunday flea market is a veritable sea of vintage Sicilian finds.

Mercato del Capo (p54) Plump olives, pungent cheese and voluptuous vegetables fill this popular Palermo market.

Mercatino delle Pulci (p203) Modica's monthly antiques fair draws both serious collectors and curious rookies.

Month by Month

TOP EVENTS

Festa di Sant'Agata, February

Carnevale, February–March

Pasqua (Easter), March–April

Ciclo di Rappresentazioni Classiche, May–June

Taormina Arte, June–September

January

Hot on the heels of the New Year comes Epiphany (6 January). On Etna and Monte Mufara in the Madonie it's ski season, while many coastal resort towns are firmly shut.

February

Temperatures aren't exactly balmy, but citrus orchards are heavy with fruit, and almond blossoms begin to appear in Agrigento. Carnevale also heats up in places like Acireale and Sciacca.

Carnevale

During the week before Ash Wednesday, many towns stage carnivals. The most flamboyant are in Sciacca (www.sciaccarnevale.it) and Acireale (www.carnevaleacireale.com).

Festa di Sant'Agata

One million Catanians follow a silver reliquary of St Agata through the city streets. This festival takes place from 3 to 5 February and is accompanied by spectacular fireworks.

Sagra del Mandorlo in Fiore

Performances of drama and music among the almond blossoms in the Valley of the Temples on the first Sunday in February (www.sagradelmandorloinfiore.com).

March

Weather in March is capricious, alternating between sun, wind and rain. Easter Week brings marzipan lambs to bakery windows and marks the opening date for many seasonal businesses.

Pasqua (Easter)

Holy Week is marked by solemn processions and passion plays. The most famous are in Trapani, Enna, Scicli, Lipari and Erice.

April

Markets overflow with wild strawberries, artichokes and fava beans. Weather is moody; it can be chilly or blissfully springlike.

La Processione dei Misteri

For four days, Trapani's 20 traditional *maestranze* (guilds) parade life-sized wooden statues of the Virgin Mary and other Biblical figures through the streets, accompanied by a band that plays dirges to the slow, steady beat of a drum.

May

Many places on outer islands are just opening for the season. With wildflowers blooming, this is a glorious season for walking on the Aeolians or in the Vendicari and Zingaro reserves.

Ciclo di Rappresentazioni Classiche

Combining classical intrigue with an evocative setting, the Cycle of

Classical Plays, held from mid-May to mid-June, brings Syracuse's 5th-century-BC amphitheatre to life with performances from Italy's acting greats (www.indafondazione.org).

Infiorata

At Noto's big annual jamboree, held around the third Sunday in May, the highlight is the decoration of Via Corrada Nicolaci, with works of art made entirely from flower petals (www.infioratadinoto.it).

June

Great month for walking in the mountains. Beaches are crowded on weekends but still not at peak capacity. Summer ferry schedules start at month's end, bringing an influx of visitors to the islands.

Taormina Film Fest

Hollywood big shots arrive in Taormina in mid-June for six days of film screenings and press conferences at the Teatro Greco (www.taorminafilmfest.it).

Taormina Arte

Opera, dance, theatre and live-music performances are staged at the Teatro Greco from June to September, with big-name performers from all over the world (www.taormina-arte.com).

July

School is out and Sicilians everywhere are headed away from cities to mountains or beaches for summer holidays. Prices and temperatures rise.

Festino di Santa Rosalia

Palermo's biggest annual festival celebrates Santa Rosalia, the patron saint of the city. The multiday party culminates with the saint's relics being paraded through the city, followed by celebratory fireworks on the waterfront (www.santarosaliapalermo.it).

August

Hot, expensive and crowded. Everyone is on holiday and many businesses and restaurants close for part of the month.

Ferragosto

After Christmas and Easter, Ferragosto, on 15 August, is Italy's biggest holiday. It marks the Feast of the Assumption, but even before Christianity the Romans honoured their gods on Feriae Augusti. Beaches are jam-packed and city attractions open for limited hours only.

Palio dei Normanni

Piazza Armerina's medieval pageant (between 12 and 14 August) commemorates Count Roger's taking of the town from the Moors in 1087 (www.paliodeinormanni.it).

September

Warm weather and sea but without the summer crowds. Hotel prices drop from their midsummer peak. Prime time for diving on Ustica.

Festival Internazionale del Cuscus

San Vito Lo Capo's famous fish couscous is celebrated annually at this 10-day event. The multicultural festivities involve musicians and chefs from around the world (www.couscousfest.it).

October

Businesses in the outer islands begin to curtail services, even as the chestnut harvest and wild mushroom seasons begin in earnest on Mt Etna and in the Madonie and Nebrodi Mountains.

November

Chilly, rainy weather creeps in, and many accommodations in beach and island communities close for winter. Opera season in Palermo and Catania is in full swing.

December

The days of alfresco living are firmly at an end. December is chilly although impending Christmas festivities help warm things up.

Natale

During the weeks preceding Christmas, many churches set up cribs or nativity scenes known as *presepi;* these are particularly notable in Caltagirone and Erice.

Itineraries

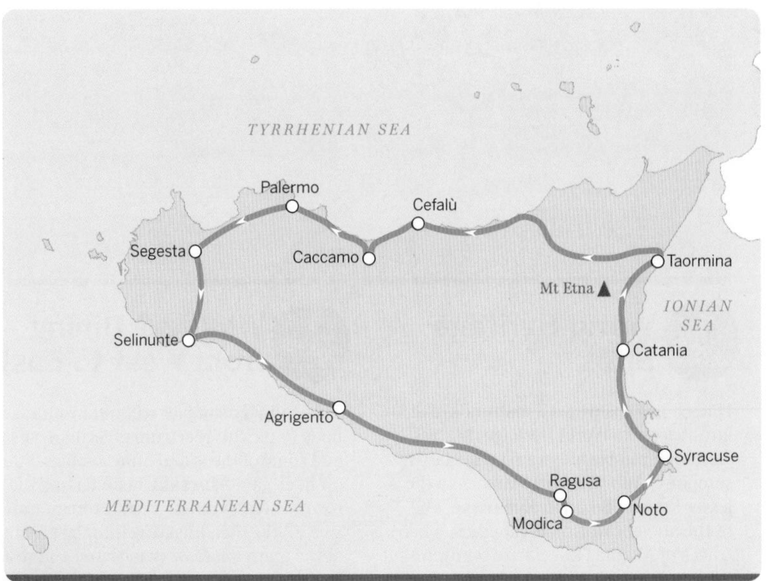

Only the Best

This two-week circle tour offers an introduction to Sicily's varied wonders – ancient archaeological sites, baroque hill towns, Arab-Norman churches and castles, volcanoes and beaches.

Begin in **Palermo**, where you can pick up a hire car for your circumnavigation of the island. After spending some time exploring the capital's diversity of architectural treasures, head southwest to the temples at **Segesta**, **Selinunte** and **Agrigento**. Next, cut east across the island to the Unesco-listed Val di Noto, where the baroque beauties of **Ragusa**, **Modica** and **Noto** are all obligatory stops. From here it's on to **Syracuse**, a highlight of any trip to Sicily: split your time here between the pedestrian-friendly ancient island city of Ortygia and the vast classical ruins of the Parco Archeologico. Continue up the coast to bustling **Catania** and circle **Mt Etna** to reach **Taormina**, a town whose abundant attractions include its ancient Greek theatre and the gorgeous beaches just below. Finally, loop back to Palermo via **Cefalù** – where the beautiful beach and 12th-century cathedral will vie for your attention – and **Caccamo**, home to one of Sicily's most spectacularly sited Norman castles.

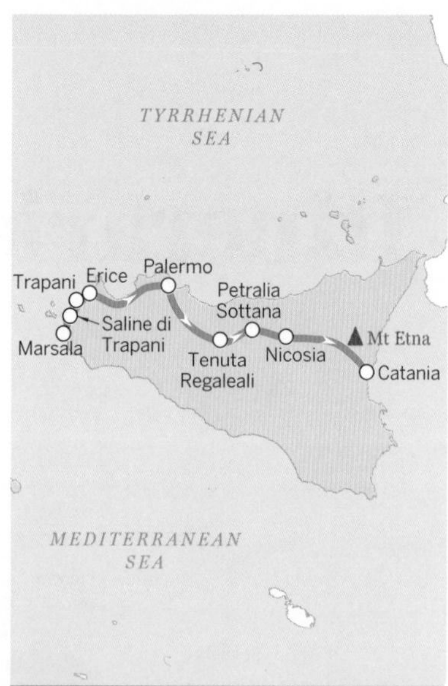

7 DAYS World Heritage Sites

Unesco has enshrined a multitude of Sicilian sites on its World Heritage list; this weeklong ramble offers a representative sampling, from the world-famous to the lesser-known. Begin in **Syracuse**, one of the ancient world's great cities, where traces of Magna Graecia are omnipresent – from papyrus-fringed Fontana Aretusa to the amphitheatres, altars and caves of the Parco Archeologico. Next head west to the **Necropoli di Pantalica** – an eerie assemblage of Bronze Age tombs built into limestone cliffs – before continuing to the captivating Val di Noto. The late-baroque towns of **Noto**, **Modica** and **Ragusa** are the superstars here, but it's also worth seeking out the small villages of **Scicli** and **Palazzolo Acreide** and the famed ceramics centre of **Caltagirone**, with its grand staircase of 142 distinctively tiled steps. Continue west to **Villa Romana del Casale**, whose dazzling Roman mosaic floors depict bikini-clad gymnasts and prancing wild African beasts. Finish at Sicily's most magnificent archaeological site: **Agrigento**'s Valley of the Temples, with its Doric sanctuaries spectacularly perched on a ridgetop near the Mediterranean coast.

7 DAYS Wining & Dining from West to East

This culinary sampler will treat your taste buds to the full spectrum of Sicilian cuisine and some of the island's finest wines. Start off in elegant **Marsala**, taste-testing the town's sweet wine on a cellar tour at Cantine Florio, then lingering into the evening at the many *enoteche* (wine bars) and restaurants in the pedestrian-friendly centre. Next morning, stop in at the **Saline di Trapani**, which have supplied salt to Sicilian tables for centuries, before lunching on legendary fish couscous in **Trapani** and enjoying dessert with a breathtaking view in **Erice**, renowned for its marzipan fruit, nougat and other nut-based sweets. Next stop is **Palermo**, whose colourful markets, street food, irresistible bakeries and countless fine eateries are highlights of any Sicilian food trip. Head south for a cooking course at the 400-hectare **Tenuta Regaleali**, one of Sicily's leading wine producers, then skirt the southern edge of the Madonie and Nebrodi Mountains, sampling the local black pork, ricotta, pecorino, mushrooms and hazelnuts in pretty hill towns like **Petralia Sottana** and **Nicosia**. Last, stop in for tastings of local honey, pistachios and Etna DOC wine on the flanks of **Mt Etna** before enjoying a final evening in cosmopolitan **Catania**.

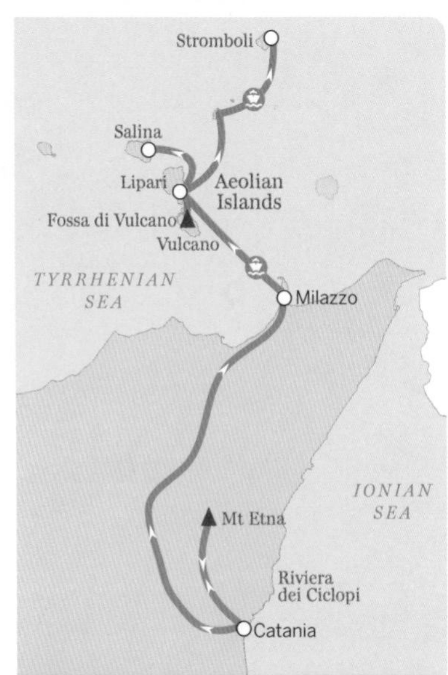

4 DAYS Mountain Retreats

Discover Sicily's more traditional side along the beautiful back roads of the Madonie and Nebrodi Mountains, a world apart from the coastal resorts just below. Relax into your journey in picture-perfect **Cefalù**, where you can lounge on the beach and enjoy panoramic coastal views from the ruined Norman citadel. Follow the coast east to **Castel di Tusa**, famous for its avant-garde collection of open-air sculptures, then turn inland and climb towards the lost-in-time mountain town of **Mistretta**. After detouring to explore the medieval village of **Nicosia**, continue south to **Enna**, a handsome hill town that marks Sicily's geographic centre – a fact best appreciated from atop the fortified walls of the Castello di Lombardia. Snake back north through Gangi into the heart of the **Parco Naturale Regionale delle Madonie**, a magnificent natural landscape dotted with hazelnut orchards, ash forests and photogenic hilltop towns. Linger a couple of days along the mountains' western edge to explore the old stone churches of **Petralia Soprana** and **Petralia Sottana**, the Targa Florio automobile race museum at **Collesano** and the castle at **Castelbuono** before rejoining the coast at Cefalù.

7 DAYS Smoke & Fire: Volcanic Sicily

Sicily's trio of active volcanoes – Mt Etna, Vulcano and Stromboli – form the dramatic backdrop for this tour of northeastern Sicily. Start in **Catania**, a city built of lava from the devastating volcanic eruption of 1669. Your first logical step is to climb the volcano that did all the damage, **Mt Etna**. As legend would have it, it was from Etna's lofty heights that the Cyclops hurled his stones at the fleeing Odysseus – you can still see their jagged forms along the **Riviera Dei Ciclopi** coastline, where traditional fishing villages have been reinvented as summer resorts. From here, circumnavigate Etna's western flank via Paternò, Biancavilla, Bronte and Randazzo and continue north to **Milazzo**, where you can catch a ferry to **Lipari**, the largest of the Aeolian Islands. Read up on the archipelago's fiery past at Lipari's Museo Archeologico, then island-hop across to the verdant island of **Salina**, whose twin extinct cones are one of Sicily's most harmonious sights. Those looking for something a little more 'active' can climb smoking **Fossa di Vulcano**, with its sulphur-belching crater and gloopy mudbaths, or scale the 'lighthouse of the Mediterranean', **Stromboli**, an eternal lava-lamp whose eruptions continually light up the night sky.

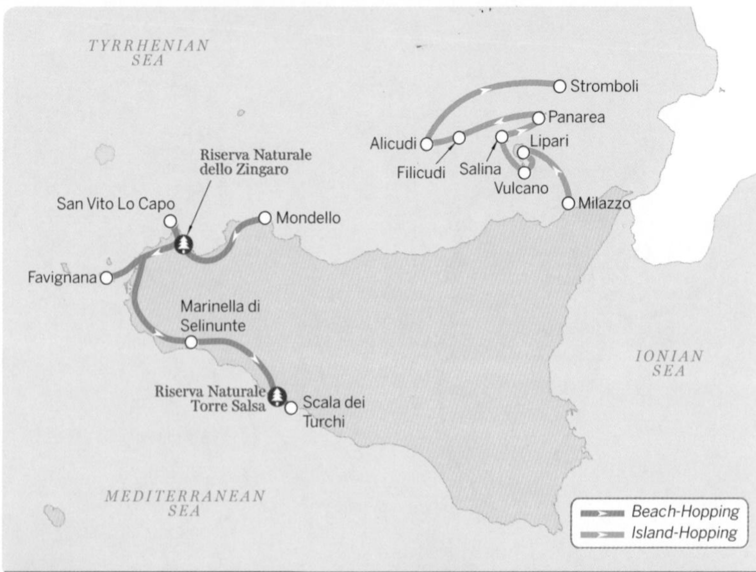

Beach-Hopping

Island-Hopping

Starting in Palermo and ending just west of Agrigento, this tour takes in the prettiest beaches of western Sicily, from family-friendly coastal resorts to wild stretches of shoreline protected in two of the island's loveliest nature preserves. Unpack your beach towel for the first time at **Mondello**, a summer playground just west of Palermo, whose deep roots as a coastal resort are reflected in its showy Liberty-era pier and summer villas. From here, it's an easy trip west to the Golfo di Castellammare, where the idyllic beach of **San Vito Lo Capo** offers an urban counterpoint to the scenic walking trails and sparkling coves of **Riserva Naturale dello Zingaro**. Next, hop the 30-minute ferry from Trapani to the Egadi Islands, and relax for a day or two beside the aquamarine waters of **Favignana**'s eastern beaches before resuming your journey along Sicily's Mediterranean coast. The last leg east towards Agrigento includes stopovers to ogle ancient Greek temples from the beach at **Marinella di Selinunte**, to stroll the vast, untrammelled sands of **Riserva Naturale Torre Salsa** and to sunbathe or dive off the blindingly chalk-white cliffs of **Scala dei Turchi**.

Leave the car behind and settle into a slower rhythm on this island-hopping adventure through the Aeolian Islands – seven volcanic beauties with seven distinct personalities, all connected by ferry and hydrofoil to Sicily's north coast. Begin by cruising across the Tyrrhenian from **Milazzo** to **Lipari,** home to the Aeolians' only sizeable town. Here you can split your time between urban attractions and excursions to the beaches and walking trails that lie just beyond town. From Lipari, frequent hydrofoils fan out to all the remaining islands. Your next destination should be **Vulcano**, a mere 10 minutes from Lipari, where you can explore black-sand beaches, soak in mud baths and climb the island's smoking crater on an easy day trip. Next, set your compass north for lush green **Salina**, home to Malvasia vineyards, Sicily's most famous capers and some enjoyable, slow-paced window-shopping in the low-key villages of Malfa and Santa Marina Salina. Eventually you'll feel called to explore the outer islands: chic, whitewashed **Panarea;** remote **Filicudi** with its hilltop ruin of a Bronze Age village; *way* off-the-beaten-track **Alicudi**; and the most spectacular of all, actively erupting **Stromboli**.

Plan Your Trip

Eat & Drink Like a Local

If food isn't already one of your prime motivations for visiting Sicily, it should be! Over the centuries Sicilian chefs have drawn culinary inspiration from mainland Italy, North Africa and countless other sources, adding tasty and unexpected indigenous twists to create one of the world's most unique and magnificent cuisines.

Food Experiences

Meals of a Lifetime

Osteria Nero D'Avola (p164) Owner Turi Siligato regales guests with tales of personally fishing and foraging for his ever-changing menu.

Osteria La Bettolaccia (p93) Sample Trapani's inimitable couscous, served with a delectable seafood broth, steps from the fish market.

Ristorante La Madia (p242) Every dish on Michelin-starred Madia's multi-course tasting menu is an exquisite work of art.

Bistrot Bella Vita (p193) An obsession with quality, seasonality and organic produce drives the kitchen at this easy-to-miss marvel.

Cooking Classes

Serious epicureans can learn their way around the Sicilian kitchen at one of the island's cooking schools.

Cooking with the Duchess (p56) Gregarious, multilingual duchess Nicoletta Polo Lanza opens the tiled kitchen of her 18th-century seaside *palazzo* (mansion) for half-day Sicilian cooking courses. After taking students to shop in Palermo's markets and pick herbs in her backyard garden, she shares secrets of the island's multifaceted cuisine, from street food to classic main courses to gorgeous desserts.

The Year in Food

While *sagre* (local food festivals) go into overdrive in autumn, there's never a bad time to raise your fork in Sicily.

Spring (March–May)

Asparagus, artichokes and little wild strawberries flood the local market stalls, and Easter specialities fill bakery windows. Tuna and swordfish both come into season.

Summer (June–August)

Time for aubergine, peppers, berries and seafood by the sea. Beat the heat Sicilian style with gelato on a brioche, or fresh mulberry *granita* (crushed ice made with fresh fruit).

Autumn (September–November)

Food festivals galore, wine-harvest season and a perfect time to visit the mountains for gems such as chestnuts, hazelnuts, mushrooms and wild game.

Winter (December–February)

Time for Christmas treats such as *buccellati* – dough rings stuffed with minced figs, raisins, almonds, candied fruit and/or orange peel.

Anna Tasca Lanza Cooking School (p225) Affiliated with one of Sicily's leading wine producers, this fabulous school in the middle of the Sicilian countryside has been around since 1989. Classes are taught at a century-old agricultural estate, with all ingredients sourced from the family garden or surrounding farms. Courses run from one to five days, with the option of overnight stays and additional food-related excursions to vineyards, permaculture gardens or the famous sweet shop of Maria Grammatico in Erice.

La Corte del Sole Cooking Lessons (p193) These half-day lessons are offered by the chef at the pretty Corte del Sole *agriturismo*, tucked between the baroque town of Noto and the beautiful coastline of the Riserva Naturale Oasi Faunistica di Vendicari.

Cheap Treats

Panelle Fried chickpea-flour fritters, often served in a sesame roll with *crocché* (fried potato dumplings made with cheese, parsley and eggs): find this classic Sicilian street food at Palermo's Friggitoria Chiluzzo (p65) or Mercato di Ballarò (p54).

Sfincione A spongy pizza-like Sicilian treat made with tomatoes, onions and (sometimes) anchovies; try it at I Banchi (p209) in Ragusa or Francu U Vastiddaru (p64) in Palermo.

Arancini Rice balls stuffed with meat or cheese, coated with breadcrumbs and fried; bite into a blissfully big one at Catania's Spinella (p174) or Palermo's Touring Café (p64).

Dare to Try

Pani ca muesa A roll filled with calf's spleen, *caciocavallo* cheese, a drizzle of hot lard and a squeeze of lemon juice; track it down at Rocky Basile's streetside cart in Mercato della Vucciria (p54), Palermo.

Stigghiola Seasoned and barbecued skewers of lamb or kid intestines, served from street-food stalls in Mercato della Vucciria (p54).

Spaghetti ai ricci Pasta in an orange-tinted sauce made from the reproductive organs of sea urchins; Ristorante Del Golfo (p90) in Castellammare del Golfo is a good place to try this.

'Mpanatigghi Sweet biscuits filled with chocolate, spices and – wait for it – minced beef! Taste them if you dare at Dolceria Bonajuto (p205) in Modica.

THE ARK OF TASTE

The Ark of Taste is an international catalogue of endangered food products drawn up by the Slow Food Foundation for Biodiversity. It aims to protect indigenous edibles threatened with extinction by industrialisation, globalisation, hygiene laws and environmental dangers, and actively encourages their cultivation for consumption. Foods included in the list must be culturally or historically linked to a specific region, locality, ethnicity or traditional production practice, and must also be rare. There are 38 Sicilian foods on the list, ranging from Pantelleria capers and Zibibbo grapes to Favignana tuna roe, Iblei Mountains thyme honey and the Etna silver goat. For a full list, go to www.slowfoodfoundation.com.

Local Specialities

Palermo

Snack in street markets on the local classic *pane e panelle* (a chickpea fritter sandwich with optional potato croquettes, fried aubergine and lemon), or sit down to a restaurant meal of *pasta con le sarde* (pasta with sardines, pine nuts, raisins and wild fennel) followed by *involtini di pesce spada* (thinly sliced swordfish fillets rolled up and filled with breadcrumbs, capers, tomatoes and olives).

Western Sicily

Savour this region's marked North African influence with a plate of *couscous di pesce alla trapanese* (fish couscous in a broth spiced with saffron, parsley and garlic) or a *bric* (savoury Tunisian pastry filled with tuna or shrimp). Top your pasta with *pesto alla trapanese* (made with fresh tomatoes, basil, garlic and almonds), and be sure to tour Marsala's world-renowned wine cellars.

Tyrrhenian Coast

Seafood is king along the coast, but some of the region's most interesting cuisine lies inland. The Madonie and Nebrodi Mountains are recognised throughout Sicily for their delicious hazelnuts, chestnuts, wild mushrooms, fresh sheep's milk ricotta,

Above: *Pasta alla Norma* (pasta topped with aubergine, basil, fresh ricotta and tomatoes)

Right: *Arancini* (deep-fried rice balls)

MICHELE TONINELLI/SHUTTERSTOCK ©

provola cheese and *suino nero* (pork from local black pigs).

Aeolian Islands

With seven islands to choose from, you'll never run out of seafood. You'll also want to try *pasta all'eoliana,* with a sauce that incorporates the islands' renowned capers and olives, and sip the smooth and sweet Malvasia dessert wine grown on verdant Salina island. Other local treats include *pane cunzato* (sandwiches piled high with tuna, ricotta, aubergine, capers and olives) and delicious *granita.*

Ionian Coast

Hit Catania for one of Sicily's most beloved first courses, *pasta alla Norma* (pasta topped with aubergine, basil, fresh ricotta and tomatoes), and if you're passing through Messina, don't miss *agghiotta di pesce spada* (swordfish with pine nuts, sultanas, capers, olives and tomatoes). Several other regional specialities are grown on Mt Etna's volcanic slopes, including Bronte pistachios, Zafferana Etnea honey and Etna DOC wine.

SICILIAN SWEET TREATS

Most traditional Sicilian dishes fall into the category of *cucina povera* (cooking of the poor), featuring cheap and plentiful ingredients such as pulses, vegetables and bread. Supplemented by fish (locally caught and still relatively inexpensive), this diet is still widely embraced today, but differs in one major respect to that of previous generations – the inclusion of decadent desserts.

The two most beloved are *cassata siciliana* (a mix of ricotta, sugar, candied fruit and chocolate that is flavoured with vanilla and maraschino liqueur, encased by sponge cake and topped with green icing) and *cannoli* (crisp tubes of fried pastry dough filled with creamy ricotta and sometimes decorated with a maraschino cherry, candied fruit, grated chocolate or ground nuts). You'll find both on restaurant menus across the island.

Syracuse & the Southeast

Celebrate the earthy flavours of the southeast with *macco di fave* (fava bean puree with wild fennel) or *lolli con le fave* (hand-rolled pasta with fava beans), and don't miss *ravioli di ricotta al sugo di maiale* (ricotta ravioli with a pork-meat *ragù*). The Syracuse region is famous for its lemons, blood oranges and tomatoes, and Ragusa is home to the excellent Ragusano DOP cheese. Local desserts include Modica's spiced chocolate creations and Noto's fine gelati.

Central Sicily

The only place in Sicily without a coastline: the interior hill towns around Enna build their menus around meat, sausages and wild game, accompanied by mushrooms and fresh vegetables such as fava beans and wild asparagus. If you're here in September or October, don't miss the region's delicious yellow-and-red-streaked Leonforte peaches.

Mediterranean Coast

Seafood takes centre stage along Sicily's southwestern shoreline, most notably in the busy fishing port of Sciacca. Inland, the region's sun-baked fields and orchards produce excellent almonds, Canicatta grapes, Ribera oranges and Nocellara del Belice olives.

How to Eat & Drink

When to Eat

Sicilians love to eat at virtually any time of day. The three set meals are interspersed with breaks for coffee, street snacks and early-evening *aperitivi.*

➡ *Colazione* (breakfast) – Many Sicilians eat the standard Italian breakfast of coffee with *cornetti* (croissants filled with cream or marmalade), *brioche* or *fette bicottate* (packaged dry toast), but they also enjoy a couple of sweet alternatives in summertime: *brioche e gelato* (a sweet roll filled with ice cream) and *granita con panna* (flavoured crushed ice, often topped with whipped cream).

➡ *Pranzo* (lunch) – Traditionally the biggest meal of the day, especially on Sundays. A full *pranzo* typically lasts at least two hours, with antipasti, a *primo* (first course), *secondo* (second course), *contorni* (side dishes), fruit, wine, water and dessert. Standard restaurant hours are from noon to 2.30pm, though most Sicilians eat after 1pm.

➡ *Aperitivi* (pre-dinner drink) – Sicilians enjoy post-work drinks between 5pm and 8pm, often at outdoor tables when weather permits. At many places, the price of your drink includes an offering of snacks.

➡ *Cena* (dinner) – The courses available at dinnertime are the same as at lunch, though you'll be hard-pressed to finish two meals of this size in a single day. In restaurants it's always perfectly permissible to order just a *primo* or *secondo*. Another less-substantial alternative is pizza, which is widely served in the evenings throughout Sicily. Standard restaurant hours are from 7.30pm to 11pm, though locals don't arrive in earnest until 9pm or later.

LOOK OUT FOR

➡ Interdonato lemons – natural hybrid of lemon and citron with a slightly bitter taste.

➡ Almonds from Noto – intense and aromatic nuts from ancient trees.

➡ Pistachios from Bronte – emerald-green nuts with an intense flavour and unctuous texture.

➡ Black pork from the Nebrodi Mountains – can be enjoyed in succulent ham, sausages and bacon.

➡ Capers from Salina – known for their firmness, perfume and uniform size.

➡ Ricotta infornata – ricotta cheese baked in a stone oven, eaten fresh or used for grating.

Where to Eat

Sicilian eateries range from the humblest of street-side stalls to top-of-the-line gourmet restaurants, with plenty of options in between. Here's a breakdown of the most common places to eat. Menus for most places are posted by the door.

➡ Trattoria – often family-run, this is a less formal restaurant serving regional specialities, with a focus on traditional pasta, fish and meat dishes. Many of Sicily's best eateries fall into this category.

➡ *Ristorante* (restaurant) – can be anything from a conservative hotel-based establishment with crisp white linen and formal service to a trendy up-and-coming eatery. Restaurants tend to serve a wider selection of dishes and charge higher prices than trattorias.

➡ *Osteria* – historically a tavern focused on wine, the modern version is usually an intimate, relaxed trattoria or wine bar offering a handful of dishes from a verbal menu.

➡ Pizzeria – a top place for a cheap feed, a cold beer and a buzzing, convivial vibe. Most open only at night.

➡ *Enoteca* (wine bar) – wines are the clear focus, but most places also serve a limited menu of deli-style snacks or simple meals.

➡ *Agriturismo* – in rural areas, this is an eatery on a country estate or working farm where much of the produce is cultivated on-site.

➡ *Friggitoria* – these street-food venues range from portable carts pushed through local markets to hole-in-the-wall eateries with small kitchens and limited, informal seating. The common denominator is the emphasis on simple fried snacks and the ultra-low prices, usually no more than a euro or two.

➡ *Tavola calda* (literally 'hot table') – a simple canteen-style eatery serving pre-prepared pasta, meat and vegetable dishes, along with snacks and *panini* (bread rolls with simple fillings).

➡ Bar-*caffè* – typically varying its functions depending on the time of day, a bar-*caffè* will serve coffee and *cornetti* (Italian croissants) in the morning, drinks in the afternoon and evening, and sweet and savoury snacks all day long. Many also serve ice cream.

➡ *Pasticceria* (pastry shop) – typically serves a wide selection of pastries and cakes, including classic Sicilian treats such as *cannoli* and *cassata*. Some have a *caffè* attached, others do not.

➡ *Gelateria* (ice-cream shop) – one of the best reasons to come to Sicily, generally with a vast rainbow of flavours. Don't miss *brioche e gelato* (ice cream served on a roll), a common Sicilian treat.

Menu Decoder

While tourist-oriented restaurants sometimes provide bilingual menus, you'll be better off learning some Italian food

'Mpanatigghi (Modican pastries stuffed with minced meat, almonds, chocolate, cloves and cinnamon)

terminology. Here are a few key terms that will help you decipher Sicilian menus.

➡ *Menu a la carte* – choose whatever you like from the menu.

➡ *Menu di degustazione* – tasting menu, usually consisting of six to eight 'tasting size' courses.

➡ *Menu turistico* – the dreaded 'tourist menu', a fixed-price, multicourse affair that often signals mediocre fare aimed at gullible tourists.

➡ *Piatto del giorno* – dish of the day.

➡ *Nostra produzione* or *fatta in casa* – made in-house, used to describe anything from pasta to olive oil to *liquori* (liqueurs).

➡ *Surgelato* – frozen, usually used to denote fish or seafood that has not been freshly caught.

➡ *Antipasti* – hot or cold appetisers; for a tasting plate of mixed appetisers, request an *antipasto misto.*

➡ *Primi* – first courses of pasta, rice, couscous or soup.

➡ *Secondi* – second courses of *pesce* (fish) or *carne* (meat).

➡ *Contorni* – side dishes of *verdura* (vegetables) or *insalata* (salad) intended to accompany your main course.

➡ *Dolci* – sweets (many Sicilian menus also use the English word dessert).

➡ *Frutta* – fresh fruit, served in more traditional eateries as the epilogue to your meal.

COFFEE, SICILIAN STYLE

Sicilians take their coffee seriously, and order it in the following ways.

Espresso A tiny cup of very strong black coffee; usually called a *caffè* or *caffè normale.*

Caffè macchiato An espresso with a dash of milk.

Cappuccino Espresso topped with hot foaming milk; only drunk at breakfast or in the mid-morning.

Caffè latte Coffee with milk that is steamed but not frothed; an extremely milky version is called a *latte macchiato* (stained milk); again, only drunk in the morning.

Caffè freddo The local version of an iced coffee.

Plan Your Trip

Outdoor Activities

With its favourable climate and gorgeous mix of landscapes, Sicily offers an appealing setting for outdoor activities. Whatever is on your personal wish list for a Mediterranean vacation – hiking, swimming, boating, diving, snorkelling, birdwatching, rock climbing – Sicily has what you're after.

Don't Miss Experiences

Diving & Snorkelling

Explore the underwater wonders of Lipari, Filicudi, Ustica or Isola Bella.

Volcano Viewing

Watch Stromboli's nocturnal fireworks from the summit or a boat, or teeter on the edges of Etna.

Birdwatching

Witness the annual passage of flamingos, herons and other migratory birds among the salt pools near Trapani.

Sailing Trips

Explore the coastlines, beaches and hidden coves around Syracuse and the Riserva Naturale dello Zingaro.

Guided Nature Walks

Climb into the Madonie Mountains above Cefalù to see traditional ricotta-making over an open wood fire.

Hiking

Aeolian Islands

The enchantment of the Aeolian Islands lies in the archipelago's strikingly diverse yet interconnected landscapes. Each of the seven volcanic islands has its own personality, with beautiful trails and tantalising views to its sister islands across the sea. Motorised traffic is limited everywhere (virtually nonexistent on some islands), making for some of Italy's most tranquil walking.

Highlights include the following:

Stromboli One of the world's classic volcano hikes, the guided trek up 924m Stromboli (p147) at sunset is a magical experience, with the crater's fireworks juxtaposed against the darkening sky.

Lipari Wildflower-strewn coastal bluffs drop abruptly into the Mediterranean on the spectacular Pianoconte to Quattropani (p136) hike.

Vulcano As much an olfactory as a visual experience, the climb to 391m Fossa di Vulcano (p140) brings you face-to-face with sulphurous fumes from the steaming crater, complemented by beautiful views of the other Aeolians lined up to the north.

Salina Climb through ferns and verdant pine forest to the Aeolians' highest point, Monte Fossa delle Felci (p143; 962m), enjoying magnificent views of vineyards, the Lingua salt lagoon, and the symmetrically arrayed cones of Filicudi and Alicudi.

Panarea Loop walks of varying length converge on Punta del Corvo (p146), Panarea's 421m summit.

Filicudi Take the easy 10-minute hike from the port to Filicudi's Bronze Age settlement, Villaggio Preistorico (p146), or the longer jaunt to the abandoned village of Zucco Grande (p153).

Alicudi For end-of-the-world tranquillity, jump ship at the Aeolians' westernmost island and follow the donkeys up stone staircases to Filo dell'Arpa (p154), where unbroken Mediterranean views stretch clear to the horizon.

Mount Etna

From Piano Provenzano (p181) on Etna's northern slopes, trails lead to Pizzi Deneri and the Volcanic Observatory at 2800m, or up to the main crater at 3200m. Both offer spectacular views of the Peloritani, Nebrodi and Madonie mountain ranges and the Valle del Bove. Further down, there's lovely walking in the pine, birch and larch trees of the Pineta Ragabo.

The ascent of the southern slopes begins at Rifugio Sapienza (p256; 1923m), from where you can take the Funivia dell'Etna (p181) cable car and walk 2km up to the volcano's four craters.

Madonie & Nebrodi Mountains

Revolving around the hulking mass of Pizzo Carbonara (1979m), the Monti Madonie (Madonie Mountains) are threaded with an extensive trail network. Walkers here enjoy remarkable solitude as they pass through oak-chestnut forests, stone-walled mountain villages and montane meadows where shepherds still make ricotta over wood fires. Highlights include the climb from Piano Battaglia to the summit of **Pizzo Carbonara**, the flower-strewn mountain meadows of **Piano Catarineci**, the **Sentiero degli Abies Nebrodensis**, which showcases the last 30 surviving examples of the critically endangered Sicilian fir, and the **Sentiero degli Agrifogli Giganti** with its centuries-old oaks and maples and giant (15m-high) holly bushes.

Spiaggia dei Conigli (p236), Lampedusa

TOP TREKS

Piano Battaglia (p123) Walk among wildflowers to the Madonie's highest peak.

Mt Etna (p181) Hike the picturesque slopes of Europe's most famous volcano.

Riserva Naturale dello Zingaro (p88) Visit museums of local culture as you hike the 7km coastal path north of Scopello.

Valle dell'Anapo (p196) Explore this dramatic limestone gorge pockmarked with Bronze Age and Iron Age necropolises.

Castello Punta Troia, Marettimo (p102) Zigzag along coastal bluffs from a whitewashed island village to a lonely castle dramatically perched atop a rocky outcrop.

Riserva Naturale Oasi Faunistica di Vendicari (p201) Scan for flamingos and roseate spoonbills as you navigate boardwalks through these gorgeous coastal wetlands.

East of the Madonie lie the Monti Nebrodi (Nebrodi Mountains), another sparsely populated landscape that is home to the *cavallo sanfratellano* (a horse once used by medieval Lombard knights, introduced to Sicily under the Normans). Centres of activity for hikers include the **Rocche del Crasto**, dramatic limestone peaks that rise steeply above the towns of Alcara Li Fusi and Longi, and a 70km section of the **Sentiero Italia** (Italy's 6166km national hiking trail).

Other Hiking

Prime spots for walking range from the Valle dell'Anapo and the Vendicari wetlands in southeastern Sicily to the Zingaro and Monte Cofano nature reserves and the island of Marettimo in western Sicily.

Organised Walks

Two excellent companies offering week-long guided walks with a strong Sicilian cultural component are Carmelina Ricciardello's Sicilian Experience (p119) and Anita Iaconangelo's **Italian Connection** (www.italian-connection.com). Other local agencies include Gruppo Guide Alpine Etna Nord (p181) and Gruppo Guide Alpine Etna Sud (p183) on Mt Etna, Nesos (p136) in the Aeolian Islands, Natura Sicula (p199) in Syracuse and Vai Col Trekking Sicilia (p124) in the Nebrodi Mountains.

Diving & Snorkelling

Ustica

Divers from around the world come to explore Ustica's magnificent underwater sites. The island's western shores are home to a protected marine reserve, which is divided into three zones. Highlights include the underwater archaeological trail off **Punta Cavazzi**, where artefacts including anchors and Roman amphorae can be admired. Other popular dive sites are the **Scoglio del Medico**, an outcrop of basalt riddled with caves and gorges that plunge to great depths; and **Secca di Colombara**, a magnificent rainbow-coloured display of sponges and gorgonias.

The island's many dive centres organise itineraries and hire out equipment.

Aeolian Islands

There are good dives off most of the Aeolians, with some of the best surrounding the main island of Lipari. Another highlight is the Museo Archeologico Sottomarino area off Filicudi, where the sunken wrecks of nine ancient Greek and Roman ships provide fabulous diving opportunities.

Diving operators in the Aeolians include La Gorgonia (p136) on Lipari, Saracen (p141) on Vulcano, Amphibia (p146) on Panarea, La Sirenetta (p150) on Stromboli and Apogon (p153) and I Delfini (p153) on Filicudi.

Other Diving & Snorkelling

About an hour west of Palermo, the Riserva Naturale dello Zingaro is great for diving. Cetaria Diving Centre (p85) in Scopello organises guided dives in the waters off the nature reserve between April and October, visiting underwater caves and shipwrecks; it also offers boat excursions with snorkelling.

Near Taormina, the WWF-protected reserve of Isola Bella (p164) also has some good diving. Nike Diving Centre (p164) offers diving equipment and lessons, along with snorkelling excursions and stand-up paddleboarding.

Beaches & Swimming

With 14 offshore islands and nearly 1500km of coastline on the Ionian, Tyrrhenian and Mediterranean Seas, Sicily has beaches for every taste. The deep blue, turquoise and emerald-green waters that lap the shoreline are clean and warm throughout the summer and autumn months, with swimming conditions at their best from June through early October. Beaches range from pebbly to sandy, and from crowded bathing *lidos* where you can rent sun loungers and umbrellas to expanses of nearly deserted sand.

BEST BEACHES

San Vito Lo Capo (p85) Join the sun worshippers by the electric turquoise waters of this perennial summer holiday destination.

Spiaggia dei Conigli (p236) This sandy beauty in the remote Pelagic Islands regularly wins awards as one of the world's finest beaches.

Scala dei Turchi (p237) A dazzling white outcropping shaped like a staircase, with beaches on either side, perfect for wading or diving off the rocks.

Spiaggia di Cefalù (p114) A lovely, family-friendly expanse of sand backed by a dramatic promontory and one of Sicily's prettiest medieval towns.

Torre Salsa (p237) Perfect for fans of wild, unspoiled coastline, this off-the-beaten-track gem is part of a WWF-administered nature reserve.

Isola Bella (p164) Facing the island preserve of the same name, this pebbly beach below Taormina is tucked into a supremely picturesque cove.

Sailing & Kayaking

Boat trips of all kinds can be organised along Sicily's coast and in the outer islands.

Sailing Team (p192) explores the beaches and nature reserves south of Syracuse by sailboat.

Buena Vida (www.buenavida.it) San Vito Lo Capo–based company that runs sailing and other boat excursions to the Riserva Naturale dello Zingaro and the Egadi Islands.

Sicily in Kayak (p141) offers kayaking tours around Vulcano and the other Aeolians, ranging from half a day to an entire week. A number of other operators on the Aeolians organise round-the-island and inter-island boat trips exploring the islands' sea grottoes and secluded swimming spots.

Birdwatching

Given its prime position on the migratory flight path between Africa and Europe, Sicily is a great place for birdwatching. Spring (April) and autumn (September) are the best seasons.

Several companies offer birdwatching tours in Sicily, including the UK-based **Nature Trek** (www.naturetrek.co.uk) and **Limosa Holidays** (www.limosaholidays.co.uk).

Hot spots here include the following:

Riserva Naturale Oasi Faunistica di Vendicari (p201) The wetlands are home to flamingos, herons, spoonbills, cranes, ducks, cormorants and collared pratincoles.

Riserva Naturale dello Zingaro (p88) This nature reserve has more than 40 species, including the rare Bonelli eagle, hawks, buzzards, kestrels, swifts and Imperial crows, as well as the endemic 'Greek Partridge of Sicily'.

Parco Regionale dei Nebrodi (p124) The park has some 150 species of birds, among them endemic species such as the Sicilian marshtit, birds

Above: Hiking, Vulcano (p140)

Right: Sailboats and kayakers on the water near Syracuse (p185)

BATHE YOURSELF IN MUD

People spend many euros on beauty treatments, but Sicilians only have to hop over to the island of Vulcano or the beach of Eraclea Minoa to dip into a healing, beautifying and overall health-enforcing mud bath.

Vulcano's Laghetto di Fanghi (p140) is a large pool of gloopy, sulphurous mud that has long been considered excellent treatment for skin disorders and arthritis. Get your oldest bikini on (the smell of sulphur will *never* leave the fabric) and relax for a while – apply a mud face mask while you're at it. Finish off with a natural spa bath (hot bubbling springs in a small natural seawater pool).

Across the island, near Agrigento, you'll see green people emerging from the beach of Eraclea Minoa. Sunbathers here flock to the beach's natural mud rock, scraping the mud and spreading it all over their bodies and faces – a wonderful natural skin treatment. Let it dry on your skin and wash it off with a refreshing swim in the sea. What could be better?

of prey including buzzards, kestrels, peregrine falcons and golden eagles, and wetland species such as grebes, coots, dippers and the kingfishers.

Mozia (p98) This tiny island is a haven for many species, including flamingos, herons, storks and cranes, as well as grey herons.

Lingua (p143) Salina's lagoon attracts huge numbers of migrating birds in April; scores of Eleonora's falcons *(Falco eleonorae)* return to nest here.

Cycling

There's no great cycling tradition in Sicily, and you'll see far fewer cyclists here than in northern Italy. Still, it can be a great way to see the countryside, particularly in spring and autumn when the weather is not too hot. Some cities, including Syracuse and Noto, have recently instituted low-cost bike sharing systems, and cycling is also an excellent way of getting around offshore islands such as Favignana, where there are numerous rental outlets.

Given the lack of infrastructure for cyclists, one attractive option is to join an organised tour. Sicilian agencies include Etna Touring (p182), which leads mountain-bike trips on Mt Etna, and Agrigento-based **Coast2Coast** (www.coast2coast.it), which offers a variety of road- and mountain-bike trips throughout Sicily. International companies offering weeklong bike tours in Sicily include **Backroads** (www.backroads.com), **VBT** (www.vbt.com) and **Butterfield & Robinson** (www.butterfield.com).

Rock Climbing

Arrampicata (climbing) is increasingly popular in Siciy. San Vito Lo Capo is the island's rock-climbing capital, luring climbers with its variety of challenging crags and the San Vito Climbing Festival (p88), a four-day event held annually in mid-October. Other leading destinations include Mt Etna, the limestone pinnacles of Rocche di Crasto in the Nebrodi Mountains, and multiple sites in the Madonie Mountains including Monte D'Oro outside Collesano, La Rocca di Sciara near Caltavuturo, Rocca di Sant'Otiero near Petralia Sottana and Passo Scuro outside Castelbuono.

Skiing

Sicily will never compete with the Alps or even the Appenines as a ski destination, but for curiosity value, there's nothing like hitting the slopes at the island's two ski mountains, Mt Etna and Monte Mufara in the Monti Madonie.

You can ski Mt Etna (both downhill and cross-country) between December and March. There are five pistes at Nicolosi Nord on Etna's southern slopes and seven at Linguaglossa on the northern side. For details, see www.etnasci.it.

At Piano Battaglia (www.pianobattaglia.it), in the heart of the Madonie Mountains, Sicily's other ski area operates annually from January to mid-March. The twin slopes of Mufara and Mufaretta offer 4km of runs, all served by a pair of ski lifts newly revamped in 2015.

Plan Your Trip

Travel with Children

Few places are as friendly to children as Sicily. Families are welcomed at restaurants, cafes and hotels, and staff are generally diligent in accommodating your needs. Family-friendly attractions abound (beaches, ice-cream shops, puppet theatres), and you'll benefit from family discounts on transport along with free children's admission at many sites.

Best Regions for Kids

Aeolian Islands

Island-hopping by boat will appeal to the explorer in any kid – as will climbing Stromboli's steaming cone for a nightly dose of volcanic fireworks.

Southeastern Sicily

Flamingos along the Vendicari coast and Sicilian puppet shows with funny battle scenes will captivate kids of all ages, while open spaces like Syracuse's Piazza del Duomo help squirmy toddlers get the wiggles out.

Tyrrhenian Coast

Long sandy beaches at Cefalù make for happy family times, and the steeply perched Norman castle at Caccamo is perfect for medieval role-playing.

Western Sicily

Enjoy stress-free beach days swimming and cycling on Favignana, discover ancient cave art on Levanzo, or ride the funicular up to Erice to sample sugary almond sweets.

Ionian Coast

Whether you're splashing on the beach below Taormina, climbing Europe's tallest

Practical Tips

When to Go

Spring, early summer and autumn are generally best for families with small children. High summer temperatures can make life miserable for little ones – although good beaches and the occasional gelato should make this more bearable.

Before You Go

- Car seats for infants and children are available from most car-rental firms, but you should always book them in advance.
- Stock up on sun cream even in spring and autumn, when it can still be quite warm in Sicily.
- Insect repellent (especially for mosquitoes) is highly recommended.
- For more information see Lonely Planet's *Travel with Children* book.

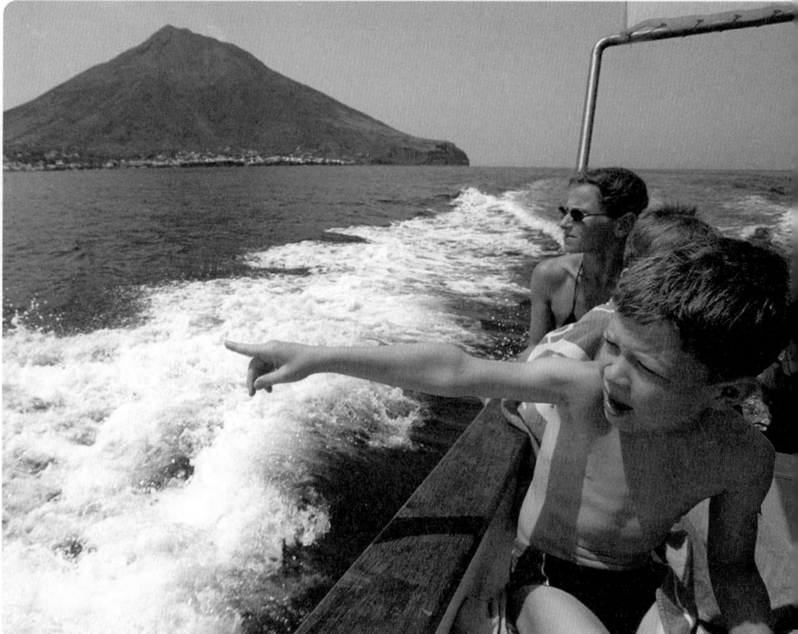

Children on a boat near Stromboli (p147)

volcano or getting grossed out by giant fish heads in Catania's market, the Ionian Coast creates lasting memories for everyone.

Sicily for Kids

Dining Out

Eating in Sicily should be a breeze. In restaurants, high chairs are usually available and it's perfectly acceptable to order a *mezza porzione* (half portion) off the normal menu for little ones. Even the fussiest of kids will enjoy the island's abundant fresh fruit, savoury snacks like *arancine* (fried, stuffed rice balls) or basics like pizza and pasta with a tomato sauce – while more adventurous eaters will be able to 'expand' their palate with varied seafood, fish, meat and veggie dishes. Gelati, *granite* (crushed ice with various flavours) and the many fantastic Sicilian *dolci* (desserts) will be fought over by the entire family.

Attractions

Sicily and its smaller offshore islands offer plenty of ways to keep the family engaged, be it the mix of history and nature at the Valley of the Temples in Agrigento, the many beaches and islands, vibrant street markets at Palermo and Catania, or a simple *passeggiata* (evening stroll) with the locals, ice cream in hand. Teenagers will be able to break up lazy days with swimming and organised boat trips, while activity-seeking families have three volcanoes to climb and lots of snorkelling and diving options. Norman castles and ancient ruins are scattered around the island and are ripe for exploration.

Entertainment

Away from the beaches, smaller kids can be kept entertained at the local main square – the piazzas are usually equipped with fun rides and, well, other kids! Traditional puppet shows are a great way to introduce your children to local culture – it helps if they're into battles!

Safety

While it's generally safe for kids to run around small town squares, keep an eye on the scooters that sometimes zip in and out – pedestrian areas are something of a relative concept in Sicily.

Family-Friendliness

Family life is highly valued in Sicily. Babies will be cooed over, and children of all ages will generally be welcomed. Breastfeeding is common, and attitudes are relaxed.

Children's Highlights

Desserts

Gelateria Ciccio Adelfio (p65), Palermo Everyone loves gelato, especially for breakfast, when it's served in a sweet bun at classic shops like this one!

Da Alfredo (p144), Salina, Aeolian Islands On a hot day, there's nothing yummier and more refreshing than a *granita*, topped with a dollop of whipped cream just for fun.

La Rinascente (p93), Trapani Meet the *cannoli*-maker and watch him fill yours on the spot as you anticipate that first crunchy, creamy bite.

In & On the Water

Spiaggia di Cefalù (p114) For sheer family fun in the sun, this long sandy beach east of Palermo is hard to beat.

Ustica (p82), Palermo Region Water-loving families and older kids and teenagers can snorkel and dive to their heart's desire on this island just off Palermo.

Scala dei Turchi (p237) Young kids can frolic in the shallow water near Agrigento.

Grotta del Bue Marino (p43), Filicudi Visit this spectacular sea grotto by boat.

The Outdoors

Stromboli Crater (p147), Aeolian Islands A glimpse of Stromboli's glowing innards on a night climb is any kid's fairy-tale vision of a volcano come true.

Fossa di Vulcano (p140), Aeolian Islands Follow the pongy path to this steaming, sulphur-spewing crater, known to the Romans as Vulcan's forge.

Castello di Caccamo (p118) Storm the ramparts of this and other Norman castles across the island.

Ruins of Selinunte (p108) This sprawling ruined city has temples, piles of ancient rubble and wide open spaces for kids to explore, plus a beach just below.

Azienda Agrituristica Bergi (p249), Castelbuono Enjoy animals, swimming pools and lots of space while overnighting at this and other *agriturismi* (farm stays) around the island.

Arts & Sicilian Culture

Piccolo Teatro dei Pupi (p192), Syracuse Watch brave knights defeat evil monsters in a traditional puppet play.

Farm Cultural Park (p233), Favara Creative teens will appreciate the edgy installations at this unique artists' community.

Villa Romana del Casale (p222), Piazza Armerina At this ancient Roman hunting villa, mosaics of lions, tigers and youthful gymnasts will capture many young imaginations.

Passeggiata Search out carousels, cafes and convivial company of every age during the evening stroll.

What to Expect

- Admission to many cultural sites is free for under-10s or under-18s (particularly EU citizens).
- On trains, the *offerta familia* allows a discount of 50% for children under 15 and 20% for other family members if you are travelling in a group of two to five people (see www.trenitalia.com for conditions).
- You can stock up on nappies, baby formula and sterilising solutions at pharmacies and supermarkets.
- Fresh cow's milk is sold in bars that have a '*Latteria*' sign and in supermarkets.

ACCOMMODATION

Generally, apartment rental is easy to find and works best for families who want to self-cater. Many hotels and *pensioni* (guesthouses) offer reduced rates for children or will add an extra bed or cot on request (usually for an extra 30% or so). *Agriturismi* (farmstays) are excellent for children because they're always in a natural setting, with big gardens and fields around them, and usually have an animal or two on site.

Regions at a Glance

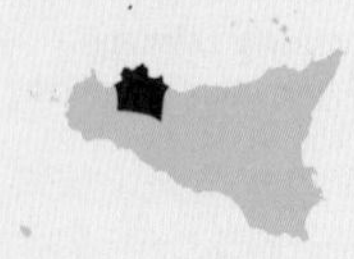

Palermo

Art & Architecture
Food
Nightlife

Cultural Treasure Chest

Palermo has everything from Byzantine mosaics to Arab-Norman palaces to exuberant rococo chapels. This city is full of surprises: verses from the Koran scrawled on church columns, Arabic marble inlay beside glimmering images of an all-powerful Christ, and baroque domes atop medieval foundations.

Culinary Capital

From appetisers such as *sarde in beccafico* (pine-nut-and-raisin-stuffed sardines rolled in breadcrumbs) to the world's most scrumptious *cannoli,* every menu page is worth lingering over. Don't limit yourself to restaurants – stroll through the city's bustling markets and discover its superb street food.

Puppets & Prima Donnas

Nights out in Palermo can mean many things: live music at one of Italy's great opera houses, medieval tales performed by exquisite hand-crafted puppets, an evening soak in a Moorish steam bath, or bar-hopping the buzzing late-night streets.

p48

Western Sicily

History
Outdoors
Food & Wine

Ancient Eyries

For an idyllic natural setting, few ruins can match Segesta and Selinunte; where hilltop temples sit in splendid, moody isolation, peeking through fields of tall grass and wildflowers. Erice's Norman castle comes close, though, perched on a spectacular hilltop that's been coveted by everyone from the Phoenicians to the ancient Greeks.

Fun in the Sun

Whether you're climbing San Vito's crags, hiking the trails of Marettimo and the Zingaro, or cycling and sunbathing on Favignana, western Sicily offers endless supplies of outdoorsy fun.

Saracen Seasonings

North African influences have always been close at hand in western Sicily, as reflected in the seductively spiced fish couscous that appears on every menu. Some of Sicily's finest wines are also produced here, most notably around Marsala and Erice.

p84

Tyrrhenian Coast

Beaches
Hill Towns
Food

Sea & Sand

Dotted with pretty resort towns such as Cefalù and Castel di Tusa, the Tyrrhenian Coast becomes a jam-packed beach playground every summer.

Mountain Retreats

Old stone villages like Castelbuono, Mistretta and Petralia Sottana hunker down against the Nebrodi and Madonie Mountains' high slopes, offering a welcome home base to outdoors enthusiasts who are increasingly discovering the region's charms.

Fabulous Fungi

Kiss seafood goodbye and prepare to be impressed by the entirely different cuisine of the Nebrodi and Madonie Mountains. Wild mushrooms and roast meats, notably from the indigenous *suino nero* (black pig), are mainstays of the menu, as are local hazelnuts, chestnuts, ricotta and *provola* cheese.

p111

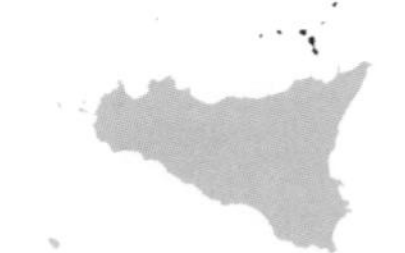

Aeolian Islands

Outdoors
Food & Wine
Volcanoes

Natural Paradise

If stunning coastal beauty is your idea of paradise, you've come to the right place. Each of the seven Aeolians has its own natural charms, with enough diving, swimming, kayaking, walking and climbing to satisfy outdoors enthusiasts of all stripes.

Island Flavours

Fresh seafood figures prominently in the Aeolians' divine cuisine, along with local capers and olives. The island of Salina is famous for its honey-sweet Malvasia wine, available at shops and restaurants throughout the archipelago.

Smoke & Fire

Yes, most of the Aeolians' volcanoes are now extinct. But Vulcano and Stromboli just keep on smoking, the former luring visitors with its therapeutic mud baths, the latter with its awe-inspiringly fiery eruptions.

p129

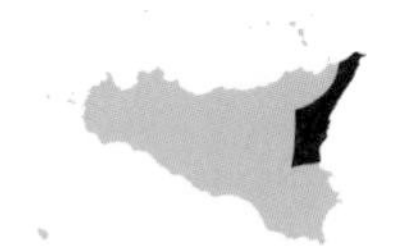

Ionian Coast

Volcanoes
Festivals
Food & Wine

Volcano Views

Mt Etna's spellbinding form dominates this stretch of coast from every imaginable angle, looming on the horizon at the end of Catania's busy boulevards, peeking through the stage at Taormina's Greek theatre, providing four-season outdoor recreation and feeding local agriculture with its fertile volcanic soil.

Fabulous Festivals

This place really knows how to throw a party. Taormina buzzes all summer long with world-class festivals of film, theatre, music and dance, while winter revellers are lured into the streets by Acireale's Carnevale and Catania's massive Festa di Sant'Agata.

Markets & Vineyards

Foodies will find plenty to love in this corner of Sicily, from the acclaimed Etna DOC wine to Catania's colourful fish and produce markets.

p155

Syracuse & the Southeast

Architecture
History
Food

Baroque Beauty

Devastated by a 1693 earthquake, southeastern Sicily's hill towns rose like a phoenix from the ashes, adopting the appealing baroque aesthetic you see today in the Unesco-listed towns of Noto, Modica, Ragusa and their smaller sisters throughout the southeast.

Ancient Greek Echoes

Modern-day Syracuse still glows with the glory of its Greek past, in the repurposed temple columns of Ortygia's cathedral, the papyrus-fringed pool at the heart of town and the cycle of Greek dramas that still draws crowds to the city's ancient amphitheatre each summer.

Sweet Temptations

From Modica's chocolates to Noto's *granite* (crushed ice made with various flavours) to the wine-flavoured ice creams of Ragusa, this is a region that any sweet tooth will love.

p184

Central Sicily

Hill Towns
History
Shopping

Norman Strongholds

Bearing traces of their Norman past, Central Sicily's hill towns float like islands in the sky above the surrounding landscape. The regional capital of Enna lords over them all from its prime position at Sicily's geographic centre.

Roman Splendour

The world's most extensive and best-preserved late-Roman mosaic floors are shining brighter than ever thanks to recent renovations. Look for them in the ancient Villa Romana del Casale outside Piazza Armerina.

Ceramics Central

Ceramics lovers beware! Caltagirone's dozens of artisans' shops, ceramics museum, and whimsical 142-step staircase covered top to bottom in hand-painted tiles may seduce you into an acquisitive frenzy.

p212

Mediterranean Coast

History
Beaches
Food

Transcendent Temples

Agrigento's unparalleled array of ancient temples, coupled with the superb collection of artefacts at the nearby archaeological museum, constitutes Sicily's greatest classical legacy.

White Cliffs, Wild Sands

Stellar beach-going spots dot the coast west of Agrigento, including the long, unspoiled shoreline of Riserva Naturale Torre Salsa, the golden sands of Eraclea Minoa and the stunning white rock formation called Scala dei Turchi, at its best when illuminated by the setting sun.

Superb Seafood

You can eat well all along this coast, but at no place better than Sciacca, where seafood is delivered straight from the boat into the kitchens of the many port-side restaurants.

p227

On the Road

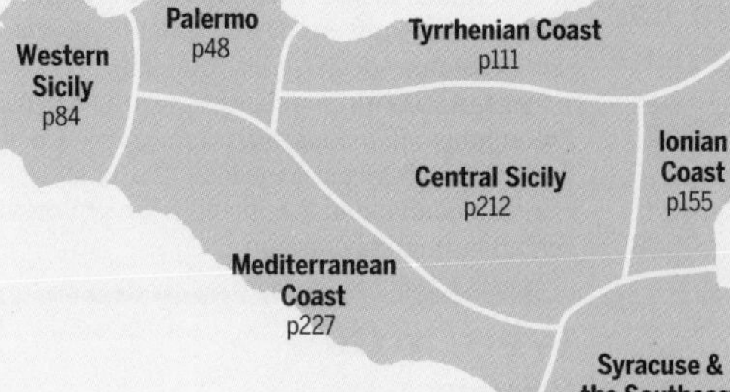

Aeolian Islands
p129
Palermo
p48
Western
Sicily
p84
Tyrrhenian Coast
p111
Ionian
Coast
p155
Central Sicily
p212
Mediterranean
Coast
p227
Syracuse &
the Southeast
p184

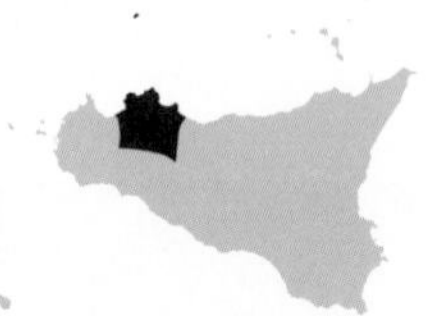

Palermo

Includes ➡

Best Places to Eat

- Bisso Bistrot (p64)
- Trattoria al Vecchio Club Rosanero (p64)
- Gagini (p66)
- Il Maestro del Brodo (p66)
- Trattoria Ai Cascinari (p64)

Best Places to Sleep

- BB22 Palace (p246)
- Stanze al Genio Residenze (p246)
- B&B Amelie (p246)
- Butera 28 (p246)
- Grand Hotel Piazza Borsa (p247)

Why Go?

Flamboyant, guarded, feisty yet staunchly aristocratic, Palermo is a seething mass of contradictions. Pock-marked buildings, broken pavements and decrepit infrastructure reveal deep political and economic cracks, and yet all are easy to overlook when you enter a church full of luminously beautiful Byzantine mosaics, wander along a street of stately baroque *palazzi* (palaces) or eavesdrop on the genial banter between canny stall owners and bargain-hunting housewives at a street market. Palermo is a cryptic creature, a city where nefarious neglect and soul-stirring beauty have always linked arms, where preconceptions are concurrently affirmed and subverted, where light and shade stir impressions that bury deep under your skin.

Beyond Palermo is a string of worthy day-trip destinations. Among these is the mosaicked magnificence of Monreale Cathedral, beach-loving Mondello, the pristine marine reserve of Ustica island, and the inland town of Corleone, home to a defiant anti-mafia museum.

When to Go

Palermo

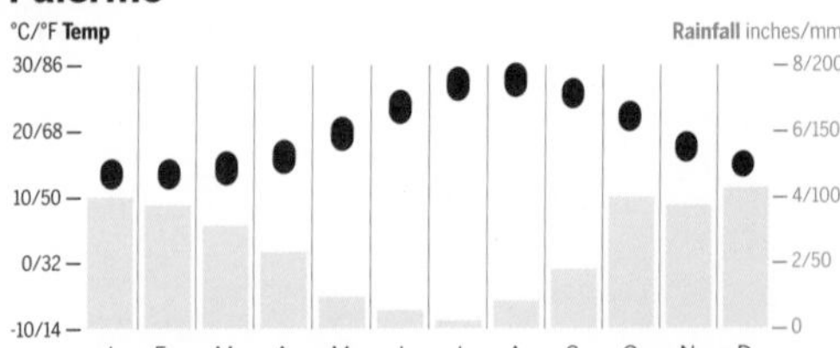

Apr & May Lower prices and pleasant weather combine to make springtime a perfect season for visiting Palermo.

July Join the throngs in celebration of Santa Rosalia. Summer performances fill the open-air Teatro di Verdura.

Sep & Oct Optimal late-season diving conditions without the crowds in the crystal-clear waters off Ustica.

Palermo Highlights

1 Cappella Palatina (p53) Basking in Palermo's heady multicultural past amid Byzantine mosaics and Arabic marble-work.

2 Teatro Massimo (p67) Demanding an encore at one of Europe's opera house belles.

3 Mercato di Ballarò (p54) Diving into a gut-rumbling torrent of buxom produce, heady aromas and hollering market vendors.

4 Museo Archeologico Regionale (p61) Pondering the art and tastes of the ancients at this archaeological treasure trove.

5 Galleria Regionale della Sicilia (p56) Catching up on centuries of Sicilian art in a magnificent *palazzo*.

6 Orto Botanico (p60) Finding refuge from the traffic and crowds among trees and sleepy cats in this raffish oasis.

7 Museo delle Maioliche (p57) Enjoying a private tour of rare and precious maiolica tiles at this under-the-radar treasure.

PALERMO

☎091 / POP 678,500

For millennia at the crossroads of civilisations, Palermo delivers a heady, heavily spiced mix of Byzantine mosaics, Arabesque domes and frescoed cupolas. This is a city at the edge of Europe and at the centre of the ancient world, a place where souk-like markets rub against baroque churches, where date palms frame Gothic palaces and where the blue-eyed and fair have bronze-skinned cousins.

Centuries of dizzying highs and crushing lows have formed a complex metropolis. Here, crumbling staircases lead to gilded ballrooms and guarded locals harbour hearts of gold. Just don't be fooled. Despite its noisy streets, Sicily's largest city is a shy beast, rewarding the inquisitive with citrus-filled cloisters, stucco-laced chapels and vintage stores filled with the threads of faded aristocrats. Add to this Italy's biggest opera house and an ever-growing number of vibrant, new-school eateries and bars and you might just find yourself suddenly, unexpectedly in love.

Sights

Palermo has its share of engaging museums, historic palaces and richly decorated churches, most of which lie in the historic neighbourhoods of La Kalsa, Vucciria, Il Capo and Albergheria. This said, Palermo's most uplifting and engaging experiences come from simply walking through these neighbourhoods' streets and their jumble of patchwork architecture, unexpected piazzas and street markets.

Most museums offer a discounted entry price for EU citizens under the age of 18.

Around the Quattro Canti

The busy intersection **Quattro Canti** (Four Corners), marks the centre of the old city. Just off it are a handful of must-see sights, in particular the 16th-century Fontana Pretoria and 12th-century church of La Martorana.

Quattro Canti MONUMENT

(Piazza Vigliena; Map p58) Officially titled Piazza Vigliena, the elegant intersection of Corso Vittorio Emanuele and Via Maqueda is better known as the Quattro Canti. Marking the epicentre of the old city, the junction is framed by a perfect circle of curvi-linear facades that disappear up to the blue vault of the sky in a clever display of perspective. Each facade lights up in turn throughout the course of the day, landing it the nickname *Il Teatro del Sole* (Theatre of the Sun).

Echoing the style of late-Renaissance Rome and constructed in the early 17th century, the Quattro Canti's four symmetrical facades are the work of royal architect Giulio Lasso. Each corner is divided in three classical orders: Doric at the bottom, Ionic in the middle and Composite at the top. The decorative elements were left in the capable hands of architect Mariano Smiriglio, whose other projects in town include the baroque reworking of the **Chiesa di Santa Maria di Valverde** (Map p58; Largo Cavalieri di Malta; ⏲9am-1pm Mon-Sat). Statues adorn each of the three tiers, representing the seasons at the bottom, Spanish sovereigns in the middle, and female Palermitan saints at the top.

La Martorana CHURCH

(Chiesa di Santa Maria dell'Ammiraglio; Map p58; ☎345 8288231; Piazza Bellini 3; adult/reduced €2/1; ⏲9.30am-1pm & 3.30-5.30pm Mon-Sat, 9-10.30am Sun) On the southern side of Piazza Bellini, this luminously beautiful 12th-century church was endowed by King Roger's Syrian emir, George of Antioch, and was originally planned as a mosque. Delicate Fatimid pillars support a domed cupola depicting Christ enthroned amid his archangels. The interior is best appreciated in the morning, when sunlight illuminates magnificent Byzantine mosaics.

In 1433 the church was given over to an aesthetically challenged order of Benedictine nuns – founded by Eloisa Martorana, hence its nickname – who tore down the Norman apse, reworked the exterior in a fussy baroque fashion and demolished most of the stunning mosaics executed by Greek artisans, replacing them with the gaudy baroque ornamentation of their own frescoed chapel. The few remaining original mosaics include two magnificent portraits, one representing George of Antioch, crouched behind a shield at the feet of the Virgin Mary, and one of Roger II receiving his crown from Christ (the only portrait of him to survive in Sicily).

Mussolini returned the church to the Greek Orthodox community in 1935, and Greek Mass is still celebrated here.

★**Fontana Pretoria** SQUARE

(Map p58; Piazza Pretoria) Fringed by imposing churches and buildings, Piazza Pretoria is dominated by the over-the-top Fontana

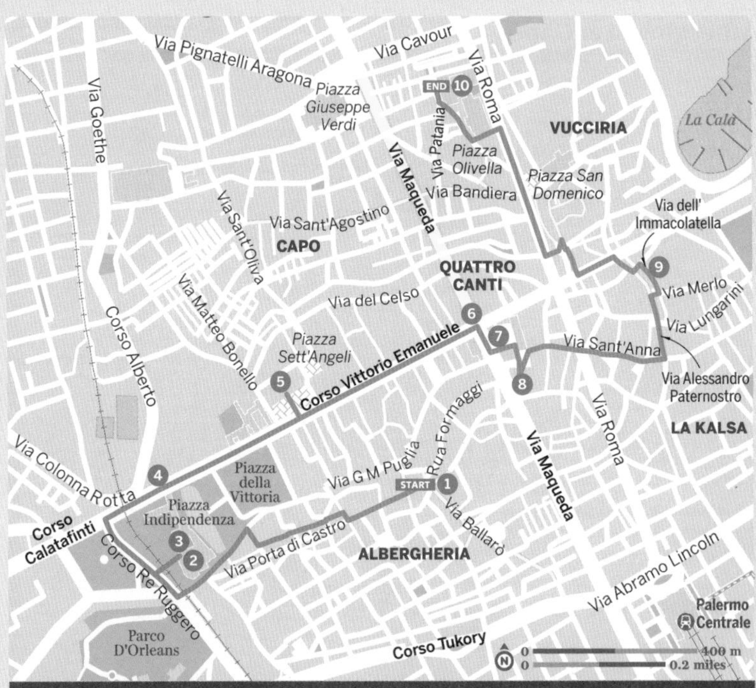

City Walk Historic Palermo

START MERCATO DI BALLARÒ
END MUSEO ARCHEOLOGICO REGIONALE
LENGTH 4.2KM; SIX TO SEVEN HOURS

Dense but compact, central Palermo is best explored on foot. This tour covers some of the city's most enticing assets.

Pique your appetite with an early morning trundle through the 1 **Mercato di Ballarò** (p54) then head west along Via Porta di Castro to the sparkling 2 **Cappella Palatina** (p53) and adjoining 3 **Palazzo dei Normanni** (p53). Head back east along Corso Vittorio Emanuele, through the Mannerist-style city gate of 4 **Porta Nuova** to the architectural fusion that is the 5 **Cattedrale di Palermo** (p55). The cathedral's finest quality is its exterior, so take it in and continue further east on Corso Vittorio Emanuele; when you hit the intersection with Via Maqueda you're at the 6 **Quattro Canti** (p50), Palermo's most beautiful junction. If you're feeling peckish or thirsty, Bisso Bistro awaits at its northwest corner.

Replenished, head south on Via Maqueda to 7 **Piazza Pretoria** (p50) and its epic Tuscan fountain. Exit the square from its southeast corner to reach Piazza Bellini and its cross-cultural architectural mash-up. It's here that you'll find 12th-century 8 **La Martorana** (p50) and its glittering Byzantine mosaics. Take time to appreciate their mastery before continuing east on Discesa dei Giudici. Cross busy Via Roma, continue east on Via Sant'Anna, turning left into Via Paternostro. The street passes pretty Piazza San Francesco d'Assisi. Look into the 16th-century 9 **Oratorio di San Lorenzo** (p57), adorned with the remarkable rococo stuccowork of Giacomo Serpotta before continuing north on Via Paternostro to Corso Vittorio Emanuele. Cross the street and continue north on Via Pannieri. The street spills into a small square that's home to the morning Mercato della Vucciria, famously depicted in Renato Guttuso's 1974 painting *La Vucciria*, now housed in Palermo's Museo dell'Inquisizione. Ascend the steps alongside Chiesa di Sant'Antonio to Via Roma and end your saunter at the nearby 10 **Museo Archeologico Regionale** (p61), home to one of southern Italy's finest classical art collections.

Albergheria & Capo

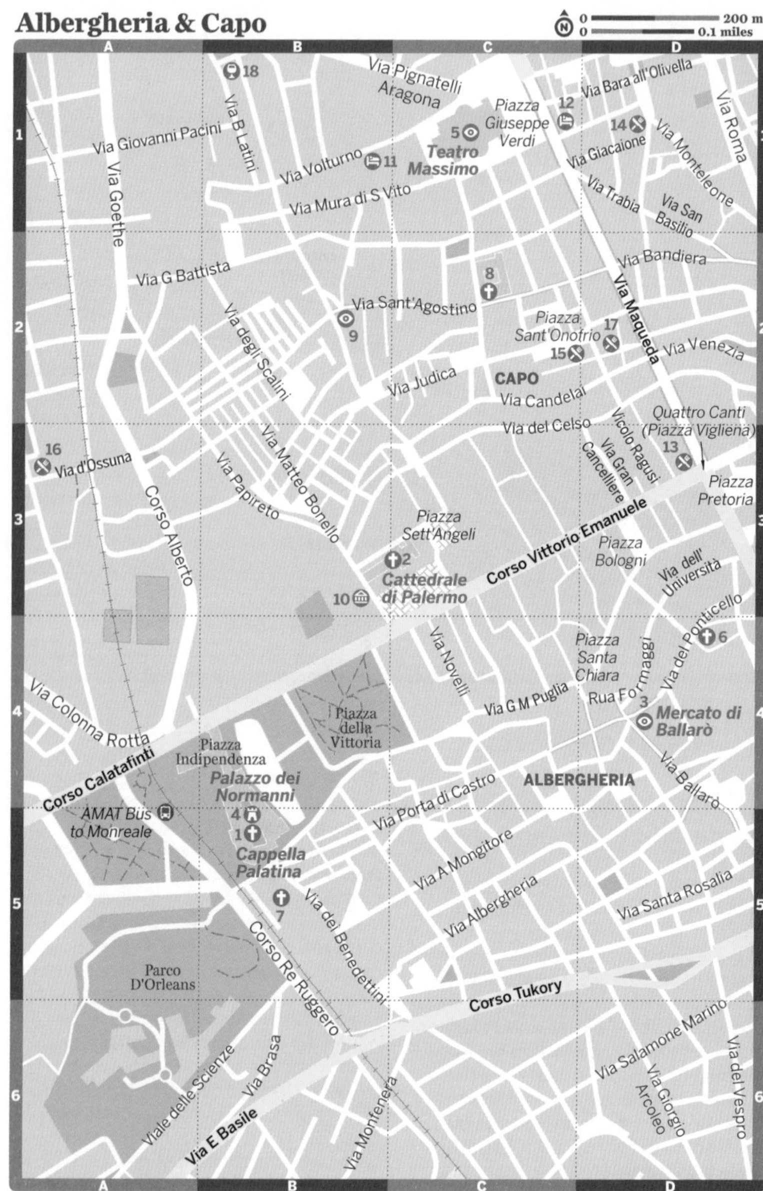

Pretoria, one of Palermo's major landmarks. The fountain's tiered basins ripple out in concentric circles, crowded with nude nymphs, tritons and leaping river gods. Such flagrant nudity proved a bit much for Sicilian churchgoers, who prudishly dubbed it the Fontana della Vergogna (Fountain of Shame).

Designed by the Florentine sculptor Francesco Camilliani between 1554 and 1555 for the Tuscan villa of Don Pedro di Toledo, the fountain was bought by Palermo in 1573

Albergheria & Capo

Top Sights
1 Cappella Palatina B5
2 Cattedrale di Palermo C3
3 Mercato di Ballarò D4
4 Palazzo dei Normanni B5
5 Teatro Massimo C1

Sights
6 Chiesa del Gesù D4
7 Chiesa di San Giovanni degli Eremiti B5
8 Chiesa di Sant'Agostino C2
9 Mercato del Capo B2
10 Museo Diocesano di Palermo B3

Sleeping
11 A Casa di Amici B&B B1
12 Massimo Plaza Hotel C1

Eating
13 Bisso Bistrot D3
14 FUD D1
15 Pizzeria Frida C2
16 Trattoria Ai Cascinari A3
17 Trattoria al Vecchio Club Rosanero D2

Drinking & Nightlife
18 Enoteca Butticè B1

Entertainment
Teatro Massimo .... (see 5)

and proudly positioned in front of the Palazzo Pretorio (Municipal Hall) in a bid to outshine the newly crafted Fontana di Orione installed in Messina.

Chiesa Capitolare di San Cataldo CHURCH
(Map p58; Piazza Bellini 3; €2.50; ⏲9.30am-12.30pm & 3-6pm) This 12th-century church in Arab-Norman style is one of Palermo's most striking buildings. With its dusky-pink bijou domes, solid square shape, blind arcading and delicate tracery, it illustrates perfectly the synthesis of Arab and Norman architectural styles. The interior, while more austere, is still beautiful, with its inlaid floor and lovely stone-and-brickwork in the arches and domes.

The building was founded in the 1150s by Maio of Bari (William I's emir of emirs, or chancellor), but Maio's murder in 1160 meant it was never finished – hence the lack of additional adornment within.

Piazza Bellini SQUARE
(Map p58) The disparate architectural styles and eras of the buildings adorning this magnificent piazza should by rights be visually discordant, but in fact contribute to a wonderfully harmonious public space. The piazza's eastern edge is adorned by the delightful **Teatro Bellini** (Bellini Theatre).

Albergheria

Once inhabited by Norman court officials, Albergheria has been a poor and ramshackle quarter since the end of WWII – indeed, you can still see wartime bomb damage scarring some buildings. The area is now home to a growing immigrant population that has revitalised the streets with its aspirations. Albergheria's east side is home to Palermo's busiest street market, the Mercato di Ballarò, as well as the beautiful Chiesa del Gesù. By far the biggest tourist draws here, however, are the Palazzo dei Normanni and its exquisite chapel, Cappella Palatina, both at the far western edge of the neighbourhood, a manageable 1km walk away.

★**Palazzo dei Normanni** PALACE
(Palazzo Reale; Map p52; ☎091 626 28 33; www.federicosecondo.org; Piazza Indipendenza 1; adult/reduced Fri-Mon €8.50/6.50, Tue-Thu €7/5; ⏲8.15am-5.45pm Mon-Sat, to 1pm Sun) Home to Sicily's regional parliament, this venerable palace dates to the 9th century. However, it owes its current look (and name) to a major Norman makeover, during which spectacular mosaics were added to its royal apartments and magnificent chapel, the Cappella Palatina. Visits to the apartments, which are off-limits from Tuesday to Thursday, take in the mosaic-lined **Sala dei Venti**, and **Sala di Ruggero II**, King Roger's 12th-century bedroom.

★**Cappella Palatina** CHAPEL
(Palatine Chapel; Map p52; www.federicosecondo.org; Piazza Indipendenza; adult/reduced Fri-Mon €8.50/6.50, Tue-Thu €7/5; ⏲9am-5pm Mon-Sat, 8.30-9.40am & 11.15am-1pm Sun) Designed by Roger II in 1130, this extraordinary chapel is Palermo's top tourist attraction. Located on the mid-level of Palazzo dei Normanni's three-tiered loggia, its glittering gold mosaics are complimented by inlaid marble floors and a wooden *muqarnas* ceiling, the latter a masterpiece of Arabic-style honeycomb carving reflecting Norman Sicily's cultural complexity.

DON'T MISS

STREET MARKETS

Palermo's historical ties with the Arab world and its proximity to North Africa reverberate in the noisy street life of the city's ancient centre, and nowhere is this stronger than in its markets.

Each of the city's four historic quarters claims its own street market, but the Vucciria, Ballarò and Capo are the 'Big Three' in terms of popularity and history.

The **Mercato della Vucciria** (Map p58; Piazza Caracciolo; 7am-8pm Mon, Tue, Thu-Sat, to 1pm Wed) is the most dishevelled of the three, with rough-edged customers, a small number of stalls selling produce and old junk, and often-grumpy stallholders. Infinitely more vibrant is the **Mercato di Ballarò** (Map p52; 7am-8pm Mon, Tue, Thu-Sat, to 1pm Wed & Sun), filled with stalls peddling household goods, clothes and foodstuffs of every possible description – this is where many Palermitans do their daily shop. The **Mercato del Capo** (Map p52; Via Sant'Agostino; 7am-8pm Mon, Tue, Thu-Sat, to 1pm Wed & Sun), which extends through the tangle of lanes and alleyways of the Albergheria and Capo quarters respectively, is the most atmospheric of all. Here, meat carcasses sway from huge metal hooks, glistening tuna and swordfish are expertly dismembered, and anchovies are filleted. Long and orderly lines of stalls display pungent cheeses, tubs of plump olives and a huge array of luscious fruits and voluptuous vegetables.

The markets are busiest in the morning. Remember: keep an eye on your belongings while exploring.

Note that queues are likely, and that you'll be refused entry if you're wearing shorts, a short skirt or a low-cut top.

The chapel's well-lit interior is simply breathtaking. Every inch is inlaid with precious stones, giving the space a lustrous quality. These exquisite mosaics were mainly the work of Byzantine Greek artisans brought to Palermo by Roger II in 1140 especially for this project. They capture expressions, detail and movement with extraordinary grace and delicacy, and sometimes with enormous power – most notably in the depiction of Christ the Pantocrator and Angels on the dome. The bulk of the mosaics recount the tales of the Old Testament, though other scenes recall Palermo's pivotal role in the Crusades. Some of the mosaics are later and less-assured additions, for instance the Virgin and Saints in the main apse under Christ the Pantocrator. Fortunately, these don't detract too much from the overall achievement.

It's not only the mosaics you should be gazing at – don't miss the painted wooden ceiling featuring *muqarnas*, a decorative device resembling stalactites that is unique in a Christian church (and, many speculate, a sign of Roger II's secret identity as a Muslim). The walls are decorated with handsome marble inlay that displays a clear Islamic aesthetic, and the carved marble in the floor is stunning: marble was as precious as any gemstone in the 12th century, so the floor's value at the time of its construction is almost immeasurable by today's standards.

There's a lot to take in, so once inside don't let the attendants hurry you through. Note also that the chapel is sometimes used for weddings, in which case it closes at 4.15pm.

Chiesa di San Giovanni degli Eremiti CHURCH

(Map p52; 091 651 50 19; Via dei Benedettini 16; adult/reduced €6/3; 9am-6.30pm Mon-Sat, to 1pm Sun) This remarkable, five-domed remnant of Arab-Norman architecture occupies a magical little hillside in the middle of an otherwise rather squalid neighbourhood. Surrounded by a garden of citrus trees, palms, cacti, rosemary bushes and ruined walls, it's built atop a mosque that itself was superimposed on an earlier chapel. The peaceful Norman cloisters outside offer lovely views of the Palazzo dei Normanni.

Chiesa del Gesù CHURCH

(Casa Professa; Map p52; Via del Ponticello; requested donation €2; 7-11.30am & 5-6.30pm Mon-Sat, 7am-12.30pm Sun, closed afternoon Aug) Also known as Casa Professa, this is one of Palermo's most breathtaking churches. The Jesuits first built a church on this site between 1564 and 1578. Incorporated into a larger church in 1633, the building was significantly restored after suffering major bomb damage in WWII. While the church's facade displays relative restraint typical of the late 16th century, its transept, apses and dome burst with 17th-century baroque extravagance. The dome's vault is decorated with a fresco attributed to Pietro Novelli.

Il Capo

Directly north of the Albergheria quarter, Il Capo is another web of interconnected streets and blind alleys. As impoverished as its neighbour, it too has a popular street market, the Mercato del Capo, which runs the length of Via Sant'Agostino and terminates at Porta Carini, one of Palermo's oldest town gates. The centrepiece of the quarter is the imposing monastery of Chiesa di Sant'Agostino, which ran the region in medieval times.

★Cattedrale di Palermo CATHEDRAL
(Map p52; 091 33 43 73; www.cattedrale.palermo.it; Corso Vittorio Emanuele; cathedral free, tombs €1.50, treasury & crypt €2, roof adult/reduced €5/3, all-inclusive ticket adult/reduced €7/5; cathedral 7am-7pm Mon-Sat, 8am-7pm Sun, royal tombs, treasury & roof 9.30am-5pm) A feast of geometric patterns, ziggurat crenellations, maiolica cupolas and blind arches, Palermo's cathedral has suffered aesthetically from multiple reworkings over the centuries, but remains a prime example of Sicily's unique Arab-Norman architectural style. The interior, while impressive in scale, is essentially a marble shell whose most interesting features are the **royal Norman tombs** (to the left as you enter), the **treasury** (home to Constance of Aragon's gem-encrusted 13th-century crown) and the panoramic views from the **roof**.

Construction began in 1184 at the behest of Palermo's archbishop, Walter of the Mill (Gualtiero Offamiglio), an Englishman who was tutor to William II. Walter held great power and had unlimited funds at his disposal, but with the building of the magnificent cathedral at Monreale he felt his power diminishing. His solution was to order construction of an equally magnificent cathedral in Palermo. This was erected on the location of a 9th-century mosque (itself built on a former chapel); a detail from the mosque's original decor is visible at the southern porch, where a column is inscribed with a passage from the Koran. The cathedral's proportions and the grandeur of its exterior became a statement of the power struggle between Church and throne occurring at the time, a potentially dangerous situation that was tempered by Walter's death (in 1191), which prevented him from seeing (and boasting about) the finished building.

Since then the cathedral has been much altered, sometimes with great success (as in Antonio Gambara's 15th-century three-arched portico that took 200 years to complete and became a masterpiece of Catalan Gothic architecture), and sometimes with less fortunate results (as in Ferdinando Fuga's clumsy dome, added between 1781 and 1801). Thankfully Fuga's handiwork did not extend to the eastern exterior, which is still adorned with the exotic interlacing designs of Walter's original cathedral. The south-western facade was laid in the 13th and 14th centuries, and is a beautiful example of local craftsmanship in the Gothic style. The cathedral's entrance – through Gambara's three magnificent arches, which are currently hidden behind scaffolding and a huge car advert – is fronted by gardens and a statue of Santa Rosalia, one of Palermo's patron saints. A beautiful painted intarsia decoration above the arches depicts the tree of life in a complex Islamic-style geometric composition of 12 roundels that show fruit, humans and all kinds of animals. It's thought to date back to 1296.

To the left as you enter the cathedral, the Monumental Area harbours several royal Norman tombs, which contain the remains of two of Sicily's greatest rulers: Roger II (rear left) and Frederick II of Hohenstaufen (front left), as well as Henry VI and William II. The cathedral's treasury houses a small collection of Norman-era jewels and religious relics. Most extraordinary is the fabulous 13th-century crown of Constance of Aragon (wife of Frederick II), made by local craftsmen in fine gold filigree and encrusted with gems. More bizarre treasures include the tooth and ashes of Santa Rosalia, kept here in silver reliquaries.

Museo Diocesano di Palermo MUSEUM
(Map p52; 091 607 72 15; www.museodiocesanopa.it; Via Matteo Bonello 2; adult/reduced €4.50/3; 9.30am-1.30pm Sun & Tue-Fri, 10am-6pm Sat) Palermo's Diocesan Museum is home to an important collection of artworks. The basement hosts a medley of sculptures from the 15th to 18th centuries, including works by Renaissance artists Francesco Laurana and Antonello Gagini. The newly opened first floor occupies 10 halls of the old Archbishop's Palace, furnished with Italian and Flemish paintings from the 16th to 19th

centuries. Don't miss the Sala Beccadelli, capped by a mid-15th-century ceiling and the Cappella Borremans, lavished with 18th-century frescoes by Flemish painter Guglielmo Borremans.

The museum houses works by Pietro Novelli, Sicily's most significant painter of the early 17th century, including *Compianto di Cristo morto* (Lamentation of Christ), a masterpiece reflecting the influence of both Caravaggio and Van Dyck. Also of particular interest is the *Veduta della Cattedrale di Palermo* (View of Palermo Cathedral), which offers a rare depiction of the exterior of the medieval church before its 18th-century alterations, which included the addition of the dome.

Chiesa di Sant'Agostino CHURCH
(Church of Saint Augustine; Map p52; Via Sant' Agostino; ⌚8am-noon & 4-6pm Mon-Sat, to noon Sun) The centrepiece of the Capo quarter is the Chiesa di Sant'Agostino and its adjoining Augustinian monastery, which ran the region in medieval times. A glorious rose window embellishes the church's late-13th-century facade. Inside, a 17th-century makeover saw the addition of stuccowork by the great Giacomo Serpotta, though, admittedly, this is not his finest work.

The adjoining monastery is home to a delightful cloister. Although the cloister dates from the 16th century, two mullioned windows on one side survive from its 14th-century incarnation.

La Kalsa

Plagued by poverty, La Kalsa has long been one of the city's most notorious neighbourhoods. A recent program of urban regeneration, however, has seen many of its long-derelict *palazzos* being restored and long-abandoned streets speckled with petite bohemian bars, trendy eateries and boutique hotels. It's also here that you'll find some of Palermo's top cultural sights, including art repositories Galleria Regionale della Sicilia, Galleria d'Arte Moderna and the time-warped luxury of Palazzo Mirto.

★Galleria Regionale della Sicilia MUSEUM
(Palazzo Abatellis; Map p58; ☎091 623 00 11; www.regione.sicilia.it/beniculturali/palazzoabatellis; Via Alloro 4; adult/reduced €8/4; ⌚9am-6.30pm Tue-Fri, to 1pm Sat & Sun) Housed in the stately 15th-century Palazzo Abatellis, this art museum – widely regarded as Palermo's best – showcases works by Sicilian artists from the Middle Ages to the 18th century. One of its greatest treasures is *Trionfo della Morte* (Triumph of Death), a magnificent fresco (artist unknown) in which Death is represented as a demonic skeleton mounted on a wasted horse, brandishing a wicked-looking scythe while leaping over his hapless victims.

Represented at the heart of the painting, under Death's horse, are the vain and pampered aristocrats of Palermo, while the poor and hungry look on from the side. The huge image, carefully restored, has been given its own space on the ground level to maximise its visual impact.

The gallery is full of countless other treasures, which collectively offer great insight into the evolution of Sicilian art. Among these is Antonello da Messina's enigmatic 15th-century masterpiece *L'Annunciata* (Virgin Annunciate), with its refined balance of Italian and Flemish influences.

The exhibition space itself was designed to fill this gorgeous Catalan Gothic *palazzo* in 1957 by Carlo Scarpa, one of Italy's leading architects.

Museo dell'Inquisizione MUSEUM
(Map p58; Piazza Marina 61; adult/reduced €8/3; ⌚10am-7pm Mon-Fri, to 5pm Sat & Sun Apr-Oct, 9.30am-6.30pm Mon-Fri, to 5pm Sat & Sun Nov-Mar, last entry 1hr before closing) Housed in the lower floors and basements of 14th-century Palazzo Chiaromonte Steri, this fascinating museum explores the legacy of the Inquisition in Palermo. Thousands of 'heretics' were detained here between 1601 and 1782; the honeycomb of former cells has been painstakingly restored to reveal multiple layers of their graffiti and artwork (religious and otherwise). Visits are by guided

COOKING WITH THE DUCHESS

Food, history and literature simmer together at **Cooking with the Duchess** (www.butera28.it/cooking-with-the-duchess.php; day course per person €150), a cooking course conducted by Duchess Nicoletta Polo Lanza Tomasi in a seafront palace, which was once home to writer Giuseppe Tomasi de Lampedusa. The course includes a morning shopping trip to the market and the creation of a four-course lunch, devoured with matching wines. The day concludes with a tour of the *palazzo*.

THE GENIUS OF GIACOMO SERPOTTA

Giacomo Serpotta (1656–1732) is widely considered the greatest Sicilian artist of the late baroque and rococo period, catapulting stuccowork in Italy from a mere craft to a dizzying high art. Born to a sculptor in Palermo's La Kalsa district, the artist would establish an international reputation for his bewitching, life-like figures, often positioned in unorthodox and asymmetrical ways to create a striking sense of realism and perspective. Complimenting his imaginative approach was a technical brilliance that saw Serpotta develop a polishing technique able to grace his stuccowork with a marble-like lustre.

To view his artistic evolution, pay a visit to the oratories of Santa Cita (p61), San Lorenzo and San Domenico (p61) in chronological order. Santa Cita's interior bursts with the freshness of Serpotta's creativity, which includes cherubs stretching out a stucco canvas depicting the battle of Lepanto. The artist's growing prowess sizzles in the Oratorio di San Lorenzo, whose meticulous details include an extraordinary statue of a breastfeeding *Carità* (Charity) and a sea of playful *putti* (cherubs) adorning the walls. Serpotta reaches his artistic maturity in the Oratorio di San Domenico. Here, confident statements include the depiction of allegorical figures as dames dressed in lace and ostrich feathers; a representation considered highly innovative at the time.

tour only, conducted in English and Italian and depart every 30 to 60 minutes from the ticket desk.

Religiously themed graffiti includes a depiction of Christ being tortured by Spanish soldiers and images of local protector saints San Rocco and Santa Rosalia. Works of a more profane nature include hearts pierced with arrows or instruments of torture, elaborate maps of Sicily where other prisoners were invited to add missing details, an inquisitor holding the scales of justice, and a caricature of another inquisitor astride a defecating horse adjacent to the latrine.

The tour also takes in two works by noted Sicilian modern artist Renato Guttuso: first, a copy of his graphic depiction of the strangulation murder of inquisitor De Cisneros by the handcuffed 22-year-old prisoner Diego La Mattina; and Guttuso's original, masterful 1974 painting of the Vucciria market. Figures depicted in the latter work include the artist, his wife and Guttuso's much younger lover.

Museo delle Maioliche MUSEUM

(Stanze al Genio; Map p58; ☎340 0971561; www.stanzealgenio.it; Via Garibaldi 11; adult/reduced €7/5; ⏲by appointment) Lovers of handpainted Italian maiolica should make a beeline for this unique museum, which contains a superlative private collection of circa 5000 tiles, most from Sicily and Naples, and spanning the 15th to 20th centuries. Amassed over three decades by founder Pio Mellina, the tiles fill the walls and floors of the lovingly restored 16th-century Palazzo Torre-Piraino, itself a work of art with vaulted and frescoed ceilings.

Oratorio di San Lorenzo CHAPEL

(Map p58; Via dell'Immacolatella 5; €3; ⏲10am-6pm) The late-16th-century Oratory of St Lawrence features glorious stuccowork by master rococo sculptor Giacomo Serpotta. Capturing scenes from the lives of St Lawrence and St Francis, the work is kept in fine company by an Antonino Grano–designed marble floor and exquisite side benches with ivory and mother-of-pearl inlaying. Above the altar is a reproduction of Caravaggio's *The Nativity with St Francis and St Lawrence,* stolen from here in 1969 and still one of the FBI's top 10 unsolved art crimes.

Galleria d'Arte Moderna MUSEUM

(Map p58; ☎091 843 16 05; www.gampalermo.it; Via Sant'Anna 21; adult/reduced €7/5; ⏲9.30am-6.30pm Tue-Sun) This lovely, wheelchair-accessible museum is housed in a sleekly renovated 15th-century *palazzo,* which metamorphosed into a convent in the 17th century. Divided over three floors, the wide-ranging collection of 19th- and 20th-century Sicilian art is beautifully displayed. There's a regular program of modern-art exhibitions here, as well as an excellent bookshop and gift shop. English-language audio guides cost €4.

The collection includes everything from 19th-century monumental historical genre paintings to futuristic romps from the early 20th century. Works are dedicated largely to Sicily and Palermo in their subject matter, with themes and landscapes that will be familiar to anyone who's already toured the island and will serve as inspiration for newcomers just embarking on their Sicilian

Vucciria & La Kalsa

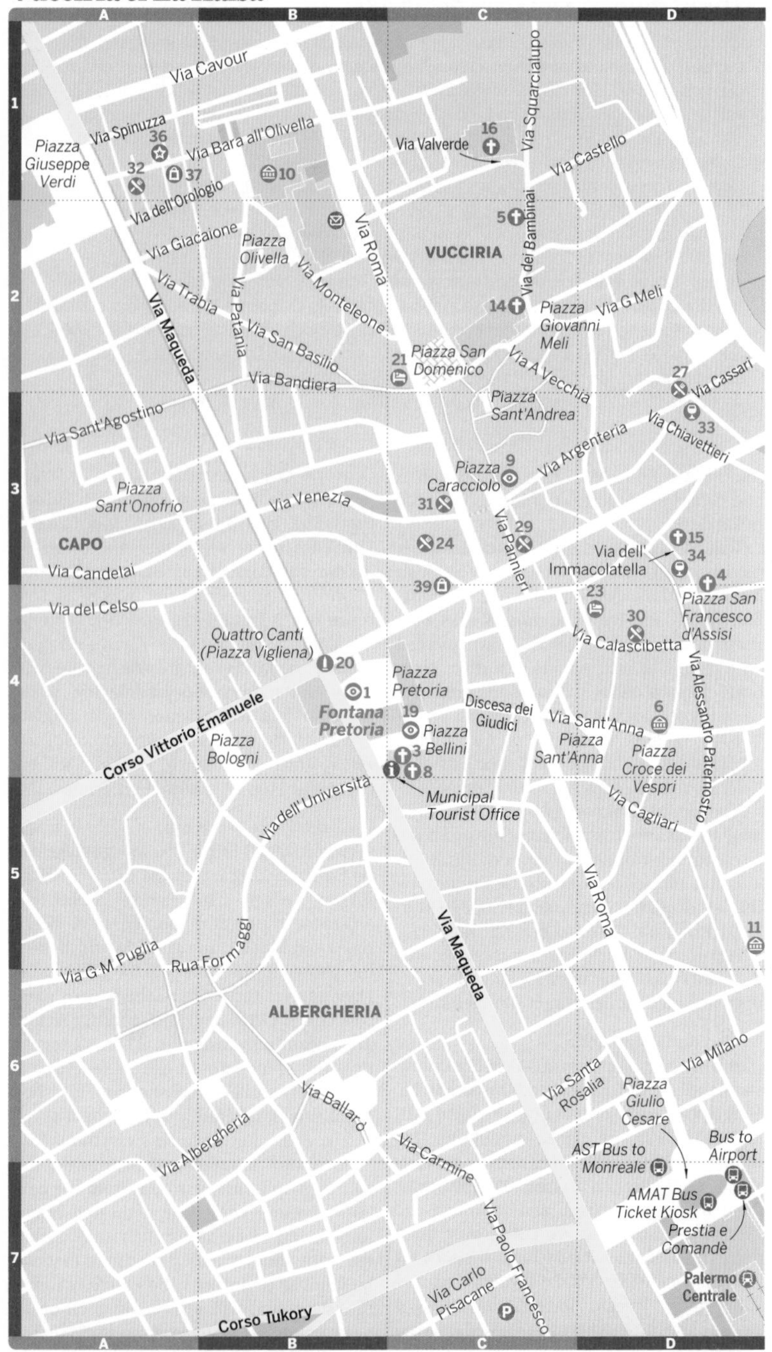

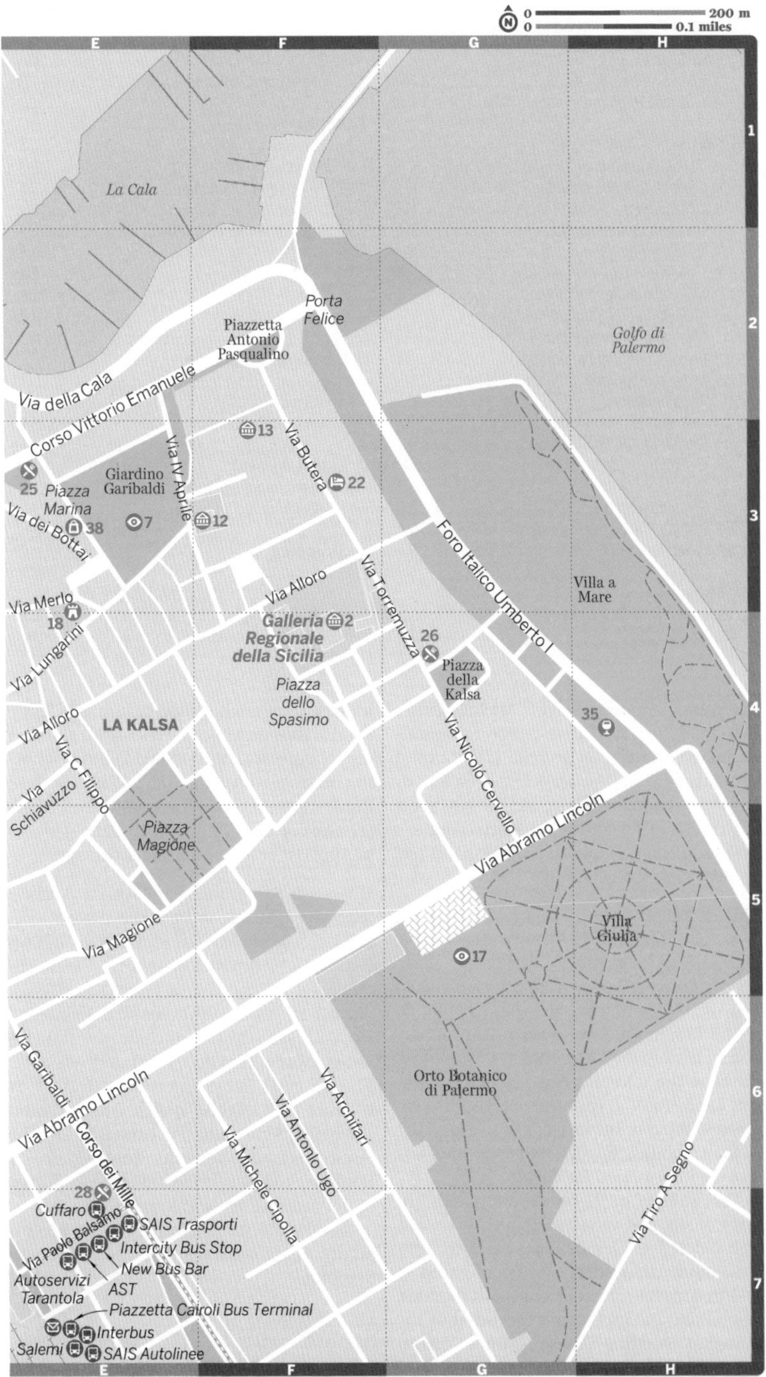
0 200 m
0 0.1 miles
La Cala
Porta Felice
Piazzetta Antonio Pasqualino
Golfo di Palermo
Via della Cala
Corso Vittorio Emanuele
Via IV Aprile
Via Butera
Giardino Garibaldi
Piazza Marina
Via dei Bottai
Via Alloro
Via Torremuzza
Foro Italico Umberto I
Villa a Mare
Via Merlo
Via Lungarini
Galleria Regionale della Sicilia
Piazza dello Spasimo
Piazza della Kalsa
LA KALSA
Via Alloro
Via C Filippo
Via Schiavuzzo
Via Nicolò Cervello
Via Abramo Lincoln
Piazza Magione
Via Magione
Villa Giulia
Via Garibaldi
Via Abramo Lincoln
Corso dei Mille
Via Archifari
Via Antonio Ugo
Via Michele Cipolla
Orto Botanico di Palermo
Via Tiro A Segno
Via Paolo Balsamo
Cuffaro
SAIS Trasporti
Intercity Bus Stop
New Bus Bar
AST
Autoservizi Tarantola
Piazzetta Cairoli Bus Terminal
Interbus
Salemi
SAIS Autolinee
PALERMO

Vucciria & La Kalsa

Top Sights
1 Fontana Pretoria B4
2 Galleria Regionale della Sicilia F4

Sights
3 Chiesa Capitolare di San Cataldo C4
4 Chiesa di San Francesco d'Assisi D3
5 Chiesa di Santa Maria di Valverde C2
6 Galleria d'Arte Moderna D4
7 Giardino Garibaldi E3
8 La Martorana C4
9 Mercato della Vucciria C3
10 Museo Archeologico Regionale B1
11 Museo delle Maioliche D5
12 Museo dell'Inquisizione F3
13 Museo Internazionale delle Marionette F3
14 Oratorio di San Domenico C2
15 Oratorio di San Lorenzo D3
16 Oratorio di Santa Cita C1
17 Orto Botanico G5
18 Palazzo Mirto E3
19 Piazza Bellini C4
20 Quattro Canti B4

Sleeping
21 BB22 Palace C2
22 Butera 28 F3
23 Grand Hotel Piazza Borsa D4
Stanze al Genio Residenze (see 11)

Eating
24 Ferro di Cavallo C3
25 Francu U Vastiddaru E3
26 Friggitoria Chiluzzo G4
27 Gagini D2
28 Gelateria Ciccio Adelfio E7
29 Il Maestro del Brodo C3
30 Osteria Ballarò D4
31 Touring Café C3
32 Trattoria Basile A1

Drinking & Nightlife
33 Bocum Mixology D3
34 Botteghe Colletti D3
35 Kursaal Kalhesa H4

Entertainment
36 Teatro dei Pupi di Mimmo Cuticchio A1

Shopping
37 Il Laboratorio Teatrale A1
38 Mercatino Antiquariato Piazza Marina E3
39 Mercurio Vintage C4

adventure. Examples include Michele Catti's *Ultime foglie* (Last Leaves; 1906), a beautiful image of a wet Viale della Libertá on a late autumn day; Antonio Leto's *Saline di Trapani,* depicting the reflective salt pools of western Sicily; Ettore de Maria Bergler's *Taormina;* and Gennaro Pardo's paintings of the temples at Selinunte.

Palazzo Mirto PALACE

(Map p58; ☎091 616 75 41; www.regione.sicilia.it/beniculturali/palazzomirto; Via Merlo 2; adult/reduced €6/3; ⏲9am-6pm Tue-Sat, to 1pm Sun) Just off Piazza Marina, this *palazzo* is one of the few in Palermo open to the public. Dating back to the 17th century, the building served as the Palermo residence of the Filangeri family for four centuries, and offers visitors a glimpse of the lavish, lost world of the Sicilian nobility. English-language booklets provide information for visitors.

The walls of its 21 rooms are covered in acres of silk and velvet wallpaper, with vast embroidered wall hangings, frescoed ceilings, gaudy chandeliers and floors paved in coloured marbles, maiolica tiles and mosaics. Memorable rooms include the tiny but extravagant Salottino Cinese (Chinese Salon) full of black lacquer, silken wallpaper and a rather conceited ceiling painting of European aristos viewing the room from above. It also features a leather-walled Fumoir (Smoking Salon), with walls of colourfully dyed Cordovan leather, and the Salottino di Diana (Lounge of Diana), with a swivelling statue of Apollo that leads to a secret passageway.

Chiesa di San Francesco d'Assisi CHURCH

(Map p58; Piazza San Francesco d'Assisi; ⏲7-11.30am & 4-6pm Mon-Sat, 7am-1pm & 4-6.30pm Sun) On a picture-perfect piazza, the much-amended Chiesa di San Francesco d'Assisi dates back to the 13th century. Remnants from its early history include the Romanesque facade, striking portal and left apse. The church's most interesting feature is the rare arch of the Cappella Mastrantonio (Chapel of Mastrantonio), carved in 1468 by Francesco Laurana and his protégé Pietro da Bonitate, and one of the only true examples of Renaissance art in Palermo.

Also notable are sculptures by the Gagini family, Giambattista Ragusa and Giacomo Serpotta.

Orto Botanico GARDENS

(Map p58; ☎091 2389 1236; www.ortobotanico.unipa.it; Via Abramo Lincoln 2; adult/reduced €5/2;

⏲9am-8pm May-Aug, to 7pm Apr & Sep, to 6pm Mar & Oct, to 5pm Nov-Feb) Laid out by Léon Dufourny and Venanzio Marvuglia, this raffish, sub-tropical paradise shelters massive fig trees, tall palms and dazzling hibiscus bushes, an avenue of bizarre-looking bottle and soap trees, as well as coffee trees, papaya plants and sycamores. It's a soothing haven of silence and fascinating botany, with shaded pathways, the odd dog and a large herb garden focused on Mediterranean plants.

Giardino Garibaldi GARDENS
(Map p58; Piazza Marina; ⏲24hr) Surrounded on all sides by elegant *palazzi*, gentrified Piazza Marina is Palermo's quietest piazza, and its small Giardino Garibaldi encloses Palermo's oldest tree, a venerable 25m-high, 150-year-old *ficus benjamin*. Dedicated to Garibaldi, the square has witnessed its fair share of bloody executions. These days, the square is better known for its popular Sunday flea market.

Vucciria

The shabby Vucciria neighbourhood is known throughout Sicily for its Mercato della Vucciria, the inspiration for Sicilian painter Renato Guttuso's most important work, *La Vucciria* (1974).

Once the heart of poverty-stricken Palermo and a den of crime and filth, the Vucciria illustrated the almost medieval chasm that existed between rich and poor in Sicily up until the 1950s. Though it's still quite shabby, the quarter is one of Palermo's most fascinating areas to explore, with most of its interesting buildings in the vicinity of the imposing 17th-century Chiesa di San Domenico.

Museo Archeologico Regionale MUSEUM
(Map p58; ☎091 611 68 07; www.regione.sicilia.it/beniculturali/salinas; Piazza Olivella 24; ⏲9.30am-6.30pm Tue-Fri, to 1pm Sat & Sun) Situated in a Renaissance monastery, this splendid, wheelchair-accessible museum houses some of Sicily's most valuable Greek and Roman artefacts, including the museum's crown jewel, a series of original decorative friezes from the temples at Selinunte. Undergoing renovations since 2010, the museum's ground floor is open so far, with the first floor set to reopen in late 2016 and the second floor opening at an undetermined future date. In the meantime, visitors have access to its gracious, fountain-studded courtyard, citrus-filled cloister and a selection of ancient sarcophagi, statues and pottery.

Beyond the decorative friezes from Selinunte, other important finds in the museum's collection include a Phoenician sarcophagus from the 5th century BC, Greek carvings from Himera, the Hellenistic *Ariete di Bronzo di Siracusa* (Bronze Ram of Syracuse), Etruscan mirrors and the largest collection of ancient anchors in the world.

Oratorio di Santa Cita CHAPEL
(Map p58; www.ilgeniodipalermo.com; Via Valverde; admission €4, joint ticket incl Oratorio di San Domenico €6; ⏲9am-6pm) This 17th-century chapel showcases the breathtaking stuccowork of Giacomo Serpotta, who famously introduced rococo to Sicilian churches. Note the elaborate *Battle of Lepanto* on the entrance wall. Depicting the Christian victory over the Turks, it's framed by stucco drapes held by a cast of cheeky cherubs modelled on Palermo's street urchins. Serpotta's virtuosity also dominates the side walls, where sculpted white stucco figures hold gilded swords, shields and a lute, and a golden snake (Serpotta's symbol) curls around a picture frame.

This chapel is associated with four other nearby churches, collectively known as the Tesori della Loggia (Treasures of the Loggia). Three of the churches (Santa Cita, San Giorgio dei Genovesi and Santa Maria di Valverde) are free; a combined ticket (available here) offers a small discount on admission to the remaining chapel, the Oratorio di San Domenico.

Oratorio di San Domenico CHAPEL
(Map p58; www.ilgeniodipalermo.com; Via dei Bambinai 2; admission €4, joint ticket incl Oratorio di Santa Cita €6; ⏲9am-6pm) Dominating this small chapel is Anthony Van Dyck's fantastic blue-and-red altarpiece, *The Virgin of the Rosary with St Dominic and the Patronesses of Palermo*. Van Dyck completed the work in Genoa in 1628, after leaving Palermo in fear of the plague. Also gracing the chapel are Giacomo Serpotta's amazingly elaborate stuccoes (1710–17), vivacious and whirling with figures. Serpotta's name meant 'lizard' or 'small snake', and he often included these signature reptiles in his work; see if you can find one!

New City

North of Piazza Giuseppe Verdi, Palermo's streets widen, the buildings lengthen, and the shops, restaurants and cafes become more elegant (and more expensive). Glorious

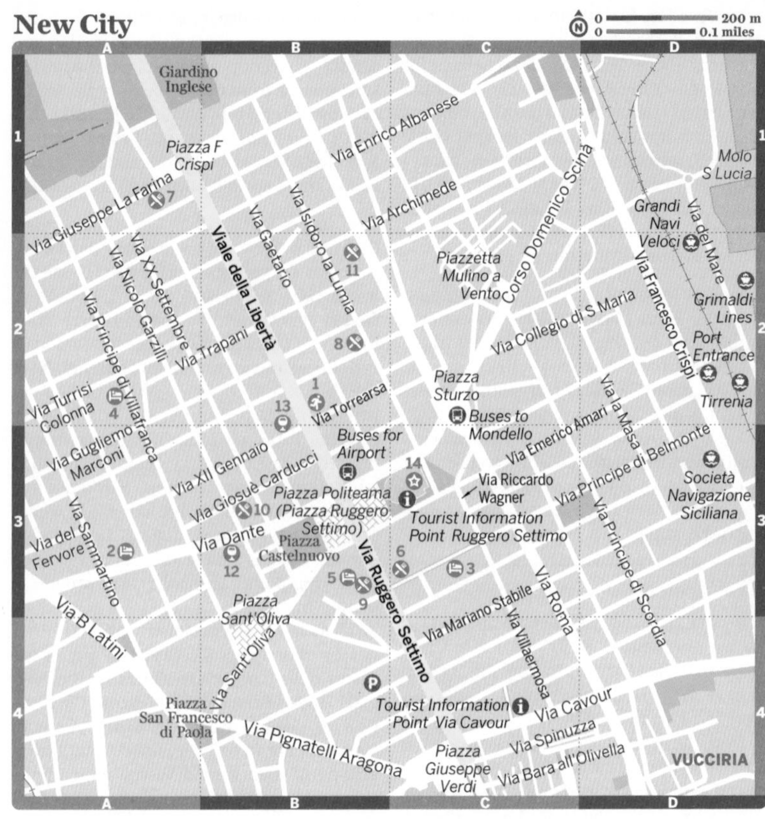

New City

Activities, Courses & Tours
1 Hammam B2

Sleeping
2 A Casa di Amici Hostel A3
3 B&B Amélie C3
4 Hotel Principe di Villafranca A2
5 Palazzo Pantaleo B3

Eating
6 Antico Caffè Spinnato C3
7 Bioesserì A1
8 Cucina Papoff B2
9 I Cuochini B3
10 Pasticceria Cappello B3
11 Pasticceria Fratelli Magrì B2

Drinking & Nightlife
12 Enoteca Buonivini B3
13 Pizzo & Pizzo B2

Entertainment
14 Teatro Politeama Garibaldi C3

neoclassical and Liberty examples from the last golden age in Sicilian architecture give the city an exuberant, belle-époque feel in stark contrast to the narrow, introspective vibe of the historic quarter. Head here for trendy *aperitivo* (pre-dinner drinks) sessions, high-end retail therapy and rousing symphonies at the Teatro Politeama Garibaldi.

★ **Teatro Massimo** THEATRE

(Map p52; tour reservations 091 605 32 67; www.teatromassimo.it; Piazza Giuseppe Verdi; guided tours adult/reduced €8/5; 9.30am-5.30pm) Taking over 20 years to complete, Palermo's neoclassical opera house is the largest in Italy and the second-largest in Europe. The closing scene of *The Godfather: Part*

III, with its visually arresting juxtaposition of high culture, crime, drama and death, was filmed here and the building's richly decorated interiors are nothing short of spectacular. Guided 30-minute tours are offered throughout the day in English, Italian, French, Spanish and German.

Outside the City Centre

Villa Malfitano VILLA

(☎091 682 05 22; www.fondazionewhitaker.it/villa.html; Via Dante 167; adult/reduced €9/6; ⏰9am-3pm Mon-Sat) A showcase of Liberty architecture, set in a 9-hectare (22-acre) formal garden planted with rare and exotic species, this villa is most notable for its whimsical interior decoration, which includes a 'Summer Room' with walls painted to resemble a conservatory, and a music room draped with 15th-century tapestries illustrating the *Aeneid*. It's a 20-minute walk west from Piazza Castelnuovo.

The villa was built in 1886 by Joseph Whitaker, a member of the entrepreneurial English business dynasty that made a fortune in the Marsala trade in Sicily in the 19th century. Joseph and his wife Tina were leading figures in Palermo's high society and entertained their belle-époque buddies here in lavish style, even hosting King Edward VII in 1907 and George V in 1925.

Catacombe dei Cappuccini CATACOMB

(www.catacombepalermo.it; Piazza Cappuccini; adult €3, child under 8yr free; ⏰9am-1pm & 3-6pm, closed Sun afternoon Nov-Mar) These catacombs house the mummified bodies and skeletons of some 8000 Palermitans who died between the 17th and 19th centuries. Earthly power, gender, religion and professional status are still rigidly distinguished, with men and women occupying separate corridors, and a first-class section set aside for virgins. From Piazza Indipendenza, it's a 1.2km walk west along Via Cappuccini.

Activities

Hammam BATHHOUSE

(Map p62; ☎091 32 07 83; www.hammam.pa.it; Via Torrearsa 17d; €40; ⏰women only 2.30-8.30pm Mon & Wed, 11.30am-8.30pm Fri, men only 4-8pm Tue, 11.30am-8pm Sat, couples & mixed groups 2.30-8.30pm Thu) For a sybaritic experience, head to this marble-lined Moorish bathhouse, where you can indulge in a soak, a steamy sauna and a vigorous scrub-down. There's a one-off charge (€10) for slippers and an exfoliating glove. A variety of massages and other treatments are available for an additional charge. Bookings are strongly recommended.

Tours

Streat Palermo WALKING

(www.streatpalermo.it; 45min tour per person adult/reduced €39/30) Organised by Palermitan local Marco Romeo, these walking tours make a grand circuit of the city's street-food stalls, as well as offering glimpses into the city's history. The street food 'passport', allowing you to keep track of the places you've visited, is a nice touch.

Palermo Street Food WALKING

(www.palermostreetfood.com; 3hr tour per person €30) Led by an enthusiastic group of young Palermitans, these walking tours offer insight into Palermo's celebrated street food as well as its architecture and art. Tours are conducted in the morning and evening, the morning option including an exploration of historic produce markets. Book tours at least 48 hours in advance.

Sicilia Letteraria WALKING

(☎091 625 40 11, 327 6844052; www.parcotomasi.it; 2½hr tour €8.50; ⏰by arrangement) This organisation runs literary walks and excursions, including a walking tour focused on Sicilian novelist Giuseppe Tomasi di Lampedusa and his literary showpiece *Il Gattopardo* (The Leopard). The tour – which runs at least twice monthly – is usually in Italian. Private tours (€20 per person) are available in English.

Festivals & Events

Festino di Santa Rosalia RELIGIOUS

(U Fistinu; www.santarosaliapalermo.it; ⏰10-15 Jul) Palermo's biggest annual festival celebrates patron saint Santa Rosalia, beloved for having saved the city from a 17th-century plague. The most colourful festivities take place on the evening of 14 July, when the saint's relics are paraded aboard a grand chariot from the Palazzo dei Normanni through the Quattro Canti to the waterfront, where fireworks and general merriment ensue.

Eating

While Palermo's restaurant scene may not rival that of Sicily's Michelin-star-studded southeast, expect to find everything from heirloom trattorias serving faithful classics like *bucatini con le sarde* (pasta mixed with sardines, wild fennel, raisins, pine nuts and breadcrumbs), to next-gen hotspots tweaking nonna's recipes. Hit the markets and street-food stalls for delicious bargain bites, and the *pasticcerie* (pastry shops) for staples including *frutta martorana* (fruit-shaped marzipan).

★Trattoria al Vecchio Club Rosanero SICILIAN €

(Map p52; ☎091 251 12 34; Vicolo Caldomai 18; meals €14; ⏲1-3.30pm Mon-Sat, plus 8.15-10.30pm Thu-Sat; 📶) A veritable shrine to the city's football team (*rosa nero* refers to the team's colours, pink and black), cavernous Vecchio Club scores goals with its bargain-priced, flavour-packed grub. Fish and seafood are the real fortes here; if it's on the menu, order the *caponata e pesce spada* (caponata with swordfish), a sweet-and-sour victory. Head in early to avoid a wait.

★Bisso Bistrot BISTRO €

(Map p52; ☎328 1314595, 091 33 49 99; Via Maqueda 172; meals €14-18; ⏲9am-midnight Mon-Sat) Frescoed walls, exposed ceiling beams and reasonably priced, lip-smacking appetisers, *primi* (first courses) and *secondi* (main courses) greet diners at this swinging, smart-casual bistro. Located at the north-west corner of the Quattro Canti, its fabulous edible offerings cover all bases, from morning *cornetti* (croissants) to lunch and dinner meat, fish and pasta dishes (the latter are especially good). Solo diners will appreciate the front bar seating.

Tip: if heading in for dinner, arrive before 7.30pm or prepare for a decent wait.

Trattoria Ai Cascinari SICILIAN €

(Map p52; ☎091 651 98 04; Via d'Ossuna 43/45; meals €20-25; ⏲12.30-2.30pm Tue-Sun, plus 8-10.30pm Wed-Sat) Yes, it's a bit out of the way, but Ai Cascinari, 1km north of the Cappella Palatina, is a long-standing Palermitan favourite, and deservedly so. It's especially enjoyable on Sunday afternoons, when locals pack the labyrinth of back rooms and waiters perambulate non-stop with plates of scrumptious seasonal antipasti, fresh seafood and desserts from Palermo's beloved Cappello and Scimone *pasticcerie*.

FUD BURGERS €

(Map p52; ☎091 611 21 84; www.fud.it; Piazza Olivella 4; burgers €5.90-8.90, salads €8.50-10.90; ⏲noon-3.30pm & 7pm-1am; 📶) A slick, pumping combo of concrete walls, filament bulbs and communal tables, FUD gives fast food a Slow Food makeover. Offerings include salads and pizzas, both playing second fiddle to the cult-status burgers, built from scratch using prime local produce. Wash down the goodness with a Sicilian craft beer, then scan the shelves for take-home treats, from local jams and almonds to FUD's own wine.

In the warmer months, nab a table on the square, home to baroque beauty Chiesa di San Ignazio all'Olivella.

Pizzeria Frida PIZZA €

(Map p52; www.fridapizzeria.it; Piazza Sant'Onofrio 37; pizzas €4-13; ⏲7.30pm-midnight, closed Tue) With footpath tables under umbrella awnings on a low-key Capo piazza, this local favourite makes thin-crust pizzas in a variety of shapes, including *quadri* (square, picture-frame-shaped pizzas) and *vulcanotti* (named after famous volcanoes and looking the part). Toppings include Sicilian specialties like tuna, capers, pistachios, mint, aubergines and fresh ricotta.

Touring Café CAFE €

(Map p58; ☎091 32 27 26; Via Roma 252; arancino €1.70; ⏲6.15am-11pm Mon-Fri, to midnight Sat & Sun) Don't let the gleaming Liberty-style mirrored bar and array of picture-perfect pastries distract you. You come here for the *arancine,* great fist-sized rice balls stuffed with *ragù,* spinach or butter, and fried to a perfect golden orange.

I Cuochini STREET FOOD €

(Map p62; Via Ruggero Settimo 68; snacks from €0.70; ⏲8.30am-2.30pm Mon-Sat, plus 4.30-7.30pm Sat) Hidden inside a little courtyard off Via Ruggero Settimo, this long-standing Palermitan favourite specialises in low-cost snacks, including delicious *arancinette* and divine *panzerotti* (stuffed fried dough pockets). The latter come in countless delectable varieties: ricotta and mint, squash blossoms and cheese, mozzarella, cherry tomatoes and anchovies, just to name a few.

Francu U Vastiddaru STREET FOOD €

(Map p58; Corso Vittorio Emanuele 102; sandwiches €1.50-3.50; ⏲8am-1am) Palermitan street food doesn't get any better or cheaper than the delicious *panini* (sandwich) hawked from this hole-in-the-wall sandwich shop just off Piazza Marina. Options range from the classic *panino triplo,* (with chickpea fritters, potato croquettes and aubergine) to the owner's trademark *panino vastiddaru*

SWEET TREATS

Palermo is justly famous for its sweet treats, from the delicate crunch of freshly filled *cannoli* (pastry shells with a sweet filling) to the velvety comfort of *cassata* (a concoction of sponge cake, cream, marzipan, chocolate and candied fruit). For a calorific revelation, loosen your belt and head straight to one of these cult-status pit-stops.

Pasticceria Fratelli Magrì (Map p62; ☎091 58 47 88; www.pasticceriamagri.com; Via Isidoro Carini 42; pastries from €1.70; ⊙7am-9pm Thu-Tue) Yes, the made-from-scratch *cannollo* and *cassata* are just gorgeous, but this third-generation *pasticceria* (pastry shop) in the new city also peddles lesser-known classics, including the *patata* (sponge pastry with custard, marzipan and almond paste) and *torta savoia,* a multi-layered chocolate and hazelnut cake.

Pasticceria Cappello (Map p62; ☎091 611 37 69; www.pasticceriacappello.it; Via Giosuè Carducci 19; desserts from €1.70; ⊙7.30am-9.30pm Thu-Tue) The *setteveli* (seven-layer chocolate cake) was invented at this bakery-cafe and has long since been copied all over Palermo. Order a serve but leave room for the dreamy *delizia di pistacchio,* a granular pistachio cake topped with creamy icing and a chocolate medallion. The *cornetti* (croissants) here are glossy, fresh and perfect for a lighter start to the day.

Gelateria Ciccio Adelfio (Map p58; ☎091 616 15 37; Corso dei Mille 73; gelato from €1; ⊙7am-midnight) A quick walk from the train station, this old-school gelateria lures tongues from across town. Go local and have your ice cream sandwiched in a brioche (€2). From classic flavours like pistachio, *torrone* (nougat) or *cannolo*, to more daring concoctions like Mars (an icy take on the chocolate bar), the gelato here is fabulously fresh, consistent and an utter bargain.

Antico Caffè Spinnato (Map p62; ☎091 749 51 04; www.spinnato.it; Via Principe di Belmonte 107-15; pastries from €0.80; ⊙7am-1am Sun-Fri, to 2am Sat; 📶) While the sugary bites here may not quite rival Magrì, Cappello or Ciccio Adelfio, this 1860 veteran offers a taste of the old-world cafe society that once thrived in Palermo. Settle in at a sidewalk table or in its snug interior for a lingering *caffè e torta* (coffee and cake) session, or go straight for a cooling spritz.

(with roast pork, salami, emmental cheese and spicy mushrooms).

Friggitoria Chiluzzo STREET FOOD €
(Map p58; Piazza della Kalsa; sandwiches €1.50-2; ⊙8am-5pm Mon-Sat) There's a lot to be said for simplicity, like sitting on beer crates in the shadow of a baroque church and chowing down on cheap, delicious local street food. This beloved street vendor makes some of Palermo's best *pane e panelle* (sesame bread with chickpea fritters). Add some *crocchè* (potato croquettes), fried aubergine and a squeeze of lemon and call it lunch!

Trattoria Basile TRATTORIA €
(Map p58; ☎091 33 56 28; Via Bara all'Olivella 76; meals €9-14; ⊙noon-3.30pm Mon-Sat) Cheap, tasty, home-style grub awaits at cafeteria-style Basile. Pay first, take a number at the window for your pasta or main course, then sidle over and choose three antipasti. While scoffing down your appetisers, listen for your number – they'll bellow it out (in Italian) when your order is ready. For your own sanity, avoid the 1pm to 2pm rush hour.

Ferro di Cavallo TRATTORIA €
(Map p58; ☎091 33 18 35; www.ferrodicavallopalermo.it; Via Venezia 20; meals €17; ⊙12.30-3pm Mon-Sat, plus 7.30-11.30pm Wed-Sat) Tables line the footpath and caricatures of the owners beam down from bright-red walls at this bustling family-run trattoria, in business since 1944. While some locals claim that standards have slipped, the place remains a solid standby for Sicilian classics like *pasta con le sarde*. Head in early or prepare to wait.

Bioesserì HEALTH FOOD €€
(Map p62; ☎091 765 71 42; www.bioesseri.it; Via Giuseppe La Farina 4; pizza €8.50-13.50, meals €28; ⊙7.30am-11pm Mon-Thu, to 11.30pm Fri, 8.30am-11.30pm Sat, to 11pm Sun; 📶) Join on-point locals at this fresh, stylish Milanese import, decked out in leather banquettes and upcycled crates turned into furniture. Part

cafe, part upmarket grocery store, its virtuous bites tap all bases, from vegan *cornetti*, smoothies and soy-milk *budini* (puddings), to spelt-flour pizzas and innovative dishes like leek-and-potato soup with liquorice powder, or black squid-ink quinoa.

Osteria Ballarò SICILIAN €€

(Map p58; ☎091 791 01 84; www.osteriaballaro.it; Via Calascibetta 25; meals €30-45; ⏰12.15-3.15pm & 7-11.30pm) A slinky, buzzing restaurant-cum-wine bar, Osteria Ballarò marries an atmospheric setting with sterling, Slow Food island cooking. Bare stone columns, exposed brick walls and vaulted ceilings set an evocative scene for arresting *crudite di pesce* (local sashimi) and seafood *primi*, elegant local wines and memorable Sicilian *dolci* (sweets). Reservations recommended. Slow Food recommended.

Il Maestro del Brodo TRATTORIA €€

(Map p58; ☎091 32 95 23; Via Pannieri 7; meals €22-31; ⏰noon-3pm Tue-Sun, plus 7.30-11pm Fri & Sat) This no-frills trattoria in the Vucciria offers delicious soups, an array of ultrafresh seafood and a sensational antipasto buffet featuring a dozen-plus homemade delicacies: *sarde a beccafico* (stuffed sardines), aubergine *involtini* (roulades), smoked fish, artichokes with parsley, sun-dried tomatoes, olives and more.

Cucina Papoff SICILIAN €€

(Map p62; ☎091 58 64 60; www.cucinapapoff.it; Via Isidoro La Lumia 32; meals €27-37; ⏰7.30-11.15pm Mon-Sat) Celebrate all things surf at Cucina Papoff, where stone walls, grand arched doorways and carved wooden ceilings set an elegant mood for seafood feasts. Dishes burst with flavour, whether it's succulent prawns fried in chickpea flour, fresh ravioli filled with crustaceans, or a surprisingly seductive pairing of octopus and potatoes. If it's on the menu, let lemon mousse be your epilogue.

Gagini ITALIAN €€€

(Map p58; ☎091 58 99 18; www.gaginirestaurant.com; Via dei Cassari 35; meals €45, 4/8-course degustation menu €55/85; ⏰1-3pm & 8-11pm; 📶) Expect sharp professionals and serious gastronomes at Gagini's rustic, candlelit tables. In the kitchen is young-gun chef Gioacchino Gaglio, whose passion for season, region and new-school thinking delivers

DON'T MISS

PALERMO'S STREET FOOD

Bangkok, Mexico City, Marrakesh, Palermo: clued-in gastronomes around the world know that Sicily's capital is one of the world's street-food capitals. The mystery is simply how Palermo is not the obesity capital of Europe given just how much noshing goes on! Palermitans are at it all the time: when they're shopping, commuting, discussing business, romancing...basically at any time of the day. What they're devouring is the *buffitieri* – little hot snacks prepared at stalls and designed for eating on the spot.

Kick off the morning with *pane e panelle,* Palermo's famous chickpea fritters – great for vegetarians and a welcome change from a sweet custard-filled croissant. You might also want to go for some *crocchè* (potato croquettes, sometimes flavoured with fresh mint), *quaglie* (literally translated as quails, they're actually aubergines/eggplants cut lengthwise and fanned out to resemble a bird's feathers, then fried), *sfincione* (a spongy, oily pizza topped with onions and caciocavallo cheese) or *scaccie* (discs of bread dough spread with a filling and rolled up into a pancake). In the warmer months, locals find it difficult to refuse a freshly baked brioche jammed with ice cream or *granita* (crushed ice mixed with fresh fruit, almonds, pistachios or coffee).

From 4pm onwards the snacks become decidedly more carnivorous and you may just wish you hadn't read the following translations: how about some barbecued *stigghiola* (goat intestines filled with onions, cheese and parsley), for example? Or a couple of *pani ca meusa* (breadroll stuffed with sautéed beef spleen). You'll be asked if you want it *'schietta'* (single) or *'maritata'* (married). If you choose *schietta,* the roll will only have ricotta in it before being dipped into boiling lard; choose *maritata* and you'll get the beef spleen as well.

You'll find stalls and kiosks selling street food all over town, especially in Palermo's street markets.

marvels like Sicilian tempura with citrus granita, *tagliolini* (thick spaghetti) with Enna saffron, scampi and escarole cream, and honey-scented *baccalà* (salted cod) with black chickpeas, spiced shoots and roasted chestnuts. Book ahead.

Drinking & Nightlife

Lively clusters of bars can be found along Via Chiavettieri in the Vucciria neighbourhood (just northwest of Piazza Marina), also home to Via Paternostro and its duo of arty, bohemian bars. You'll also find bars in the Champagneria district due east of Teatro Massimo, centred on Piazza Olivella, Via Spinuzza and Via Patania. Higher-end drinking spots are concentrated in Palermo's new city. In summer, many Palermitans decamp to seaside Mondello.

★Enoteca Buonivini WINE BAR
(Map p62; Via Dante 8; ⏲9.30am-1.30pm & 4pm-midnight Mon-Thu, to 1am Fri & Sat) Serious oenophiles flock to this bustling, urbane *enoteca* (wine bar), complete with bar seating, courtyard and a generous selection of wines by the glass. There's no shortage of interesting local drops, not to mention artisan cheese and charcuterie boards, beautiful pasta dishes and grilled meats. When you're done, scan the shelves for harder-to-find craft spirits (Australian gin, anyone?) and Sicilian gourmet pantry essentials.

Bocum Mixology COCKTAIL BAR
(Map p58; ☎091 33 20 09; www.bocum.it; Via dei Cassari 6; ⏲6pm-1.30am Tue-Sun) All hail Bocum, Palermo's first proper cocktail bar. While the ground-floor cantina is a fine spot for cognoscenti wines and DOP *salumi* (charcuterie), the real magic happens upstairs. Here, on your right, lies the mixology lounge, where skilled hands shake and stir seamless, nuanced libations. Add flickering candlelight and crackling jazz, and you have yourself one rather bohemian Palermo evening.

Botteghe Colletti BAR
(Map p58; Via Alessandro Paternostro; ⏲5pm-2am) Red theatrical curtains, old wooden cabinets and flickering candles in old gin bottles: this snug bar pulls a mixed-aged crowd of artists, students and general bohemians, clutching drinks, nibbling on *aperitivo* bites and spilling out onto the atmospheric street. Order a smoked Negroni, strike up a conversation or while away the hours with a game of chess.

Pizzo & Pizzo WINE BAR
(Map p62; ☎091 601 45 44; www.pizzoepizzo.com; Via XII Gennaio 1; ⏲12.30-3.30pm & 7.30-11.30pm Mon-Sat) Sure, this sophisticated wine bar is a great place for *aperitivo* (think complimentary morsels like cucumber topped with ricotta mousse, spicy orange marmalade, mustard seed and pistachio), but the buzzing, grown-up atmosphere and the tempting array of cheeses, cured meats and smoked fish might just convince you to stick around for dinner.

Best of all, staff are happy to open most bottles in stock, even if you're just after a glass.

Enoteca Butticè WINE BAR
(Map p52; ☎091 251 53 94; www.enotecabuttice.it; Piazza San Francesco di Paola 12; ⏲6pm-midnight Mon-Sat; 📶) Chipped concrete floors, old sewing machines turned tables and a gramophone turned lamp: welcome to one of Palermo's most eclectic (and best) wine bars, where chatty crowds pour onto the street and the blackboard is never short of intriguing Old and New World drops. Food options include simple pasta dishes, though the place is best for a pre-dinner swill.

Kursaal Kalhesa BAR
(Map p58; ☎091 616 00 50; www.facebook.com/kursaalkalhesa; Foro Umberto I 21; ⏲8pm-12.30am Tue & Wed, to 2am Thu, to 3am Fri-Sun) Don't be fooled by the nondescript entrance, embedded in Palermo's massive sea walls – slip inside and Kursaal Kalhesa opens up like an ancient church, complete with high stone vaults. A lounge bar, restaurant and club in one, it's best for pre-dinner drinks or a live music gig, the latter usually served up Thursday to Sunday and followed by DJ sets.

Entertainment

Palermo's cultural offerings include world-class opera, ballet and symphonies. More unusual concert venues include churches and historic villas. In the summer, outdoor music and ballet concerts are held at the Teatro di Verdura. Numerous pubs and bars across the city offer live music, spanning anything from rock and blues to jazz and funk. For something truly unique, catch a Sicilian puppet show.

DON'T MISS

SICILIAN MARIONETTE THEATRE

Sicily's most popular form of traditional entertainment is the *opera dei pupi* (rod-marionette theatre), and the best place to attend a performance is in Palermo.

Marionettes were first introduced to the island by the Spanish in the 18th century and the art form was swiftly embraced by locals, enthralled with the re-enacted tales of Charlemagne and his heroic knights Orlando and Rinaldo. Effectively the soap operas of their day, these puppet shows expounded the deepest sentiments of life – unrequited love, treachery, thirst for justice and the anger and frustration of the oppressed. Back then, a puppet could speak volumes where a person could not.

There are traditionally two types of *opera dei pupi* in Sicily: Palermitan (practised in Palermo, Agrigento and Trapani) and Catanese (in Catania, Messina and Syracuse). Carved from beech, olive or lemon-tree wood, the marionettes stand some 1.5m high, have wire joints and wear richly coloured costumes. The knights are clad in metal suits of armour that make the figures shine and resonate when they engage in swordfights with bloodthirsty Saracen warriors or mythical monsters.

Good puppeteers are judged on the dramatic effect they can create – lots of stamping feet, thundering and a gripping running commentary – and on their speed and skill in directing the battle scenes. Nowadays the *opera dei pupi* has been relegated to folklore status, maintained by a few companies largely for the benefit of tourists and children. The best places to attend a performance are at the **Museo Internazionale delle Marionette** (Map p58; ☎091 32 80 60; www.museomarionettepalermo.it; Piazzetta Antonio Pasqualino 5; adult/reduced €5/3; ⏲9am-1pm & 2.30-6.30pm Mon-Sat) or at the **Teatro dei Pupi di Mimmo Cuticchio** (Map p58; ☎091 32 34 00; www.figlidartecuticchio.com; Via Bara all'Olivella 95; adult/reduced €10/5), a theatre run by the Associazione Figli d'Arte Cuticchio (check its website for performance times).

★Teatro Massimo OPERA

(Map p52; ☎box office 091 605 35 80; www.teatromassimo.it; Piazza Giuseppe Verdi) Ernesto Basile's six-tiered art-nouveau masterpiece is Europe's second-largest opera house and one of Italy's most prestigious, right up there with La Scala in Milan, San Carlo in Naples and La Fenice in Venice. With lions flanking its grandiose columned entrance and an interior gleaming in red and gold, it stages opera, ballet and music concerts from September to June. Opera tickets range from around €20 to €125.

Teatro Politeama Garibaldi PERFORMING ARTS

(Map p62; ☎091 607 25 11; Piazza Ruggero Settimo) This grandiose theatre is a popular venue for opera, ballet and classical music, staging afternoon and evening concerts. It's home to Palermo's symphony orchestra, the Orchestra Sinfonica Siciliana (www.orchestrasinfonicasiciliana.it).

Teatro di Verdura PERFORMING ARTS

(☎091 605 33 53; Viale del Fante 70; ⏲Jul & Aug) A summer-only program of mostly opera and popular music (including prolific national and international acts) in the lovely gardens of the Villa Castelnuovo, about 6km north of the city centre. Adding to the whimsy is a delightful open-air bar that opens during shows.

Shopping

In the new city, Via della Libertà is lined with high-end Italian and international fashion stores. More atmospheric is the city's historic centre, where crumbly streets harbour anything from puppet-making workshops to vintage shops selling mid-century Sicilian couture. For fresh edibles, hit Mercato di Ballarò or Mercato del Capo. Come Sunday morning, trawl the Mercatino Antiquariato Piazza Marina for Sicilian antiques and decorative objects.

★Mercurio Vintage VINTAGE

(Map p58; Corso Vittorio Emanuele 231; ⏲9.30am-1pm & 4-7.30pm) What was a Liberty-era jewellery store is now a treasure trove of valuable vintage threads, shoes and decorative items, including ceramics, jewellery and couture from past and present Sicilian designers. Dig up anything from Chanel satin heels and Céline silk scarves, to Antonio D'Anna '70s platform heels or a Giovanna

Valenti brocade top. A small selection of men's items includes coats and silk ties.

The store is usually closed on Sunday afternoons from October to March.

Mercatino Antiquariato Piazza Marina MARKET

(Map p58; Piazza Marina; ⏲7am-2pm Sun) Palermo's best-loved flea market takes over Piazza Marina and surrounding streets every Sunday morning. Those with a sharp eye can find some real treasures among the stalls of books, retro records and Catholic kitsch, including vintage Italian glassware and jewellery, Sicilian ceramics, recycled sculptures, coffee sets, even the odd art deco armchair. Head in early for the best finds.

Il Laboratorio Teatrale ARTS & CRAFTS

(Map p58; ☎091 32 34 00; Via Bara all'Olivella 40; ⏲10am-1pm & 4-7pm Tue-Sat) A true artists' workshop, this enchanting space is where the Cuticchio family constructs puppets for its famous theatre across the street. High-quality puppets dating from the mid-1800s to the present are displayed here, and are available for purchase by serious enthusiasts.

Orientation

Palermo is large but easily walkable – if you can brave crossing the street, that is. Lively Via Maqueda is its central street, extending from the train station in the south and then changing name to Via Ruggero Settimo at Piazza Giuseppe Verdi, the gateway to the new city. At Piazza Castelnuovo (also commonly known as Piazza Politeama), it continues into Viale della Libertà, a grand boulevard lined with 19th-century apartment blocks.

Via Maqueda is bisected by Corso Vittorio Emanuele (also known as Via Vittorio Emanuele), running east to west from the port of La Cala to the cathedral and Palazzo dei Normanni. The intersection of Via Maqueda and Corso Vittorio Emanuele is the Quattro Canti (Four Corners), which divides historic Palermo into four traditional quarters: La Kalsa (southeast), Vucciria (northeast), Il Capo (northwest) and Albergheria (southwest). These quarters contain the majority of Palermo's sights.

Parallel to Via Maqueda is another major thoroughfare, Via Roma. A one-way system moves traffic north up Via Roma from the train station and south down Via Maqueda. The stretch of Via Maqueda from Corso Vittorio Emanuele to Piazza Giuseppe Verdi is pedestrian-only from 10am to 7am (from 8am on Sundays), a move that has revitalised the street, with an increase in foot traffic and new food and retail outlets. In mid-2016, a similar trial was planned for Via Roma between Corso Vittorio Emanuele and Via Cavour to the north.

Information

DANGERS & ANNOYANCES

Contrary to stereotypes, Palermo is a relatively safe city with low rates of violent crime. That said, it pays to follow a few basic rules. Wear handbags across your body and away from the street to avoid moped-riding thieves from snatching it. Be aware of your possessions in crowded areas, especially city buses and markets. Avoid poorly lit and deserted streets at night, especially those around the train station and the Kalsa district.

EMERGENCY

For an ambulance, call ☎118 or ☎091 666 55 28.

Police (Questura; ☎091 21 01 11; Piazza della Vittoria 8) Palermo's main station.

INTERNET ACCESS

Free wi-fi is available at many restaurants, cafes and bars in Palermo, and most hotels and B&Bs offer guests free, reliable wi-fi. The city also hosts numerous free wi-fi hotspots, including at Piazza Pretoria, Piazza Bellini, Piazza Bologni and Piazza San Domenico.

MEDICAL SERVICES

Hospital (Ospedale Civico; ☎091 666 11 11; www.arnascivico.it; Piazza Nicola Leotta; ⏲24hr) Emergency facilities.

POST

Main Post Office (Map p58; ☎091 753 53 92; Via Roma 322; ⏲8.20am-7pm Mon-Fri, to 12.30pm Sat) Smaller branch offices can be found at the train station (Map p58; Palermo Centrale Train Station; ⏲8.20am-1.30pm Mon & Tue, to 7pm Wed-Fri, to 12.30pm Sat) and on Piazza Verdi.

TOURIST INFORMATION

Municipal Tourist Office (Map p58; ☎091 740 80 21; http://turismo.comune.palermo.it; Piazza Bellini; ⏲8am-8pm Mon-Thu, to 6.30pm Fri, 9am-7pm Sun) The main branch of Palermo's city-run information booths. Other locations include Piazza Ruggero Settimo (Map p62; Teatro Politeama Garibaldi, Piazza Ruggero Settimo; ⏲8.30am-1.30pm Mon-Fri), Via Cavour (Map p62; Via Cavour; ⏲8.30am-6.30pm Mon-Fri, 9am-7pm Sun), the Port of Palermo and Mondello, though these are only intermittently staffed, with unpredictable hours.

Tourist Information – Falcone-Borsellino Airport (☎091 59 16 98; ⏲8.30am-7.30pm Mon-Fri, to 6pm Sat) Downstairs in the arrivals hall.

Getting There & Away

AIR

Falcone-Borsellino Airport (☎800 541880, 091 702 02 73; www.gesap.it) is at Punta Raisi, 35km northwest of Palermo on the A29 motorway. There are regular flights between Palermo and most mainland Italian cities.

BOAT

Numerous ferry companies operate from Palermo's **port** (Map p62; ☎091 604 31 11; cnr Via Francesco Crispi & Via Emerico Amari), just east of the New City.

Grandi Navi Veloci (Map p62; ☎010 209 45 91, 091 58 74 04; www.gnv.it; Calata Marinai d'Italia) Runs ferries to Civitavecchia (from €73), Genoa (from €90), Naples (from €44) and Tunis (from €72).

Grimaldi Lines (Map p62; ☎091 611 36 91, 081 49 64 44; www.grimaldi-lines.com; Via del Mare) Runs ferries to Salerno (from €43, 10 to 12 hours) and Tunis (from €35, 11 to 13½ hours) twice weekly, and to Livorno (from €49, 18 hours) thrice weekly.

Liberty Lines (☎0923 87 38 13; www.libertylines.it; Molo Vittorio Veneto) Runs hydrofoils to Ustica Wednesday to Monday year-round (from €24.45, 1½ hours, one to two daily).

Società Navigazione Siciliana (Siremar; Map p62; ☎ferry bookings 090 36 46 01, hydrofoil bookings 0923 87 38 13; www.siremar.it; Via Francesco Crispi 118, Palermo) Operates one daily car-ferry service between Ustica and Palermo (€18.35 one way, three hours), as well as one to three hydrofoil services daily (€25 one way, 1½ hours).

Tirrenia (Map p62; ☎892123; www.tirrenia.it; Calata Marinai d'Italia) Sails to Cagliari (from €41, 12 hours, Saturday only) and Naples (from €49, 10 hours, daily). From mid-July to early September, ferries to Cagliari sail on Wednesday and Sunday, not on Saturday.

BUS

Offices for all bus companies are located within a block or two of Palermo Centrale train station. The two main departure points are the **Piazzetta Cairoli bus terminal** (Map p58; Piazzetta Cairoli), just south of the train station's eastern entrance, and the **Intercity bus stop** (Map p58) on Via Paolo Balsamo, two blocks due east of the train station. Check locally with your bus company to make sure you're boarding at the appropriate stop.

Salemi (Map p58; ☎091 772 03 47; www.autoservizisalemi.it), Segesta, **SAIS Autolinee** (Map p58; ☎800 211020, 091 616 60 28; www.saisautolinee.it; Piazzetta Cairoli Bus Station) and **Interbus** (Map p58; ☎091 616 79 19; www.interbus.it) tickets are sold at the main bus terminal building at Piazzetta Cairoli. **AST** (Azienda Siciliana Trasporti; Map p58; ☎091 680 00 11; www.aziendasicilianatrasporti.it) and **Autoservizi Tarantola** (Map p58; ☎0924 310 20; www.tarantolabus.it) tickets can be purchased from the **New Bus Bar** (Map p58; ☎091 617 30 24; Via Paolo Balsamo 32). **Cuffaro** (Map p58; ☎091 616 15 10; www.cuffaro.info) tickets are purchased from the Cuffaro ticket office at Via Paolo Balsamo 13, opposite New Bus Bar.

Societá Autolinee Licata (SAL; ☎0922 40 13 60; www.autolineesal.it) runs between Palermo's Falcone-Borsellino Airport at Punta Raisi and Agrigento (€12.60, 2¾ hours, three daily Monday to Saturday).

CAR & MOTORCYCLE

Palermo is accessible on the A20–E90 toll road from Messina, and from Catania (A19–E932) via Enna. Trapani and Marsala are also easily accessible from Palermo by motorway (A29), while Agrigento and Palermo are linked by the SS121, a good state road through the interior of the island.

TRAIN

Regular services leave from **Palermo Centrale train station** (Piazza Giulio Cesare; ⏲6am-9pm) to Messina (from €12.80; three to 3¾ hours, eight to 14 daily), Catania (from €13.50, 2¾ to 5½ hours, five to 10 daily) and Agrigento (€9, two hours, six to 10 daily), as well as to nearby towns such as Cefalù (from €5.60, 45 minutes to one hour, nine to 10 daily). There are also Intercity trains to Reggio di Calabria, Naples and Rome.

Inside the station are ATMs, toilets and left-luggage facilities (first five hours €6 flat fee, next seven hours €0.90 per hour, all subsequent hours €0.40 per hour; office staffed 8am to 8pm).

Getting Around

TO/FROM THE AIRPORT

Prestia e Comandè (Map p58; ☎091 58 63 51; www.prestiaecomande.it; one-way/return €6.30/11) runs an efficient half-hourly bus service between 5am and 12.15pm that transfers passengers from the airport to the centre of Palermo, dropping people off outside the **Teatro Politeama Garibaldi** (Map p62; Via Dante) and Palermo Centrale train **station** (Map p58). To find the bus, follow the signs past the downstairs taxi rank and around the corner to the right. Tickets for the journey, which takes anywhere from 35 to 50 minutes depending on traffic, cost €6.30 one-way or €11 return and are purchased on the bus. Return journeys to the airport run between 4am and 10.30pm with the same frequency and pick up points.

(Continued on page 79

Sicilian Architecture

Architecture lovers will find themselves in heaven in Sicily. There is hardly a town that isn't graced with at least one mini-masterpiece. The unique style of Sicilian baroque is a feast for the senses, and there are Classical temples, shimmering mosaics, Byzantine churches and Norman forts to explore.

Contents

Above Cappella Palatina (p53)

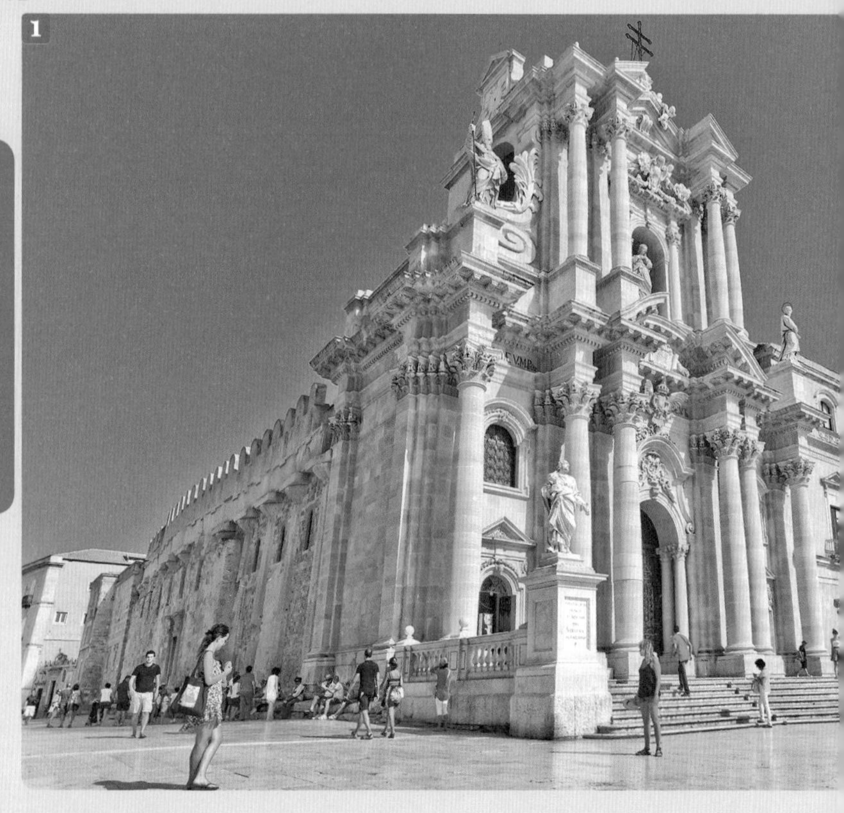
1

Baroque Cathedrals

The sight of Sicily's baroque cathedrals is one of the foremost reasons for visiting the island. Ranging from reformed ancient temples to whirling mixtures of baroque and neoclassical, each of these churches gives its city centre a unique lushness and grandeur.

Duomo

Syracuse's flamboyant cathedral (p185) lords it over the city's beautiful showpiece square. Its sumptuous facade is typically baroque, but the columns that run down the sides tell of a former life as a temple to the Greek goddess Athena.

Cattedrale di San Nicolò

In Noto, a town noted for its sublime baroque buildings, the spectacular Cattedrale di San Nicolò (p197) trumps the lot. Standing in monumental pomp at the top of a grandiose staircase, it stylishly fuses the best of baroque and neoclassical architecture.

Cattedrale di San Giorgio

Fans of the TV series *Inspector Montalbano* might recognise Ragusa's towering baroque cathedral (p206), often used as a backdrop. The work of Sicily's grand baroque maestro Rosario Gagliardi,

EDDY GALEOTTI/SHUTTERSTOCK ©

RODKARV/SHUTTERSTOCK ©

1. Duomo (p185), Syracuse **2.** Cattedrale di Sant'Agata (p170), Catania **3.** Cattedrale di San Giorgio (p206), Ragusa

MARCO OSSINO/SHUTTERSTOCK ©

it's a masterclass in overstated style and unrestrained passion.

Chiesa di San Giorgio

A commanding presence, Modica's great church (p202) looms over the town's serpentine streets and bustling medieval centre. Its monumental facade is a stunning example of baroque on a grand scale while the echoing interior drips with silver and gold.

Cattedrale di Sant'Agata

The highlight of Catania's centre is its wedding-cake cathedral (p170). Dedicated to the city's patron saint, Agata, it's unique among Sicily's baroque churches for its black-and-white tones, a reflection of the volcanic stone used in its construction.

SICILIAN BAROQUE

After being devastated by an earthquake in 1693, Sicily was presented with an opportunity to redesign many of its cities and experiment with a new architectural style that was taking Europe by storm: baroque. A backlash against the pared-down classical aesthetic of the Renaissance, this new style was dramatic, curvaceous and downright sexy – a perfect match for Sicily's unorthodox and exuberant character. Aristocrats in towns such as Noto, Modica, Ragusa, Catania and Syracuse rushed to build baroque *palazzi* (palaces), many decorated with the grotesque masks and *putti* (cherubs) that had long been a hallmark of the island's architecture. Even the church got into it, commissioning ostentatious churches and oratories aplenty.

ELISA LOCCI/SHUTTERSTOCK ©

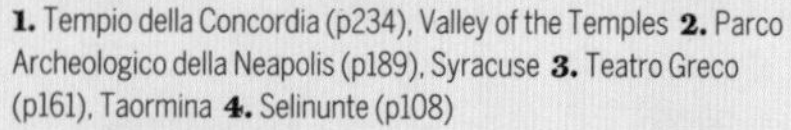

1. Tempio della Concordia (p234), Valley of the Temples **2.** Parco Archeologico della Neapolis (p189), Syracuse **3.** Teatro Greco (p161), Taormina **4.** Selinunte (p108)

JTB PHOTO/UIG VIA GETTY IMAGES ©

Classical Masterpieces

Sicily is renowned for its classical masterpieces, from the perfectly preserved temples at Agrigento, Segesta and Selinunte to the ancient Greek theatres of Syracuse and Taormina.

Valley of the Temples

The model for Unesco's logo and one of the world's best-preserved Greek temples, Tempio della Concordia is the star turn of stunning Agrigento. The ruins (p234) are what's left of Akragas, once the fourth-largest city in the ancient world.

Parco Archeologico della Neapolis

A major power in ancient times, Syracuse boasts one of Sicily's great classical monuments – Teatro Greco (p190), a supremely well-preserved Greek amphitheatre. In the theatre's shadow, you can explore caves where slaves once laboured.

Selinunte

You don't have to be an archaeologist to be bowled over by the Greek temples at Selinunte (p108). They are beautifully set against a sunny seaside backdrop that looks particularly fabulous in spring, when wildflowers set the scene ablaze with colour.

Segesta

Standing in proud isolation amid rugged, green hills, the ruins of ancient Segesta (p90) are an unforgettable sight. Pride of place goes to the stately 5th-century-BC temple – but don't miss the amphitheatre, dramatically gouged out of the hillside.

Taormina

Enjoying spectacular views of snowcapped Mt Etna and the Ionian Sea, Taormina's Teatro Greco (p161) makes the perfect venue for the town's summer film and arts festivals.

Inspiring Mosaics

Among the treasures left behind by Sicily's many invaders is the island's wealth of exquisite mosaics. Representing everything from biblical themes to wild African animals, these date to the Roman, Byzantine and Arab-Norman periods.

Cappella Palatina

Sicily's greatest work of Arab-Norman art is this sparkling mosaic-encrusted chapel (p53) in the Palazzo dei Normanni in Palermo. Every inch of the arched interior is emblazoned with golden mosaics and biblical figures. Precious inlaid marble and an Arabic-style carved wooden ceiling complete the picture.

Villa Romana del Casale

This villa (p222) in Piazza Armerina is home to some of the world's finest Roman mosaics. Buried for centuries under a layer of mud, they stand out for their scale, use of colour, and scenes of mythological monsters and bikini-clad girls working out with weights.

Duomo di Cefalù

The robust, fortress-like exterior of Cefalù's hulking Norman cathedral (p114) guards one of Sicily's most celebrated mosaics: the depiction of Christ Pantocrator in the apse. Dating to the mid-12th century, it's a remarkably lifelike depiction of a severe man with drawn cheeks and a dark beard.

La Martorana

A favourite venue for local weddings, Palermo's most popular medieval church (p50) is a treasure trove of Byzantine mosaics.

Cattedrale di Monreale

An outstanding example of Norman architecture, Monreale's famous cathedral (p80) harbours a dazzling interior of Byzantine-influenced mosaics depicting stories from the Old Testament.

1. La Martorana (p50), Palermo **2.** Sala delle Dieci Ragazze (p2 Villa Romana del Casale **3.** Cattedrale di Monreale (p80), Monre

2

EYE UBIQUITOUS/UIG VIA GETTY IMAGES ©

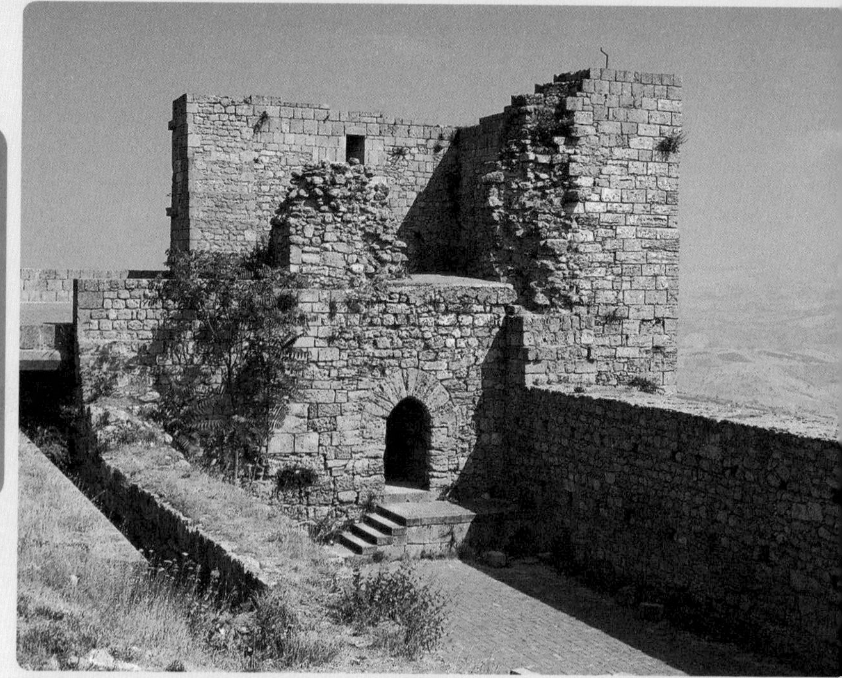

Castello di Lombardia (p214), Enna

Captivating Castles

Sicily's castles have played a vital role in the island's history, serving as forts during the Norman era, when most of them were built. They continue to tower over landscapes and cities, and are some of the island's most impressive sights. Some are even said to be still holding ancient ghosts captive!

Palazzo dei Normanni

This palace (p53) in Palermo has long been the nerve centre of island power. It housed one of Europe's most glittering courts and is now the seat of Sicily's regional government.

Castello di Lombardia

As impressive as this formidable 14th-century castle (p214) in Enna is, the real highlight is the sweeping panorama that unfolds from the top of Torre Pisana, the tallest of the castle's six remaining towers. As far as the eye can see, great swaths of rolling green countryside stretch off in all directions.

Castello di Caccamo

One of Italy's largest castles, Caccamo's impregnable fort (p118) served as a Norman stronghold and then a base for the powerful 14th-century Chiaramonte family. It's protected by a series of forbidding walls and ingenious fortifications, and commands magnificent views.

Castello dei Ventimiglia

An evocative sight, the enormous castle (p119) that gives Castelbuono its name is said to be haunted. Every month the ghost of a long-dead queen runs the lengths of its corridors, which now host a small museum and art gallery.

(Continued from page 70)

Due to track work, the **Trinacria Express** (☎ 091 704 40 07; one-way ticket €6.30) train is currently running between the airport and Palermo Notarbartolo train station, located in the New City. Normal services to Palermo Centrale station are expected to resume by the end of 2016. In the meantime, the Prestia e Comandè airport shuttle bus is a much more convenient option to reach the city.

There is a taxi rank outside the arrivals hall and the fare to/from Palermo is between €35 and €45, depending on your destination in the city.

All the major car-hire companies are represented at the airport.

CAR & MOTORCYCLE

When making a booking, ask your hotel about parking; many hotels have a *garage convenzionato*, a local garage that offers special rates to their guests (typically between €12 and €20 per day).

Alternatively, you'll need to find a legal space on the city's streets or piazzas. For spaces marked by blue lines, you must get a ticket from a machine (usually every day except Sunday; see the hours of operation posted at the machine nearest your vehicle). For spaces with signs stating a maximum parking time but with no ticket machine in evidence, you'll need to purchase a form called a *scheda* – available from tobacconists – and place it on your dashboard, first making sure to scratch off the circles corresponding to the time and date you parked there. If you neglect to do this, or if you park longer than the time allowed, you may be fined.

PUBLIC TRANSPORT

Palermo's orange, white and blue city buses, operated by **AMAT** (☎ 091 35 01 11, 848 800817; www.amat.pa.it), are frequent but often overcrowded and slow. The free map handed out at Palermo tourist offices details the major bus lines; most stop at the train station.

Tickets, valid for 90 minutes, cost €1.40 and can be pre-purchased from *tabaccherie* (tobacconists) or the AMAT bus **booth** (Map p58) on Piazza Giulio Cesare just outside Palermo Centrale train station, or €1.80 on board the bus. A day pass costs €3.50. Once you board the bus, ensure to validate your ticket in the machine.

TAXI

Taxis are expensive in Palermo, and heavy traffic can make matters worse. Official taxis should have a *tassametro* (meter), which records the fare; check for this before embarking. Hailing a passing taxi on the street is not customary; rather, you'll need to phone ahead for a taxi or wait at one of the taxi ranks at major travel hubs such as the train station, Piazza Politeama, Teatro Massimo and Piazza Independenza.

BUSES FROM PALERMO

COMPANY	DESTINATION	PRICE (€)	DURATION (HR)	FREQUENCY
AST	Ragusa	13.50	4	4 daily Mon-Fri, 3 Sat, 2 Sun
AST	Modica	13.50	4½	4 daily Mon-Fri, 3 Sat, 2 Sun
Autoservizi Tarantola	Segesta	7	1¼	3 daily Mon-Sat Apr-Oct
Cuffaro	Agrigento	9	2	8 daily Mon-Fri, 6 Sat, 3 Sun
Interbus	Syracuse	13.50	3½	2 to 3 daily
SAIS Autolinee	Enna	9	1¾	2 daily Sun-Fri, 1 Sat
SAIS Autolinee	Messina	15	2¾	6 daily Mon-Fri, 3 Sat & Sun
SAIS Autolinee	Catania	12.50	2¾	12 daily Mon-Sat, 9 Sun
SAIS Trasporti (p121)	Petralia Soprana	10.30	2	3 daily Mon-Sat, 2 Sun
SAIS Trasporti	Petralia Sottana	10.30	1¾	3 daily Mon-Sat, 2 Sun
SAIS Trasporti	Polizzi Generosa	9.30	1¼	3 daily Mon-Sat, 2 Sun
SAIS Trasporti	Cefalù	5.70	1	6 daily Mon-Fri, 5 Sat
SAIS Trasporti	Rome	36	12	1 daily (overnight service)
Salemi	Mazara del Vallo	9	2	12 daily Mon-Fri, 9 Sat, 4 Sun
Salemi	Marsala	9.40	2¼	5 to 7 daily
Salemi	Trapani's Birgi airport	11	1¾	5 to 7 daily

PALERMO REGION

Palermo is in turn exhilarating and exhausting, and after a few days visitors often find that they need a respite from its noisy, dirty and crowded streets. Fortunately, there are plenty of options for an easy urban escape.

Mondello

☎ 091

In the summer months, it sometimes seems as if the entire population of Palermo has packed a beach towel and a pair of D&G shades and decamped to this popular beach resort, 11km north from the centre of town.

Originally a muddy, malaria-ridden port, Mondello only really became fashionable in the 19th century, when the city's elite flocked here in their carriages, thus warranting the huge Liberty-style pier that dominates the seafront and kicking off a craze for building opulent summer villas. Most of the beaches are private (two loungers and an umbrella cost around €15 to €22 per day), but there is also a wide swath of public beach crammed with swimmers, pedalos and noisy jet skis.

Eating

Seafood restaurants and snack stalls have colonised the *lido* (beach; Viale Regina Elena) and the main piazza hosts numerous cafes with outdoor seating. One of Sicily's trendiest restaurants, **Bye Bye Blues** (☎ 091 684 14 15; www.byebyeblues.it; Via del Garofalo 23; 6-courses €60; ⏲ 1-2.30pm & 8-10.30pm Tue-Sun), is located a few streets back from the beach.

Getting There & Away

Catch **AMAT bus** 806 (€1.40, 20 minutes, every 10 to 20 minutes between 5.45am and 10.30pm, fewer services on Sunday) from Piazza Sturzo (Map p62). The last bus back to Palermo departs Mondello at 11pm.

Monreale

☎ 091 / POP 39,410 / ELEV 310M

Overlooking Palermo and the Tyrhennian Sea, the hillside town of Monreale is home to one of Sicily's greatest cultural treasures, the Cattedrale di Monreale.

Sights

★ **Cattedrale di Monreale** CATHEDRAL
(☎ 091 640 44 03; Piazza del Duomo; admission to cathedral free, north transept, Roano chapel & terrace €4, cloisters adult/reduced €6/3; ⏲ cathedral 8.30am-12.45pm & 2.30-5pm Mon-Sat, 8-10am & 2.30-5pm Sun, cloisters 9am-6.30pm Mon-Sat, to 1pm Sun) Inspired by a vision of the Virgin and determined to outdo his grandfather Roger II, who was responsible for the cathedral in Cefalù and the Cappella Palatina in Palermo, William II set about building the Cattedrale di Monreale, 8km southwest of Palermo. Incorporating Norman, Arab, Byzantine and classical elements, the cathedral is considered the finest example of Norman architecture in Sicily. It's also one of the most impressive architectural legacies of the Italian Middle Ages.

Although the cathedral's mosaicists hailed from Sicily and Venice, the stylised influence of the Byzantines pervades their work. Completed in 1184 after only 10 years' work, their shimmering masterpieces depict biblical tales, from the creation of man to the Assumption, in 42 different episodes. The beauty of the mosaics cannot be overstated – you have to see for yourself Noah's ark perched atop the waves or Christ healing a leper infected with large leopard-sized spots. The story of Adam and Eve is wonderfully portrayed, with a grumpy-looking, post-Eden-eviction Eve sitting on a rock while Adam labours in the background. The large mosaic of Christ, dominating the central apse, is stunning. Binoculars make viewing the mosaics easier, although they are still impressive to the naked eye. For a guide to the various scenes, print out the handy key and map at www.seepalermo.com/monrealekeyprint.htm.

Adjacent to the cathedral is the entrance to the **cloister**, which illustrates William's love of Arab artistry. This tranquil courtyard is an ode to Orientalism, with elegant Romanesque arches supported by an array of slender columns alternately decorated with shimmering mosaic patterns. Each capital is unique, and taken together they represent a sculptural record of medieval Sicily. Especially interesting is the capital of the 19th column on the west aisle, depicting William II offering the cathedral to the Madonna.

For a bird's-eye view of the cloister, its geometric garden and the cathedral's mountainous surrounds, climb the stairs to the cathedral's terrace, accessed from inside the cathedral.

Eating

You'll find numerous trattorias and restaurants of varying quality in the vicinity of the cathedral. As a general rule, avoid places

Around Palermo

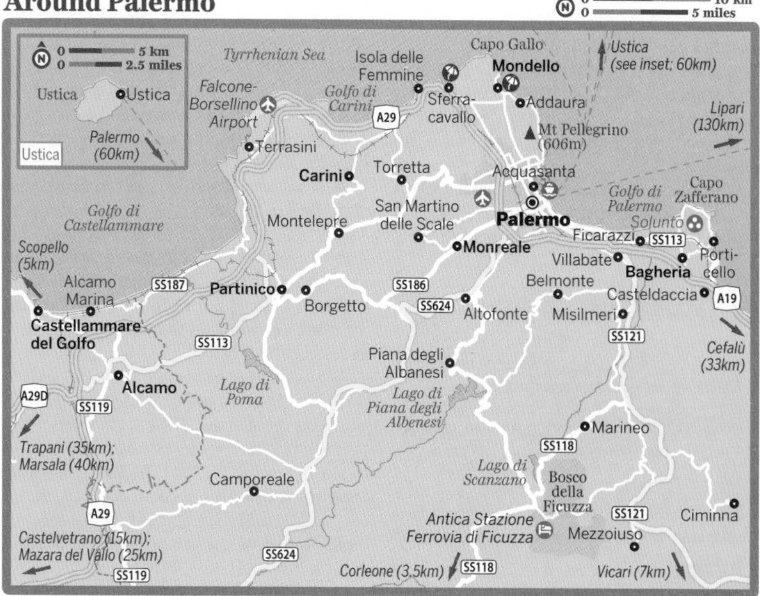

offering a *menu turistico* (tourist menu), which usually signals mediocre meals. Two conveniently located restaurants popular with locals and clued-in foodies are meat-geared **Bricco & Bacco** (☎091 641 77 73; www.briccoebacco.it; Via D'Acquisto 13; meals €25-35; ⏲12.30-3.30pm & 7.45pm-midnight Tue-Sun) and seafood-focused **Ciambra** (☎091 640 67 17; Via Rosolino Pilo 1; meals €25-35; ⏲noon-2.30pm & 7-11.30pm Tue-Sun; 📶).

Getting There & Away

To reach Monreale, take **AMAT bus** 389 (€1.40, 30 to 40 minutes, roughly every 75 minutes) from Piazza Indipendenza in Palermo (Map p52). The bus will drop you off at Via Fontana del Drago, from where the cathedral is a 450m uphill walk along either Via Palermo or Via D'Acquisto.

Alternatively, you can catch an **AST bus** (Map p58) for Monreale from in front of Palermo Centrale train station (€2.40, 40 minutes, hourly Monday to Saturday).

Corleone

☎091 / POP 11,200 / ELEV 600M

Having suffered centuries of poverty and possessing a well-documented history as a Mafia stronghold, the town of Corleone – 60km from Palermo and best known through Francis Ford Coppola's classic *Godfather* trilogy – has been trying to reinvent itself over the last decade. For travellers, the one reason to head here is for CIDMA, an absorbing anti-Mafia museum.

Sights

CIDMA MUSEUM

(Centro Internazionale di Documentazione sulla Mafia e Movimento Antimafia; ☎340 4025601, 091 845 242 95; cidmacorleone@gmail.com; Via Giovanni Valenti 7; admission Jun-Aug €5, price varies other times; ⏲by arrangement) Corleone's small anti-Mafia museum recounts the terrifying history of Sicily's Cosa Nostra crime syndicate, focusing on the brave efforts of the anti-Mafia campaigners and judges who spoke out against organised crime rather than succumbing to the Mafia-promoted culture of omertà (silence). Visits are by guided-tour only, available in English, Italian and Spanish. Call or email ahead to reserve a space, as tour frequency and the availability of multilingual guides vary.

A huge 'No Mafia' sign greets visitors at the entrance, as does a poignant quote from murdered anti-Mafia judge Giovanni Falcone about the unbearable but necessary sacrifice demanded by fighting this just cause. Three rooms are visited: the first holds the very documents from the groundbreaking maxi-trials of 1986–87; the second exhibits photos by photojournalist Letizia Battaglia, who documented Mafia crimes in the 1970s and 1980s; and the third displays photos of Mafia bosses, the men of justice who fought them and people who have lost loved ones.

The museum is located in a cobbled street just off Piazza Garibaldi, a 450m walk up Via Francesco Bentivegna from Piazza Falcone e Borsellino.

Getting There & Away

AST (p70) buses travel between Palermo and Corleone (€5.40, 1½ hours, nine daily). In Corleone, passengers are dropped off at Piazza Falcone e Borsellino. Check return bus times as services are infrequent. Also, be back at the bus stop 15 minutes before the official departure time as buses sometimes leave early.

Ustica

091 / POP 1370

This tiny island floats alone almost 60km north of Palermo in the Tyrrhenian Sea. Part of the Aeolian volcanic chain, the land mass is actually the tip of a submerged volcano. Blazing pink-and-red hibiscus flowers and prickly green cacti punctuate the island's black, volcanic-rock. Ustica's shoreline is littered with dramatic grottoes and the surrounding waters – protected within Area Marina Protetta Isola di Ustica (Island of Ustica Protected Marine Area) – are kept sparkling and clean by an Atlantic current, resulting in an underwater wonderland of fish and coral. Indeed, the reserve is host to half of the marine species present in Mediterranean waters.

Palermitans flock here in July and August, so consider visiting in June and September to enjoy the beautiful coastline and grottoes without the crowds. Note that between October and Easter most of the island's services close down during the week and ferry services from the mainland can be cancelled in bad weather.

Activities

Diving

Divers from all over the world come to Ustica between May and October to explore its magnificent underwater sites. Highlights include the **underwater archaeological trail** off Punta Cavazzi, where artefacts such as anchors and Roman amphorae can be admired. Other popular dive sites are the **Scoglio del Medico**, an outcrop of basalt riddled with caves and gorges that plunge to great depths; and **Secca di Colombara**, a magnificent rainbow-coloured display of sponges and gorgonias.

There are numerous dive centres that offer dive itineraries and hire equipment. Among them, **Diving Center Ustica** (335 8210017; www.usticadiving.it; Contrada Piano Cardoni; one snorkel/dive incl equipment €20/55) – affiliated with Hotel Diana – stands out as the lone operator managed by local residents born and raised on Ustica.

Area Marina Protetta Isola di Ustica is divided into three zones. Zone A extends along the west flank of the island from the promontory north of Punta Spalmatore to Punta Megna and as far as 350m offshore. You can swim within its boundaries at designated spots, but fishing and boating are prohibited. Two of the island's most beautiful natural grottoes – the **Grotta Segreta (Secret Grotto)** and the **Grotta Rosata (Pink Grotto)** – are located here.

Zone B extends beyond Zone A from Punta Gavazzi to Punta Omo Morto and as far as 4.8km offshore; swimming and underwater photography are permitted within its boundaries, as is hook-and-line fishing. Zone C applies to the rest of the coast; swimming and boating are allowed and national fishing regulations apply. Always check your itinerary with a dive centre or the marine national park headquarters before you dive.

Hiking

Ustica's compact size makes it ideal for walking, with a number of walking trails available.

For a grand tour of the coastline, start by following the signposted **Sentiero del Mezzogiorno** south from town. The trail soon curves west, skirting high bluffs and traversing occasional patches of pine forest before eventually rejoining the coast at Ustica's western lighthouse (simply called **Faro** on local maps). From the lighthouse, continue north on foot or by local bus to **Cappella della Madonna della Croce**, an 18th-century white adobe church high on the hillside. Here another footpath splits off, following the northern coastal bluffs to the **Villaggio Preistorico**, a rather poorly maintained remnant of a Bronze Age village. Finish the loop by following the main road back into town. The whole circuit takes between three and four hours.

Another scenic trail passes through pine woods to the summit of **Guardia di Mezzo** (248m), before descending to the best part of the coast at **Spalmatore**, where it's possible to swim in natural rock pools.

Closer to town, shorter walking paths lead to the **Rocca della Falconiera**, a defensive tower above the church; to the lookout point above the lighthouse at **Punta Omo Morto**; and to the **Torre Santa Maria**, a Bourbon-era tower just south of the town centre. Ask at the tourist office for directions.

Eating

Ustica is famous for its tiny, dark lentils. The smallest variety grown in Italy, they're revered by top-tier chefs across the country. Other specialties include capers and fresh seafood. The island's fruits and vegetables are renowned for their intense flavour, attributed to Ustica's rich volcanic soil.

Between October and Easter, most of Ustica's restaurants close down during the week.

Da Umberto SICILIAN **€€**
(☎091 844 95 42; Via della Vittoria 7; meals €25-35; ⊙noon-2pm & 7-11pm) Popular with Slow Food fans, this veteran restaurant is lovingly run by the Tranchina family. In the kitchen is matriarch Giovanna, whose allegiance to seasonal and local ingredients drives beautiful, nostalgic dishes like *minestra con tenerumi, fiori di zucca e caciocavallo* (soup of cucuzza leaves, zucchini flowers and caciocavallo cheese) and *polpettine di finocchio selvatico in agrodolce* (wild-fennel patties in sweet-and-sour sauce).

Ristorante Giulia SEAFOOD **€€**
(☎091 844 90 07; Via San Francesco 16; meals €25-35; ⊙8pm-midnight June–mid-Sep) Just north of Ustica's central square, this family-run eatery is renowned for its fresh, local seafood, put to mouthwatering work in dishes like *zuppa di scorfano* (scorpion-fish soup), *spaghetti con l'aragosta* (spaghetti with lobster) and delicate *polpette di pesce* (fish patties). If you're lucky enough to be around when it's open, work up an appetite and make a beeline for it.

Information

Area Marina Protetta di Ustica (Marine National Park; ☎091 844 94 56; www.parks.it/riserva.marina.isola.ustica; Piazza Umberto I 11; ⊙9am-noon & 5-7pm mid-June–mid-Oct) The Marine Reserve Visitors Centre is in the centre of the village and can advise on activities, boat trips and dive centres.

VisitUstica (☎338 7414970; www.visitustica.it; Piazza Umberto I; ⊙10am-1pm & 5-7pm Mon-Sun Jun-Sep) On Ustica's main square; offers info on the island and the marine reserve.

Getting There & Away

Società Navigazione Siciliana (p70) operates one daily car-ferry service between Ustica and Palermo (€18 one way, three hours), as well as one to three daily hydrofoil services (€25 one way, 1½ hours).

Liberty Lines (p70) runs hydrofoils between Ustica and Palermo Wednesday to Monday year-round (from €24, 1½ hours, one to two daily). Liberty Lines also operates a Naples–Ustica hydrofoil service on Saturdays from June to early September (€91 one way, 4¼ hours).

Climbing the hill through Ustica's church square, look for both companies' ticket offices on your left.

Getting Around

Measuring a modest 8.7 sq km, Ustica is easy to explore on foot.

A local bus (€1.20) makes regular circuits of the island, leaving every 45 to 60 minutes in each direction. If you're after your own wheels, **Ricarica ARA** (☎091 844 96 05, 338 1100972; Banchina Barresi) rents out 50cc and 125cc scooters.

In summertime, **Bicincittà** (☎800 75 55 15; www.bicincitta.com) provides rental bikes that can be picked up and dropped off at two sites around the island using cash or credit card. Rental per day is €15.

Western Sicily

Includes ➡

Why Go?

Sicily's windswept western coast has beckoned invaders for millennia. Its richly stocked fishing grounds, hilltop vineyards and coastal saltpans were coveted by the Phoenicians, Greeks, Romans and Normans, all of whom influenced the region's landscape and culture. Even the English left their mark, with 18th-century entrepreneurs lured here and made rich by one of the world's most famous sweet wines, marsala.

Today, this part of the island is coming into its own as an off-the-beaten-track destination, perfect for those who savour slow travel. There's an amazingly diverse range of experiences to be had here. Standout attractions include the ancient ruins of Segesta and Selinunte, the hilltop village of Erice and the Golfo di Castellammare, with its stunning juxtaposition of sea and mountain scenery. Adding to western Sicily's appeal are its unique local cuisine and proximity to Palermo and Trapani international airports.

Best Places to Eat

- ➡ Il Veliero (p102)
- ➡ Osteria La Bettolaccia (p93)
- ➡ Syráh (p88)
- ➡ Da Vittorio (p110)
- ➡ San Lorenzo Osteria (p105)

Best Places to Sleep

- ➡ Pensione Tranchina (p247)
- ➡ Il Profumo del Sale (p248)
- ➡ Melia Resort Dimore Storiche (p249)
- ➡ Marettimo Residence (p248)
- ➡ Hotel Elimo (p248)

Road Distances (km)

	Marsala	Scopello	Segesta	Selinunte
Scopello	75			
Segesta	50	30		
Selinunte	45	70	60	
Trapani	30	35	30	95

GOLFO DI CASTELLAMMARE

The stunning promontory between Castellammare del Golfo and Monte Cofano (659m) is perhaps the most beautiful in all of Sicily. The small coastal city of Castallammare is the most accessible destination on this stretch of coast, but those prepared to be a bit more adventurous will discover the unspoiled Riserva Naturale dello Zingaro a short distance to the northwest; here, the wild coastal landscape is dotted with tempting swimming coves and quaint settlements built around historic *baglios* (manor houses) and *tonnare* (tuna-processing plants). Added to all this are the ancient ruins of Segesta, only a short drive inland, and the popular beach town of San Vito Lo Capo at the promontory's northwestern tip.

Scopello

☎0924 / POP 385

The hamlet of Scopello couldn't be any more charming if it tried. Built around an 18th-century *baglio* (manor house) fortified with a high wall and huge gates, its white houses and smooth-stone streets look like they belong in a 1950s Italian movie. In fact, the historic *tonnara* on the shore below is a popular film location – the 2004 Hollywood blockbuster *Ocean's Twelve* was filmed here, as was an episode of the *Inspector Montalbano* TV series.

Favourite pastimes in Scopello include sipping a coffee on the main piazza, hiking in the nearby Riserva Naturale dello Zingaro and swimming in one of Sicily's most idyllic coves, Spiaggia dei Faraglioni, which is next to the *tonnara*.

Try to avoid Scopello in August, when it becomes unpleasantly crowded.

Sights & Activities

Spiaggia dei Faraglioni BEACH

(www.tonnaradiscopello.com; €3; ⏲9am-7pm) Overlooking incredibly blue waters, this pebbly but stupendously picturesque beach sits next to an old tuna factory at the foot of dramatic rock formations (one of which is crowned by a medieval tower), just below the town of Scopello. The beach is private property, so you'll have to pay admission, plus a parking fee, and abide by other restrictions – no beach umbrellas or photos of the *tonnara*, which is for the private use of the owners and their guests.

Cetaria Diving Centre DIVING

(☎368 3864808, 0924 54 11 77; www.cetaria.it; Via Ciro Menotti 4, Scopello; ⏲Apr-Oct) With more than 15 years of experience, this diving centre in Scopello organises dives and underwater tours of the Zingaro nature reserve between April and October, visiting underwater caves and two shipwrecks; they also offer boat excursions and snorkelling.

Eating

You'll find a good mix of eateries within 200m of the grand cobbled courtyard at the centre of town – including bakeries, pizzerias and a terrace restaurant serving pricier Sicilian fare with spectacular views.

If you're staying at Pensione Tranchina (p247), be sure to take advantage of its fabulous home-cooked meals. Unfortunately, the *pensione* doesn't cater for outsiders unless one of its own guests opts to skip dinner; interested non-guests are welcome to check around 5pm to see if a table has opened up.

Bar Nettuno SICILIAN €€

(☎0924 54 13 62; Baglio Isonzo 13; meals €30-40; ⏲9am-late) Tucked into the cobbled courtyard at the heart of Scopello, this bar has an outdoor terrace that's perfect for late-afternoon drinks, but it also serves excellent food – from *arancine* (stuffed rice balls) and *pane cunzatu* (open-faced Sicilian sandwiches) to full seafood meals featuring grilled octopus, tuna with pistachios or pasta with clam sauce. Service sometimes suffers during busy periods.

Getting There & Away

Scopello is 10km northwest of Castellammare del Golfo via the SS187 and the SP63.

Autoservizi Russo (☎0924 3 13 64; www.russoautoservizi.it) runs buses between Castellammare del Golfo and Scopello (€2.70, 20 minutes, four daily except Sunday).

San Vito Lo Capo

☎0923 / POP 4635

Occupying the tip of Capo San Vito is the seaside town of San Vito Lo Capo, full of beachcombers and sun worshippers in summer. San Vito is renowned for its crescent-shaped sandy beach, one of the prettiest in Sicily, where limpid turquoise and ultramarine waters are juxtaposed against the dramatic mountain backdrop of Monte Monaco.

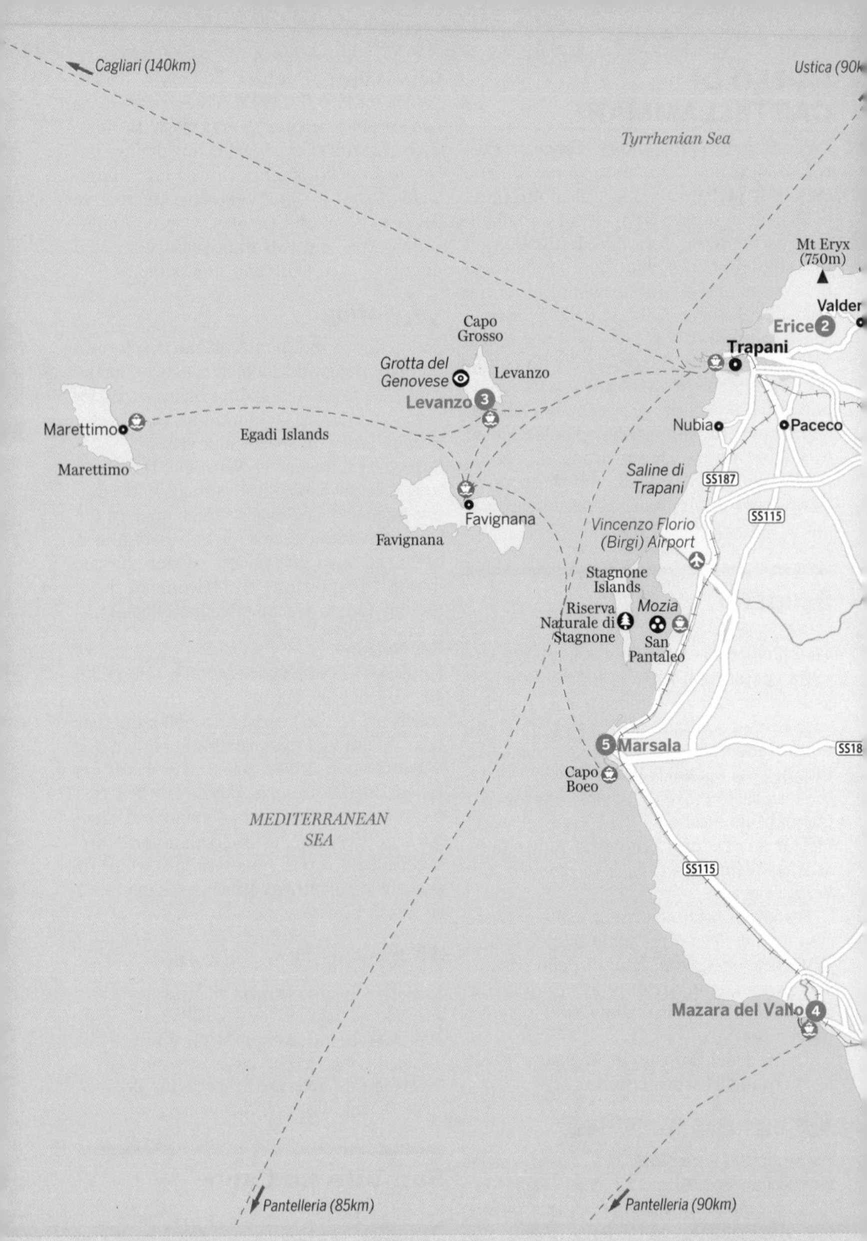

Cagliari (140km)
Ustica (90k
Tyrrhenian Sea
Mt Eryx (750m)
Valder
Erice 2
Capo Grosso
Trapani
Grotta del Genovese
Levanzo
Levanzo 3
Marettimo
Egadi Islands
Nubia
Paceco
Marettimo
Saline di Trapani
SS187
SS115
Favignana
Favignana
Vincenzo Florio (Birgi) Airport
Stagnone Islands
Riserva Naturale di Stagnone
Mozia
San Pantaleo
5 Marsala
SS18
Capo Boeo
MEDITERRANEAN SEA
SS115
Mazara del Vallo 4
Pantelleria (85km)
Pantelleria (90km)

Western Sicily Highlights

1 **Segesta** (p90) Contemplating one of the world's most perfect classical temples atop an idyllic hillside.

2 **Castello di Venere** (p97) Planning your next move while surveying western Sicily's stunning landscape from Erice's Norman castle.

3 **Grotta del Genovese** (p101) Exploring ancient cave art on the island of Levanzo.

4 **La Casbah** (p106) Admiring hand-painted wall tiles and stopping in for fish couscous in the narrow lanes of Mazara del Vallo's old Saracen quarter.

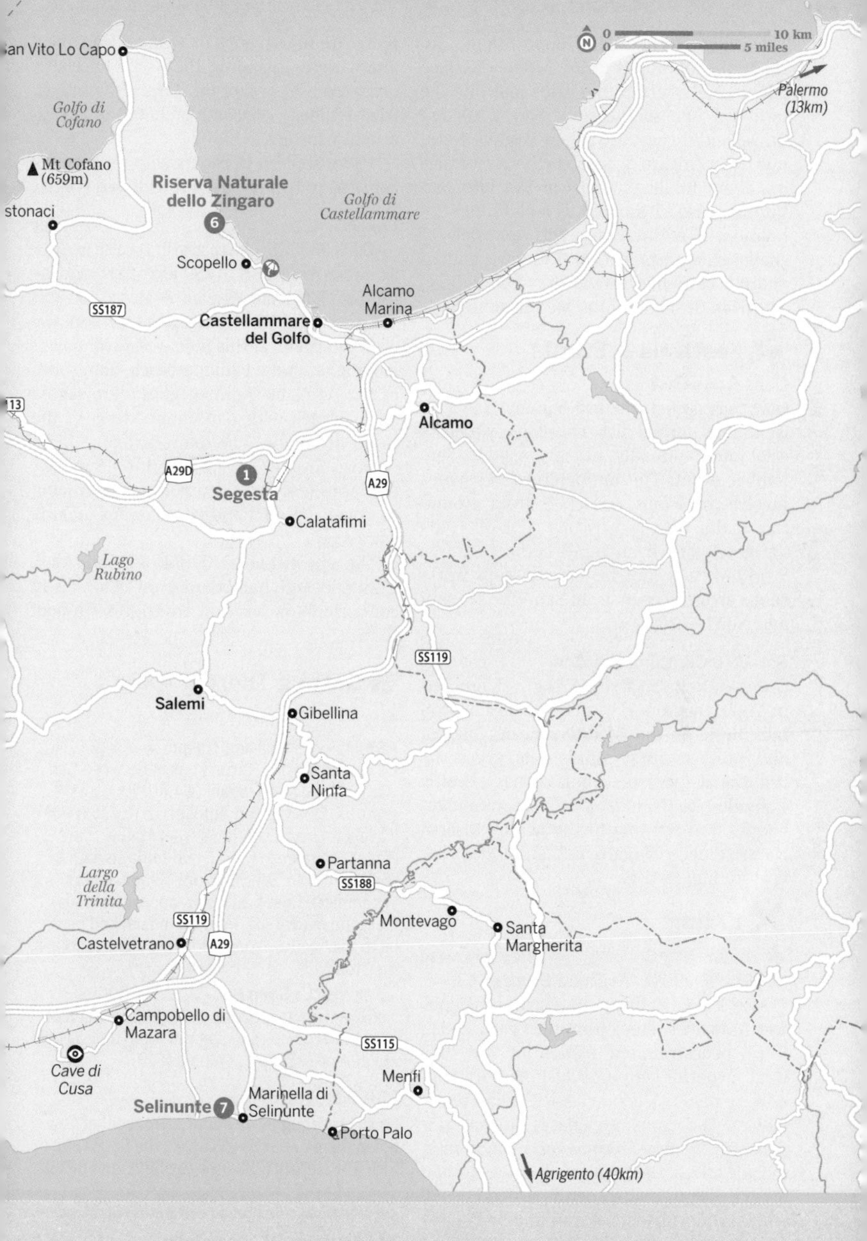

5 **Marsala** (p103) Joining the evening *passeggiata* (evening stroll) through the marble-paved streets, then people-watching over aperitifs at a streetside *enoteca* (wine bar).

6 **Riserva Naturale dello Zingaro** (p88) Walking the coastal trails near Scopello, stopping to visit museums of local history and culture along the way.

7 **Selinunte** (p108) Getting a sense of historical perspective as you roam through gargantuan piles of crumbled columns on the seaside bluffs.

Excellent local hiking opportunities include the 3km ascent of Monte Monaco (about 2½ hours round trip; look for the trailhead just southeast of San Vito) and the splendid coastal trails of Riserva Naturale dello Zingaro, whose northern entrance lies about 10km southeast of San Vito. San Vito has also blossomed as a climbing destination in recent years, with a variety of challenging crags just outside town and an autumn climbing festival drawing enthusiasts from throughout the Mediterranean.

Festivals & Events

Cous Cous Fest FOOD
(www.couscousfest.it; mid–late Sep) San Vito is famous for its fish couscous, which is celebrated annually at this six-day September event. The multicultural festivities involve musicians and chefs from around the world, with a couscous cook-off (Italy against teams from other countries), free World Music concerts, and couscous workshops given by chefs from San Vito, Trapani and North Africa.

San Vito Climbing Festival OUTDOORS
(www.sanvitoclimbingfestival.it/eng) Launched in 2009, this four-day, mid-October festival bills itself as the Mediterranean's biggest and most exciting multisports event. Its traditional focus on climbing has recently expanded to include kayaking, mountain biking, trail running in the nearby Riserva Naturale dello Zingaro, and an outdoor adventure film festival.

Eating

★**Syráh** MODERN SICILIAN €€
(0923 97 20 28; Via Savoia 5; meals €30-45; noon-3pm & 7.30-11pm) Offering prime people-watching a few steps from the beach in San Vito's pedestrianised restaurant row, this local favourite shows off chef Vito Cipponeri's creative twists on classic Sicilian ingredients. Audacious appetisers (mixed raw fish with Modica chocolate and lemon marmalade) share the menu with couscous and other delicious mains such as seafood ravioli with shrimp, artichokes and tuna roe.

Al Ritrovo SICILIAN €€
(0923 97 56 56; www.alritrovo.it; Viale Cristoforo Colombo 314, Castelluzzo; meals €30-40; 12.30-2pm & 7.30-10pm) Acclaimed by the international Slow Food organisation, this roadside eatery 8km south of San Vito features couscous prominently on the menu. However, there are also plenty of seafood and meat alternatives, including the house speciality *gran frittura con pescato del golfo* (mixed fried seafood), all complemented by an excellent wine list.

There are also 13 rooms with modern decor (€49 to €99 per person with half board).

Pocho SEAFOOD €€
(0923 97 25 25; www.pocho.it; Località Isulidda; fixed-price meals €38; 7.30-10pm daily mid-Jun–mid-Sep, 7.30-10pm Wed-Sat & Mon, 12.30-3pm Sun rest of year) Dinner is a feast for both the eyes and palate at this hotel-restaurant overlooking dramatic Isulidda beach, 2km south of San Vito. In summer, guests are seated on a terrace with panoramic views of the Golfo di Cofano. The daily-changing menu revolves around local seafood; on Sundays, chef Marilù serves a couscous tasting menu, preceded by an optional couscous-making workshop.

The adjacent hotel (double with breakfast from €80, with half board from €120) has 12 comfortable rooms and an impressive pool terrace.

Getting There & Away

BUS

AST (Azienda Siciliana Trasporti; 0923 2 10 21; www.astsicilia.it) runs buses between San Vito Lo Capo and Trapani (€4.60, 1½ hours, eight to 10 daily), and Autoservizi Russo (p85) travels to/from Palermo's train station and Piazza Politeama (€9.40, two to three hours, two Monday to Saturday, one Sunday, more in summer). Buses arrive at/depart from Via Piersanti Mattarella, near the beach and parallel to Via Savoia – look for street signs marking the stops.

San Vito Lo Capo Bus (328 8009095; www.sanvitolocapobus.com) offers convenient direct van transfers to San Vito from the airports at Palermo (€22) and Trapani (€19).

CAR & MOTORCYCLE

San Vito is roughly 45 minutes from either Castellammare del Golfo (43km via the SS187 and SP16) or Trapani (37km via the SP20 and SP16).

Riserva Naturale dello Zingaro

Saved from development by local protests, the tranquil **Riserva Naturale dello Zingaro** (0924 35 108; www.riservazingaro.it; adult/reduced €5/3; 7am-7.30pm Apr-Sep, 9am-5pm Oct-Mar) was established in 1981 as Sicily's first nature

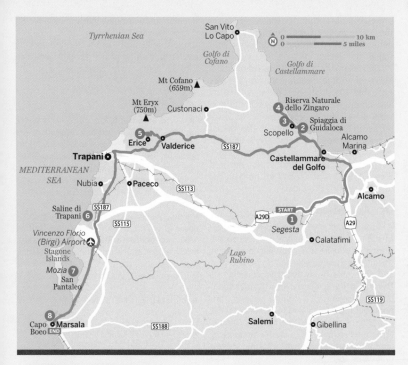

Driving Tour
Best of the West

START SEGESTA
END MARSALA
LENGTH 109KM; ONE TO THREE DAYS

This tour weaves together two ancient archaeological sites, a coastal nature reserve, a medieval hilltop town, and one of Sicily's prime wine-growing regions. While the route can be driven as a one-day rental-car loop (the start point is only 30 minutes from either Palermo or Trapani airport), it's more rewarding to spread the journey over two or three days.

Start at 1 **Segesta** (p90), just off the A29D autostrada. One of Sicily's most evocative ancient sites, Segesta consists of a perfectly preserved, hauntingly beautiful Doric temple at the edge of a precipitous gorge, and a hilltop amphitheatre with views clear out to the Mediterranean.

From here, meander north to the dazzling blue-green waters of 2 **Spiaggia di Guidaloca**. Stop for a dip here, or continue north to 3 **Scopello** (p85), where you can swim in the shadow of some supremely photogenic *faraglioni* (rock spires). Alternatively, take a day hike into the 4 **Riserva Naturale dello Zingaro** (p88), Sicily's oldest nature reserve, just 2km further north.

Double back to the SS187, which winds lazily through vineyards before climbing a dizzying set of switchbacks to 5 **Erice** (p96). Perched high above a fairy-tale coastal landscape, this hilltop has been prized by every civilisation that's passed through, from the Elymians to the Normans to the day-trippers who come now to sample its fabulous views and addictive sweets.

Next descend to the 6 **Saline di Trapani** (p98), a mirror-like landscape of salt pools and windmills that has been a centre for salt production since ancient times. From here take a short boat ride to the island of 7 **Mozia** (p98), home to one of Europe's finest Phoenician archaeological sites.

Back on the 'mainland', it's a short jaunt down to 8 **Marsala** (p103), capital of one of Sicily's great wine-producing regions. Tour the Marsala cellars at Florio, then settle in for aperitifs and dinner among the glimmering stone-paved streets of the historic centre.

preserve. It has become the star attraction on the gulf, drawing an ever-growing number of nature-lovers and outdoors enthusiasts, both Italian and foreign.

The reserve is a hiker's paradise and a haven for wildlife, including the rare Bonelli's eagle and 40 other bird species. Wild carob and bright yellow euphorbia dust the hillsides, along with 700 other species of Mediterranean flora – some unique to this stretch of coast – while hidden coves such as Marinella Bay provide tranquil swimming spots.

The park's main entrance is 2km north of Scopello, with a secondary entrance 12km south of San Vito Lo Capo.

Activities

A stunning 7km coastal walk (four hours return, not counting stops) runs between the reserve's Scopello and San Vito entrances, passing several fine beaches, a visitor centre and four museums: the **Museo delle Attività Marinare**, housed in a former tuna-processing plant, with exhibits ranging from photos of local fishermen to treatises on the importance of tuna to the ancient Greeks; Museo della Cultura Contadina, documenting the Zingaro's farming traditions; **Museo della Manna**, explaining how sap from local ash trees is processed into the ancient delicacy known as manna; and **Museo Naturalistico**, featuring displays on the Zingaro's flora and fauna.

Additional hikes, including several trails inland, are detailed on park maps, which can be picked up freely at the park's Scopello entrance, or downloaded from the website.

Various organisations around the park organise guided walks – see the park's visitor centre for a list.

Getting There & Away

The closest towns to the reserve are Scopello (2km to the south) and San Vito Lo Capo (12km to the north). From either town, take the SP63 until it dead-ends at the park entrance. There is no public transport to the park.

Castellammare del Golfo

0924 / POP 15,140

Founded by the Elymians as the port for nearby Segesta, the small coastal city of Castellammare del Golfo has a pleasant harbour that is overlooked by the remains of a much-modified Saracen castle and surrounded by sandy beaches, making it a popular summer holiday destination for Sicilians. Beyond the harbour itself, however, the city is a rather sprawling and lacking in charm, making nearby Scopello and San Vito Lo Capo more appealing for an extended stay.

Eating

★Ristorante Del Golfo SEAFOOD €€€
(0924 3 02 57; www.ristorantedelgolfo.it; Via Segesta 153; meals €35-55; noon-3pm & 7-11pm, closed Tue Oct-May) This perennial Castellammare favourite serves seafood delights such as *scampi marinati all'arancia* (prawns marinated in orange juice), *linguine gamberi pistacchio e bottarga* (pasta with shrimp, pistachios and cured fish roe) or *pesce in crosta di sale alla griglia* (grilled fish encrusted with Trapani's famous salt). Save room afterwards for *cassatelle* – deep-fried pastries filled with sweet ricotta, lemon rind and chocolate.

Getting There & Away

BUS

Buses depart from Via della Repubblica. Autoservizi Russo (p85) runs services to Piazza Politeama and the central train station in Palermo (€6.40, 1½ hours, six daily Monday to Saturday, one on Sunday), as well as services to Scopello (€2.70, 20 minutes, four daily except Sunday) and San Vito Lo Capo (€6.40, 1¼ hours, three daily Monday to Saturday, one on Sunday). Extra buses operate in July and August. Azienda Siciliana Trasporti (p88) runs buses to Trapani (€4.30, one to 1¼ hours, four daily Monday to Saturday).

CAR & MOTORCYCLE

Castellammare del Golfo is only 44km from Palermo's Falcone-Borsellino (Punta Raisi) airport via the A29 autostrada.

TRAIN

The train station is an inconvenient 3km out of town, although there is a shuttle bus (€1.50). Trains run four times daily (three on Sunday) to Trapani (€8.70, 1¾ to two hours).

SEGESTA

Set on the edge of a deep canyon amid desolate mountains, the 5th-century BC ruins of **Segesta** (0924 95 23 56; adult/reduced €6/3; 9am-7.30pm Apr-Sep, 9am-1hr before sunset Oct-Mar) are one of the world's most magical ancient sites.

Long before the arrival of the Greeks, Segesta was the principal city of the Elymians, an ancient civilisation claiming descent from the Trojans that settled in Sicily in the Bronze Age. The Elymians were in constant conflict with Greek Selinunte, whose destruction (in 409 BC) they pursued with bloodthirsty determination. More than 100 years later the Greek tyrant Agathocles slaughtered over 10,000 Elymians and repopulated Segesta with Greeks.

Little remains of ancient Segesta today, save its hilltop theatre and never-completed Doric temple, yet the ruins' remarkable state of preservation and the majesty of their rural setting combine to make this one of Sicily's enduring highlights.

Sights

Doric Temple RUINS

Segesta's centrepiece is its remarkably well-preserved Doric temple, dating from around 430 BC. Standing in splendid isolation amid fields of wildflowers and grasses, it has retained all of its columns, topped by a perfectly intact entablature and pediment – though the missing roof and lack of fluting on the columns indicate that it was never completed. On windy days the 36 giant columns are said to act like an organ, producing mysterious notes. It's a five-minute walk uphill from the ticket office.

Greek Theatre RUINS

Crowning the summit of Monte Bàrbaro, this 3rd-century BC Greek theatre is Segesta's most prominent ruin after its famous Doric temple. The theatre commands sweeping views north to the Golfo di Castellammare (with a rather incongruous-looking modern autostrada snaking its way across the valley in the foreground). A shuttle bus (€1.50) climbs to the theatre half-hourly along the 1.5km access road from Segesta's ticket booth. Return to the parking lot via a lovely 30-minute downhill footpath with fine temple views.

Getting There & Away

BUS

Tarantola (0924 3 10 20; www.tarantolabus.com) runs buses to Segesta from Trapani's main bus station (one way/return €4/6.60, 40 to 50 minutes each way). The most convenient departures leave Trapani at 8am, 10am and noon, returning from Segesta at 11.10am, 1.10pm and 4.10pm.

Tarantola also runs an 8.50am bus to Segesta from Via Balsamo near Palermo's train station (one way/return €7/11.20, 80 minutes each way), returning from Segesta to Palermo at 11.45am and 3.40pm. This service runs Monday to Saturday from April to October; buses only run on Monday from November to March.

Note that the above buses do not run on Sundays or holidays.

CAR & MOTORCYCLE

The Segesta exit is clearly marked off the A29D autostrada between Trapani (32km to the west) and Palermo (76km to the east).

TRAPANI

0923 / POP 69,180

Hugging the harbour where Peter of Aragon landed in 1282 to begin the Spanish occupation of Sicily, the sickle-shaped spit of land occupied by Trapani's old town once sat at the heart of a powerful trading network that stretched from Carthage to Venice. Traditionally the town thrived on coral and tuna fishing, with some salt and wine production. These days, Trapani's port buzzes with ferry traffic to the Egadi Islands and Pantelleria, and the adjacent historic centre is a popular place to stroll, for both locals and travellers awaiting their next boat.

Sights

Although the narrow network of streets in Trapani's historic centre is Moorish, the city takes most of its character from the fabulous 17th- and 18th-century baroque of the Spanish period. Prime examples include the **Cattedrale di San Lorenzo** (Corso Vittorio Emanuele; 8am-4pm) on pedestrianised Corso Vittorio Emanuele, and the striking **Palazzo Senatorio** (cnr Corso Vittorio Emanuele & Via Torrearsa) at the eastern end of the same street, along with the **Palazzo Riccio di Morana** (Via Garibaldi) and **Palazzo Fardella Fontana** (Via Garibaldi) on nearby Via Garibaldi. The best time to explore this area is in the early evening, when the *passeggiata* is in full swing.

Chiesa del Purgatorio CHURCH

(0923 56 28 82; Via San Francesco d'Assisi; voluntary donation requested; 7.30am-noon & 4-7pm Mon-Sat, 10am-noon & 4-7pm Sun) Just off the *corso* in the heart of the city, this church houses the impressive 18th-century *Misteri*, 20 life-sized wooden effigies depicting the story of Christ's Passion, which take centre stage during the city's dramatic Easter Week processions every year. Explanatory panels

Trapani

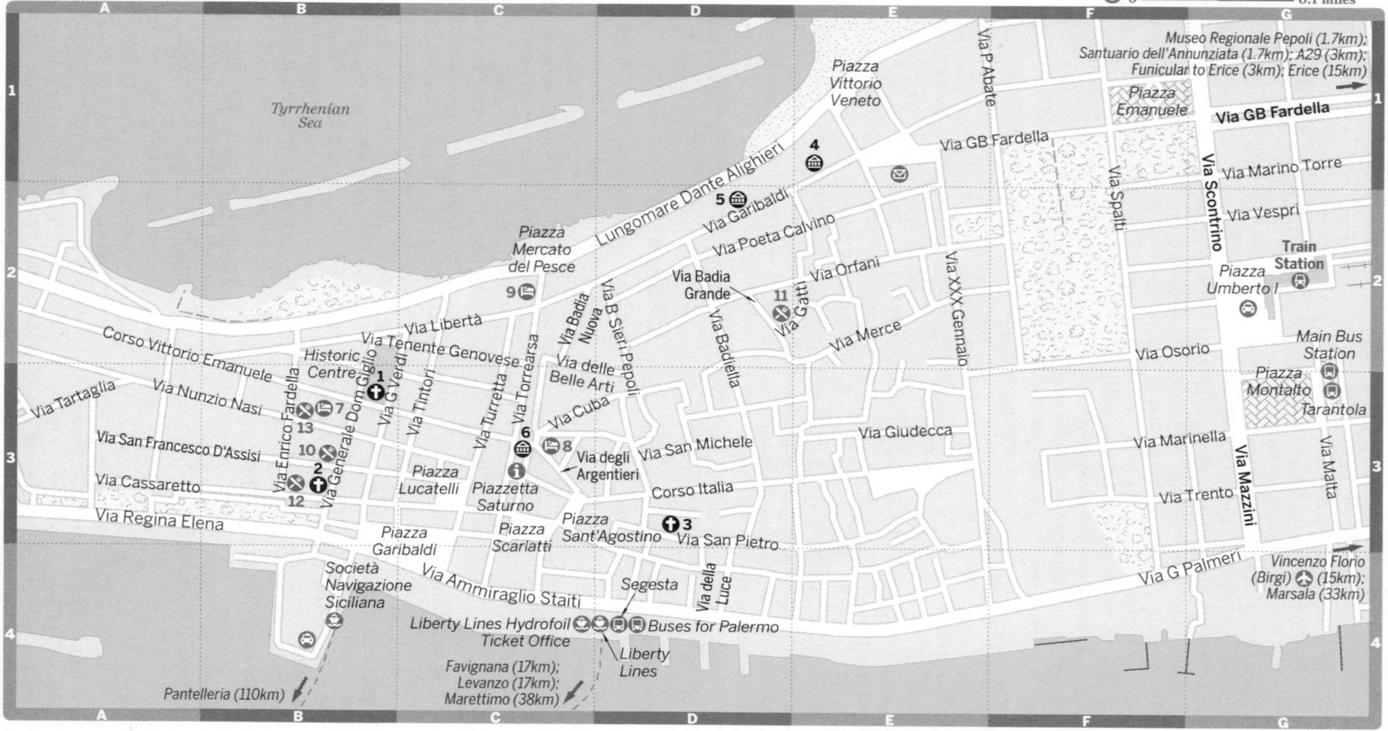

0 200 m
0 0.1 miles
Museo Regionale Pepoli (1.7km); Santuario dell'Annunziata (1.7km); A29 (3km); Funicular to Erice (3km); Erice (15km)
Tyrrhenian Sea
Piazza Vittorio Veneto
Via P Abate
Piazza Emanuele
Via GB Fardella
Via GB Fardella
Via Spalti
Via Scontrino
Via Marino Torre
Via Vespri
Train Station
Piazza Umberto I
Lungomare Dante Alighieri
Via Garibaldi
Via Poeta Calvino
Via Orfani
Via XXX Gennaio
Via Badia Grande
Via Gatti
Via Merce
Via Osorio
Main Bus Station
Piazza Montalto
Tarantola
Piazza Mercato del Pesce
Via Libertà
Via Badia Nuova
Via B Sieri Pepoli
Via Badiella
Corso Vittorio Emanuele
Via Tenente Genovese
Historic Centre
Via delle Belle Arti
Via Tartaglia
Via Nunzio Nasi
Via Enrico Fardella
Via Generale Dom Giglio
Via G Verdi
Via Tintori
Via Turretta
Via Torrearsa
Via Cuba
Via Giudecca
Via Marinella
Via Mazzini
Via Malta
Via San Francesco D'Assisi
Via San Michele
Via degli Argentieri
Via Cassaretto
Piazza Lucatelli
Piazzetta Saturno
Corso Italia
Via Trento
Via Regina Elena
Piazza Garibaldi
Piazza Scarlatti
Piazza Sant'Agostino
Via San Pietro
Via G Palmeri
Vincenzo Florio (Birgi) (15km); Marsala (33km)
Società Navigazione Siciliana
Via Ammiraglio Staiti
Segesta
Via della Luce
Liberty Lines Hydrofoil Ticket Office
Buses for Palermo
Liberty Lines
Favignana (17km); Levanzo (17km); Marettimo (38km)
Pantelleria (110km)
1
2
3
4
5
6
7
8
9
10
11
12
13

Trapani

Sights
1 Cattedrale di San Lorenzo.................. B3
2 Chiesa del Purgatorio.......................... B3
3 Chiesa di Santa Maria del Gesù.......... D3
4 Palazzo Fardella Fontana...................... E1
5 Palazzo Riccio di Morana..................... D2
6 Palazzo Senatorio................................. C3

Sleeping
7 Ai Lumi B&B... B3
8 Albergo Maccotta................................. C3
9 La Gancia... C2

Eating
10 Caupona Taverna di Sicilia.................. B3
11 La Rinascente...................................... D2
12 Osteria La Bettolaccia......................... B3
13 Tavernetta Ai Lumi.............................. B3

in English, Italian, French and German help visitors to understand the story behind each figure.

Some of the statues are originals; others are copies of statues that were destroyed by WWII Allied bombings or irreparably damaged after being dropped by their bearers during a procession (the statues are heavy and unwieldy, and mishaps sometimes occur).

Each statue was commissioned and is now carried by members of a particular profession. For example, *Jesus Before Herod* was commissioned by the Millers and Bakers Guild; *Jesus Entombed,* by the Pasta-Makers Guild; and *The Whipping,* by the Bricklayers and Stonemasons Guild. One of the figures, *The Ascent of Calvary,* isn't claimed by a particular guild, but is instead accompanied by the Trapanese people at large.

Museo Nazionale Pepoli MUSEUM
(☎ 0923 55 32 69; www.comune.trapani.it/turismo/pepoli.htm; Via Conte Pepoli 180; adult/reduced €6/3; ⏰ 9am-5.30pm Mon-Sat, to 12.30pm Sun) In a former Carmelite monastery, this museum houses the collection of Conte Pepoli, who devoted his life to salvaging Trapani's local arts and crafts, most notably the garish coral carvings – once all the rage in Europe, before Trapani's offshore coral banks were decimated. The museum also has a good collection of Gagini sculptures, silverwork, archaeological artefacts and religious art.

Don't miss Andrea Tipa's gaudy 18th-century *presepe* (Nativity scene or crèche) made of alabaster, coral, shells and other marine material, or the significantly less ornate but far more beautiful coral carvings by Fra' Matteo Bavera. Other highlights include an extraordinary *cassetta reliquaria* (relic box) from the workshop of Alberto and Andrea Tipa and remnants of painted tile floors from the Chiesa di Santa Maria delle Grazie (featuring fishing scenes) and the Chiesa di Santa Lucia (with scenes of Trapani's city centre).

Chiesa di Santa Maria del Gesù CHURCH
(Via San Pietro; ⏰ 8am-1pm) This Catalan-Gothic church in the historic centre houses the exquisite *Madonna degli Angeli* (Madonna of the Angels), a glazed terracotta statue by Andrea della Robbia.

Eating

Trapani's unique position on the sea route to Tunisia has made couscous (or *cuscus,* as it is sometimes spelled here) something of a speciality, particularly when served *alla trapanese* (accompanied by a soup of seafood, garlic, chilli, tomatoes, saffron, parsley and wine, to be ladled over the couscous according to individual taste). Another irresistible staple is *pesto alla trapanese* (pesto made from fresh tomatoes, basil, garlic and almonds), eaten with *busiate,* a small hand-twirled pasta.

La Rinascente PASTRIES €
(☎ 0923 2 37 67; Via Gatti 3; cannoli €2; ⏰ 9am-1.30pm & 3-7pm Mon, Tue, Thu & Fri, 7.30am-2pm Sat & Sun) When you enter this bakery through the side door, you'll feel like you've barged into someone's kitchen – and you have! Thankfully, owner Giovanni Costadura's broad smile will quickly put you at ease, as will a taste of his homemade *cannoli,* which he'll fill for you on the spot.

★ **Osteria La Bettolaccia** SICILIAN €€
(☎ 0923 2 16 95; www.labettolaccia.it; Via Enrico Fardella 25; meals €35-45; ⏰ 12.45-3pm Mon-Fri, plus 7.45-11pm Mon-Sat) Unwaveringly authentic, this Slow Food favourite just two blocks from the ferry terminal is the perfect place to try *cous cous con zuppa di mare* (couscous with mixed seafood in a spicy fish sauce, with tomatoes, garlic and parsley). Even with its newly expanded dining room, it can still fill up, so book ahead.

Caupona Taverna di Sicilia SEAFOOD €€
(☎ 340 3421335, 0923 54 66 18; Piazza Purgatorio 32; meals €25-36; ⏰ 1-2.15pm & 8-11.30pm Wed-Mon) Fresh fish rules the menu at this fabulous family-run spot two blocks from the

LA PROCESSIONE DEI MISTERI

Since the 18th century, the citizens of Trapani – represented by 20 traditional *maestranze* (guilds) – have begun a four-day celebration of the Passion of Christ on the Tuesday before Easter Sunday by parading a remarkable, life-sized wooden statue of the Virgin Mary through the town's streets. Over the course of the next three days, nightly processions of the remaining *Misteri* (life-sized wooden statues) make their way through the old quarter and port to a specially erected chapel in Piazza Lucatelli, where the icons are stored overnight. Each procession is accompanied by crowds of locals and a Trapanese band, which plays dirges to the slow, steady beat of a drum.

The high point of the celebration is on Friday afternoon, when the 20 guilds emerge from the Chiesa del Purgatorio and descend the steps of the church, carrying each of the statues, to begin the 1km-long procession up to Via Giovanni Battista Fardella; the procession then returns to the church the following morning. The massive crowds that gather to witness the slow march often reach a peak of delirious fervour that is matched only by that of the Semana Santa parades in Seville, Spain.

To witness the procession, you'll need to book your accommodation well in advance. At other times, the figures are on display in the Chiesa del Purgatorio (p91). For more information, check out www.processionemisteritp.it (in Italian, Spanish and French only).

port. Chef Rosi cooks and husband Claudio works the tables, serving up superb couscous and colourful seafood classics like *pesce spada alla pantesca* (swordfish in a sauce of tomatoes, garlic, parsley, olives and capers). Save room for the monster-sized *cannoli* (enough to feed two people easily).

Tavernetta Ai Lumi SICILIAN €€

(☎0923 87 24 18; www.ailumi.it; Corso Vittorio Emanuele 75; meals €30-40; ⏰1-3pm & 7.30-11pm, closed Tue Oct-May) Converted from an 18th-century stable block, this tavern's rustic interior features exposed brickwork, heavy wooden furniture and huge arches, complemented by a delightful sidewalk terrace in the heart of historic Trapani. Fresh seafood rules the menu, along with Trapanese classics like *cuscusu di pesce* (fish couscous) and *caserecce al pesto trapanese* (tube-shaped pasta with crushed almonds, garlic, basil and tomatoes).

ℹ Information

Hospital (Ospedale Sant'Antonio Abate; ☎0923 80 91 11; www.asptrapani.it; Via Cosenza) Five kilometres east of the centre.

Police (Questura; ☎0923 59 81 11; Piazza Vittoria Veneto 1) Trapani's main police station.

Post Office (Piazza Vittorio Veneto 11; ⏰8.30am-7pm Mon-Fri, to 12.30pm Sat)

Tourist Office (☎0923 54 45 33; sport.turismo.spettacolo@comune.trapani.it; Piazzetta Saturno; ⏰9am-9pm Jun-Sep, to 5.30pm Mon & Thu, to 2pm Tue, Wed & Fri Oct-May) Just north of the port, Trapani's tourist office offers city maps and information.

ℹ Getting There & Away

Trapani's busy port is the main embarkation point for the Egadi archipelago and the remote Moorish island of Pantelleria. Nearby Vincenzo Florio (Birgi) Airport is well served by cut-rate flights from mainland Italy and the rest of Europe.

AIR

Sicily's third-busiest airport, **Vincenzo Florio airport** (Birgi Airport; TPS; ☎0923 61 01 11; www.airgest.it), is 16km south of Trapani at Birgi. **Ryanair** (☎899 018880; www.ryanair.com) serves two-dozen destinations throughout Italy and Europe, including Bologna, Brussels, Frankfurt, Milan and Rome. **Alitalia** (☎06 6 56 40; www.alitalia.com) offers twice-daily flights to the island of Pantelleria.

BOAT

Trapani's ferry terminal is opposite Piazza Garibaldi. **Società Navigazione Siciliana** (Siremar; ☎090 36 46 01; www.siremar.it; Ferry Terminal) and **Traghetti delle Isole** (☎0923 2 24 67; www.traghettidelleisole.it) both operate year-round car ferries to Pantelleria (€34, 5¾ to six hours, one to two daily). Società Navigazione Siciliana also runs year-round ferries to the Egadi Islands of Favignana (€9.70, one to 1½ hours, three daily), Levanzo (€9.70, one to 1½ hours, three daily) and Marettimo (€14.60, three hours, one daily).

Hydrofoils dock a few blocks east of the ferry terminal along Via Ammiraglio Staiti. **Liberty Lines** (☎0923 87 38 13; www.libertylines.it; Via Ammiraglio Staiti) runs more than a dozen hydrofoils daily to Favignana (€11.80, 20 to 40 minutes) and Levanzo (€11.80, 25 to 50 minutes), with at least four of these continuing to

Marettimo (€18.80, one to 1½ hours). Liberty Lines also operates summer-only, Saturday-morning hydrofoils to Ustica (€32.50, 2½ hours) and Naples (€108, seven hours). Get tickets at the ticket office just west of the docks. Note that hydrofoil tickets purchased for same-day travel cost €1.50 less.

BUS

Segesta (☎0923 2 19 56, 0923 2 84 04; www.buscenter.it) runs express buses connecting Trapani with Palermo (€9.60, two hours, at least hourly between 5.30am and 8pm) from its stop near the hydrofoil docks. Buy tickets at **Egatour** (☎0923 2 17 54; www.egatourviaggi.it; Via Ammiraglio Staiti 13), directly opposite the bus stop.

All other intercity buses arrive and depart from Trapani's **main bus station** (☎0923 2 00 66; Piazza Montalto). Tickets can be bought from the bar in the station building. AST (p88) serves Erice (€2.90, 40 minutes to one hour, four to six daily), San Vito Lo Capo (€4.60, 1½ hours, eight to ten daily), Marsala (€3.60, 1¼ hours, four Monday to Saturday) and Mazara del Vallo (€5.30, 1¾ hours, three Monday to Saturday).

Tarantola (p91) operates a service to Segesta (€6.60 round trip, 40 to 50 minutes each way, five to six daily), while **Lumia** (☎0923 2 17 54, 0922 2 04 14; www.autolineelumia.it) goes to Sciacca (€9, 2¼ hours) and Agrigento (€11.90, 3½ hours) three times Monday to Friday, twice on Saturday, and once on Sunday.

Buses run less frequently on Sundays and holidays, and from October to May.

TRAIN

From Trapani's train station, 1km east of the centre on Piazza Umberto, 10 daily trains (five on Sunday) run to Marsala (€3.80, 25 to 40 minutes) and Mazara del Vallo (€5.10, 55 minutes). For Palermo, the bus is a much faster and more direct option.

ℹ Getting Around

Tickets for local buses operated by **ATM** (Azienda Trasporto e Mobilità; ☎0923 55 95 75; www.atmtrapani.it) – valid for 90 minutes – cost €1.20 at *tabacchi* (tobacco shops) or €1.40 if purchased on board the bus.

TO/FROM THE AIRPORT

From Birgi airport, departing from a curbside bus stop just outside the arrivals hall, AST (p88) runs buses (€4.90, 20 minutes) to Trapani's port and main bus station on Piazza Montalto approximately every hour from 8.30am to 12.30am, and also offers regular service to Mazara del Vallo (€4, three daily).

There are also direct buses from Birgi airport to Marsala operated by AST (€2.70, 45 minutes, four daily except Sunday) and Salemi (€2.50, 30 minutes, five to six daily). **Salemi** (☎0923 98 11 20; www.autoservizisalemi.it) teams up with **Terravision** (☎0923 48 23 71; www.terravision.eu) to provide direct bus service to Palermo's Piazza Politeama and train station (€11, 1¾ to two hours, five to six daily); buy tickets online or from Terravision's office directly adjacent to the rental-car counters in Birgi's arrivals hall.

A taxi between Birgi and Trapani costs €30 to €35.

BICYCLE

Cycling is an easy and pleasant way to explore the Saline di Trapani, the flat landscape of salt pools and windmills just south of town. **Bike Shop** (☎388 2518505; www.bikeshoptp.it; Via Verdi 5; bicycle hire per 24hr €8; ⏲9am-8pm), conveniently placed near Trapani's port, rents out bikes at very reasonable rates.

BUS

Two free city buses (numbers 1 and 2) operated by ATM make circular trips through Trapani, connecting the bus station, the train station and the port. Tickets for ATM's other local buses – valid for 90 minutes – cost €1.20 at *tabacchi*

STRADA DEL VINO E DEI SAPORI ERICE DOC

Representing over a dozen local wine producers, the Associazione Strada del Vino e dei Sapori Erice DOC (www.stradadelvinoericedoc.it) celebrates the Erice DOC (Denominazione di Origine Controllata; Controlled Origin Denomination) wine that is produced in the province of Trapani.

The Erice DOC appellation recognises several indigenous grape varieties from the region, including Catarratto, Nero d'Avola, Grillo, Insolia, Frappato, Perricone and Zibibbo. These grapes owe their distinctive flavour to the fact that they're grown in vineyards that lie between an altitude of 250m and 500m, but are also located close to the sea.

As you drive around western Sicily, you'll see plenty of Erice DOC wine route signs, but bear in mind that it's not always the easiest route to follow. Signposts are intermittent and the number of wineries regularly open to the public is limited – for tastings, the award-winning **Fazio** (☎0923 81 17 00; www.casavinicolafazio.it; Via Capitano Rizzo 39, Fulgatore; ⏲9.30am-1pm & 2.30-5pm Mon-Fri) is a dependable choice.

(tobacco shops) or €1.40 if purchased on board the bus.

CAR & MOTORCYCLE

There are plenty of parking spaces at the port and near the train station. Purchase tickets from the machines on the street (prices range from €0.50 to €0.80 per hour, with rates increasing as you get closer to the city centre).

Long-term parking for visitors to the Egadi Islands (€7 per day) can be found in a fenced lot off Via dei Grandi Eventi, about 1km east of the port. ATM runs a free shuttle bus from the parking lot back to the port (lines 2A and 2B), but posted hours are rather unreliable.

TAXI

Taxi ranks are located at the ferry terminal and on Piazza Umberto I, just outside the train station.

AROUND TRAPANI

Erice

☎0923 / POP 28,355 / ELEV 751M

Erice watches over the port of Trapani from the legendary mountain of Eryx, situated a giddy 750m above sea level. It's a mesmerising walled medieval town whose mountain charm is enhanced by the unpredictable weather that can take you from sunny afternoon to foggy evening in the space of a few minutes.

The town has sweeping views of the sea and the valley below, and is home to Sicily's most famous pastry shop, Maria Grammatico.

Erice has a notorious history as a centre for the cult of Venus (Astarte to the Phoenicians and Aphrodite to the Greeks). The mysterious Elymians claimed descent from Venus' famous Trojan son, Aeneas, who mentions the sanctuary as a holy landmark in the *Aeneid*. Acolytes here practised the peculiar ritual of sacred prostitution, with the prostitutes accommodated in the temple itself. Despite countless invasions, the sacred site long remained inviolate – no need to guess why!

Sights

Virgil once compared Eryx to Mt Athos for its altitude and spiritual pre-eminence. Not that the town resembles a sanctuary today – temples and convents have given way to carpet shops selling the town's famous *frazzate* (bright rugs made from colourful rags) and innumerable souvenir stalls. Still, Erice is about wall-hugging alleys, votive niches and secret courtyards, all of which are best appreciated in the evenings and early mornings after the battalions of day-trippers leave.

DON'T MISS

MARIA GRAMMATICO

This **pasticceria** (☎0923 86 93 90; www.mariagrammatico.it; Via Vittorio Emanuele 14; pastries from €2; ⊙9am-10pm May, Jun & Sep, to 1am Jul & Aug, to 7pm Oct-Apr) is owned and run by Sicily's renowned septuagenarian pastry chef Maria Grammatico, subject of Mary Taylor Simeti's book *Bitter Almonds*.

In the early 1950s, Maria's father died suddenly of a heart attack. Her impoverished mother, pregnant with a sixth child, decided to send Maria, aged 11, and her younger sister to the cloistered San Carlo orphanage in Erice to learn the art of pastry-making from the nuns. There, the children toiled in brutally hard conditions – beating sugar mixtures for six hours at a time, rising before dawn to prime the ovens, shelling kilos of almonds and surviving on an unrelenting diet of meatless pasta and vegetable gruel. At 22, Maria left the orphanage after having a nervous breakdown and started making sweets and pastries to survive. The rest, as they say, is history.

The world-famous *pasticceria*, with its shady courtyard out back, and the associated **Caffè Maria** (www.caffe-maria-erice.it; Via Vittorio Emanuele 4; ⊙8.30am-9pm Oct-May, to midnight Jun-Sep), with its panoramic upstairs terrace, are good places to take a break as you wander around Erice. At either place you can sample Sicilian treats such as *cannoli* filled with fresh ricotta; green *cassata* cakes made of almonds, sugar, vanilla, buttermilk curd and candied fruit; perfectly formed marzipan fruits; lemon-flavoured *cuscinetti* (small fried pastries); and *buccellati* (hard, fig biscuits) twisted around fig, cinnamon and clove comfit. At Easter, the shop is filled with super-cute almond-citron baby lambs that are made to celebrate Erice's *I Misteri* celebration. Be warned that the produce here uses more sugar than is usual – your dentist would certainly not approve!

Erice

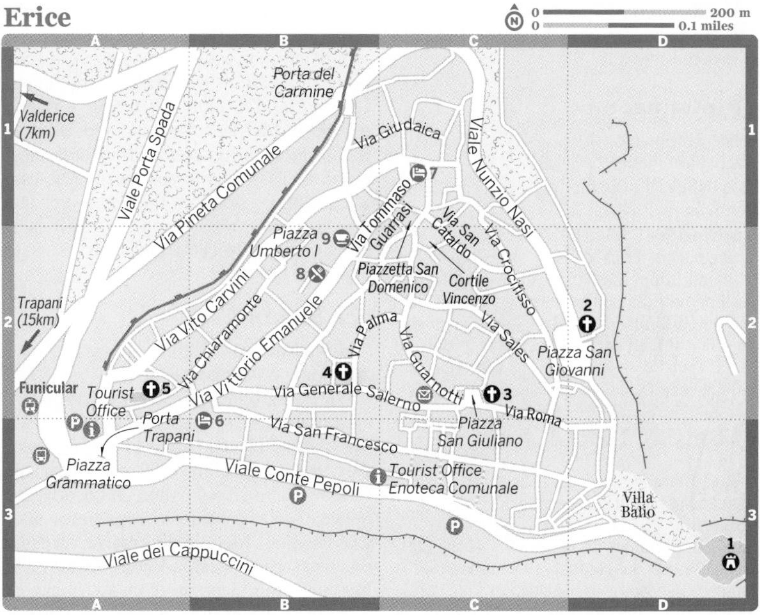

Castello di Venere CASTLE

(☎366 6712832; www.fondazioneericearte.org/castellodivenere.php; Via Castello di Venere; adult/reduced €4/2; ⊙10am-1hr before sunset daily Apr-Oct, 10am-4pm Sat, Sun & holidays Nov-Mar) This 12th- to 13th-century Norman castle was built over the Temple of Venus, long a site of worship for the ancient Elymians, Phoenicians, Greeks and Romans. Nowadays the castle's rooms are off-limits, but visitors can explore the grassy interior courtyard, filled with ruined foundations and flanked by an impressive stone wall allegedly built by Daedalus. Stealing the show are the spectacular vistas extending to San Vito Lo Capo on one side and the Saline di Trapani on the other.

To arrange midweek visits in winter, phone at least 24 hours in advance.

Duomo CATHEDRAL

(Via Chiaramonte; €5; ⊙10am-1hr before sunset Apr-Oct, 10am-12.30pm Nov-Feb, 10am-4pm Mar) Of Erice's 60-odd churches, the Duomo is the most interesting. It was built in 1312 by order of a grateful Frederick III, who had sheltered in Erice during the Sicilian Vespers uprising (1282–1314). The interior was remodelled in neo-Gothic style in 1865, but the 15th-century side chapels were conserved. Views from atop the 28m-high **Campanile**, with its mullioned windows, are impressive.

> **Erice**
>
> **Sights**
> 1 Castello di Venere D3
> 2 Chiesa di San Giovanni D2
> 3 Chiesa di San Giuliano C2
> 4 Chiesa di San Martino B2
> 5 Duomo A2
>
> **Sleeping**
> 6 Hotel Elimo B3
> 7 Hotel San Domenico C1
>
> **Eating**
> 8 Maria Grammatico B2
>
> **Drinking & Nightlife**
> 9 Caffè Maria B2

Tickets purchased here also grant admission to three other local churches: **San Martino** (Via Pietro Salerno 8; ⊙10am-6pm Apr-Oct, to 8pm Jul & Aug, earlier closing Nov-Mar), **San Giuliano** (Via Roma; ⊙10am-6pm Apr-Oct, to 8pm Jul & Aug, earlier closing Nov-Mar) and **San Giovanni** (Via San Giovanni 4; ⊙10am-6pm Apr-Oct, to 8pm Jul & Aug, earlier closing Nov-Mar).

Eating

Erice is famous throughout Sicily for its *dolci ericini* (almond sweets); as a result, you'll find as many pastry shops as restaurants in the historic centre. Given the town's status as a tourist magnet, price-to-quality ratio is not always the greatest.

Information

Police Station (Questura; ☎0923 55 50 00; Piazza Grammatico; ⏲24hr)

Post Office (Via Guarnotti 7; ⏲8.15am-1.30pm Mon-Fri)

Tourist Office (☎348 6912335; www.facebook.com/EriceTourism; Porta Trapani; ⏲10am-1.30pm Tue-Sat, 10.30am-1.30pm Sun mid-Apr–mid-Oct) Main information booth adjacent to the Porta Trapani parking lot; subsidiary office at the Enoteca Comunale (☎0923 86 93 88; Viale Conte Pepoli 11; ⏲3-6pm Mon-Sat mid-Apr–mid-Oct).

Getting There & Away

BUS

There is a regular **AST** (Azienda Siciliana Trasporti; ☎0923 2 10 21; www.astsicilia.it) bus service to/from Trapani (€2.90, 40 minutes to one hour, six daily Monday to Saturday, four Sunday). All buses arrive and depart from Porta Trapani stop at the foot of Erice's old town.

CAR & MOTORCYCLE

Paid parking is available next to Porta Trapani and along Viale Conte Pepoli. There's a ticket machine adjacent to the main Porta Trapani lot.

FUNICULAR

The best way to travel between Erice and Trapani is on the **funicular** (Funivia; ☎0923 56 93 06, 0923 86 97 20; www.funiviaerice.it; one way/return €5.50/9; ⏲1-8pm Mon, 8.10am-8pm Tue-Fri, 9am-9pm Sat, 10am-8pm Sun). The funicular station in Erice is just below, and across the street from, Porta Trapani. To reach the funicular station in Trapani, catch bus 21 or 23 from Via GB Fardella down to the eastern end of Via Alessandro Manzoni (where Trapani ends and Erice begins); bus schedules and route maps are on the Funivia website.

Saline di Trapani

Along the coast between Trapani and Marsala lies this evocative landscape of *saline* (shallow salt pools) and decommissioned *mulini* (windmills). The salt from these marshes is considered Italy's finest and has been big business for centuries; today, only a cottage industry remains, providing for Italy's more discerning dinner tables. The best time to visit is summer, when the sun turns the saltpans rosy pink and makes the salt heaps shimmer. In winter, the heaps – covered with tiles and plastic tarpaulins to keep out the rain – are considerably less picturesque.

The most attractive stretches of coast are protected within two wetland preserves: Riserva Naturale Saline di Trapani e Paceco to the north near Trapani, and **Riserva Naturale di Stagnone** to the south near Marsala. The latter encompasses San Pantaleo island – home to the noted archaeological site of Mozia – and the larger Isola Lunga, which protects the shallow waters of Stagnone lagoon.

Sights

Riserva Naturale Saline di Trapani e Paceco PARK

(☎327 5621529, 0923 86 77 00; www.salineditrapani.it) Administered by the World Wildlife Fund, this nature reserve protects the northern section of the Saline di Trapani near the small settlement of Nubia. With advance notice, WWF guides can sometimes offer free two-hour tours of the reserve, focusing on migratory waterfowl from February to May and from September to November, or accompanying visitors to observe the salt harvest from July to September. Tours are usually scheduled on Wednesdays, Fridays or Saturdays; phone at least a week ahead to check availability.

Mozia ARCHAEOLOGICAL SITE

(San Pantaleo) Located on the tiny island of San Pantaleo, ancient Mozia (also known as Motya or Mothia) was one of the Mediterranean's most important Phoenician settlements. Established in the 8th century BC and coveted for its strategic position, Mozia is today the world's best-preserved Phoenician site.

The entire island was bought by the ornithologist and amateur archaeologist Joseph Whitaker (1850–1936) in the early 20th century and bequeathed to the Joseph Whitaker Foundation by his daughter Delia on her death in 1971. Joseph, who was a member of an English family that gained great wealth from the Marsala trade, built a villa here and spent decades excavating the island and assembling a unique collection of Phoenician artefacts, many of which are now on display in the museum that bears his name.

The fields around the museum are strewn with ruins from the ancient Phoenician settlement. Visitors can wander at will around the island to explore these, following a network of trails punctuated with helpful maps and information displays. Excavations include the ancient port and dry dock, where you can see the start of a Phoenician road – now approximately 1m underwater – that once linked San Pantaleo with the mainland. There's also a bar-cafe serving drinks and snacks.

Whitaker Museum MUSEUM
(☎0923 71 25 98; www.fondazionewhitaker.it; San Pantaleo; adult/reduced €9/5; ⏲9.30am-6.30pm Apr-Oct, 9am-3pm Nov-Mar) This museum on San Pantaleo island, 10km north of Marsala, houses a unique collection of Phoenician artefacts assembled over decades by amateur archaeologist Joseph Whitaker. Its greatest treasure is *Il Giovinetto di Mozia*, a 5th-century-BC Carthaginian-influenced marble statue of a young man. To get here, drive or bike to the Mozia dock 10km north of Marsala and catch one of the half-hourly, 10-minute ferries operated by Mozia Line.

Museo del Sale MUSEUM
(☎0923 86 70 61; www.museodelsale.it; Via Chiusa, Nubia; adult/reduced €2.50/1.50; ⏲9.30am-7.30pm May-Sep, 10am-5pm Oct-Apr, closed Jan & Feb) Set amid the salt pools 9km south of Trapani, this simple family-run museum in a historic windmill offers a wonderful perspective on Trapani's salt-producing industry. Historic photos of salt workers are labeled to show the division of labour, from the skilled elders who maintained the windmills to the young boys who hauled water as apprentices. Guides occasionally regale visitors with haunting renditions of old salt workers' melodies, interspersed with explanations of the tools and mechanisms used locally to extract salt.

Museo Saline Ettore e Infersa MUSEUM
(☎0923 73 30 03; www.salineettoreinfersa.com; Contrada Ettore Infersa 55; adult/reduced €7/2.50; ⏲9am-8.30pm Apr-Oct, by appointment Nov-Mar) The southernmost of the region's two salt museums is housed in a beautifully restored 16th-century windmill opposite the Mozia boat dock, just 10km north of Marsala. It has displays about the history of salt production in the area, including a film in multiple languages. From 4pm to 6pm on Wednesday and Saturday afternoons in summer, you can see the windmill in action.

Drinking & Nightlife

Mamma Caura BAR
(☎0923 96 60 36; www.mammacaura.it; Contrada Ettore Infersa; ⏲noon-10pm) After an afternoon touring the Saline, this is a gorgeous place to kick back and contemplate the beauty of this unique landscape over a beer or *aperitivi*. The ample outdoor terrace has picture-postcard views of the salt pools and windmills silhouetted against the setting sun. Lunch and dinner are also served, though you'll generally eat better in nearby Marsala (p105).

Getting There & Away

Access to the Saline di Trapani is via the SP21 (the Via del Sale or Salt Road) between Trapani and Marsala.

To reach Mozia, you'll need to take one of the boats operated by **Mozia Line** (☎0923 98 92 49, 338 7860474; www.mozialine.com; round-trip adult/reduced €5/2.50; ⏲9.15am-6.30pm) from its dock opposite San Pantaleo island, about 20km south of Trapani and 10km north of Marsala.

EGADI ISLANDS

Easily accessible by hydrofoil from Trapani or Marsala, the Egadi Islands (Isole Egadi) are popular destinations for swimming, diving, eating and general relaxation.

For centuries, the Egadi islanders have lived from the sea, as the prehistoric cave paintings on Levanzo illustrate. In 241 BC, when the islands were a key Carthaginian stronghold, one of the Punic Wars' most critical battles was fought at Cala Rossa (Red Cove, so named for the amount of Carthaginian blood spilt). When the Arabs took Sicily, they used the islands as a stepping-stone, fortifying them heavily to prevent anyone else following suit.

In 1874, Genovese bankers sold the islands to the Florio family, who established a branch of their lucrative tuna industry here, bringing great prosperity to the islands. Unfortunately, the surrounding waters have been terribly overfished, causing a dent in the local economy. The islands only became part of the Italian state in 1937.

Favignana

POP 4230

The largest of the Egadi Islands is butterfly-shaped Favignana, which is dominated by Monte Santa Caterina (287m) to the west. You can easily explore the island's eastern half on a bicycle, as the terrain here is almost completely flat. Around the coast, deep gouges in the cliffs are reminders of tufa quarrying that occurred in the past; many of these have now been reclaimed by the crystal-clear waters and are atmospheric swimming spots.

Sights

The first thing you'll see as you step off the boat is the **Ex Stabilimento Florio della Tonnara**, Favignana's historic tuna factory.

Favignana town's other significant building, **Palazzo Florio**, was built in 1876 for Vincenzo's son Ignazio, who purchased the Egadis in 1874. It now houses the tourist office, among other things.

The best beaches are on the southern side of the island at **Miramare** and **Lido Burrone**. The latter is a dreamy place for a swim, with a long, graceful stretch of sand lapped by clear aquamarine waters and backed by nice views of Monte Santa Caterina. On the north side, the bays at **Cala Rossa** and **Scalo Cavallo** are also lovely swimming spots.

Ex Stabilimento Florio delle Tonnare di Favignana e Formica MUSEUM
(☎324 5631991; www.facebook.com/exstabilimentofloriofavignana; Via Amendola 29; adult/reduced €6/3; ⊙hours vary) Vincenzo Florio Sr (1799–1886), a brilliant Palermitan businessman who had made his name in the sulphur, shipping and Marsala industries, also invented a way of steam-cooking and preserving canned tuna that revolutionised the fish-packing industry and cemented the success of his family's business empire. This *tonnara*, one of many the Florios ran around Sicily, operated until 1977; since 2010 it has operated as a museum.

The museum focuses on the Egadi Islands' fishing industry, displaying tuna boats, nets and stacks of vintage tuna tins from the Florio factory's heyday. A silent video documents the cannery's history and tuna fishing traditions in the seas around Favignana, including the island's famous Mattanza. Hours vary depending on the availability of volunteer staff; call ahead for details. Optional guided tours (occasionally available in English) are included in the ticket price.

Eating & Drinking

Osteria del Sotto Sale OSTERIA €€
(☎329 7726127; www.sottosale.com; Via Vittorio Emanuele 19, Favignana; meals €30-45; ⊙noon-4pm & 6.30pm-midnight Apr-Oct) The atmosphere is

LA MATTANZA

One of the Egadi Islands' most ancient traditions, the *mattanza* (ritual tuna slaughter) has come to a halt in recent years due to the ever-decreasing number of tuna swimming into local waters.

For centuries schools of bluefin tuna have used the waters around western Sicily as a mating ground. Locals can recall the golden days of the Egadis' fishing industry, when it was not uncommon to catch giant breeding tuna of between 200kg and 300kg. Fish that size are rare these days and the annual catch is increasingly smaller due to the worldwide commercial overfishing of tuna. Climate change also appears to have disrupted the tuna's normal breeding and migration cycle in recent years.

Traditionally, the *mattanza* occurred in late May or early June. Fishermen would organise their boats and nets in a complex formation designed to channel the tuna into a series of enclosures, which culminated in the *camera della morte* (chamber of death). Once enough tuna were imprisoned, the fishermen closed in and the *mattanza* began. It was a bloody affair – with up to eight or more fishermen at a time sinking huge hooks into a tuna and dragging it aboard. Anyone who has seen Rossellini's classic film *Stromboli* will no doubt recall the *mattanza* scene, one of the most famous accounts of this ancient tradition.

The number of tuna caught by this method was relatively small and sustainable – the fact that the *mattanza* took place for around 900 years without overfishing is testament to this. Problems arose with the increase in commercial fishing in the 1960s: tuna were caught year-round, and deep waters were exploited using long-line fishing and indiscriminate means such as drift and gill nets. Anything that passed by was caught, and thus the Mediterranean's fish resources were depleted. Despite the waning tuna population, La Mattanza was reinvented as a tourist attraction for several years, but even that was finally discontinued in 2007.

These days, fishing with drift nets is officially prohibited by the European Union, and catches are subject to strict quotas, in the hope of reviving the tuna's fortunes.

casual-chic at this welcoming *osteria* (tavern) with indoor and outdoor seating on Favignana's main pedestrian street. An offshoot of the more upscale Sotto Sale restaurant around the corner, it specialises in creative cuisine made with classic Sicilian ingredients: *busiate* (corkscrew-shaped pasta) with mussels and fava beans, tuna burgers, and desserts like ricotta cake flavoured with citrus and chocolate.

Il Pakkaro SEAFOOD **€€**
(☎328 0613380, 0923 3 24 41; Piazza Matrice, Favignana; meals €25-30; ⏲noon-3pm & 7-11pm) An atmospheric spot for an affordable meal, this trattoria in Favignana's central piazza serves tasty, unpretentious pasta and seafood dishes on vinyl tablecloths festooned with dolphins. Try the *busiate* with shrimp, pistachios and fish roe, or sample their island twist on *pasta alla carbonara* (with tuna instead of pancetta), followed by plates of grilled tuna, yellowtail or calamari.

Sotto Sale MODERN SICILIAN **€€€**
(☎320 8432916; www.facebook.com/sottosalefavignana; Via Garibaldi 7, Favignana; meals €50-55; ⏲7.30pm-midnight) Favignana's favourite spot for a romantic dinner, Sotto Sale caters to a sophisticated crowd with beautifully presented nouvelle Sicilian cuisine. Expect appetisers like tuna tartare with swordfish roe, wild fennel and oranges, followed by flambeed octopus or risotto studded with *gamberi rossi di Mazara* (Mazara del Vallo's famous red shrimp) – all served in an intimate, low-lit dining room.

New Albatros BAR
(☎346 7576883; Via Vittorio Emanuele 25, Favignana; ⏲noon-midnight) Strategically placed for people-watching at the corner of Favignana's main square, this bar serves drinks and snacks along with an eclectic mix of reggae, rock and blues, while a steady parade of locals and tourists – everyone from posing fashionistas to carefree kids pushed on their parents' bikes – waltzes past during the evening *passeggiata*. There's occasional live music on summer evenings.

Information

Guardia Medica (☎0923 92 12 83; Via delle Fosse, Favignana) Round-the-clock medical assistance.

Police Station (☎0923 92 16 70; Piazza Europa, Favignana)

Tourist Office (☎0923 92 54 43; www.welcometoegadi.it; Palazzo Florio, Favignana; ⏲9.30am-1.30pm & 3-6pm Jun-Sep, 9.30am-1.30pm Apr, May & Oct) Helpful office on the ground floor of the elegant Palazzo Florio, one block from the hydrofoil dock. Supplies information on diving and boating operators, accommodation and excursions.

Getting There & Away

Liberty Lines (p94) runs year-round hydrofoils to Favignana from Trapani (€11.80, 30 to 40 minutes), with summer-only service from Marsala (€11.80, 30 minutes). Inter-island hydrofoils to Levanzo (€7.30, 10 minutes) and Marettimo (€11.90, 30 to 40 minutes) also operate year-round.

Getting Around

BICYCLE & SCOOTER

Bike or scooter is the best way to get around Favignana, giving you access to all the little coves and beaches dotting the island. The port area is swarming with places offering bikes, scooters and motorbikes for hire. Bicycle hire ranges from €6 to €10 per day, depending on season; scooters run €25 to €50, and cars €40 to €80. One of the most convenient places to rent is **Egadi Booking** (☎392 8395774; www.egadibooking.com), right on the hydrofoil dock.

BUS

Tarantola (☎0924 3 10 20; ticket/day pass €1.10/3) operates three bus routes around the island, all of which originate at a stop on the *lungomare* (seafront promenade) 200m east of the hydrofoil dock. Schedules are posted at Favignana's tourist office and at the bus stop.

Levanzo

There are two main reasons to visit Levanzo: to examine the prehistoric cave paintings at the Grotta del Genovese, and to spend some time swimming off the island's pebbly beaches.

Sights

★**Grotta del Genovese** CAVE
(☎339 741 88 00, 092 392 40 32; www.grottadelgenovese.it; guided cave tour €10, incl transport one-way/round trip €18/22.50; ⏲tours 10.30am daily, extra tour 2.30pm or 3pm Jul & Aug) Between 6000 and 10,000 years old, the Upper Palaeolithic wall paintings and neolithic incised drawings at the Genovese Cave were discovered in 1949 by Francesca Minellono, a painter from Florence who was holidaying on Levanzo. Mostly featuring animals, the later ones also include men and tuna. Visits

to the grotto are by guided tour only, and reservations are required.

The all-inclusive tour takes two hours; transport is by boat if weather conditions are favourable – otherwise, it's by 4WD, with a steep but scenic 700m descent on foot from the parking area to the cave. You can also reach the grotto by foot from the port (1½ hours each way), or walk one way and take a jeep or boat the other. Advance booking of the cave visit is imperative, regardless of how you get there.

Activities

Three spots on the island offer great swimming. To get to **Faraglione**, walk 1km along the road west of town until you see a couple of rocks sticking out of the water just offshore. For something quieter and more remote, take the 4km cross-island trail to **Capo Grosso** on the far northern shore, where there is also a lighthouse.

Alternatively, take a right out of town and walk along the dirt road. The road forks 300m past the first bend; take the rocky path down towards the sea and keep going until you get to **Cala Minnola**, a small bay with crystal-clear water where, outside the month of August, you can swim in peace and tranquillity.

Eating

Ristorante Paradiso SEAFOOD €€
(0923 92 40 80; www.albergoparadiso.eu; Via Lungomare 8; meals €30-45; Apr-Oct) With its charming terrace overlooking the port, this is a pleasant place to snack on *antipasti* (€12) or *lasagne alla marinara* (seafood lasagne) while awaiting the hydrofoil. Sadly, the owners take undue advantage of their monopoly on the island's restaurant business, with rather surly service and unduly high prices for other menu items, including water (€3) and cover charge (€3).

Getting There & Away

Liberty Lines (p94) runs year-round hydrofoils to Levanzo from Trapani (€11.80, 25 to 50 minutes), and summer-only service from Marsala. Inter-island hydrofoils to Favignana (€7.30, 10 minutes) and Marettimo (€11.90, 25 minutes) also operate year-round.

Marettimo

The wildest, westernmost and least developed of the Egadi Islands, Marettimo is a collection of green mountain peaks and whitewashed houses dipping into a little harbour packed with bobbing fishing boats. With the overfishing of tuna affecting fishermen's incomes, villagers are increasingly focusing on the economic potential of tourism, and more accommodation options have cropped up in recent years; however, this doesn't mean that you'll ever find Marettimo packed with tourists – indeed, the island still virtually shuts down in winter, and remains sleepier than its neighbours even in peak summer season.

There's only one road on the island, and the main mode of motorised transport is electric carts, making this a prime destination for walkers. Fanning out in all directions from the town centre, a well-marked trail network leads quickly into unspoilt nature, climbing through fragrant pine forests to dramatic coastal lookouts, then descending again to remote beaches.

Activities

Three of the most popular trails are the hike north from town to the crumbling Norman castle perched on the lonely promontory of **Punta Troia**, the short climb west to **Case Romane**, where the remains of Roman houses share the stage with a spare, whitewashed Byzantine church, and the longer hike following the island's southwestern shores to the secluded beach at **Cala Nera**. At various points along the trail, well-placed picnic benches invite hikers to take a shady break.

Marettimo is also a perfect place for relaxation and swimming – other good beaches include **Cala Sarda** on the south coast and stunning **Cala Bianca** at the island's northwest corner.

Eating

★**Trattoria Il Veliero** SEAFOOD €€
(0923 92 32 74; Via Umberto 22; meals €30; noon-2pm & 7-9.30pm Mar-Oct) Just north of the hydrofoil dock, this family-run waterfront eatery is a seafood-lover's fantasy. Chef-owner Peppe Bevilacqua goes to the market daily, picking out the freshest catches. Superbly prepared Sicilian classics like *pasta con le sarde* (pasta with sardines) and *fritto misto* (fried shrimp and calamari) share the menu with octopus salad, tuna carpaccio, perfectly grilled fish and countless other delights.

Getting There & Away

Liberty Lines (p94) runs year-round hydrofoils to Marettimo from Trapani (€18.80, 1¼ hours), Levanzo (€11.90, 25 to 40 minutes) and Favignana (€11.90, 25 to 50 minutes), with summer-only service from Marsala (€18.80, 1¼ hours).

THE SOUTHWEST

Marsala

☎0923 / POP 83,065

Many know about its sweet dessert wines, but few people realise what a charmer the town of Marsala is. Though its streets are paved in gleaming marble, lined with stately baroque buildings and peppered with graceful piazzas, Marsala has pleasures that are simple – a friendly *passeggiata* most nights, plenty of aperitif options and family-friendly restaurants aplenty.

Marsala was founded by the Phoenicians who escaped from Mozia after it was defeated in 397 BC by an army led by Dionysius I of Syracuse. They settled here on Capo Lilibeo, calling their city Lilybaeum and fortifying it with 7m-thick walls that ensured it was the last Punic settlement to fall to the Romans. In AD 830 it was conquered by the Arabs, who gave it its current name Marsa Allah (Port of God).

Sights

Museo Archeologico Baglio Anselmi MUSEUM

(☎0923 95 25 35; Lungomare Boeo 30; adult/reduced €4/2; ⏲9am-7.30pm Tue-Sat, to 1.30pm Sun & Mon) Marsala's finest treasure is the partially reconstructed remains of a Carthaginian *liburna* (warship) sunk off the Egadi Islands during the First Punic War. Displayed alongside objects from its cargo, the ship's bare bones provide the only remaining physical evidence of the Phoenicians' seafaring superiority in the 3rd century BC, offering a glimpse of a civilisation extinguished by the Romans. As of mid-2016, the ship was undergoing restoration work but scheduled to reopen to the public in 2017.

Among the objects found on board the ship and displayed here are ropes, cooking pots, corks from amphorae, a brush, olive stones, a sailor's wooden button and even a stash of cannabis. In an adjacent room are other regional archaeological artefacts including a marble statue known as *La venere di lilybaeum* (The Venus of Lilybaeum) and some mosaics from the 3rd and 5th centuries AD.

Museum visitors can also explore the adjacent **Insula Romana**, a vast archaeological site that encompasses the remains of a 3rd-century Roman villa and a well-preserved Decumanus Maximus (Roman ceremonial road) paved with giant stones.

Complesso Monumentale San Pietro MUSEUM

(☎0923 71 87 41; Via Ludovico Anselmi Correale; ⏲9am-1pm & 4-8pm Tue-Sat, 9am-1pm & 4.30-7.30pm Sun) FREE Housed in a beautifully restored 15th-century convent, this arts centre is home to an intriguing complex of small museums. Most noteworthy is the upstairs space devoted to Giuseppe Garibaldi, who landed in Marsala on 11 May 1860 with his

THE SWEET SMELL OF SUCCESS

Fresh out of sherry country in southern Spain, John Woodhouse's 'sweet nose' knew a business opportunity when he smelled it. The English soap merchant swiftly based himself in Marsala aiming to market its wine to the seemingly insatiable sweet palate of 18th-century England, but had to grapple with one problem: how was he to get the wine to England without it going bad? He added a dash of pure alcohol and, *voilà*, Marsala's fortified wine was born.

The real success of the wine came when the British Navy used it as an alternative to port in order to supply the sailors' ration of one glass of wine per day. Lord Nelson placed a huge order in 1800, and soon other entrepreneurs wanted to get in on the action. Benjamin Ingham and his nephew, Joseph Whitaker, set up the first rival winery, exporting to the USA and Australia in 1806. The third big producer was canny Vincenzo Florio, who already owned the Egadi Islands and their lucrative tuna plants. All of the wineries were eventually bought by Cinzano in the 1920s, which merged them under the Florio label. In 1988, Cinzano sold the company to Illva Saronno, which now operates three labels: Florio, Duca di Salaparuta and Corvo.

For more information on Marsala and the wineries that produce it today, see www.stradavinomarsala.it.

Marsala

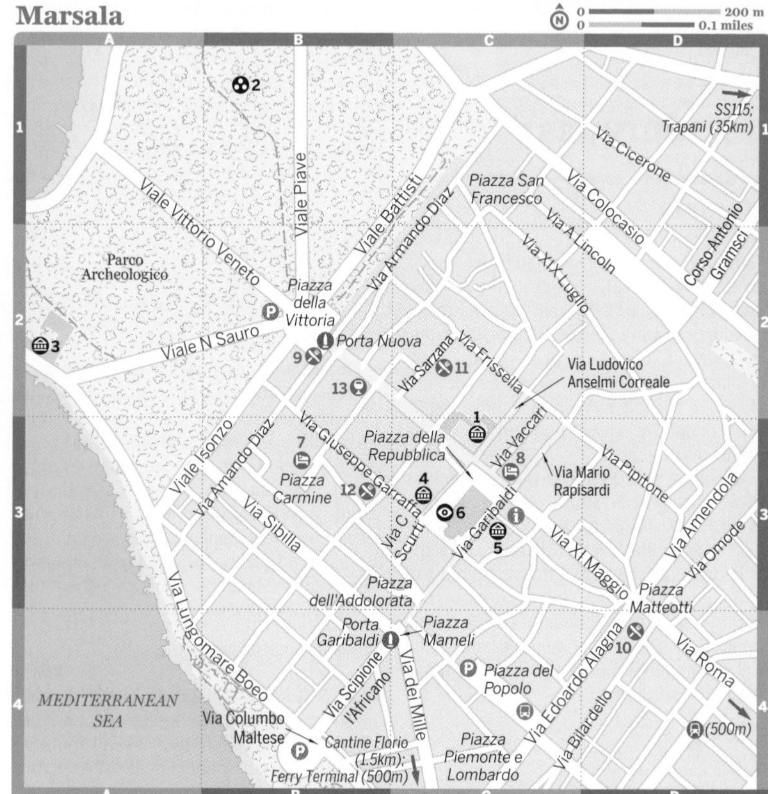

army of 1000 redshirts in the first stage of their successful campaign to conquer the kingdom of the Two Sicilies. The Garibaldi collection includes weapons, documents, uniforms and portraits but unfortunately lacks interpretive labels in English.

Other museums include a small collection of local archaeological finds and a space devoted to Marsala's unique Easter Thursday procession. On the upper floor, close to the courtyard entrance, you'll find the Museo dei Pupi, which displays Marsala-designed puppets and their theatrical backdrops.

Piazza Della Repubblica PIAZZA

Marsala's most elegant piazza is dominated by the imposing Chiesa Madre. Just across the way, on the eastern side of the square, is the arcaded **Palazzo VII Aprile** (Piazza Della Repubblica), formerly known as the Palazzo Senatorio (Senatorial Palace) and now the town hall.

Museo degli Arazzi Fiamminghi MUSEUM

(☎0923 71 13 27; Via Giuseppe Garraffa 57; adult/reduced €4/2; ⏱9am-1pm & 4-6pm Tue-Sun) Tapestry fans should check out this tiny museum just behind Marsala's Chiesa Madre. The eight 16th-century Flemish tapestries on display were woven in Brussels for Spanish King Philip II.

Activities

Cantine Florio WINE-TASTING

(☎0923 78 11 11; www.duca.it/cantineflorio; Via Vincenzo Florio 1; tours adult/reduced €13/5; ⏱9am-6pm Mon-Fri, to 1pm Sat, English-language tour by advance reservation 9.30am & 4.30pm Mon-Fri, 9.30am Sat) These venerable wine cellars just east of town open their doors to visitors to explain the Marsala-making process and the fascinating history of local viticulture. Afterwards, visitors can sample the goods in Florio's spiffy tasting room (tastes of four wines, accompanied by hors d'oeuvres, are

Marsala

Sights

1 Complesso Monumentale San Pietro ... C3
2 Insula Romana ... B1
3 Museo Archeologico Baglio Anselmi ... A2
4 Museo degli Arazzi Fiamminghi ... C3
5 Palazzo VII Aprile ... C3
6 Piazza Della Repubblica ... C3

Sleeping

7 Hotel Carmine ... B3
8 Il Profumo del Sale ... C3

Eating

9 Assud ... B2
10 Il Gallo e l'Innamorata ... D4
11 Quimera ... C2
12 San Lorenzo Osteria ... B3

Drinking & Nightlife

Ciacco Putia Gourmet ... (see 6)
13 Enoteca della Strada del Vino di Marsala ... B2

included in the tour price). Take bus 16 from Piazza del Popolo.

Other producers in the same area include Pellegrino, Donnafugata, Rallo, Mavis and Intorcia.

Eating

The historic centre between Via Garibaldi and Porta Nuova is packed with classy restaurants, interspersed with more casual eateries serving *panini* (sandwiches) and *taglieri* (meat and cheese boards) accompanied by glasses of local wine.

Quimera SANDWICHES €
(☎349 6783243; www.facebook.com/quimerapub; Via Sarzana 34-36; sandwiches & salads from €5; ⏲7.30am-3pm & 6.30pm-2am Mon-Sat, 6.30pm-2am Sun) Smack in the middle of the pedestrianised centre, this is Marsala's hotspot for artisanal beers, gourmet sandwiches and meal-sized salads, all served with a smile by friendly young owners.

Assud MODERN SICILIAN €€
(☎0923716652; www.facebook.com/ASSUDCucinaMeridionale; Via Armando Diaz 66; meals €25-35; ⏲noon-3pm & 6.30-11pm Tue-Sun) Good wines accompany the short but sweet menu at this cosy eatery straddling Marsala's historic walls. The nightly evolving mix of antipasti, *primi* and *secondi* (three to four in each category) might include anything from seafood couscous to a *tris di arancine* (three re-imagined versions of Sicily's classic rice balls, filled respectively with meat, eggplant and ricotta, and squid ink).

San Lorenzo Osteria SICILIAN €€
(SLO; ☎0923 71 25 93; www.osteriasanlorenzo.com; Via Garraffa 60; meals €30-40; ⏲7.30-11pm Wed-Mon, plus 12.30-2.30pm Sun; 📶) With roots as a wedding-catering business, this stylish eatery is a class act all round – from the ever-changing menu of fresh seafood dishes scrawled daily on the blackboard to the interior's sleek modern lines to the gorgeous presentation of the food.

Il Gallo e l'Innamorata SICILIAN €€
(☎0923 195 44 46; www.osteriailgalloelinnamorata.com; Via Bilardello 18; meals €25-35; ⏲12.30-2.30pm & 7.30-10.30pm Tue-Sun) Warm-orange walls and arched stone doorways lend an artsy, convivial atmosphere to this Slow Food–acclaimed eatery. The à la carte menu is short and sweet, featuring a few well-chosen dishes each day, including the classic *scaloppine al Marsala* (veal cooked with Marsala wine and lemon).

Drinking & Nightlife

As one of Sicily's viticultural capitals, Marsala is naturally teeming with *enoteche* (wine bars), most of them concentrated near Via XI Maggio in the historic centre.

Ciacco Putia Gourmet WINE BAR
(☎347 6315684; www.ciaccoputia.it; Via Cammareri Scurti 3; ⏲11.30am-3pm & 5.30-11.30pm Mon-Sat) Run by an English-speaking Sicilian-Tuscan couple, this sweet little *enoteca* is a great place to sample quality Marsala wines accompanied by locally sourced *salumi* (cold cuts) or snacks like *panini* with *burrata* (cheese made from mozzarella and cream), lemon and anchovies. Just as appealing is the setting, in an attractive square directly opposite the showy 18th-century baroque facade of the Chiesa del Purgatorio.

Enoteca della Strada del Vino di Marsala WINE BAR
(☎0923 71 34 89; www.enotecastradavinomarsala.it; Via XI Maggio 32; ⏲11am-2am Tue-Sun) Sponsored by the local association of Marsala wine merchants, this atmospheric wine bar in the heart of the pedestrian zone has tables invitingly spread under the arcades of its interior courtyard. It's a good place to sample a variety of local vintages, starting at €3 per glass.

Information

Police Station (Questura; 0923 71 88 11; Via Giuseppe Verdi 1; 24hr)

Post Office (Via Roma 167; 8am-6.30pm Mon-Sat)

Tourist Office (0923 99 33 38, 0923 71 40 97; ufficioturistico.proloco@comune.marsala.tp.it; Via XI Maggio 100; 8.30am-1.30pm & 3-8pm Mon-Fri, to 1.30pm Sat) Spacious office with comfy couches right off the main square; provides a wide range of maps and brochures.

Getting There & Away

BOAT

From June to early September, Liberty Lines (www.libertylines.it) operates five daily hydrofoils between Marsala and Favignana (€11.80, 30 minutes), with connections to the other Egadi Islands.

BUS

From Marsala's bus terminal at Piazza del Popolo (off Via Mazzini in the centre of town), **AST** (Azienda Siciliana Trasporti; www.aziendasicilianatrasporti.it) travels to Mazara del Vallo (€2.90, 25 to 45 minutes, three daily except Sunday) and Trapani (€3.60, one hour, four daily except Sunday) via Birgi Airport (€2.70).

Lumia (www.autolineelumia.it) runs to Agrigento (€10.10, 2¾ hours) and Sciacca (€7, 1½ hours) three times Monday to Friday, twice on Saturday, and once on Sunday from its stop in Piazza Caprera.

Salemi (0923 98 11 20; www.autoservizisalemi.it) also runs five to six daily buses to Palermo (€11, 2¼ to 2½ hours) from its stop on Viale Fazio near the train station.

TRAIN

The best way to travel along this stretch of coast is by train. There are 10 trains daily (four on Sunday) to Trapani (€3.80, 25 to 40 minutes) and Mazara del Vallo (€3.10, 20 minutes). To reach Marsala's historic centre from the train station, walk 800m up Via Roma, which meets Via XI Maggio at Piazza Matteotti.

Mazara del Vallo

0923 / POP 51,800

Vaguely redolent of a North African *kasbah* (and still bearing the Casbah name), Mazara's historic quarter is a labyrinth of narrow streets, sprinkled with magnificent baroque and Norman-period buildings. It's small enough that you won't ever really get lost, and the dilapidated old buildings give it a rugged charm.

Mazara was one of the key cities of Saracen Sicily and the North African influence is still strongly felt here – the town has one of the highest percentages of immigrants in Italy, with hundreds of people from Tunisia and Maghreb arriving annually to work on Mazara's fishing fleet.

In summer, Mazara is inundated with holidaymakers who head straight to Tonnarella beach, on the western side of the city.

Sights

Mazara's streets and alleys are decorated with colourful hand-painted tiles, a subtle touch that adds to the pleasure of randomly strolling through town.

La Casbah HISTORIC SITE
At the northwest corner of the historic centre, this multicultural maze of narrow streets was once the heart of the Saracen city. The main thoroughfare was Via Bagno, which still has its *hammam* (public baths). Today, the area is rundown but interesting, in large part because it retains a strong Arab connection through the Tunisian immigrants who now live here.

Piazza della Repubblica PIAZZA
Mazara's central piazza is an attractive space edged by elegant buildings, including the **Cattedrale del San Salvatore** (hours vary) FREE, the two-storey **Seminario dei Chierici** (dating from 1710) and, on the opposite side of the square, the 18th-century **Seminario Vescovile**, with its impressive 11-arched portico. Unfortunately, the 1970s office tower on the west side of the square is a visual affront of the highest order.

Chiesa di Sant'Ignazio CHURCH
(Piazza Plebiscito) This early 18th-century church collapsed in the 1930s, but its roofless remains make a photogenic detour, with their circular colonnade of twin columns backed by a vine-draped stone wall.

Castle RUINS
(Piazza Mokarta) Just in from the waterfront, the ragged remains of Count Roger's Norman castle have definitely seen better days, but their forlorn ruination is wonderfully atmospheric at night (when they are floodlit).

Eating

Mazara is Sicily's largest fishing centre, with many restaurants specialising in seafood. Be sure to try the local *gambero rosso di Mazara* (Mazara red shrimp), a delicacy renowned throughout Sicily. In the

DON'T MISS

THE SATYR THAT ROSE FROM THE SEA

The jewel in Mazara's crown, **Museo del Satiro** (☎0923 93 39 17; Piazza Plebiscito; adult/reduced €6/3; ⏲9am-7.45pm) revolves around its central exhibit, a bronze statue known as the *Satiro danzante* (Dancing Satyr), hauled from the watery depths by local fisherfolk in the late 1990s. The sculpture depicts a bacchanalian satyr dancing wildly like a whirling dervish, arms outstretched, head flung back, the centrifugal force evident in his flowing hair. Originally, the statue would have been used in Dionysian processions; today it commands its own form of no-less-passionate worship here.

The museum is located in the deconsecrated shell of the Chiesa di Sant'Egidio. On entering, make sure you watch the 25-minute video before looking at anything else. In Italian, with English subtitles, the film tells the story of a group of fishermen who were working their nets 40km off the shores of Tunisia in 1997 when they pulled up the bronze leg of a statue. Time elapsed and they continued to fish in the same area, wondering if they would ever find the rest of the statue. Extraordinarily, they did so the next year – a rare original casting from the Hellenistic era. In the film the boat's captain, overcome by romanticism, recounts the dramatic rescue. What followed was a 4½-year period of painstaking restoration, during which time Mazara strenuously tussled with the powers in Rome to ensure the return of the satyr, which only came home in 2003.

back streets of La Casbah, you'll also find a number of places serving excellent fish couscous.

Eyem Zemen TUNISIAN €
(☎347 386 99 21; Via Porta Palermo 36; meals €20-25; ⏲11am-3.30pm & 7pm-midnight) For a taste of Tunisia, try this delightful hole-in-the-wall in the heart of La Casbah, marked by a bilingual Italian-Arabic sign. Tunisian owner Fatiha serves grilled Mazara prawns, kebabs, roast mutton, multiple varieties of couscous (with vegetables, seafood, meat or wild fennel), and *brik* (savoury tuna- or shrimp-filled pastries). In warm weather, dine alfresco at tables on the adjacent piazza.

Service can be a bit slow, so come prepared to linger – ideally sticking around long enough to enjoy Tunisian pastries with toasted pine nuts and mint tea after your meal.

La Bettola SEAFOOD €€
(☎0923 94 64 22; www.ristorantelabettola.it; Via Maccagnone 32; meals €30-45; ⏲1-3pm & 7.30-11pm Thu-Tue) Over the past 4½ decades, chef-owner Pietro Sardo has established a reputation as one of Sicily's top chefs. At this renowned seafood eatery, just around the corner from Mazara's train station, he continues to create sensational and often unexpected flavour combinations like citrus-scented lobster or red mullet and ricotta-filled tortellini, followed by his famous *cassata* for dessert.

ℹ Information

Hospital (Ospedale Civico A Ajello; ☎0923 65 79 41; Via Salemi 175; ⏲24hr)

Police Station (☎0923 93 44 11; Via Sansone 56)

Tourist Office (☎0923 94 46 10; www.comune.mazaradelvallo.tp.it; Via XX Settembre 5; ⏲9am-1pm & 4-8pm) Municipal government info centre, just off the *lungomare* (seafront promenade), next to the castle.

ℹ Getting There & Away

BUS

Mazara's **bus station** (Via Salemi) is next to the train station. **Salemi** (☎0923 98 11 20; www.autoservizisalemi.it) goes to Palermo (€9, two hours) five to six times daily. **Lumia** (☎0922 2 04 14, 0923 2 17 54; www.autolineelumia.it) runs to Agrigento (€9.20, 2¼ hours) and Sciacca (€5.80, one hour) three times Monday to Friday, twice on Saturday, and once on Sunday. **AST** (www.aziendasicilianatrasporti.it) travels to/from Marsala (€2.90, 25 to 45 minutes, three daily except Sunday) and Trapani (€5.30, 1¾ to 2¼ hours, three daily except Sunday).

CAR & MOTORCYCLE

Mazara is an easy, 90-minute drive down the A29 autostrada from Palermo. Coming from Agrigento (116km, 1½ hours) or Sciacca (56km, 45 minutes), take the SS115 west and join the A29 at Castelvetrano. The SS115 from Marsala (23km, 35 minutes) is slower and more congested.

TRAIN

There are 10 daily trains (four on Sunday) from Mazara to Marsala (€3.10, 20 minutes) and Trapani (€5.10, 55 minutes).

Selinunte

The ruins of **Selinunte** (☎0924 4 62 77; adult/reduced €6/3; ⏰9am-6pm Apr-Oct, to 5pm Nov-Mar) rank among the most impressive and captivating archaeological sites in Sicily.

Selinos (as it was known to the Greeks) was once one of the richest and most powerful cities in the world, with over 100,000 inhabitants and an unrivalled temple-building program. The most westerly of the Greek colonies, it was established by a group of settlers from nearby Megara Hyblaea in 628 BC who had been attracted by its wonderful location atop a promontory between two major rivers (now silted up), the Modione and Cottone, the latter forming a secure natural harbour. The plains surrounding the site were overgrown with celery (*selinon* in Greek), which served as inspiration for the new colony's name.

Today this vast complex of fields and ruined temples beside the Mediterranean is a delightful place to wander, especially in springtime, when the wildflowers are in full bloom.

History

Originally allied with Carthage, Selinunte switched allegiance after the Carthaginian defeat by Gelon of Syracuse at Himera in 480 BC. Under Syracusan protection it grew in power and prestige. The city's growth resulted in a litany of territorial disputes with its northern neighbour, Segesta, which ended abruptly in 409 BC when the latter called for Carthaginian help. Selinunte's former ally happily obliged and arrived to take revenge.

Troops commanded by Hannibal utterly destroyed the city after a nine-day siege, leaving only those who had taken shelter in the temples as survivors; they were spared not out of a sense of humanity but because of the fear that they might set fire to the temples and prevent their looting. In a famous retort to the Agrigentan ambassadors who sought to negotiate for the survivors' lives, Hannibal replied that as they hadn't been able to defend their freedom, they deserved to be slaves. One year later, Hermocrates of Syracuse took over the city and initiated its recovery, though it soon fell back under Carthaginian control. Around 250 BC, with the Romans about to conquer the city, its citizens were relocated to Lilybaeum (Marsala), the Carthaginian capital in Sicily, but not before they destroyed as much as they could. What they left standing, mainly temples, was finished off by an earthquake in the Middle Ages.

The city was forgotten until the middle of the 16th century, when a Dominican monk identified its location. Excavations began in 1823, courtesy of two English archaeologists, William Harris and Samuel Angell, who uncovered the first metopes.

Sights

Selinunte's ruins are spread out over a vast area dominated by the hill of Manuzza – the location of the ancient city proper. The site deserves a visit of at least three hours to do it justice.

The entrance and ticket office are near the eastern temples, adjacent to a large parking lot about 200m off the SP115dir. Just beyond the ticket booth you'll find a kiosk renting **electric carts** (☎380 3907485;

OFF THE BEATEN TRACK

CAVE DI CUSA

Most of the buttery yellow stone used to construct the great temples of Selinunte was hewn at **Cave di Cusa** (☎0924 4 62 77; adult/reduced €2/1; ⏰9am-6pm Mon-Sat, to 1pm Sun), ancient Greek quarries. The setting is charming – overgrown and wild, it's dotted with olive trees and wildflowers. Huge column drums forever awaiting transport to Selinunte are scattered around, and if you look carefully you will come across two carved columns ready for extraction. When removed, the columns would have been transported to Selinunte across wooden logs by oxen or slaves.

The site is about 17km northwest of Selinunte. Head 4km north on SS115dir, then 9km west on SP56 to Campobello di Mazara; from Campobello, follow the series of signposted backroads 4km further to reach the site. From Mazara del Vallo, take the SS115 11km east to Campobello di Mazara, then follow the signs 4.5km south to Cave di Cusa.

There's officially a €2 admission fee, though staffing at the entrance gate is intermittent. Free admission is also occasionally granted to visitors holding a ticket for the Selinunte ruins issued within the preceding three days.

Selinunte

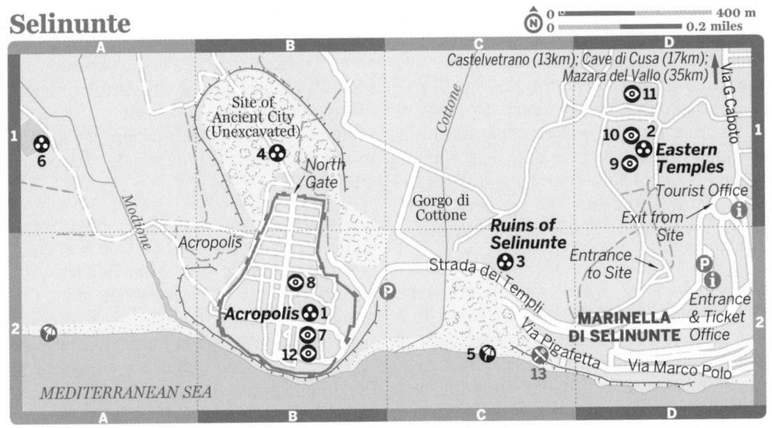

Selinunte

Top Sights

1 Acropolis B2
2 Eastern Temples D1
3 Ruins of Selinunte C2

Sights

4 Ancient City B1
5 Lido di Zabbara C2
6 Sanctuary of Malophoros A1
7 Temple A B2
Temple B .... (see 1)
Temple C .... (see 1)
8 Temple D B2
9 Temple E D1
10 Temple F D1
11 Temple G D1
12 Temple O B2

Eating

13 Lido Zabbara C2

hire €3-12 depending on number of sites visited) to help mobility-impaired visitors get around.

★Eastern Temples ARCHAEOLOGICAL SITE
The eastern temples are the most stunning of all Selinunte's ruins, crowned by the majestic **Temple E**. Built in the 5th century BC and reconstructed in 1958, Temple E stands out due to its completeness; as you walk from the ticket office, it's the first structure you'll come to.

Temple G, the northernmost temple, was built in the 6th century BC and, although never completed, was one of the largest temples in the Greek world. Today it is a massive pile of impressive rubble – as is its counterpart directly to the south, **Temple F**.

★Acropolis ARCHAEOLOGICAL SITE
(Strada dei Templi) The Acropolis, the heart of Selinunte's political and social life, occupies a slanted plateau overlooking the now-silted-up Gorgo di Cottone. Huddled in the southeastern part are five temples (A, B, C, D and O). Virtually the symbol of Selinunte, **Temple C** is the oldest temple on the site, built in the middle of the 6th century BC.

The stunning metopes found by Harris and Angell were once a part of this formidable structure, as was the enormous Gorgon's mask that once adorned the pediment; both of these can be viewed in the Museo Archeologico Regionale in Palermo. Experts believe that the temple was dedicated to Apollo.

Northernmost of the remaining temples is **Temple D**, built towards the end of the 6th century BC and dedicated to either Neptune or Venus.

The smaller **Temple B** dates from the Hellenistic period and could have been dedicated to the Agrigentan physiologist and philosopher Empedocles, whose water-drainage scheme saved the city from the scourge of malaria (a bitter irony for William Harris, who contracted the disease during the initial excavations and died soon after).

The two other temples, **Temple A** and **Temple O**, closest to the sea, are the most recent, built between 490 and 480 BC. They are virtually identical in both style and size, and it's been suggested that they might have been dedicated to the twins Castor and Pollux.

Sanctuary of Malophoros ARCHAEOLOGICAL SITE
Walk west about 20 minutes from the acropolis across the now-dry river Modione (formerly the Selinon), then up a dirt path, and

you'll reach the ravaged ruins of the temple dedicated to Demeter, the goddess of fertility. Amid the debris, two altars can be made out; the larger of the two was used for sacrifices.

Although they're not much to look at, these are some of the most important finds of the site as they provide an insight into the social history of Selinunte. Thousands of votive offerings to Demeter have been found in the area (nearly 12,000), including stelae crowned with real human heads.

Ancient City ARCHAEOLOGICAL SITE

Occupying the hill of Manuzza, to the north of the acropolis, the Ancient City, where most of Selinunte's inhabitants lived, is the least excavated of all the sites. Exploration of the area has only begun in recent years, and evidence suggests that survivors of the destruction of 409 BC may have used the city as a necropolis.

Lido di Zabbara BEACH

No visit to Selinunte is complete without a walk along this attractive stretch of beach below the archaeological site, which affords marvellous views back up to the clifftop temples. A path once led here from the acropolis parking area, but it has now been fenced off, so the only access is via the beachfront town of Marinella di Selinunte.

Eating

Avoid the tourist cafes around the archaeological site's car park and head for the coast at Marinella di Selinunte or Porto Palo, where you'll find some attractive seafood eateries along the beachfront.

Lido Zabbara BUFFET €

(0924 4 61 94; Via Pigafetta, Marinella di Selinunte; buffet per person €12; noon-3pm Mar-early Nov, plus 7.30-10.30pm Jun-Sep) For tasty, reasonably priced food near the ruins, head straight for this low-key eatery on the beachfront. Affable long-time owner Jòjò welcomes temple-weary travellers to his delightful outdoor terrace for grilled fish of the day and a varied buffet of two-dozen items, including many salads and vegetables. Afterwards, rent umbrellas and sun loungers and stick around to sunbathe.

★ **Da Vittorio** SEAFOOD €€

(0925 7 83 81; www.ristorantevittorio.it; Via Friuli Venezia Giulia, Porto Palo; meals €30-45; 12.30-2.30pm & 7-10pm) Travellers with their own vehicles should consider detouring 15km east of Selinunte to this venerable eatery on the Porto Palo beachfront. In business for five decades, Da Vittorio has earned a reputation as one of western Sicily's best spots for fresh seafood. The front-row view of crashing breakers is wonderful any time of day, but especially at sunset.

Rooms are available upstairs for anyone too stuffed to drive home (single €50 to €60, double €80 to €90).

La Pineta SEAFOOD €€

(0924 4 68 20; Via Punta Cantone, Marinella di Selinunte; meals €25-35; 9am-10.30pm) You couldn't ask for a nicer setting than this beachfront eatery at the edge of the Foce del Belice nature preserve at Marinella's far eastern edge. It's especially nice at sunset, or in the evening when the whole place is aglow with bamboo torches. Grilled fish is the speciality, complemented by simple pasta dishes for those on tighter budgets.

Information

Tourist Office (Azienda Provinciale di Turismo; 0924 4 62 51; 8am-6pm Mon-Fri, 9am-1pm & 2-6pm Sat) On the roundabout just outside Selinunte's main car park, this office supplies a photocopied map of the ruins with multilingual text, plus bus timetables to Castelvetrano and points beyond, including Agrigento.

Getting There & Away

BUS

Autoservizi Salemi (0924 8 18 26; www.autoservizisalemi.it/tratte/selinunte) runs regular buses between Marinella di Selinunte and Castelvetrano's train station (€1.50, 25 to 35 minutes, seven Monday to Saturday year-round, four Sunday July and August only), where you can make onward rail connections to Mazara, Marsala, and Trapani. For eastbound travellers, **Lumia** (0922 2 04 14; www.autolineelumia.it) runs buses from Castelvetrano to Agrigento (€8.60, two hours, three Monday to Friday, two Saturday, one Sunday).

CAR & MOTORCYCLE

Coming from Palermo and other points north, take the Castelvetrano exit off the A29 and follow the signs (briefly east on the SS115, then south on the SS115dir). If you're driving from Agrigento, take the SS115 west for about 85km, then exit onto the SS115dir south. The turn-off for the ruins is clearly signposted, on the northwestern outskirts of the coastal town of Marinella di Selinunte.

TRAIN

There are 10 daily trains (four on Sunday) from Castelvetrano to Mazara del Vallo (€3.10, 20 minutes), Marsala (€4.30, 40 minutes) and Trapani (€6.20, 1¼ hours).

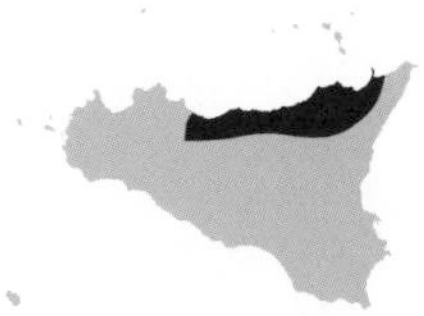

Tyrrhenian Coast

Includes ➡

Best Places to Eat

- Bottega Ti Vitti (p116)
- A Fuoco Lento (p122)
- Nangalarruni (p121)
- A Castellana (p118)
- Osteria Bacchus (p116)

Best Places to Sleep

- Azienda Agrituristica Bergi (p249)
- Dolce Vita (p249)
- Albergo Il Castello (p250)
- Casa Migliaca (p250)

Why Go?

The coastal stretch between Palermo and Milazzo is packed with dramatic beach and mountain scenery, and appealing coastal towns like Cefalù and Castel di Tusa – but once summer rolls around, it's holiday central, characterised by crowded roads and beaches. Somehow neither this, nor the ever-growing proliferation of concrete buildings marring the coastline, can dissuade locals from coming here for their annual vacation and having a whale of a time.

Few sun-worshippers head inland from these sybaritic summer playgrounds to visit the nearby Madonie and Nebrodi Mountains, but those who do are swiftly seduced. These superb natural landscapes enfold hilltop villages where the lifestyle is traditional, the sense of history palpable and the mountain cuisine exceptional, featuring wild forest mushrooms, *suino nero* (pork from local black pigs), and ricotta straight from the sheep.

Road Distances (km)

	Caccamo	Castelbuono	Cefalù	Milazzo
Castelbuono	75			
Cefalù	50	20		
Milazzo	185	135	130	
Petralia Sottana	90	35	60	175

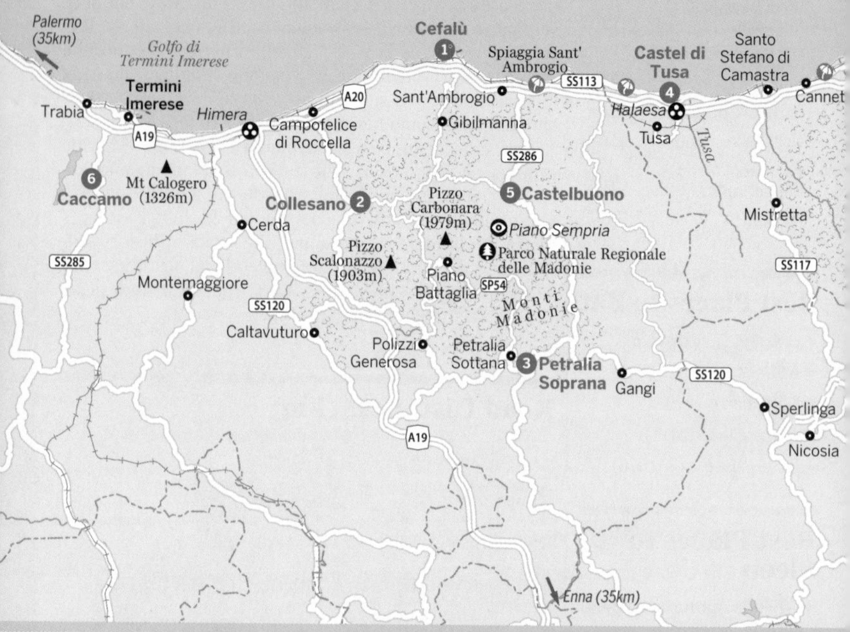

Tyrrhenian Coast Highlights

1. **Cefalù** (p114) Choosing the glitter that suits you best – the sparkling gold mosaics of the Duomo or the fashion-conscious beach scene a few paces away.

2. **Museo Targa Florio** (p123) Reliving the glory days of Italy's greatest road race in this little Collesano museum.

3. **Petralia Soprana** (p121) Whiling away a chilly mountain evening by the blazing fire in a pizzeria.

4. **Castel di Tusa** (p125) Celebrating the summer solstice at the hilltop pyramid, the newest installation in

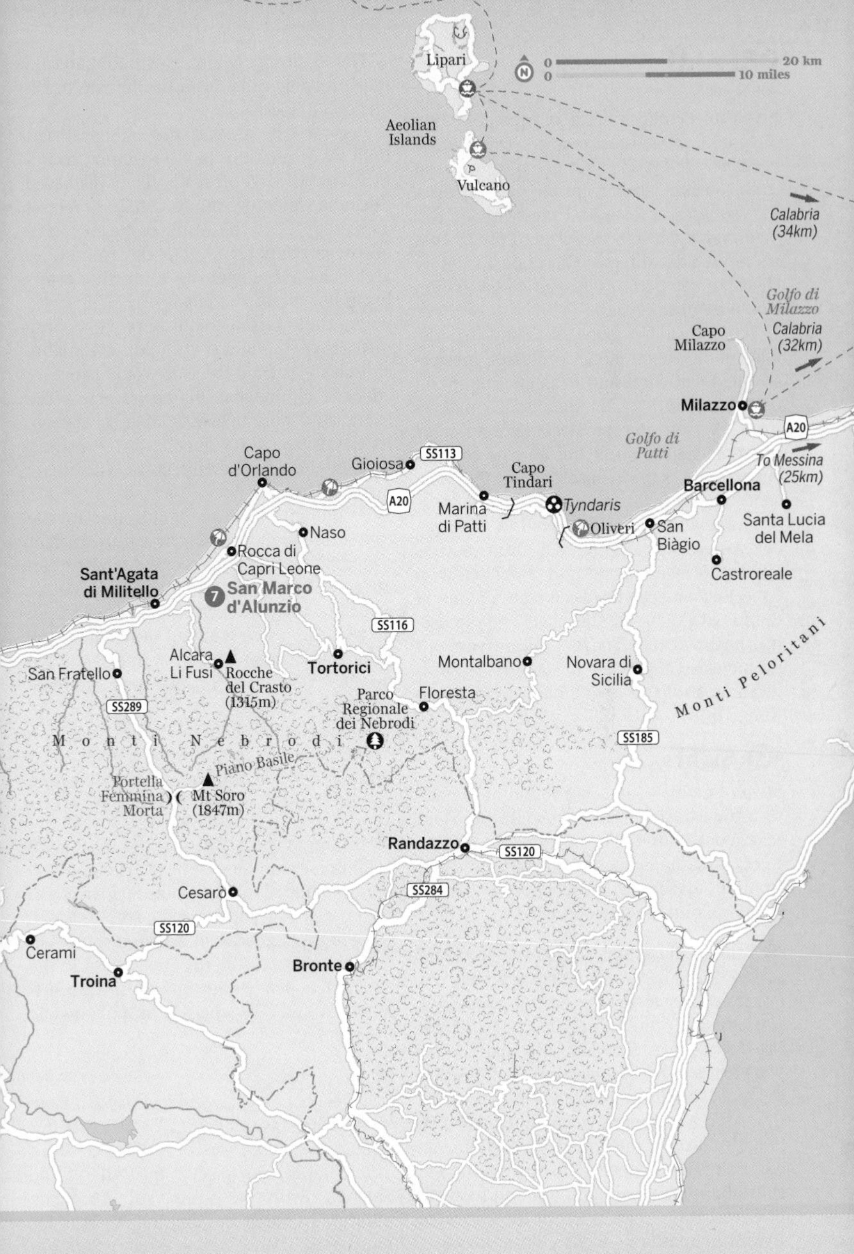

Castel di Tusa's innovative Fiumara d'Arte project.

5 Castelbuono (p118) Visiting a bakery to try a sweet taste of manna, an ancient delicacy made from the sap of local ash trees.

6 Caccamo (p118) Enjoying bird's-eye views of rugged hills and the distant Tyrrhenian from the imposing Norman castle.

7 San Marco d'Alunzio (p125) Seeing if you can count all the churches without running out of fingers and toes.

CEFALÙ

POP 14,450 / ☎0921

Beautiful Cefalù offers a rare combination of tourist attractions: one of Sicliy's finest beaches side-by-side with one of its greatest Arab-Norman architectural masterpieces. The squares, streets and churches of this medieval town are so postcard-pretty that it's no wonder director Giuseppe Tornatore chose to set parts of his much-loved film *Cinema Paradiso* here.

You won't be alone in admiring Cefalù's honey-hued stone buildings, mosaic-adorned cathedral and dramatic mountain backdrop; during summer, holidaymakers from all over Europe flock here to relax in resort hotels, stroll the narrow cobbled streets and sun themselves on the long sandy beach.

The town is perfectly suited to slow, pedestrianised exploration. The little port is lined with fishing boats and populated with fisherfolk who can be observed maintaining their boats, mending their nets and discussing the day's catch. The *lungomare* (seafront promenade) is popular for the *passeggiata* (evening stroll), as is the main street, Corso Ruggero.

Sights

Most of Cefalù's sights are found in the historic town centre around Corso Ruggero and Piazza del Duomo. The only exception is La Rocca – to appreciate the magnificent views from this ancient eyrie you'll need to brave a steep walk up the mountainside.

★Duomo di Cefalù — CATHEDRAL

(☎092 192 20 21; www.cattedraledicefalu.com; Piazza del Duomo; cloisters adult/reduced €3/2; ⏱duomo 8am-6pm Apr-Oct, 8am-1pm & 3.30-5pm Nov-Mar, cloisters 10am-1pm & 3-6pm Apr-Oct, 10am-1pm Mon-Fri, by arrangement Sat Nov-Mar) Cefalù's cathedral is one of the jewels in Sicily's Arab-Norman crown, only equalled in magnificence by the Cattedrale di Monreale and Palermo's Cappella Palatina. Filling the central apse, a towering figure of Christ All Powerful is the focal point of the elaborate Byzantine mosaics – Sicily's oldest and best preserved, predating those of Monreale by 20 or 30 years.

In his hand, a compassionate-looking Christ holds an open Bible bearing a Latin and Greek inscription. Other mosaic groups include the Virgin with Four Archangels dressed as Byzantine officials.

The 16 interior columns with Roman capitals probably came from the Tempio di Diana on La Rocca.

Legend tells us that the cathedral was built by Roger II in the 12th century to fulfil a vow to God after his fleet was saved during a violent storm off Cefalù. In fact, it was more likely the result of Roger's tempestuous relationship with the Palermitan archbishopric. Eager to curb the growing influence of the papacy in Sicily (with whom the Palermo archbishopric had close ties), Roger thought that building a mighty church so far from Palermo would prove an effective reminder of his power across the island and pose a disincentive to any potential usurpers. It's thus hardly surprising that the cathedral's architecture is distinctly fortress-like.

To the left of the main entrance are the cathedral's **cloisters**, which feature ancient columns supporting graceful Arab-Norman arches. The finely carved capitals depict a mix of religious and secular images, all detailed on a free handout available at the ticket desk – among the most interesting are the depictions of acrobats, a pair of crocodiles and Noah's Ark.

You can enjoy the view of the cathedral's soaring twin pyramid towers, framed by La Rocca, over a morning coffee or evening aperitif in the Piazza del Duomo.

★Spiaggia di Cefalù — BEACH

Cefalù's crescent-shaped beach is one of the most popular along the whole Sicilian coast. In summer it is packed, so be sure to arrive early to get a good spot. Though some sections require a ticket, the area closest to the old town is public and you can hire a beach umbrella and deck chair for approximately €15 per day.

★La Rocca — VIEWPOINT

(adult/reduced €4/2; ⏱8am-7pm May-Sep, 9am-4pm Oct-Apr) Looming over Cefalù, this imposing rocky crag was once the site of an Arab citadel, superseded in 1061 by the Norman castle whose ruins still crown the summit. To reach the top, follow signs for Tempio di Diana, taking Vicolo Saraceni off Corso Ruggero or Via Giuseppe Fiore off Piazza Garibaldi. The 30- to 45-minute route climbs the Salita Saraceni (p115), a winding staircase, through three tiers of city walls before emerging onto rock-strewn upland slopes with spectacular coastal views.

The windswept summit appears a suitable home for the race of giants that are said to have been Sicily's first inhabitants. There are stunning views of the town below and the ruined 4th-century BC Tempio di Diana.

Bastione Capo Marchiafava VIEWPOINT
For fabulous sea views in the heart of Cefalù, make your way to this 17th-century fortification, off Via Bordonaro.

Lavatoio HISTORIC SITE
(Via Vittorio Emanuele) FREE Descend the curving stone steps to this picturesque cluster of 16th-century wash basins, built over a spring that was well known in antiquity.

Salita Saraceni HISTORIC SITE
An enormous staircase, the Salita Saraceni, winds up through three tiers of city walls in a 30- to 45-minute climb to the summit of La Rocca. From here you have wonderful views of the town below. The steps are to the right of the Banco di Sicilia on Piazza Garibaldi. From here the way is clearly signposted.

Museo Mandralisca MUSEUM
(0921 42 15 47; www.fondazionemandralisca.it; Via Mandralisca 13; adult/reduced €6/4; 9am-7pm, closed Mon Nov-Feb) This small, privately owned museum showcases a collection amassed by parliamentarian, archaeologist and natural-history buff, Baron Mandralisca (1809–64). The rather faded displays of Greek ceramics and Arab pottery are of marginal interest compared to Antonello da Messina's splendid *Ritratto di un uomo ignoto* (Portrait of an Unknown Man; 1465), considered one of the most distinctive portraits of the Italian Renaissance.

Acquired by the Baron after he discovered it being used as a makeshift cupboard door in Lipari, da Messina's painting depicts a man with an enigmatic smirk, almost as captivating and thought provoking as the Mona Lisa's – albeit without the attendant hype.

Il Castello RUINS
(La Rocca) Apart from a few loose rocks there is nothing left of Il Castello, a Norman castle that once crowned the rocky peak above Cefalù, or the Arab citadel.

Tempio di Diana RUINS
(La Rocca; 24hr) Dating to the 4th century BC, the Tempio di Diana's crumbling remains provide a romantic getaway for young lovers.

Tours

Visit Sicily Tours BOATING
(0921 92 50 36; www.visitsicilytours.com; Corso Ruggero 83; boat tours €30-80; Apr-Oct) This agency offers 3½-hour boat tours of the coastline surrounding Cefalù, with stops for swimming and snorkelling. Fresh fruit and soft drinks are included in the price. Full-day trips to the Aeolian Islands (Lipari, Vulcano, Panarea and Stromboli) are also offered, including transfers to the port from any Cefalù hotel.

Eating

Despite being packed with restaurants, Cefalù does not generally offer great value for money. If all you're after is a passable meal with a beautiful view, you'll find plenty of seafront terrace restaurants along Via Bordonaro in the old town centre.

TOP TRAVEL THEMES – TYRRHENIAN COAST

Archaeological Sites Abandon your deck chair and umbrella for a few mornings to soak up history rather than the sun while visiting the ruins of ancient settlements such as Tyndaris (p127) and Halaesa (p126).

Churches Every town, however small, seems to have a lavishly decorated church gracing its main piazza. Start a survey of the best at the magnificent Duomo di Cefalù (p114).

Fabulous Fortresses This coast has been fortified against possible invaders for millennia. Check out three of the region's most sensationally sited strongholds at Caccamo (p118), Milazzo (p126) and Cefalù.

Monti Madonie Take a driving tour (p120) through the Madonie mountains, visiting historic hilltop villages and dining in acclaimed restaurants along the way.

Slow Food Discover the delights of local food products, dishes and traditions when eating your way through the Madonie and Nebrodi regional parks.

Cefalù

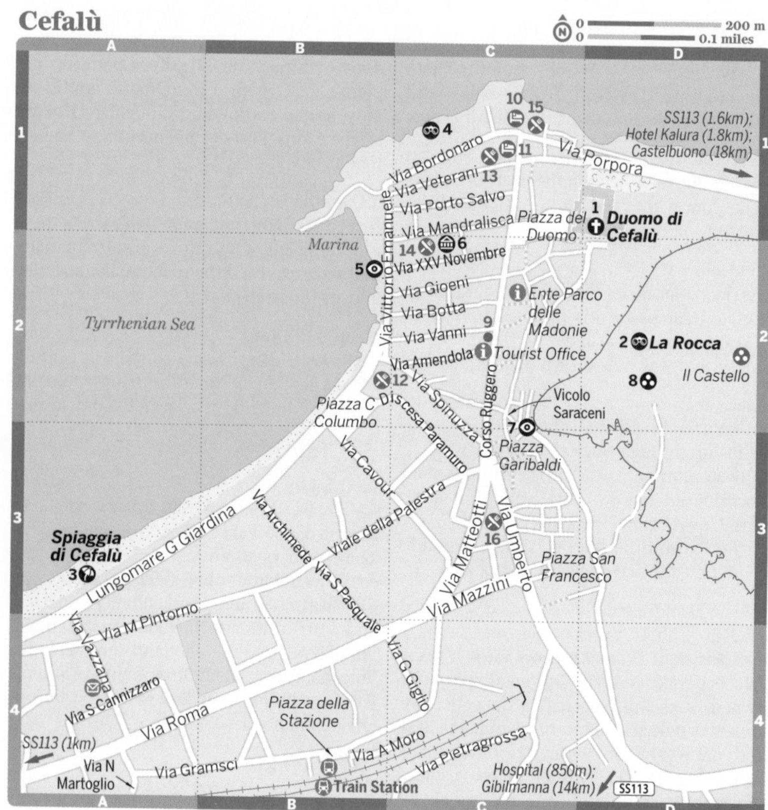

★Bottega Ti Vitti PIZZA €

(☎0921 92 26 42; www.bottegativitti.com; Lungomare Giardina 7; pizza, salads & burgers €5-12; ⏲10am-midnight, closed Tue Nov-Apr) This casual waterfront spin-off of the more formal restaurant Ti Vitti serves pizzas, salads and inventive 'Sicilian burgers' made with top-of-the-line local ingredients – such as Piacentino Ennese, sheep's-milk cheese with saffron and black pepper, in place of cheddar. It's a great spot to watch the sunset while sampling Sicilian wines and microbrews and snacking on local cheese and meat platters.

★Osteria Bacchus SICILIAN €€

(☎320 1449452; Belvedere di Sant'Ambrogio 2, Sant'Ambrogio; meals €25-35; ⏲noon-2pm & 7.30-10pm) Far from the madding crowd that descends on Cefalù each summer, this family-run restaurant in nearby Sant'Ambrogio boasts a relaxed and breezy terrace perched high above the sea. It's a great place to linger over spectacular meals of freshly caught fish, *tagliatelle alle vongole e cozze* (ribbon pasta with fresh clams and mussels), Sicilian appetisers or beautifully presented steaks.

Look for it at the entrance to Sant'Ambrogio village, 7km east of Cefalù, off the SS113 coastal highway.

La Tavernetta PIZZA, SEAFOOD €€

(☎0921 42 25 10; www.la-tavernetta.com; Corso da Presidiana; pizza €6-10, meals €30-35; ⏲noon-11.30pm Tue-Sun) Tucked away in the marina (called Porto Turistico) east of the historic centre, this is a favourite among locals for its first-rate seafood and pizzas. The pasta with swordfish, eggplant, tomatoes and mint is magnificent.

Ti Vitti SICILIAN €€

(☎0921 92 15 71; www.ristorantetivitti.com; Via Umberto I 34; meals €35-45; ⏲noon-3pm & 6.30-

Cefalù

Top Sights

1 Duomo di Cefalù D1
2 La Rocca D2
3 Spiaggia di Cefalù A3

Sights

4 Bastione Capo Marchiafava C1
5 Lavatoio B2
6 Museo Mandralisca C2
7 Salita Saraceni C2
8 Tempio di Diana D2

Activities, Courses & Tours

9 Visit Sicily Tours C2

Sleeping

10 Dolce Vita C1
11 La Plumeria C1

Eating

12 Bottega Ti Vitti B2
13 La Botte C1
14 La Galleria C2
15 Locanda del Marinaio C1
16 Ti Vitti C3

11pm Wed-Mon) Named after a Sicilian card game, this fine restaurant specialises in fresh-from-the-market fish dishes, locally sourced treats such as *basilisco* mushrooms from the nearby Monte Madonie, and some of the best *cannoli* you'll find anywhere in Sicily. For something more casual, head to its affiliated pizzeria, Bottega Ti Vitti, whose waterfront setting is perfect for sunset *aperitivi*.

La Galleria SICILIAN, CAFE **€€**
(☎0921 42 02 11; www.lagalleriacefalu.it; Via Mandralisca 23; meals €30-40; ⊙12.30-3pm & 7.30-11pm Fri-Wed) This is about as hip as Cefalù gets. Functioning as a restaurant, cafe and occasional gallery space, La Galleria has an informal vibe, a bright internal courtyard and an innovative menu that mixes standard *primi* and *secondi* with a range of all-in-one dishes (€14 to €16) designed to be meals in themselves.

Locanda del Marinaio SEAFOOD **€€**
(☎0921 42 32 95; Via Porpora 5; meals €30-40; ⊙noon-2.30pm & 7-11pm Wed-Mon) Fresh seafood rules the chalkboard menu at this upscale eatery along the old town's main waterfront thoroughfare. Depending on the season, you'll find dishes such as red tuna carpaccio with toasted pine nuts, shrimp and zucchini on a bed of velvety ricotta, or grilled octopus served with thyme-scented potatoes, all accompanied by an excellent list of Sicilian wines.

La Botte SICILIAN **€€**
(☎0921 42 43 15; www.labottecefalu.com; Via Veterani 20; meals €25-35; ⊙12.30-2.30pm & 7.30-11.30pm Tue-Sun) This small, family-run restaurant just off Corso Ruggero serves a good choice of antipasti, seasonally driven pasta dishes and seafood-dominated mains. The €26 fixed menu of three fish courses plus a side dish offers good value.

Information

Ente Parco delle Madonie (☎0921 92 33 27; www.parcodellemadonie.it; Corso Ruggero 116; ⊙8am-6pm Mon-Sat) Knowledgeable staff supply information about the Parco Naturale Regionale delle Madonie.

Hospital (☎0921 92 01 11; www.fondazionesanraffaelegiglio.it; Contrada Pietrapollastra; ⊙24hr) On the main road out of town in the direction of Palermo.

Police (Questura; ☎0921 92 60 11; Via Roma 15)

Post Office (Via Vazzana 2; ⊙8.30am-7pm Mon-Fri, to 12.30pm Sat) Just in from the *lungomare*.

Tourist Office (☎0921 42 10 50; strcefalu@regione.sicilia.it; Corso Ruggero 77; ⊙9am-7.30pm Mon-Fri, 8am-2pm Sat) English-speaking staff, lots of leaflets and good maps.

Getting There & Away

BUS

Buses depart from the stop outside the train station regularly from Monday to Saturday, with occasional Sunday services. **SAIS** (☎091 617 11 41; www.saistrasporti.it) travels to Palermo (€5.70, one hour, five Monday to Saturday) and Castelbuono (€2.60, 40 minutes, five Monday to Saturday).

CAR & MOTORCYCLE

Cefalù is situated just off the A20-E90 toll road that travels between Messina and Palermo. Finding a car park can be a nightmarish challenge in summer. The most convenient spots are next to the train station or along the *lungomare* (€1 per hour).

To hire a bike, Vespa or motorbike, try **Scooter for Rent** (☎092 142 04 96; www.scooterforrent.it; Via Vittorio Emanuele 57; per day/week 50cc Vespa €35/175, mountain bike €10/45; ⊙9am-noon & 4-6pm).

TRAIN

Frequent trains runs to Palermo (from €5.60, 55 minutes), Milazzo (from €8.70, 1½ to 2¼ hours) and virtually every other town on the coast.

Exiting the station, turn right down Via Gramsci to reach Via Matteotti, which leads directly into the old town centre. If heading for the beach, turn left from the station into Via Gramsci, turn right down Via N Martoglio, then take Via Vazzana, which will bring you to the western end of the *lungomare*.

CACCAMO

POP 8215 / ☎091

Lorded over by its imposing Norman castle, this hilltop town is a popular day trip from both Cefalù and Palermo. Though the area was settled in ancient times, Caccamo was officially founded in 1093, when the Normans began building their fortress on a rocky spur of Monte San Calogero. The castle was enlarged by the noble Chiaramonte family in the 14th century and is now one of Italy's largest and most impressive, with walls and fortifications that originally included ingenious traps for any intruder who might have breached the outer perimeter.

Sights

Castello di Caccamo CASTLE

(☎091 814 92 52; adult/reduced €4/free; ⊙9am-1pm & 3-7pm Sat-Mon, 8.30am-1.30pm & 3-8pm Tue-Fri) Originally constructed by the Normans in the 11th century, Caccamo's clifftop castle is one of the most dramatically sited in all of Sicily. Beyond the castle's first gate, a ramp leads to a broad courtyard that gives access to several monumental, sparsely decorated rooms, from which you can enjoy magnificent views of the surrounding countryside.

Chiesa Madre CHURCH

(Piazza Duomo; ⊙9am-1pm & 3-8pm) Nestled in the shadow of the castle, downhill from Corso Umberto I, picturesque Piazza Duomo is home to this 11th-century cathedral dedicated to St George. Remodelled twice (in 1477 and 1614), the cathedral's sacristy has some lovely carvings of the *Madonna con bambino e angeli* (Madonna with Child and Angels) and *Santi Pietro e Paolo* (Sts Peter and Paul), both by Francesco Laurana.

Eating

A Castellana SICILIAN **€**

(☎091 814 86 67; www.castellana.it; Piazza dei Caduti 4; set menu €24; ⊙noon-2.30pm & 7-10pm Tue-Sun) Located in the grain stores of the castle, this Slow Food–acclaimed eatery has a panoramic terrace for summer dining and is renowned for its assured treatment of classic Sicilian dishes. You can order à la carte or opt for an excellent-value set menu comprising four courses plus coffee.

Getting There & Away

Caccamo is on the SS285 between Palermo and Agrigento. **Randazzo** (☎091 814 82 35; www.autolineerandazzo.it) runs buses to/from Cefalù (€4.60, 70 minutes, one daily), Palermo (€4.60, 70 minutes, three daily) and Termini Imerese (€2.70, 30 minutes, six daily). There are no Sunday services.

PARCO NATURALE REGIONALE DELLE MADONIE

After spending time jostling with armies of sun-seeking holidaymakers on the overdeveloped coast, savvy visitors abandon their deckchairs and head to the hills to savour the spectacular scenery and tranquil surrounds of the 400-sq-km Madonie regional park.

An outdoorsy paradise that's perfectly suited to slow, culturally rich travel, the Monti Madonie (Madonie Mountains) are crowned by Pizzo Carbonara – at 1979m the highest mountain in Sicily after Mt Etna – and the regional park takes in farms, hilltop towns and ski resorts.

Spring here sees spectacular spreads of wildflowers carpeting the mountain slopes; autumn brings wild mushrooms and richly coloured foliage; winter prompts downhill action on the ski slopes; and June through August offers an escape from the coastal crowds.

This is an area where people live and work, not just a nature reserve, meaning that you can combine hiking with visits to historic hilltop towns and meals in some fine restaurants.

Castelbuono

POP 9010 / ☎0921 / ELEV 423M

The charming capital of the Madonie is set amid ancient manna ash and chestnut forests. It owes much of its building stock and character to the Ventimiglias, a powerful noble family who ruled the town between the 14th and 16th centuries.

WORTH A TRIP

SANT'AMBROGIO

For a behind-the-scenes peek at village life in the Madonie foothills, head to the small town of Sant'Ambrogio, perched on a steep hillside above the sparkling Tyrrhenian, 7km east of Cefalù. Here you'll find veteran walking guide Carmelina Ricciardello, who has devoted her life to developing sustainable tourism along this stretch of coast.

Born in Sicily and raised in Australia, Carmelina moved back to Sant'Ambrogio as an adult and created her own walking tour company, **Sicilian Experience** (☎349 5763215; www.sicilianexperience.com; Via Mastro Nino Incaprera 37, Sant'Ambrogio), focused on sharing Sicily's cultural wealth with English-speaking visitors. Tours range from day trips to watch local shepherds making ricotta over the wood fire, to displays of medieval Arabic falconry techniques in the high meadows of the Madonie, to multiday, village-to-village hiking adventures.

Beyond running her own business, Carmelina has worked to develop a sustainable tourist economy for others in Sant'Ambrogio, creating opportunities for locals to rent out apartments, offer wine tasting and cooking courses, or lead visitors on horse and donkey treks in the nearby mountains. All of these ventures serve to keep Sant'Ambrogio culturally vibrant without sacrificing its traditions or its small-town tranquility – making this a pleasant counterpoint to the more frenetic beach scene in nearby Cefalù.

Sights

Castello dei Ventimiglia CASTLE

(☎0921 67 71 26, 0921 67 12 11; www.museocivico.eu; Piazza Castello; adult/reduced €4/2; ⌚9.30am-1pm & 3.30-7pm Tue-Fri, 10am-1.30pm & 3.30-7pm Sat & Sun) Originally known as the Castello del Buon Aere (Castle of Good Air), the enormous castle that soars above Castelbuono's golden patchwork of houses gave the town its name and is its most distinctive landmark. Built by Francesco I Ventimiglia in 1316, it features displays on local archaeology and Castelbuono's history.

Popular legend has it that the castle is haunted by the 14th-century Queen Constance Chiaramonte, who is said to run along the corridors, regular as clockwork, on the first Tuesday of the month. At the heart of the fortress is the Cappella di Sant'Anna (Chapel of St Anne), which dates from 1683 and is decorated with marvellous stuccowork from the school of renowned Sicilian sculptor Giacomo Serpotta. It houses the supposed skull of the saint in a silver urn.

Museo Naturalistico Francesco Minà Palumbo MUSEUM

(☎0921 67 71 74; www.museominapalumbo.it; Via Roma 72; adult/reduced €2/1; ⌚9am-1pm & 3-7pm Tue-Sun) Named after the naturalist Francesco Minà Palumbo (1814–99), this unassuming museum is housed in the former convent of Santa Venera. It's home to a collection of artefacts that gives an exhaustive insight into the botany, natural history, minerals and archaeology of the Madonie mountains.

Festivals & Events

Funghi Fest FOOD

(☎0921 67 38 56) For three days in late October, thousands of fungus fans descend on Castelbuono to pick wild mushrooms in the Parco Regionale delle Madonie, taste mushroom-based recipes from celebrity chefs, and celebrate the harvest season with music and special events.

Eating

Castelbuono's rustic regional cuisine showcases fruits of the Madonie such as *funghi di bosco* (forest mushrooms) and *cinghiale* (wild boar).

Fiasconaro PASTRIES €

(☎0921 67 12 31; www.fiasconaro.com; Piazza Margherita 10; pastries from €1; ⌚6.30am-midnight Thu-Tue, 9am-1pm & 3.15-8pm Wed) Home of the local speciality, *mannetto* (manna cake), this much-loved *pasticceria* on the main street leading to the castle is also packed with treats such as homemade gelato, buttery *cornetti* (croissants), decadently sweet *cassata siciliana* (sponge cake with cream, marzipan, chocolate and candied fruit) and the unusual *testa di Turco* (Turk's head; blancmange with puff pastry in the middle).

The *pasticceria* is on one side of the road and the Fiasconaro cafe is opposite – it's perfectly acceptable to purchase your

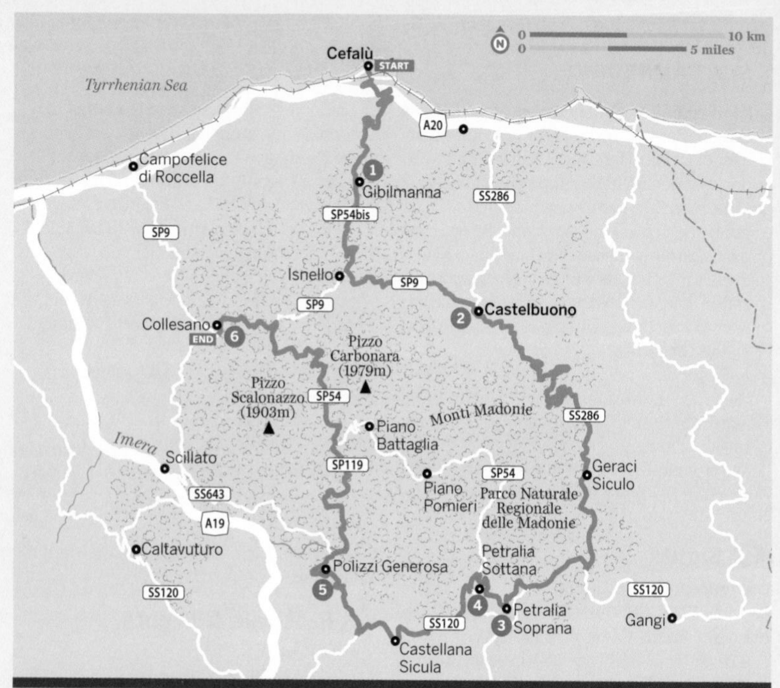

Driving Tour
Monti Madonie

START CEFALÙ
END COLLESANO
LENGTH 113KM; ONE TO THREE DAYS

This tour takes in the most picturesque towns in the Madonie mountains and rewards leisurely exploration; to see everything in one day is possible, but it will be tiring.

From Cefalù, follow the winding SP54bis for approximately 15km to the 1 **Santuario di Gibilmanna**, spectacularly perched 800m above sea level on the slopes of Pizzo Sant'Angelo (1081m). Here, in the 17th century, the Virgin Mary reputedly restored sight to two blind worshippers and speech to a person who couldn't speak. The miracle was later confirmed by the Vatican, and the church has since become one of Sicily's most important shrines. The views over the Madonie from the belvedere out front are spectacular.

From Gibilmanna, head 18km southeast on the SP9 to 2 **Castelbuono** (p118), presided over by its magnificent 14th-century castle. Stop in at Pasticceria Fiasconaro in the heart of town for a taste of *mannetto* (manna cake), a sweet delicacy made using the sap of the local flowering ash trees, then take the winding SS286 to the picturesque mountain town of 3 **Petralia Soprana** (p121). The road, intermittently fringed by dense forest, is relentlessly sinuous but offers wonderful views over the valleys.

After lunching in Petralia Soprana or its prett[y] sister town of 4 **Petralia Sottana** (p122), follow the SS120 for 19km to 5 **Polizzi Generosa**, nestled at the entrance to the Imera Valley. Named *generosa* (generous) by Frederick II in the 1230s, the town is now best known as a trekking base for the Madonie, and is riddled with churches that are often shrouded in mist. It's also home to a pastry known as the *sfoglio:* sweet dough filled with artisanal sheep's milk cheese, cinnamon, chocolate and sugar.

Your last stop is medieval 6 **Collesano** (p123), 26km northwest on the SP119 and SP54 (or take the SS643 and SP54; both routes afford splendid mountain views). Don't miss the Targa Florio museum, which celebrates the history of the Madonie's storied mountain road race and make sure you stick around town for a hearty mountain dinner at delightful Casale Drinzi.

sweet treat at the *pasticceria* and take it to the cafe.

A Rua Fera PIZZA €
(☎0921 67 67 23; www.aruafera.it; Via Roma 71; pizzas €5-9, meals €25; ⏰12.30-3pm & 7-11pm Wed-Mon) Stone walls, beamed ceilings, tile floors and delightful smoky aromas contribute to the rustic atmosphere at this cosy pizzeria-trattoria. Along with wood-fired pizzas, you'll find tempting pasta dishes such as *pappardelle fresche con funghi di stagione* (fresh pappardelle noodles with seasonal mushrooms).

★**Nangalarruni** SICILIAN €€
(☎0921 67 12 28; www.hostarianangalarruni.it; Via delle Confraternite 10; fixed menus €25-32; ⏰12.30-3pm & 7-10pm, closed Wed Nov-Mar) Famous throughout Sicily for its delicious dishes featuring forest mushrooms and wild boar, Giuseppe Carollo's eatery deserves equal renown for its splendid Sicilian wine selection, displayed on the shelves of the cosy wood-beamed dining room. Spike your appetite with an array of local cheeses, then move on to mains featuring fresh ricotta, locally sourced vegetables and roast meats.

Information

Pro Loco (☎389 6893810; www.prolococastelbuono.it; Piazza Margherita; ⏰9.30am-1pm & 3:30-7pm) In Castelbuono's main square, a three-minute walk from the castle; offers information on Castelbuono and the Madonie in general.

Getting There & Away

Castelbuono is 23km southeast of Cefalù via the SS113 and SS286. If travelling along the A20 autostrada, take the Pollina/Castelbuono exit.

SAIS Trasporti (☎091 617 11 41; www.saistrasporti.it) runs buses to Castelbuono from Palermo (€8.60, 1¾ hours, three to five Monday to Saturday, one Sunday) and Cefalù (€2.60, 40 minutes, six daily Monday to Saturday, one Sunday).

Petralia Soprana

POP 3375 / ☎0921 / ELEV 1147M

Beautifully positioned at the top of a hill above a treeline of pines, Petralia Soprana (from the Italian word *sopra,* meaning 'above') is one of the best-preserved small towns in north-central Sicily, full of picturesque stone houses and curling wrought-iron balconies brimming with geraniums. It's also the highest village in the Madonie. There's not much for visitors to do except wander around the narrow cobbled lanes, visit a couple of churches and soak up the sweeping views from the town's belvederes.

Sights

Chiesa Santi Pietro e Paolo CATHEDRAL
(Piazza del Popolo; ⏰9am-12.30pm & 4-7pm) The town's cathedral, located on Piazza del Popolo, off Piazza dei Quattro Cannoli, was consecrated in 1497 and has an elegant 18th-century portico and a 15th-century *campanile* (bell tower). It is dedicated to Sts Peter and Paul.

Chiesa di Santa Maria di Loreto CHURCH
(Via Loreto; ⏰9am-12.30pm & 4-7pm) The most beautiful of Petralia Soprana's many churches is the 18th-century Chiesa di Santa Maria di Loreto, at the end of Via Loreto, off the main square, Piazza del Popolo (follow the signs to Da Salvatore). Inside is an altarpiece by Gagini and a Madonna by Giacomo Mancini. To the right of the church through an arch is the **U Castru belvedere**, with views across the valley and to Etna on a clear day.

Eating

★**Da Salvatore** TRATTORIA, PIZZERIA €
(☎0921 68 01 69; Piazza San Michele 3; pizzas €4-8, meals €17-25; ⏰1-3pm & 8-11pm Wed-Mon Mar-Oct, 8-11pm Fri-Sun Nov-Feb) Salvatore Ruvutuso, his wife Maria and two children run this Slow Food–acclaimed trattoria with its summertime sidewalk seating and wonderfully cosy interior dining room. Kick off with a delicious selection of antipasti including frittata, superb *caponata* (cooked vegetable salad) and pungent *provola delle Madonie,* then choose from a daily menu that usually features a rustic pasta, vegetable soup or fragrant stew.

Pizzas are only served in the evening. The restaurant is tucked into a little square near the Chiesa di Santa Maria di Loreto – just follow the signs. Note: no credit cards.

Lu Carmè SICILIAN €
(☎0921 64 11 35; www.lucarme.it; Via Pergola 12; meals €20-25; ⏰12.30-3pm & 7.30-10.30pm Thu-Tue) Just below Petralia Soprana's main square, this new family-run venture may look rather sterile at first glance, but step inside to discover well-prepared, reasonably priced mountain treats like wild-mushroom risotto, goat stew, or mixed grills of veal,

pork and mutton. Upstairs, Bar Lombardo makes the best *granite* (Italian ices) in town, using locally harvested figs, lemons, mulberries and pomegranates.

★ A Fuoco Lento SICILIAN **€€**
(☎338 2890100; www.lalocandadicadi.it/afuoco lento.htm; Borgo Cipampini; meals incl house wine €30-35) It's worth driving down to Cipampini, 10km below Petralia Soprana, to eat at this intimate stone-walled gem of a restaurant. Chef-owners Diego and Patrizia seat only 30 people each evening for multicourse dinners that include wood-fired bread with pecorino cheese and homemade rose jam, regional cold cuts, ricotta-mint fritattas, Madonie pork with apples and ginger, local wine and much more.

Guests are encouraged to linger and talk, and on occasion, play the piano in the corner of the room.

Getting There & Away

BUS

SAIS Trasporti (p121) operates two to three daily buses from Palermo to Petralia Soprana (€10.30, two hours).

CAR & MOTORCYCLE

To reach Petralia Soprana from Petralia Sottana, drive up Corso Paolo Agliata to Piazza Umberto and follow the winding narrow road leading uphill through the arch at the right-hand side of the Chiesa Madre, veering right at the first fork.

There is limited free car parking in Piazza del Popolo. Alternatively, park on the side of the road leading uphill into town.

Petralia Sottana

POP 2870 / ☎0921 / ELEV 1000M

Below Petralia Soprana, the town of Petralia Sottana (from the Italian *sotto,* meaning 'under') is the gateway to the regional park and the headquarters of the **Ente Parco delle Madonie** (☎0921 68 40 11; www.parcodelle madonie.it; Corso Paolo Agliata 16, Petralia Sottana). The park office, located in the foyer of the Museo Civico Antonio Collisani, supplies maps and walking itineraries for the Madonie along with brochures and information about Petralia Sottana itself. The town is also worth a wander for its collection of picturesque stone churches and towers.

Sights

Petralia Sottana is dominated by its main street, Corso Paolo Agliata, which is a popular shopping strip during the day and hosts the town's surprisingly busy *passeggiata* in the early evening. Like Petralia Soprana, the town possesses a number of handsome churches, including the baroque **Chiesa di San Francesco** on the Corso and the 17th-century **Chiesa Madre** at the end of the Corso on Piazza Umberto. The *campanile* of the latter is the town's major landmark. On the road leading to Petralia Soprana is the **Chiesa di Santissima Trinità alla Badia**, which has a handsome marble altarpiece carved by Giandomenico Gagini.

Museo Civico Antonio Collisani MUSEUM
(☎0921 64 18 11; www.comune.petraliasottana.pa.it; Corso Paolo Agliata 100; adult/reduced €2/1;

OFF THE BEATEN TRACK

CROSSING THE NEBRODI MOUNTAINS

Several charming routes wind across the Nebrodi ranges, weaving through tiny mountain hamlets and steep, forested slopes. The SS116 starts at Capo d'Orlando on the coast and climbs to Floresta (1275m), the highest village in the park, where you can stop for local olives, cheeses and meats at Alimentari Giuseppe Calabrese on the main square. From here, the road makes a spectacular descent to Randazzo, with unforgettable views of Mt Etna.

Cutting through the heart of the park is the enchanting SS289, which links Sant'Agata di Militello with Cesarò in the interior. Along the route is San Fratello, a typical Nebrodi town originally founded by Roger I's third wife, Adelaide di Monferrato, for her Lombard cousins (hence the strange local dialect).

If you're coming from the Monti Madonie, a pretty highland route into the Nebrodi is the SS120. Starting from Petralia Sottana, head east through the gorgeous hill towns of Gangi, Sperlinga and Nicosia, then turn north on the SS117 to Mistretta. The landscape is especially picturesque in springtime, when the high rolling hills are covered in wildflowers. On clear days, there are good distant views of Mt Etna to the southeast.

⏲8.30am-2pm & 3.30-6.30pm Mon-Fri, 9.30am-12.30pm & 4-7pm Sat & Sun) Focusing on the archaeology and geology of the Madonie, this small museum has an impressive display of fossils found in the area and is worth a visit.

Information

Tourist Office (☎0921 64 18 11; Corso Paolo Agliata 100; ⏲8.30am-2pm & 3.30-6.30pm Mon-Fri, 9.30am-12.30pm & 4-7pm Sat & Sun) Helpful office with a good collection of maps and books about history, wildlife and walking in the Madonie.

Getting There & Away

BUS

SAIS Trasporti (p121) operates two to three daily buses from Palermo to Petralia Sottana (€10.30, 1¾ hours).

CAR & MOTORCYCLE

Petralia Sottana is on the SS120. If coming from Palermo via the A19 autostrada, exit at Tremonzelli.

There is a car park overlooking the valley directly opposite the junction of the SS120 and Corso Paolo Agliata (Petralia's main street). You'll find a second car park around the back side of the Chiesa Madre – drive through the arch just above the church, take the first left-hand fork and look for it on the left-hand side.

Piano Battaglia

More Swiss than Sicilian, the little ski resort at Piano Battaglia (www.pianobattaglia.it) is dotted with chalets that play host to an ever-growing number of Sicilian downhill skiers in winter.

The Mufara (northern slopes) skiing complex goes up to heights of 1840m and serves 3.5km of runs, while the Mufaretta (southwest slope) reaches 1680m, with a run about 500m long. A pair of ski lifts, newly revamped in 2015, whisks skiers to the top. Cross-country skiing and snowboarding are also popular here.

With the advent of spring, Piano Battaglia becomes an equally good walking, climbing and mountain-biking destination, with plenty of signposted paths and a profusion of wildflowers. One popular walk starts at the Rifugio Piero Merlino (p250) and heads north-northwest, taking in Pizzo Scalonazzo (1903m) and Pizzo Carbonara to end in an area of oak woodland at Piano Sempria (1300m). The *rifugio* can help you with itineraries and guides.

Eating

Ristoro dello Scoiattolo SICILIAN €
(☎349 6439987; meals €20; ⏲noon-3pm) Perched at 1600m, near the base of the Mufara ski slope, this rustic restaurant is Piano Battaglia's perennial favourite spot to indulge in reasonably priced, hearty mountain fare. Cosy up by the fireplace or enjoy panoramic vistas from the outdoor deck.

Getting There & Away

From Petralia Sottana, it's a twisty 19km climb along the SP54 to Piano Battaglia. To get here from Collesano (22km) or Castelbuono (36km), take the SP9 to the SP54 south.

Collesano

POP 4050 / ☎0921 / ELEV 917M

The upper reaches of this charming medieval town are dominated by the pink-and-cream Basilica San Pietro on Corso Vittorio Emanuele and the weathered remains of a nearby Norman castle. Like Castelbuono, the town was once governed by the Ventimiglias and retains an aristocratic air.

Sights

There are a number of churches worthy of a visit, including the frescoed 15th-century **Duomo** (aka Santa Maria la Nuova), the 12th-century **Chiesa di St Maria la Vecchia**, the 17th-century **Chiesa di St Maria del Gesù** and the early-16th-century **Chiesa di St Giacomo**.

Museo Targa Florio MUSEUM
(☎0921 66 46 84; targaflorio.it/musei; Corso Vittorio Emanuele 3; adult/reduced €2/1; ⏲9am-noon Tue-Sun) This unique little museum displays photographs and memorabilia documenting the Targa Florio, the world's oldest sports-car racing event. Established by wealthy automobile enthusiast Vincenzo Florio in 1906, then discontinued in 1977 due to safety concerns, the 72km race along the Monti Madonie's treacherous narrow roads was intensely challenging, with countless hairpin bends testing both the driver's skill and the car's performance.

A plaque in the museum's first room chronicles the names and car models of all the winners throughout the event's seven-decade history (in case you're wondering, Porsche won the most times, followed closely by Alfa Romeo).

Eating

★ Casale Drinzi SICILIAN €

(☎0921 66 40 27; www.casaledrinzi.it; SP9, Contrada Drinzi; pizzas €3.50-9, meals €18-23; ⊙noon-2pm & 7.30-10pm Mar-Jan) This wooden chalet in the hills immediately above Collesano is one of the Madonie's gems – one whiff of the delicious aromas emanating from the kitchen and you'll know you've come to the right place. The menu features hearty mountain specialities like stewed pork with artichokes and smoked ham alongside other rustic favourites featuring Slow Food–recognised regional ingredients.

Items not to be missed when available include the *degustazione di antipasti* (a plate of stuffed zucchini flowers, deep-fried ricotta, lardo-topped bruschetta and chargrilled local onions), *pappardelle al sugo di selvaggina* (homemade pasta ribbons with a game sauce) and *fagiolo Badda Nera* (beans grown in the area around Polizzi Generosa). Pizzas are added to the menu at night – a good reason to book into the on-site B&B (singles/doubles €40/60).

Getting There & Away

Collesano is 23km west of Castelbuono via the SP9. **AST** (Azienda Siciliana Trasporti; ☎091 680 00 38; www.aziendasicilianatrasporti.it) runs three to five buses from Palermo to Collesano (€6, 1¼ to 1¾ hours) Monday through Saturday.

DON'T MISS

BEST BEACHES

Stake a claim to a sandy patch of paradise at the following resorts and throw yourself into the swing of the Sicilian summer scene.

Cefalù (p114) This wildly popular resort town balances magnificent cultural attractions with a beach scene that is as renowned as Taormina's.

Oliveri (p127) This sandy stretch of beach beneath the ancient settlement of Tyndaris hosts fewer holidaymakers than many of its neighbours.

Capo D'Orlando (p126) Uninterrupted sand stretches west of the point, dramatic rocky shoreline to the east, and a ruined castle presides above it all.

PARCO REGIONALE DEI NEBRODI

Encompassing the Monti Nebrodi (Nebrodi Mountains) of northeastern Sicily, the Nebrodi Regional Park (www.parcodeinebrodi.it) was established in 1993 and constitutes the single largest forested area in Sicily, dotted with remote and traditional villages that host few visitors. The forest here ranges in altitude from 1200m to 1500m; the park's highest peak is Monte Soro (1847m), and the Lago di Biviere is a lovely natural lake supporting herons and stilts.

The lovely, off-the-beaten-track park encompasses an undulating landscape of beech, oak, elm, ash, cork, maple and yew trees that shelter the remnants of Sicily's wildlife: porcupines, San Fratello horses and wildcats, as well as a healthy population of birds of prey including golden eagles, lanner and peregrine falcons and griffon vultures. The high pastures have always been home to hard-working agricultural communities that harvest mushrooms and hazelnuts, churn out creamy ricotta and graze cows, sheep, horses, goats and pigs.

Activities

Vai Col Trekking Sicilia WALKING

(☎349 7362863; www.vaicoltrekkingsicilia.com) Certified environmental guide Attilio Caldarera runs this recommended agency, which organises day trips and multiday walking excursions in the Parco Regionale dei Nebrodi.

Information

There are visitor centres in **Alcara Li Fusi** (☎0941 79 39 04; Via Ugo Foscolo 1, Alcara Li Fusi), **Cesarò** (☎095 773 20 61; Via Bellini 79, Cesarò), **Mistretta** (☎0921 38 14 75; Via Aversa 26, Mistretta), **Bronte** (☎338 2993077; Castello di Nelson, Bronte) and **Randazzo** (☎095 799 16 11; Corso Umberto 197, Randazzo) and smaller information points in several other towns throughout the park. All keep irregular hours and most staff speak Italian only. For more information, see www.parks.it/parco.nebrodi or www.parcodeinebrodi.it.

Getting There & Away

The best way to explore the park is by car, as bus services are few and far between.

Interbus (☎091 34 20 55; www.interbus.it) operates buses from Messina to Cesarò (€9.20, three hours, one daily Monday to Saturday), Mistretta (€9.60, 2¼ hours, one daily Monday to Friday) and Randazzo (€7, two hours, two daily Monday to Saturday). It also offers service between the coastal town of Santo Stefano di Camastra and Mistretta (€2.70, 35 minutes, four daily Monday to Friday, two daily on weekends).

San Marco d'Alunzio

POP 2030 / ☎0941 / ELEV 550M

This spectacularly situated hilltop town, 9km from the coast, was founded by the Greeks in the 5th century BC and then occupied by the Romans, who named it Aluntium and built structures such as the **Tempio di Ercole** (Temple of Hercules) at the town's entrance. A Norman church, now roofless, was subsequently built on the temple's red marble base.

Southeast of the town is the trekking base, **Longi**, and southwest is **Alcara Li Fusi**, a small village situated beneath the impressive **Rocche del Crasto** (1315m), a nesting site of the golden eagle.

Sights

Virtually all of San Marco d'Alunzio's older buildings and its 22 churches were made using locally quarried marble. At the top of the hill are the scant remains of the first **castle** built by the Normans in Sicily.

Chiesa di Santa Maria delle Grazie CHURCH

(Via Aluntina; hours vary) The most impressive of San Marco d' Alunzio's churches is Chiesa di Santa Maria delle Grazie, where there's a Domenico Gagini statue of the *Madonna con bambino e San Giovanni* (Madonna with Child and St John) from 1481.

Museo della Cultura e delle Arti Figurative Bizantine e Normanne MUSEUM

(Museum of Byzantine & Norman Culture & Figurative Art; ☎0941 79 77 19; Badia Nica, Via Ferraloro; adult/reduced €2.50/1.50; 9am-1pm & 3.30-7.30pm) Next to the 16th-century Chiesa di San Teodoro, in a restored 16th-century Benedictine monastery, is a lovely space showing fresco fragments from the town's churches and a somewhat motley collection of columns, capitals and other bits and pieces from the Greek, Roman, Byzantine and Norman periods, most of them excavated in the surrounding area.

Information

Tourist Office (☎0941 79 73 39; www.sanmarco-turismo.it; Via Aluntina; 9am-1pm year-round, plus 3-7pm Oct-Apr, 3.30-7.30pm May, Jun & Sep, 4-8pm Jul & Aug) In the square opposite the Chiesa Madre.

Getting There & Away

From the coastal SS113 just east of Sant'Agata di Militello, turn onto the squiggly SP160, which makes the steep 7km ascent to San Marco d'Alunzio.

Camarda e Drago (☎0941 70 22 70; www.camardaedrago.it) runs three to four buses from Sant'Agata's train station to San Marco d'Alunzio (45 minutes) Monday through Saturday.

Mistretta

POP 4820 / ☎0921

Located on the western border of Nebrodi Regional Park, and accessed via the SS117 from Santo Stefano di Camastra, is the charming hilltop time capsule of Mistretta. The streets here have hardly changed over the past 300 years, and most of the locals look as if they've been around for almost as long. Little disturbs the mountain quietude, making this a pleasant retreat for nature-lovers.

Information

Tourist Office (Pro Loco Mistretta; ☎334 935 55 22; www.prolocomistretta.it; Via Libertà 267)

COASTAL RESORT VILLAGES

Castel di Tusa

POP 2980 / ☎0921

Named after the castle that now lies in ruins 600m above it, this small coastal resort about 25km east of Cefalù is best known for the controversial **Fiumara d'Arte**, an open-air sculpture park featuring a collection of contemporary artworks scattered along the *fiumara* (riverbed) of the Tusa River. The most recent, and most impressive, installation is the **Piramide 38° Parallelo**, a gleaming rust-coloured steel pyramid high on a hilltop above the sea, now a regular gathering point for solstice celebrations.

From Castel di Tusa's beach, a small road leads inland to the parent village of Tusa. Between the coastal resort and the village, about 3km up from the coast, you'll see a signpost for the ancient Greek ruins of Halaesa.

Sights

Halaesa RUINS

(☎0921 33 45 31; ⏰9am-1hr before sunset) FREE Beautifully positioned on a hillside, and accessed through a small olive grove, the scant remnants of this Greek city founded in the 5th century BC command fine views of the surrounding countryside and – in good weather – the Aeolian Islands. The most conspicuous ruins are those of its agora and its massive, rusticated walls. A small museum displays finds from the site. Downhill near the site entrance are the remains of a Colombarium, a 2nd-century Roman necropolis with some well-preserved stonework.

Getting There & Away

Just 800m east of the town centre, Castel di Tusa station (labeled Tusa on the Trenitalia website) is serviced by trains from Milazzo (€7.90, 1½ to 1¾ hours, eight daily) and Palermo (€6.90, 1¼ to 1½ hours, eight daily).

Capo d'Orlando

POP 13,305 / ☎0941

The busiest resort town on the coast after Cefalù, Capo d'Orlando was founded – legend tells us – when one of Charlemagne's generals, a chap called Orlando, stood on the *capo* (headland) and declared it a fine place to build a castle. The ruins of this structure are still visible. In 1299 Frederick II of Aragon was defeated here by the rebellious baron Roger of Lauria, backed up by the joint forces of Catalonia and Anjou. More-recent rebels include the town's shopkeepers and traders, who made a name for themselves in the 1990s with their stand against the Mafia's demands for *pizzo* (protection money).

Visitors come here for the beaches, both sandy and rocky, that are on either side of town. The best swimming is to the east.

Information

Tourist Office (☎0941 91 81 34; www.turismocapodorlando.it; Lungomare Andrea Doria; ⏰9am-1pm & 3-7pm Sep-Jun, 9am-1pm & 5-9pm Jul & Aug) On the waterfront, just west of the point.

Getting There & Away

The best way to get here is by train from Milazzo (from €5.10, 45 minutes), Cefalù (from €5.10, 45 minutes) or Palermo (from €9, two to 2½ hours).

MILAZZO

POP 31,800 / ☎090

Hardly Sicily's prettiest town, Milazzo is hemmed in on its eastern perimeter by industrial development that can make even the most open-minded visitor run for the nearest hydrofoil. Indeed, the prime reason for setting foot in this town is to get to the Aeolian Islands. But, away from the refineries and busy dock, Milazzo has a pretty *Borgo Antico* (Old Town), and the isthmus that juts out to the north is an area of great natural beauty dotted with rocky coves, well worth a visit for those with time to spare.

Sights

★**Capo Milazzo** WATERFRONT

If you have a car, don't miss the scenic drive north along Strada Panoramica to see the gorgeous, rugged coastline of Capo Milazzo. At the end of the isthmus is a lighthouse; park in the nearby lot, from where short walks lead to the Santuario Rupestre di San Antonio da Padova and the Piscina di Venere (p128).

Alternatively, you can arrange a boat trip (ask at the tourist office) around the rocky cape to Baia del Tonno on the western side of the isthmus.

Castello di Milazzo CASTLE

(☎090 922 12 91, guided tours 328 8316110; www.compagniadelcastellomilazzo.it; Salita Castello; adult/reduced €5/3.50, Sun guided tour adult/reduced €5/2; ⏰8.30am-1.30pm & 3.30-6.30pm Tue-Sun) Originally the site of a Greek acropolis, then an Arab-Norman citadel, Milazzo's enormous castle was built by Frederick II in 1239, expanded by Charles V of Aragon and stormed by Garibaldi's troops in 1860. The whole of Milazzo once fitted within its massive walls. Nowadays it's a lovely site to clamber around, full of flowers and crumbling fortifications, with dreamy views of the bay and the Aeolians from atop the Torre Normanna, the castle's oldest and highest part.

The castle grounds, enclosed within late-15th-century Aragonese outer walls, contain the city's Duomo Vecchio (old cathedral) and the ruins of the Palazzo dei Giurati (the old town hall). To get here, climb the Salita Castello, which rises up through the atmospheric old town. Guided tours (available in English with advance notice) are offered at 4.30pm on Sunday afternoons throughout the summer.

WORTH A TRIP

CAPO TINDARI

At Capo Tindari, just off the autostrada between Milazzo and Cefalù, a historic church, Santuario della Madonna del Tindari, and an ancient Greco-Roman site, Tyndaris, make an interesting detour. Coming from the east, turn off the autostrada at Oliveri and follow signs for Tindari/Tyndaris. If you're coming from the west, the site is 12km from Marina di Patti on the SS113. Drivers must park in the paid lot at the foot of the hill, then walk (15 minutes) or take the shuttle bus (€1 return, five minutes) up to the sanctuary and the ruins.

Santuario della Madonna del Tindari (Sanctuary of the Madonna of Tindari; ☎0941 36 90 03; www.santuariotindari.it; ⏲6.45am-12.30pm & 2.30-7pm Mon-Sat, 6.45am-12.45pm & 2.30-8pm Sun) This enormous church can be seen from miles around: it sits right on Capo Tindari, its dome glistening in the sun. A sanctuary was built here in the 16th century to house the icon of the Bruna Madonnina del Tindari (Black Madonna of Tindari), but the current garishly decorated building mainly dates from the 20th century. The inscription underneath the icon reads *Nigra sum, sed hermosa* (I am black, but beautiful).

Tyndaris (☎0941 36 90 23; adult/reduced €6/3; ⏲9am-1hr before sunset) This ancient Greek holy place was founded by Dionysis of Syracuse after his victory over the Carthaginians in 396 BC. The secluded ruins (a basilica, agora, Roman house and Greek theatre) are set on the cliff edge amid prickly pears, olives and cypress trees. In summer you can clearly see the Aeolian Islands and the lovely Oliveri lagoon in the bay below. There's also a small museum displaying artefacts excavated at the site.

Santuario Rupestre di San Antonio da Padova RUINS

(Capo Milazzo) The evocative remains of this 13th-century church sit astride a cactus-covered hillside overlooking Capo Milazzo's crystal-clear waters. It was here that San Antonio da Padova famously sought refuge after a January 1221 shipwreck. Between the 16th and 18th centuries the original church was significantly spruced up with new altars and marble bas-reliefs, before falling into its current ruined state.

Antiquarium di Milazzo MUSEUM

(☎090 922 34 71; Via Impallomeni; ⏲9am-7pm Tue-Sat, to 1pm Sun & Mon) FREE Housed just below the castle in the 16th-century Quartiere degli Spagnoli defensive barracks, this 10-room museum displays treasures dating from neolithic times to the Byzantine era, amassed over seven decades of local archaeological digs. The collection is strong on household ceramics and funerary urns, with an emphasis on the Greek and prehistoric periods.

Eating

There's a good mix of eateries, from sidewalk pizzerias to fancy fish restaurants, along the waterfront just north of the port – convenient even for those just grabbing a quick bite between ferries.

Pane, Mortadella e Champagne SANDWICHES €

(☎090 922 32 60; Via Francesco Crispi 85; sandwiches €2-5; ⏲noon-midnight) A great place for *aperitivi* or afternoon snacks, this hole-in-the-wall deli with sidewalk seating is opposite the waterfront, 500m north of the ferry terminal. They build sandwiches to order from top-quality *salumi* (cold cuts), *formaggi* (cheeses) and other savoury ingredients, accompanied by a good selection of Sicilian wines.

★Al Bagatto SICILIAN €€

(☎090 922 42 12; www.locandadelbagatto.com/restaurant.php; Via Massimiliano Regis 11; meals €25-35; ⏲7.30pm-midnight Mon-Sat) Three decades after opening as one of the region's first wine bars, this place is still thriving under affable chef-owner Chiara Surdo. Mellow music and lighting and a fabulous wine list complement a Slow Food–celebrated menu of dishes made fresh on the spot with local ingredients, from divine beef carpaccio to tube-shaped pacchero pasta with Nebrodi black pork *ragù*.

If you don't score a table, join the local bohemian set and prop yourself at the bar to enjoy a delicious plate of antipasto with a glass of wine.

Toto Passami L'Olio OSTERIA €€

(☎090 240 30 18; www.totopassamilolio.it; Via Impallomeni 69-71; meals €35-45; ⏲11.30am-4pm &

DON'T MISS

VENUS' SWIMMING POOL

Out at the very tip of Capo Milazzo, **Piscina di Venere** (Venus' Pool; Capo Milazzo) is a gorgeous rock-fringed pool that makes an idyllic spot for swimming and sunbathing. Accessed by a 15-minute walk from the Capo Milazzo parking lot through a landscape of olive groves, cactus and stone walls, its tranquil turquoise waters are separated by a small ring of rocks from the ultramarine Mediterranean just beyond.

7.30-11pm Thu-Tue;) Welcoming visitors with its bright front terrace and soundtrack of traditional Sicilian music, this intriguing newcomer specialises in creative, locally sourced dishes built around sometimes obscure ingredients, with plenty of vegan and vegetarian options. Everything is beautifully presented, from faux *cannoli* filled with anchovy-cauliflower cream, to lentil soup with wild fennel and caper leaves, to spit-roasted rabbit with tuna 'bacon'.

Some may find it a bit precious, while others will appreciate the enthusiasm of the young chef-owners, old friends who genuinely enjoy sharing their passion for bringing traditional Sicilian ingredients into the 21st century.

Doppio Gusto SEAFOOD **€€€**
(090 924 00 45; www.ristorantedoppiogusto.it; Via Luigi Rizzo 44; meals €40-55; 12.30-2.30pm & 7.30-10.30pm Tue-Sun) For stellar seafood just paces from the port, this upscale eatery with a devoted local following is the obvious choice. Service can be a bit stiff and formal, but food quality is exceptional, with everything fresh off the boat. Stay cool in the air-conditioned interior or watch the world go by under the awning out front.

Information

Hospital (Ospedale Giuseppe Fogliani; 090 9 29 01; Villaggio Grazia; 24hr)

Police (Questura; 090 923 03 11; Via Municipio 1)

Tourist Office (090 922 28 65; strmilazzo@regione.sicilia.it; Piazza Caio Duilio 19-22; 8am-2pm Mon-Fri, plus 3.30-6.30pm Tue & Thu) Milazzo's tourist office is just a few blocks north of the hydrofoil dock.

Getting There & Away

BOAT

Milazzo is the primary point of departure for ferries and hydrofoils to the Aeolian Islands, with three companies providing year-round service. The main operators – **Liberty Lines** (0923 87 38 13; www.libertylines.it), **Società Navigazione Siciliana** (Siremar; 090 36 46 01; www.siremar.it) and **NGI** (Navigazione Generale Italiana; 800 250000; www.ngi-spa.it) – have ticket offices along Via dei Mille opposite the port.

BUS

Buses depart from Piazza della Repubblica near the port. **Giuntabus** (090 67 57 49; www.giuntabustrasporti.com) runs frequently to/from Messina (€4.20, 50 minutes, 18 daily Monday to Friday, 15 on Saturday, three on Sunday), where you can make onward connections to Catania (€9.30).

CAR & MOTORCYCLE

Milazzo is situated just off the A20-E90 toll road that travels between Messina and Palermo.

If you want to leave your car in Milazzo while you island-hop, private garages charge around €12 per day. A less expensive alternative is to park on the street in spaces marked with blue lines; buy scratch-off parking tickets (€5 per 24hr, available at tobacconists) for as many days as you'll be gone and place them all visibly on your car's dashboard. Short-term street parking (€0.70 per hour) is also available in the same spaces. For a partial list of garages, see www.parcheggiomilazzoportogarage.blogspot.it.

TRAIN

Regular services travel to Palermo (from €11.30, 2½ to 3¾ hours, 13 daily), Cefalù (€8.70, 1¾ to 2¼ hours) and Messina (€3.80, 20 to 35 minutes, hourly).

Getting Around

BUS

AST bus 5 runs between the train station and port (€1.20, 10 minutes) half hourly between 6am and 9pm. Bus 6 runs between the port and Capo Milazzo (€1.20, 15 minutes) every 90 minutes or so between 7.50am and 5.10pm. Note that these buses operate Monday through Saturday only; Sunday and holiday service remained indefinitely suspended at the time of research. Tickets (valid for two hours) can be bought inside the train station or at local tobacconists (including the shop with the AST sign opposite the quayside bus stop).

TAXI

A taxi from the station to the port will cost approximately €12 to €15.

Aeolian Islands

Includes ➡

Best Places to Eat

- ➡ Ristorante La Canna (p154)
- ➡ Trattoria Da Pina (p141)
- ➡ Porto Bello (p144)
- ➡ Le Macine (p138)
- ➡ Punta Lena (p150)

Best Places to Sleep

- ➡ B&B Al Salvatore di Lipari (p251)
- ➡ Hotel Ravesi (p252)
- ➡ Casa del Sole (p252)
- ➡ Casa delle Stelle (p251)
- ➡ Diana Brown (p251)

Why Go?

Rising out of the cobalt-blue seas off Sicily's northeastern coast, the Unesco-protected Aeolian Islands (Vulcano, Lipari, Salina, Panarea, Stromboli, Filicudi and Alicudi) are a little piece of paradise, a magical outdoor playground offering thrills and spills at every turn. Stunning waters provide sport for swimmers, sailors and divers, while trekkers can climb hissing volcanoes and gourmets can sip honey-sweet Malvasia wine.

The obvious base is Lipari, the largest and liveliest of the seven islands, but it's by no means the only option. Salina boasts excellent accommodation and good transport links, while Stromboli and Vulcano entertain nature lovers with awe-inspiring volcanic shenanigans and black-sand beaches. Ultra-chic Panarea offers luxurious living at lower prices in low season, while Filicudi and Alicudi have an end-of-the-line appeal that's irresistible for fans of off-the-beaten-track adventure.

Road/Sea Distances (km)

	Lipari	Messina	Milazzo	Santa Maria Salina
Messina	50			
Milazzo	35	40		
Santa Maria Salina	20	80	65	
Stromboli	45	75	70	45

Aeolian Islands Highlights

1. **Lipari** (p133) Digging through five millennia of history at the archaeological museum.
2. **Salina** (p142) Savouring local wine and capers on the Aeolians' lushest island.
3. **Stromboli** (p147) Watching the volcano erupt at sunset.
4. **Panarea** (p146) Lounging poolside on a sunny whitewashed terrace on the island, or exploring its constellation of five offshore islets on a day trip.
5. **Filicudi** (p153) Diving in search of sunken Greek and Roman ships off Capo Graziano.
6. **Vulcano** (p140) Holding your nose and covering your body with sulphurous ooze in the island's other-worldly mud baths.
7. **Alicudi** (p154) Escaping to this isolated outpost, where fishermen still run the show and donkeys sometimes seem to outnumber tourists.

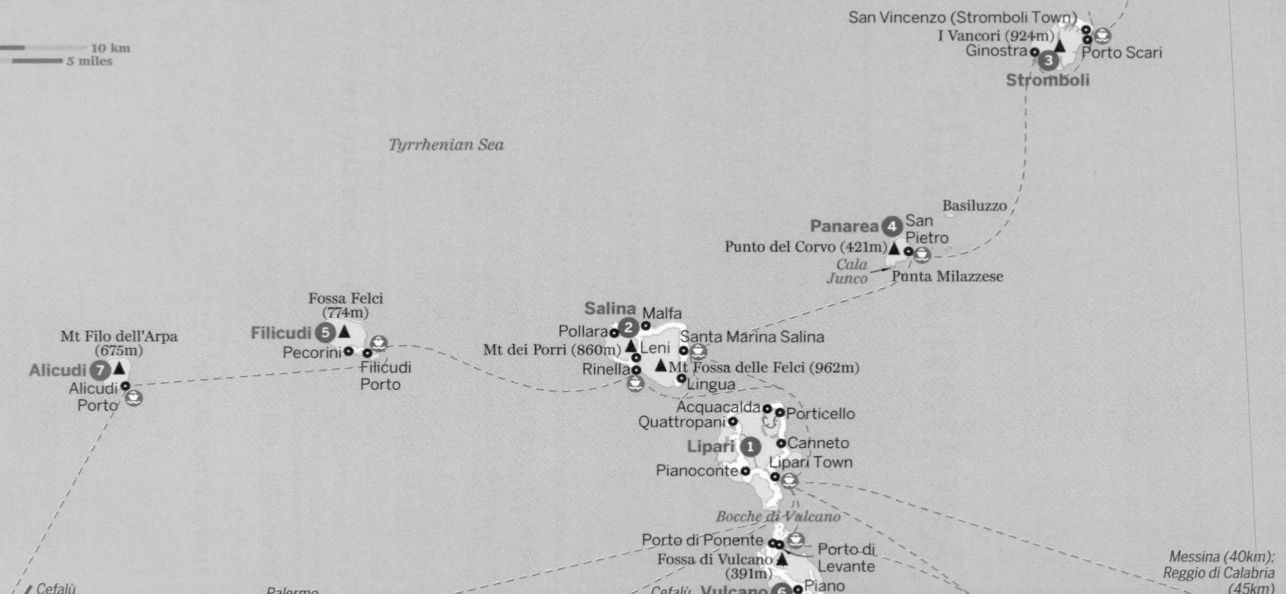

Getting There & Away

Almost all visitors to the Aeolians come by sea. The main point of departure is Milazzo on the Sicilian 'mainland', from where there are regular year-round car ferries and hydrofoils. Lipari is the Aeolians' main point of arrival and its transport hub, with connections to all the other islands. Services are most frequent between June and September and much reduced in winter, when heavy seas can affect schedules. Ferries are cheaper, less frequent and much slower than hydrofoils, although they are less vulnerable to bad weather.

AIR

The only way to reach the Aeolians by air is to take a helicopter. Panarea-based **Air Panarea** (☎ 090 983 44 28; www.airpanarea.com) operates transfers to the Aeolians year-round from points in Sicily, including Catania, Palermo and Taormina, and from the Italian mainland (Rome, Naples, Salerno, Reggio di Calabria). Prices cover the entire six-seat helicopter and vary according to departure point and destination; for details, contact Air Panarea via its online form.

BOAT

Liberty Lines (☎ 0923 87 38 13; www.libertylines.it) operates all hydrofoils to the islands, including summer-only services from Palermo that make stops on all seven islands. Check the Liberty Lines website for up-to-the-minute schedules.

Ferry service from Milazzo (cheaper but slower and less frequent than hydrofoil service) is provided by **Società Navigazione Siciliana** (Siremar; ☎ 090 36 46 01; www.siremar.it) and **NGI Traghetti** (☎ 090 928 40 91; www.ngi-spa.it).

From Naples, Società Navigazione Siciliana runs twice-weekly car ferries to the islands, while **SNAV** (☎ 081 428 55 55; www.snav.it) operates daily, summer-only hydrofoils.

BUS

Travellers arriving at Catania's Fontanarossa airport can reach the Aeolians fairly easily, thanks to regular shuttle bus services. **Eoliebooking** (☎ 090 981 42 57; www.eoliebooking.com/navetta) runs direct shuttles from Catania's Fontanarossa airport to Milazzo's hydrofoil dock (€25 per person, minimum two people, 1¾ hours, up to eight departures daily). **Giuntabus** (☎ 090 67 57 49; www.giuntabustrasporti.com) runs a slightly slower but less expensive bus service along the same route, with a transfer in Messina (€13.50, 2½ to 3¾ hours, 10 departures Monday to Friday, fewer on weekends).

LIPARI

POP 12,635

Lipari is the largest, busiest and most accessible of the Aeolian Islands. Visitors arriving from the mainland will likely experience it as a relaxing introduction to island life; on the other hand, if you've just come from the outer Aeolians, it may feel a bit like the big city!

The main focus is Lipari Town, the archipelago's principal transport hub and the nearest thing that islanders have to a capital city. A busy little port with a pretty, pastel-coloured seafront and plenty of accommodation, it makes the most convenient base for island hopping. Away from the town, Lipari reveals a rugged and typically Mediterranean landscape of low-lying *macchia* (dense Mediterranean shrubbery), silent, windswept highlands, precipitous cliffs and dreamy blue waters.

History

Named after Liparus, the father-in-law of Aeolus (the Greek god of the winds), Lipari was settled in the 4th millennium BC by the Stentinellians, Sicily's first known inhabitants. These early islanders developed a flourishing economy based on obsidian, a glassy volcanic rock used to make primitive tools.

HYDROFOILS TO THE AEOLIAN ISLANDS

FROM	TO	COST (€)	DURATION	FREQUENCY
Messina	Lipari	27.80	1½-2¾hr	4 daily in summer, 1 daily in winter
Milazzo	Alicudi	30.70	3hr	2-3 daily
Milazzo	Filicudi	25.25	2½hr	2-3 daily
Milazzo	Lipari	18.80	1hr	13-17 daily
Milazzo	Panarea	20.80	1½-2½hr	3-7 daily
Milazzo	Salina	20.55	1½hr	12 daily
Milazzo	Stromboli	23.95	1¼-3hr	3-7 daily
Milazzo	Vulcano	18	45min	12-16 daily

Lipari Town

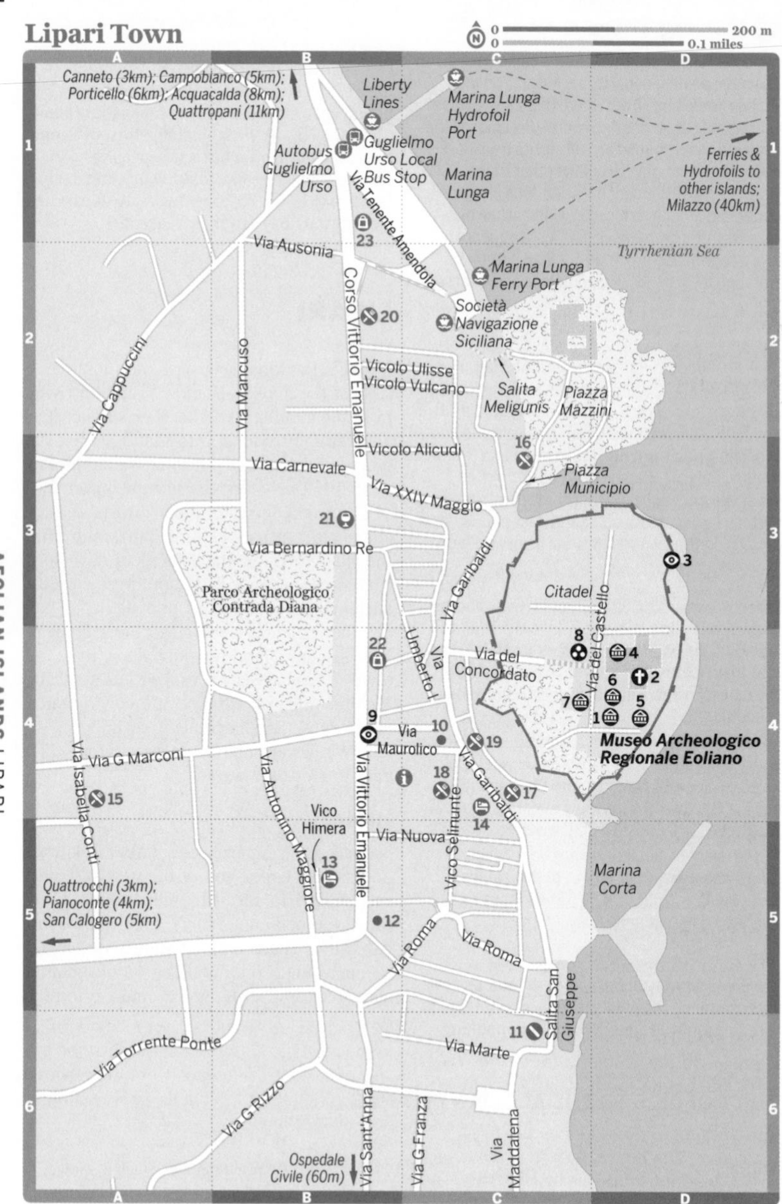

Commerce continued under the Greeks, but the arrival of the Romans in the 3rd century BC signalled the end of the islanders' good fortunes. The Roman authorities were in a vengeful mood after the islanders had sided against them in the First Punic War, and reduced the island to a state of poverty through punitive taxation.

Over the ensuing centuries, volcanic eruptions and pirate attacks – most famously in 1544, when Barbarossa burnt Lipari Town to the ground and took off with most of its

Lipari Town

Top Sights
1 Museo Archeologico Regionale Eoliano D4

Sights
2 Cattedrale di San Bartolomeo D4
3 Citadel D3
4 Museo Archeologico Eoliano (Sezione Classica) D4
5 Museo Archeologico Eoliano (Sezione Epigrafica) D4
6 Museo Archeologico Eoliano (Sezione Preistorica) D4
7 Museo Archeologico Eoliano (Sezione Vulcanologica) C4
8 Parco Archeologico C4
9 Town Centre B4

Activities, Courses & Tours
10 Da Massimo/Dolce Vita C4
11 Diving Center La Gorgonia C6
12 Nesos B5

Sleeping
13 Diana Brown B5
14 Enzo Il Negro C4

Eating
15 E Pulera A4
16 Filippino C3
17 Gilberto e Vera C4
18 Kasbah C4
19 La Cambusa C4
20 L'Officina del Cannolo B2

Drinking & Nightlife
21 Cafè La Precchia B3

Shopping
22 Fratelli Laise B4
23 La Formagella B1

female population – kept the islanders in a state of constant fear.

Unremitting poverty ensured large-scale emigration, which continued until well into the 20th century, leaving the island remote and unwanted. During Italy's fascist period in the 1930s, Mussolini used Lipari Town's castle to imprison his political opponents. Things gradually started to improve with the onset of tourism in the 1950s, and now Lipari sits at the heart of one of Sicily's most revered holiday destinations.

Sights

Lipari Town

Although it's the main tourist centre in the Aeolians, Lipari Town hasn't yet sold its soul, and it retains a charming, laid-back island vibe. There are few sights beyond the soaring clifftop citadel and archaeological museum, but it's lovely to stroll the labyrinthine alleyways with the sun on your face and nothing to do but enjoy the relaxed atmosphere. The best approach to the citadel is Via del Concordato, a stairway that leads up from Via Garibaldi to the Cattedrale di San Bartolomeo.

★Museo Archeologico Regionale Eoliano MUSEUM

(☎090 988 01 74; www.regione.sicilia.it/beniculturali/museolipari; Via Castello 2; adult/reduced €6/3; ⏲9am-6.30pm Mon-Sat, to 1pm Sun) A must-see for Mediterranean history buffs, Lipari's archaeological museum boasts one of Europe's finest collections of ancient finds. Especially worthwhile are the **Sezione Preistorica**, devoted to locally discovered artefacts from the Neolithic and Bronze Ages to the Greco-Roman era, and the **Sezione Classica**, the highlights of which include ancient shipwreck cargoes and the world's largest collection of miniature Greek theatrical masks.

The museum is divided into several sections, each housed in a separate building. Start in the Sezione Preistorica in the Palazzo Vescovile (Bishop's Palace) next to the Cattedrale. A plethora of artefacts displayed in chronological order provides a fascinating insight into the development of the island's earliest cultures. Among the first items on display are finely sculpted tools made from the obsidian on which Lipari's early economy was based – telling evidence of the relative sophistication of the island's prehistoric civilisation. Prehistoric finds from the other islands are housed in a small pavilion directly in front of the Palazzo Vescovile.

On the other side of the cathedral is the Sezione Classica. Highlights here include finds from Lipari's 11th-century BC necropolis, including a sizeable collection of burial urns. There's also a staggering array of amphorae salvaged from shipwrecks off the coasts of Panarea, Filicudi and Lipari itself. Upstairs are impressive displays of decorated vases and the museum's treasured collection of Greek theatrical masks. On this same floor you'll find a number of statuettes –

Lipari Island

the one of *Andromeda con bambino* (Andromeda with Child) is particularly beautiful – along with some elegant jewellery and a collection of polychromatic vases decorated by an artist simply known as Il Pittore Liparoto (the Lipari Painter; 300–270 BC).

Other sections worth a quick look are the **Sezione Epigrafica** (Epigraphic Section), across the road from the Sezione Preistorica, which has a small garden littered with engraved stones and a room of Greek and Roman tombs; and the **Sezione Vulcanologica** (Vulcanology Section), which illustrates the Aeolians' volcanic geology.

Note that the museum **ticket office** is about 100m north of the museum entrance.

Town Centre AREA

One of Lipari Town's great pleasures is simply wandering its streets, lapping up the laid-back island atmosphere. Lipari's liveliest street is **Corso Vittorio Emanuele**, a cheerful thoroughfare lined with bars, cafes, restaurants and delis. The street really comes into its own in early evening, when it's closed to traffic and the locals come out for their *passeggiata* (evening stroll).

Another atmospheric area is **Marina Corta**, down at the end of Via Garibaldi, a pretty little marina ringed by popular bars and restaurants.

Citadel CITADEL

After the pirate Barbarossa rampaged through in 1544, murdering most of Lipari's men and enslaving the women, the island's Spanish overlords fortified Lipari by constructing a citadel (also known as the castle) around the town centre. The town has since moved downhill, but much of the citadel's impregnable wall structure survives; it's an impressive sight, especially when seen from below.

Cattedrale di San Bartolomeo CHURCH

A fine example of 17th-century baroque architecture, this church was built to replace the original Norman cathedral destroyed by Barbarossa. Little remains of the 12th-century original except a section of Benedictine cloister to the right of the main entrance. The interior features a silver statue of St Bartholomew (1728), Lipari's patron saint, with his flayed skin tucked under his arm.

Parco Archeologico RUINS

In the sunken area opposite Lipari's cathedral, you can see the remains of a series of circular huts, the oldest of which date to the 17th century BC. Nearby, at the southern end of the citadel, you'll find some Greek sarcophagi adjacent to an open-air amphitheatre that was built in 1978.

Around Lipari

Lipari's main sights, most notably the archaeological museum, are in Lipari Town, and there's enough going on that you could conceivably never leave the city limits. However, to find the best swimming and hiking spots and enjoy some sensational views, it's well worth exploring the island's rugged hinterland.

★Quattrocchi VIEWPOINT

Lipari's best coastal views are from a celebrated viewpoint known as Quattrocchi (Four Eyes), 3km west of town. Follow the road for Pianoconte and look on your left as you approach a big hairpin bend about 300m beyond the turn-off for Spiaggia Valle i Muria. Stretching off to the south, great, grey cliffs plunge into the sea, while in the distance plumes of sinister smoke rise from the dark heights of neighbouring Vulcano.

★Spiaggia Valle i Muria BEACH

Lapped by clean waters and surrounded by sheer cliffs, this dark, pebbly beach on Lipari's southwestern shore is a dramatically beautiful swimming and sunbathing spot. From the signposted turn-off, 3km west of Lipari town toward Pianoconte, it's a steep 25-minute downhill walk; come prepared with water and sunscreen. In good weather, Lipari resident **Barni** (☎339 8221583, 349 1839555) sells refreshments from his rustic cave-like beach bar, and provides memorably scenic boat transfers to and from Lipari's Marina Corta (€5/10 one-way/return).

The turn-off is easily reached by car, scooter or local bus from Lipari town. The path down to the beach starts as a paved road, but eventually narrows to a dirt trail, passing through a rugged landscape of long grass, flowers and cacti. Slogging back up the hill is a real workout, so it's preferable to arrange return boat transit with Barni beforehand. Navigating through the *faraglione* (rock towers) of Lipari's western shore at sunset, with Vulcano's crater smoking on the horizon, is an unforgettable experience, and the perfect way to return home after a long day on the beach.

Spiaggia di Canneto BEACH

The nearest beach to Lipari Town, and the most popular swimming spot on the island, is the long, pebbly strip at Canneto, 3km north of town on the other side of a jutting headland.

Spiaggia della Papesca BEACH

(Spiaggia Bianca) Beyond Campobianco, near the abandoned pumice mines at Porticello, this pebble beach is nicknamed Spiaggia Bianca in reference to the layers of white pumice dust that once covered it. These have been slowly washed away by the rough winter seas, leaving it a dark shade of grey. However, residual pumice still gives the sea a limpid turquoise colour here.

Campobianco MINE

A few kilometres north of the beach at Canneto lies the Campobianco quarry, where huge gashes of white rock streak down the green hillside. These are the result of extensive pumice quarrying, which was an important local industry until 2000, when Unesco called for curtailment of mining operations as a condition for granting World Heritage status to the Aeolians.

Activities

Hiking

Away from the more obvious coastal pleasures, there's some lovely hiking on Lipari, especially along the rugged northern and western coastlines. Most walks involve fairly steep slopes, although the summer heat is as likely to wear you down as the terrain. Take all the usual precautions: a hat,

THREE PERFECT DAYS

Pamper Yourself on Salina

The Aeolians' greenest island struts its stuff at meal times with garden-fresh produce, abundant seafood and locally grown Malvasia wine. Hotels here are among the islands' cushiest, too. Wake up late to cappuccino with a sea view, indulge in a *ciclo benessere* (spa treatment) at **Hotel Signum** (p252) in Malfa, pack a picnic to photogenic **Pollara** (p142) or visit one of the local vineyards, then dine at **Porto Bello** (p144), **La Pinnata del Monsù** (p144) or any of the island's other standout restaurants.

Scale a Pair of Active Volcanoes

It's not every day you can climb two active volcanoes in less than 24 hours. Here's how: catch an early morning hydrofoil from Lipari to Vulcano, and reach the island's steam-belching **summit** (p140) by midmorning, before the heat and hordes of day-trippers arrive. Return to Lipari's **Marina Corta** (p134) for lunch, then hop on a tour boat to Stromboli in time to join your trekking party in the late afternoon. By sunset, you'll be oohing and aahing over the stunning fireworks of Europe's most active **volcano** (p147). Trek back down for pizza in the piazza, then ride a boat home to your familiar Lipari bed.

Island-Hop Till You Drop

No matter what island you wake up on, a boat tour can expand your horizons in a hurry. Local operators typically offer tours to multiple islands in a single day, offering a taste of the Aeolians' varied personalities even to those with limited time.

sunscreen, plenty of water, and try to avoid the midday sun.

★Pianoconte to Quattropani HIKING
This three- to four-hour hike starts from Pianoconte's school (5km west of Lipari Town), descending toward the sea along a paved road, which eventually narrows to a trail. Levelling out along the coastal bluffs, a relatively flat section skirts Lipari's western shoreline, affording fabulous views of Salina, Vulcano, Filicudi and Alicudi, before climbing steeply to the town of Quattropani.

As you descend from Pianoconte, you'll pass the old Roman baths of **San Calogero**, famous in antiquity for the thermal spring that flowed at a constant temperature of 60°C. Climbing back to Quattropani, you'll also pass the **Old Kaolin Mine**, where the hillside is still visibly scarred. The trail can just as easily be hiked in the opposite direction, starting just south of the town of Quattropani. Either way, the strenuous climbs and steep descents are rewarded with spectacular coastal scenery. Both ends of the trail can be reached by local bus – on the way there, ask the driver to let you off at the trailhead; returning, look for the official bus stop in either Pianoconte or Quattropani.

Quattropani to Acquacalda WALKING
The pleasant hour-long downhill stroll from Quattropani to Acquacalda follows a paved but lightly travelled road hugging Lipari's north shore, affording spectacular views of Salina and a distant Stromboli. Take the bus to Quattropani (€1.90), then simply proceed downhill on the main road 5km to Acquacalda, where you can catch the bus (€1.55) back to Lipari Town.

Monte Pilato HIKING
At Lipari's northeastern corner, Monte Pilato is a mountain of pumice and obsidian formed by a volcanic explosion in AD 700. A 2km trail leads to its summit (476m), starting from Ristorante Da Lauro in the town of Acquacalda. Up top, there's a nice view of the fields of solidified obsidian known as Rocche Rosse (Red Rocks).

Nesos HIKING
(☎090 981 48 38; www.nesos.org; Corso Vittorio Emanuele 24) Run by conservation biologist Pietro Lo Cascio, this recommended local environmental organisation publishes the excellent hiking guide *15 Walks in the Aeolian Islands* – available in English, German, French and Italian, and scheduled for an updated edition with three dozen new hikes in 2017. It also leads guided walks on Lipari and throughout the Aeolians (€10, plus boat fare if travelling beyond Lipari).

Diving

Diving Center La Gorgonia DIVING
(☎090 981 26 16; www.lagorgoniadiving.it; Salita San Giuseppe; per dive with own/rented equipment €35/55, courses €60-750) This outfit offers courses, boat transport, equipment hire and general information about scuba diving and snorkelling around Lipari. See the website for a complete price list.

Tours

A boat tour around Lipari is a good way of seeing the island, and the only way of getting to some of the more inaccessible swimming spots. Lipari's high concentration of tour operators also makes it a great base from which to embark on day trips to the outer Aeolian islands.

Numerous agencies in town offer tours. Prices vary depending on the season, but as a rough guide allow €20 for a tour of Lipari and Vulcano, €45 to visit Filicudi and Alicudi, €45 for a day trip to Panarea and Stromboli, or €80 for a late afternoon trip to Stromboli with a guided trip up the mountain at sunset and a late night return to Lipari. Tour companies generally operate from March to October.

Da Massimo/Dolce Vita BOATING
(☎090 981 30 86; www.damassimo.it; Via Maurolico 2) One of Lipari's best-established agencies, well-positioned on a side street between Corso Vittorio Emanuele and Via Garibaldi. Specialises in sunset hikes to the top of Stromboli, returning by boat to Lipari the same evening. Also hires boats and dinghies.

DON'T MISS

THE AEOLIANS' BEST HIKES

- **Stromboli Crater** (p147)
- **Pianoconte to Quattropani** (p136)
- **Fossa di Vulcano** (p140)
- **Zucco Grande** (p153)
- **Filo dell'Arpa** (p154)
- **Punta del Corvo** (p146)

Festivals & Events

Easter RELIGIOUS

Heartfelt and theatrical, Lipari's traditional Easter celebrations begin on Palm Sunday with the **Via Crucis**, a candle-lit procession from Piazza Mazzini to the citadel, culminating in a re-enactment of the crucifixion. On Good Friday, groups of barefoot penitents accompany statues of Christ around town in an atmosphere of funereal silence.

Easter Day is more light-hearted, with two processions, one headed by the resurrected Jesus and the other by the Virgin Mary, meeting in Marina Corta to fireworks and noisy rejoicing.

Eating

Lipari Town

Lipari's town centre is packed with restaurants, bars, cafes and gelaterias; many line the edges of Corso Vittorio Emanuele and Via Garibaldi, the twin thoroughfares running north-south between Marina Lunga and Marina Corta, while others are tucked enticingly into side alleys along the way.

Gilberto e Vera SANDWICHES €

(☎090 981 27 56; www.gilbertoevera.it; Via Garibaldi 22; half/full sandwich €3.50/5; ⊙8am-2.30pm & 4pm-midnight mid-Mar–mid-Nov) Still run by the friendly couple who founded it 35 years ago (ably assisted by daughter Alessia), this beloved shop sells two dozen varieties of sandwiches, many named for now-grown locals who used to stop by here on their way to school. It's the perfect stop for morning hiking and beach-hopping provisions, or afternoon snacks on the street-side terrace.

L'Officina del Cannolo SEAFOOD €€

(☎090 981 34 70; www.officinadelcannolo.com; Corso Vittorio Emanuele 214; meals €34-37; ⊙noon-3pm & 7-10.30pm Mar-Dec) This stylish newcomer outshines other restaurants on Lipari's main drag with the quality of its fresh-caught local fish, incorporated into appetisers (tuna burgers), *primi* (homemade pasta with swordfish, capers, mint and wild fennel) and *secondi* (seared yellowtail in a pistachio crust); but the real show-stopper is their namesake *cannoli,* made with creamy ricotta from Vulcano and a light crunchy shell.

E Pulera MODERN SICILIAN €€

(☎090 981 11 58; www.pulera.it; Via Isabella Conti; meals €30-45; ⊙7pm-midnight late Apr–mid-Oct) With its serene garden setting, low lighting, tile-topped tables and exquisite food – from tuna carpaccio with blood oranges and capers for dinner to *cassata* (sponge cake, ricotta, marzipan, chocolate and candied fruit) served with sweet Malvasia wine for dessert – E Pulera makes an upscale but relaxed choice for a romantic dinner.

DON'T MISS

DIVING SPOTS AROUND LIPARI

Lipari's got some spectacular spots for divers to explore. The folks at Diving Center La Gorgonia (p136) can point you to the following spots and many more:

Punta Castagna (difficult; depth 10m to 40m) A spectacular dive with a 10m white pumice platform interrupted by multicoloured channels.

Secca del Bagno (difficult; depth 40m to 45m) A breathtaking collection of colourful walls that are swathed with schools of technicolour fish.

Pietra Menalda (medium; depth 18m to 40m) See the homes of octopuses, eel, groupers and other sea critters on the southern side of the island.

Pietra del Bagno (all levels; 20m to 40m) Circumnavigate the Bagno rock, while witnessing colourful rock surfaces and sea life.

La Parete dei Gabbiani (medium; 20m to 45m) A black-and-white dive: black lava rock streaked with white pumice stone, hiding cracks that are home to lobsters.

Filippino SICILIAN €€

(☎090 981 10 02; www.filippino.it; Piazza Mazzini; meals €30-50; ⊙noon-3pm & 7pm-midnight, closed Mon Oct-Mar) In business for over a century, Filippino is a mainstay of Lipari's culinary scene, considered by many the island's finest restaurant. Housed in an elegant glass pavilion adjacent to the citadel, its army of white-coated waitstaff serves a dizzying array of Sicilian classics and home-grown innovations, from savoury fish stews to jasmine mousse for dessert. Dress appropriately and make a booking.

Kasbah MODERN SICILIAN, PIZZA €€

(☎090 981 10 75; www.kasbahcafe.it; Vico Selinunte 45; pizzas €6-8, meals €33-35; ⊙7-11.30pm

Mar-Nov) Tucked down narrow Vico Selinunte, with a window where you can watch the chefs at work, this place serves everything from fancy pasta, fish and meat dishes to simple wood-fired pizzas (try the Kasbah, with smoked swordfish, rocket, lemon and black pepper). The stylish dining room with its grey linen tablecloths is complemented by a more casual outdoor terrace.

La Cambusa TRATTORIA €€
(☎349 4766061; www.lacambusalipari.it; Via Garibaldi 72; meals €25-30; ⏲12.30-3pm & 7.30-10pm Easter-Oct) Old seafaring prints and a menu of traditional fish staples give this little trattoria the cosy air of a retired fisherman's house. Diners crowd the street-side tables and cosy interior for unpretentious classics such as *spaghetti ai pesce spada* (with swordfish, tomatoes, capers and olives) and *sarde a beccafico* (lightly fried sardines stuffed with breadcrumbs, raisins, pine nuts and parsley).

Around Lipari

The lion's share of restaurants are concentrated in Lipari Town, but you'll also find a few in outlying communities such as Canneto, Pianoconte and Acquacalda. Many restaurants close during the winter season between late October and Easter.

Papisca SICILIAN €
(☎090 981 23 62; Via Marina Garibaldi 67, Canneto; snacks €2-9; ⏲9am-midnight, closed Thu Nov–mid-Jun) On the waterfront in Canneto, this bar-cafe is beloved among locals for its reasonably priced snacks (*arancini,* frittatas, *pasta al forno,* breaded anchovies), perfect for enjoying with a cold Messina beer on the front terrace. Save room for their famous gelati and *granite* (flavoured ices), or end your meal Aeolian-style with a glass of Malvasia wine accompanied by sesame cookies.

★**Le Macine** SICILIAN €€
(☎090 982 23 87; www.lemacine.org; Via Stradale 9, Pianoconte; meals €30-40; ⏲noon-2.30pm & 7-10pm daily May-Sep, Sat & Sun Oct-Apr) This country restaurant in Pianoconte, 4.5km from Lipari Town, comes into its own in summer, when meals are served on the terrace. Seafood and fresh vegetables star in dishes such as swordfish cakes with artichokes, shrimp-filled ravioli or fish in *ghiotta* sauce (with olive oil, capers, tomatoes, garlic and basil). Call ahead to request their free shuttle service from Lipari.

Drinking & Nightlife

Marina Corta is the most scenic spot to people-watch while chilling out over a cool drink; grab a sidewalk seat at one of the touristy bars lining the waterfront square. Corso Vittorio Emanuele is the other big hot spot for early evening *aperitivi.*

Cafè La Precchia BAR
(☎090 981 13 03; www.cafelaprecchia.com; Corso Vittorio Emanuele 191; ⏲noon-2am) If you fancy a late-night drink or simply want a prime people-watching perch during the *passeggiata,* pull up a chair at this hugely popular bar. It has an enormous menu of drinks, from *cafe frappe* to cocktails and wine, and stays open until the small hours. Occasional live music adds to the party atmosphere.

Shopping

La Formagella FOOD & DRINKS
(☎090 988 07 59; Corso Vittorio Emanuele 250; ⏲8am-8.30pm Mar-Oct) You simply can't leave the Aeolian Islands without a small pot of capers and a bottle of sweet Malvasia wine. You can get both, along with meats, cheeses and other delicious goodies, at this gourmet grocery-deli just around the corner from the hydrofoil dock.

Fratelli Laise FOOD & DRINKS
(☎090 981 27 31; www.fratellilaise.com; Corso Vittorio Emanuele 118; ⏲9am-1pm & 4-7pm) About two-thirds of the way down from Marina Lunga to Marina Corta, a lush, technicolour fruit display announces the presence of this traditional greengrocer, piled high with wines, sweets, *anis* (aniseed) biscuits, pâtés, capers and olive oils. It's an excellent place to find food gifts to bring home – or simply to stock up on picnic provisions.

Information

Ospedale Civile (☎090 988 51 11; Via Sant'Anna) First-aid and emergency services.

Police Station (☎090 981 13 33; Via Marconi)

Tourist Office (☎090 988 00 95; infopoint eolie@regione.sicilia.it; Via Maurolico 17; ⏲9am-1pm & 4.30-7pm Mon, Wed & Fri, 9am-1pm Tue & Thu) Lipari's sporadically staffed office provides information covering all the Aeolian Islands.

Getting There & Away

The main port is Marina Lunga, where you'll find ticket offices for hydrofoil operator **Liberty Lines** (☎ 090 981 24 48; www.libertylines.it), and ferry operators NGI and **Società Navigazione Siciliana** (Siremar; ☎ 090 981 10 17; www.siremar.it). Hydrofoils run frequently to the mainland port of Milazzo (€17.30, one hour) and to the other Aeolian islands: Vulcano (€7.30, 10 minutes), Santa Marina Salina (€10.30, 20 minutes), Panarea (€11.90, one hour), Stromboli (€19.30, 1½ to 1¾ hours), Filicudi (€16.20, one to 1¼ hours) and Alicudi (€20.05, 1½ to two hours). There's also occasional hydrofoil service to Messina (€26.30, 1½ to 2¾ hours, four daily in summer, one daily in winter). Ferry service is less expensive but much slower and less frequent.

In summer (late May through early September), SNAV (p131) also offers daily hydrofoil service from Naples to Lipari (from €58, 6½ hours).

Getting Around

The island is small enough that a grand circuit only takes about an hour by car or scooter. If you've got more time on your hands, you can also make your way around on public buses.

BUS

Autobus Guglielmo Urso (☎ 090 981 10 26; www.ursobus.com/orariursobus.pdf) runs buses all over the island from its bus stop opposite the Marina Lunga hydrofoil dock. One main route serves the island's eastern shore, from Lipari Town to Canneto (five minutes) and Acquacalda (20 minutes); another runs from Lipari Town to the Quattrocchi viewpoint and the western highland settlements of Pianoconte and Quattropani. Individual tickets range in price from €1.90 to €2.40. If you're making multiple trips, you'll save money by buying a ticket booklet (six/10/20 tickets for €10/14/28). Service is limited to nonexistent on Sundays.

CAR & MOTORCYCLE

Lipari is not big – only 38 sq km – but to explore it in depth it can be helpful to have your own wheels. The seafront road circles the entire island, a journey of about 30km. Various outfits opposite the Marina Lunga hydrofoil dock rent out bikes, scooters and cars, including **Da Marcello** (☎ 090 981 12 34; www.noleggiodamarcello.com; Via Sottomonastero) and **Da Luigi** (☎ 090 988 05 40; www.noleggiolipari.it; Marina Lunga; ⏰ 8am-8pm). Allow about €10 per day for a bike, between €15 and €40 per day for a scooter, and from €30 to €70 per day for a small car.

VULCANO

POP 715

With its visibly smoking crater and vile sulphurous fumes, Vulcano makes an indelible first impression. The island's volcanic nature has long been impressing visitors: the ancient Romans believed it to be the chimney of the fire god Vulcan's workshop, and today it remains famous for its therapeutic mud baths and hot springs. The main drawcard, however, remains the Fossa di Vulcano (Gran Cratere), the steaming volcano that towers over the island's northeastern shores.

Vulcano's most obvious attractions – climbing the crater, strolling over to the mud baths and the black beaches at Porto di Ponente – are easily managed on a day trip from Lipari. Visitors who linger and explore beyond touristy Porto di Levante will discover a whole different island, swimming off Gelso's volcanic beaches, kayaking the wild coast or enjoying the rural tranquillity of the central plateau, filled with vegetable gardens, birdsong and a surprising amount of greenery.

Sights

★Capo Grillo VIEWPOINT

For spectacular sea and island views without the physical exertion of climbing Fossa di Vulcano, follow the signposted road to Capo Grillo, about 7km southeast of Vulcano

MUD-BATH TIPS

- Don't stay in longer than 10 or 15 minutes – the water and mud is slightly radioactive. Pregnant women should avoid it altogether.
- Don't use your favourite fluffy towel or one you've 'borrowed' from a hotel – most hotels will provide a special *fanghi* towel on request.
- If you have a sulphite allergy, stay away.
- Remember to remove watches and jewellery.
- Take flip-flops or sandals – there are hot air vents that can scald your feet.
- Wear a swimsuit you don't mind destroying: once the smell gets in, it's easier to buy a new one than to get rid of the pong.

port, near the mid-island settlement of Piano. From here you'll get breathtaking perspectives on Lipari and Salina, with Panarea, Stromboli and Filicudi floating off in the distance.

Spiaggia Sabbia Nera BEACH

Vulcano's beach scene is centred on this smooth strip of black sand at Porto di Ponente, about 10 minutes' walk beyond the mud pools on the western side of the peninsula. One of the few sandy beaches in the Aeolians, it's a scenic spot, curving around a bay of limpid, glassy waters out of which rise jutting *faraglioni* (rock towers).

From the beach, a road traverses a small isthmus to **Vulcanello** (123m), a bulb of land that was spewed out by a volcanic eruption in 183 BC. Here you'll find the famous **Valle dei Mostri** (Valley of the Monsters), a group of wind-eroded dark rocks that have formed grotesque shapes.

Gelso AREA

On the island's southern coast, Gelso is a minuscule but picturesque port with a family-run restaurant and a couple of black-sand beaches that rarely get very crowded. In summer there's a bus service to get there, but you'll be much better off hiring a car or scooter, as services are limited and it's a 15km walk back if you get stranded.

West of the port a trail runs a few hundred metres to the 18th-century church of **Santa Maria delle Grazie** and an abandoned **lighthouse**. Just uphill (north) from the port, a steep dirt track (pedestrians only) branches off to **Spiaggia dell'Asina** (Donkey Beach), a crescent of black sand giving onto inviting waters. A second beach, **Spiaggia Cannitello**, is surrounded by lush, almost tropical greenery. Both beaches have rudimentary bar-cafes, where you can hire sun lounges and umbrellas.

Activities

★ Fossa di Vulcano HIKING

Vulcano's top attraction is the straightforward trek up its 391m volcano (no guide required). Start early if possible and bring a hat, sunscreen and water. Follow the signs south along Strada Provinciale, then turn left onto the zigzag gravel track that leads to the summit. It's a 30- to 60-minute climb to the lowest point of the volcano's rim (290m), where you'll be rewarded with fine views of the steaming crater encrusted with red and yellow crystals.

It's well worth lingering up top and climbing another 15 minutes around to the southern rim for stunning views of the other Aeolian islands lined up on the northern horizon, with the gaping crater in the foreground. The truly ambitious can descend steeply to the crater floor (but beware of hot steam vents and the accompanying toxic fumes).

Laghetto di Fanghi HOT SPRINGS

(www.termevulcano.it; €3, shower/towel €1/2.60; 7am-10pm Jul & Aug, 9am-6.30pm late Mar-Jun & Sep-early Nov) Backed by a *faraglione* (rock tower) and stinking of rotten eggs, Vulcano's harbourside pool of thick, coffee-coloured sulphurous gloop isn't exactly a five-star beauty farm. But the warm (28°C) mud is considered an excellent treatment for rheumatic pains and skin diseases, and rolling around in it can be fun if you don't mind smelling funny for a few days. Keep the mud away from your eyes (as the sulphur is acidic and can damage the cornea) and hair.

Once you have had time to relax in the muddy water, get some soft clay from the bottom of the pool and apply it to your body and face. Wait for the clay mask to dry, wash it off in the pool, then run to the natural spa around the corner, where there are hot, bubbling springs in a small natural seawater pool.

Diving Centre Saracen DIVING
(☎347 7283341; www.scuolasubpalermo.it; Resort Mari del Sud, Via Porto Ponente; snorkelling €35, dives incl equipment from €50; ⏲Easter-Oct) This local dive centre offers a range of dives, plus snorkelling excursions that focus on Vulcano's many marine caves and subterranean hot springs. It also sponsors the Vulcano Dive Festival (p141) in late June.

Sicily in Kayak KAYAKING
(☎329 5381229; www.sicilyinkayak.com) This outfit offers half-day kayaking tours around Vulcano and Lipari (9.30am to 12.30pm or 2.30pm to 5.30pm), as well as stand-up paddleboard courses and guided excursions.

Tours

In summer you can take boat tours of the island from the port for €15 to €20 per person; local operators set up in kiosks. Highlights to look out for include the **Grotta del Cavallo**, a sea cave known for its light effects, and the **Piscina di Venere**, a natural swimming pool set in its own rocky amphitheatre.

Festivals & Events

Vulcano Dive Festival SPORTS
(www.vulcanodivefestival.it) Over a four-day weekend in late June, this festival draws divers for daily explorations of Vulcano's submarine landscape, courses in underwater photography and marine biology, and nightly entertainment.

Eating

Eateries near the port tend to be touristy and overpriced. If you have time, it's well worth exploring further afield.

Malvasia SANDWICHES €
(☎090 985 22 27; www.ristorantemalvasiavulcano.it; Via degli Eucaliptus; sandwiches from €8; ⏲noon-2pm & 7-11pm late Apr-early Oct) After years selling open-faced sandwiches from a cart near Vulcano's port, jovial owner Maurizio Pagano opened this inviting new restaurant and wine bar in 2015. Bask on the sunny front patio and enjoy his trademark *pane cunzatu eoliano* (tuna, olives, capers, tomatoes and buffalo-milk mozzarella on olive oil-drenched toasted bread), or go for daily specials of fresh-grilled fish and meat.

★**Trattoria da Pina** SEAFOOD €€
(☎368 668555; Gelso; meals €25-30; ⏲late Apr–mid-Oct) With its outdoor porch overlooking the black-sand beach at Vulcano's southern tip, this down-to-earth trattoria, with sea-blue tablecloths, serves up fresh-caught fish in a wonderful end-of-the-line setting. Two local men do the fishing, and their mothers do the cooking.

La Forgia Maurizio SICILIAN €€
(☎339 1379107; Strada Provinciale 45, Porto di Levante; meals €30-35; ⏲12.30-3pm & 7-11pm; 🌶) Maurizio, owner of this devilishly good restaurant between the port and the volcano, spent 20 winters in Goa, India. Eastern influences sneak into his menu of Sicilian specialities, and several items are vegan- or vegetarian-friendly. Check out the multicourse tasting menu (€30 including wine, water and dessert), finished off with *liquore di kumquat e cardamom,* Maurizio's homemade answer to *limoncello* (lemon liqueur).

Maria Tindara SICILIAN €€
(☎090 985 30 04; Strada Provinciale 38, Piano; meals €25-35; ⏲noon-2pm & 7.30-9.30pm) On Vulcano's fertile central plateau, 7km south of the port, this family-run restaurant serves delicious *caponata* (sweet-and-sour vegetable salad) and homemade pasta alongside mountain specialities such as grilled lamb. With locals hanging out at the bar up front, it's a pleasant antidote to Porto di Levante's tourist-thronged eateries. Snacks of local cheese and capers (€7) are also offered to refuel hungry hikers and cyclists.

Orientation

Boats dock at the Porto di Levante. From here it's a short walk – bear right as you exit the harbour area – to the *fanghi* (mud baths), hidden behind a small hillock of rocks. Continuing beyond the mud pools, the road leads to Porto di Ponente, where you'll find a number of hotels and Spiaggia Sabbia Nera (Black Sand Beach), a long stretch of black sand. For the Fossa di Vulcano, bear left as you disembark and continue approximately 1km along the base of the volcano until you see the *'accesso al cratere'* sign on your left indicating the way up.

Information

Emergency Doctor (335 7662988; Via Favaloro, Porto di Levante; 24hr)

Police (090 985 21 10; Strada Provinciale)

Getting There & Around

Of the seven Aeolian islands, Vulcano is closest to the mainland, meaning that hydrofoil service here is especially frequent, with departures every hour or so; all Lipari-bound boats from Milazzo or Messina stop here first.

BICYCLE

Bikes can be hired from **Sprint da Luigi** (090 985 22 08, 347 7600275; www.vulcano-luigi-rent.com; Porto di Levante; bicycle/scooter/car rental per day from €5/20/40), who can also organise island tours.

BOAT

Vulcano is an intermediate stop between Milazzo (ferry/hydrofoil €9.80/€15.40, two hours/45 minutes) and Lipari (ferry/hydrofoil €4.70/€7, 25 minutes/10 minutes), with frequent service in both directions. Beyond Lipari, most boats continue to the outer Aeolian Islands.

Alternatively, you can travel from Naples to Vulcano aboard the biweekly ferry (from €55, 14½ to 16½ hours) operated by **Società Navigazione Siciliana** (Siremar; 090 36 46 01; www.siremar.it), or the daily, summer-only hydrofoil (from €58, 6¼ hours) operated by SNAV (p131).

Ticket offices are near the dock at Porto di Levante.

BUS

Scaffidi Bus (338 6961723, 090 985 30 73) runs buses around the island. There's year-round service from Porto di Levante to Porto di Ponente (€1.90), Piano (€2.40) and Capo Grillo (€2.40, 20 minutes, five Monday to Saturday, two Sunday). From mid-June to mid-September, buses also run to Gelso (€2.70, 40 minutes, around three daily). There's a timetable posted at the main bus stop, at the beginning of Strada Provinciale near the hydrofoil dock. Buy tickets on the bus. If you're going to the beaches at Gelso, ask the driver to let you off at the dirt track.

CAR & MOTORCYCLE

Sprint da Luigi Rent some wheels from this well-signposted outfit near the port. Multilingual owners Luigi and Nidra offer tips for exploring the island and also rent out an apartment (€40 to €70) in Vulcano's tranquil interior.

TAXI

Santi (366 3028712; www.taxivulcanosantitour.com) Provides taxi service as well as guided trips around the island. Call ahead to negotiate rates.

SALINA

POP 2600

In delightful contrast to the exposed volcanic terrain of the other Aeolians, Salina – the archipelago's second largest island – boasts a lush, verdant landscape thanks to its natural freshwater springs. Woodlands, wildflowers, thick yellow gorse bushes and serried ranks of grape vines carpet its hillsides, while high coastal cliffs plunge into the breaking waters below.

Named for the *saline* (salt works) of Lingua at the island's southeastern edge, Salina is shaped by two extinct volcanoes, Monte dei Porri (860m) and Monte Fossa delle Felci (962m), the Aeolians' two highest peaks. These form a natural barrier in the centre of the island, ensuring that the sleepy villages around the perimeter retain their own individual character. Tourism is most evident in the main port of Santa Marina Salina; elsewhere there's a distinct sense that the rest of the world is a long way away. If that sounds good, you'll love Salina.

Sights

Santa Marina Salina VILLAGE

Salina's main port, Santa Marina is a typical island settlement with steeply stacked whitewashed houses rising up the hillside. The principal street is **Via Risorgimento**, a lively pedestrian-only strip lined with cafes and boutiques. It's not a big place, and there are no specific sights, but it makes an ideal base for exploring the rest of the island.

Malfa VILLAGE

Tumbling down the hillside to a small shingle beach, this settlement on Salina's north coast is the island's largest, though you'd never guess it from the tranquil atmosphere. About halfway between the town entrance and the sea is the main church square, focal point of Malfa's laid-back social life, from which sloping lanes fan up and down the hillsides.

Pollara VILLAGE

Don't miss a trip to sleepy Pollara, sandwiched dramatically between the sea and the steep slopes of an extinct volcanic crater on Salina's western edge. The gorgeous beach here was used as a location in the 1994 film *Il Postino,* although the land access route to the beach has since been closed due to landslide danger.

You can still descend the steep stone steps at the northwest end of town and swim across to the beach, or simply admire the spectacular view, with its backdrop of volcanic cliffs.

Lingua VILLAGE

Three kilometres south of Santa Marina Salina, the tiny village of Lingua is a popular summer hang-out, with a couple of hotels, a few trattorias and a small beach. Its main feature is the **salt lagoon**, which sits under an old lighthouse at the end of the village. The centre of the summer scene is seafront Piazza Marina Garibaldi.

Until quite recently the salt works were an important local employer, but now the lagoon only provides sustenance for the migrating birds that pass through in spring and autumn en route to and from Africa. Lingua's most famous business venture these days is Da Alfredo (p144), a bar-gelateria famous across Sicily for its flavourful *granite*.

Rinella VILLAGE

This tiny hamlet on the south coast is Salina's second port, regularly served by hydrofoils and ferries. Pastel-coloured houses huddle around the waterfront, and there are a couple of decent swimming spots nearby. If the sandy beach by the village centre gets too cramped, follow the path to Punta Megna, from where you can access the pebbly **Spiaggia Pra Venezia**.

Museo dell'Emigrazione Eoliana MUSEUM

(Aeolian Emigration Museum; ☎392 2694313; www.museisicilianiemigrazione.it; Via Fontana 4, Malfa; ⏲10am-noon & 5-8pm May-Oct, by appointment Nov-Apr) FREE This small museum, tucked behind the church on the main road above Malfa, documents the emigration of thousands of residents from Salina and the other Aeolian Islands to Australia and the Americas in the late 19th and early 20th centuries.

Activities

★Monte Fossa delle Felci HIKING

For jaw-dropping views, climb to the Aeolians' highest point, Monte Fossa delle Felci (962m). The two-hour ascent starts from the **Santuario della Madonna del Terzito**, an imposing 19th-century church at Valdichiesa, in the valley separating the island's two volcanoes. Up top, gorgeous perspectives unfold on the symmetrically arrayed volcanic cones of Monte dei Porri, Filicudi and a distant Alicudi.

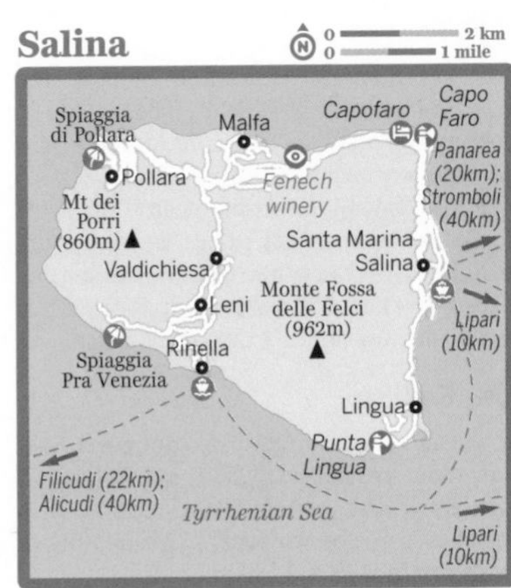

From the sanctuary – an important place of pilgrimage for islanders, particularly around the Feast of the Assumption on 15 August – you can follow a signposted track up through pine and chestnut woodlands and fields of ferns, all the way to the top. Along the way you'll see plenty of colourful flora, including wild violets, asparagus and a plant known locally as *cipudazza* (Latin *Urginea marittima*), which was sold to the Calabrians to make soap, but is used locally as mouse poison!

Once you've reached the summit (the last 100m are particularly tough), the views are breathtaking, particularly looking west towards Filicudi and Alicudi and also from the southeast ridge where you can look down over the Lingua salt lagoon and over to Lipari and Vulcano. To get to the trailhead by public transport, take the bus from Santa Marina Salina to Malfa, then change for a Rinella-bound bus and ask the driver to let you off at Valdichiesa.

★Signum Spa SPA

(Salus Per Aquam; ☎090 984 42 22; www.hotelsignum.it; Via Scalo 15, Malfa; €30, treatments extra; ⏲10am-8pm Apr-Sep) Enjoy a revitalising hot spring soak or a cleansing sweat in a traditional adobe-walled steam house at Hotel Signum's fabulous spa. The complex includes several stylish spa baths on a pretty flagstoned patio, and blissful spaces where you can immerse your body in salt crystals, get a massage or pamper yourself with natural essences of citrus, malvasia and capers.

Tours

Some of the best swimming spots in the area are only accessible by sea, so you'll need to sign up for a boat tour or hire a boat for yourself. **Salina Relax Boats** (☎345 2162308; www.salinarelaxboats.com; Via Roma 86, Santa Marina Salina) offers various tours of Salina and the other islands, costing between €60 and €70 per person; it also hires out boats and runs a water-taxi service.

Eating

Malvasia wine and fat, juicy capers are Salina's twin specialities, which you'll find on virtually every menu. Island cuisine also benefits from the widespread availability of fresh produce from local gardens.

★Da Alfredo SANDWICHES €
(Piazza Marina Garibaldi, Lingua; granite €2.60, sandwiches €9-13; ⏲8am-11pm Jun-Sep, 10am-6pm Oct-May) Straddling a sunny waterfront terrace in Lingua, Alfredo's place is renowned Sicily-wide for its *granite*. For an affordable lunch, try their *pane cunzato*, open-faced sandwiches loaded with smoked tuna carpaccio, citrus, wild fennel, almond-caper pesto, ricotta, tomatoes, capers, olives and more; split one with a friend – they're huge!

Al Cappero SICILIAN €
(☎090 984 39 68; www.alcappero.it; Pollara; meals €22-27; ⏲noon-2pm Easter-May, noon-2pm & 7.30-10pm Jun–mid-Sep; 🌿) This family-run place in Pollara, with a sprawling outdoor terrace, specialises in old-fashioned Sicilian home-cooking, including several vegetarian options. It also sells home-grown capers and rents out simple rooms down the street (€350 to €550 per week).

★Porto Bello SEAFOOD €€
(☎090 984 31 25; www.portobellosalina.com; Via Lungomare 2, Santa Marina Salina; meals €30-50; ⏲noon-2.30pm & 7-11pm Easter-Oct, by reservation Nov-Easter) For Santa Marina's best seafood, don't miss this award-winning restaurant with a terrace overlooking the harbour, run by the same family since 1978. In low season, make a beeline for their excellent value tourist menu (€15), featuring the house speciality *pasta al fuoco* (fiery pasta with hot peppers) and *secondi* of grilled fish or squid stewed in Malvasia wine.

La Pinnata del Monsù TRATTORIA €€
(☎328 9225889; Via Sorgente 1A, Malfa; meals €25-35; ⏲noon-2pm & 7.30-10pm mid-Apr–Oct) With a sunny terrace overlooking the vineyards and the sea at Malfa's southern edge, this newish trattoria (opened in 2014) serves up superbly rendered Sicilian classics such as *caponata*, *busiate* (corkscrew-shaped tube pasta) with squid and wild fennel, and *cannoli* filled on the spot with fresh ricotta from nearby Vulcano.

A Cannata SICILIAN €€
(☎090 984 31 61; Via Umberto I 13, Lingua; meals €30-35; ⏲12.30-2.30pm & 7.30-10pm) Seafood caught fresh daily by owner Santino, accompanied by local vegetables, is served in the

MALVASIA

Salina's good fortune is its freshwater springs. It is the only island of the Aeolians with natural water sources, the result of which is the startling greenery. The islanders have put this to good use, producing their own style of wine, Malvasia. It is thought that the Greeks brought the grapes to the islands in 588 BC, and the name is derived from Monemvasìa, a Greek city.

The wine is still produced according to traditional techniques using the Malvasia grape and the now-rare red Corinthian grape. The harvest generally occurs in the second week of September when the grapes are picked and laid out to dry on woven cane mats. The drying process is crucial: the grapes must dry out enough to concentrate the sweet flavour but not too much, which would caramelise them.

The result is a dark-golden or light-amber wine that tastes, some say, of honey. It is usually drunk in very small glasses and goes well with cheese, sweet biscuits and almond pastries.

In recent years, Salina's wineries have also started producing some excellent dry Malvasia whites that go nicely with seafood; you'll find these on menus around Salina and throughout the archipelago.

WINERIES

Salina's vineyards produce some excellent wines, and sampling the island's famous Malvasia is one of the great pleasures of travelling here. Signposted off the main road in Malfa you'll find three of the best wineries: **Fenech** (☎090 984 40 41; www.fenech.it; Via Fratelli Mirabilo 41), **Marchetta** (☎090 984 40 48; www.vinidisalina.it; Via Umberto I, No 9, Malfa) and **Virgona** (☎090 984 44 30; www.malvasiadellelipari.it; Via Bandiera 2, Malfa). Other important Malvasias are produced at the luxurious Capofaro (p252) resort on the 5-hectare Tasca d'Almerita estate between Malfa and Santa Marina, and at **Hauner** (☎090 984 31 41; www.hauner.it; Via Umberto I, Lingua), near the town of Lingua at Salina's southeast corner. Some of these wineries will let you stop in for a taste if you call ahead. Alternatively, you'll find local Malvasias well represented on restaurant wine lists around the island.

sun-filled seafront pavilion at this unassuming but excellent restaurant, run by the same family for nearly four decades. Expect dishes such as squid-ink risotto, *maccheroni* (macaroni) with aubergine, pine nuts, mozzarella and ricotta, fresh grilled fish, sautéed wild fennel, almond *semifreddi* (a light frozen dessert) and local Malvasia wine.

'nni Lausta MODERN SICILIAN €€
(☎090 984 34 86; Via Risorgimento, Santa Marina Salina; meals €30-40; ⊙noon-11pm Easter-Oct) This stylish modern eatery with its cute lobster logo builds its menu around freshly caught fish and other locally sourced ingredients, with 80% of the produce originating in its own garden. The downstairs bar is popular for aperitifs and late-night drinking.

Drinking & Nightlife

★**Maracaibo** BAR
(☎331 6244981; Punta Scario, Malfa; ⊙8am-11pm late May-Sep) This palm-thatched beach bar on the rocky shoreline of Punta Scario (just below Malfa town) makes a dreamy spot for a sunset drink. Friendly owners Francesco and Doroty also rent out loungers (€3), beach umbrellas (€4) and kayaks (single/double €4/6).

Orientation

Most boats dock at Santa Marina Salina, the island's biggest settlement. The town's main street, Via Risorgimento, runs parallel to the seafront one block back from the port. Salina's other main settlements are: Lingua, 3km south of Santa Marina Salina; Malfa, on the northern coast; inland Leni; and Rinella, a tiny fishing hamlet on the southern coast. Note that many hydrofoils stop in at Rinella as well as Santa Marina Salina.

Information

Emergency Doctor (☎090 984 40 05; ⊙24hr)
Police Station (☎090 984 30 19; Via Lungomare, Santa Marina Salina)

Getting There & Around

Salina has two ferry ports: Santa Marina on the island's east shore, and tiny Rinella on the south shore. Most boats from Lipari will stop at Rinella en route to Filicudi and Alicudi, while those bound for Panarea and Stromboli will typically stop at Santa Marina Salina. Some stop at both ports.

BICYCLE

Hire mountain bikes from **Antonio Bongiorno** (☎338 3791209; www.rentbongiorno.it; Via Risorgimento 222, Santa Marina Salina), one block uphill from Santa Marina's hydrofoil dock.

BOAT

Liberty Lines (☎092 387 38 13; www.libertylines.it) runs frequent hydrofoils to Santa Marina Salina from Lipari (€10.30, 20 to 40 minutes), Vulcano (€11.90, 40 minutes to one hour) and Milazzo (€19.05, 1½ to two hours). Less frequent services connect Santa Marina with Stromboli, Panarea, Filicudi and Alicudi. Liberty Lines also offers daily sailings to/from Messina (€30.35, 2¼ to three hours, three daily in summer, one in winter). Some of these services call at Rinella en route. The ticket office is on the square 100m north of the hydrofoil dock.

Alternatively, you can travel from Naples to Santa Marina Salina aboard the biweekly ferry (from €52, 10¾ hours) operated by **Società Navigazione Siciliana** (Siremar; ☎090 98 60 16; www.siremar.it), or the daily, summer-only hydrofoil (from €58, 5¾ hours) operated by SNAV (p131).

BUS

CITIS (☎090 984 41 50; www.trasportisalina.it) provides dependable local bus service year-round. There are bus stops near the ports in Santa Marina and Rinella, and timetables are posted around the island.

Direct buses run from Santa Marina to Lingua (€1.90, five to 10 minutes), Malfa (€1.90, 15 to 20 minutes), Valdichiesa (€2.40, 25 minutes), Leni (€2.70, 30 minutes) and Rinella (€2.70, 40 minutes). From Santa Marina to Pollara (€2.40, 25 minutes to 1½ hours), a change of buses in Malfa is always required. Service to all destinations is more frequent in July and August; see schedules online.

CAR & MOTORCYCLE

Antonio Bongiorno (p145) hires scooters (from €20 per day) and cars (from €50 per day).

PANAREA

POP 240

Exclusive and expensive, Panarea is the smallest and most fashionable of the Aeolians, attracting international jet-setters and Milanese fashionistas for a taste of *dolce far niente* (sweet nothing). In summer, luxury yachts fill the tiny harbour and flocks of day-trippers traipse around the car-free whitewashed streets of San Pietro, the port and principal settlement. Panarea is a strictly summer-only destination with very little going on outside the tourist season – in fact, arrive between November and Easter and you'll find most places closed.

Sights

All of the island's main sights are within easy striking distance of San Pietro. North of town lie the tiny community of **Ditella** and the rocky beach at Spiaggia Fumarola. South is the village of **Drautto**, followed by sandy Spiaggetta Zimmari, the prehistoric village, and the crystal-clear waters of Cala Junco.

Villaggio Preistorico ARCHAEOLOGICAL SITE

Dramatically sited on Punta Milazzese, an elevated headland surrounded by the sea, these round foundations of 23 stone huts are the only vestiges of a prehistoric village dating back to the 14th century BC. Pottery found here shows distinctly Minoan influences, lending credence to the theory that the islanders maintained trading ties with the Cretans. The village is about a 45-minute walk south of San Pietro; from Spiaggetta Zimmari, climb the steep series of steps, then follow the signs.

★Cala Junco BEACH

Near Panarea's prehistoric village, about 45 minutes south of San Pietro, steps lead down to this gorgeous little cove with a rock-strewn beach and dreamy aquamarine waters.

Spiaggetta Zimmari BEACH

This small stretch of brown sand backed by a steep overgrown dune, about 20 minutes on foot south of San Pietro, is Panarea's only sandy beach and gets packed in summer.

Spiaggia Fumarola BEACH

To the north of San Pietro, this stone beach, with full-on views of Stromboli, is reached via a steep, winding descent north of Ditella. Outside peak months this is an isolated spot ideal for a quiet swim, but in July and August, the sun-seekers move in en masse and the ringing of mobile phones becomes incessant.

Offshore Islands ISLAND

Five islets off Panarea's eastern shore can be toured by boat. Nearest to Panarea is **Dattilo**, which has a pretty little beach called Le Guglie. The isle of **Lisca Bianca** also offers good swimming on a small white beach. North of Dattilo, **Basiluzzo** is the largest of the five islets, given over to the cultivation of capers. To hire a boat for the journey, check the seafront kiosks at San Pietro or try **Nautilus** (☎333 4233161; www.panarea.com/nautilus; Via Drautto) at Drautto, south of San Pietro.

The remaining islands are **Lisca Nera** and **Bottaro**, the latter being nothing more than a protruding rock, On the seabed beneath the narrow channel between Lisca Bianca and Bottaro lies the **wreck** of a 19th-century English ship. Divers can hire scuba equipment and organise dives at **Amphibia** (☎335 6138529; www.amphibia.it; Via San Pietro) in San Pietro.

Activities

Panarea offers a nice mix of activities, both on the mainland and offshore. Its largely traffic-free streets and small network of trails make it an appealing walking destination in spring and fall.

Punta del Corvo HIKING

At 421m, this rocky outcropping is Panarea's highest point and a popular day-hiking destination. Two trails (marked 1 and 2 on local maps) converge here, and can be combined into a scenic full-island circuit. Allow about four hours for the full round trip, and be ready for some steep climbs and descents. From up top, there are spectacular views of all six of the neighbouring Aeolian islands.

Eating

Panarea has a plethora of seafood restaurants near the port, including many with nice views across the water to Stromboli. A few additional eateries are scattered along the narrow lanes leading north to Ditella and south to Drautto.

Da Francesco SICILIAN €€
(☎090 98 30 23; www.dafrancescopanarea.com; Via San Pietro; meals €28-35; ⊙noon-2.30pm & 7-10pm Mar-Nov) Up a short flight of stairs from the port (follow the signs), Da Francesco is a laid-back trattoria with a straightforward fish-focused menu and fine sea views toward Stromboli from its upstairs terrace. Try the speciality: *spaghetti alla disgraziata* (with tomatoes, aubergines, chilli, capers, olives and ricotta). Simple rooms are also available (singles €35 to €70, doubles €70 to €140).

Trattoria da Paolino SICILIAN €€
(☎090 98 30 08; Via Iditella 75; meals €26-32; ⊙12.30-3pm & 7.30-10pm Easter–mid-Oct) For four decades, Paolino has been serving an ever-changing menu of top quality, home-style Aeolian specialities on his breezy blue-and-white terrace overlooking the sea, a 10-minute walk north from the harbour. Tuna figures prominently on the menu (smoked, *sott'olio,* or mixed with pine nuts and wild fennel in *pasta magna magna*) alongside plenty of other fish, pasta and vegetable dishes.

Getting There & Away

Hydrofoils and ferries dock in the main settlement of San Pietro.

In summer **Liberty Lines** (☎090 98 33 44; www.libertylines.it) runs up to seven hydrofoils daily to/from Stromboli (€12.60, 30 minutes), Lipari (€11.90, 25 minutes to one hour) and Milazzo (€19.30, 1½ to 2½ hours). In winter, there are fewer services.

Società Navigazione Siciliana (Siremar; ☎090 98 30 07; www.siremar.it) also runs ferries to all these destinations; ferries cost less than the hydrofoil, but take about twice as long.

The quickest way to reach Panarea from the Italian mainland is via the summer-only hydrofoil from Naples operated by SNAV (p131) (from €58, five hours, late May through early September).

Ticket offices for all companies are at the port in San Pietro.

Getting Around

Cars are not allowed on Panarea, but you won't need one as the island is small enough to get around on foot. The preferred mode of transport is golf carts. To arrange a taxi contact **Pantaxi** (☎333 3138610) or **Panarea Taxi** (☎338 4931207).

STROMBOLI

POP 400

For many the most captivating of the Aeolians, Stromboli conforms perfectly to one's childhood idea of a volcano, with its symmetrical, smoking silhouette rising dramatically from the sea. It's a hugely popular day-trip destination, but to best appreciate its primordial beauty, languid pace and the romance that lured Roberto Rossellini and Ingrid Bergman here in 1949, you'll need to give it at least a couple of days.

Volcanic activity has scarred and blackened much of the island, but the northeastern corner is inhabited, and it's here that you'll find the island's famous black beaches and the main settlement sprawled attractively along the volcano's lower slopes. Despite the picture-postcard appearance, life here is tough: food and drinking water have to be ferried in, there are no roads across the island, and until relatively recently there was no electricity in Ginostra, the island's second settlement on the west coast.

Sights

★Stromboli Crater VOLCANO
For nature lovers, climbing Stromboli is one of Sicily's not-to-be-missed experiences. Since 2005 access has been strictly regulated: you can walk freely to 400m, but need a guide to continue any higher. Organised treks depart daily (between 3.30pm and 6pm, depending on the season), timed to reach the summit (924m) at sunset and to allow 45 minutes to observe the crater's fireworks.

The climb itself takes 2½ to three hours, while the descent back to Piazza San Vincenzo is shorter (1½ to two hours). All told, it's a demanding five- to six-hour trek up to the top and back; you'll need to have proper walking shoes, a backpack that allows free movement of both arms, clothing for cold and wet weather, a change of T-shirt, a handkerchief to protect against dust (wear glasses not contact lenses), a torch (flashlight), 1L to 2L of water and some food. If you haven't got any of these, Totem Trekking (p150) hires out all the necessary equipment, including

Stromboli

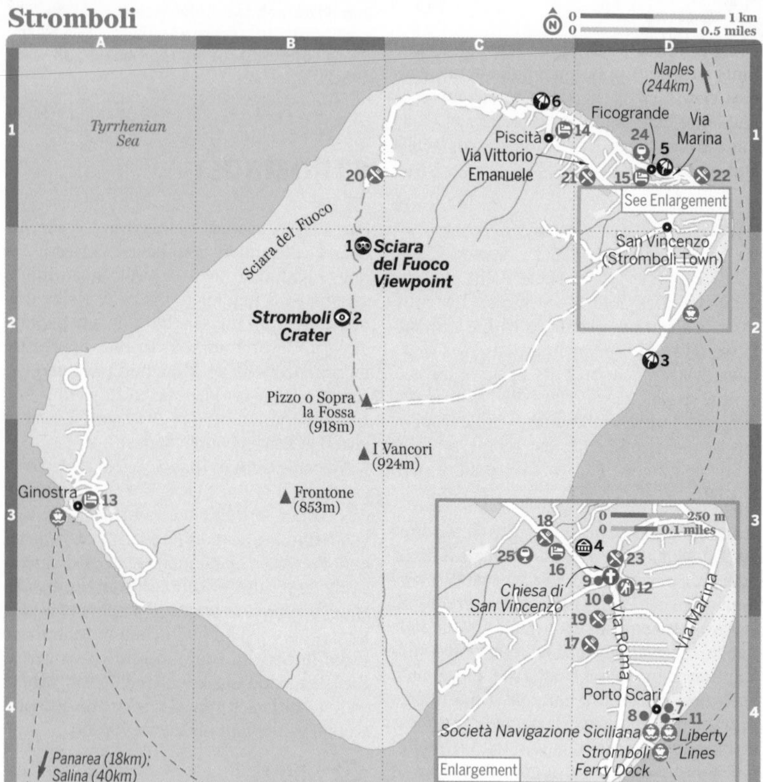

Stromboli

Top Sights

1 Sciara del Fuoco Viewpoint B2
2 Stromboli Crater B2

Sights

3 Forgia Vecchia D2
4 Red House D3
5 Spiaggia di Ficogrande D1
6 Spiaggie di Piscità C1

Activities, Courses & Tours

7 Antonio Caccetta D4
8 Il Vulcano a Piedi D4
La Sirenetta Diving .... (see 15)
9 Magmatrek D3
10 Quota 900 .... D3
11 Società Navigazione Pippo D4
Stromboli Adventures .... (see 9)
12 Totem Trekking D3

Sleeping

13 B&B Luna Rossa A3
14 Casa del Sole C1
15 La Sirenetta Park Hotel D1
16 Pensione Aquilone C3

Eating

17 Ai Gechi D4
18 La Bottega del Marano C3
19 Lapillo Gelato D4
20 L'Osservatorio B1
21 Pardès D1
22 Punta Lena D1
23 Ritrovo Ingrid D3

Drinking & Nightlife

24 La Tartana Club D1
25 Locanda del Barbablù C3

boots (€6), backpacks (€5), hiking poles (€4), torches (€3) and windbreakers (€5).

★**Sciara del Fuoco Viewpoint** VIEWPOINT
(Path of Fire) An alternative to scaling Stromboli's summit is the hour-long climb to this viewpoint (400m, no guide required), which directly overlooks the Sciara del Fuoco (the blackened laval scar running down Stromboli's northern flank) and offers fabulous if more distant views of the crater's explosions. Bring plenty of water, and a torch if walking at night. The trail (initially a switchbacking road) starts in Piscità, 2km west of Stromboli's port; halfway up, you can stop for pizza at L'Osservatorio (p150).

During active periods, explosions occur every 20 minutes or so and are preceded by a loud belly-roar as gases force hot magma into the air. After particularly strong eruptions, you can watch as red-hot rocks tumble down the seemingly endless slope, creating visible splashes as they plop into the sea. For best viewing, come on a still night, when the livid red Sciara and exploding cone are dramatically visible.

Arriving here around sunset will allow you to hike one direction in daylight, then stop for dinner and more volcano-gawking at L'Osservatorio on the way back down. Making the trek just before dawn is also a memorable experience, as you'll likely have the whole mountain to yourself. From Piscità it takes about 30 minutes to get to L'Osservatorio, and another half hour to reach the viewpoint. Be prepared – the climb gets steep towards the end.

Red House HISTORIC BUILDING
(Via Vittorio Emanuele 22) This rusty-red house is where Ingrid Bergman and Roberto Rossellini lived together while filming *Stromboli, Terra di Dio* in 1949. Their liaison provoked a scandal in the film world, as both were married to other people at the time. Descending from San Vincenzo church on Stromboli's main square, look for a plaque marking the house on the right-hand side.

You can't actually go inside, but it's interesting to see the scene of such a famous romance.

Spiaggia di Ficogrande BEACH
Stromboli's black sandy beaches are the best in the Aeolian archipelago. The most accessible and popular swimming and sunbathing is at Ficogrande, a strip of rocks and black volcanic sand about a 10-minute walk northwest of the hydrofoil dock.

Forgia Vecchia BEACH
About 300m south of the port, Forgia Vecchia, is a long stretch of black pebbles curving around a tranquil bay and backed by the volcano's green slopes.

Spiaggie di Piscità BEACH
Backed by rugged bluffs, this moderate-sized stretch of black-sand beach lies 2km west of Stromboli's port, at the edge of the small whitewashed settlement of Piscità.

Chiesa di San Vincenzo CHURCH
(Piazza San Vincenzo) A major Stromboli landmark, San Vincenzo is the island's main church. In mid- to late afternoon, the square out front becomes a gathering point for trekkers preparing to climb the volcano.

Activities

To climb to the top of Stromboli you'll need to go on an organised trek. Maximum group size is 20 people, and although there are usually multiple groups on the mountain, spaces can still fill up. To avoid disappointment, book early – if possible a week or more before you want to climb. The standard fee for group climbs is €28 per person.

Magmatrek HIKING
(☎090 986 57 68; www.magmatrek.it; Via Vittorio Emanuele) Has experienced, multilingual (English-, German- and French-speaking) guides that lead daily treks up the volcano (maximum group size of 20 people). It can also put together tailor-made treks for individuals or groups.

Quota 900 HIKING
(☎090 98 62 51; www.quota900stromboli.it; Via Roma) Between the port and the church, this relative newcomer leads excursions to Stromboli's craters and rents out equipment.

Stromboli Adventures HIKING
(☎090 98 62 64; www.stromboliadventures.it; Via Vittorio Emanuele) Staffed by year-round residents, this well-established smaller agency to the right of the church leads daily treks up to Stromboli's craters.

Il Vulcano a Piedi HIKING
(☎090 98 61 44, 349 2126428; www.ilvulcanoapiedi.it; Via Pizzillo) A reputable outfit led by Stromboli native Nino Zerilli, a certified Alpine

guide with over 25 years of experience leading tours on Stromboli.

Totem Trekking HIKING
(☎090 986 57 52; www.totemtrekkingstromboli.com; Piazza San Vincenzo 4; ⏰9.30am-1pm & 3.30-7pm) Totem Trekking hires out hiking equipment, including boots (€6), backpacks (€5), hiking poles (€4), torches (€3), fleece jackets (€5) and windbreakers (€5).

La Sirenetta Diving DIVING
(☎338 8919675, 347 5961499; www.lasirenettadiving.it; Via Mons di Mattina 33; ⏰late May–mid-Sep) Offers diving courses and accompanied dives, opposite the beach at La Sirenetta Park Hotel.

Tours

One of the most popular ways of viewing Stromboli's nocturnal fireworks is to take a boat tour of the island. **Società Navigazione Pippo** (☎090 98 61 35, 338 9857883; pipponav.stromboli@libero.it; Porto Scari) and **Antonio Caccetta** (☎090 98 60 23; Vico Salina 10) are among the numerous outfits running boat tours out of Porto Scari. The two most popular itineraries are a three-hour round-the-island daytime cruise (€25), including an hour of free time to explore Ginostra and a swimming break at Strombolicchio (the rock islet jutting out of the water off the north coast), and a 1½-hour sunset excursion (€20) to watch the Sciara del Fuoco explosions from the sea.

Eating

Eating out in Stromboli can be pricey, as many food items have to be shipped in. Seafood is ubiquitous, while pizza provides a more wallet-friendly alternative.

Lapillo Gelato GELATERIA €
(Via Roma; gelato from €2.50; ⏰10am-1pm & 3.30pm-midnight Jun–mid-Sep, 3.30-9pm mid-Sep–May) On the main street between the port and the church, this artisanal gelateria is a great place to fuel up with homemade ice cream before making the big climb. The pistachio flavour is pure creamy bliss.

La Bottega del Marano DELI €
(Via Vittorio Emanuele; snacks from €2; ⏰8.30am-1pm & 4.30-8pm Mon-Sat) The perfect source for volcano-climbing provisions or a self-catering lunch, this reasonably priced neighbourhood grocery – at a bend in the road five minutes west of the trekking agency offices – has a well-stocked deli case full of meats, cheeses, olives, artichokes and sun-dried tomatoes, plus shelves full of wine and awesomely tasty fresh-baked focaccias.

L'Osservatorio PIZZA €
(☎090 945 08 56, 338 1097830; pizzas €7-12; ⏰10.30am-late) Sure, you could eat a pizza in town, but come on – you're on Stromboli! Make the 45-minute, 2km uphill trek west of town to this pizzeria and you'll be rewarded with exceptional volcano views from an expansive panoramic terrace, best after sundown.

Ritrovo Ingrid CAFE, PIZZERIA €
(☎090 98 63 85; Piazza San Vincenzo; pizza from €7; ⏰8am-3am Jul & Aug, to 1am Sep-Jun) A Stromboli institution, the panoramic terrace of this all-purpose cafe-gelateria-pizzeria is busy throughout the day as islanders come for their morning cappuccino, tourists pop in for an ice cream and trekkers compare notes over an evening pizza.

★**Punta Lena** SICILIAN €€
(☎090 98 62 04; Via Marina 8; meals €35-40; ⏰12.15-2.30pm & 7-10.30pm early May–mid-Oct) For a romantic outing, head to this family-run waterfront restaurant with cheerful blue decor, fresh flowers, lovely sea views and the soothing sound of waves lapping in the background. The food is as good as you'll get anywhere on the island, with signature dishes including fresh seafood and *spaghetti alla stromboliana* (with wild fennel, cherry tomatoes and breadcrumbs).

Pardès SICILIAN €€
(☎338 671 43 83; Via Vittorio Emanuele 81; meals €25-35; ⏰noon-2.30pm & 6-10pm Easter-Oct; 📶) Run by friendly father-daughter team Sergio and Vanina, this wine bar-cafe dishes up small but delicious serves of homemade soup, pasta and local fish, accompanied by veggies from the adjacent garden. There's pleasant seating on a back terrace with direct views up to the volcano, plus Sicilian wines, and beer on tap.

Ai Gechi SEAFOOD €€
(☎338 3577559; www.facebook.com/trattoriagechistromboli; Vico Salina 12, Porto Scari; meals €30-35; ⏰noon-3pm & 7-11pm Easter–mid-Oct) Follow the trail of painted lizards to this great hideaway, down an alley off Via Roma. Flanked by a towering cactus, the shaded verandah of a whitewashed Aeolian house serves as the dining area, eclectically decorated with ship lamps and a whale skeleton

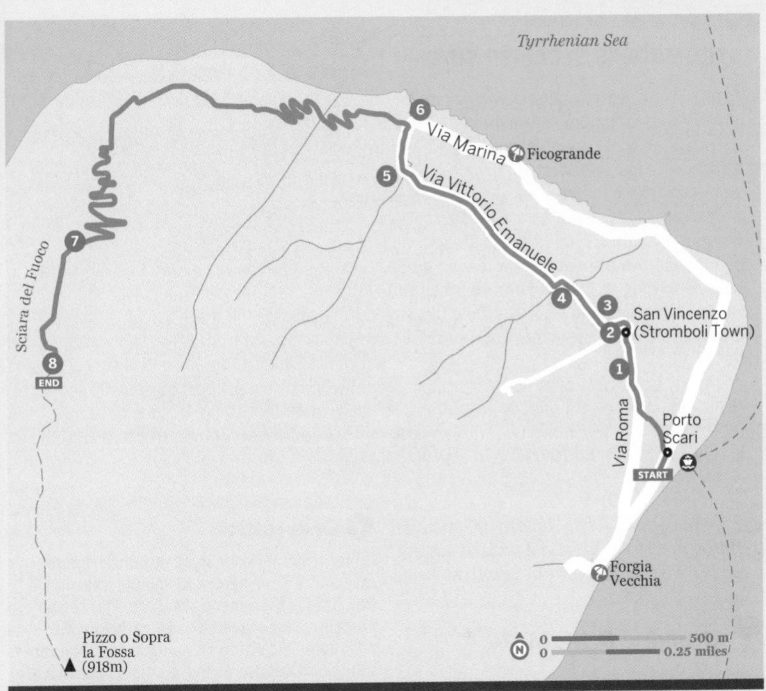

Walking Tour
Stromboli & the Sciara del Fuoco

START STROMBOLI HYDROFOIL PORT
END SCIARA DEL FUOCO
LENGTH 4KM; TWO HOURS ONE WAY

Offering an alternative to the classic guided hike up to Stromboli's craters, this self-guided jaunt takes you through the whitewashed streets of Stromboli town before climbing halfway up the mountain for dramatic perspectives on the volcano's eruptions from below. You're allowed to hike this trail unaccompanied, as the viewpoint sits below the 400m 'restricted' level.

Leave the port two to three hours before sundown. This allows you to arrive at the viewpoint around sunset to watch the volcano's fireworks juxtaposed against the darkening sky. Make sure to bring a torch (flashlight); it's absolutely essential for the return hike.

From the port, walk up Via Roma toward Stromboli's main square, stopping in for homemade ice cream at 1 **Lapillo Gelato** (p150). After passing Stromboli's main church, 2 **Chiesa di San Vincenzo** (p149), continue downhill to the 3 **Red House** (p149), site of Ingrid Bergman and Roberto Rossellini's torrid love affair while filming *Stromboli: Terra di Dio* in 1949. A few hundred metres further on, as the main road jogs briefly left, look for 4 **La Bottega del Marano** (p150), a neighbourhood grocery with a great deli where you can pick up trail snacks and water.

About 2km from your starting point, pass 5 **Chiesa di Piscità** on your left. Here you can take an optional five-minute detour down to the black sand beach of 6 **Piscità** (p149), tucked into a rocky cove, before retracing your steps and returning along the main road to a left-hand turnoff with signs for L'Osservatorio. Start climbing gradually, paralleling the sea at first, then following a series of switchbacks to 7 **L'Osservatorio** (p150) pizzeria.

From the pizzeria to the viewpoint the climb is much steeper. Arriving at the 8 **Sciara del Fuoco viewpoint** (p149), prepare to be amazed! The sight of the volcano's explosive eruptions, followed by cascades of red-hot rock crashing down the lava-blackened mountainside into the sea is stunning. Linger past nightfall, as the volcano's orange glow becomes more dramatic with the waning light.

OFF THE BEATEN TRACK

STROMBOLI'S SLEEPIER SIDE

To see Stromboli's less touristy side, hop off the ferry at **Ginostra**, a tiny village on the island's western shore. There are only 30 year-round residents here, but you can sleep overnight at B&B Luna Rossa (p253) or ask around about the several other local *affittacamere* (rental rooms) in town. Foodwise, Ginostra has a couple of small grocery stores and three restaurants serving local seafood.

It's possible to climb from Ginostra to Stromboli's crater, but this is a physically demanding approach due to the steeper ascent and constant exposure to sunlight coming in from the west. Experienced guide Mario Pruiti, who lives in Ginostra, arranges trips according to demand and weather conditions; contact Magmatrek (p149) in Stromboli to see if he's got anything planned during your visit. If there's a big enough group, prices per person are comparable to the classic ascent from Stromboli (€28 to €35).

Liberty Lines runs occasional hydrofoils from Stromboli's main port to Ginostra (€9.10, 10 minutes, three daily in summer, one daily in winter). Hydrofoils from Lipari (€19.10, 50 minutes to two hours), Santa Marina Salina (€17.80, 50 minutes to 1½ hours) and Panarea (€11.90, 25 minutes) also stop here.

the owner discovered nearby. Gorgeous traditional seafood is served with a slightly modern twist, backed by an excellent local wine list.

Drinking & Nightlife

Locanda del Barbablù BAR
(☎090 98 61 18; www.barbablu.it; Via Vittorio Emanuele 17; ⏰7-11pm Easter-Oct) This dusky-pink Aeolian inn houses the island's classiest drinking spot, with the same owner and staff since 1985. It's a fashionable port of call for the August aperitif set, with a lively bar, rustic-chic decor and an excellent list of Sicilian wines.

La Tartana Club BAR
(☎090 98 60 25; Via Marina, Ficogrande; ⏰9.30am-2am late Jun-early Sep) Rub elbows with the likes of Dolce and Gabbana and the president of Italy at this chic resto-bar, a long-standing favourite of Stromboli's beautiful people. La Tartana hits its stride every evening when a refined crowd gathers for aperitifs at the piano bar and couples romance each other over cocktails at candlelit tables on the seafront terrace.

Regulars also flock here to read the morning paper over coffee at breakfast time, graze at the casual lunch buffet or indulge in La Tartana's trademark dessert, *coppa Stromboli*, a volcano-shaped mass of chocolate, sweet cream and hazelnut ice cream studded with candied cherries and doused in a lava flow of strawberry syrup.

Orientation

Boats arrive at Porto Scari, downhill from the main town. From here, a 10-minute walk up Via Roma leads to the central square, Piazza San Vincenzo, where guided hikes gather in late afternoon. Via Vittorio Emanuele continues another 2km westwards to the smaller community of Piscità. Note that there is no street lighting on Stromboli except in a couple of main streets and on Piazza San Vincenzo, so bring a torch (flashlight).

Information

Emergency Doctor (☎090 98 60 97; Via Vittorio Emanuele; ⏰24hr)

Police Station (☎090 98 60 21; Via Picone) On the left as you walk up Via Picone toward Via Roma.

Getting There & Around

Stromboli is the easternmost of the Aeolians, meaning that ferry and hydrofoil services are less frequent than to islands in the centre of the archipelago, and stormy weather is more likely to disrupt service. If you're only coming here to climb the volcano, note that many private boat operators in Lipari offer package deals including round-trip transport plus a guided excursion to the craters.

There are no cars on Stromboli, just scooters, electric carts and three-wheeler vehicles known locally as *ape*. Many hotels will provide free transport to and from the dock if you call ahead. Walking on the island is easy and pleasant.

BOAT

Liberty Lines (☎090 98 60 03; www.libertylines.it) offers daily hydrofoil service to Panarea

(€12.60, 30 minutes), Santa Marina Salina (€17.80, one to 1¼ hours), Lipari (€19.30, one to two hours) and Milazzo (€22.45, 2¼ to three hours). There are up to eight daily services in high season, but this falls to two a day in winter.

Società Navigazione Siciliana (Siremar; ☎090 98 60 16; www.siremar.it) also runs car ferries from Stromboli to Naples (from €44.50, 10 hours) and Milazzo (from €16.45, 6¾ hours), as well as to Lipari (€12.90, 3½ hours) and the other Aeolians. In bad weather the service is often disrupted or cancelled altogether, as Stromboli's dock is smaller than others on the Aeolians. Ticket offices are at the port.

The quickest way to reach Stromboli from the Italian mainland is via the summer-only hydrofoil from Naples operated by SNAV (p131; from €58, 4½ hours, late May through early September).

CAR & MOTORCYCLE

You can hire scooters from **Giovanni 'Il Catanese'** (☎090 98 63 37; Lungomare; scooter per day €20); look for him about 800m north of the hydrofoil dock (150m north of the ENEL building), on the waterfront road toward Ficogrande.

TAXI

For taxi service, in this case a golf-cart style vehicle, call **Sabbia Nera Taxi** (☎090 98 63 90).

FILICUDI

POP 235

Among the prettiest and least developed of the Aeolian Islands, Filicudi is also one of the oldest, dating back to tectonic activity 700,000 years ago. Shaped like a snail when seen from some angles, the island entices visitors with its rugged coastline lapped by crystal clear waters and pitted by deep grottoes. The island has just a few small villages.

Sights

Attractions include the dazzling **Grotta del Bue Marino** on the island's western edge, and **Scoglio della Canna** (Cane Reef), a dramatic 71m *faraglione* (rock tower) off Filicudi's northwestern shore.

Prehistoric Village ARCHAEOLOGICAL SITE

Follow the main road 10 minutes southeast of the port toward Capo Graziano, where a marked trail branches off and climbs to the lichen-covered stone foundations of 27 Bronze Age huts on a terraced hillside. Discovered in 1952, they date to 1700 BC, 300 years before Panarea's Punta Milazzese. It's an extremely evocative spot, with dramatic sea and island views and newly installed bilingual signs providing historical context.

From the village you can descend to Filicudi's only real beach, a stony affair that offers the easiest swimming on the island – if you want to take a dip elsewhere, you'll have to clamber down some jagged rocks or rent a boat.

Activities

Offshore from Capo Graziano lies the **Museo Archeologico Sottomarino** area, where the sunken wrecks of nine ancient Greek and Roman ships provide fabulous diving opportunities. The island also boasts a small network of hiking trails, including the multihour climb to **Fossa Felci** (774m) at the centre of the island.

★**Lidalina** BEACH

(☎349 3617577; www.filicudi.it/lidalina.php; ⊙9.30am-midnight Jul–mid-Sep) Run by delightful British-American couple Alina and Antonio, this dreamy spot at the far end of Pecorini Mare's waterfront rents out loungers and umbrellas so you can soak up the sun between dips all afternoon, snacking on Aeolian classics such as *caponata* and *granite* or sipping *aperitivi* at sundown; loungers cost €13, including transfer from Filicudi's hydrofoil dock.

Zucco Grande HIKING

A beautiful 60- to 90-minute uphill hike from the port leads to Zucco Grande, a village on Filicudi's northeast flank that's been largely abandoned, though a few enterprising villagers have begun renovating some of the ruined homes. The trail winds along flower-covered hillsides high above the sea, with spectacular views back to Capo Graziano and the port.

I Delfini OUTDOORS

(☎090 988 90 77, 340 1484645; www.idelfinifilicudi.com; Pecorini) At this all-purpose agency, Nino Terrano organises dives, rents out diving equipment and scooters, and offers boat trips around the island, pointing out local attractions along the way. He can usually be found at Pecorini's small marina.

Apogon Diving Center DIVING

(☎347 3307185; www.apogon.it; Hotel Phenicusa, Filicudi Porto; dives from €35) Based at Hotel Phenicusa near the hydrofoil dock, this local dive centre provides everything you need to explore Filicudi's watery depths.

Eating

Most accommodations have their own restaurants serving fresh seafood. There are also a couple of low-key eateries down by the port.

★Ristorante La Canna SEAFOOD €€
(☎090 988 99 56, 336 926560; www.lacannahotel.it; meals €25-27; ⌚1-2.30pm & 8-10pm) Delicious traditional Sicilian seafood is accompanied by fresh produce from the surrounding gardens at this hillside restaurant, adjacent to the hotel of the same name. It's up a steep set of steps from the harbour. Non-hotel guests should reserve ahead.

La Sirena Restaurant SEAFOOD €€
(☎090 988 99 97; www.pensionelasirena.it; meals €30-45; ⌚12.30-2.30pm & 7.30-10pm late Apr-Sep) Nothing beats dining on La Sirena's pretty tiled terrace in tiny seaside Pecorini Mare. Pull up a straw-seated chair at a little wooden table, admire the front-row view of colourful boats, rocky beach and sparkling Mediterranean and feast on fresh local seafood preceded by appetisers such as tuna and neonata fritters or *carbonara di pesce* (spaghetti with fish-based carbonara sauce).

Getting There & Away

Liberty Lines (☎0923 87 38 13; www.libertylines.it) runs hydrofoils from Filicudi to Alicudi (€11.90, 25 minutes), Rinella (Salina; €11.30, 25 minutes), Santa Marina Salina (€13.60, 40 minutes) and Lipari (€16.20, 1¼ hours). Service is considerably less frequent than elsewhere in the archipelago. NGI (www.ngi-spa.it) and Società Navigazione Siciliana (www.siremar.it) also run occasional car ferries to/from Filicudi.

ALICUDI

POP 105

If your goal is to really get away from it all, Alicudi just might be your dream destination. As isolated a place as you'll find in the entire Mediterranean basin, its main settlement has minimal facilities and no roads. Transportation here means boats and mules – you'll see the latter hauling goods up and down the steep stone steps from the port the minute you disembark.

Outside summer season, Alicudi is the kind of place where you have to ask around for rooms, and where the evening's chief entertainment may be watching fishermen unload and clean fish. By day it offers prime opportunities for off-the-beaten-track hiking or peaceful sunbathing – the best spots are south of the port, where you'll have to clamber over boulders to reach the sea. The waters are crystal clear and there's nothing to disturb you save the occasional hum of a fishing boat.

Activities

Filo dell'Arpa HIKING
A two-hour trek up a relentlessly steep but pretty series of stone staircases leads to Alicudi's central peak (675m); simply follow the blue arrows painted on the walls. A pretty church, **Chiesa di San Bartolo**, marks the hike's midpoint. At the T-intersection up top where the trail dead ends at a stone wall, turn left to circle the crater of the extinct volcano or right to continue on the main trail to the dramatic cliffs at Alicudi's western edge.

Near the summit you'll also find the **Timpone delle Femmine**, huge fissures where women are said to have taken refuge during pirate raids.

Make sure you wear sturdy shoes and bring plenty of water as there is virtually no shade along the way.

Eating

There's are a couple of bars down by the port, supplemented by Hotel Ericusa's restaurant during its short opening season. The rest of the year, accommodations can arrange meals with local fishing families; ask when booking your room.

Silvio & Gabriella Taranto SEAFOOD €
(☎090 988 99 22; meals €20) Numbering among Alicudi's few year-round residents are this local fisherman and his wife, who can arrange simple but tasty home-cooked meals any time of year. Call at least a day ahead to reserve. They're just a block south and a block uphill from the boat dock, next door to Marcella & Isabella's *affittacamere* (rental rooms).

Getting There & Away

Liberty Lines (☎0923 87 38 13; www.libertylines.it) runs two to four daily hydrofoils from Alicudi to Filicudi (€11.90, 25 minutes), Rinella (Salina; €16.20, 55 minutes), Santa Marina Salina (€18.30, 1¼ hours) and Lipari (€20.05, 1¾ hours).

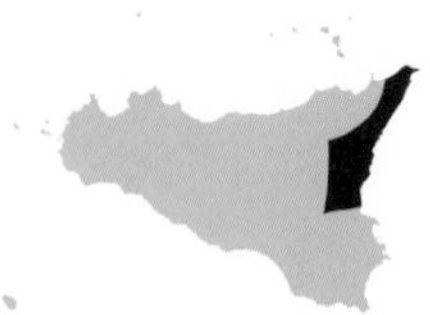

Ionian Coast

Includes ➡

Best Places to Eat

- Il Barcaiolo (p164)
- Osteria Nero D'Avola (p164)
- Mè Cumpari Turiddu (p174)
- Pescheria Fratelli Vittorio (p174)
- Shalai (p256)

Best Places to Sleep

- B&B Crociferi (p255)
- B&B Habitat (p255)
- Hotel Villa Belvedere (p254)
- Casa Turchetti (p254)
- Shalai (p256)

Why Go?

The Ionian Coast is studded with enough Sicilian icons to fill a souvenir tea towel. It's here that you'll find the skinny Strait of Messina, mighty Mt Etna and the world's most spectacularly located ancient Greek theatre. Catania is the region's centre, a shabby, swinging city packed with students, bars and nightlife. Its black-and-white baroque is World Heritage–listed, while its hyperactive fish market is one of Sicily's most appetising sights. Halfway up a rocky mountainside, regal Taormina is sophisticated and exclusive, a favourite of holidaying VIPs and day-tripping tourists. Brooding menacingly on the city's doorstep, Mt Etna offers unforgettable hiking, both to the summit craters and around the woods that carpet its lower slopes. Etna is also a wine area, dotted with vines and celebrated wineries. With a car and a little planning, the mountain sets a stunning scene for hunting out the perfect vintage.

Road Distances (km)

	Acireale	Catania	Messina	Nicolosi
Catania	15			
Messina	85	95		
Nicolosi	20	15	100	
Taormina	40	50	50	60

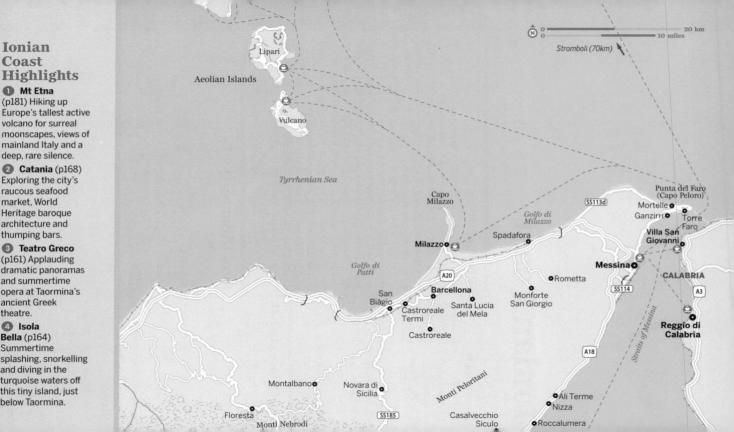

Ionian Coast Highlights

1 Mt Etna (p181) Hiking up Europe's tallest active volcano for surreal moonscapes, views of mainland Italy and a deep, rare silence.

2 Catania (p168) Exploring the city's raucous seafood market, World Heritage baroque architecture and thumping bars.

3 Teatro Greco (p161) Applauding dramatic panoramas and summertime opera at Taormina's ancient Greek theatre.

4 Isola Bella (p164) Summertime splashing, snorkelling and diving in the turquoise waters off this tiny island, just below Taormina.

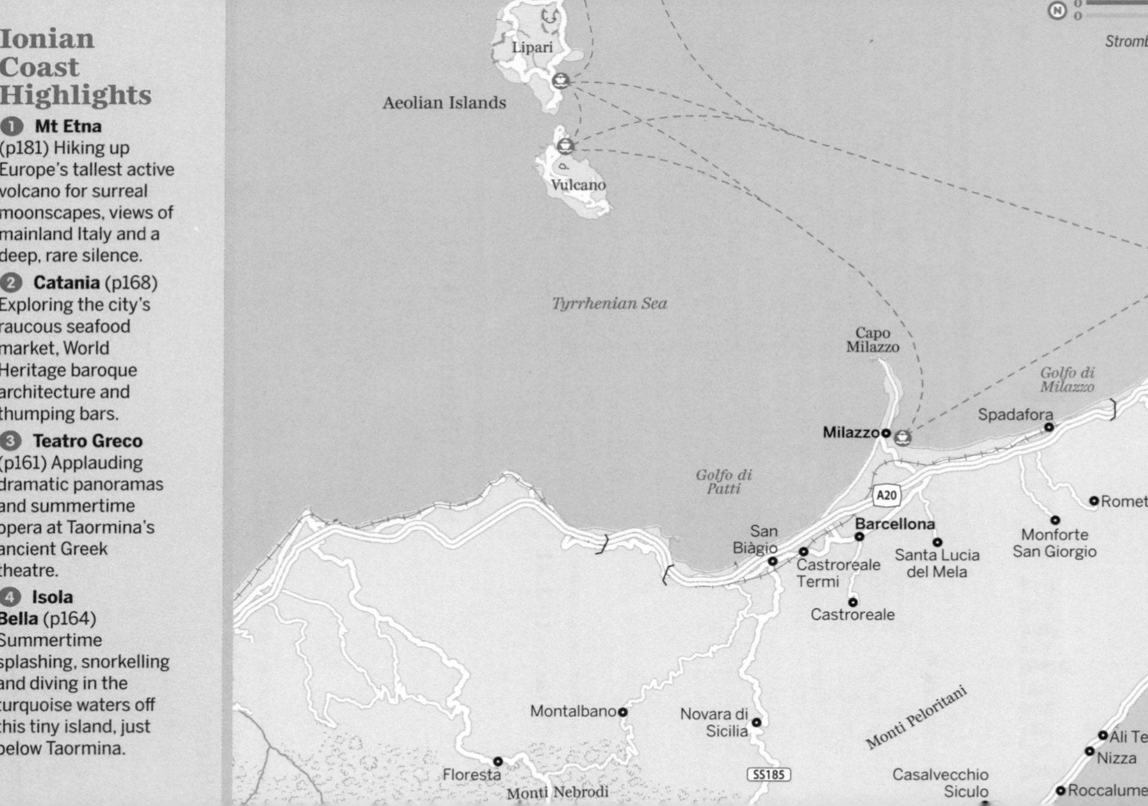

5 Planeta Feudo di Mezzo (p182) Sampling extraordinary *vino* at one of Etna's most revered wineries, just outside Passopisciaro.

6 Trattoria La Grotta (p178) Lazy seaside feasting at a much-loved trattoria, set snugly in the tiny coastal village of Santa Maria la Scala.

MESSINA

090 / POP 240,215

Just a few kilometres from the Italian mainland, Messina sits on a curved harbour at the northernmost point of Sicily's Ionian Coast. For centuries it has been a major transport hub and today it's an important gateway to and from the island.

First impressions aren't especially flattering. But look beyond the traffic, graffiti and vacant storefronts and you'll find a city of wide boulevards and elegant turn-of-the-

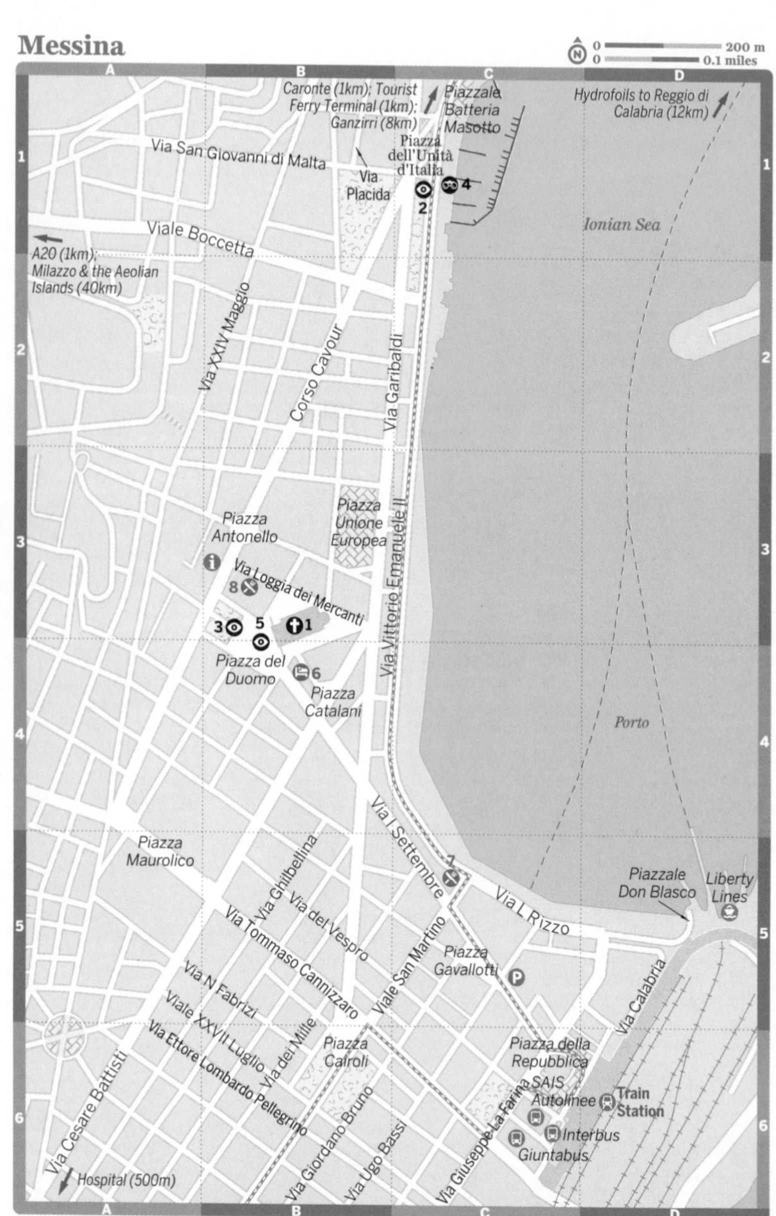

century buildings. Messina is home to one of Sicily's finest cathedrals, an engaging art museum and local swordfish celebrated by gourmets across the island. Historical monuments are thin on the ground, however, the result of a devastating earthquake in 1908 and a mass bombing in WWII.

Sights

Duomo CATHEDRAL

(Piazza del Duomo; cathedral 7am-12.30pm & 3.30-7.30pm Mon-Sat, 8am-1pm & 3.30-7.30pm Sun, cathedral museum 10.30am-1pm Mon-Sat) Messina's one great sight is the Norman Duomo (or at least a faithful replica of it). One of Sicily's finest cathedrals, its treasures include an impressive carved altar and a grand inlaid organ, the second largest in Italy. Originally built in the 12th century and accidentally burnt to the ground in 1254, the cathedral was destroyed again in the earthquakes of 1783 and 1908, as well as by an incendiary WWII bomb in 1943.

Very little remains of the original structure, except for the striped marble inlay, the tracery of the facade and the arresting Catalan Gothic portal. Treasures such as the famous Manta d'Oro (Golden Mantle), used to 'cloak' holy pictures during religious celebrations, are kept in the Museo della Cattedrale, accessed from inside the cathedral.

Piazza Del Duomo SQUARE

Piazza del Duomo is home to Messina's cathedral and its curious *campanile* (bell tower). Soaring 60m into the sky, the tower incorporates an astronomical clock, said to be the world's largest. Built in Strasbourg in 1733, it strikes at noon, setting in motion a procession of bronze automata that sets off a comical roaring lion and crowing cockerel. Facing the tower is the marble **Fontana di Orione** (1553). Created by Florentine sculptor Giovanni Angelo Montorsoli (pupil to Michelangelo), it commemorates Orion, the mythical founder of Messina.

Nearby on Piazza Catalani, the 12th-century Chiesa della Santissima Annunziata dei Catalani is a fine example of Arab-Norman construction.

Museo Regionale MUSEUM

(090 36 12 92; Viale della Libertà 465; adult/reduced €8/4; 9am-7pm Mon-Sat, to 1pm Sun) Set for expansion in late 2016, Museo Regionale houses a considerable art collection. Top billing goes to the *San Gregorio* (St Gregory) polyptych by local boy Antonello da Messina (1430–79). Although in pretty shabby condition, its five panels are wonderfully figurative. Scan the walls for da Messina's *Madonna con bambino e santi* (Virgin with Child and Saints), as well as two splendid works by Caravaggio (1571–1610): *L'Adorazione dei pastori* (Adoration of the Shepherds) and *Risurrezione di Lazzaro* (Resurrection of Lazarus).

To get here, pick up a tram at Piazza Cairoli and take a ride up the sickle-shaped harbour. Halfway along, you'll see the 16th-century **Fontana del Nettuno** (Neptune's Fountain) in the middle of two busy roads, and the colossal golden statue, the **Madonnino della Lettera**, towering over the port. Carry on to the end of the line for the Museo Regionale.

Eating

Messina is famous for its quality *pesce spada* (swordfish), which is typically served *agghiotta*, with pine nuts, sultanas, garlic, basil and tomatoes. It's also lauded for its *granita con panna* (granita served with cream), considered by many to be the best in Sicily.

Fratelli La Bufala PIZZA, ITALIAN €

(090 66 25 13; www.fratellilabufala.eu; cnr Via Vittorio Emanuele II & Viale San Martino; pizzas €4-8, dishes €7-17; 12.30-3.30pm & 7.30pm-12.30am;) Contemporary, light-filled and bustling, this successful Naples' chain churns out bubbling, doughy, Neapolitan-style pizzas to famished suits, friends and the odd nun. The menu's star-turn is buffalo mozzarella and buffalo meat, available in numerous other dishes, from antipasto platters and pasta dishes to grilled meats. Beyond these are fresh, satisfying salads and a decent number of flesh-free options.

Messina

Sights

1 Duomo....B3
2 Fontana del Nettuno....C1
3 Fontana di Orione....B3
4 Madonna della Lettera....C1
5 Piazza Del Duomo....B4

Sleeping

6 B&B del Duomo....B4

Eating

7 Fratelli La Bufala....C5
8 Osteria Del Campanile....B3

DON'T MISS

LOCAL SPECIALITIES

Swordfish (Messina) You'll find *pesce spada* (swordfish) on menus across Sicily, but the best are caught in the Strait of Messina between May and July.

Pasta alla Norma (Catania) Named after a Bellini opera, this is a rich, classic Catania dish of fried aubergine (eggplant), tomato and salted ricotta.

Wine (Mt Etna) Grapes grown on Etna go into Etna DOC, one of Sicily's best-known wines.

Honey (Zafferana Etnea) This small town on Etna's eastern slopes is celebrated for its honey, made from a range of local flowers.

Mussels (Ganzirri) Diners head up here from Messina to dine on *cozze* (mussels) cultivated in a salt lake.

Osteria Del Campanile SICILIAN €€
(☎ 090 71 14 18; www.osteriadelcampanile.com; Via Loggia dei Mercanti 9; meals €25; ⌚noon-3pm & 7pm-midnight Tue-Sun) With its warm wooden interior and prime location – just behind the Duomo – this cosy hostelry is a good bet for classic coastal cuisine. The menu features all the usual suspects – pasta with seafood, grilled meat and fish.

ℹ Information

Hospital (Ospedale Piemonte; ☎ 090 22 21; Viale Europa 45) Has a casualty department.

Police Station (☎ 090 36 61 11; Via Placida 2) Messina's main police station.

Tourist Office (☎ 090 67 29 44; www.comune.messina.it/turismo; Corso Cavour; ⌚8am-5.30pm Mon-Fri, usually also 8am-5.30pm Sat & 8am-1pm Sun summer) Friendly English-speaking staff with good information about Messina. The office is located on Via Cavour, which borders Piazza del Duomo.

ℹ Getting There & Away

BOAT

Messina is the main point of arrival for ferries and hydrofoils from the Italian mainland. Detailed timetable information is available online at www.trasportisullostretto.it.

Caronte & Tourist (☎ 090 36 46 01, 800 627414; www.carontetourist.it) Runs frequent car ferries to/from Villa San Giovanni (passenger/car €2.50/37, 25 minutes). From Tuesday to Sunday it also runs one daily service to/from Salerno (passenger/car €34/30, nine hours). Car ferries run to/from a ferry terminal around 1km north of Piazza dell'Unità d'Italia.

Liberty Lines (☎ 0923 87 38 13; www.libertylines.it; Via Vittorio Emanuele II) Runs hydrofoils to/from Reggio Calabria (passenger €3.50, 30 minutes, 16 daily Monday to Friday, six daily Saturday and Sunday). Services leave from the dock just to the north of Messina's train station.

BUS

All long-distance bus companies run services from Piazza della Repubblica, right outside the train station.

Giuntabus (☎ 090 67 57 49; www.giuntabus.com; Piazza della Repubblica) Runs a service to Milazzo (€4, 50 minutes, 15 daily Monday to Saturday, three Sunday) for connections to the Aeolian Islands.

Interbus (☎ 090 66 17 54; www.interbus.it; Piazza della Repubblica 16) Runs to Taormina (€4.30, 1½ to 1¾ hours, three to five daily Monday to Friday, four Saturday, one Sunday).

SAIS Autolinee (☎ 090 77 19 14, 800 211020; www.saisautolinee.it; Piazza della Repubblica 11) Serves Palermo (€13, 2¾ hours, at least four daily Monday to Friday, three Saturday and Sunday), Catania (€8.40, 1½ hours, 23 daily Monday to Friday, 13 Saturday, nine Sunday) and Catania airport (€9.30, two hours, 15 Monday to Friday, nine Saturday, eight Sunday).

CAR & MOTORCYCLE

For Palermo, Milazzo (connections to the Aeolian Islands), Taormina, Catania and Syracuse, turn right from the docks and follow Via Vittorio Emanuele II along the waterfront up to Piazza dell'Unità d'Italia. Here, double back on Corso Cavour and turn right into Viale Boccetta, following the green A20 autostrada (motorway) signs.

Car hire is available at **Hertz** (☎ 090 34 44 24; www.hertz.it; Via Garibaldi 128) and **Sicilcar** (☎ 339 4484484, 090 4 69 42; www.sicilcar.net; Via Garibaldi 187).

TRAIN

As a rule buses are a better bet than trains, particularly to Milazzo and Taormina, but there are several daily trains to Catania (from €7.60, 1½ to two hours), Syracuse (from €10.50, 2½ to three hours) and Palermo (€12.80, three to 4½ hours).

ℹ Getting Around

CAR & MOTORCYCLE

If you have no luck parking on the street (blue lines denote pay-and-display meter parking), there's a useful multistorey car park, **Parcheg-**

gio Cavallotti (Via I Settembre; 1/3/24hr €1/2.50/6; ⏲5am-11.30pm Mon-Sat), near Piazza Cairoli. You will need to purchase a parking ticket from the ground-floor ticket office once you have parked your car. Scratch the time of arrival on the ticket and display it on your dashboard.

TRAM

An electric tram runs from Piazza Cairoli via the train station up to the Museo Regionale. Buy tickets (€1.70 return) from *tabacchi* (tobacco shops).

AROUND MESSINA

Punta del Faro

From Messina the coast curves around to Sicily's most northeasterly point, **Punta del Faro** (also called Capo Peloro), just 3km across the water from the Italian mainland. South of the cape is the lakeside town of **Ganzirri**, a popular summer hang-out and pretty setting for a fish dinner. On the other side of the cape, **Mortelle** is the area's most popular summer resort, where the Messinese go to sunbathe and hang out.

Eating

Mussels *(cozze)* are the local speciality on Punta del Faro and the molluscs are cultivated in the peninsula's salty lake waters. The area is also a good spot to tuck into fresh *vongole* (clams), *pesce spada* (swordfish) and *stoccafisso* (stockfish).

La Napoletana SEAFOOD **€€**
(☎090 39 10 32; Via Lago Grande 29; meals €30-35; ⏲Thu-Tue) A family-run restaurant housed in a neoclassical villa, La Napoletana is a good place to try the speciality of Punta del Faro – locally cultivated mussels. The restaurant specialises in local seafood, so, mussels aside, expect plenty of clams, swordfish and stockfish.

Getting There & Away

The easiest way to explore Punta del Faro is by car. From Messina, take the SP43, a picturesque coastal road that leads to Ganzirri and, beyond it, Mortelle. From Ganzirri, local streets lead to the adjacent neighbourhood of Torre Faro and the very tip of the peninsula.

TAORMINA

☎0942 / POP 11,085 / ELEV 204M

Spectacularly perched on the side of a mountain, Taormina is one of Sicily's most popular summer destinations, a chi-chi resort town popular with holidaying high-rollers and those wanting a taste of Sicilian dolce vita.

Granted it's unashamedly touristy and expensive, but the town merits a couple of days for its stunning ancient theatre, people watching and breathtaking vistas.

Founded in the 4th century BC, Taormina enjoyed great prosperity under the Greek ruler Gelon II and later under the Romans, but fell into quiet obscurity after being conquered by the Normans in 1087. Its reincarnation as a tourist destination dates to the 18th century, when northern Europeans discovered it on the Grand Tour. Among its fans was DH Lawrence, who lived here between 1920 and 1923.

Taormina gets extremely busy in July and August and virtually shuts down between November and Easter. Ideally, head up in April, May, September or October.

Sights

★**Teatro Greco** RUINS
(☎0942 2 32 20; Via Teatro Greco; adult/reduced €10/5; ⏲9am-1hr before sunset) Taormina's premier sight is this perfect horseshoe-shaped theatre, suspended between sea and sky, with Mt Etna looming on the southern horizon. Built in the 3rd century BC, it's the most dramatically situated Greek theatre in the world and the second largest in Sicily (after Syracuse). In summer, it's used to stage international arts and film festivals. In peak season the site is best explored early in the morning to avoid the crowds.

Villa Comunale PARK
(Parco Duchi di Cesarò; Via Bagnoli Croce; ⏲9am-midnight summer, 9am-sunset winter) To escape the crowds, wander down to these stunningly sited public gardens. Created by Englishwoman Florence Trevelyan in the late 19th century, they're a lush paradise of tropical plants and delicate flowers, punctuated by whimsical follies. You'll also find a children's play area.

Corso Umberto I AREA
Taormina's chief delight is wandering this pedestrian-friendly, boutique-lined thoroughfare. Start at the tourist office in **Palazzo Corvaja** (Largo Santa), which dates back to the 10th century before heading

Taormina

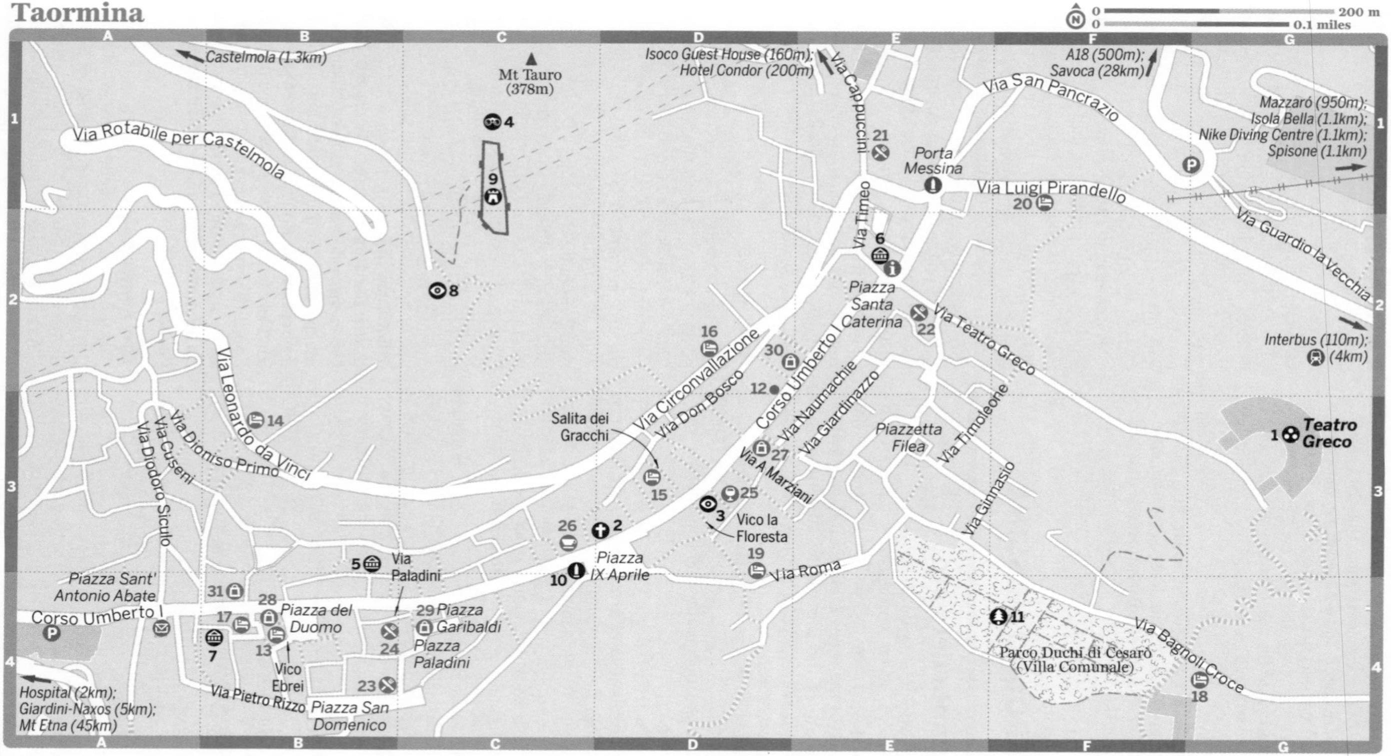

Castelmola (1.3km)
Mt Tauro (378m)
Isoco Guest House (160m);
Hotel Condor (200m)
A18 (500m);
Savoca (28km)
Mazzaró (950m);
Isola Bella (1.1km);
Nike Diving Centre (1.1km);
Spisone (1.1km)
Via Rotabile per Castelmola
Via Cappuccini
Via San Pancrazio
Porta Messina
Via Luigi Pirandello
Via Guardio la Vecchia
Via Timeo
Piazza Santa Caterina
Via Teatro Greco
Interbus (110m);
(4km)
Teatro Greco
Via Leonardo da Vinci
Via Circonvallazione
Via Don Bosco
Salita dei Gracchi
Corso Umberto I
Via Naumachie
Via Giardinazzo
Piazzetta Filea
Via Timoleone
Via Ginnasio
Via Dioniso Primo
Via Cuseni
Via Diodoro Siculo
Via A Marziani
Vico la Floresta
Piazza IX Aprile
Via Paladini
Via Roma
Piazza Sant' Antonio Abate
Corso Umberto I
Piazza del Duomo
Piazza Garibaldi
Piazza Paladini
Vico Ebrei
Via Pietro Rizzo
Piazza San Domenico
Parco Duchi di Cesarò (Villa Comunale)
Via Bagnoli Croce
Hospital (2km);
Giardini-Naxos (5km);
Mt Etna (45km)
200 m
0.1 miles

Taormina

Top Sights
1 Teatro Greco G3

Sights
2 Chiesa San Giuseppe D3
3 Corso Umberto I D3
4 Monte Tauro C1
5 Palazzo Ciampoli B3
6 Palazzo Corvaja E2
7 Palazzo Duca di Santo Stefano B4
8 Santuario Madonna della Rocca C2
9 Saracen Castle C1
10 Torre dell'Orologio C3
11 Villa Comunale F4

Activities, Courses & Tours
12 SAT D2

Sleeping
13 Al Duomo B4
14 Casa Cuseni B3
15 Casa Turchetti D3
16 Hostel Taormina D2
17 Hotel del Corso B4
18 Hotel Villa Belvedere G4
19 Hotel Villa Schuler D3
20 Villa Nettuno F1

Eating
21 L'Arco dei Cappuccini E1
22 Minotauro E2
23 Osteria Nero D'Avola B4
Osteria RossoDivino .... (see 17)
24 Tischi Toschi B4

Drinking & Nightlife
25 Morgana D3
26 Wunderbar Caffè C3

Shopping
27 Carlo Mirella Panarello D3
28 Dieffe B4
29 Kerameion C4
30 La Torinese D2
31 Pafumi B4

southwest for spectacular panoramic views from **Piazza IX Aprile**. Facing the square is the early-18th-century **Chiesa San Giuseppe** (☎0942 2 37 66; Piazza IX Aprile; ⏲usually 8.30am-8pm). Continue west through **Torre dell'Orologio**, the 12th-century clock tower, into **Piazza del Duomo**, home to an ornate baroque fountain (1635) that sports Taormina's symbol, a two-legged centaur with the bust of an angel.

You're now in the Borgo Medievale, the oldest quarter of town. On the eastern side of Piazza del Duomo is the 13th-century **cathedral**. It survived much of the Renaissance-style remodelling undertaken throughout the town by the Spanish aristocracy in the 15th century. Just north of the Corso is the 14th-century **Palazzo Ciampoli** (Salita Ciampoli 9), now the Hotel El Jebel. Just to the south (and near Porta Catania) stands the **Palazzo Duca di Santo Stefano**, a 13th-century palace once home to the De Spuches, a noble family of Spanish origin. It's now used as a functions space, but its Norman Gothic windows and Arab accents make it one of Taormina's architectural pin-ups.

Castelmola VILLAGE

For eye-popping views of the coastline and Mt Etna, head for this cute hilltop village above Taormina, crowned by a ruined castle. If you're reasonably fit, head up on foot (one hour) for a good workout and sweeping panoramas. Alternatively, take the hourly Interbus service (one way/return €1.90/3, 15 minutes). While you're up here, stop in for almond wine at **Bar Turrisi** (☎0942 2 81 81; www.barturrisi.com; Piazza Duomo, Castelmola; ⏲9am-2am Mon-Sun; 📶), a four-level bar with some rather cheeky decor.

Monte Tauro VIEWPOINT

The short 20-minute climb to the top of Monte Tauro (378m) is not exactly Himalayan, but it is steep and the final steps are quite hard work. Your reward is a breathtaking view over Taormina's rooftops, the Teatro Greco and, beyond, to the coast.

From Via Circonvallazione, a signposted path leads up past the tiny **Santuario Madonna della Rocca**. Founded by the abbot Francesco Raineri in around 1640, the church is built inside a grotto. According to legend, the Virgin Mary and baby Jesus appeared to a young shepherd who had taken refuge in the grotto during a sudden storm. The lofty panorama from the church's terrace is almost as heavenly, taking in Taormina and the deep-blue Ionian Sea beyond. Further up the mountain lie the windswept ruins of a Saracen **castello** (castle), once the site of Taormina's ancient Greek acropolis. You can't actually get to the castle – a locked gate blocks the path – but it's the views, rather than the sights, that are the real attraction.

Activities

Acquaterra ADVENTURE

(☎095 50 30 20; www.acquaterra.com) Runs kayaking, rafting and river-tubing excursions on the Alcantara river near Taormina.

BEACHES NEAR TAORMINA

The nearest beach to Taormina is **Lido Mazzarò**, accessible by **funivia** (Cable Car; Via Luigi Pirandello; ticket/day pass €3/10; ⏲ every 15min 9am-1.30am Mon, from 8am Tue-Sun summer, 7.45am-8pm Tue-Sun winter) from Via Luigi Pirandello. It's a popular pebbly beach, well serviced with umbrellas and deck chairs for hire (from about €10 per day).

To the south of Mazzarò, and an easy walk past the Sant'Andrea hotel, is **Isola Bella** (adult/reduced €4/2), a tiny island set in a stunning cove, which was once home to Florence Trevelyan; it's her house that sits in silent solitude on top of the rocky islet. There's wonderful snorkelling in the crystalline waters or you can hire a boat and pootle around the rocky bays. If you prefer your adventures underwater, **Nike Diving Centre** (☎339 1961559; www.diveniketaormina.com; Spiaggia dell'Isola Bella) offers a range of packages from its base at the northern end of the beach.

For a real sandy beach you will have to go to **Spisone**, just beneath the autostrada exit. It's about a 2km walk north from the Mazzarò cable car station.

SAT BUS TOURS

(☎0942 2 46 53; www.satexcursions.it; Corso Umberto 73) One of a number of agencies that organises day trips to Mt Etna (from €35), Syracuse (€45), Noto (€45), Palermo (€55) and Agrigento (€55).

Festivals & Events

Taormina Opera Festival MUSIC

(www.taorminafestival.org) Taormina's Greek Theatre makes an evocative setting for opera at this annual fest, running from mid-July to early September.

Taormina FilmFest FILM

(www.taorminafilmfest.it) Hollywood big shots arrive in mid-June for a week of film screenings, premieres and press conferences at the Teatro Greco.

Taormina Arte PERFORMING ARTS

(☎0942 2 11 42; www.taormina-arte.com; ⏲ Jun-Sep) This world-class festival delivers opera, dance, theatre and music concerts with an impressive cast of international names.

Eating

There's no getting around it – eating in Taormina is expensive. Prices are universally higher here than in the rest of Sicily, and service is not always what it should be. That said, there are some excellent restaurants serving quality local produce and wines, popular with locals and discerning visitors. Avoid touts and tourist menus and make reservations at the more exclusive and popular places, up to four days ahead in the summer.

Minotauro PASTRIES €

(☎0942 2 47 67; Via di Giovanni 15; pastries from €1, cannoli €2.50; ⏲9am-8.30pm, to midnight summer) Tiny Minotauro has an epic reputation for its calorific, made-from-scratch treats. Scan the counters for old-school tempters, from artful marzipan and sticky *torrone* (nougat) to *paste di mandorla* (almond biscuits) with fillings like orange or pumpkin. Top billing goes to the silky ricotta *cannoli*, filled fresh to order and pimped with pistachio, cinnamon and candied orange.

★ **Il Barcaiolo** SICILIAN €€

(☎0942 62 56 33; www.barcaiolo.altervista.org; Via Castellucci 43, Spiaggia Mazzarò; meals €33-45; ⏲1-2.30pm & 7-10.45pm May-Sep, to 10pm rest of year) You'll need to book five days ahead come summer, when every *buongustaio* (foodie) and hopeless romantic longs for a table at this fabulous trattoria. Set snugly in a boat-fringed cove at the northern end of Mazzarò beach, it's celebrated for its sublimely fresh seafood, from sweet *gamberi rossi marinati agli agrumi* (raw Mazzara shrimps served with citrus fruits) to *sarde a beccaficu* (stuffed sardines).

Leave room for the homemade *cassata* or deliciously naughty chocolate-and-orange mousse.

★ **Osteria Nero D'Avola** SICILIAN €€

(☎0942 62 88 74; www.osterianerodavola.it; Piazza San Domenico 2b; meals €32-47; ⏲12.30-3pm & 7-11pm Tue-Sun Sep-Jun, 7pm-midnight Jul & Aug) Not only does affable owner Turi Siligato fish, hunt and forage for his smart *osteria*, he'll probably greet you at your table, share anecdotes about the day's bounty and play a few tunes on the piano. Here, seasonality, local producers and passion underscore arresting dishes like the signature *cannolo di limone Interdonato* (thinly sliced Interdonato lemon with roe, tuna, tomato and chives).

An impressive wine list showcases local drops, with staff usually happy to open most bottles, even if you're only after a glass.

L'Arco dei Cappuccini SICILIAN €€
(☎0942 24 893; Via Cappuccini 5; meals €30-45; ⏰12.30-2.30pm & 5-11.30pm Thu-Tue, only dinner mid-Jul–Aug, also open Wed Aug, closed Nov–mid-Dec & early Jan–mid-Mar) If you demand your seafood ridiculously fresh, reserve a table at this superlative local favourite. The *crudo* antipasto makes for a showstopping prologue, followed by beautifully balanced dishes like *fettuccine cernia* (pasta with grouper) and an earthy *pasta con le sarde* (spaghetti with sardines, raisins, pine nuts and fennel) in which every ingredient sings. Service is kind and gracious.

Tischi Toschi SICILIAN €€
(☎339 3642088; Via Paladini 3; meals €30-45; ⏰12.30-2.30pm & 7.30-10.30pm, closed Mon lunch May-Oct, closed Mon Nov-Apr) With only a handful of tables, this family-run, Slow Food–acclaimed trattoria offers a level of creativity and attention to detail that's generally lacking in touristy Taormina. The limited menu changes regularly based on what's in season, and is filled with less-common regional specialities, from succulent stewed rabbit with olives, carrots, pine nuts and celery, to heavenly wild-fennel 'meatballs'.

Add in a charming front patio and you'll understand why booking is advisable.

Osteria RossoDivino SICILIAN €€€
(☎0942 62 86 53; www.osteriarossodivino.com; Vico Spuches 8; meals €37-55; ⏰7pm-2am Jul-Sep, noon-3pm & 7pm-midnight Wed-Mon Oct-Jun, closed Feb) With seating on an intimate, candlelit courtyard, this coveted nosh spot (book ahead!) is the passion project of siblings Jacqueline and Sara Ragusa. The day's offerings – written on a blackboard – are dictated by the season, the local fishermen's catch, and the siblings' own morning market trawl. Expect anything from heavenly anchovy tempura (the secret: mineral water in the batter) to fragrant seafood couscous.

Attention to detail extends to the wine list, a showcase for smaller local producers and natural wines.

Drinking & Nightlife

Taormina's nightlife revolves around the town's numerous bars and cafes, mostly located on or just off the main pedestrian strip of Corso Umberto I. Most venues have outdoor seating for alfresco posing.

★ **Morgana** COCKTAIL BAR
(☎0942 62 00 56; www.morganataormina.it; Scesa Morgana 4; ⏰7.30pm-late Apr-Oct, closed Tue Nov & Dec) This so-svelte cocktail-lounge sports a new look every year, with each concept inspired by Sicilian culture, artisans and landscape. It's the place to be seen, whether on the petite dance floor or among the prickly pears and orange trees in the dreamy, chi-chi courtyard. Fuelling the fun are gorgeous libations, made with local island ingredients, from wild fennel and orange to sage.

Wunderbar Caffè CAFE
(☎0942 62 50 32; www.wunderbarcaffe.it; Piazza IX Aprile 7; ⏰9am-late; 📶) A Taormina landmark since the dolce vita 1960s, this glamorous and achingly expensive cafe has served them all – Tennessee Williams, who liked to watch 'the squares go by', Greta Garbo, Richard Burton and Elizabeth Taylor. With tables spread over the vibrant piazza and jacketed waiters taking the orders, it is still very much the quintessential Taormina watering hole.

Shopping

Shopping is a popular pastime in Taormina, particularly on pedestrianised Corso Umberto I. Lining the street is a mix of high-end fashion, shoes and accessories, quality ceramic goods, lace and linen tableware, antique furniture, as well as local culinary deli treats and wine.

Dieffe FASHION & ACCESSORIES
(www.dieffetaormina.com; Corso Umberto I 226; ⏰10am-10pm summer, 10.30am-8pm rest of year) A bastion of 'Made in Italy', this easy-to-miss boutique offers sharp edits of men's threads, shoes and accessories from unique local and mainland designers. Expect anything from hand-painted leather belts from Sicilian artist Salvatore Montanucci, to handcrafted shoes from Le Marche's Galizio Torresi and beautifully detailed linen shirts from Tuscany's Osvaldo Trucchi. A must for lovers of idiosyncratic Italian style.

Kerameion CERAMICS
(☎339 2079032; www.kerameion.com; Corso Umberto I 198; ⏰9am-1pm & 2.30-8pm Mon-Sat, 9am-1pm Sun) Local artist Marco Monforte runs this shop specialising in colourful Sicilian tiles and made-to-order ceramics.

Pafumi JEWELLERY
(☎0942 5 60 66; Corso Umberto I 251; ⏰9.30am-1.30pm & 2.30-9pm) Made in Sicily and not sold anywhere off the island, the colourful

earrings, bracelets and pendants of the Isola Bella jewellery line are reason enough to browse at this shop near Porta Catania. Other Italian lines are also well represented.

Carlo Mirella Panarello CERAMICS, ACCESSORIES
(Corso Umberto I 122; ⌚9am-1pm & 4-8pm) This eclectic shop is a fun place to browse for citrus-themed ceramics, as well as jewellery, bags and hats. The store does not break for lunch from April to September.

La Torinese FOOD & DRINKS
(☎0942 2 31 43; www.latorinesetaormina.it; Corso Umberto I 59; ⌚9.30am-1pm & 4-8.30pm) Stock up on local olive oil, capers, marmalade, honey and wine. Smash-proof bubble wrapping helps to bring everything home in one piece.

Information

Hospital (Ospedale San Vincenzo; ☎0942 57 92 97; Contrada Sirina) Downhill, 2km from the centre.

Police Station (☎0942 61 02 01; Corso Umberto I 219) On Taormina's main pedestrian strip.

Post Office (☎0942 21 30 11; Piazza Sant'Antonio Abate)

Tourist Office (☎0942 2 32 43; Palazzo Corvaja, Piazza Santa Caterina; ⌚8.30am-2.15pm & 3.30-6.45pm Mon-Fri year-round, also 8.30am-2.15pm & 3.30-6.45pm Sat Apr-Oct, 9am-1pm Sun Jun-Oct) Has plenty of practical information, including transport timetables and a free map.

Getting There & Away

BUS

Bus is the easiest way to reach Taormina. The bus station is on Via Luigi Pirandello, 400m east of Porta Messina, the northeastern entrance to the old town. **Interbus** (www.interbus.it; Via Luigi Pirandello) services leave daily for Messina (€4.30, 55 minutes to 1¾ hours, up to six daily), Catania (€5.10, 1¼ hours, up to 16 daily) and Catania airport (€8.20, 1½ hours, up to 12 daily). It also runs services to Castelmola (€1.90, 15 minutes, up to 11 daily).

CAR & MOTORCYCLE

Taormina is on the A18 autostrada and the SS114. The historic centre is closed to nonresident traffic and Corso Umberto I is closed to all traffic. You can hire cars and scooters at **California Car Rental** (☎0942 2 37 69; www.californiarentcar.com; Via Bagnoli Croce 86; Vespa per day/week €40/250, Fiat Panda €65/309) near Villa Comunale. Reckon on €40/65 per day for a Vespa/Fiat Panda.

Some top-end hotels offer limited parking, otherwise you'll have to leave your car in one of three car parks outside the historic centre: **Porta Catania** (per 24hr €15), **Porta Pasquale** (per 24hr €14) or **Lumbi** (per 24hr €13.50). All three are within walking distance of Corso Umberto I, though Lumbi (the furthest) runs a free shuttle bus up to the centre.

TRAIN

There are frequent trains to and from Messina (from €4.30, 40 minutes to 1¼ hours) and Catania (€4.30, 35 minutes to one hour), but the awkward location of Taormina's station (a steep 4km below town) is a strong disincentive. If you do arrive this way, catch a taxi (€15) or an Interbus coach (€1.90, 20 minutes, roughly one to three an hour) up to town. Note that train frequency is reduced on Sunday.

AROUND TAORMINA

Giardini-Naxos

☎0942 / POP 9525

The unpretentious resort of Giardini-Naxos is a popular alternative to more expensive Taormina. Action is centred on a long parade of hotels, bars, pizzerias and souvenir shops strung along the beach. It heaves in summer but outside of the high season (Easter to October) there's nothing going on and you won't miss much if you pass it by.

Sights

Beach BEACH
Giardini's long beach (mainly sand and coarse grey pebbles) curves around the crescent-shaped bay between Capo Taormina and Capo Schisò, a lick of prehistoric lava at the southern end. There is a small *spiaggia libera* (free beach), but most of it is given over to *lidos* (private beach clubs). Expect to pay around €16 for entry, which includes sun lounge and umbrella rental.

Eating

You'll find numerous pizzerias, *trattorie* and restaurants along (and just off) the *lungomare* (seafront promenade).

L'Acquario SEAFOOD €€
(☎0942 5 62 84; www.lacquariodegustazione.com; Via Vittorio Emanuele 66; tasting menu €45; ⌚noon-2pm & 7-11pm Mon-Sun) Locals head to this smart, welcoming nosh spot for fantastically fresh seafood, cooked with finesse and presented with playful whimsy. It's hard to resist the oysters, though these are merely a prelude to inspired, seasonal dishes which might pair Acquerello rice with pumpkin,

WORTH A TRIP

GOLE ALCANTARA

Located 15km inland from Giardini-Naxos, **Gole Alcantara** (☎0942 98 50 10; www.golealcantara.com; €10; ⏲8am-sunset) is a vertiginous 25m-high natural gorge bisected by the freezing waters of the Alcantara river (the name is derived from the Arabic *al qantara*, meaning bridge). Characterised by its weirdly symmetrical rock formations – created when a red-hot lava flow hit the water and splintered the basalt into lava prisms – it's a spectacular sight well worth searching out.

The gorge is now part of the Gole Alcantara Parco Botanico e Geologico, which is within the Parco Fluviale dell'Alcantara regional park. It's out of bounds between November and March due to the risk of flash flooding, but is open during the rest of the year. To get to the bottom there's a lift near the car park or a 224-step staircase some 200m or so uphill from the lift. Once down by the river, you can hire waders to splash around in the icy waters or simply sunbathe on the surrounding banks. Note that heavy crowds in summer can make this spot feel somewhat less wild and serene, though the 3.5km of nature trails in the area provide the opportunity to explore further afield.

Interbus runs here from Taormina (€3.20, one hour, up to five daily).

mozzarella, red Mazzara prawns and Iranian caviar, or make *branzino* (seabass) sing in a delicate coat of pistachio crumbs.

Information

Tourist Office (☎0942 25 10 10; Via Tysandros 54; ⏲8.30am-2.15pm & 3.30-6.45pm Mon-Fri, 9am-12.45pm & 4-6.15pm Sat Easter-Oct, 8.30am-2.15pm Mon-Fri & 3.30-6.45pm Wed Nov-Easter) Provides accommodation lists and handy maps.

Getting There & Away

BUS

Interbus (☎0942 62 53 01; www.interbus.it) Regular services run between Giardini-Naxos and Taormina's bus station (€1.90, roughly one to three hourly) stopping at the train station en route.

TRAIN

Giardini shares its train station with Taormina. It's situated at the northern end of the seafront, about 10 minutes' walk from the town centre. There are frequent trains to and from Messina (from €4.30, 40 minutes to 1¼ hours) and Catania (€4.30, 35 minutes to one hour). Reduced frequency on Sunday.

Savoca

☎0942 / POP 1745 / ELEV 330M

Hidden away in the hills above Santa Teresa di Riva, Savoca is a tiny village with Hollywood credentials. Francis Ford Coppola filmed part of *The Godfather* here, the village standing in for Corleone. One of the locations used was **Bar Vitelli** (☎334 9227227; Piazza Fossia 7; ⏲9am-midnight summer, to 7.30pm rest of year), a rickety bar near the village entrance. It was here that a love-struck Michael Corleone (Al Pacino) asks the wrong man about Apollonia Vitelli, the beautiful woman who had caught his eye. Order a granita (with a side of *biscotti* for dipping) and devour it on the bar's front patio. From here you can see the 14th-century Chiesa di Santa Lucia, where Michael marries Apollonia.

With its gated walls, rustic stone cottages and haunting churches, the village seems unchanged since medieval times.

Sights

Catacomb CATACOMB
(☎380 6948408; Via Cappuccini 10; admission by donation; ⏲9.30am-7.30pm Apr-Oct, to 5pm Wed-Sun Nov-Mar) Located beneath a 17th-century Capuchin monastery, Savoca's small catacomb is considered one of Sicily's most significant. Its mummified corpses date back to the 17th and 18th centuries and represent some of the town's bigwigs. Among them is monk Bernardo della Limina, located second from left in the middle row facing the stairs. Considered a miracle-performing, quasi-saint, his patchwork garment was sewn using fabric donated by the faithful.

Other original garments include beautiful silks, a testament to Savoca's once-thriving silk production industry.

Information

For more information about the village, ask at the small **tourist office** (☎0942 76 11 25; http://turismo.comune.savoca.me.it; Via Pineta; ⏲9am-1pm & 3-7pm).

Getting There & Away

You will need a car to reach Savoca. From Taormina, take the A18/E45 towards Messina and exit for Roccalumera. Follow the signs for Catania/Savoca, which lead you southbound through Santa Teresa di Riva on the SS114 before leading you inland and uphill on the SP19 for 4km to Savoca.

CATANIA

095 / POP 315,600

For all the noise, chaos and scruffiness that hit the visitor at first glance, Catania has a strong magnetic pull. This is Sicily at its most youthful, a city packed with cool and gritty bars, abundant energy and an earthy spirit in sharp contrast to Palermo's aristocratic airs.

Catania's historic core is a Unesco-listed wonder, where black-and-white *palazzi* tower over sweeping baroque piazzas. One minute you're scanning the skyline from a dizzying dome, the next contemporary art in an 18th-century convent. Beneath it all are the ancient ruins of a town with over 2700 candles on its birthday cake. Indeed, food is another local forte. This is the home of Sicily's iconic *pasta alla Norma* and the extraordinary La Pescheria market.

Keeping an eye on it all is Catania's sky-scraping frenemy, Mt Etna, a powerful presence that adds another layer of intensity and beauty to Sicily's second-biggest city.

History

Catania, or Katáne as it was once called, was originally founded by the Chalcidians in 729 BC and grew to become a major regional power in the 4th and 5th centuries BC. In subsequent centuries it was ruled by a succession of foreign powers (first the Romans, then the Byzantines, Saracens and Normans) but by the mid-17th century it had once again become a prosperous commercial centre. In the late 1600s, however, disaster struck. Twice. First, Mt Etna erupted in 1669, engulfing the city in boiling lava, then, in 1693, a huge earthquake rocked the region, leaving 12,000 people dead.

Out of the ashes arose the city that stands today. Under the supervision of architects Giovanni Vaccarini and Stefano Ittar, a new street grid was created incorporating spacious squares and streets of differing widths, all designed to provide escape routes and greater shelter in case of another eruption. Indeed, Catania cleverly snatched victory from the jaws of defeat, erecting grandiose *palazzi* and churches out of the very volcanic rock that Etna had rained on it.

In modern times, years of neglect left many of the city's great buildings on the verge of decay but renovations in the early 2000s restored many of them to their former glory.

Sights

★La Pescheria MARKET

(Via Pardo; 7am-2pm Mon-Sat) Catania's raucous fish market, which takes over the streets behind Piazza del Duomo every workday morning, is street theatre at its most thrilling. Tables groan under the weight of decapitated swordfish, ruby-pink prawns and trays full of clams, mussels, sea urchins and all manner of mysterious sea life. Fishmongers gut silvery fish and high-heeled housewives step daintily over pools of blood-stained water. It's absolutely riveting. Surrounding the market are a number of good seafood restaurants.

★Teatro Massimo Bellini THEATRE

(095 715 09 21; www.teatromassimobellini.it; Via Perrotta 12; guided tours adult/reduced €6/3; tours 9.30am-noon Tue-Sat) A few blocks northeast of the *duomo*, is Catania's dashing opera. Completed in 1890 and made for homegrown composer Vincenzo Bellini, the building's interiors are suitably lavish, from the stucco-and-marble extravagance of the foyer (known as the *ridotto*) to the glory of the theatre itself, wrapped in four tiers of gilded boxes. The theatre's painted ceiling, by Ernesto Bellandi, depicts scenes from four of Bellini's best-known operas.

★Complesso Monumentale Monastero delle Benedettine CHURCH

(www.benedettineviacrociferi.it; cnr Via Teatro Greco & Via Crociferi; adult/reduced incl Museo Arte Contemporanea Sicilia €5/3.50; 10am-7pm Mon-Sat, 10.30am-7pm Sun Apr-Sep, reduced hours rest of year) The Complesso Monumentale Monastero delle Benedettine covers three adjacent sites: a Benedictine convent, the **Chiesa di San Benedetto** and the **Museo Arte Contemporanea Sicilia** (MACS; 095 715 22 07; www.museomacs.it; Via San Francesco 30; adult/reduced €3.50/2, free with Complesso Monumentale Monastero delle Benedettine ticket; 10am-7pm Fri-Wed Apr-Sep, 9am-6pm Fri-Wed Oct-Mar) across the street. Top billing goes to the church, built between 1704 and 1713 and adorned with splendid stucco, marble and a late-18th-century altar made of Sicilian jasper. Captivating artworks include Giovanni Tuccari's glorious ceiling frescoes and a rather graphic depiction of St Agatha being tortured in front of a curious sultan.

Piazza del Duomo SQUARE

A Unesco World Heritage Site, Catania's central piazza is a set piece of contrasting lava and limestone, surrounded by buildings in the unique local baroque style and crowned by the grand Cattedrale di Sant'Agata (p170). At its centre stands **Fontana dell'Elefante** (Piazza del Duomo) (1736), a naive, smiling black-lava elephant dating from Roman times and surmounted by an Egyptian obelisk. Another fountain at the piazza's southwest corner, **Fontana dell'Amenano**, marks the entrance to Catania's fish market.

Legend has it that the elephant belonged to the 8th-century magician Eliodorus, who reputedly made his living by turning people into animals. The obelisk itself is said to possess magical powers that help ease Mt Etna's volatile temperament. Much younger is the 19th-century Amenano fountain. Created by Neapolitan sculptor Tito Angelini, the splash-happy piece commemorates the Amenano River, which once ran above ground and on whose banks the Greeks first founded the city of Katáne.

Via Crociferi STREET

A lovely, tranquil spot for a morning stroll, Via Crociferi is one of Catania's most attractive streets, famous for its exuberant baroque churches and imposing 18th-century *palazzi*.

Arco di San Benedetto (Via Crociferi), built by the Benedictines in 1704, marks the beginning of Via Crociferi. According to legend, the arch was built in a single night to defy a city ordinance against its construction on the grounds that it was a seismic liability.

Parco Archeologico Greco Romano RUINS

(☎095 715 05 08; Via Vittorio Emanuele II 262; adult/reduced incl Casa Liberti €6/3; ⊙9am-7pm Mon-Sat, to 1.30pm Sun) West of Piazza del Duomo lie Catania's most impressive ancient ruins: the remains of a 2nd-century Roman Theatre and its small rehearsal theatre, the Odeon. The ruins are evocatively sited in the thick of a crumbling residential neighbourhood, with vine-covered buildings that appear to have sprouted organically from the half-submerged stage. Adjacent to the main theatre is the **Casa Liberti**, an elegantly restored 19th-century apartment now home to two millennia worth of artefacts discovered during the excavation of the site.

Via Etnea STREET

It's not difficult to see how Catania's main shopping street got its name – on a clear day you can see Mt Etna rising majestically at the end of it. Via Etnea runs straight from Piazza del Duomo up to the foothills below Etna. Lined with department stores, bars and pavement cafes, it's busy at most times but heaves on Saturday afternoons, when shoppers pile in from the suburbs to strut, schmooze and update their wardrobes.

At its southern end, Piazza dell'Università is an atmospheric spot to take stock over a coffee and cake. On the other side of the square is **Palazzo dell'Università**, the Vaccarini-designed building that houses the city university. On the eastern flank is another Vaccarini edifice, **Palazzo Sangiuliano**.

To escape the madding crowds, continue up to the lovely **Giardino Bellini** (⊙6am-11pm summer, to 10pm spring & autumn, to 9pm winter) where you can relax on a bench in the shady gardens and admire views up to that volcano.

Chiesa Badia di Sant'Agata CHURCH

(☎348 7967711; www.badiasantagata.wordpress.com; Via Vittorio Emanuele II 182; dome €3; ⊙9.30am-12.30pm Tue-Sun, plus 5-8pm Fri & Sat & 7-8.30pm Sun) With an elegant concave-convex facade reminiscent of Borromini, this 18th-century church was designed by Palermitan architect Giovanni Battista Vaccarini. The architect's death in 1768 saw Nicolò Daniele take over completion of the interior, his own contributions including the dramatic Carrara marble floor and amber-coloured altars in Castronovo marble. The pièce de résistance, however, is the spectacular, 360-degree panorama from the dome, which takes in the city's rooftops and domes, and a brooding Mt Etna to the north.

Monastero dei Benedettini di San Nicolò l'Arena MONASTERY

(☎095 710 27 67; www.monasterodeibenedettini.it; Piazza Dante 32; grounds free, guided tours adult/reduced €7/4; ⊙8.30am-8pm Mon-Fri, to 2pm Sat, guided tours hourly 9am-5pm Mon-Sun, 11am-6pm daily Aug) The Monastero dei Benedettini di San Nicolò l'Arena is one of Europe's largest monasteries. Built in 1703 and now part of the city university, it's home to two grand internal cloisters and one of Sicily's most important libraries. Daily guided tours visit the cloisters and library, as well as other areas usually closed to the public. Alternatively, you can view the cloisters on your own from the surrounding corridors.

Catania

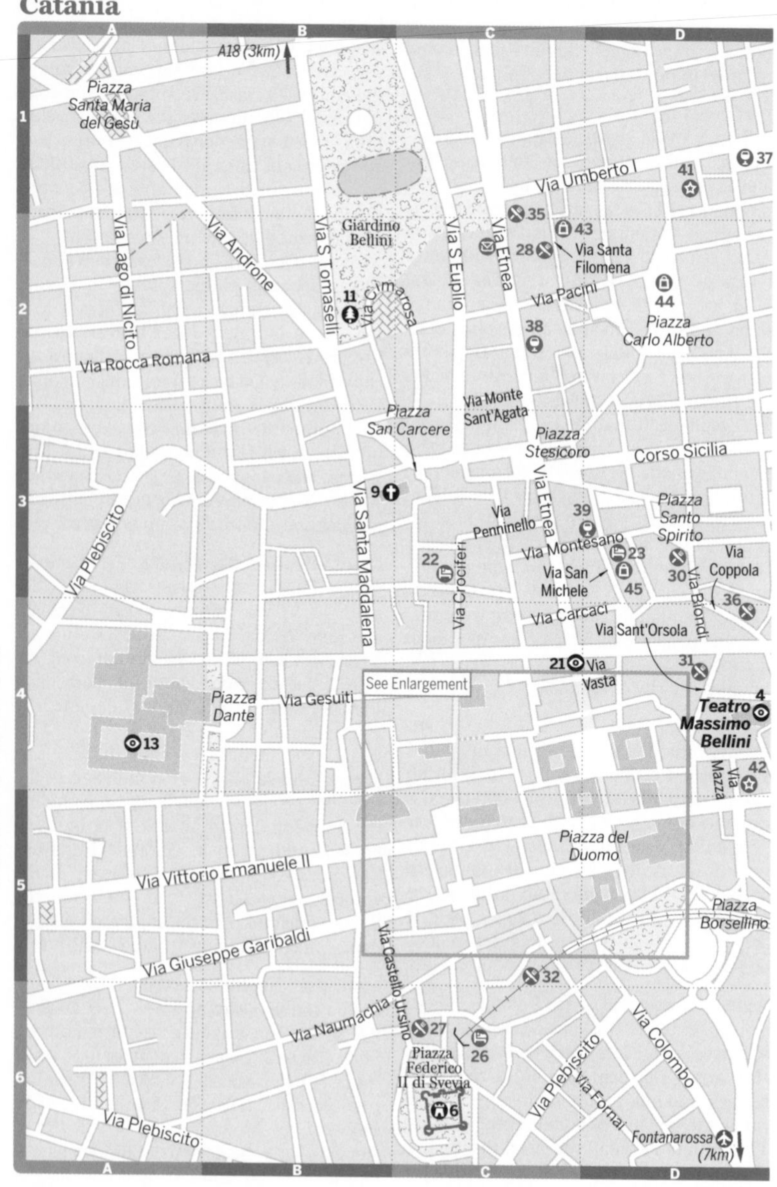

Cattedrale di Sant'Agata CATHEDRAL
(095 32 00 44; Piazza del Duomo; 7am-noon & 4-7pm Mon-Sat, 7.30am-12.30pm & 4.30-7pm Sun) Inside the vaulted interior of this cathedral, beyond its impressive marble facade sporting two orders of columns taken from the Roman amphitheatre, lie the relics of the city's patron saint. Its other famous resident is the world-famous Catanian composer Vincenzo Bellini, his remains transferred here in 1876, 41 years after his death in France. Consider visiting the **Museo Diocesano**

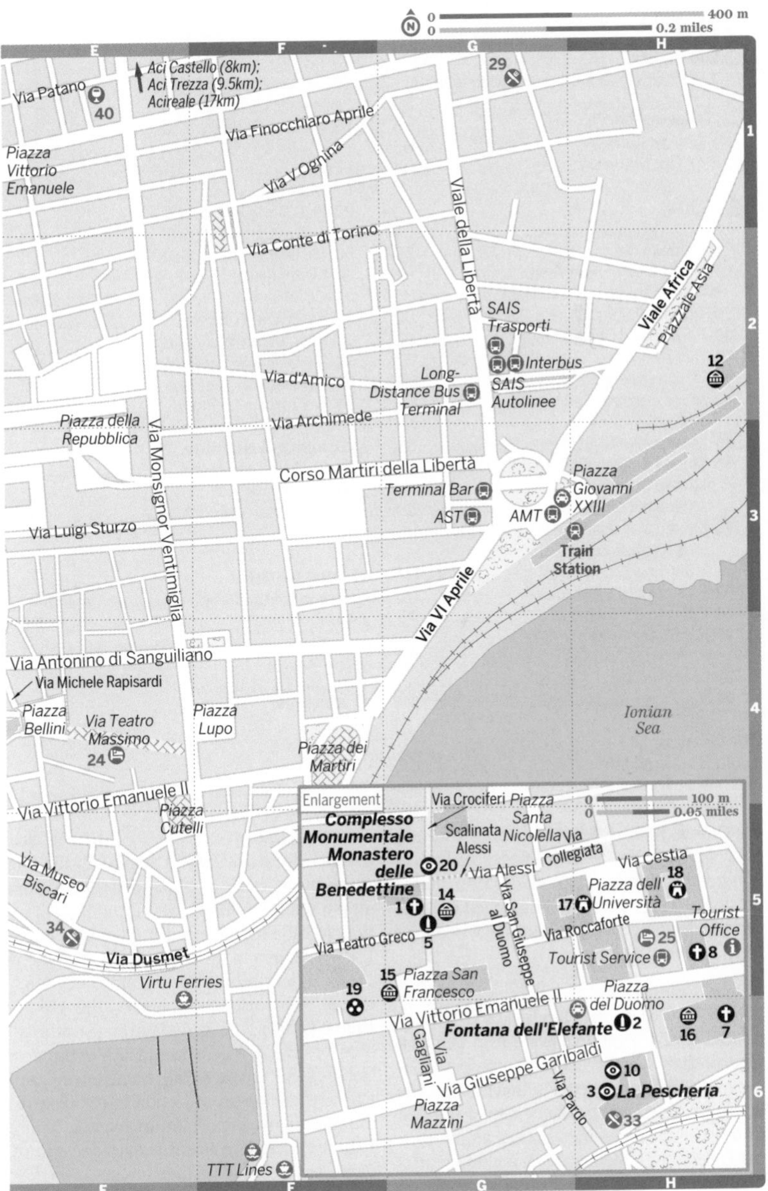

(☎095 28 16 35; www.museodiocesanocatania.com; Piazza del Duomo; adult/reduced museum only €7/4, museum & baths €10/6; ⏲9am-2pm Mon, Wed & Fri, 9am-2pm & 3-6pm Tue & Thu, 9am-1pm Sat) next door for access to the Roman baths directly underneath the church.

The young virgin Agata resisted the advances of the nefarious Quintian (AD 250) and was horribly mutilated (her breasts were hacked off and her body rolled in hot coals). You can actually visit the dungeons where these atrocities were committed under

Catania

Top Sights

1 Complesso Monumentale Monastero delle Benedettine G5
2 Fontana dell'Elefante H6
3 La Pescheria H6
4 Teatro Massimo Bellini D4

Sights

5 Arco di San Benedetto G5
6 Castello Ursino C6
7 Cattedrale di Sant'Agata H6
8 Chiesa Badia di Sant'Agata H5
9 Chiesa di Sant'Agata al Carcere B3
10 Fontana dell'Amenano H6
11 Giardino Bellini B2
12 Le Ciminiere H2
13 Monastero dei Benedettini di San Nicolò l'Arena A4
14 Museo Arte Contemporanea Sicilia G5
15 Museo Belliniano G5
Museo Civico .... (see 6)
Museo del Cinema .... (see 12)
16 Museo Diocesano H6
Museo Storico dello Sbarco in Sicilia .... (see 12)
17 Palazzo dell'Università H5
18 Palazzo Sangiuliano H5
19 Parco Archeologico Greco Romano F6
Piazza del Duomo .... (see 2)
20 Via Crociferi G5
21 Via Etnea C4

Sleeping

22 B&B Crociferi C3
23 B&B Faro D3
24 B&B Habitat E4
25 Ostello degli Elefanti H5
26 Palazzu Stidda C6

Eating

27 Da Antonio C6
28 FUD Bottega Sicula C2
29 Le Tre Bocche G1
30 Mè Cumpari Turiddu D3
31 Millefoglie D4
32 Ostello C5
Pasticceria Caprice .... (see 26)
33 Pescheria Fratelli Vittorio H6
34 Sicilia In Bocca Alla Marinara E5
35 Spinella C1
36 Trattoria di De Fiore D4

Drinking & Nightlife

37 Chiosco Giammona D1
38 Etnea Roof C2
39 Razmataz D3
40 Ritz E1

Entertainment

41 Arena Argentina D1
42 Enola Club D4
Teatro Massimo Bellini .... (see 4)
Zo .... (see 12)

Shopping

43 Boudoir 36 .... C2
44 La Fiera D2
45 Tabaré D3

the **Chiesa di Sant'Agata al Carcere** (☎338 1441760; Piazza San Carcere; ⏰10am-noon Tue-Sat) behind the Roman amphitheatre on Piazza Stesicoro. The saint's jewel-drenched effigy is ecstatically venerated on 5 February in one of Sicily's largest festivals.

Museo Belliniano MUSEUM

(☎095 715 05 35; Piazza San Francesco 3; adult/reduced €5/2; ⏰9am-7pm Mon-Sat, to 1pm Sun) One of Italy's great opera composers, Vincenzo Bellini was born in Catania in 1801. The house he grew up in has since been converted into this museum, which houses an interesting collection of memorabilia, including original scores, photographs, pianos once played by Bellini, and the maestro's death mask.

In his short life (he died aged 34), Bellini composed 10 operas, including the famous trio: *La sonnambula* (The Sleepwalker), *I puritani* (The Puritans) and *Norma*, which has since been immortalised as the name of Sicily's most famous pasta dish – *pasta alla Norma*.

Castello Ursino CASTLE

(Piazza Federico II di Svevia) Catania's forbidding 13th-century castle once guarded the city from atop a seafront cliff. However, the 1669 eruption of Mt Etna changed the landscape and the whole area to the south was reclaimed by the lava, leaving the castle completely landlocked. The castle now houses the **Museo Civico** (☎095 34 58 30; Castello Ursino, Piazza Federico II di Svevia; adult/reduced €6/3; ⏰9am-7pm Mon-Fri, to 8.30pm Sat & Sun), home to the valuable archaeological collection of the Biscaris, Catania's most important aristocratic family. Exhibits include colossal classical sculpture, Greek vases and some fine mosaics.

Le Ciminiere MUSEUM

(☎095 401 22 32; Viale Africa) Le Ciminiere is a modern museum complex housed in a converted sulphur refinery. The most interesting of its museums is the **Museo Storico dello Sbarco in Sicilia** (☎095 53 35 40; Le Ciminiere, Viale Africa; adult/reduced €4/2; ⏰10am-

5.45pm Tue-Sun Jun-Aug, 9am-4.45pm Tue-Sun Sep-May), which illustrates the history of the WWII Allied landings in Sicily. Also noteworthy is the **Museo del Cinema** (☎095 401 19 28; Le Ciminiere, Viale Africa; adult/reduced €4/2; ⏱10am-6pm Tue-Sun Jun-Aug, 9am-5pm Tue-Sun Sep-May), which explores the evolution of movie making and features movie posters, memorabilia and vintage cinema equipment. Museums aside, Le Ciminiere is also home to performance space Zo (p175).

Festivals & Events

If visiting Catania in February or early March, don't miss Carnevale (p178), one of Sicily's biggest festivals in nearby Acireale.

Festa di Sant'Agata RELIGIOUS

(www.festadisantagata.it) In Catania's biggest religious festival (3 to 5 February), one million Catanians follow the Fercolo (a silver reliquary bust of St Agata) along the main street of the city accompanied by spectacular fireworks.

Eating

Eating out in Catania is a real pleasure, whether by market stalls at La Pescheria or on trendy Via Santa Filomena. There's a huge choice of snack bars, *trattorie* and restaurants, including vegetarian and vegan-friendly options. The city's street food is also superb. Classic bites include *arancini* (fried rice balls), *cartocciate* (bread stuffed with ham, mozzarella, olives and tomato) and *pasta alla Norma*, all invented right here.

★Da Antonio TRATTORIA €

(☎095 218 49 38; www.facebook.com/TrattoriaDaAntonio; Via Castello Ursino 59; meals €20; ⏱7.30-11pm daily, plus 12.30-3pm Tue-Sun) Humble yet quietly sophisticated, Da Antonio spoils food-lovers with well-priced, beautifully cooked food served by knowledgeable waitstaff. Despite having made inroads onto the tourist radar, it's still the kind of place where well-dressed local families come for Sunday lunch. The antipasti (to sample various offerings ask for an *assaggio*) and *primi* are particularly good, especially those dishes showcasing local fish and homemade pasta.

Trattoria di De Fiore TRATTORIA €

(☎095 31 62 83; Via Coppola 24/26; meals €15-25; ⏱7pm-12.30am Mon, 1pm-12.30am Tue-Sun) For over 50 years, septuagenarian chef Rosanna has been recreating her great-grandmother's recipes, including the best *pasta alla Norma* you'll taste anywhere in Sicily. Service can be excruciatingly slow, but for patient souls this is a rare chance to experience classic Catanian cooking from a bygone era. Don't miss Rosanna's trademark *zeppoline* (sugar-sprinkled ricotta-lemon fritters) at dessert time. Occasionally closed Mondays in winter.

Rosanna says her grandmother referred to *pasta alla Norma* as *pasta Mungibeddu* in honour of Mt Etna (Mungibeddu being the traditional Sicilian name for Catania's famous volcano): tomatoes represented Etna's red lava, aubergine the black cinders, ricotta the snow and basil leaves the mountain vegetation.

Millefoglie VEGETARIAN €

(☎331 2505331; Via Sant'Orsola 12; dishes €6-8; ⏱12.45-3pm Mon-Sat, closed Sat May-Oct; 📶🌿) Delicious, flesh-free grub awaits at little Millefoglie, a shabby-chic, whitewashed eatery with wooden floors, communal tables

TOP TOURS & TRAILS

Etna Touring (p182) You can explore Mt Etna on your own, but going with a guide ensures that you won't miss anything or accidentally stumble into a fuming crater.

Gole Alcantara (p167) A renowned beauty spot, this deep rocky canyon is bisected by the freezing Alcantara river. In summer you can wade through the waters, sunbathe or walk along the surrounding nature trails.

Sail ahoy Take a boat tour to explore the caves and black volcanic rocks of the Riviera dei Ciclopi, the popular stretch of coastline north of Catania. Inquire at Catania's tourist office (p176) for more information.

Isola Bella (p164) This picture-perfect bay offers the best swimming near Taormina, as well as excellent diving courtesy of Nike Diving Centre.

Ferrovia Circumetnea (FCE; ☎095 54 11 11; www.circumetnea.it; Via Caronda 352a, Catania) If you prefer to keep some distance between yourself and Etna's volatile craters, jump on a train and tour the small towns that circle the volcano's base.

and an open kitchen. The morning's market produce dictates the menu, which might feature vibrant wholewheat *casarecce* (twisted pasta) with zucchini, fava beans, peas, pecorino, lemon zest and basil, or chocolate mousse with chilli and strawberries. A few vegan dishes usually dot the menu.

Ostello SICILIAN, PIZZA €
(☎095 723 30 10; Piazza Currò 6; pizza €6-10, meals €20; ⊙noon-4pm & 8pm-12.30am, pizzas until 2am; ✎) Pub-like Ostello personifies Catania: grungy, youthful and arty. Hunker down among students, professors and backpackers for decent bulgur-and-vegetable patties, couscous, burgers, pizzas (except on Tuesday) and classic pasta dishes. There's even a vegan lunch on Sundays (€12). You'll find the best table for two downstairs in a natural grotto, complete with gurgling stream (book it in advance and wear warm clothes). DJs hit Ostello's decks on Wednesday nights, with live jazz on Thursday from 9.30pm.

FUD Bottega Sicula BURGERS €
(☎095 715 35 18; www.fud.it; Via Santa Filomena 35; burgers, panini & pizzas €5-10; ⊙noon-3pm & 7pm-1am; ⓦ) With sharp service and pavement seating on trendy Via Santa Filomena, this hip, back-alley eatery epitomises youthful Catania's embrace of 'Sicilian fast food', made with high-quality, locally sourced ingredients, from Sicilian cheeses to Nebrodi black pork. With wry humour, every burger and *panino* on the menu is spelled using Italian phonetics, from the 'cis burgher' (cheeseburger) to the rustic 'cauntri' (country) sandwich.

Neapolitan-style pizzas are also available.

Spinella PASTRIES €
(☎095 32 72 47; Via Etnea 300; snacks from €1.80; ⊙7.30am-10.30pm; ⓦ) The Slow Food movement especially recommends Spinella's traditional sweets – try the *frutta martorana* (marzipan sweets shaped like fruits and vegetables) and *olivette di sant'Agata* (olive-shaped sweets typically made only in January and February, for the festival of St Agatha). If you don't fancy a sit-down lunch but want something tasty on the hoof, Spinella serves one of Catania's best *arancini*.

★Mè Cumpari Turiddu SICILIAN €€
(☎095 715 01 42; Piazza Santo Spirito 36-38; meals €22-30; ⊙bistro 11am-1am, restaurant noon-12.30am; ⓦ) Old chandeliers, recycled furniture and vintage mirrors exude a nostalgic air at this quirky bistro-restaurant-providore, where tradition and modernity meet to impressive effect. Small producers and Slow Food sensibilities underline sophisticated, classically inspired dishes like ricotta-and-marjoram ravioli in a pork sauce, soothing Ustica lentil stew or a playful 'deconstructed' *cannolo*. There's a fabulous selection of Sicilian cheeses, lighter bistro grub and cakes.

Pescheria Fratelli Vittorio SEAFOOD €€
(☎339 7733890; Via Dusmet 1; meals €25-40; ⊙11am-3pm & 7pm-midnight Tue-Sun, closed Sun dinner) Cats would kill for a table at Fratelli Vittorio, a cult-status eatery whose counter glistens with Catania's freshest fish and seafood. It's not surprising given that co-owner Giovanni is a fishmonger, handpicking the best ingredients from the nearby market. For a decadent overview, opt for the *degustazione di antipasti del giorno*, or feel the love in the generous *zuppa di pesce* (seafood soup).

If there's still room, finish with a serve of *fedora*, a sweet concoction of ricotta, chocolate chips and toasted almonds.

Cutilisci MODERN SICILIAN €€
(☎095 37 25 58; www.cutilisci.it; Via San Giovanni li Cuti 67-69; pizzas €6.50-14, meals €25-30; ⊙1-3pm & 7.45pm-midnight Wed-Mon, 7.45pm-midnight Tue; ⓦ✎👪) When the weather is good, the tables are out on the small pavement terrace at Cutilisci, a much-loved waterfront restaurant in the harbour of San Giovanni li Cuti. Wholesome ingredients and global influences define the menu, whose offerings include swordfish steak with orange and fennel salad and a barley, spelt and vegetable tabbouleh. A taxi from the city centre will cost around €15 one-way.

On weekends in August, the restaurant sometimes only opens for dinner.

Sicilia In Bocca Alla Marinara SEAFOOD €€
(☎095 250 02 08; Via Dusmet 35; meals €30-35; ⊙1-3pm & 7.30pm-midnight) Catania's 14th-century sea walls provide the *suggestivo* (evocative) setting for this popular restaurant. With the smell of the sea breezing in, surf is the obvious choice, from a delicious swordfish carpaccio with citrus-fruit dressing to classic *pasta ca' muddica* (with anchovy and toasted breadcrumbs). Sit in the lively brick-arched dining hall or enjoy views of the Duomo from the upstairs terrace.

Le Tre Bocche TRATTORIA €€€
(☎095 53 87 38; Via Mario Sangiorgi 7; meals €35-45; ⊙two sittings daily, 8.30pm & 10.30pm, plus 1-3pm

Sun) A fantastic Slow Food–recommended trattoria that takes pride in the freshest seafood and fish – so much so, they have a stand at La Pescheria market. Short pasta comes with wonderful sauces such as *bottarga* (fish roe) and artichoke, spaghetti are soaked in sea urchins or squid ink, and risotto is mixed with courgette and king prawns.

The antipasti buffet offers fish carpaccios and marinated prawns, and the *secondi* are best for indulging in *ricciola* (yellowtail) baked with potatoes or sea bream cooked in sea water.

Drinking & Nightlife

Not surprisingly for a busy university town, Catania has great nightlife. There are dozens of cafes, bars and live-music venues across town but hubs include Piazza Bellini (a student favourite), Via Montesano, Via Penninello and Via Alessi. Opening hours are generally from around 9pm to 2am, although things often don't hot up until around midnight.

★Ritz COCKTAIL BAR
(www.facebook.com/ritzcatania; Via Pantano 54; 7.30pm-2am Tue-Sun) New-kid Ritz is a svelte, clued-up spot that takes its libations seriously. Divided into Aperitif, Anytime, Dinner, After Dinner and Long Drink & Muddle, cocktails are made with passion and precision, from punchy Aviations to a very local Etna Kir (spumante Brut rosé, Etna cherry-liqueur, hazelnut crust). There's a small, interesting selection of craft beers and a range of bites, including decent pizzas.

★Razmataz BAR
(095 31 18 93; Via Montesano 17; 8.30am-late;) Wines by the glass, draught and bottled beer and an ample cocktail list are offered at this delightful wine bar with tables invitingly spread out across the tree-shaded flagstones of a sweet backstreet square. It doubles as a cafe in the morning, but really gets packed with locals from *aperitivo* time onward.

If you're hungry, scan the backboard for a decent selection of light meals (from €4), including spinach and gorgonzola quiche and a cheese platter.

Etnea Roof ROOFTOP BAR
(095 250 51 11; UNA Palace Hotel, Via Etnea 218; 10.30am-midnight) You'll be toasting to the view at Una Hotel's rooftop garden bar, a grown-up hideaway with a sucker-punch view of Etna. Ponder its power on the succulent-fringed terrace or retreat to one of the softly lit lounges inside. A good time to head up is from 7.30pm, when €15 buys you an alcoholic libation and free reign of the decent *aperitivo* buffet.

Chiosco Giammona KIOSK
(Piazza Vittorio Emanuele III; 8am-4am) Hit this pretty, Liberty-era *chiosco* (drinks kiosk) for a made-to-order *seltz,* a nonalcoholic mix of fizzy water, freshly squeezed lemon juice and natural fruit syrup. Purists opt for the unsweetened *seltz limone e sale* (with lemon and salt). Those who like it *dolce* (sweet) can choose from a number of fruit syrups, including *mandarino* (mandarin) and *tamarindo* (tamarind).

Other drinks sold include beer and coffee.

Entertainment

Arena Argentina CINEMA
(095 32 20 30; www.cinestudio.eu; Via Vanasco 10; adult/reduced €3/2; Jun-early Oct) For local cinephiles, summer means sultry outdoor film nights at Arena Argentina. Head up for mainly cult and art-house flicks, from *Purple Rain* and *Labyrinth* to newer releases like *Mad Max: Fury Road* and *The Danish Girl.* Warning: films are usually dubbed in Italian.

Teatro Massimo Bellini THEATRE
(095 730 61 11; www.teatromassimobellini.it; Via Perrotta 12) Catania's premier theatre is named after the city's most famous son, composer Vincenzo Bellini. Sporting the full red-and-gilt fitout, it stages a year-round season of opera and an eight-month program of classical music from November to June. Tickets, which are available online, start at around €20 and can rise to over €100 for a seat in the stalls.

Zo PERFORMING ARTS
(095 816 89 12; www.zoculture.it; Piazzale Asia 6;) Housed in Catania's former sulphur works, Zo serves up contemporary art and performance from Italy and beyond. Its eclectic program of events ranges from club nights, concerts and dance performances, to installations, theatre workshops and the occasional film screening. The venue also houses a hip bar with decent drinks and bites (including vegetarian dishes). Check the website for upcoming events.

Enola Club JAZZ
(340 5188431; Via Mazza 14) The godfather of Catania's jazz scene, the Enola Club attracts

big-name Italian and international artists to its pocket-sized stage, while also trumpeting new and emerging local talent. Like all self-respecting jazz clubs, it's a tight squeeze with a fairly nondescript decor, but that in no way diminishes the hot, steamy atmosphere.

Shopping

Boudoir 36 BEAUTY
(☎095 715 23 58; www.boudoir36.it; Via Santa Filomena 36; ⏰6-10pm Tue-Sat) Engineer by day, fragrance maestro by night, Antonio Alessandria indulges his passion for scents at his lavish little perfumery. You won't find mainstream brands here, just serious, cognoscenti wonders from the likes of New York's Aedes de Venustas and Paris' The Different Company and Parfum d'Empire. Botanical body wash, balms, hair care and room sprays are also available.

Tabaré ART
(☎338 7509597; Via San Michele 24; ⏰10am-8pm Mon-Sat, 3-8pm Sun) Tabaré sells the wares of five female Catanian artisans. Marisa Casaburi creates whimsical models and sculptures in papier maché, Carla Marletta turns recyclables into photo frames, while Ljubiza Mezzatesta's notebooks will have you itching to jot. Then there's Lina Lizzio's funky jewellery and Giovanna Cacciola's graphic tees. The small upstairs gallery serves up rotating exhibitions of local, unisex artists the women personally love.

La Fiera MARKET
(Piazza Carlo Alberto; ⏰8am-1pm Mon-Fri, to 7pm Sat) Every morning except Sunday, Piazza Carlo Alberto (just off Via Etnea) is flooded by the chaos of La Fiera. Not dissimilar to a Middle Eastern kasbah, the market peddles everything from curvaceous aubergines and oranges, to bootleg CDs and knock-off designer bags.

Information

Airport Tourist Office (☎095 723 96 82; ⏰8am-8.15pm Mon-Sat) In the Arrivals hall.

Catania Pass (www.cataniapass.it; 1-/3-/5-day pass individual €12.50/16.50/20, family €23/30.50/38) Discount pass offering free or reduced admission to museums and unlimited use of public transport. The pass can be purchased at numerous outlets, including the tourist information office at Catania Airport, the main tourist office off Piazza del Duomo and participating museums including the Museo Civico, Museo Belliniano and Museo Diocesano.

Hospital (Ospedale Santo Bambino; ☎095 743 63 06; www.policlinicovittorioemanuele.it/ospedale-santo-bambino; Via Tindaro 2) Has a 24-hour emergency department.

Police (Questura; ☎095 736 71 11; Piazza Santa Nicolella 8) Police station just off Via Etnea.

Post Office (Via Etnea 215) Post office on central Catania's main strip.

Tourist Office (☎095 742 55 73; www.comune.catania.it; Via Vittorio Emanuele 172; ⏰8am-7.15pm Mon-Sat) Very helpful city-run tourist office.

Getting There & Away

AIR

Catania Fontanarossa airport (☎095 723 91 11; www.aeroporto.catania.it) is Sicily's busiest and located 7km southwest of the city centre. Airlines include Alitalia, Lufthansa, Turkish Airways, easyJet and Ryanair. Year-round destinations include Naples, Rome, Bologna and Milan, as well as London (Gatwick and Luton), Paris (Charles de Gaulle and Orly), Zürich, Munich, Cologne/Bonn, Stuttgart, Hamburg, Berlin (Tegel) and Malta.

Shuttle-bus service **Alibus** (www.amt.ct.it) runs to the airport from numerous stops in central Catania, including the train station (€4, 30 minutes, every 25 minutes). Tickets can be purchased on board (carry the correct change). A **taxi** (p177) will cost around €18 to €22.

BOAT

Catania's **ferry terminal** lies at the southeast edge of the historic centre. From here, **TTT Lines** (☎095 34 85 86, 800 627414; www.tttlines.com) runs a nightly ferry service to Naples. Fares per person for a *poltrona* (airline-type armchair) start from €13.50. A double cabin starts from €126. Journey time is roughly 12 hours.

From May through September, **Virtu Ferries** (☎095 703 12 11; www.virtuferries.com) runs daily ferries from Pozzallo (south of Catania) to Malta (1¾ hours). Fares vary depending on length of stay in Malta (same-day adult return €87 to €138, open return €115 to €163). Coach transfer between Catania and Pozzallo (€10 each way) adds two hours to the journey. In Catania, the Virtu Ferries ticket office is at the port.

BUS

All long-distance buses leave from a **terminal** (Via Archimede) 250m north of the train station, with ticket offices across the street on Via D'Amico. As a rule, buses are quicker than trains for most destinations.

Interbus (☎ 095 53 27 16; www.interbus.it; Via d'Amico 187) Runs to Syracuse (€6.20, 1½ hours, 18 daily Monday to Friday, 10 Saturday, seven Sunday) and Taormina (€5.10, 1¼ hours, 11 to 16 daily), Ragusa (€8.60, two hours, six to 13 daily) and Piazza Armerina (€9.20, 1¾ hours, two to five daily).

SAIS Autolinee (☎ 800 211020, 095 53 61 68; www.saisautolinee.it; Via d'Amico 181) Serves Palermo (€12.50, 2¾ hours, 12 daily Monday to Saturday, nine Sunday), Messina (€8.40, 1½ hours, 23 daily Monday to Friday, 14 Saturday, 11 Sunday) and Enna (€8, 1½ hours, seven daily Monday to Friday, six Saturday, three Sunday).

SAIS Trasporti (☎ 090 601 21 36; www.saistrasporti.it; Via d'Amico 181) Runs to Agrigento (€13.40, three hours, nine to 14 daily) and overnight to Rome (€40, one daily, 10½ hours).

Tourist Service (☎ 095 820 42 81; www.touristservice2006.com; Via Vittorio Emanuele 130) Operates hop-on, hop-off tourist buses from Catania to Aci Castello and Aci Trezza. Tickets cost €15 and are valid all day. Buses depart hourly (every 90 minutes in the winter) from Catania's Via Vittorio Emanuele, right next to Piazza del Duomo.

CAR & MOTORCYCLE

Catania is easily reached from Messina on the A18 autostrada as well as from Palermo on the A19. From the autostrada, signs for the city centre direct you to Via Etnea.

TRAIN

Frequent trains depart from Catania Centrale station on Piazza Papa Giovanni XXIII. Destinations include Messina (from €7.60, 1¼ to two hours), Syracuse (from €6.90, 1¼ hours) and Palermo (from €13.50, three hours). Train services are significantly reduced on Sunday.

Getting Around

BUS

Several useful **AMT** (☎ 800 018696, 095 751 91 11; www.amt.ct.it) city buses terminate in front of Catania Centrale train station, including buses 1-4 and 4-7 (both running roughly hourly from the station to Via Etnea). Also useful is bus D, which runs from Piazza Borsellino (just south of the Cattedrale di Sant'Agata, or *duomo*) to the local beaches. Tickets, from *tabacchi* (tobacconists) cost €1 and last 90 minutes. A two-hour combined bus-metro ticket costs €1.20.

AST (☎ 095 723 05 11; www.aziendasicilianatrasporti.it; Via Sturzo 232) runs to many smaller towns around Catania, including Acireale (€2.70). It also connects Catania to Rifugio Sapienza on Mt Etna. AST tickets can be purchased at Terminal Bar, opposite Catania Centrale train station.

CAR & MOTORCYCLE

Choosing to drive in town means you will have to deal with the city's complicated one-way system – for example, you can only drive along Via Vittorio Emanuele II from west to east, while the parallel Via Giuseppe Garibaldi runs from east to west.

Parking is extremely difficult in the city centre. If you're bringing your own car, consider staying at a hotel or B&B with parking facilities; if you're hiring a car, the advice is to pick up the car as you leave town and return it when you re-enter.

METRO

Catania's one-line metro currently has only six stops, all on the periphery of town. For tourists, it's mainly useful as a way of getting from Catania Centrale station to the Circumetnea train that circles Mt Etna. A 90-minute metro ticket costs €1. A two-hour combined metro-bus ticket costs €1.20.

TAXI

For a taxi, call **Radio Taxi Catania** (☎ 095 33 09 66; www.radiotaxicatania.org). You'll find taxi ranks at the train station and at the northwest corner of Piazza del Duomo.

RIVIERA DEI CICLOPI

Extending north of Catania, the Riviera dei Ciclopi is an attractive stretch of coastline that draws no shortage of beach-seeking *catanesi* (Catanians). Until quite recently it was a desperately poor area of isolated fishing villages, but tourism has given it a much needed impetus and it is now a lively summer stomping ground. While many of the beaches are rocky, the swimming is excellent, and the area's booty of restaurants, bars, nightclubs and accommodation keeps punters reveling long after their last dip.

The coast owes its name to a Homeric legend according to which the towering black rocks that rise out of the sea – actually great hunks of solidified lava – were thrown by the blinded Cyclops, Polyphemus, in a desperate attempt to stop Odysseus escaping. Volcanic activity has created dramatic coastal features, including gorgeous grottoes and dizzying cliffs smothered in thick, lush vegetation.

Acireale

☎ 095 / POP 52,700

The main town on the Riviera, Acireale is set on a series of lava terraces that drop to the sea about 17km north of Catania. Although it's not exactly undiscovered, it remains largely tourist free, a mystery given its stately baroque centre and imposing public buildings. Taking this easy 2km downhill is Santa Maria la Scala, a tiny fishing village seemingly made for perfect seafood lunches.

And while Acireale has long been known for its thermal waters, its modern claim to fame is its spectacular Carnevale festivities, bursting into life each February.

Sights

To eye-up Acireale's most impressive architecture, start in Piazza Duomo, a grandiose square surrounded on three sides by monumental buildings. On the western flank is the **cathedral** (Piazza Duomo; ⏲8am-noon & 4.30-8.30pm), built in the early 1600s and topped by towering conical-capped spires. Inside, the echoing vaults and chapels are richly frescoed.

Next to the cathedral, the **Basilica dei Santi Pietro e Paolo** (Piazza Duomo; ⏲8am-noon & 4-7.30pm) displays a typically elaborate 18th-century facade. To the right of it, the **Palazzo Municipale** impresses with its wrought-iron balconies and imposing central portal.

From the piazza, Via Ruggero Settimo leads south to Piazza Lionardo Vigo and the gorgeous **Basilica di San Sebastiano** (Piazza Lionardo Vigo; ⏲8.30am-12.30pm & 4-8pm), one of the town's finest baroque buildings. Guarded by statues of Old Testament characters, the basilica lifts the spirit with its luminous facade, whimsically lined with *putti* (cherubs). Inside, splendid frescoes recount episodes from the life of St Sebastian.

Nearby, the streets around Piazza Marconi host Acireale's noisy *pescheria* (fish market).

Teatro-Museo dell'Opera dei Pupi THEATRE

(☎347 8061464; www.operadeipupi.com; Via Nazionale 195; ⏲9am-noon & 4-7.30pm summer, 9am-noon & 3-6pm winter) FREE Acireale has a long tradition of puppet theatre and you can learn all about it at Teatro-Museo dell'Opera dei Pupi. Guided tours of the museum are in Italian, although English-language information is available on request. From July to September, it also runs twice-weekly puppet shows (Thursday and Sunday), with tickets costing between €5 and €15. If you don't have your own wheels and wish to visit the museum, you can request a pick-up from Acireale train station (charged separately).

Santa Maria la Scala VILLAGE

There are two reasons to make the 2km downhill walk to this minute fishing village. One is the walk itself, which, once you've crossed the main road, is a lovely country stroll with gorgeous coastal views. The other is to feast on super-fresh seafood at one of the delightful trattorias.

To get to the village, which consists of little more than a tiny harbour, a church, some houses and a black beach, follow Via Romeo down from Piazza Duomo, cross the main road and keep going.

Festivals & Events

Carnevale CARNIVAL

(www.carnevaleacireale.com) The best time to visit Acireale is during February's Carnevale, when the town puts on one of the best spectacles in Sicily. The stars of the show are the elaborately decorated floats, some bedecked in Technicolor flower displays, others carrying huge papier-mâché caricatures of local celebrities. All around bands play, costumed dancers leap about and confetti rains.

The exact dates vary each year, but you can get details on the event's comprehensive website. And if you miss it first time round, don't worry, there's a rerun, albeit on a smaller scale, in early August.

Eating

Trattoria La Grotta TRATTORIA €€

(☎095 764 81 53; Via Scalo Grande 46, Santa Maria la Scala; meals €30-35; ⏲1-2.30pm & 8-10.30pm Wed-Mon) Book ahead for a memorable, finger-licking experience at La Grotta, the best of Santa Maria la Scala's restaurants. As you enter you'll pass the fish counter, where your order is picked out and weighed before going in the pot. Your work done, settle in (the dining area is atmospherically set in the body of a cave) and eagerly await your superb seafood feast.

Tip: fortes include the *insalata di mare* (seafood salad), a mouth-watering medley of prawns, calamari and octopus, and the sensational grilled fish.

L'Oste Scuro SEAFOOD €€

(☎095 763 40 01; Piazza Lionardo Vigo 5-6; meals €30-35; ⏲12.30-3.30pm & 7pm-midnight) With the shouts of the nearby fish market ringing in the air and views to the Basilica di San Sebastiano, this is a setting for a filling fish meal. Tuck into the seafood classic *pasta con gamberi, zucchini e zafferano* (pasta with prawns, courgettes and saffron) followed by a towering sauté of mussels and clams.

La Taverna TRATTORIA €€
(☎346 4066148; Via Ercole 4; pizzas from €5, meals €25-30; ⊙noon-3pm & 7pm-midnight Fri-Wed) A straight-up trattoria serving old-school Sicilian grub. Given its location in the middle of the fish market, it's at its best at lunch when hungry locals pop in for grilled catch of the day or *calamari arrosto* (roast squid). Seafood is the obvious choice, but it also does some decent non-fish dishes; try the *pasta con funghi porcini* (pasta with porcini mushrooms).

Information

Tourist Office (☎095 89 52 49; Via Romeo 2; ⊙8am-2pm & 3-9pm Mon-Thu, 8am-1pm & 3-9pm Fri & Sat)

Getting There & Away

BUS

AST (p177) buses run frequently between Catania and Acireale (€2.70, 50 minutes, half-hourly to hourly) Monday to Saturday. Interbus (p177) also runs buses to Acireale from Catania (€2.70, 50 minutes, four to five daily Monday to Saturday, one Sunday) and Taormina (€4, 70 minutes, three to four daily Monday to Saturday, one Sunday)

CAR & MOTORCYCLE

If driving from Catania, head north along the SS114 coastal road. Alternatively, take the A18 tollway and exit for Acireale.

TRAIN

Trains to Acireale run one to three times hourly from Catania (€2.50, 10 to 15 minutes). From Taormina, trains to Acireale run once or twice hourly (€3.80, 25 to 45 minutes). Frequency is significantly reduced on Sunday. Acireale train station is inconveniently located 2km south of the city centre, making buses a better option.

Aci Trezza

☎095

A few kilometres south of Acireale, the small fishing village of Aci Trezza has a lively seafront and a number of good restaurants. Offshore, a series of surreal, jagged basalt rocks, the **Scogli dei Ciclopi**, rise out of the sea. These are the mythical missiles that the blinded Cyclops, Polyphemus (who lived in Etna), is supposed to have thrown at the fleeing Odysseus. Aci Trezza is also celebrated as the setting of *I Malavoglia,* Giovanni Verga's 19th-century literary masterpiece of life in a poor, isolated fishing community.

Sights & Activities

The principal activity in Aci Trezza is hanging out on the seafront, sunbathing in the day – wooden platforms are set up over the black volcanic rocks – and waltzing up and down after dark. You can enjoy the spectacle from one of the *lungomare* (seafront promenade) bars.

To explore the coast's caves, coves and bays, there are a number of operators at the port offering boat tours. One such, **Vaporetto Polifemo** (☎331 3148624; www.vaporettopolifemo.it; boat trips from €12), runs daily excursions along the coast.

Eating & Drinking

L'Osteria dei Marinari SEAFOOD €€
(☎095 27 79 21; Lungomare Ciclopi 185; meals €25-35; ⊙noon-3pm & 7-11pm) While the service can sometimes be patchy, the food here satisfies. This is where locals come for fresh fish and seafood, tucking into tried-and-tested staples like refreshing *insalata di polpo* (octopus salad), squid-ink risotto and a simply gorgeous *frittura di calamari* (fried calamari). Book ahead in the summer.

Banacher CLUB
(☎095 27 10 24; www.banacher.com; Via XXI Aprile 79) This is one of the Riviera's largest nightclubs, with multiple dance floors, a swimming pool and various club nights catering to the young and not so young.

Café de Mar CAFE
(☎095 27 61 29; Lungomare Ciclopi 119; ⊙8pm-late) Directly opposite the iconic Faraglioni, with white sofas and armchairs scattered across a palm-shaded garden, this bar-lounge-restaurant hybrid is a fine spot to kick back with a spritz and indulge in a little people-watching. Peckish punters have a range of options, including pizzas, burgers, salads and cheeses.

Getting There & Away

If driving from Catania, head north on the SS114.

AMT (p177) city bus 534 (€1, hourly) runs to Aci Trezza from Catania's Piazza Borsellino. A more expensive option is the Tourist Service (p177) hop-on, hop-off bus (daily ticket €15), which also runs from Catania to Aci Castello and Aci Trezza. The bus stop is directly opposite the ticket office.

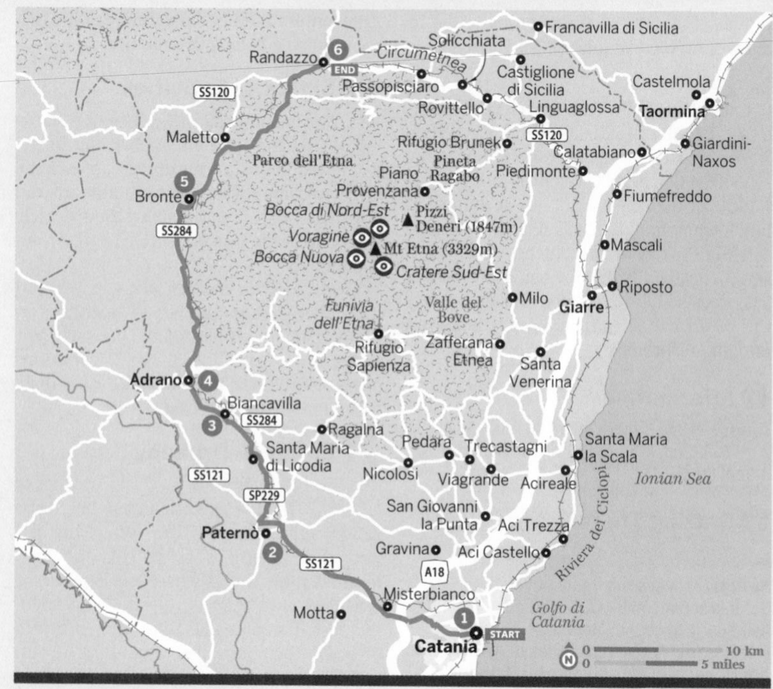

Driving Tour
Etna's Western Flank

START CATANIA
FINISH RANDAZZO
LENGTH 78KM / ONE DAY

The five small towns on the western side of the Parco dell'Etna offer a wonderful escape. Tourism has largely passed by these towns and each has a unique character.

Heading west out of 1 **Catania** on the SS121 brings you to 2 **Paternò**, a scruffy workaday town built around an 11th-century Norman *castello* (castle). Built in 1072 as a defence against the Saracens, the castle has been rebuilt over the centuries and now all that remains is the keep. But most impressive are the sweeping views up to Etna.

Continuing on the SP229 you'll pass huge *fichi d'india* (prickly pears) and orange groves (and piles of litter) on the way to 3 **Biancavilla**, a small town founded by Albanian refugees in 1480 but now typically Sicilian with many baroque churches. The market town of 4 **Adrano**, 3km further, boasts a robust Norman *castello* rising from a huge fortified base, commissioned by Count Roger II in the late 11th century. It now houses a small museum. Nearby, on Via Catania, you can see the remains of Adranon, a 4th-century-BC Greek settlement.

The SS284 heads directly north through acres of nut groves to 5 **Bronte**, famous throughout Italy for its pistachios (make sure you try a pistachio ice cream from the main strip, Corso Umberto). Beyond Bronte, the road leads through an increasingly rugged landscape, interspersed with chunks of lava flow, as it heads up to 6 **Randazzo**, the most interesting of Etna's towns.

Heavy bombing in WWII meant that much of the town's grey medieval centre had to be reconstructed. The main sights are the three crenellated churches, Cattedrale di Santa Maria, Chiesa di San Nicolò and Chiesa di San Martino, which in the 16th century took turns to act as the town cathedral. Round off the day with dinner at San Giorgio e Il Drago, a Slow Food–recommended trattoria with outdoor seating in the historic centre.

Aci Castello

☎095 / POP 18,725

Marking the beginning, or end, of the Riviera dei Ciclopi, the small town of Aci Castello lies 9km from central Catania, making it an easy day trip from the city, even by public transport. Swim off and tan on the volcanic rocks, otherwise, the main attraction is the *castello* set atop an immense black rock.

Sights

Castello CASTLE

(☎320 4339691; adult/reduced €3/1.50; ⏰9am-1pm & 4-8pm Jun–mid-Sep, 9am-1pm & 3-7pm Mar-May & mid-Sep–Oct, 9am-1pm & 3-5pm Nov-Feb) Built in the 13th century, this dark, brooding Norman castle sits over an earlier Arab fortification. It's in surprisingly good shape considering its age, and hosts a small museum with a collection of geological rock samples and bizarre prehistoric skulls. The castle appears to be grafted atop the Rocca di Acicastello, a vast, black volcanic rock. The rock is considered a vulcanological rarity, having emerged from an underwater fissure.

Getting There & Away

If driving from Catania, head north on the SS114.

AMT (p177) city bus 534 (€1, hourly) runs to Aci Castello from Catania's Piazza Borsellino. A more expensive option is the Tourist Service (p177) hop-on, hop-off bus (daily ticket €15), which also runs from Catania to Aci Castello and Aci Trezza.

MOUNT ETNA

ELEV 3329M

Dominating the landscape of eastern Sicily, Mt Etna is a massive brooding presence. At 3329m it is Italy's highest mountain south of the Alps and the largest active volcano in Europe. It's in an almost constant state of activity and eruptions occur frequently, most spectacularly from the four summit craters, but more often, and more dangerously, from the fissures and old craters on the mountain's flanks. This activity, which is closely monitored by 120 seismic activity stations and satellites, means that it is occasionally closed to visitors.

Since 1987 the volcano and its slopes have been part of a national park, the **Parco dell'Etna**. Encompassing 590 sq km and some 21 towns, the park's varied landscape ranges from the severe, snowcapped mountaintop to lunar deserts of barren black lava, beech woods and lush vineyards where the area's highly rated DOC wine is produced.

Activities

Walking

Mt Etna's southern slope is the most accessible and popular gateway for those wanting to ascend the volcano, and the starting point for getting up to the crater area is **Rifugio Sapienza** (1923m), a small cluster of souvenir shops and bars based around the eponymous mountain refuge (p256). From here there are various options for heading up towards the peak.

The easiest is to take the **Funivia dell'Etna** (☎095 91 41 41; www.funiviaetna.com; return €30, incl bus & guide €63; ⏰9am-4.15pm Apr-Nov, to 3.45pm Dec-Mar) up to 2500m and then a minibus to the Torre del Filosfo at 2920m. Alternatively, you can forego the minibus and walk from the upper cable-car station. It's quite a steep 2km walk and you should allow yourself up to four hours to get back in time for the return cable car. Another option is to walk all the way from Rifugio Sapienza, but this is a strenuous climb that will take about four hours (less on the way down). Note that in windy weather the cable-car service is suspended and replaced by a minibus.

There are four craters at the top: Bocca di Nord-Est (northeast crater), Voragine, Bocca Nuova and Cratere Sud-Est (southeast crater). The two you're most likely to see are Cratere Sud-Est, one of the most active, and Bocca Nuova. How close you can get will depend on the level of volcanic activity. If you're hiking without a guide, always err on the side of caution as the dangers around the craters are very real. To the east of the crater area, the Valle del Bove, a massive depression formed after a cone collapsed several thousand years ago, falls away in a precipitous 1000m drop.

Piano Provenzana WALKING

The gateway to Etna's quieter and more picturesque northern slopes is Piano Provenzana (1800m), a small ski station about 16km up from Linguaglossa. From July to October, **Gruppo Guide Alpine Etna Nord** (☎095 777 45 02; www.guidetnanord.com) runs jeep tours from here to 2900m, from where the craters are (strenuously) reached on foot. The trek back to Piano Provenzana affords spectacular views.

Further down the volcano, there's lovely summer walking in the pine, birch and larch trees of the **Pineta Ragabo**, a vast wood accessible from the Mareneve road between Linguaglossa and Milo.

Note that you'll need your own car to get to Piano Provenzana and the Pineta Ragabo, as no public transport passes this way.

Cycling

If cycling is your thing, there are some fine (albeit tough) trails around the mountain; you can hire bikes from **Etna Touring** (☎095 791 80 00; www.etnatouring.com; Via Roma 1, Nicolosi) in Nicolosi for €15 per day, as well as organise guided rides on request.

Skiing

Sicily is an unlikely skiing destination but you can do both downhill and cross-country here between December and March. The state of the slopes and how many lifts are working depends on the latest volcanic activity – check the current situation at www.etnasci.it.

In decent conditions there are five pistes on the southern side of the mountain and three on the northern side. A daily ski pass costs €30.

WINE, OIL & HONEY TASTING

Mt Etna is an important wine area, producing Etna DOC, one of 23 Sicilian wines to carry the Denominazione di Origine Controllata denomination.

There are numerous wineries in the area where you can taste the local *vino*. The volcano's picturesque northern slopes are home to highly acclaimed estate **Planeta Feudo di Mezzo** (☎0925 195 54 60; winetour@planeta.it; Contrada Sciara Nuova, Passopisciaro). Located 3.2km southwest of Passopisciaro (look for the 'Planeta' sign on the SS120 in town), it also produces exquisite olive oils: two single origins and a bolder blend. Degustations take place in a historic pressing room. Choose from a simple degustation of four wines and three oils (€15 per person), one with accompanying cheeses and charcuterie (€30) or a multicourse lunch (€40 to €50). Bookings should be made at least a day ahead, especially for lunch. Basic degustations are sometimes available with an hour's notice.

Also in Passopisciaro is **Vini Calcagno** (☎095 92 38 48; www.vinicalcagno.it; Via Regina Margherita 157, Passopisciaro), a small, fourth-generation family enterprise especially noted for its rose. While it doesn't have a dedicated *cantina* (cellar door) just yet, the family does offer tours of its century-old vines and degustations of its wines and olive oils (with accompanying charcuterie) in one of their old pressing cabins (€15 per person). Degustations should be booked at least one day in advance.

From Passopisciaro, the SS120 leads to big-gun winery **Patria Vini** (www.vinipatria.it; SS120, Solicchiata), 1.5km to the east. Of the area's wineries producing vintages, its degustations (€12 per person, with snacks) offer a tour of the site, including the fascinating bottling plant. Patria's on-site amphitheatre hosts occasional performances; see its Facebook page for upcoming events.

Of course, Etna is not all *vino e olio* (wine and oil). On its eastern slopes, the small town of **Zafferana Etnea** has a long tradition of apiculture, producing up to 35% of Italy's honey. For a taste, visit **Oro d'Etna** (☎095 708 14 11; Via San Giacomo 135, Zafferana Etnea; ⌚8.30am-6.30pm Mon-Sun), where you can try honey made from the blossoms of orange, chestnut and lemon trees.

The newly launched **Treno dei Vini dell'Etna** (Etna Wine Train; www.circumetnea.it; ticket adult/child 5-12 €23/10) is a handy way to explore the area's wineries without a car. The train runs on selected dates from May to November, leaving Riposto train station at 9.10am, arriving in Randazzo at 10.20am, from where a hop-on, hop-off 'Wine Bus' service continues to a number of wineries and towns on Etna's northern slopes.

The bus runs every two hours, giving time to lunch at a winery or explore the towns along the way. Tickets can be purchased at Circumetnea train stations, aboard the Wine Bus or from retail outlets displaying the 'Around Etna' sign. An optional coupon (€12) allows for a wine degustation at selected wineries and wine bars. From mid-June to September, a second train departs Riposto at 11.25am.

Note that in the summer, the Wine Train departs from Piedimonte Etneo station, with a bus transfer available to/from Randazzo. See the website for more details.

Tours

There are many operators offering guided tours up to the craters and elsewhere on the mountain, and even if your natural inclination is to avoid them, they are well worth considering. The guides know the mountain inside out, and are able to direct you to the most spectacular points, as well as explain what you're looking at. They also offer a valuable safety precaution. Tours typically involve some walking and 4WD transport.

Recommended reliable operators include **Etna Sicily Touring** (☎095 723 75 54, 392 5090298; www.etnasicilytouring.com), **Escursioni sull'Etna** (☎340 5780924), **Etna Experience** (☎349 3053021, 095 873 87 56; www.etnaexperience.com) and **Gruppo Guide Alpine Etna Sud** (☎389 3496086, 095 791 47 55; www.etnaguide.com).

Prices vary depending on the tour you take, but you should bank on spending from around €45 per person for a half-day tour (usually morning or sunset) and from about €65 for a full day.

Eating

Mt Etna's slopes are dotted with *trattorie*, restaurants and *agriturismi* (farm-stays), many serving rustic, turf-based local fare. Numerous wineries also offer local charcuterie, cheese or more substantial local fare as part of their wine and olive oil degustations, which usually require booking at least a day ahead.

Agriturismo San Marco SICILIAN €
(☎389 4237294; www.agriturismosanmarco.com; Rovittello; meals €23; ⏲1.30-3.30pm Mon-Sun, reservations required) Find your way to this welcoming *agriturismo* (farm-stay) near Rovittello for authentic farmhouse food in a lovely bucolic setting. À la carte offerings are ditched for a set daily menu of soulful, rustic grub that might include a *primo* of fresh pasta with meaty *ragú* or a *secondo* of succulent grilled meat. Bookings are required, but you'll need to call for directions anyway.

Antico Orto Dei Limoni SICILIAN €€
(☎095 91 08 08; www.ortolimoni.it; Via Grotte 4, Nicolosi; pizzas from €5, set menu €27; ⏲1-3pm & 7.30-11pm Wed-Mon) There can be few better ways of rounding off a day in the mountains than with a meal at this delightful Nicolosi restaurant. Occupying a converted wine and oil press, it specialises in tried-and-tested country fare. It's all good but the house antipasto (a mix of creamy ricotta, salami and marinated vegetables) is a standout.

Also try the excellent pasta with *ragù*, peas and mushrooms. If you're really hungry, go for the pharaonic set menu, which at €28 is excellent value.

Orientation

The two main approaches to Etna are from the north and south. The southern route, signposted as Etna Sud, is via Nicolosi and Rifugio Sapienza, 18km further up the mountain. The northern approach, Etna Nord, is through Piano Provenzana, 16km southwest of Linguaglossa.

Information

Parco dell'Etna (☎095 82 11 11; www.parcoetna.ct.it; Via del Convento 45, Nicolosi; ⏲9am-2pm & 4-7.30pm) Offers specialist information about Mt Etna, including climbing and hiking information. About 1.3km north of the centre of Nicolosi.

Proloco Linguaglossa (☎095 64 30 94; www.prolocolinguaglossa.it; Piazza Annunziata 5, Linguaglossa; ⏲9am-1pm & 4-7pm Mon-Sat, 9am-noon Sun) Local tourist office on Etna's northern side, with maps, brochures and general information on the area.

Nicolosi Tourist Office (☎095 91 44 88; Piazza Vittorio Emanuele 32, Nicolosi; ⏲9am-1.30pm Mon-Fri, plus 4-6pm Wed & Thu) Tourist office in the centre of Nicolosi, with information on Mt Etna and surrounds.

Getting There & Away

BUS

AST (☎095 723 05 11; www.aziendasicilianatrasporti.it) runs a daily bus from Catania to Rifugio Sapienza (return €6.60) via Nicolosi, leaving from Piazza Papa Giovanni XXIII (opposite Catania's main train station) at 8.15am and arriving at Rifugio Sapienza at 10.15am. The return journey leaves Rifugio Sapienza at 4.30pm, arriving in Catania at 6.30pm.

CAR & MOTORCYCLE

Nicolosi is about 17km northwest of Catania on the SP10. From Nicolosi it's a further 18km up to Rifugio Sapienza. For Linguaglossa, take the A18 autostrada from Catania, exit at Fiumefreddo and follow the SS120 towards Randazzo.

TRAIN

Slow train Ferrovia Circumetnea (p173) follows a 114km trail around the base of the volcano from Catania to Riposto. Affording great views, the service stops off at a number of small towns on the way, including Bronte and Randazzo. From Catania it takes two hours to reach Randazzo (one way/return €5.20/8.20) in the mountain's northern reaches.

Syracuse & the Southeast

Includes ➡

Best Places to Eat

- Ristorante Duomo (p209)
- La Cialoma (p201)
- Don Camillo (p194)
- Bistro Bella Vita (p193)
- Ristorante Vicari (p200)

Best Places to Sleep

- Hotel Gutkowski (p256)
- Nòtia Rooms (p257)
- Casa Gelsomino (p258)
- Casa Talía (p258)
- La Corte del Sole (p257)

Why Go?

Home to Magna Graecia's most magnificent ancient city and some of Italy's most glorious baroque towns, Sicily's southeast is the island's top draw.

The temptation is to stay in Syracuse, sipping *granite* (flavoured ice) in cinematic piazzas and sunning yourself on the seafront, but drag yourself away and you'll be falling head over heels for Sicily's most beautiful towns. Top billing goes to Noto, Modica and Ragusa, each one a feast of architectural flourishes and gastronomic delights – ice cream in Noto, chocolate in Modica and one of Sicily's finest restaurants in Ragusa. All three towns rose from the rubble of an earthquake in 1693 to become luminous examples of Sicilian baroque, a style that lends the region a cohesive aesthetic appeal.

Then there is the region's countryside, a sun-bleached canvas of sleepy backroads lined with carob trees, epic rocky ravines studded with prehistoric tombs, and tranquil, sandy beaches backed by bird-rich greenery.

Road Distances (km)

	Modica	Noto	Pachino	Ragusa
Noto	40			
Pachino	40	25		
Ragusa	15	50	55	
Syracuse	75	40	55	85

SYRACUSE & AROUND

Syracuse

0931 / POP 122,500

More than any other city, Syracuse encapsulates Sicily's timeless beauty. Ancient Greek ruins rise out of lush citrus orchards, cafe tables spill onto dazzling baroque piazzas, and honey-hued medieval lanes lead down to the sparkling blue sea. It's difficult to imagine now but in its heyday this was the largest city in the ancient world, bigger even than Athens and Corinth. Its 'Once upon a Time' begins in 734 BC, when Corinthian colonists landed on the island of Ortygia and founded the settlement, setting up the mainland city four years later. Almost three millennia later, the ruins of that then-new city constitute the Parco Archeologico della Neapolis, one of Sicily's greatest archaeological sites. Across the water from the mainland, Ortygia remains the city's most beautiful corner, a casually chic, eclectic marvel with an ever-growing legion of fans.

Sights

Ortygia

A labyrinth of atmospheric alleyways and refined piazzas, Ortygia is really what Syracuse is all about. Skinny lanes are lined with attractive *palazzi,* vibrant eateries and cafes, and the central square, Piazza del Duomo, is one of Sicily's most spectacular. The entire mini-peninsula is framed by beautiful houses and walls that look out onto the sea; there is swimming off the rocks in the summer months and incredible views all year round. Get away from the tourist crowds and explore the mesmerising maze of la Giudecca, Ortygia's old Jewish Quarter. The area, accessed by way of Ponte Nuovo, is best explored on foot.

★**Piazza del Duomo** PIAZZA

(Map p188) Syracuse's showpiece square is a masterpiece of baroque town planning. A long, rectangular piazza flanked by flamboyant *palazzi,* it sits on what was once Syracuse's ancient acropolis (fortified citadel). Little remains of the original Greek building but if you look along the side of the Duomo, you'll see a number of thick Doric columns incorporated into the cathedral's structure.

To the north of the Duomo, over Via Minerva, **Palazzo Municipale** (Map p188; Palazzo Senatoriale) is home to Syracuse city council. Built in 1629 by the Spaniard Juan Vermexio, it is nicknamed 'Il Lucertolone' (the Lizard) after the architect's signature – a small lizard carved into a stone on the left corner of the cornice. On the other side of the Duomo, the elegant, 17th-century **Palazzo Arcivescovile** (Archbishop's Palace; Map p188; Piazza del Duomo) is home to the **Biblioteca Alagoniana** and some rare 13th-century manuscripts.

Over the square, in the northwestern corner, is the **Palazzo Beneventano del Bosco** (Map p188), which sports a pretty 18th-century facade, while at its southern end is the **Chiesa di Santa Lucia alla Badia** (Map p188; 0931 6 53 28; Via Santa Lucia alla Badia 2; by donation; 11am-4pm Tue-Sun), home to Caravaggio's arresting masterpiece, *Il seppellimento di Santa Lucia* (Burial of St Lucy), painted in Syracuse between 1608 and 1609.

★**Duomo** CATHEDRAL

(Map p188; Piazza del Duomo; adult/reduced €2/1; 9am-6.30pm Mon-Sat Apr-Oct, to 5.30pm Nov-Mar) Built on the skeleton of a 5th-century BC Greek temple to Athena (note the Doric columns still visible inside and out), Syracuse's cathedral became a church when the island was evangelised by St Paul. Its most striking feature is the columned baroque facade (1728–53) added by Andrea Palma after the 1693 earthquake. A statue of the Virgin Mary crowns the rooftop, in the same spot where a golden statue of Athena once served as a beacon to homecoming Greek sailors.

The original temple was renowned throughout the Mediterranean, in no small part thanks to Cicero, who visited Ortygia in the 1st century BC. Note the interesting baptismal font to the right as you enter; it consists of an ancient Greek *krater* (large vase) adorned by seven 13th-century bronze lions.

Castello Maniace CASTLE

(Map p188; Piazza Federico di Svevia; adult/reduced €4/2; 9am-1.30pm) Guarding the island's southern tip, Ortygia's 13th-century castle is a lovely place to wander, gaze out over the water and contemplate Syracuse's past glories. The castle grounds house two exhibitions, one shedding light on the fortress' evolution through the centuries, the other displaying archaeological objects from the site, including Norman-era ceramics and some curious-looking ceramic hand grenades

Syracuse & the Southeast Highlights

1 **Syracuse** (p185) Exploring the mighty Greek ruins, ancient Jewish ritual bath and vibrant island street life of this ancient town.

2 **Noto** (p197) Taking in scoops of gelato and swirls of baroque in this World Heritage beauty.

3 **Modica** (p202) Feasting on cult-status chocolate and bombastic churches in this dramatically situated town.

4 **Ragusa** (p206) Falling for beautiful, twisting streets and whirling baroque architecture in Ragusa's historic heart.

5 **Riserva Naturale Oasi Faunistica di Vendicari** (p201) Being lulled by golden rays and aqua waves on the sandy, tranquil beaches of this wild reserve.

6 **Marzamemi** (p201) Seaside lunching and piazza-side sunning in this pretty, peeling fishing village.

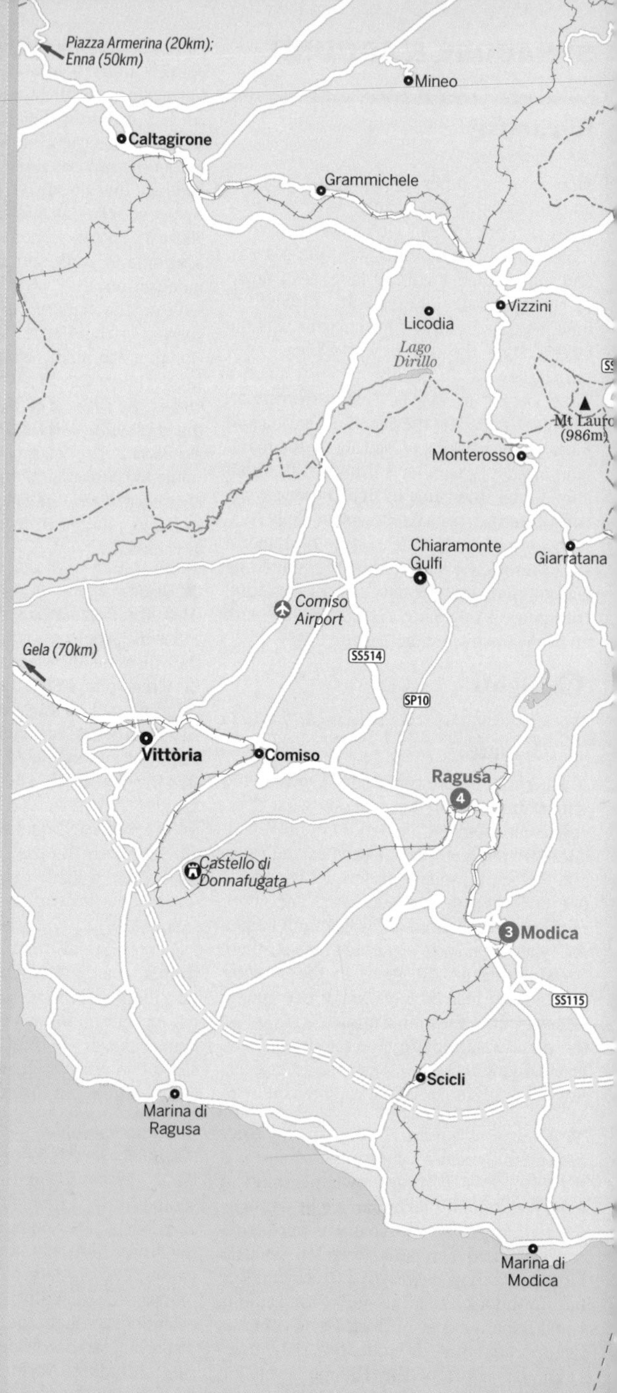

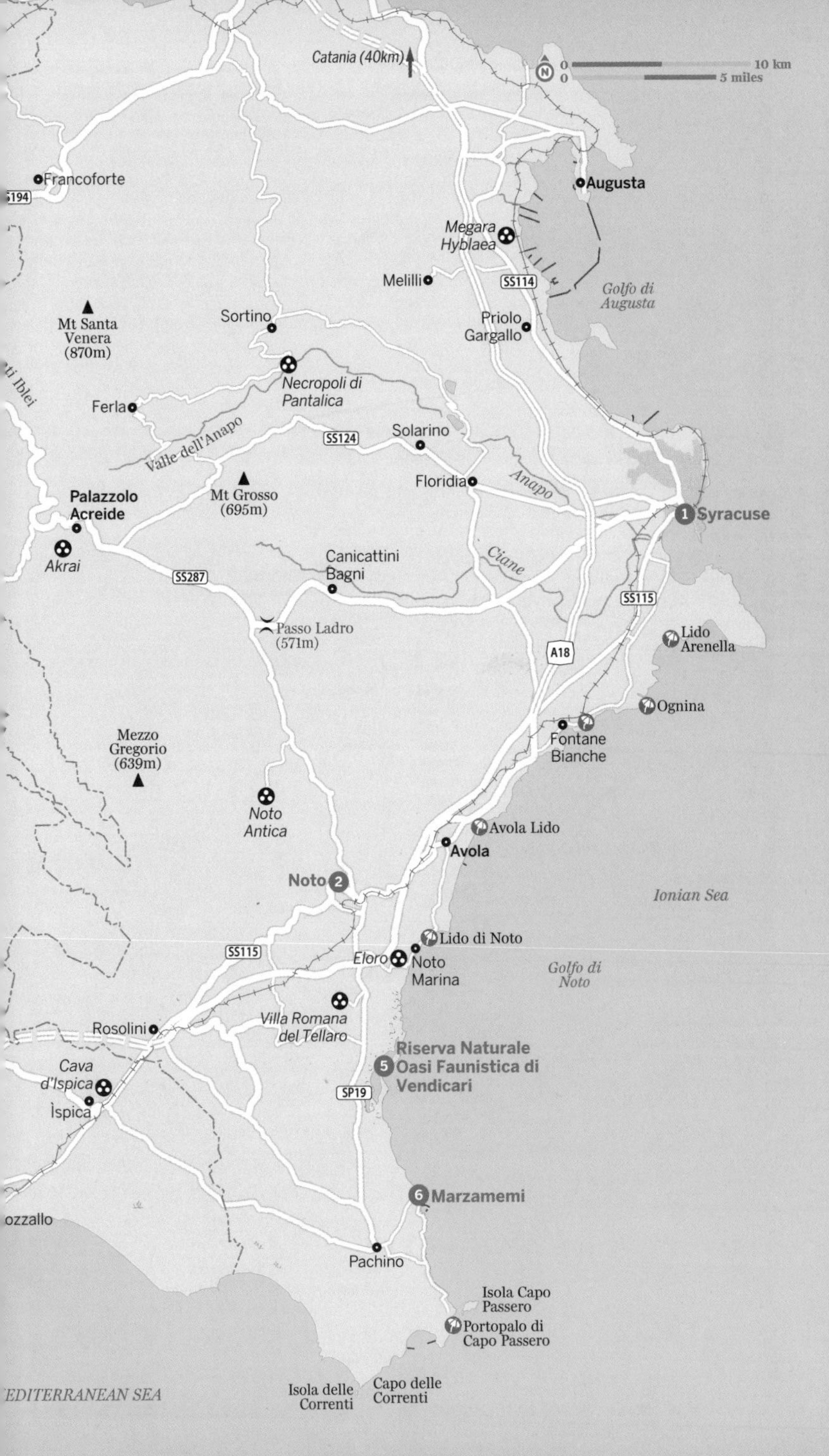

Catania (40km)
0 10 km
0 5 miles
Francoforte
Augusta
Megara Hyblaea
Melilli
SS114
Golfo di Augusta
Mt Santa Venera (870m)
Sortino
Priolo Gargallo
Necropoli di Pantalica
Ferla
Valle dell'Anapo
SS124
Solarino
Floridia
Anapo
Mt Grosso (695m)
Palazzolo Acreide
Akrai
1 Syracuse
Canicattini Bagni
Ciane
SS287
SS115
Passo Ladro (571m)
Lido Arenella
A18
Ognina
Fontane Bianche
Mezzo Gregorio (639m)
Noto Antica
Avola Lido
Avola
Noto 2
Ionian Sea
Lido di Noto
SS115
Eloro
Noto Marina
Golfo di Noto
Villa Romana del Tellaro
Rosolini
Riserva Naturale
5 Oasi Faunistica di Vendicari
Cava d'Ispica
Ìspica
SP19
6 Marzamemi
Pachino
Isola Capo Passero
Portopalo di Capo Passero
Isola delle Correnti
Capo delle Correnti

Ortygia

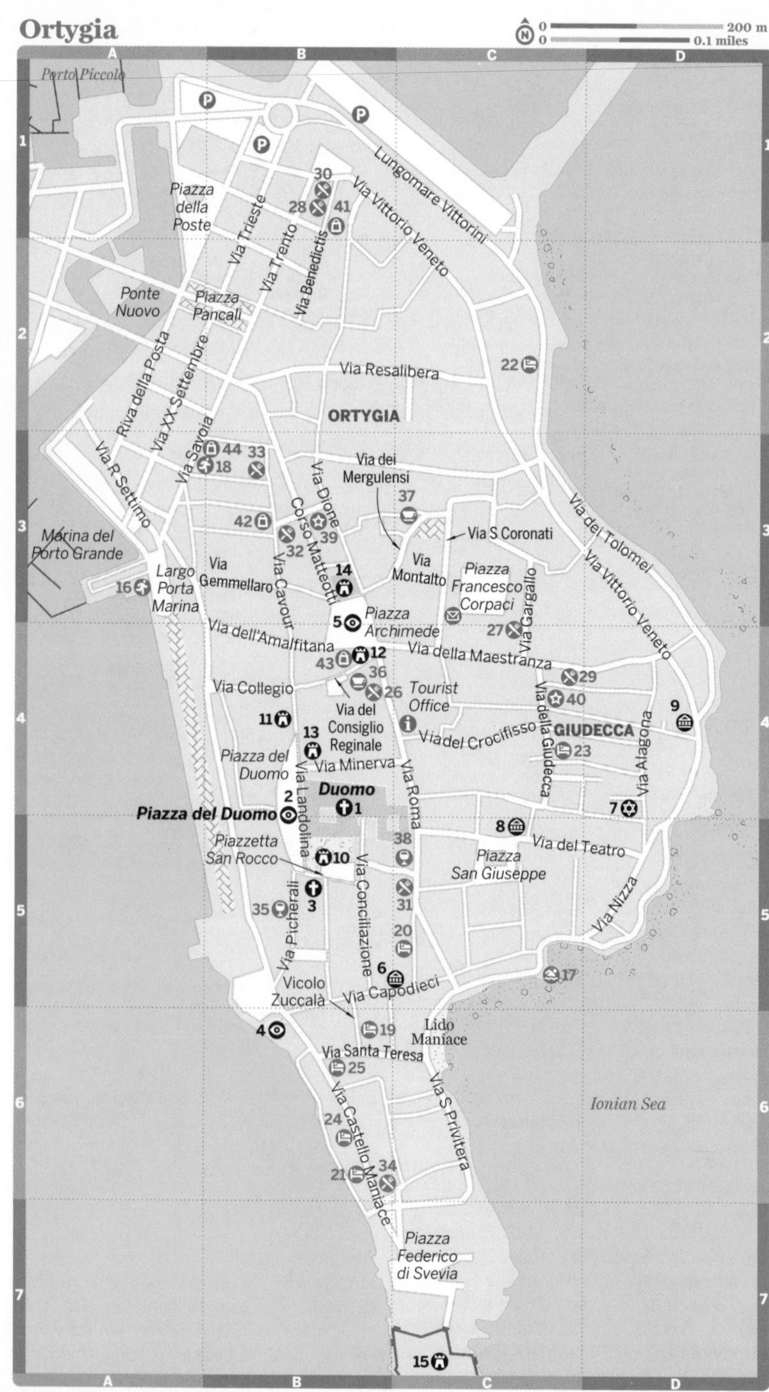

0 200 m
0 0.1 miles
Porto Piccolo
Piazza della Poste
Ponte Nuovo
Piazza Pancali
Lungomare Vittorini
Via Vittorio Veneto
Via Trieste
Via Trento
Via Benedictis
Riva della Posta
Via XX Settembre
Via Savoia
Via R Settimo
Via Resalibera
ORTYGIA
Via dei Mergulensi
Via Dione
Corso Matteotti
Via S Coronati
Via dei Tolomei
Marina del Porto Grande
Largo Porta Marina
Via Gemmellaro
Via Cavour
Via Montalto
Piazza Francesco Corpaci
Via Gargallo
Piazza Archimede
Via dell'Amalfitana
Via della Maestranza
Via Collegio
Via del Consiglio Reginale
Tourist Office
Via del Crocifisso
GIUDECCA
Via della Giudecca
Via Alagona
Piazza del Duomo
Via Minerva
Via Landolina
Via Roma
Duomo
Piazzetta San Rocco
Via del Teatro
Piazza San Giuseppe
Via Nizza
Via Picherali
Via Conciliazione
Vicolo Zuccalà
Via Capodieci
Lido Maniace
Via Santa Teresa
Via S Privitera
Via Castello Maniace
Ionian Sea
Piazza Federico di Svevia

Ortygia

Top Sights
1 Duomo ... B4
2 Piazza del Duomo ... B4

Sights
3 Chiesa di Santa Lucia alla Badia ... B5
4 Fontana Aretusa ... B6
5 Fontana di Artemide ... B3
6 Galleria Regionale di Palazzo Bellomo ... C5
7 Miqwe ... D4
8 Museo Aretuseo dei Pupi ... C5
9 Museo del Papiro ... D4
10 Palazzo Arcivescovile ... B5
11 Palazzo Beneventano del Bosco ... B4
12 Palazzo Lanza-Bucceri ... B4
13 Palazzo Municipale ... B4
14 Palazzo Platamone ... B3
15 Taleet ... C7

Activities, Courses & Tours
Biblios Cafè ... (see 36)
16 Compagnia del Selene ... A3
17 Forte Vigliena ... C5
18 Sailing Team ... A3

Sleeping
19 B&B Aretusa Vacanze ... B6
20 B&B dei Viaggiatori, Viandanti e Sognatori ... C5
21 Henry's House ... B6
22 Hotel Gutkowski ... C2
23 La Via della Giudecca ... C4
24 Palazzo Bianco ... B6
25 Palazzo del Sale ... B6

Eating
26 A Putia delle Cose Buone ... B4
27 Bistrot Bella Vita ... C4
28 Caseificio Borderi ... B1
29 Don Camillo ... C4
30 Fratelli Burgio ... B1
31 Moon ... C5
32 Sicilia in Tavola ... B3
33 Sicily ... B3
34 Taberna Sveva ... B6

Drinking & Nightlife
35 Barcollo ... B5
36 Biblios Cafè ... B4
37 Movimento Centrale ... C3
38 Solaria Vini & Liquori ... C5

Entertainment
39 Fondazione Inda ticket office ... B3
40 Piccolo Teatro dei Pupi ... C4

Shopping
41 Antico Mercato ... B1
42 Fish House Art ... B3
43 Massimo Izzo ... B4
44 Terracotta Ceramiche di Caltagirone ... B3

from the 16th century. Opening times are subject to change.

Galleria Regionale di Palazzo Bellomo GALLERY
(Map p188; ☎0931 6 95 11; www.regione.sicilia.it/beniculturali/palazzobellomo; Via Capodieci 16; adult/reduced €8/4; ⊙9am-7pm Tue-Sat, to 1pm Sun) Housed in a 13th-century Catalan-Gothic palace, this art museum's eclectic collection ranges from early Byzantine and Norman stonework to 19th-century Caltagirone ceramics. In between there's a good range of medieval religious paintings and sculpture, as well as a fetching couple of 18th-century Sicilian carriages.

Museo del Papiro MUSEUM
(Map p188; ☎0931 2 21 00; www.museodelpapiro.it; Via Nizza 14; adult/reduced €5/2; ⊙10am-7pm Tue-Sat, to 2pm Sun May-Sep, 9.15am-2pm Tue-Sun Oct-Apr) Ortygia's Museo del Papiro offers a fine collection of papyrus documents and products, boats and an English-language film about the nifty material's history. That Syracuse has a museum dedicated to papyrus is hardly coincidental; the papyrus plant grows in abundance around the nearby Ciane River, and was used to make paper in the 18th century.

Mainland Syracuse

Although not as picturesque as Ortygia, the mainland city is home to a number of fascinating archaeological sights. The most compelling is the Parco Archeologico della Neapolis northwest of the city centre, but you'll also find plenty of interest at the city's renowned archaeological museum, the Museo Archeologico Paolo Orsi. Underground, an extensive network of catacombs dates from the Roman era.

★**Parco Archeologico della Neapolis** ARCHAEOLOGICAL SITE
(Map p190; ☎0931 6 62 06; Viale Paradiso 14; adult/reduced €10/5, incl Museo Archeologico €13.50/7; ⊙8.30am-1.45pm Mon, last entry 12.45pm, 8.30am-7.30pm Tue-Sun, last entry 6pm) For the classicist, Syracuse's real attraction is this archaeological park, home to the pearly

Syracuse

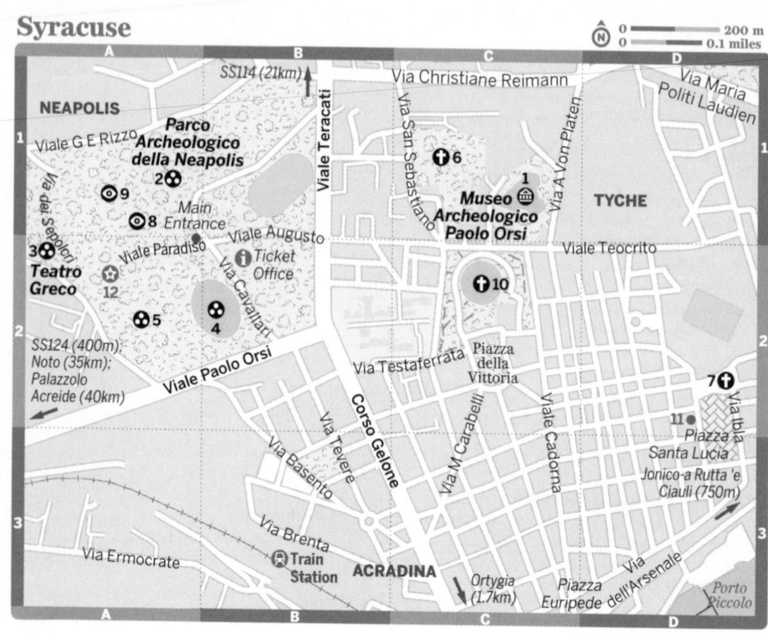

Syracuse

Top Sights

1 Museo Archeologico Paolo Orsi C1
2 Parco Archeologico della Neapolis A1
3 Teatro Greco A2

Sights

4 Anfiteatro Romano B2
5 Ara di Gerone II A2
6 Basilica & Catacombe di San Giovanni C1
7 Basilica di Santa Lucia al Sepolcro D2
8 Latomia del Paradiso A1
9 Orecchio di Dionisio A1
10 Santuario della Madonna delle Lacrime C2

Activities, Courses & Tours

11 Natura Sicula D2

Entertainment

12 Fondazione Inda ticket booth A2

white 5th-century-BC **Teatro Greco** (Map p190; Parco Archeologico della Neapolis). Hewn out of the rocky hillside, this 16,000-capacity amphitheatre staged the last tragedies of Aeschylus (including *The Persians*), first performed here in his presence. In late spring it's brought to life with an annual season of classical theatre.

Beside the theatre is the mysterious **Latomia del Paradiso** (Garden of Paradise; Map p190; Parco Archeologico della Neapolis), a deep, precipitous limestone quarry out of which stone for the ancient city was extracted. Riddled with catacombs and filled with citrus and magnolia trees, it's also where the 7000 survivors of the war between Syracuse and Athens in 413 BC were imprisoned. The **Orecchio di Dionisio** (Ear of Dionysius; Map p190; Parco Archeologico della Neapolis), a 23m-high grotto extending 65m back into the cliffside, was named by Caravaggio after the tyrant Dionysius, who is said to have used the almost perfect acoustics of the quarry to eavesdrop on his prisoners.

Back outside this area you'll find the entrance to the 2nd-century **Anfiteatro Romano** (Map p190; Parco Archeologico della Neapolis), originally used for gladiatorial combats and horse races. The Spaniards, little interested in archaeology, largely destroyed the site in the 16th century, using it as a quarry to build Ortygia's city walls. West of the amphitheatre is the 3rd-century-BC **Ara di Gerone II** (Altar of Hieron II; Map p190; Parco Archeologico della Neapolis), a monolithic sacrificial altar to Heron II, where up to 450 oxen could be killed at one time.

To reach the park, take Sd'A Trasporti minibus 2 (€1, 15 minutes) from Molo Sant'Antonio, on the west side of the main bridge into Ortygia. Alternatively, walking from Ortygia will take about 30 minutes. If driving, park on Viale Augusto (tickets are available at the nearby souvenir kiosks).

The **ticket office** (Map p190; Parco Archeologico della Neapolis) is located near the corner of Via Cavallari and Viale Augusto, opposite the main site.

★Museo Archeologico Paolo Orsi MUSEUM
(Map p190; ☎0931 48 95 11; www.regione.sicilia.it/beniculturali/museopaoloorsi; Viale Teocrito 66; adult/reduced €8/4, incl Parco Archeologico €13.50/7; ⊙9am-6pm Tue-Sat, to 1pm Sun) About 500m east of the archaeological park, this modern museum contains one of Sicily's largest and most interesting archaeological collections. Allow plenty of time to investigate the four sectors charting the area's prehistory, as well as Syracuse's development from foundation to the late Roman period.

Basilica di Santa Lucia al Sepolcro CHURCH, CATACOMB
(Map p190; ☎0931 6 46 94; www.kairos-web.com; Piazza Santa Lucia; church free, guided tour of catacombs & Sepolcro adult/reduced €8/5; ⊙church 8.30am-noon & 4-6.30pm, 8.30-10.30am Sun, guided tours of catacombs & Sepolcro 10am-5pm Mon-Sat) The northern end of Piazza Santa Lucia, one of the city's biggest squares, is dominated by the Basilica di Santa Lucia al Sepolcro. The current 17th-century building stands on the site where the city's patron saint, Lucia, an aristocratic girl who devoted herself to saintliness after being blessed by St Agatha, was martyred in 304. In fact, the marble column to the right of the main altar is believed to be the very spot where the saint's life was taken.

The church is an impressive sight with its columned portico, Norman portal (a remnant of the previous Norman church) and 18th-century octagonal chapel known as the Sepolcro. The chapel is home to a reputedly miraculous sculpture of St Lucia. Created by Tuscan sculptor Gregorio Tedeschi in the 17th century, the saint's marble face, hands and feet famously perspired for three consecutive days in May 1735.

Lurking beneath the church is an impressive network of **catacombs**, used by the early Christians for burials. Both the Sepolcro and catacombs can be visited on 40-minute guided tours (in Italian and English).

According to Roman law, Christians were not allowed to bury their dead within the city limits (which, during the Roman occupation, did not extend beyond Ortygia), so the early Christians used the outlying district of Tyche for burials, accessing underground aqueducts unused since Greek times. New tunnels were carved out, and the result was a labyrinthine network of burial chambers.

Basilica & Catacombe di San Giovanni CHURCH, CATACOMB
(Map p190; ☎0931 6 46 94; www.kairos-web.com; Via San Sebastiano; guided tour adult/reduced €8/5; ⊙9.30am-12.30pm & 2.30-5.30pm Tue-Sun) The city's most extensive catacombs lie beneath the Basilica di San Giovanni, itself a pretty, truncated church that served as the city's cathedral in the 17th century. It is dedicated to the city's first bishop, St Marcian, who was tied to one of its pillars and

LEGENDARY FOUNTAINS

Fresh water has been bubbling up at the **Fontana Aretusa** (Map p188; Largo Aretusa) since ancient times when it was the city's main water supply. The fountain, now the place to hang out on summer evenings, is a monumental affair set around a pond full of papyrus plants and grey mullets.

Legend has it that Artemis, the mythical goddess of hunting, transformed her beautiful handmaiden Aretusa into the spring to protect her from the unwelcome attention of the river god Alpheus. In her watery guise, Aretusa fled from Arcadia under the sea, hotly pursued by Alpheus, their waters mingling as she came to the surface in Ortygia.

Artemis is the star turn of **Fontana di Artemide** (Fontana di Diana; Map p188; Piazza Archimede), the 19th-century fountain that's the highlight of Piazza Archimede, a handsome square that's circled by imposing Catalan Gothic *palazzi*, including **Palazzo Lanza-Bucceri** (Map p188; Piazza Archimede) and **Palazzo Platamone** (Map p188; Piazza Archimede), now home to the Banca d'Italia.

DON'T MISS

LA GIUDECCA

Simply walking through Ortygia's tangled maze of nougat-coloured alleys is an atmospheric experience, especially down the narrow lanes of **Via Maestranza**, the heart of the old guild quarter, and the quickly gentrifying Jewish ghetto of Via della Giudecca. At the Alla Giudecca hotel you can visit an ancient Jewish **miqwe** (Ritual Bath; Map p188; 0931 2 22 55; Via Alagona 52; tours in English & Italian €5; tours 9am-7pm late-Mar–Oct, reduced hours rest of year) some 20m below ground level. Blocked up in 1492 when the Jewish community was expelled from Ortygia, the baths were rediscovered during renovation work at the hotel.

A short walk away, Syracuse's much-loved puppet theatre, the **Piccolo Teatro dei Pupi** (Map p188; 0931 46 55 40; www.pupari.com; Via della Giudecca 17; 6 times weekly Apr-Oct, fewer Nov-Mar) stages puppet shows re-enacting traditional tales involving magicians, love-struck princesses, knights and dragons. See the website for a calendar of performances. The puppet workshop is at Via della Giudecca 19, while just down the road, the small **Museo Aretuseo dei Pupi** (Map p188; 0931 46 55 40; Palazzo Midiri-Cardona, Piazza San Giuseppe; adult/reduced €3/2; 11am-6pm Mon-Sat summer, 11am-1pm & 4-6pm Mon-Sat winter) chronicles Sicily's rich history of puppet theatre.

flogged to death in 254. The church and eerie catacombs are only accessible on 30- to 40-minute guided tours (available in English), which depart regularly from the site's ticket office.

Activities

Sailing Team BOATING

(Map p188; 093 16 08 08; www.sailingteam.biz; Via Savoia 14; day trip for 6-8 people from €350) For an unforgettable experience, book a boat trip on one of the sailing boats rented out by Sailing Team. Trips set off down the south coast to explore beaches and pristine nature reserves.

Compagnia del Selene BOATING

(Map p188; 347 1275680; www.compagniadelselene.it; Foro Vittorio Emanuele II; 50min tour per adult/under 10yr €10/free) This sailing outfit takes passengers around Ortygia on a ride that offers splendid views of the city. Passengers have the option of enjoying lunch, *aperitivo* or dinner on board (booked ahead), while in the summer months, tours include a sightseeing-and-swimming combo and an evening cruise.

Boat Trip BOATING

(368 3170711; per person €12) A popular diversion between March and November is a boat trip up the Ciane, a mythical river dedicated to the nymph Ciane. The river habitat – a tangle of lush papyrus – is the only place outside North Africa where papyrus grows wild. From town follow signs to Palazzolo Acreide. The turn-off for the boat tour is marked by a road sign labelled 'Tours Boat Ciane'.

Forte Vigliena SWIMMING

(Map p188) Flanked by the crenellated walls of Forte Vigliena along Ortygia's eastern waterfront, this platform surrounded by flat rocks is a favourite local hang-out for swimming and sunbathing in the summer months.

Lido Arenella SWIMMING

(www.lidomaniace.it) Serious beach bunnies make the short trip south from Ortygia to Arenella, where sandy, blue-flag beaches await. Be warned, though, that it gets very busy here, particularly on summer weekends. Catch bus 23 from Corso Umberto I.

Festivals & Events

Ciclo di Rappresentazioni Classiche THEATRE

(Festival of Greek Theatre; www.indafondazione.org) Syracuse boasts the only school of classical Greek drama outside Athens, and in May and June it hosts live performances of Greek plays (in Italian) at the Teatro Greco, attracting Italy's finest performers. Tickets (€26 to €69) are available online, from the **Fondazione Inda ticket office** (Map p188; office 0931 48 72 00, tickets 800 542644; www.indafondazione.org; Corso Matteotti 29; 10am-1pm Mon-Sat) in Ortygia or at the **ticket booth** (Map p190; 10am-6.30pm) outside the theatre.

Festa di Santa Lucia RELIGIOUS

On 13 December, the enormous silver statue of the city's patron saint wends its way from the cathedral to Piazza Santa Lucia accompanied by fireworks.

Eating

Ortygia is the best place to eat. Its postcard-pretty streets heave with bustling trattorias, romantic restaurants and hip cafes and bars. While some are obvious tourist traps, many are not, and you'll have no trouble finding somewhere to suit your style. Most places specialise in surf, so expect plenty of seafood pasta and grilled catches-of-the-day.

★Caseificio Borderi SANDWICHES €
(Map p188; Via Benedictis 6; sandwiches €5; 6am-4pm Mon-Sat) No visit to Syracuse's market is complete without a stop at this colourful deli near Ortygia's far northern tip. Veteran sandwich-master Andrea Borderi stands out front with a table full of cheeses, olives, greens, herbs, tomatoes and other fixings and engages in nonstop banter with customers while creating free-form sandwiches big enough to keep you fed all day.

Fratelli Burgio SICILIAN €
(Map p188; 0931 6 00 69; www.fratelliburgio.com; Piazza Cesare Battisti 4; panini €3.50-6, platters €12-20; 7am-3.30pm Mon-Sat;) A hybrid deli, wine shop and eatery edging Ortygia's market, trendy Fratelli Burgio is all about artisanal grazing. Consider opting for a *tagliere*, a wooden platter of artful bites, from velvety cow-milk mousse with chargrilled aubergine, to zesty *caponata* (sweet-and-sour vegetables). If you're europinching, fill up on one of the gourmet *panini*, stuffed with a range of seasonal veggies, herbs, cured meats and cheeses.

Sicily PIZZA €
(Map p188; 392 9659949; www.sicilypizzeria.it; Via Cavour 67; pizzas €4.50-12; 7pm-midnight Tue-Sun) Experimenting with pizzas is something you do at your peril in culinary-conservative Sicily. But that's what they do, and do well, at this funky retro-chic pizzeria. So if you're game for wood-fired pizzas topped with more-ish combos like sausage, cheese, Swiss chard, pine nuts, sun-dried tomatoes and raisins, this is the place for you.

Sicilia in Tavola SICILIAN €
(Map p188; 392 4610889; Via Cavour 28; meals €20-30; 12.30-2.30pm & 7.30-10.30pm Tue-Sun) One of the longest established and most popular eateries on Via Cavour, this snug, simple trattoria has built its reputation on delicious homemade pasta and seafood. To savour both at once, tuck into the *fettuccine allo scoglio* (pasta ribbons with mixed seafood) or the equally fine prawn ravioli, paired with sweet cherry tomatoes and chopped mint. Reservations recommended.

★Bistrot Bella Vita ITALIAN €€
(Map p188; 0931 46 49 38; Via Gargallo 60; sweets €1.50, meals €25; cafe 7.30am-midnight, restaurant noon-2.30pm & 7-10.45pm Tue-Sun) Owned by affable Lombard expat Norma and her Sicilian pastry-chef husband Salvo, this casually elegant cafe-restaurant is one of Ortygia's rising stars. Stop by for good coffee (soy milk available) and made-from-scratch *cornetti, biscotti* and pastries (try the sour orange-and-almond tart). Or book a table in the intimate back dining room, where local, organic produce drives beautifully textured, technically impressive dishes.

★Moon VEGAN €€
(Map p188; 0931 44 95 16; www.moonortigia.com; Via Roma 112; meals €18-30; 11am-midnight Wed-Mon late-Apr–Oct, 6pm-midnight Wed-Mon Nov–mid-Jan & mid-Feb–late Apr;) If vegan fare usually makes you yawn, subvert your thinking at boho-chic Moon. A cast of mostly organic and biological ingredients beam in decadent, intriguing dishes that might see a tower of thinly sliced pears interlayered with a rich, soy-based cashew cream cheese, or chickpea and tofu conspiring in a smokey *linguine alla carbonara* as wicked as the original.

From the contemporary art and sculptural lighting, to the upcycled furniture, everything at Moon is for sale, which also doubles as a performance space, serving up

TOP COURSES

Italian cookery classes Brush up your cooking skills with a three-hour lesson at **La Corte del Sole** (0931 82 02 10; www.lacortedelsole.it; Contrada Bucachemi, Lido di Noto; 3hr lesson per person €70; 9.30am-12.30pm Tue-Sat, closed Aug) hotel, near Lido di Noto.

Learn the language In Syracuse, **Biblios Cafè** (Map p188; 0931 6 16 27; www.biblioscafe.it; Via del Consiglio Regionale 11) runs language courses enlivened by shopping trips to the local market, cooking lessons and visits to local wine producers.

weekly theatre and music performances on its small backstage.

A Putia delle Cose Buone SICILIAN €€
(Map p188; ☎0931 44 92 79; www.aputiadellecosebuone.it; Via Roma 8; meals €18-30; ⊙12.45-3pm & 7-11pm; ✍) From the whimsical lanterns to the benches draped in colourful pillows, this little bolthole feels welcoming from the word go. Then there's the food: creative, reasonably priced Sicilian dishes that make ample use of local seafood, veggies and extra-virgin olive oil (labelled EVO on the menu). Salads, vegan and vegetarian options also abound. Service is friendly, and there's pavement seating in warm weather.

Jonico-a Rutta 'e Ciauli SICILIAN €€
(☎0931 6 55 40; Riviera Dionisio il Grande 194; pizza €4.50-9, meals €25-35; ⊙12.30-2.30pm & 7-11.30pm, closed Tue Oct-May; 📶) It's a long and not particularly enticing hike to this seafront restaurant, but once you're there you'll appreciate the effort. On warm days, the terrace is utter bliss, the sound of crashing waves below a suitable soundtrack to competent, regional dishes like *spaghetti alla palermitana* (with sardines, fennel and raisins) and *orata all'arancia* (sea bream cooked in orange juice).

Taberna Sveva SICILIAN €€
(Map p188; ☎0931 2 46 63; Piazza Federico di Svevia; meals €25-30; ⊙6.30-11.30pm Mon-Sun Jun-Sep, noon-3pm & 7-10.30pm Thu-Tue Oct-May) Away from the main tourist maelstrom, charming Taberna Sveva occupies a quiet corner of Ortygia. On warm summer evenings the outdoor terrace is the place to sit, with alfresco tables set out on a tranquil cobbled square in front of Syracuse's 13th-century castle. Flavours are old-school Sicilian, so expect plenty of tuna and swordfish and some wonderful pasta. Slow Food recommended.

★**Don Camillo** MODERN SICILIAN €€€
(Map p188; ☎0931 6 71 33; www.ristorantedoncamillo.it; Via Maestranza 96; degustation menus €35-70; ⊙12.30-2.30pm & 8-10.30pm Mon-Sat; 📶✍) One of Ortygia's most elegant restaurants, Don Camillo specialises in sterling service and innovative Sicilian cuisine. Pique the appetite with mixed shellfish in a thick soup of Noto almonds, swoon over the swordfish with orange-blossom honey and sweet-and-sour vegetables, or (discreetly) lick your whiskers over an outstanding *tagliata di tonno* (tuna steak) with red-pepper 'marmalade'. A must for Slow Food gourmands.

Drinking & Nightlife

A vibrant university town, Syracuse has a lively cafe culture, with many bars and cafes spilling over Ortygia's gorgeous streets. Piazzetta San Rocco is a popular spot, as is the seafront around Fontana Aretusa.

Biblios Cafè CAFE
(Map p188; www.biblioscafe.it; Via del Consiglio Reginale 11; ⊙noon-9pm Wed-Mon Apr-Oct, 10am-2pm & 5-10pm Wed-Mon Nov-Mar) This beloved bookshop-cafe organises a whole range of cultural activities, including wine-tasting, literary readings, creative workshops and language courses. It's also a great place to drop in any time of day, for coffee or *aperitivi* or just to mingle.

Movimento Centrale CAFE
(Map p188; www.movimentocentrale.net; Via dei Mergulensi 33; ⊙9am-11pm Fri-Wed) This hip little cafe-cum-bike-shop serves drinks, juices and healthy snacks, and offers a 10% discount to people who arrive by bike.

Barcollo BAR
(Map p188; Via Pompeo Picherali 10; ⊙7pm-3am; 📶) Hidden away in a flamboyant baroque courtyard, sultry Barcollo lures with its fresh flowers, flickering tealights and chi-chi outdoor deck. *Aperitivo* is served daily between 7pm and 10pm (there's an *aperitivo* buffet on Sunday), with DJ sets on Friday and Sunday, and live music on Saturday.

Solaria Vini & Liquori WINE BAR
(Map p188; ☎0931 46 30 07; www.vini-siciliani.it; Via Roma 86; ⊙11.30am-2.30pm & 6pm-1am Mon-Sat; 📶) A wonderfully old-school *enoteca* (wine shop), with rows of rustic wooden tables and dark bottles lined up on floor-to-ceiling shelves. Stop by for a glass of wine or two, well paired with *vino*-friendly bites including cheese, olives, prosciutto, anchovies, sardines and *crocchè* (potato croquettes). The wine list is extensive and predominantly local, with French vintages and Champagnes thrown in for Gallic flair.

Shopping

Browsing Ortygia's quirky boutiques is great fun. Good buys include papyrus paper, ceramics and handmade jewellery. While shops are peppered across the island, you'll find a concentration of interesting boutiques and galleries on Via Cavour and Via Roma.

Fish House Art ARTS & CRAFTS

(Map p188; ☎339 7771364; www.fishhouseart.it; Via Cavour 29-31; ⏲10am-1pm & 4-8pm Mon-Sat) The theme is marine at Fish House Art, a quirky gallery and shop swimming with whimsical, beautifully crafted objects inspired by the sea. It's a showcase for both emerging and established Italian artisans, whose wares span anything from richly hued fish made of hand-blown glass, to curious, recycled-metal creatures and wearable art.

Massimo Izzo JEWELLERY

(Map p188; ☎0931 2 23 01; www.massimoizzo.com; Piazza Archimede 25; ⏲4-8pm Mon, 9am-1pm & 4-8pm Tue-Sat) The flamboyant jewellery of Messina-born Massimo Izzo is not for wallflowers. Bursting with life and whimsy, his creations are bold and idiosyncratic, making clever use of Sciacca coral, gold and precious stones. Best of all, the handmade pieces are often inspired by themes close to the Sicilian heart: the sea, theatre and classical antiquity.

Terracotta Ceramiche di Caltagirone CERAMICS

(Map p188; ☎0931 196 26 36; www.terracottasicilia.it; Via Savoia 18; ⏲9.30am-1pm & 4.30-8pm Mon-Sat) This is where the cognoscenti (including Dolce & Gabbana) head for beautiful ceramics from Caltagirone, a central Sicilian town famed for its ceramic production. Fusing classical motifs and bold, contemporary style, its stock includes iconic *teste di Moro* (Moor heads) and conversation-piece vases and bowls in rich, luscious colours.

Antico Mercato MARKET

(Map p188; Via de Benedictis; ⏲8am-1pm Mon-Sat) Near the harbour is Syracuse's produce market, a gut-rumbling sea of red-canopied stalls bursting with just-caught mussels, oysters, octopus and shellfish. You'll also find fragrant, just-baked bread, seasonal fruit and vegetables and luscious local pastries – in short, all the ingredients for a DIY Sicilian feast.

Orientation

Syracuse's main sights are concentrated in two areas: Ortygia, and 2km across town at the Parco Archeologico della Neapolis. Ortygia, Syracuse's historic centre and most atmospheric neighbourhood, is an island joined to the mainland by a couple of bridges. It is well signposted and has a useful car park (Parcheggio Talete). If coming by bus, you'll be dropped off at the bus terminal in front of the train station. From here it's about a 1km walk to Ortygia – head straight down Corso Umberto. Alternatively, catch grey minibus 1, which loops around the island every half hour or so, making stops at a number of convenient locations. Via Roma is Ortygia's main thoroughfare.

Information

Hospital (Ospedale Umberto I; ☎0931 72 41 11; Via Testaferrata 1) Hospital located just east of the Parco Archeologico.

Police Station (☎0931 6 51 76; Piazza San Giuseppe 6) Ortygia's police station.

Post Office (Map p188; Via dei Santi Coronati 22; ⏲8.20am-1.30pm Mon-Fri, to 12.30pm Sat) Post office in Ortygia.

Tourist Office (Map p188; ☎0931 46 29 46, 800 055500; www.provincia.siracusa.gov.it; Via Roma 31; ⏲8am-8pm Mon-Sat, 9am-noon Sun) City maps and brochures.

Getting There & Away

BUS

Buses are generally faster and more convenient than trains, with long-distance buses arriving and departing from the **bus terminal** (Corso Umberto I), just 180m southeast of the train station.

Interbus runs buses to Noto (€3.60, one hour, four daily Monday to Friday, two daily Saturday and Sunday), Catania (€6.20, 1½ hours, 18 daily Monday to Friday, nine Saturday, seven Sunday) and its airport, and Palermo (€13.50, 3¼ to 3½ hours, two to three daily). You can buy tickets at the kiosk by the bus stops.

FLYING INTO SOUTHEASTERN SICILY

Catania Fontanarossa (www.aeroporto.catania.it), 62km north of Syracuse and easily reached on the A18 motorway, is the closest major airport. It's served by numerous airlines with connections to many Italian cities and destinations across Europe. **Interbus** (☎0931 6 67 10; www.interbus.it) runs frequent services between the airport and Syracuse (€6.20, 1¼ hours). It also runs direct services to Noto (€8.40, 1½ to 2¾ hours) and Ragusa (€8.60, 1¾ hours). Reduced service on Sunday; check times on the Interbus website.

A small number of flights to Italian and European cities also fly from the much smaller **Comiso Airport** (☎0932 96 14 67; www.aeroportodicomiso.eu), 27km northwest of Ragusa.

AST (☎0931 46 27 11; www.aziendasiciliana trasporti.it) routes include Palazzolo Acreide (€4.30, 1½ hours, six daily Monday to Saturday). Tickets are available at the train station bar.

CAR & MOTORCYCLE

The dual-carriageway SS114 heads north from Syracuse to Catania, while the SS115 runs south to Noto and Modica. While the approach roads to Syracuse are rarely very busy, traffic gets increasingly heavy as you enter town and can be pretty bad in the city centre.

If you're staying in Ortygia, the best place to park is the **Talete parking garage** (Parcheggio Talete; Map p188) on Ortygia's northern tip, which charges a 24-hour maximum of €10 (payable by cash or credit card at the machine). Molo Sant'Antonio on the mainland, just across the bridge from Ortygia, is another option.

Note that most of Ortygia is a limited traffic zone, restricted to residents and those with special permission. On-street parking is hard to find during the week, and less so on Sunday when it's often free.

TRAIN

From Syracuse's **train station** (Via Francesco Crispi) up to 11 trains depart daily for Catania (from €6.90, one to 1½ hours) and Messina (from €10.50, 2½ to 3½ hours). Some go on to mainland Italy.

There are also trains to Noto (€3.80, 30 to 35 minutes, eight daily Monday to Saturday) and Ragusa (€8.30, 2¼ to 2½ hours, three daily Monday to Saturday).

Getting Around

BICYCLE

Syracuse's bike-sharing program, **GoBike** (☎366 6917046; per day €10, or annual subscription €10, first 30min free, additional hour €1) allows visitors to pick up and return bikes at 10 locations around town. Register and pay fees at any location, including the train station.

BUS

Syracuse is home to an innovative system of grey electric minibuses operated by **Sd'A Trasporti** (www.siracusadamare.it; ticket/day pass/week pass €1/3/10). To reach Ortygia from the bus and train stations, catch minibus 1, which loops around the island every half hour or so, making stops at a number of convenient locations. To reach Parco Archeologico della Neapolis, take minibus 2 from Molo Sant'Antonio (just west of the bridge to Ortygia). Be warned that during the **Ciclo di Rappresentazioni Classiche** (p192) festival, minibus 2 can get extremely crowded, with lengthy delays. For route maps see Sd'A Trasporti's website.

THE SOUTHEAST

Valle Dell'Anapo, Ferla & Necropoli di Pantalica

Around 40km northwest of Syracuse is the World Heritage–listed Necropoli di Pantalica, a significant Iron Age and Bronze Age necropolis. Situated on a huge plateau, the site is surrounded by the beautifully wild and unspoilt landscape of the Valle dell'Anapo (Anapo Valley), a deep limestone gorge created by the Anapo and Calcinara rivers and laced with walking trails (paths marked 'B' are slightly more challenging).

The valley is accessible from Sortino. From Syracuse, you can also head northwest on the SS124 towards Palazzolo Acreide. After about 36km, turn off right towards Ferla. The signposted road plunges steeply to the floor of the valley, where you can leave your car by the Forestry Commission hut and walk through the woodlands on foot. Continuing about 5km up from the valley floor you come to Ferla, a small town with an attractive baroque centre, and another 11km beyond that the Necropoli di Pantalica.

Sights

Necropoli di Pantalica ARCHAEOLOGICAL SITE

(Via Pantalica) FREE On a huge plateau above the Valle dell'Anapo is the site of Sicily's most important Iron and Bronze Age necropolis, the Necropoli di Pantalica, with more than 5000 tombs of various shapes and sizes honeycombed along the limestone cliffs. The site is terribly ancient, dating between the 13th and 8th century BC, and its origins are largely mysterious although it is thought to be the Siculi capital of Hybla, who gave the Greeks Megara Hyblaea in 664 BC.

Very little survives of the town itself other than the Anaktron or prince's palace.

Set aside half a day for the site, which is best explored with a knowledgeable guide – Pantalica Experience (p199) is a reputable operator. Don't forget to wear sensible hiking shoes and bring plenty of water.

Palazzolo Acreide

☎0931 / POP 8875 / ELEV 670M

Few people make it up to Palazzolo Acreide, but those who do find a charming, laidback town with a wealth of baroque architecture and some of the area's finest (and least publicised) ancient ruins. The original medieval town was abandoned after the 1693 earthquake, after which a new Palazzolo was built in the shadow of the Greek settlement of Akrai.

Sights

The town's central focus is **Piazza del Popolo**, which is a striking square dominated by the ornate bulk of the **Chiesa di San Sebastiano** and **Palazzo Municipale**, Palazzolo's impressive town hall. From here you can take a short walk north that will bring you to **Piazza Moro** as well as two other exquisite baroque churches, the **Chiesa Madre** and **Chiesa di San Paolo**.

These two churches, the first on the square's northern flank and the second on the southern side, form a theatrical ensemble of columns, gargoyles and fleurs-de-lis. At the top of Via Annunziata (the main road leading right out of Piazza Moro) is the fourth of the town's baroque treasures, the **Chiesa dell'Annunziata**, with a richly adorned portal of twirling columns.

Akrai ARCHAEOLOGICAL SITE

(0931 87 66 02; Colle dell'Acromonte; €4; 9am-6.30pm Apr-Oct, to 3.30pm Mon-Sat Nov-Mar) Accessed via a 20-minute uphill walk from Piazza del Popolo (or an easy drive up Via Teatro Greco), the archaeological park of Akrai is one of the area's best-kept secrets. The city of Akrai, Syracuse's first inland colony, was established to defend the overland trading route to other Greek settlements. Nowadays, its ruins are an evocative sight. The most impressive (and obvious) ruin is the **Greek theatre**, built at the end of the 3rd century BC but later altered by the Romans.

A perfect semicircle, the theatre once had a capacity of 600. Behind it are two *latomie* (quarries), later converted into Christian burial chambers. The larger of the two, **Intagliata**, has catacombs and altars cut into its sides, while the narrower one, **Intagliatella**, has a wonderful relief of a large banquet cut into the rock face.

South of the archaeological zone are a series of 3rd-century-BC stone sculptures known as the Santoni (Holy Men). It's a 15-minute walk down to the statues, but you'll need to go with a guide as the area around the statues is closed to the general public. From the ticket office, the guides usually take visitors down to the sculptures at 10.30am on Monday to Saturday from April to September (with a second trip at 4.30pm May to September). These times are always subject to change, so call ahead to confirm.

Eating

The town is home to a handful of traditional *trattorie* peddling local specialities. For a sweet pick-me-up, stop by **Pasticceria Caprice** (Map p170; 0931 88 28 46; Corso Vittorio Emanuele 21; snacks from €1.50; 7am-10pm Tue-Fri, to 11pm Sat & Sun).

Information

Tourist Office (0931 87 12 60; Piazza del Popolo; 8am-2pm Mon-Fri, plus 3-6pm Mon & Thu) In the Palazzo Municipale (Town Hall) on Piazza del Popolo.

Getting There & Away

Palazzolo is 40km west of Syracuse via the scenic SS124.

AST buses connect with Syracuse (€4.30, 45 minutes to 1¼ hours, five to six daily Monday to Saturday).

Noto

0931 / POP 23,835 / ELEV 152M

Noto is an architectural supermodel, a baroque belle so gorgeous you might mistake it for a film set. Located less than 40km southwest of Syracuse, the town is home to one of Sicily's most beautiful historic centres. The pièce de résistance is Corso Vittorio Emanuele, an elegant walkway flanked by thrilling baroque *palazzi* and churches. Dashing at any time of the day, it's especially hypnotic in the early evening, when the red-gold buildings seem to glow with a soft inner light.

Although a town called Noto or Netum has existed here for many centuries, the Noto that you see today dates to the early 18th century, when it was almost entirely rebuilt in the wake of the devastating 1693 earthquake. Creator of many of the finest buildings was Rosario Gagliardi, a local architect whose extroverted style also graces churches in Modica and Ragusa.

Sights

★**Cattedrale di San Nicolò** CATHEDRAL

(Piazza Municipio; 8am-1pm & 4-8pm) Pride of place in Noto goes to San Nicolò Cathedral, a baroque beauty that had to undergo extensive renovation after its dome collapsed

Noto

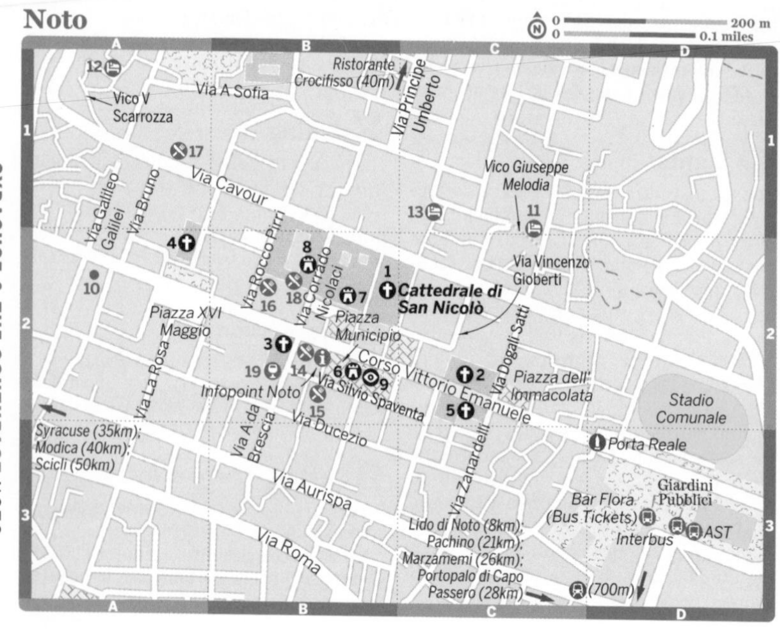

Noto

Top Sights

1 Cattedrale di San Nicolò B2

Sights

2 Chiesa del Santissimo Salvatore C2
3 Chiesa di San Carlo al Corso B2
4 Chiesa di San Domenico A2
5 Chiesa di Santa Chiara C2
6 Palazzo Ducezio B2
7 Palazzo Landolina B2
8 Palazzo Nicolaci di Villadorata B2
9 Piazza Municipio B2

Activities, Courses & Tours

10 Allakatalla A2

Sleeping

11 Melodia 3 .... C1
12 Nòtia Rooms A1
13 Ostello Il Castello C1

Eating

14 Caffè Sicilia B2
15 Dolceria Corrado Costanzo B2
16 Manna B2
17 Ristorante Il Cantuccio A1
18 Ristorante Vicari B2

Drinking & Nightlife

19 Anche gli Angeli B2

during a 1996 thunderstorm. The ensuing decade saw the cathedral scrubbed of centuries of dust and dirt before reopening in 2007. Today the dome, with its peachy glow, is once again the focal point of Noto's skyline.

Piazza Municipio PIAZZA

About halfway along Corso Vittorio Emanuele is the graceful Piazza Municipio, flanked by Noto's most dramatic buildings. To the north, sitting in stately pomp at the head of Paolo Labisi's monumental staircase is the Cattedrale di San Nicolò (p197), surrounded by a series of elegant palaces. To the left (west) is **Palazzo Landolina**, once home to the powerful Sant'Alfano family. Across the street, **Palazzo Ducezio** features a partly convex facade, its graceful arches supported by Ionic-capital columns.

Designed by Vincenzo Sinatra in the mid-18th century, the palace's lower level building was only completed in 1830, while the top floor was built in the first half of the 20th century. It now houses Noto's town hall.

Palazzo Nicolaci di Villadorata PALACE

(338 7427022; www.comune.noto.sr.it/palazzo-nicolaci; Via Corrado Nicolaci; €4; 10am-1.30pm & 2.30-7pm) The striking facade of this 18th-century palace features wrought-iron

balconies supported by a swirling pantomime of grotesque figures. Inside, the richly brocaded walls and frescoed ceilings offer an idea of the sumptuous lifestyle of Sicilian nobles, as brought to life in the Giuseppe Tomasi di Lampedusa novel *Il Gattopardo* (The Leopard).

Chiesa del Santissimo Salvatore CHURCH
(☎327 0162589; www.oqdany.it; Via Vincenzo Gioberti; by donation; ⏰10am-2pm & 3-7pm Mon-Sat, 3.30-7pm Sun) Situated towards the grand Porta Reale is the Chiesa del Santissimo Salvatore with its adjoining nunnery, reserved for the daughters of local nobility. The church's interior is the most impressive in Noto, a whimsical confection of pinks, blues, purples and gold. The fountain suspended on a wall next to the church remained after Noto's streets were lowered in 1840 to facilitate the movement of carriages.

Chiesa di San Domenico CHURCH
(Piazza XVI Maggio; by donation; ⏰10am-6pm) Towering over the tourist office on Piazza XVI Maggio is the 18th-century Chiesa di San Domenico. Considered one of Noto's finest baroque buildings, the church was designed to a Greek-cross plan by Rosario Gagliardi, who is reputedly buried here. Inside you'll find some beautiful stuccowork, inspired by St Dominic's devotion to the Madonna of the Rosary.

Chiesa di Santa Chiara CHURCH
(Corso Vittorio Emanuele; adult/reduced €2/1; ⏰10am-1pm & 3-6.30pm Mar-Jul, Sep & Oct, 9.30am-midnight Aug, 10am-noon Nov-Jan, closed Feb) Offering great views of the cathedral, this church was built by the baroque maestro Rosario Gagliardi between 1745 and 1758. The oval-plan interior is typically lavish, although the main drawcard is the panoramic view from the rooftop terrace.

Chiesa di San Carlo al Corso CHURCH
(Corso Vittorio Emanuele; clocktower €2; ⏰10am-1pm & 3-6.30pm Mar-Jul, Sep & Oct, 9.30am-midnight Aug, 10am-noon Nov-Jan, closed Feb) For sublime views of Noto's baroque skyline, climb the *campanile* (bell tower) at this church on the town's main pedestrian thoroughfare. If you suffer from vertigo, stick to admiring the handsome concave facade with its three orders of rising columns.

Tours

Allakatalla TOUR
(☎093 157 40 80; www.allakatalla.it; Corso Vittorio Emanuele 47) Allakatalla offers a wide range of organised tours, ranging from guided excursions to Syracuse to week-long jaunts around Mt Etna's vineyards and the locations used in the *Inspector Montalbano* TV series. Tours must be booked in advance.

Festivals & Events

Infiorata CARNIVAL
(www.infioratadinoto.it) Noto's big annual jamboree is the Infiorata, celebrated over three days in mid-May with music concerts, parades and the breathtaking decoration of Via Corrado Nicolaci with designs made entirely of flower petals.

Eating

Like many towns in Sicily's southeast, Noto has a vibrant food scene, with a mix of innovative, sophisticated restaurants and old-school *trattorie* serving unfussy classics. The best spots are in the *centro storico* (historic centre), within walking distance of Corso Vittorio Emanuele.

TOP TOURS

Bucolic Escapes Join the locals on a guided walk in the Syracuse countryside courtesy of local association **Natura Sicula** (Map p190; ☎328 8857092; www.naturasicula.it; Piazza Santa Lucia 24/c-d).

Follow Montalbano Follow in the footsteps of TV detective Salvo Montalbano on an **Allakatalla** tour of the series' locations: Palazzolo Acreide, Noto, Pantalica, Modica, Scicli, Donnafugata and Ragusa.

Take to the Sea Draw anchor in Syracuse and sail a yacht down the southern coast with Sailing Team (p192), stopping to explore protected wetlands and swim in turquoise seas.

Tomb Raiding Join **Pantalica Experience** (☎338 4752390; www.pantalicaexperience.altervista.org) for a customised tour of the Necropoli di Pantalica, an eerie, ancient city of the dead by a wild and rugged valley.

DON'T MISS

ICE CREAM & GRANITE

It's a heady claim, but some say Noto has the two best *gelaterie* (ice-cream shops) in the world. Facing off for the honours are **Caffè Sicilia** (☎0931 83 50 13; Corso Vittorio Emanuele 125; desserts from €2; ⏰8am-11pm Tue-Sun) and, just around the corner, **Corrado Costanzo** (☎0931 83 52 43; Via Silvio Spaventa 9; ⏰7.30am-2pm & 4-11pm Thu-Tue). Of the two, Corrado has the better ice cream – try a lick of pistachio or *amaro* (dark liqueur) flavour – but Caffè Sicilia is famous for its *granite* (drinks made of crushed ice with fruit juice). Depending on the season, you could go for *fragolini* (tiny wild strawberries) or *gelsi* (mulberry) flavours, or stick to the classic *caffè* (coffee) or *mandorla* (almond).

Both places make superb *cassata* (made with ricotta cheese, chocolate and candied fruit), *dolci di mandorle* (almond cakes and sweets) and *torrone* (nougat). Don't know which to choose? Try them all! (We won't tell your dentist, promise!)

★Manna SICILIAN €€
(☎0931 83 60 51; www.mannanoto.it; Via Rocco Pirri 15; meals €27-38; ⏰12.30-2.30pm & 7.30-10.30pm Wed-Mon Sep-Jun, 7.30-10.30pm Mon-Sun Jul & Aug; 📶) Divided into a slinky front bar and sultry back dining rooms, Manna wows with its competent, contemporary creations. Season and premium produce dictate the menu, which might see anchovy and sardine *polpettine* (patties) paired with fennel, orange and sundried tomatoes, or the ubiquitous *arancino* (fried riceballs) reinvented as a dark-chocolate and orange dessert. Staff are competent and the wine list well-versed in unique and unexpected drops.

★Ristorante Crocifisso SICILIAN €€
(☎0931 57 11 51; www.ristorantecrocifisso.it; Via Principe Umberto 48; meals €30-40; ⏰12.30-2.15pm Thu-Tue, plus 7.30-10pm Tue & Thu-Sat) Up in Noto Alta, this Slow Food–acclaimed restaurant with an extensive wine list is widely regarded as Noto's best. Sicilian classics such as *macco di fave* (broad bean purée with ricotta and toasted breadcrumbs) and *casarecce alla palermitana* (short handmade pasta with sardines and wild fennel) are complemented by juicy roast lamb, Marsala-glazed pork and pistachio- and sesame-crusted tuna.

Ristorante Il Cantuccio MODERN SICILIAN €€
(☎0931 83 74 64; www.ristoranteilcantuccio.it; Via Cavour 12; meals €32-36; ⏰12.30-2pm & 7.45-10.30pm Tue-Sun) Tucked into the courtyard of a former noble's palace, this inviting restaurant combines familiar Sicilian ingredients in inspired ways. Perennial favourites such as the exquisite *gnocchi al pesto del Cantuccio* (ricotta-potato dumplings with basil, parsley, mint, capers, toasted almonds and cherry tomatoes) are complemented by seasonally changing specials like lemon-stuffed bass with orange-fennel salad or white-wine-stewed rabbit with *caponata*.

★Ristorante Vicari MODERN SICILIAN €€€
(☎0931 83 93 22; www.ristorantevicari.it; Ronco Bernardo Leanti 9; 5-/7-course degustation menu €50/60; ⏰12.30-2pm & 7-10pm Tue-Sun, closed lunch Wed & Sun Jun-Sep) Low-slung lamps spotlight linen-clad tables at Vicari, and rightfully so. In the kitchen is up-and-coming chef Salvatore Vicari, who thrills with his whimsical takes on Sicilian produce: think sea urchin spaghetti with white-bean cream and *selicornia* (sea asparagus), tender rabbit decadently stuffed with liver pate, or ridiculously succulent octopus barbecued and smoked to perfection. Book ahead.

🍷 Drinking & Nightlife

★Anche gli Angeli LOUNGE
(☎0931 57 60 23; www.anchegliangeli.com; Via A da Brescia 2; ⏰10am-midnight Wed-Mon; 📶) Squint and you'll think you're in Rome or Milan. Urbane, sophisticated and irrefutably cool, 'Even the Angels' wears numerous hats: lounge bar, eatery, concept store and live-music venue. Occupying a string of atmospheric vaulted rooms, it's best for *vino* sessions, snacking, browsing books and take-home Sicilian delicacies, and tapping away at its live, in-house gigs.

ℹ Information

Infopoint Noto (☎339 4816218; www.notoinforma.it; Corso Vittorio Emanuele 135; ⏰10am-midnight Jul-Sep, to 7pm Apr-Jun, 10am-6pm Tue-Sun Oct-Mar) A useful tourist office, with maps, brochures and enthusiastic, multilingual staff who can also organise excursions.

Police Station (☎0931 83 52 05; Vico Brindisi 1) Near the Giardini Pubblici.

Getting There & Away

BUS

Noto's bus station is conveniently located just to the southeast of Porta Reale and the Giardini Pubblici. Buy bus tickets from **Bar Flora** (Hotel Flora, Via Pola 1), located at Hotel Flora just west of the bus stop.

AST (☎840 000323; www.aziendasiciliana trasporti.it) runs to various destinations, including Syracuse (€3.60, one hour, six daily Monday to Saturday) and Catania (€7.50, 1½ hours, six daily Monday to Saturday, two to three daily Sunday). Buses to Catania stop at Catania airport on the way.

Interbus (☎091 34 20 55, 0935 2 24 60; www.interbus.it) also runs buses to Catania (€8.40, 1½ to 2½ hours, six to seven daily Monday to Friday, three Saturday, two Sunday) and Syracuse (€3.60, one hour, four daily Monday to Friday, three Saturday, two Sunday).

CAR & MOTORCYCLE

The SS115 connects Noto with Syracuse, about 36km to the northeast.

TRAIN

Regular trains run from Syracuse (€3.80, 30 to 35 minutes, eight daily Monday to Saturday), but the station is located 1km downhill from the historic centre.

The Noto Coast

While Sicily's southeastern tip offers little in the way of excitement, its electric colours, laidback atmosphere and relative lack of development make it a relaxing day trip from Noto. From town, the SP19 heads south towards Pachino, a busy, run-of-the-mill market town surrounded by fertile vineyards. A few kilometres before it lies the altogether more charming fishing village of **Marzamemi**, which doubles as a low-key summer resort. Once in Marzamemi, a seafood meal by crashing waves or a Sicilian-inspired cocktail on the piazza does wonders for the soul.

From Marzamemi, the road follows the coast south to **Portopalo di Capo Passero**, a popular summer hang-out. The small island off the coast is **Isola Capo Passero**, with a hulking castle and nature reserve. In between Noto and the cape are several sights worth stopping at, from Roman mosaics to rugged beaches.

Sights

Riserva Naturale Oasi Faunistica di Vendicari PARK

(☎0931 46 88 79; www.riserva-vendicari.it; ⏲7am-8pm Apr-Oct, to 5pm Nov-Mar) FREE Butting onto the ruins of Eloro is a wonderful stretch of wild coastline encompassing three separate marshes and a number of sandy beaches. The most beautiful of these is Marianelli, known locally as a nudist and gay-friendly beach. From the main entrance (signposted off the Noto–Pachino road), it's about a 10-minute walk to the nearest waves, where you can pick up a path along the coast.

The reserve, which claims its own Swabian tower and an abandoned tuna-processing plant, is an important marine environment, providing sanctuary to resident and migratory birds. Among these is the black-winged stilt, the stork, wild goose and flamingo. Observation posts enable you to watch in relative comfort.

Villa Romana del Tellaro ROMAN SITE

(☎338 9733084; www.villaromanadeltellaro.com; adult/reduced €6/3; ⏲9am-6pm) Going south towards Pachino on the main SP19 brings you to this Roman villa, home to some fascinating mosaics. The villa was largely destroyed by fire in the 4th century, but painstaking excavation has brought to light fragments of the original floor mosaics, depicting hunting scenes and episodes from Greek mythology.

Eating

The best place to eat in the area is the fishing village of Marzamemi, which has an abundance of *trattorie*, mostly focused on fresh fish and seafood. Top billing goes to **La Cialoma** (☎0931 84 17 72; Piazza Regina Margherita 23, Marzamemi; meals €34-39; ⏲1-3.30pm & 8-11pm Jun-Aug, 1-3pm & 7.30-10pm rest of year, closed 2 weeks in Nov), a favourite with both local and visiting food-lovers. The town's main square is also home to locavore **Liccamúciula** (☎338 4638731; www.liccamuciula.it; Piazza Regina Margherita 2, Marzamemi; panini & salads €6-7.50; ⏲10am-10pm Mon-Thu, to 3am Fri & Sat, to midnight Sun), a cheaper cafe-bar-bookshop serving fresh, quality panini, salads and more made using quality island produce.

Getting There & Away

You will need a car to explore the area as public transport is either very limited or non existent.

Interbus (p201) runs between Noto and Pachino (€2.90, 25 minutes), but once there you will need to catch a taxi to reach Marzamemi (around €8 to €10 one-way). Interbus services between Noto and Pachino are greatly reduced on weekends.

Modica

☎0932 / POP 54,650 / ELEV 296M

With its steeply stacked medieval centre and spectacular baroque cathedral, Modica is one of southern Sicily's most atmospheric towns. But unlike some of the other Unesco-listed cities in the area, it doesn't package its treasures into a single easy-to-see street or central piazza: rather, they are spread around the town and take some discovering. It can take a little while to orientate yourself in Modica, but once you've got the measure of the bustling streets and steep staircases, you'll find a warm, genuine town with a welcoming vibe and a strong sense of pride.

An important Greek and Roman city, Modica had its heyday in the 14th century when, as the personal fiefdom of the Chiaramonte family, it was one of the most powerful cities in Sicily.

Sights

Chiesa di San Giorgio CHURCH

(Corso San Giorgio, Modica Alta; ⊙8am-12.30pm & 3.30-6.30pm) The high point of a trip to Modica – quite literally as it's up in Modica Alta – is the Chiesa di San Giorgio, one of Sicily's most extraordinary baroque churches. Considered Rosario Gagliardi's great masterpiece, it stands in isolated splendour at the top of a majestic 250-step staircase, its sumptuous three-tiered facade towering above the medieval alleyways of the historic centre.

The lavish interior, a sunlit kaleidoscope of silver, gold and egg-shell blue, encapsulates all the hallmarks of early-18th-century Sicilian baroque.

Chiesa di San Giovanni Evangelista CHURCH

(off Piazza San Giovanni, Modica Alta; ⊙hours vary) Attributed to Rosario Gagliardi and marking the top of Modica Alta is this grand baroque church. Prefaced by a sweeping staircase, the church underwent major restoration work in the 19th century, its current facade completed between 1893 and 1901. If the church is open, slip inside its elliptical interior for beautiful, neoclassical stuccowork. Nearby, at the end of Via Pizzo, a viewing balcony offers arresting views over the old town.

Corso Umberto I STREET

(Modica Bassa) Bisecting Modica Bassa, Corso Umberto I is the place to lap up Modica's lively local atmosphere. An avenue flanked by graceful palaces, churches, restaurants, bars and boutiques, it's where the locals come to strut their stuff on the evening *passeggiata*. Originally a raging river ran through town, but after major flood damage in 1902 it was dammed and Corso Umberto was built over it.

Obvious landmarks include the **Cattedrale di San Pietro** (Corso Umberto I, Modica Bassa; ⊙9am-1pm & 3.30-7.30pm Mon-Sat, 9.30am-12.30pm & 4-7.30pm Sun), an impressive church atop a rippling staircase lined with life-sized statues of the apostles, and the **Chiesa Santa Maria del Carmine** (Piazza Matteotti, Modica Bassa; ⊙9am-1pm & 3-7pm), also known as Santa Maria dell'Annunziata.

For a break from baroque, head off the *corso* to Via Grimaldi where the 12th-century **Chiesa Rupestre di San Nicolò Inferiore** (☎331 7403045; Piazzetta Grimaldi, Modica Bassa; €2.50; ⊙10am-1pm & 5-8pm Tue-Sat, 5-8pm Sun Jun-Aug, 10am-1pm & 4-7pm Tue-Sun May & Sep, reduced hours rest of year) harbours some rich Byzantine frescoes.

Back on the main street, next to the tourist office in Palazzo della Cultura, the **Museo Civico** (Corso Umberto I 149, Modica Bassa; €2.50; ⊙10am-1pm & 4-7pm Tue-Sun) houses a modest collection of archaeological finds from Modica and Cava d'Ispica, dating back to the neolithic period.

Museo del Cioccolato di Modica MUSEUM

(Corso Umberto I 149, Modica Bassa; adult/under 10yr €2.50/free; ⊙10am-8pm Mon-Sat, to 1pm Sun) Sharing the same building as the Museo Civico, this humble museum sheds light on the town's unique chocolate, from its history to its production method. You'll also find a bizarre collection of cocoa sculptures and a giant chocolate model of Italy, complete with famous icons, from Naples' Castel Nuovo to Venice's Rialto Bridge.

Festivals & Events

Festa di San Giorgio RELIGIOUS

Drums, confetti and fireworks set a hypnotic scene as a statue of Modica's patron saint is raced through the town's streets before making a victorious entrance into the Chiesa di San Giorgio. Held in April

Eating

Modica merits a stop on any Sicilian foodie trail, with both Slow Food *trattorie* and creative, high-end restaurants. The town is renowned for its grainy chocolate, produced using an ancient method. Savoury specialities include *scacce* (flat-bread dough stuffed with various fillings and folded), *buccatureddi* (half-moon shaped rolls traditionally filled with broccoli), *'mpanati* (durum-wheat focaccia traditionally stuffed with lamb), as well as ricotta-filled ravioli served in a pork sauce.

★Caffè Adamo GELATERIA €
(☎0932 94 13 08; Via Maresa Tedeschi 15-17, Modica Bassa; cup/cone from €2; ⊙6am-1am summer, to 11pm rest of year, closed Mon Sep-Jun; 📶) There is great gelato and then there's gelato made by Antonio Adamo. The affable *modinese* makes all his confections from scratch; even the Agrigento pistachios are ground on-site. The result is ice cream packed with extraordinarily natural flavour and freshness, from the cashew with salted caramel, to a dreamy raspberry-pistachio combo. Gelato aside, Antonio's *cremolate* (water ices) are also outstanding.

Osteria dei Sapori Perduti SICILIAN €
(☎0932 94 42 47; Corso Umberto I 228-230, Modica Bassa; meals €18-22; ⊙noon-3pm & 7.30-11pm Thu-Tue; 📶) Nostalgia rules the roost at bustling, affable 'Osteria of the Forgotten Flavours', right on Modica's main drag. Decked out in a jumble of old telephones and cooking utensils, it's a good spot for traditional local grub, from rustic *scacce modicane* (vegetable-stuffed flatbread) to the osteria's much-loved ricotta-filled ravioli, served in a pork *sugo* (sauce). Classic mains include nourishing *'u bollitu* (boiled veal).

La Locanda del Colonnello SICILIAN €€
(☎0932 75 24 23; www.locandadelcolonnello.it; Vico Biscari 6, Modica Alta; meals €30-35; ⊙12.30-2pm & 7.30-10pm Wed-Mon; 📶) Book ahead for a table at this Slow Food darling, hidden away in Modica Alta. Seasonality steers a menu that gives classic Sicilian flavours subtle, elegant twists. Here, succulent shrimps give earthy *zuppetta di ceci* (chickpea soup) added intrigue, while ricotta and marjoram-stuffed ravioli seduce in a rich pork *sugo* (sauce). Finish with a smooth *gelo di limone* (lemon jelly).

Fattoria delle Torri SICILIAN €€
(☎0932 75 12 86; www.fattoriadelletorri.it; Vico Napolitano 14, Modica Alta; meals €38; ⊙12.30-2.30pm & 7-10.30pm Tue-Sun, plus Mon early Jul-Aug) This is one of Modica's smartest restaurants. Housed in an elegant 18th-century *palazzo*, it has a beautiful dining area with tables set under stone arches and bay windows looking onto a small internal garden. The seafood is particularly gorgeous, especially when married with a crisp, dry white wine such as Cerasuolo di Vittoria.

★Accursio MODERN SICILIAN €€€
(☎0932 94 16 89; www.accursioristorante.it; Via Grimaldi 41, Modica Bassa; meals €40-55, tasting menus €75; ⊙12.30-2.30pm & 7.30-10.30pm Tue-Sun, closed Sun lunch in summer) While we love the modernist furniture and vintage Sicilian tiles, the real thrill at this fine-dining maverick is the food. Head chef Accursio Craparo honed his skills under the tutelage of heavyweights Pietro Leemann and Massimiliano Alajmo, resulting in boldly creative, nuanced dishes inspired by childhood memories and emblematic of new Sicilian thinking. For a well-rounded adventure, opt for a tasting menu.

Drinking & Nightlife

In the evenings, crowds flock to Corso Umberto I to stroll, hang out and eat gelato. Just behind it, skinny Via Clemente Grimaldi throngs with evening revellers of all ages, who schmooze and drink at the handful of bars dotting the street.

Rappa Enoteca WINE BAR
(Corso Santa Teresa 97-99, Modica Alta; ⊙5pm-midnight Mon-Sat) High ceilings, antique mouldings and vintage tiled floors create a delightful backdrop at this atmospheric *enoteca* in the upper town. Daily offerings, handwritten on butcher's paper, include thoughtfully chosen Sicilian wines and Italian craft beers. Match with quality cheese, olives and charcuterie for a *molto* civilised pit-stop.

Shopping

Mercatino delle Pulci MARKET
(www.mercatinodellepulcimodica.it; Viale Medaglie d'Oro, Modica Bassa; ⊙7am-3pm last Sun of month) Modica's much-loved flea market is one of the best in the region. Held on the last Sunday of the month, its rows of stalls peddle everything from vintage jewellery, tea sets, records and postcards, to old Sicilian chests, locks, chiselled coats of arms

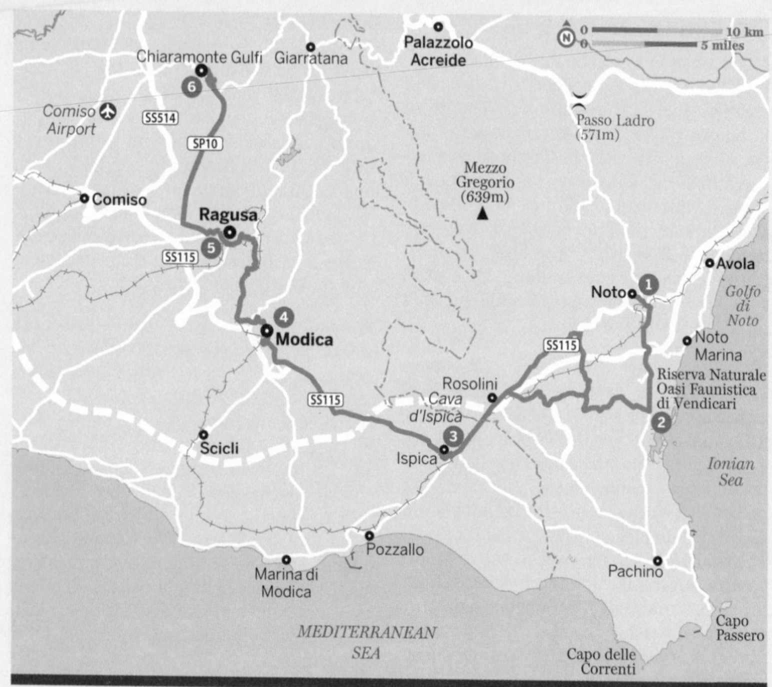

Driving Tour Baroque Towns

START NOTO
END CHIARAMONTE GULFI
LENGTH 71KM; TWO DAYS

A land of remote rocky gorges, sweeping views and silent valleys, Sicily's southeastern corner is home to the 'baroque triangle', an area of Unesco-listed hilltop towns famous for their lavish baroque architecture. This tour takes in some of the finest, all within easy driving distance of each other.

Just over 35km south of Syracuse, **1 Noto** (p197) is home to what is arguably Sicily's most beautiful street – Corso Vittorio Emanuele, a pedestrianised boulevard lined with golden baroque *palazzi*. Architecture aside, the town is also home to a number of culinary hot-spots, among them Ristorante Vicari, Ristorante Crocifisso and Manna. From Noto, pop into **2 Riserva Naturale Oasi Faunistica di Vendicari** (p201), ideal for walking around and swimming off its beaches. Continue on to Ispica, a hilltop town overlooking a huge canyon, **3 Cava d'Ispica** (p206), riddled with prehistoric tombs. Follow the SS115 for a further 18km to **4 Modica** (p202), a bustling town set in a deep rocky gorge. There's excellent accommodation and a wealth of great restaurants, so this makes a good place to stay overnight. The best of the baroque sights are up in Modica Alta, the high part of town, but make sure you have energy left for the *passeggiata* (evening stroll) on Corso Umberto I and dinner at high-end Accursio or earthy Osteria dei Sapori Perduti.

Next morning, a short, winding, up-and-down drive through rock-littered hilltops leads to **5 Ragusa** (p206), one of Sicily's nine provincial capitals. The town is divided in two – it's Ragusa Ibla that pulls the heart strings, a claustrophobic warren of grey stone houses and elegant *palazzi* that opens up onto Piazza Duomo. If you feel like lingering, consider lunching at casual hotspot I Banchi, owned by Michelin-lauded chef Ciccio Sultano. Alternatively, save your appetite for **6 Chiaramonte Gulfi** (p211), a tranquil hilltop town some 20km to the north along the SP10. Dubbed the Balcone della Sicilia (Sicily's Balcony) for its breathtaking panorama, it's famous for its coveted olive oil and blue-ribbon pork, the latter best savoured at Ristorante Majore.

and Caltagirone ceramics. Serious collectors head in early to score the most valuable finds.

Dolceria Bonajuto FOOD
(☎0932 94 12 25; www.bonajuto.it; Corso Umberto I 159, Modica Bassa; ⌚9am-8.30pm, to midnight Aug) Sicily's oldest chocolate factory is the perfect place to taste Modica's famous chocolate. Flavoured with cinnamon, vanilla, orange peel and even hot peppers, it's a legacy of the town's Spanish overlords who imported cocoa from their South American colonies. Leave room for Bonajuto's *'mpanatigghi*, sweet local biscuits filled with chocolate, spices…and minced beef!

Orientation

Modica is divided into two parts: Modica Alta (Upper Modica) and Modica Bassa (Lower Modica). Whether driving or coming by public transport you'll arrive in Modica Bassa. The main street here, Corso Umberto I, forms the bottom of the V-shaped wedge on which the historic centre sits. Most hotels and restaurants are in Modica Bassa, within easy walking distance of Corso Umberto I, although the cathedral and a number of churches are in the high town. It's a fairly tough climb to the top.

Information

Police Station (☎0932 76 92 11; Via del Campo Sportivo 481) Police station in Modica.

Tourist Office (☎346 6558227; www.comune.modica.rg.it; Corso Umberto I 141, Modica Bassa; ⌚8am-2pm & 3-7pm, closed Sun Oct-May) City-run tourist office in Modica Bassa.

Getting There & Away

BUS

Modica's bus station is at Piazzale Falcone-Borsellino at the top end of Corso Umberto I.

AST (☎0932 76 73 01; www.aziendasicilianatrasporti.it) bus routes include Noto (€4.30, 1¼ hours, six daily Monday to Saturday, two Sunday), Ragusa (€2.70, 25 minutes, up to 18 daily Monday to Friday, 13 Saturday, two Sunday) and Catania (€9, 2¼ hours, 10 daily Monday to Friday, 11 Saturday, four Sunday).

CAR & MOTORCYCLE

From Noto to Modica it's about 40km along the SS115.

Parking can be a problem, particularly if you arrive mid-morning. A good place to try is Corso Garibaldi (turn right at the Cattedrale di San Pietro). There's a free car park opposite the train station on Viale Medaglie d'Oro.

TAXI

For a taxi, call ☎392 1027894. You'll find a taxi rank on Corso Umberto I, just beside the roundabout on Piazza Principe di Napoli.

TRAIN

There are trains to Ragusa (€2.50, 25 to 30 minutes, five Monday to Saturday) and Syracuse (€7.60, 1¾ hours, four Monday to Saturday).

Around Modica

Scicli

☎0932 / POP 27,100 / ELEV 106M

About 11km southwest of Modica, Scicli is a quickly gentrifying country town with a fetching baroque centre and a pretty central piazza. The town makes regular cameos on the hit TV series *Inspector Montalbano*, and its handful of churches and eclectic museums make for a satisfying day trip from Modica.

Overlooking the place is a rocky peak topped by an abandoned church, the **Chiesa di San Matteo**. It's not too hard a walk up to the church to soak up the views over town – simply follow the yellow sign up from Palazzo Beneventano and keep going for about 10 minutes.

Sights

Antica Farmacia Cartia HISTORIC SITE
(La Farmacia di Montalbano; ☎338 8614973; www.tanitscicli.wix.com/tanitscicli; Via Francesco Mormina Penna 24; €1.50; ⌚10am-1pm & 4-8pm) Dating from 1902, this time-warped pharmacy is a sight to behold, adorned with antique apothecary jars, scales and cash register. Fans of *Inspector Montalbano* may feel a sense of déjà vu: the place has made cameo appearances in the hit TV series, earning it the sobriquet *La Farmacia di Montalbano* (The Pharmacy of Montalbano).

Museo del Costume MUSEUM
(☎334 3658158; www.museocostume.it; Via Francesco Mormina Penna 65; adult/reduced €2/1.50; ⌚10am-12.30pm & 3.30-7.30pm, to 11pm Jul & Aug) Housed in a former monastery, Scicli's Museo del Costume mainly explores the costumes and fashions of the region. The collection spans several centuries and offers atmospheric insight into the living conditions, traditions and tastes of locals through the ages. Some written information is available in English, and English-language

guided tours are offered if requested a day in advance. The museum often hosts talks, with past topics including 'The Voices of Arab Women'.

Chiesa di Santa Teresa CHURCH
(☎366 1431972; Via Santa Teresa 16; €3; ⊙10am-1.45pm & 3-7pm) This richly decorated baroque belle features 18th-century stuccowork by Pietro Cultraro. Ceiling panels capture three scenes from the life of St Teresa, while the crucifix on the left is unusual in its portrayal of Christ sans crown of thorns and with nails replaced by red roses (a symbol of the Carmelite order). Of the 16th-century frescoes on display in the nave itself, the most interesting features a very unusual inscription in Sicilianised Latin.

Eating

Nivera GELATERIA €
(☎393 8383833; Via Francesco Mormina Penna 14; gelato from €2; ⊙9.30am-1pm & 4-9.30pm Mon-Fri, to 11.45pm Sat & Sun) When the urge to lick proves irresistible, Nivera has your back. This is one of the region's top gelaterie, using seasonal, local and organic produce to create sublimely smooth confections like zingy mandarin sorbet and a silky Carrubo honey and ginger ice cream. Look out for the stars of TV series *Inspector Montalbano*, known to pop in when shooting in town.

Getting There & Away

Both the SP54 and SP42 connect Scicli to Modica, about 11km to the northeast.

From Largo Gramsci in the centre of town, AST (p205) buses run to Modica (€2.40, 25 minutes, nine to 10 daily Monday to Saturday, three Sunday), from where connections reach Ragusa and Noto. Buy bus tickets at Bar Rendo on Largo Gramsci. Note that the last bus to Modica departs Scicli at 5.50pm.

For a taxi call ☎388 0643263.

Cava d'Ispica

The town of Ispica, about 12km southeast of Modica, is located at the head of the 13km-long gorge known as **Cava d'Ispica** (☎0932 77 16 67; adult/reduced €4/2; ⊙9am-6.30pm Apr-mid-Oct, to 1.15pm Mon-Sat mid-Oct–Dec). Long used as a neolithic burial site, the caves were later transformed into cave dwellings in the Middle Ages. The gorge is tranquil and verdant and you can follow an overgrown path along the whole length of the valley.

Ragusa

☎0932 / POP 73,030 / ELEV 502M

Set amid the rocky peaks northwest of Modica, Ragusa is a town of two faces. Sitting on the top of the hill is Ragusa Superiore, a busy workaday town with sensible grid-pattern streets and all the trappings of a modern provincial capital, while etched into the hillside further down is Ragusa Ibla. This sloping area of tangled alleyways, grey stone houses and baroque *palazzi* on handsome squares is effectively Ragusa's historic centre and it's quite magnificent.

Like every other town in the region, Ragusa Ibla (the old town) collapsed after the 1693 earthquake and a new town, Ragusa Superiore, was built on a high plateau above. But the old aristocracy was loath to leave the tottering *palazzi* and rebuilt Ragusa Ibla on exactly the same spot. The two towns were merged in 1927, becoming the provincial capital at Modica's expense.

Sights

★**Ragusa Ibla** HISTORIC CENTRE
Ragusa Ibla is a joy to wander, its labyrinthine lanes weaving through rock-grey *palazzi* to open onto beautiful, sun-drenched piazzas. It's easy to get lost but you can never go too far wrong, and sooner or later you'll end up at **Piazza Duomo**, Ragusa's sublime central square.

East of the piazza, Corso XXV Aprile leads down to a second eye-catching Gagliardi church, the elliptical **Chiesa di San Giuseppe** (Piazza Pola; ⊙9am-noon & 3-7pm Jun-Sep, reduced hours rest of year), its cupola graced by Sebastiano Lo Monaco's fresco *Gloria di San Benedetto* (Glory of St Benedict, 1793). Further downhill, to the right of the entrance of the Giardino Ibleo, eye up the Catalan Gothic portal of what was once the large **Chiesa di San Giorgio Vecchio**, now mostly ruined. The lunette features an interesting bas-relief of St George killing the dragon.

At the other end of Ragusa Ibla, the **Chiesa del Purgatorio** (Piazza della Repubblica; ⊙10am-7pm Jun-Sep, reduced hours rest of year) is one of the few churches in town to have survived the great earthquake of 1693.

Cattedrale di San Giorgio CATHEDRAL
(Piazza Duomo; ⊙10am-12.30pm & 4-7pm Jun-Sep, reduced hours rest of year) At the top end of the sloping Piazza Duomo is the town's pride and joy, the mid-18th-century cathedral with a magnificent neoclassical dome and

WORTH A TRIP

CASTELLO DI DONNAFUGATA

Located 18km southwest of Ragusa is the glorious, crenellated **Castello di Donnafugata** (☎0932 61 93 33; www.comune.ragusa.gov.it; Contrada Donnafugata; ⏲9am-1pm & 2.45-5.30pm Tue, Thu & Sun, 9am-1pm Wed, Fri & Sat). Originally a medieval watchtower, the site was expanded by nobleman Vincenzo Arezzo La Rocca, Baron of Serri, who bought the estate in 1648. This expansion would subsequently form the core of the castle's 19th-century reworking. This revamp was commissioned by Corrado Arezzo de Spuches, Baron of Donnafugata, who used the palace as a rural residence. Today, the property belongs to the City of Ragusa and its sumptuous rooms and verdant grounds (which include a maze) are open to the public and well worth a visit.

The castle's newest resident is the Collezione Gabriele Arezzo di Trifiletti, an extraordinary fashion and costume collection considered one of Europe's finest. Spanning the 16th to 20th centuries (the bulk of which dates to the 18th and 19th centuries), the hoard offers a lavish overview of Sicily's once-glorious aristocratic culture. Indeed, its value led to a proposal to have it transferred to Palazzo Pitti's Costume Gallery in Florence, a suggestion swiftly quashed by the Sicilian government. The near 3000 pieces – displayed on rotation – include ball gowns, uniforms, bodices, chemises, cloaks, shawls, underwear, gloves, stockings, veils, military and ecclesiastical millinery, shoes, combs, thimbles, bags, umbrellas, cosmetic items and fans. Among the many highlights is a gown belonging to belle-époque fashion icon Donna Franca Florio; a rare hunting outfit from the late 17th century; 18th-century liveries worn by the servants of Sicilian nobility; and the very gown that inspired Claudia Cardinale's famous frock in Luchino Visconti's film *Il Gattopardo* (The Leopard; 1963).

By far the easiest way to reach the *castello* is by car. In summer, **Autotrasporti Tumino** (☎0932 62 31 84; www.tuminobus.it; Via Zama) runs one afternoon bus service (bus 3) from Ragusa to Bovio di Donnafugata, from where the castle is a further 10 minutes on foot. A second bus returns to Ragusa later in the afternoon (see the bus company's website for times). Buses do not run on Sunday or public holidays.

stained-glass windows. One of Rosario Gagliardi's finest accomplishments, its extravagant convex facade rises like a three-tiered wedding cake, supported by gradually narrowing Corinthian columns and punctuated by jutting cornices.

Giardino Ibleo GARDENS

(☎0932 65 23 74; ⏲9am-10pm Mon-Thu, to 1am Fri & Sat) At the eastern end of the old town is the Giardino Ibleo, a pleasant public garden laid out in the 19th century that is perfect for a picnic lunch.

Ragusa Superiore AREA

One of the best reasons for heading up to Ragusa's modern and less-attractive half is to walk down again. It takes about half an hour to descend the Salita Commendatore, a winding pass of stairs and narrow archways that leads down to Ragusa Ibla past the **Chiesa di Santa Maria delle Scale** (⏲10am-1pm & 3-7pm Jun-Sep, reduced hours rest of year), a 15th-century church with impressive views. To reach the Salita, follow Corso Italia eastwards and then pick up Via XXIV Maggio.

The main attraction up top is the **Duomo di San Giovanni Battista** (☎0932 62 16 58; www.cattedralesangiovanni.it; Piazza San Giovanni; belltower €2; ⏲10am-7pm, belltower 10am-12.30pm), a vast 19th-century church whose highly ornate facade is set off by Mario Spada's pretty *campanile*. Nearby, below Ponte Nuovo, the somewhat forlorn **Museo Archeologico Ibleo** (☎0932 62 29 63; Via Natalelli; ⏲9am-7pm Mon-Sat) FREE houses notable finds from the 6th-century-BC Greek settlement of Kamarina on the coast.

Festivals & Events

Ibla Grand Prize MUSIC

(www.ibla.org) A nine-day international musical festival and competition held in July, with free classical, jazz and contemporary music concerts in numerous locations across town.

FestiWall ART

(www.facebook.com/RagusaFestiWall) Ragusa's week-long street-art festival in September sees Italian and foreign artists create specially commissioned murals around the city.

Ragusa

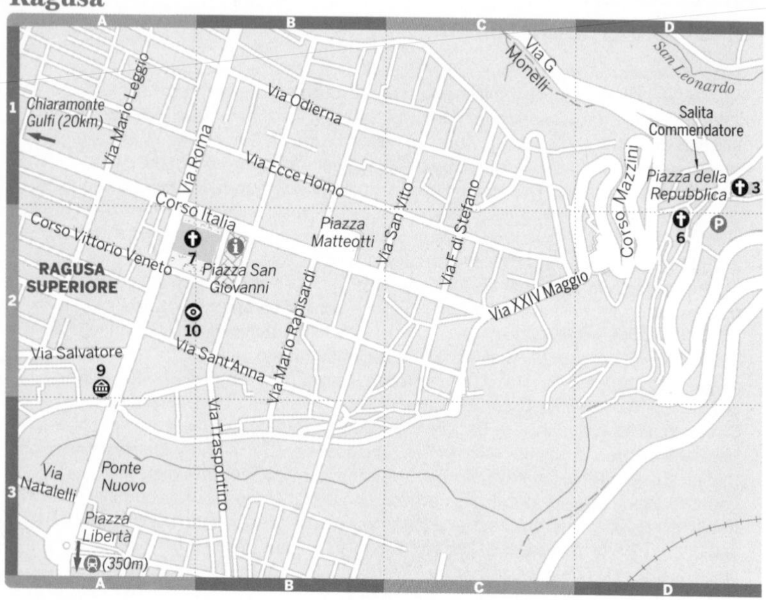

Ragusa

Eating

Ragusa has a solid selection of eateries ranging from celeb-chef fine-dining restaurants to cheerful neighbourhood trattorias. Pork is a popular local meat, appearing in typical dishes like *cavati* (shell-shaped pasta) in pork sauce and *sfogghiu* (delicate puff pastry filled with ricotta and pork sausage). Christmas brings *mucatoli* (biscuits stuffed with dried fruit).

Delicatessen in Drogheria MEDITERRANEAN €
(0932 191 05 51; Via Archimede 32; panini €3-6, dishes €4.50-9;) DID is a hip deli-cafe-bistro in one, with communal tables, bar seating and playful, '70s-style wallpaper running up the wall and ceiling. The open kitchen keeps things fresh, wholesome and scrumptious, whether it's breakfast-friendly yoghurt and smoothies, classic *panini* stuffed with biodynamic ingredients or more substantial dishes like couscous with seasonal vegetables. The chocolate, pear and ricotta cake is non-negotiable.

Gelati DiVini GELATERIA €
(0932 22 89 89; www.gelatidivini.it; Piazza Duomo 20; ice cream from €2; 10am-late) This exceptional gelateria makes wine-flavoured ice creams with Marsala, passito and muscat,

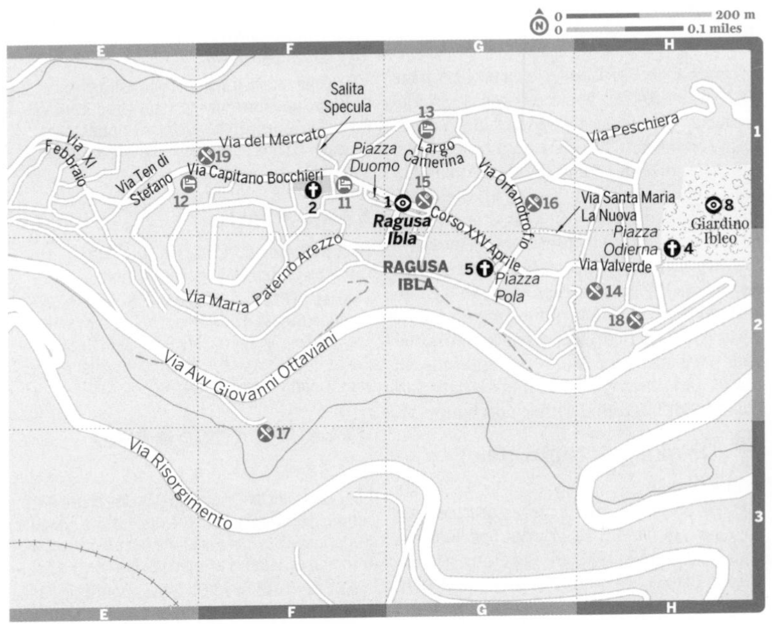

plus other unconventional offerings such as pine nut, prickly pear, watermelon, ricotta, and chocolate with spicy peppers.

Quattro Gatti SICILIAN €
(☎0932 24 56 12; Via Valverde 95; meals €18-25; ⊙7.30-11.30pm Tue-Sun) This cosy, popular Sicilian-Slovak–run eatery near the Giardino Ibleo serves a wonderful four-course fixed-price menu bursting with fresh, local flavours. The antipasti spread is especially memorable, as are the seasonally changing specials scribbled on the blackboard up front. Slovak-inspired offerings such as goulash and apple strudel round out a menu of Sicilian classics.

★I Banchi ITALIAN €€
(☎0932 65 50 00; www.ibanchiragusa.it; Via Orfanotrofio 39; panini €5-6.50, meals €28-38, 5-/9-course tasting menu €40/60; ⊙7.30am-12.30am Wed-Mon;) Michelin-star chef Ciccio Sultano is behind this contemporary, smart-casual eatery, which includes a dedicated bakery, specialist deli counter and the freedom to choose anything from *caffè* and just-baked pastries, to made-on-site gourmet *panini*, lazy wine-and-cheese sessions or more elaborate, creative dishes that put twists on Sicilian traditions (think ravioli with the pork *ragù* on the inside and ricotta on the outside).

A Rusticana SICILIAN €€
(☎0932 22 79 81; Via Domenico Morelli 4; meals €20-32; ⊙12.30-2.30pm & 7.30pm-midnight Wed-Mon) Fans of the *Inspector Montalbano* TV series will want to eat here, as it's where scenes set in the fictional Trattoria San Calogero were filmed. In reality, it's a cheerful, boisterous trattoria whose generous portions and relaxed vine-covered terrace ensure a loyal clientele. The food is defiantly *casareccia* (home-style), so expect no-frills pasta and uncomplicated cuts of grilled meat.

★Ristorante Duomo MODERN SICILIAN €€€
(☎0932 65 12 65; www.cicciosultano.it; Via Capitano Bocchieri 31; lunch menus €45-59, dinner tasting menus €125-190; ⊙12.30-4pm Tue-Sat, plus 7.30-11pm Mon-Sat) Widely regarded as one of Sicily's finest restaurants, Duomo comprises a cluster of small rooms outfitted like private parlours behind its stained-glass door, ensuring a suitably romantic ambience for chef Ciccio Sultano's refined creations. The menu abounds in classic Sicilian ingredients such as pistachios, fennel, almonds and Nero d'Avola wine, combined

in imaginative and unconventional ways. Reservations essential.

Locanda Don Serafino MODERN SICILIAN €€€
(☎0932 24 87 78; www.locandadonserafino.it/ristorante; Via Giovanni Ottaviano 13; 3-course lunch €50, meals €80, 6-/9-course tasting menu €110/145; ⏲12.45-2.30pm & 7.45-10.30pm Wed-Mon) Young-gun chef Vincenzo Candiano steers this softly lit, Michelin-starred darling, evocatively set in a series of rocky caves. Reserve a linen-draped table and settle in for top-shelf local produce and bold Sicilian reinventions – think bitter-cacao lasagne with Hyblean ricotta cheese, oven-roasted Nebrodi pancetta with fennel and aniseed puree, and sweet epilogues like delicate puff pastry with Ragusano cheese and honey.

Drinking & Nightlife

Prima Classe BAR
(☎0932 65 23 00; www.primaclassebar.com; Via Ercolano 7; ⏲7am-1.30am Mon-Sat, 5pm-1am Sun, closed Sun Jun-Sep;) Off the tourist trail, Prima Classe is where the *ragusani* play. A slick, on-point mix of concrete floors and designer Spanish lighting, it's a cafe, bar and art space in one, with rotating exhibitions, regular live music, decent drinks and fantastic *aperitivo* bites. It's also a handy coffee or lunch spot if you're near the bus station, 400m to the south.

Shopping

Le Formiche GIFTS & SOUVENIRS
(☎389 4828295; cnr Via San Massimiliano Kolbe & Via Ozanam; ⏲4.30-8.30pm Mon, 10am-1pm & 4.30-8.30pm Tue-Sat) Located in an up-and-coming pocket of the modern city, concept store 'The Ants' stocks products designed and crafted by local artists, artisans and architects. Expect to find anything from Saracen-head earrings and hand-sewn wallets, to geometric jewellery, contemporary takes on Sicilian *pupi* (puppets), satchels made from recycled materials, natural soaps, even local wines, liquors and edibles. Souvenir shopping: check.

Orientation

If you're driving, follow signs to Ragusa Ibla, where the main sights, hotels and restaurants are. Leave your car in one of the signposted car parks and walk into town. From the car park under Piazza della Repubblica it's a 10-minute walk or so to the central Piazza Duomo – follow Via Del Mercato, then Via XI Febbraio; go left up Via Ten Di Stefano then along its continuation, Via Capitano Bocchieri.

If taking public transport you will arrive in Ragusa Superiore, whose main streets are Via Roma and Corso Italia. From the upper town a local bus runs down to Giardino Ibleo in Ragusa Ibla.

Information

Police Station (☎0932 67 31 11; Via Ispettore Giovanni Lizzio) Main police station.

Tourist Office (☎0932 68 47 80; www.comune.ragusa.gov.it; Piazza San Giovanni; ⏲9am-7pm Mon-Fri, plus 9am-2pm Sat & Sun Easter–mid-Oct) Ragusa's main tourist office, with friendly, helpful staff.

Getting There & Away

BUS

Long-distance and municipal buses share a terminal on Via Zama in the upper town (Ragusa Superiore). Buy tickets at the ticket kiosk at the terminal or at cafes around the corner.

AST (☎0932 76 73 01; www.aziendasiciliana trasporti.it; Via Zama) runs regularly to Modica (€2.70, 25 minutes, 15 to 16 daily Monday to Saturday, two Sunday) and Syracuse (€7.20, three hours, two to four daily Monday to Saturday).

Interbus (www.interbus.it; Via Zama) runs to Catania (€8.60, two hours, hourly Monday to Friday, every two to three hours Saturday, every one to three hours Sunday) and Syracuse (€6.90, 2¼ hours).

CAR & MOTORCYCLE

If coming from Modica 15km away, or Syracuse some 90km to the northeast, take the SS115.

Unless your hotel has parking or can advise you on where to park, your best bet is to leave your car at the car park below Piazza della Repubblica in Ragusa Ibla; much of the old town is closed to non-residential traffic.

TRAIN

Trains run to Modica (€2.50, 20 to 30 minutes, three daily Monday to Saturday) and Syracuse (€8.30, two to 2½ hours, two daily Monday to Saturday). Some services to Syracuse require a transfer in Modica.

Getting Around

Monday through Saturday, AST's city buses 11 and 33 (€1.20) run hourly between Via Zama bus terminal and Giardino Ibleo in Ragusa Ibla. On Sunday, bus 1 makes a similar circuit.

For taxi service, call ☎0932 18 32.

Chiaramonte Gulfi

☎0932 / POP 8220 / ELEV 668M

Nicknamed *il Balcone della Sicilia* (Sicily's balcony), this delightful hilltop town offers (on a clear day) views that stretch from Gela in the south to Mt Etna in the north. Yet many visitors head here for a high of the gastronomic kind. Chiaramonte Gulfi produces a highly rated olive oil, accredited with the Denominazione d'Origine Protetta (DOP), not to mention premium pork products, from salami to *salsiccie* (sausages).

To build up an appetite, wander the knot of old medieval streets in the historic centre, crow over views that steal the breath and drop by Museo dell'Olio, the pick of the town's string of museums.

Sights

Museo dell'Olio MUSEUM

(Olive Oil Museum; ☎0932 92 82 39; www.comune.chiaramonte-gulfi.gov.it/musei; Palazzo Montesano, Via Montesano; €1; ⌚10am-1.30pm & 3-6pm Sat & Sun, by appointment only Tue-Fri) This is the most interesting of Chiaramonte Gulfi's museums. While the highlight is an olive press from 1614, there's also a collection of old farming tools and other curios relating to rural life.

Eating

It might be small, but Chiaramonte Gulfi's foodie cred is known across Italy. Pork is a staple and the town's *salumi* (charcuterie) are especially good. Seek out salami made from prized black swine from the Nebrodi Mountains. Some of it is flavoured with wild fennel, Bronte pistachios or carob. Salami made with local donkey meat is also common. The town's other revered export is extra-virgin olive oil.

Ristorante Majore SICILIAN €€

(☎0932 92 80 19; www.majore.it; Via dei Martiri Ungheresi 12; meals €20-25; ⌚9am-4pm & 6-11pm Tue-Sun) The place to buy ham, and indeed to lunch on superb pork, is Ristorante Majore, a much-acclaimed trattoria just off central Piazza Duomo. It's unpretentious and old-school, and the menu is unapologetically meaty, with signature dishes *risotto alla majore* (with pork *ragù* and local cheese) and *falsomagro alla siciliana* (pork meatballs stuffed with salami, cheese, eggs and carrot).

Getting There & Away

Chiaramonte Gulfi lies around 20km north of Ragusa. The shortest and most scenic drive between the two is on the SP10.

AST runs buses to Ragusa (€2.70, 50 minutes, four daily Monday to Thursday and Saturday, one Friday).

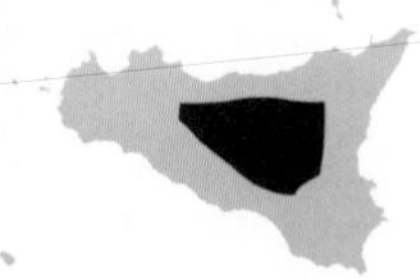

Central Sicily

Includes ➡

Best Places to Eat

- ➡ La Rustica (p215)
- ➡ Osteria al Canale (p216)
- ➡ Coria (p225)
- ➡ Il Locandiere (p224)
- ➡ Ristorante Centro Storico (p226)

Best Places to Sleep

- ➡ B&B Tre Metri Sopra Il Cielo (p259)
- ➡ Azienda Agrituristica Gigliotto (p259)
- ➡ Baglio Pollicarini (p258)
- ➡ Baglio San Pietro (p259)
- ➡ Suite d'Autore (p259)

Why Go?

Sicily's wild and empty interior is a beautiful, uncompromising land, a timeless landscape of silent, sunburnt peaks, grey stone villages and forgotten valleys. Traditions live on and life is lived at a gentle, rural pace. It's an area that encourages the simple pleasures – long lunches of earthy country food, meanders through hilltop towns, quiet contemplation over undulating vistas. It's also an area of surprising natural diversity – one minute you're driving through rolling hills reminiscent of Tuscany, the next through pockets of eucalypt bush akin to Australia.

Scattered across these landscapes are the legacies of many cultures and countless generations – windswept Greek shrines, sunbaked Norman churches and the frescoed flourishes of the baroque. It's in Villa Romana del Casale that you'll find the world's most important Roman mosaics; in tiny Morgantina, a Hellenic statue that caused a modern tug-of-war; and in Caltagirone, some of Italy's most coveted ceramics. Prepare to be pleasantly surprised.

Road Distances (km)

	Caltagirone	Caltanissetta	Enna	Nicosia
Caltanissetta	85			
Enna	60	30		
Nicosia	100	65	50	
Piazza Armerina	30	50	35	70

Central Sicily Highlights

1 Villa Romana del Casale (p222) Admiring ancient artistry at a decadent Roman villa, home to the most extraordinary Roman tile-work in existence.

2 Caltagirone (p223) Tackling Sicily's most spectacular staircase, then stocking up on the town's nationally renowned ceramics.

3 Morgantina (p220) Sitting your booty on the very steps where ancient Greeks once debated, conspired and gossiped.

4 Piazza Armerina (p219) Losing yourself in a warren of atmospheric streets and eclectic local museums.

5 Enna (p214) Exploring a whimsical cathedral, scaling a Lombard castle and soaking up spectacular views in central Sicily's busiest town.

6 Calascibetta (p217) Enjoying a little downtime and strolling through the nougat-coloured streets of a sleepy Sicilian hilltop village.

ENNA

☎0935 / POP 28,220 / ELEV 931M

Italy's highest provincial capital, Enna stands above the hills and valleys of central Sicily. The town is a dramatic sight, seemingly impregnable atop a precipitous mountain. Inside you'll discover a calm working centre with a handsome medieval core and, cloud cover permitting, some mesmerising views. There's not enough to warrant an extended stay, but it is a great place to escape the tourist pack and enjoy some cool mountain air, particularly in summer when the sun bakes everything around to a yellow crisp.

The town of Enna is split in two: the hilltop historic centre, Enna Alta, and the modern town, Enna Bassa, below. Everything of interest is up in Enna Alta.

Sights

Castello di Lombardia CASTLE

(☎0935 50 09 62; 9am-8pm Apr-Aug, to 7pm Sep & Oct, to 5pm Nov-Mar) FREE One of Sicily's most formidable castles guards Enna's highest point, at the easternmost edge of the historic centre. The original castle was built by the Saracens and later reinforced by the Normans; Frederick II of Hohenstaufen ordered that a powerful curtain wall be built with towers on every side.

The wall is still intact, but only six of the original 20 towers remain, of which the tallest is the **Torre Pisano**. Accessible from the Cortile dei Cavalieri (one of the castle's well-preserved inner courtyards), the tower delivers spectacular views over the valley to the town of Calascibetta and to Mt Etna in the northeast.

Torre di Federico II TOWER

(Viale IV Novembre; 8am-6pm) FREE Secret passageways once led to this octagonal tower, which now stands in Enna's pine-studded public gardens. Once part of the town's old defence system, it stands nearly 24m high.

Rocca Di Cerere VIEWPOINT

Just below the entrance to the castle is a huge rock, which was once home to Enna's Temple of Demeter (Ceres to the Romans), goddess of fertility and agriculture. The temple, built in 480 BC by the tyrant Gelon, is supposed to have featured a statue of King Triptolemus, the only mortal to witness the rape of Demeter's daughter Persephone.

There's not much left of the temple now, but the rocky platform, accessible by a series of steep steps, is a great place for a picnic or to take in the sunset.

Duomo CATHEDRAL

(Via Roma; 9am-1pm & 4-7pm) The Duomo is the most impressive of the historic buildings that line Via Roma, Enna's showpiece street. Built over 200 years after the original Gothic cathedral burnt down in 1446, the current cathedral is topped by a muscular 17th-century bell tower and graced with a sumptuous interior. Entry is usually through Jacopo Salemi's 16th-century side portal, which features a depiction of St Martin taking off his coat to cover the poor.

While the transept and polygonal apses offer traces of the original church, the interior is predominantly baroque, from the ornamental coffered wood ceiling and chandeliers, to the scene-stealing altar. Other points of interest include the bases of the grey basalt

Enna

columns, decorated with grotesque carvings of snakes with human heads; the pulpit and stoup, both set on Greco-Roman remains from the Temple of Demeter; 17th-century presbytery paintings by Filippo Paladino; and the altarpieces by Guglielmo Borremans.

Museo Archeologico di Palazzo Varisano MUSEUM
(☎0935 507 63 04; Piazza Mazzini 8; ⏱9am-7pm) FREE Enna's archaeological museum houses a good collection of local artefacts (labelled in Italian) excavated from throughout the region, as well as objects borrowed from the archaeological museums of both Syracuse and Agrigento. Of particular interest is the Attic-style red-and-black *krater* (drinking vase), found in the town itself and dating back to the 5th century BC.

Piazza F Crispi PIAZZA
Just off Piazza Vittorio Emanuele is another small square, Piazza F Crispi, commanding sweeping views over the valley to Calascibetta. The piazza is home to the **Fontana del Ratto di Prosperina** (Fountain of the Rape of Persephone), a monumental creation commemorating Enna's most enduring ancient legend.

Activities

Lago Di Pergusa SWIMMING
Surrounded by woodland about 9km south of town is one of Sicily's few natural lakes. It's a popular summer hang-out with some sandy beaches, big resort-style hotels and an unlikely motor-racing circuit, but out of season it's a rather forlorn place. Alas, it also has nothing to connect it to the mythical tale of Persephone, for which it's so famous.

The lake is signposted along the SS561. On public transport, take local bus 5 (€1.20) from the bus stop on Via Pergusa. You can purchase bus tickets from Coppola (p216) travel agency, right beside the bus stop.

Festivals & Events

Holy Week RELIGIOUS
The week building up to Easter is marked by solemn religious celebrations, during which the city's religious confraternities parade around in eerie capes and white hoods. The main events are on Palm Sunday, Good Friday and Easter Sunday.

Festa di Maria Santissima della Visitazione CARNIVAL
Fireworks and scantily clad farmers mark the town's patron saint's day on 2 July. Dressed in white sheets, the farmers drag an effigy of the Madonna of the Visitation through town on a cart called La Nave d'Oro (Golden Ship).

Eating

Unlike the coast, the staple here is meat, and local dishes usually involve lamb or beef and a tasty array of mushrooms and grilled vegetables. Specialities include *castrato* (charcoal-grilled castrated ram) and *polpettone* (stuffed lamb or meatballs). Soups and sausages also feature.

★La Rustica SICILIAN €
(☎0935 2 55 22; Via Aidone 28; meals €17-20; ⏱12.45-3pm & 7.30-10.30pm Mon-Sat) Slow Food stalwart La Rustica ticks all the right boxes: off the tourist trail, popular with locals and run by a couple passionate about classic local grub. While husband Gaetano tends to the vinyl-lined tables, Carmela is in the kitchen, whipping up old family recipes such as superlative *caponata* and *polpettone ripieno all'enese* (egg-stuffed meatloaf served with peas and a gorgeous tomato sauce).

Enna

Sights
1 Castello di Lombardia F2
2 Duomo D2
Fontana del Ratto di Prosperina ..... (see 4)
3 Museo Archeologico di Palazzo Varisano D2
4 Piazza F Crispi B1
5 Rocca Di Cerere F1

Eating
6 Paccamora Bio Bar B1

THE MYTH OF PERSEPHONE

The tale of Hades' capture of Demeter's daughter Persephone (also known as Proserpina) is one of the most famous Greek myths. According to Homeric legend, Hades (god of the underworld) emerged from his lair and abducted Persephone while she was gathering flowers around **Lago di Pergusa** (p215). Not knowing where her daughter had disappeared to, Demeter (goddess of the harvest) forbade the earth to bear fruit as she wandered the world looking for her. Eventually, she turned to Zeus, threatening that if he didn't return her daughter she would inflict eternal famine on the world. Zeus submitted to her threat and ordered Hades to release Persephone, though stipulating that every year she should spend six months in the underworld with Hades and six months in Sicily with her mother. Demeter still mourns during Persephone's time in the underworld, bringing winter to the world; her joy at her daughter's return is heralded by the blossoms of springtime.

Osteria al Canale SICILIAN €
(☎339 6155928, 0935 95 89 66; Via Mazzini 101, Valguarnera Caropepe; meals €20-25; ⊙noon-2.30pm & 8-10pm; 📶) Enna foodies know all about this simple village eatery, a 24km drive southeast of Enna. Lorded over by head chef Lillo Serra, its shtick is honest, locally rooted dishes such as seasoned pecorino with onion marmalade, *pasta sfoglia* (puff pastry) stuffed with seasonal veggies, and spaghetti with *pesto siciliano* (tomato, salted ricotta, basil, chilli and almonds). Dinner reservations are obligatory.

That the dining-room cabinet features a photo of Australian-born singer Tina Arena is no coincidence. Her parents hail from the village and the star herself has been known to scribble down some of Lillo's recipes.

Paccamora Bio Bar SICILIAN €
(Piazza Vittorio Emanuele 21-22; sandwiches €3.50, lunch dishes €9, dinner platter from €8; ⊙7.30am-1am Mon-Sat) With its clean lines, blond wood and shades of grey, this next-gen cafe breathes fresh thinking into Enna's main square. The focus is on the fresh, wholesome and local, from great organic coffee (non-dairy milk available), juices and wholemeal *cornetti*, to lunchtime soy-bread panini and daily specials such as spelt lasagne with carrot and artichoke. Come dinner, nibble on a tapas platter.

ℹ Information

Municipal Tourist Information Point (Castello di Lombardia; ⊙10am-1pm) In the main courtyard of Castello di Lombardia. Often also opens from 4pm to 7pm though this is never guaranteed.

Ospedale Umberto I (☎0935 51 67 54; Contrada Ferrante, Enna Bassa) Major hospital in the lower town.

Police Station (☎0935 52 21 11; Via San Giovanni 4)

Provincial Tourist Office (Infopoint; ☎0935 50 23 62; www.provincia.enna.it/infopoint.htm; Via Roma 413; ⊙9am-1pm & 3-5.30pm Mon-Fri, 9am-1pm Sun) On the main street in the historic centre.

ℹ Getting There & Away

BUS

Bus is the best way to reach Enna by public transport. Enna's official **bus station** (Viale Diaz) is in the upper town: to get to the town centre from the station, turn right and follow Viale Diaz to Corso Sicilia, turn right again and follow it to Via Sant'Agata, which leads to Via Roma, Enna Alta's main street.

Service is more frequent from the stop in Enna Bassa, 3km downhill. Hourly local buses connect Enna Bassa with the upper town, except on Sundays when it's every two hours.

SAIS Autolinee (☎0935 50 09 02; www.saisautolinee.it) runs services to Catania (€8, 1½ hours, up to nine daily Monday to Friday, six Saturday, three Sunday) and Palermo (€9, 1¾ hours, one daily Monday to Saturday). There are two daily services from Palermo to Enna on Sunday. Regular buses also run to Piazza Armerina (€3.60, 40 minutes, up to seven daily Monday to Friday, up to six Saturday, two Sunday) and Calascibetta (€1.90, 30 minutes, five to eight daily Monday to Saturday).

The **Coppola Viaggi & Turismo** (☎0935 50 20 11; Via Sant'Agata 86; ⊙9am-1pm & 4-7.30pm Mon-Fri, 9am-1pm Sat) travel agency sells bus tickets.

CAR & MOTORCYCLE

Enna is on the main Catania–Palermo A19 autostrada, about 83km from Catania, 135km from Palermo. There's handy free parking on Piazza Giovanni Rosso, right beside the Castello di Lombardia. Free parking is also available on Piazza Europa, close to Torre di Federico II.

NORTH OF ENNA

Calascibetta

0935 / POP 4530 / ELEV 691M

A densely packed maze of narrow streets set above a sheer precipice 7km north of Enna, Calascibetta was originally built by the Saracens during their siege of Enna in 951 and was later strengthened by the Norman king Roger I. The most impressive sight is the 14th-century **Chiesa Madre** (0935 3 38 49; Piazza Matrice; 9am-1pm & 3.30-7pm), Calascibetta's landmark cathedral.

The **Necropoli di Realmese** FREE, 3km northwest, is worth investigating, with some 300 rock tombs dating from 850 BC. To reach the site, head north out of town on Strada Statale 290, turn right into Strada Provinciale 80 and look for the sign marked Necropoli di Realmese (a further 700m, on your left).

Getting There & Away

SAIS Autolinee runs buses from Enna to Calascibetta (€1.90, 30 minutes, five to eight daily Monday to Saturday).

Nicosia

0935 / POP 14,035 / ELEV 724M

Set on four hills, this ancient town was once the most important of a chain of fortified Norman towns stretching from Palermo to Messina. Modern times have been tougher, and between 1950 and 1970 nearly half the town's population emigrated.

Sights

The centre of action is Piazza Garibaldi, a handsome square dominated by the elegant 14th-century facade and Catalan-Gothic campanile of the **Cattedrale di San Nicolò** (Piazza Garibaldi; 9am-noon & 4-7pm). Capped by a beautiful, painted wooden ceiling, its interior features a skilfully chiselled choir from the school of Antonello Gagini and a painting of St Bartholomew by 17th-century Tenebrist painter Jusepe de Ribera.

From the piazza, Via Salamone leads past crumbling Franco-Lombard *palazzi* to the **Basilica di Santa Maria Maggiore** (0935 64 67 16; Largo Santa Maria; 9am-noon & 4-7.30pm), a 1767 reconstruction of a 13th-century church destroyed by a landslide in 1757. Highlights include a holy water font from the late 16th century and, at the back of the chancel, a magnificent marble polyptych (1512) by the Sicilian Renaissance sculptor Antonello Gagini. In the chapel to the left are two beautifully carved wooden altar frontals from the 18th century. Back outside, the terrace offers a view of the ruins of a Norman castle, perched on a rocky crag above town.

Eating

Nicosia's most famous edible is the heavenly *nocattolo* pastry, consisting of a shortbread crust topped with cinnamon-spiced almond paste and dusted in icing sugar.

Baglio San Pietro SICILIAN €
(0935 64 05 29; www.bagliosanpietro.com; Contrada San Pietro; meals €20; noon-2.30pm & 5.30-10pm Thu-Tue) Straddling the line between country and creative (think herb and wild boar risotto followed by craft-beer panna cotta), this *agriturismo* restaurant is also well known for its delicious wood-fired porchetta (suckling pig).

Getting There & Away

The SS117 links Nicosia to the town of Leonforte 26km to the south. From here, the SS121 continues to Enna, 21km to the southwest.

Interbus (0913 4 20 55, 0935 2 24 60; www.interbus.it) runs services to Catania (€8.40, two to 2¼ hours, four daily Monday to Friday, three Saturday, one Sunday).

DON'T MISS

CENTRAL SICILY'S FESTIVE EXPERIENCES

Traditional celebrations are heartfelt in these parts and partaking in them is an unforgettable experience. You won't need to book tickets, but it pays to think ahead about accommodation.

Holy Week (p215) Plan to be in Enna for one of the town's sinister Holy Week processions, the best of which is on Good Friday.

Festa di San Giacomo (p224) Book ahead for Caltagirone's annual shindig on 24 and 25 July. The highlight is the spectacular illumination of the town's famous staircase.

Palio dei Normanni (p220) Accommodation is at a premium in Piazza Armerina from 12 to 14 August as crowds gather for the town's annual medieval pageant.

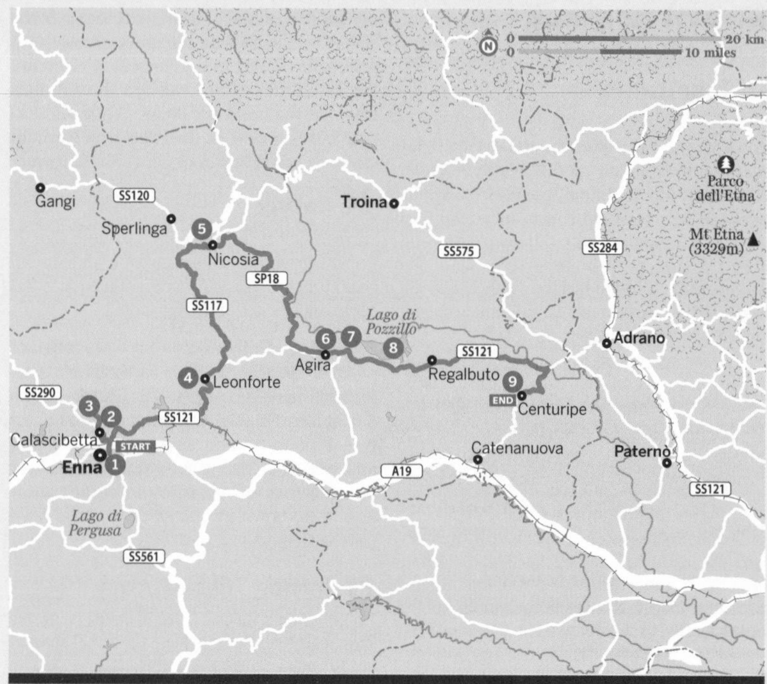

Driving Tour
Enna to Etna

START ENNA
END CENTURIPE
LENGTH 115KM; ONE OR TWO DAYS

From 1 **Enna** cross the valley and climb the 2km or so to 2 **Calascibetta**. The most impressive sight is the 14th-century Chiesa Madre, Calascibetta's landmark cathedral. Northwest 3km is the 3 **Necropoli di Realmese** (p217), boasting some 300 rock tombs dating from 850 BC.

Continuing on the SS121 from Calascibetta, the road winds and weaves 20km up to 4 **Leonforte**, an attractive baroque town once famous for horse breeding. The town's most imposing building is the Palazzo Baronale, but the drawcard is the lavish Granfonte fountain. Built in 1651 by Nicolò Branciforte, it's made up of 24 separate jets against a sculpted facade.

The next leg takes you 26km up the SS117 through dramatic scenery to 5 **Nicosia**. Set on four hills, the centre of action is Piazza Garibaldi. Check out the Cattedrale di San Nicolò, the Franco-Lombard *palazzi* and the Chiesa di Santa Maria Maggiore. Near the entrance to Nicosia, Baglio San Pietro is great for a meal break or even an overnight stop.

Push southwards along the SP18 to 6 **Agira**, another sloping hillside town capped by a medieval Norman castle. A couple of kilometres out of Agira on the SS121 the well-tended 7 **Canadian Military Cemetery** houses the graves of 490 soldiers killed in July 1943. Further on the SS121, 8 **Lago di Pozzillo** is a scenic stretch of water surrounded by hills and groves of almond trees, ideal for a picnic.

Some 13km east of Regalbuto, there's a turn-off for 9 **Centuripe**, a small town whose grandstand views of Mt Etna have earned it the nickname il Balcone di Sicilia (the Balcony of Sicily). Unfortunately, its strategic position has also brought bloodshed and the town has often been fought over. In 1943 the Allies captured the town and the Germans, realising that their foothold in Sicily had slipped, retreated to the Italian mainland.

SOUTH OF ENNA

South of Enna, the landscape becomes less dramatic, flattening out and taking on a more rural aspect as rugged mountain scenery gives way to gentle cultivated fields dotted with busy agricultural towns. The two main attractions are Piazza Armerina, celebrated for its Roman mosaics, and Caltagirone, an esteemed centre of traditional ceramic production. Both towns have decent accommodation and interesting historic centres. The remains of the Greek city of Morgantina, northeast of Piazza Armerina, are considerable and worth more than the trickle of visitors they receive.

Piazza Armerina

☎0935 / POP 22,005 / ELEV 697M

Set amid fertile farming country, this charming market town takes its name from the Colle Armerino, one of the three hills on which it is built. It is actually two towns in one: the original Piazza was founded by the Saracens in the 10th century on the slope of the Colle Armerino, while a 15th-century expansion to the southeast was redefined by an urban grid established in the 17th century. Laced with atmospheric, labyrinthine streets, the town makes a convenient base if visiting the extraordinary ancient mosaics at nearby Villa Romana del Casale.

Sights

Often overlooked by people rushing to the Villa Romana del Casale, Piazza Armerina's hilltop medieval centre is worth more than the passing glance that many people give it. The highpoint is the hilltop cathedral, a landmark for miles around, with its towering dome rising 66m.

Off Piazza Duomo is Via Monte, the arterial road of the 13th-century city. A warren of tiny alleys fan off Via Monte like the ribs of a fishbone. This is the town's most picturesque quarter and worth an aimless wander. Alternatively, take Via Floresta, beside Palazzo Trigona, to arrive at the ruins of the 14th-century Castello Aragonese.

From the cathedral, Via Cavour hairpins down to Piazza Garibaldi, the elegant heart of the old town. Overlooking the square is the late-baroque **Palazzo di Città** (Piazza Garibaldi), Piazza's former town hall (closed to the public), and the **Chiesa di San Rocco** (Piazza Garibaldi; ⏲hours vary), also known as the Fundrò, graced by a magnificent, tuff-stone portal.

Cathedral CATHEDRAL

(Piazza Duomo; ⏲8.30am-noon & 3.30-6pm) You can spot the dramatically sited dome of the huge cathedral from a few kilometres away. It rises majestically from the hilltop and the terraced houses skirt its base in descending tiers. The severe facade dates from 1719, with the dome added in 1768. Inside the airy blue-and-white interior, behind the altar, is a copy of a Byzantine painting, *Madonna delle Vittorie* (Virgin of the Victories), the original of which was supposedly presented to Count Roger I by Pope Nicholas II.

In front of the cathedral is a beautiful *belvedere* (panoramic terrace) while to the right of it is the baronial **Palazzo Trigona** (Piazza Duomo). A **statue** of Baron Marco Trigona – who financed the cathedral's construction – stands in the square.

To the side of the main church, the 44m-high **bell tower** is a leftover from an earlier 14th-century church.

Pinacoteca Comunale GALLERY

(☎0935 68 76 13; Via Monte 4; ⏲9am-6pm Tue-Sun) Piazza Armerina's small, slick public art gallery showcases mostly local artwork from the 15th to 19th centuries, including altarpieces and frescoes from long-gone churches and works by renowned local painter Giuseppe Paladino (1856–1922). Seek out the portrait of 17th-century scholar and Jesuit missionary Prospero Intorcetta. Born in Piazza Armerina and active in China, he was the first European to translate the works of Confucius into Latin.

Also of interest is the altarpiece *Sant'Andrea Avellino intercede per Piazza presso la Madonna delle Vittorie* (St Andrew Avellino intercedes for Piazza at Our Lady of Victories), which depicts Piazza Armerina as it appeared in the 17th century.

Casa Museo del Contadino MUSEUM

(☎333 9138634; Via Garibaldi 57; by donation; ⏲9am-noon & 3.30-6.30pm) A labour of love for its founder, Mario Albanese, this small but meticulously detailed ethnographic museum recreates a typical Sicilian peasant house of the 19th century. Mario's knowledge of the museum's artefacts and subject matter is impressive, and he happily offers visitors engrossing, oft-moving insight into the living conditions and sheer ingenuity of the region's rural workers (in Italian and French).

Chiesa di San Giovanni Evangelista CHURCH

(Largo San Giovanni; ⏲hours vary) Founded in the 14th century, the current Chiesa di

San Giovanni Evangelista dates back to the 18th century. Its interior is lavished with the glorious, vivid brush strokes of Dutch painter Guglielmo Borremans (1670–1744) and his students.

Festivals & Events

Palio dei Normanni CARNIVAL

(www.paliodeinormanni.it) Piazza Armerina bursts into life from 12 to 14 August, when a medieval pageant celebrates Count Roger's capture of the town from the Moors in 1087. Events kick off with the blessing of the knights on the first day, costumed parades on the second and a great joust *(quintana)* between the town's four districts on the third day.

The winning district is presented with a standard depicting Our Lady of the Victories.

Eating

Da Totò TRATTORIA €

(☎0935 68 01 53; Via G Mazzini 27; meals €24; ⊙noon-3pm & 6pm-midnight Tue-Sun) Don't let the stark white lights and bland decor put you off, this popular, affable trattoria serves excellent value-for-money food. Antipasti are of the ham, cheese and grilled veg variety, while pastas are matched with earthy sauces of porcini mushrooms or ripe local vegetables. Main courses are similarly unpretentious with grilled pepper steak a menu mainstay.

Amici Miei TRATTORIA €€

(☎0935 68 35 41; Largo Capodarso 5; pizza from €4.50, meals €25-30; ⊙7pm-midnight Tue, noon-3pm & 7pm-midnight Wed-Mon) Exposed stone walls, low wooden ceiling, wine racks and a wood-fired pizza oven set a snug vibe at this local favourite. Admittedly, the pasta dishes are little hit and miss; opt for the antipasti and pizzas instead.

Special mention should also go to the *antipasto della casa,* a fabulous platter of frittata, sliced pancetta, cheese, *caponata,* and ricotta with balsamic vinegar.

Al Fogher MODERN SICILIAN €€€

(☎0935 68 41 23; www.alfogher.sicilia.restaurant; Contrada Bellia, SS117bis; meals €50; ⊙7.30-

WORTH A TRIP

AIDONE & MORGANTINA

For a quiet rendezvous with the ancients, hit the road and shoot northeast of Piazza Armerina. A 10km drive away lies Aidone, a sleepy hilltop village whose small **archaeological museum** (☎0935 8 73 07; www.regione.sicilia.it/beniculturali/deadimorgantina; Largo Torres Truppia 1, Aidone; adult/reduced €6/3; ⊙9am-7pm Tue-Sun) is worth a stop on your way to the ancient Greek ruins of Morgantina. The museum collection includes artefacts from the Morgantina site, and has displays chronicling life in ancient times. It's also home to the long-lost *Dea di Morgantina,* an ancient statue of Venus, repatriated to Italy in 2011 from the Getty Museum in Los Angeles, California.

A 4km downhill drive from Aidone leads you to the ruins of **Morgantina** (☎0935 8 79 55; adult/reduced €6/3; ⊙2-7pm Tue-Sun Jun-Aug, 10am-5pm Tue-Sun Sep-May). The ancient town's centre is the two-storey agora (marketplace), its trapezoidal stairway used as seating during public meetings. The upper level had a market; note the walls that once divided the shops. The lower level was the site of the 1000-capacity theatre, originally built in the 3rd century BC and subsequently altered by the Romans.

To the northeast are the city's residential quarters, where the town's well-off lived, as testified by the ornate wall decorations and handsome mosaics in the inner rooms. Another residential quarter has been found behind the theatre and its considerable ruins are well worth checking out. The southwest corner of the site contains the remains of a public bath complex.

The area was originally home to Morgeti, an early Sicilian settlement founded in 850 BC on Cittadella hill. This town was destroyed in 459 BC and a new one was built on a second hill, Serra Orlando. It was an important trading post during the reign of the Syracusan tyrant Hieron II (269–215 BC), but slipped into decline after defeat by the Romans in 211 BC and was eventually abandoned. In 1955 archaeologists identified the site and began its excavation, which continues to this day.

To get to the site you'll need your own transport as no buses stop nearby.

Piazza Armerina

10.30pm Mon, noon-2.30pm & 7.30-10.30pm Tue-Sat, noon-2.30pm Sun) This is one of central Sicily's top restaurants, serving sophisticated modern cuisine to a demanding and appreciative clientele. It's about 3km out of town, but your journey is rewarded with dishes such as suckling pig with tuna-egg sauce and asparagus, or mullet served with yellow capsicum, wild rice and pistachio. Reservations required.

Equal attention is given to the wine list, which contains up to 400 labels.

Information

STS Servizi Turistici (0935 68 70 27; www.guardalasicilia.it) This helpful information point has English-speaking staff who can give you free town guides and maps of the Roman Villa (maps are often unavailable at the site itself).

Getting There & Away

BUS

Interbus (0935 2 24 60, 0913 4 20 55; www.interbus.it) runs a service to Catania (€9.20, 1¾ hours, six daily Monday to Friday, four Saturday, two Sunday). **SAIS** (800 211020, 199 244141; www.saisautolinee.it) buses connect Piazza Armerina with Enna (€3.60, 40 minutes, up to six daily Monday to Friday, up to five Saturday) and Palermo (€10.50, two hours, five daily Monday to Friday, three Saturday, two Sunday).

CAR

The SS117bis links Piazza Armerina with Enna 33km to the north. You'll find a large open-air car park in Piazza Europa, at the northeastern edge of the old city.

Piazza Armerina

Sights
1 Casa Museo del Contadino C2
2 Cathedral A2
3 Chiesa di San Giovanni Evangelista D2
4 Chiesa di San Rocco B2
5 Palazzo di Città B2
6 Palazzo Trigona A2
7 Pinacoteca Comunale A2
8 Statue of Baron Marco Trigona A2

Sleeping
9 Suite d'Autore A2

Eating
10 Amici Miei B2
11 Da Totò C2

Villa Romana del Casale

The Unesco-listed Villa Romana del Casale is central Sicily's biggest attraction for good reason: the site, situated in a wooded valley 5km southwest of the town of Piazza Armerina, is home to the finest Roman floor mosaics in existence.

Sights

★Villa Romana del Casale ARCHAEOLOGICAL SITE
(☎0935 68 00 36; www.villaromanadelcasale.it; adult/reduced €10/5; ⏲9am-6pm Apr-Oct, to 4pm Nov-Mar) Villa Romana del Casale is sumptuous, even by decadent Roman standards, and is thought to have been the country retreat of Marcus Aurelius Maximianus, Rome's co-emperor during the reign of Diocletian (AD 286–305). Certainly, the size of the complex – four interconnected groups of buildings spread over the hillside – and the 3535 sq m of astoundingly well-preserved multicoloured floor mosaics suggest a palace of imperial standing.

Following a landslide in the 12th century, the villa lay under 10m of mud for some 700 years, and was thus protected from the damaging effects of air, wind and rain. It was only when serious excavation work began in the 1950s that the mosaics, considered remarkable for their natural, narrative style, the range of their subject matter and the variety of their colour, were brought back to light.

The villa's recent restoration has covered almost the entire complex with a wooden roof (to protect the mosaics from the elements), while an elevated walkway allows visitors to view the tiled floors and the structure itself in its entirety. Architects report a dissatisfaction with the structure for the lack of light, and the shadows that obscure the colours and vivacity of the mosaics, but the condition of the mosaics has been much improved.

The site is equipped with enough informative panels (in English) for you to explore the villa autonomously. If you do want to arrange a guide, however, contact the STS Servizi Turistici (p221); otherwise you can organise one directly at the site.

➡ Thermae

To the north of the villa's **main entrance**, which leads through the remnants of a triumphal arch into an elegant **atrium** (forecourt), is the villa's baths complex. Accessible via the **palaestra** (gymnasium), which has a

Villa Romana del Casale

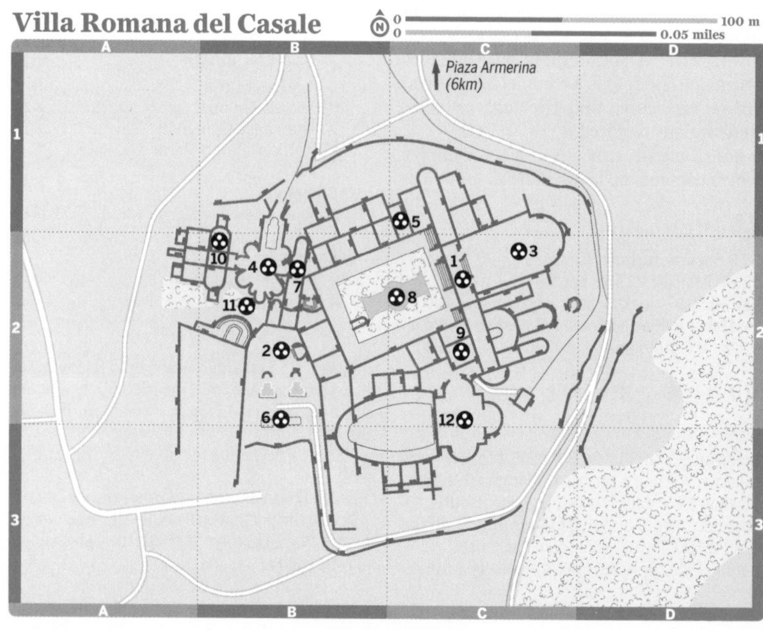

splendid mosaic depicting a chariot race at the Circus Maximus in Rome (the room is also known as the Salone del Circo or Circus Room), is the octagonal **frigidarium** (cold room), where the radiating apses contained cold plunge pools, and a **tepidarium** (warm room), where you can now see the exposed brickwork and vents that allowed hot steam into the room.

➡ Peristyle & Great Hunt

The main part of the villa is centred on the **peristyle**, a vast covered courtyard lined with amusing animal heads. This is where guests would have been received before being taken through to the **basilica** (throne room).

Of the rooms on the northern side of the peristyle, the most interesting is a dining room featuring a hunting mosaic called the **Little Hunt** – 'little' because the big hunt is over on the eastern flank of the peristyle in the **Ambulacro della Grande Caccia** (Corridor of the Great Hunt). This 64m-long corridor is emblazoned with dramatic hunting scenes of tigers, leopards, elephants, antelopes, ostriches and a rhino – animals that the Romans eventually hunted to extinction in North Africa. The first figure is resplendent in a Byzantine cape and is flanked by two soldiers, most likely Maximianus himself and two members of his personal guard.

➡ Sala delle Dieci Ragazze

(Room of the 10 Girls) Just off the southern end of the Ambulacro della Grande Caccia, in the Sala delle Dieci Ragazze, is the villa's most famous mosaic. It depicts nine (originally there were 10) bikini-clad girls working out with weights and dinky dumbbells, in preparation for the Olympic games.

Villa Romana del Casale

Sights

1 Ambulacro della Grande Caccia C2
2 Atrium B2
3 Basilica C2
4 Frigidarium B2
5 Little Hunt C1
6 Main Entrance B2
7 Palaestra B2
8 Peristyle C2
9 Sala delle Dieci Ragazze C2
10 Tepidarium B2
11 Thermae B2
12 Triclinium C2

➡ Mythical Trials

On one side of the Ambulacro is a series of apartments, the floor illustrations of which reproduce scenes from Homer and other mythical episodes. Of particular interest is the **triclinium** (banquet hall), with a splendid depiction of the labours of Hercules, where the tortured monsters are ensnared by a smirking Odysseus.

Getting There & Away

If driving to Villa Romana del Casale, follow signs along the SP15 from Piazza Armerina's town centre.

By public transport it's harder, but not impossible. Between May and September **SAVIT Autolinee** (☎ 0934 55 66 26; www.savitautolinee.it) runs eight daily buses to the site from Piaza Armerina (€1, 30 minutes), departing from Piazza Senatore Marescalchi on the hour (9am to noon and 3pm to 6pm) and returning from the villa on the half-hour.

Outside summer you will have to walk – it's downhill, not too strenuous, and takes about an hour. The walk back is only steep for the last part. Another option is to prearrange a **taxi** (☎ 329 2911435), which costs around €20 return.

Caltagirone

☎ 0933 / POP 38,830 / ELEV 608M

Hilltop Caltagirone is renowned throughout Sicily for its ceramics. The area's high-quality clay has supported production for more than 1000 years and still today the industry is an important money-spinner. The town's earliest settlers worked with terracotta, but it was the Arabs, arriving in the 10th century, who kick-started the industry by introducing glazed polychromatic colours, particularly the yellows and blues that have distinguished the local ceramics ever since.

Everywhere you go in Caltagirone you're reminded of its ceramic traditions, most emphatically at the Scalinata di Santa Maria del Monte, the town's epic, ceramic-inlaid staircase.

Caltagirone's history dates to pre-Greek times, but the town's name is Arabic in origin, a derivation of the words *kalat* and *gerun*, meaning 'castle' and 'cave'. Little remains of the town's early incarnations, as it was almost entirely destroyed by the earthquake in 1693 and subsequently rebuilt in the baroque style so typical of Sicily's southeast.

Sights

Scalinata di Santa Maria del Monte LANDMARK

Caltagirone's most evocative sight is this monumental staircase, known locally as the Scalinata di Santa Maria del Monte, which rises from Piazza Municipio to the **Chiesa di Santa Maria del Monte**, at the top of the town. Built in the early 17th century to connect the old hilltop centre with newer developments around Piazza Municipio, it was originally divided into several flights of steps separated by small squares.

These tiers were eventually unified in the 1880s to create the 142-step flight that stands today. The hand-painted maiolica tiles were a relatively recent addition, only being added in 1956. It's all very impressive, although by the time you get to the top, you'll probably be more interested in having a sit-down than admiring the tile-work. Fortunately, the huge views will quickly restore your will to move. Flanked by colourful ceramic shops, the steps are at their finest during Caltagirone's annual celebration, the **Festa di San Giacomo** (Feast of St James) on 24 and 25 July, when the entire staircase is lit by more than 4000 oil lamps. The spectacle is repeated on 14 and 15 August.

At the bottom of the staircase, **Piazza Municipio** is overshadowed by a number of grand buildings, including the **Palazzo Senatorio**, where the town senate once sat. The building is now home to a cafe.

Museo della Ceramica MUSEUM

(Regional Ceramics Museum; ☎0933 5 84 18; Via Giardini Pubblici; adult/reduced €4/2; ⏲9am-6.30pm Tue-Sun) Down from the main historic centre, this museum is the place to learn about the Sicilian ceramics industry. Exhibits, which include Greek terracotta works, medieval kitchenware and some excessively elaborate 18th-century maiolica statuettes, chronicle developments from prehistoric times to the 19th century.

Museo d'Arte Contemporanea Caltagirone MUSEUM

(☎0933 2 10 83; Via Luigi Sturzo 167; ⏲9.30am-1.30pm Mon, Tue & Thu-Sat) FREE This small, sadly forlorn museum has an engaging contemporary collection, including works by the renowned local artist Gianni Ballarò.

Giardino Pubblico GARDEN

(Via Giardini Pubblici) Next to the Museo della Ceramica, the Giardino Pubblico is a lovely place to see out the late afternoon, perhaps with an ice cream or a glass of something cool at the park bar. Manicured avenues lead down to a beautiful (if unloved) pavilion, inspired by Moorish architecture and built in the early 1950s.

Look the other way for views stretching into the distance – on a clear day, as far as Mt Etna.

Chiesa di San Francesco d'Assisi CHURCH

(Piazza San Francesco d'Assisi; ⏲hours vary) Caltagirone has an extraordinary number of churches, almost 30 in the historic centre alone. Most are baroque, dating to the building boom of the early 18th century, although some have earlier origins. One such, the Chiesa di San Francesco d'Assisi, dates to the 13th century, but now flaunts an extraordinarily flamboyant baroque facade.

Near the church, the 17th-century **Ponte San Francesco** (San Francesco Bridge) is worth a close look for its ceramic floral embellishments.

Eating

The hilltop town's specialities are earthy and rustic. Look out for *pasta cu maccu* (with puréed fava beans), *pasta chi mirangiani* (with eggplant and salted ricotta) and *piruna* (calzoni filled with spinach and other vegetables). Come Christmas, tuck into *cuddureddi ri Natali* (shortcrust pastry filled with sweet, dense *vincotto*, almonds or honey).

Bar Judica & Trieste SICILIAN €

(☎0933 2 20 21; Via Principe Amedeo 22; calzone €1.60) It's all about the street food at this unassuming neighbourhood bar, complete with pavement patio. Scan the counter for cheap, filling bites such as *pizza a taglio* (pizza by the slice), *arancini* and calzoni. The latter come in a variety of fillings, from sautéed spinach and pecorino cheese, to a combo of eggplant, mozzarella and tomato.

Two calzoni should satiate the hungriest of punters. Seal the deal with a post-prandial gelato, granita or espresso.

★Il Locandiere SEAFOOD €€

(☎0933 5 82 92; Via Luigi Sturzo 55-59; meals €30-35; ⏲12.30-2.30pm & 8-10.30pm Tue-Sun; 📶) Those in the know head to this smart little restaurant for top-quality seafood and impeccable service. What exactly you'll eat depends on the day's catch, but the fish couscous is superb and the *casarecce con ragù di tonno* (pasta fingers with tuna

DON'T MISS

COOKING COURSES & WINE TASTING

The area west of Caltanissetta is wild and remote. But if you want to get away from everything, head to beautiful **Tenuta Regaleali** (☎0921 54 40 11; www.tascadalmerita.it; Contrada Regaleali, Sclafani Bagni), near the village of Vallelunga. One of five wine-producing estates owned by the Tasca d'Almerita family, it's home to some 400 hectares of vineyards, a high-tech winery and, in a restored 19th-century building, the **Anna Tasca Lanza Cooking School** (☎0934 81 46 54; www.annatascalanza.com; Contrada Regaleali, Sclafani Bagni).

Visits to the winery are limited to guided tours (with optional tastings) for between eight and 25 people, which must be booked ahead. Cooking courses range from a day-long lesson and lunch (€170) to overnight and up to five-day packages (€1350 to €2250 per person including accommodation). Best of all, all that kneading, mixing and nibbling is laced with gorgeous glasses of vino from the winery..

sauce) a sure-fire hit. *Dolci* show-stoppers include delicious *cannoli a cucchiao* (*cannoli* with fig cream).

The mostly Sicilian wine list is long enough to please most palates.

La Piazzetta SICILIAN €€
(☎0933 2 41 78; Via Vespri 20; pizzas from €4, meals €25; ⊙12.45-3pm & 7.45-10.30pm Fri-Wed; 📶) For many locals, Saturday night means a slap-up meal at La Piazzetta, a much-loved *centro storico* (historic city centre) restaurant. That might mean a pizza and beer or something more substantial such as fresh pasta with pistachio pesto followed by a mountainous mixed grill. It's not haute cuisine, but the food is tasty, the atmosphere is convivial and the prices are honest.

Coria MODERN SICILIAN €€€
(☎0933 2 65 96; www.ristorantecoria.it; Via Infermeria 24; 3-course set lunch €30, dinner menus €45-80; ⊙12.30-2pm & 7.30-10pm Tue-Sun) Caltagirone's top restaurant is an established address on the island's fine-dining circuit. Its reputation rides on innovative, visually arresting cuisine, and while not every dish on the menu flies, the strike rate is good. Expect dishes that see grilled cod paired with plum mayonnaise, or tender beef conspiring with carob. Reservations required.

Shopping

If you're in the market for a souvenir, there are about 120 ceramics shops in town.

★Ceramiche Alessi Di Giacomo Alessi CERAMICS
(☎0933 2 19 67; www.giacomoalessi.it; Corso Principe Amedeo di Savoia 9; ⊙9.30am-1.30pm & 3.30-8pm) Giacomo Alessi is arguably Caltagirone's most famous ceramicist. Not only has his work been exhibited at the Venice Biennale, but he received a Knighthood of the Italian Republic in 2007. Inspired by classical myths, Sicilian traditions, magic, poetry and even war, he creates astounding works that masterfully balance classic and contemporary aesthetics. Even if you're not shopping, head in for a browse.

Le Maioliche di Riccardo Varsallona CERAMICS
(☎0933 2 61 67; www.maiolichevarsallona.com; Via C Colombo 33; ⊙9am-1pm & 2.30-8pm Mon-Sat) This reliably creative and innovative local ceramicist produces some interesting designs as well as the more traditional *testa di Moro* (Moor's head).

Orientation

Caltagirone is divided into an upper *(alta)* and lower *(bassa)* town, with everything of interest in the upper town. Orientate yourself around Piazza Municipio, the upper town's focal square. From here, the Scalinata di Santa Maria del Monte rises to the northeast, while shop-lined Via Vittorio Emanuele heads off west and Via Luigi Sturzo runs northeast to the Viale Regina Elena ring road. Just south of Piazza Municipio, Piazza Umberto connects with Via Roma, which runs down to the Giardino Pubblico. Buses stop in Piazza Umberto.

Information

Tourist Office (☎335 5795945; www.comune.caltagirone.ct.it; Via Duomo 15; ⊙9am-7pm Mon-Sat) Near the bottom of the Scalinata di Santa Maria del Monte.

Getting There & Away

BUS

AST (☎840 000323; www.aziendasicilianatrasporti.it) buses run to Piazza Armerina (€4.30, 1½ hours, one daily Monday to

Saturday) and Syracuse (€10.50, three hours, twice daily Monday to Saturday), and **SAIS** (☎199 244141, 800 211020; www.saisautolinee.it) runs a service to Enna (€5.80, 1¼ hours, twice daily Monday to Saturday, once daily Sunday).

CAR & MOTORCYCLE

Caltagirone is just off the SS417, the road that connects Gela on the south coast with Catania in the east. From Piazza Armerina, follow the SS117bis south and then cut across on the SS124.

If you're staying in the upper town, there's useful parking on Viale Regina Elena.

THE WESTERN INTERIOR

Bearing the scars of a history of neglect and poverty, Sicily's western interior is a bleached landscape of small, isolated towns and rolling hills. For centuries the area was divided into large *latifondi* (landed estates) owned by absentee landlords, and still today the area seems remote and largely cut off from the rest of the world. It's a tough area to travel in without your own car, although interest is mainly limited to the main city Caltanissetta and the large Regaleali wine estate.

Caltanissetta

☎0934 / POP 63,290 / ELEV 568M

One of Sicily's nine provincial capitals, Caltanissetta is the largest city in the area, a scruffy, workaday place with little obvious appeal. But if you do find yourself passing through, there's a fine central piazza and, in the suburbs, a mildly interesting archaeological museum.

The city, originally founded by the Greeks, enjoyed prosperity in the first half of the 20th century as capital of the Sicilian sulphur-mining industry and is today an important agricultural centre.

Sights

Piazza Garibaldi HISTORIC SITE

Caltanissetta's historic centre converges on Piazza Garibaldi, a handsome square flanked by the **Duomo**, the town hall and the baroque **Chiesa di San Sebastiano**. Although the Duomo sports a late-Renaissance appearance, substantial alterations made in the 19th century have ruined the overall effect. Inside, if you find the church open, are frescoes by the 18th-century Flemish artist Guglielmo Borremans.

Museo Archeologico Regionale MUSEUM

(☎0934 56 70 62; Contrada Santo Spirito; adult/reduced €4/2; ⊙9am-1pm & 3.30-7pm, closed last Mon of the month) In the suburbs, sporadically signposted from the city centre, the Museo Archeologico displays a collection of prehistoric finds from all over Sicily, including vases, tools, early Sicilian ceramics and rare terracotta figurines from the Bronze Age.

The church you'll see near the museum car park is the 12th-century **Abbazia di Santo Spirito**, one of the few surviving relics from the city's Norman period.

Eating

Hearty regional dishes include *pasta 'ncasciata* (with cauliflower and pork sausage) and *frascatula,* a thick soup usually made with broccoli, chilli, garlic, wild fennel, lard and semolina flour. Caltanissetta is also well known for its *torrone* (nougat), known locally as *'turruni.*

★**Ristorante Centro Storico** SICILIAN **€€**

(☎329 3114872; Via C Benintendi 133; ⊙12.30-3pm & 7.30-11pm Mon-Sat) Owned and run by a warm, hospitable couple, Centro Storico is all about gorgeous produce cooked with love and pride. Trust the staff's suggestions, which might include pasta with fresh sardines or an absolutely sublime *calamaro ripieno* (stuffed calamari). Desserts are equally pleasing, whether it's a *tortino al pistacchio* (pistachio tart) or a palette-reviving mint and chocolate sorbet.

Consider booking ahead, especially on Friday or Saturday nights.

Information

Tourist Office (☎0934 53 48 40; Via de Nicola 2; ⊙hours vary) Located just off the main thoroughfare of Viale della Regione. Opening times can be unpredictable.

Getting There & Away

BUS

From the bus station on Via Colajanni, **SAIS Autolinee** (☎800 211020, 199 244141; www.saisautolinee.it) runs to Enna (€4.30, 50 minutes, up to five daily Monday to Friday, three Saturday), while **SAIS Trasporti** (☎0934 56 40 72; www.saistrasporti.it) runs to Agrigento (€6.40, 1¼ hours, 15 daily Monday to Saturday, 10 Sunday).

CAR & MOTORCYCLE

If coming from Enna or the north, take the A19 autostrada to join the SS640, which passes through Caltanissetta en route to Agrigento.

Mediterranean Coast

Includes ➡

Best Places to Eat

- Ristorante La Madia (p242)
- M.A.T.E.S. (p242)
- Kalòs (p232)
- Hostaria Del Vicolo (p241)
- Aguglia Persa (p232)

Best Places to Sleep

- B&B Sotto Le Stelle (p260)
- B&B Da Lulo e Gagà (p260)
- Fattoria Mosè (p260)
- Villa Athena (p260)
- PortAtenea (p259)

Why Go?

Sicily's Mediterranean coast is a mixed bag. The main attraction of the area, the spectacular ruins of the Valley of the Temples – unparalleled across the island for their significance, expanse and beauty – are overlooked by ranks of unsightly tower blocks, giving the city of Agrigento an odd air. West of Agrigento, the development soon peters out and the landscape takes on a wilder, less contaminated aspect. Here you'll find some wonderful sandy beaches, particularly at the Riserva Naturale Torre Salsa and Eraclea Minoa, and tracts of beautiful, unspoilt countryside. The chalk cliffs of the Scala dei Turchi are a spectacular sight and there's a great beach too. Further west, the pretty spa town of Sciacca is well worth a day or two for its excellent seafood restaurants and handsome historic streets. Don't miss Favara's art neighbourhood, Farm Cultural Park, an innovative and vibrant art project that has revived a town.

Road Distances (km)

	Agrigento	Caltabellotta	Gela	Licata
Caltabellotta	60			
Gela	75	130		
Licata	45	100	30	
Sciacca	60	20	130	100

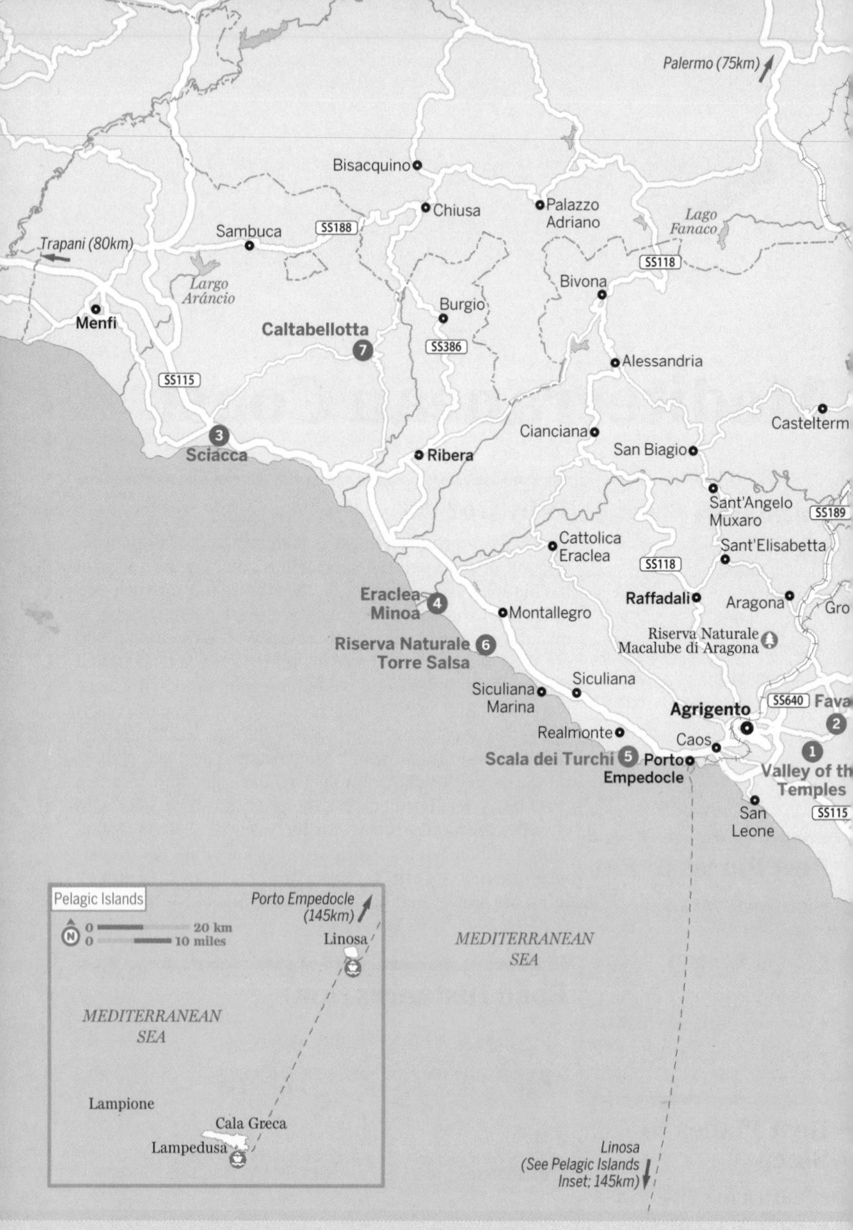

Mediterranean Coast Highlights

❶ **Valley of the Temples** (p234) Marvelling at the genius of the ancient Greeks as you wander among Agrigento's spectacular ruins.

❷ **Farm Cultural Park** (p233) Getting an alternative take on Sicilian culture at this innovative art 'neighbourhood' in Favara.

❸ **SciacCarnevale** (p239) Dancing through the streets accompanied by giant papier-mâché puppets at Sciacca's flamboyant carnival.

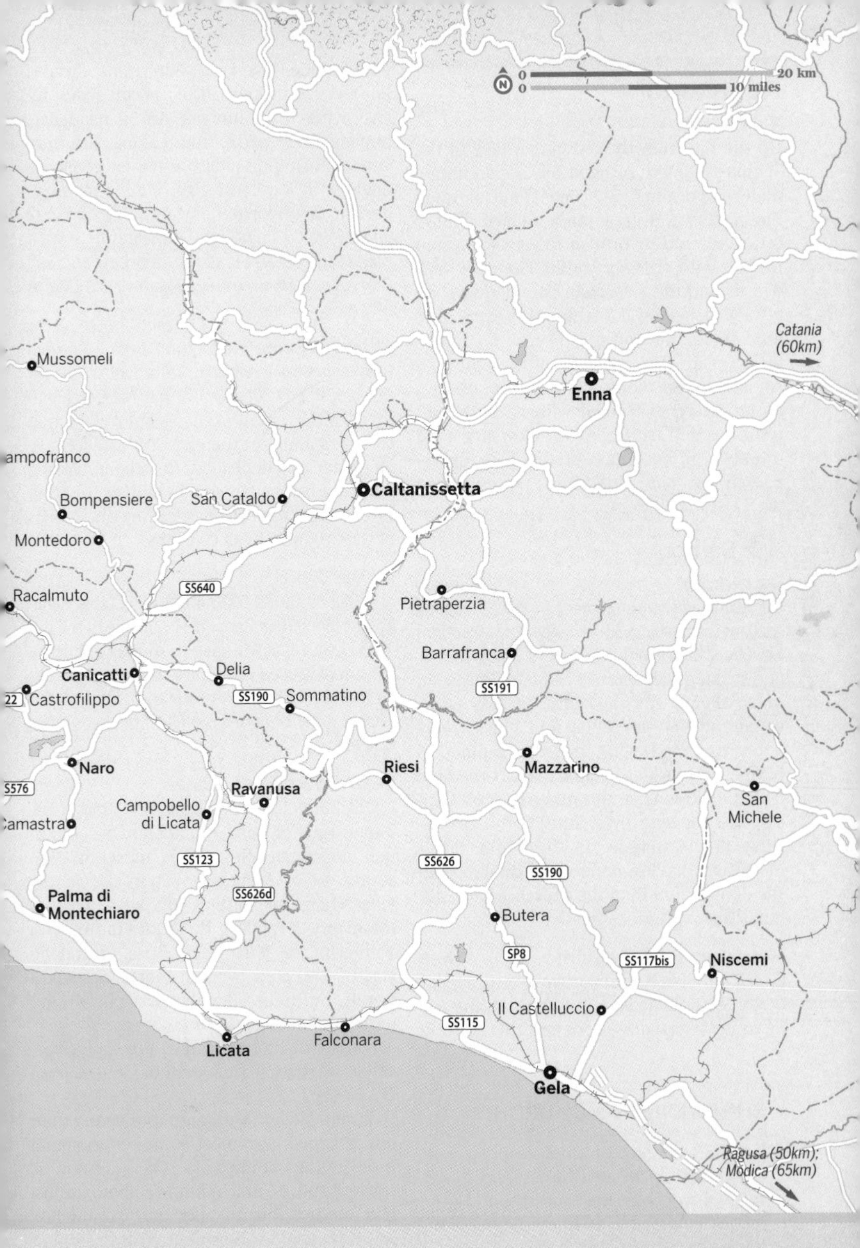

❹ **Eraclea Minoa** (p239) Exploring the ancient Greek theatre, then indulging in a natural mud scrub on the beach.

❺ **Scala dei Turchi** (p237) Contemplating sunset over the Mediterranean from the stunning white cliffs.

❻ **Riserva Naturale Torre Salsa** (p237) Experiencing the wild beauty of one of Sicily's most isolated beaches.

❼ **Caltabellotta** (p242) Soaking up dizzying views from the ruined Norman castle atop this classic hill town.

Agrigento

☎0922 / POP 59,600

Up the hill from the dazzling Valley of the Temples, modern Agrigento is not an immediately appealing prospect. Huge elevated motorways converge on a ragged hilltop centre scarred by brutish tower blocks and riddled with choking traffic. However, hidden behind this depressing outer ring is an attractive medieval kernel with some fine accommodation and a lively evening buzz.

The main thoroughfare running through Agrigento's medieval core is Via Atenea, an attractive strip lined with smart shops, trattorias and bars. Narrow alleyways wind upwards off the main street, past tightly packed *palazzi* (mansions) interspersed with historic churches.

Sights

Cathedral CATHEDRAL
(www.cattedraleagrigento.com; Via Duomo; ⏲10am-1.30pm & 3.30-7pm Apr-Oct, 10am-1pm Nov-Mar, closed Mon) The city's magnificent and striking 11th-century cathedral has been much altered over the centuries. It boasts a wonderful Norman ceiling and a mysterious letter from the Devil. Old Nick is reputed to have tried to seduce Sister Maria Crocifissa della Concezione, a nun in Agrigento's Benedictine convent, by writing to her promising all the treasure in the world. Sister Maria was having none of it, though, and she dobbed him in to the church, which still holds this mysterious missive.

Monastero di Santo Spirito CONVENT
(☎0922 20664; www.monasterosantospirito.com; Cortile Santo Spirito 9; ⏲9am-7pm) At the top of a set of steps off Via Atenea, this convent was founded by Cistercian nuns around 1290. A handsome Gothic portal leads inside, where the nuns are still in residence, praying, meditating and baking heavenly sweets, including *cuscusu* (sweet couscous made with local pistachios), *dolci di mandorla* (almond pastries) and *conchigliette* (shell-shaped marzipan sweets filled with pistachio paste). Press the doorbell and say *'Vorrei comprare qualche dolce'* ('I'd like to buy a few sweets').

Chiesa di Santa Maria dei Greci CHURCH
(www.museodiocesanoag.it; Salita Santa Maria dei Greci; ⏲10am-1.30pm & 3.30-7pm Apr-Oct, 10am-1pm Nov-Mar, closed Mon) This lovely small church stands on the site of a 5th-century Doric temple dedicated to Athena. Inside are some badly damaged Byzantine frescoes, the remains of a Norman ceiling and traces of the original Greek columns.

Museo Civico MUSEUM
(☎0922 59 03 71, 0922 40 14 50; Cortile Santo Spirito; €4; ⏲9am-1pm Mon-Fri, plus 3-7pm Tue & Thu) Upstairs at Monastero di Santo Spirito, the small Museo Civico is worth a quick visit as much for the views over the Valley of the Temples as its poorly labelled miscellany of objects.

Casa Natale di Pirandello MUSEUM
(☎0922 51 18 26; Piazzale Kaos; €2; ⏲9am-1pm & 3-7pm) Fans of Luigi Pirandello (1867–1936) will appreciate this small museum 5km southwest of Agrigento, set in the family villa where the author was born. One of the giants of modern Italian literature, and winner of the 1934 Nobel Prize, Pirandello started his career writing short stories and novels, but is best known as a playwright, author of masterpieces such as *Sei personaggi in ricerca di un autore* (Six Characters in Search of an Author) and *Enrico IV* (Henry IV).

Pirandello left Agrigento as a young man but returned here most summers to spend time at the family villa. The museum is stacked full of first editions, photographs, reviews and theatre bills, and Pirandello's ashes are kept in an urn buried at the foot of a pine tree in the garden.

Bus 1, operated by TUA (p237), makes four runs daily from Agrigento to the museum (30 minutes). Bus tickets cost €1.20 if purchased in advance from a tobacconist, or €1.70 on board the bus.

SHH! WE'RE IN A CHURCH!

A remarkable acoustic phenomenon known as *il portavoce* (the carrying voice) means even the faintest sound carries in Agrigento's cathedral, but this only seems to work in the favour of the priest standing in the apse. Should parishioners whisper in the back row near the cathedral door, the priest can hear their every word even though he's standing some 85m away!

Agrigento

Activities

Associazione Guide Turistiche Agrigento WALKING

(☎345 8815992; www.agrigentoguide.org) Agrigento's official tour guide association offers guided visits of the Valley of the Temples, Agrigento and the surrounding area in English and eight other languages.

Amici Del Cavallo HORSE RIDING

(☎328 9615224; alessandrosalsedo@gmail.com) Local riding enthusiast Alessandro Salsedo runs this agency that specialises in horse-riding tours of the Valley of the Temples and other sites around Sicily, with an emphasis on off-the-beaten-track discovery.

Temple Tour Bus BUS TOURS

(☎331 8313720; www.templetourbusagrigento.com; adult/child day ticket €15/8, night ticket €10/6, combo ticket €20/10) Painted with colourful designs to resemble a traditional Sicilian cart, this open-roofed bus offers hop-on, hop-off tours both day and night between Agrigento and the Valley of the Temples, along with optional visits to other attractions such as the Scala dei Turchi.

Agrigento

Sights

1 Cathedral ... A1
2 Chiesa di Santa Maria dei Greci ... B1
3 Monastero di Santo Spirito ... C2
Museo Civico ... (see 3)

Sleeping

4 Camere a Sud ... C2
5 PortAtenea ... C2
6 Terrazze di Montelusa ... B2

Eating

7 Aguglia Persa ... D3
8 Kalòs ... D3
9 L'Ambasciata di Sicilia ... B2
10 Naif ... C2
Sal8 ... (see 5)
11 Trattoria Concordia ... C2

Drinking & Nightlife

12 Café Girasole ... C2
13 Caffè Concordia ... A2
14 Caffè San Pietro ... C3
15 Mojo Wine Bar ... C2

Entertainment

16 Teatro Pirandello ... A2

Festivals & Events

Sagra del Mandorlo in Fiore CULTURAL
(www.sagradelmandorloinfiore.com) Encompassing food and wine tastings, concerts and folkloric events, this month-long festival runs from mid-February to mid-March, when the Valley of the Temples is cloaked in almond blossoms.

Festa di San Calògero RELIGIOUS
During this week-long festival centred on the first Sunday in July, the statue of St Calògero (who saved Agrigento from the plague) is carried through town while spectators throw spiced loaves at it.

Eating

Le Cuspidi GELATERIA €
(☎0922 59 59 14; www.lecuspidi.com; Piazza Cavour 19; gelato from €2; ⏰7.30am-1am Wed-Mon) This fabulous gelateria is the perfect antidote to Agrigento's oppressive heat. Especially scrumptious is the pistachio, flecked with nuts and super creamy.

★Aguglia Persa SEAFOOD €€
(☎0922 40 13 37; Via Francesco Crispi 33; meals €25-40; ⏰noon-3pm & 7-11pm Tue-Sun) Set in a mansion with leafy courtyard just below the train station, this place is a welcome addition to Agrigento's fine-dining scene. Opened in 2015 by the owners of Porto Empedocle's renowned Salmoriglio restaurant, it specialises in fresh-caught seafood in dishes such as citrus-scented risotto with shrimp and wild mint, or marinated salmon with sage cream and fresh fruit.

★Kalòs MODERN SICILIAN €€
(☎0922 2 63 89; www.facebook.com/ristorante.kalos; Piazzetta San Calogero; meals €30-45; ⏰12.30-3pm & 7-11pm Tue-Sun) For fine dining, head to this 'smart' restaurant just outside the historic centre. Five cute tables on little balconies offer a delightful setting to enjoy homemade pasta *all'agrigentina* (with fresh tomatoes, basil and almonds), grilled lamb chops, citrus shrimp or *spada gratinata* (baked swordfish covered in breadcrumbs). Superb desserts, including homemade *cannoli* (pastry shells with a sweet filling) and almond *semifreddi* (a light, frozen dessert), round out the menu.

Naif STEAK, SEAFOOD €€
(☎0922 187 07 35; www.facebook.com/naifsteakhouse; Via Vela 8; meals €30-40; ⏰6.30-10.30pm) In warm weather, tables spill from the interior dining room into the courtyard at this sweet eatery tucked between two side streets in the medieval centre. Billing itself as a steakhouse, Naif spoils carnivores with tempting choices – wild boar stew, roast pork glazed in Nero d'Avola wine, steak with porcini mushrooms – while also serving a perfectly respectable seafood menu.

Trattoria Concordia TRATTORIA €€
(☎0922 2 26 68; Via Porcello 8; meals €18-30; ⏰noon-3pm & 7-10.30pm Mon-Fri, 7-11pm Sat) Rough stone walls and wood-beamed ceilings lend a cosy atmosphere to this quintessential family-run trattoria, tucked up a side alley in the old town. Traditional Sicilian starters (frittata, sweet-and-sour aubergine, ricotta and olives) are complemented by tasty grilled fish and meats.

Sal8 INTERNATIONAL €€
(☎0922 66 19 90; Via Cesare Battisti 8; meals €25-40; ⏰noon-3pm & 6-11pm; 🍷) Creative cuisine complements a good drinks list at this wine bar–restaurant near the entrance to Via Atenea. Depending on the chef's whim, expect anything from sushi to seafood tagliatelle to tapas with a Sicilian twist – think shrimp and fava-bean cakes or *panelle* (chickpea fritters) served with sparkling wine. An entire section of the menu is devoted to vegan offerings.

L'Ambasciata di Sicilia SICILIAN €€
(☎0922 2 05 26; www.ristorantelambasciatadisicilia.it; Via Giambertoni 2; meals €20-35; ⏰noon-3pm & 6.30-11pm Wed-Mon) The 'Sicilian Embassy' does its utmost to improve foreign relations, plying tourists with tasty plates of traditional Sicilian fare and good seafood. In warm weather, the restaurant's big draw is its outdoor terrace across the street, which affords splendid views.

Drinking & Nightlife

Agrigento's medieval centre has a lively drinking scene. Pedestrianised Via Atenea is the place to be during the evening *passeggiata* (stroll), with bars up and down the street serving *aperitivi* (pre-dinner drinks) on sidewalk terraces. A couple of other good bars are tucked just off the main thoroughfare.

★Caffè San Pietro WINE BAR
(☎0922 2 97 42; www.spaziotemenos.it/sanpietro; Via Pirandello 1; ⏰7.30am-late Oct-Apr, from 11am May-Sep, closed Mon) This hip new cafe serves excellent coffee, Sicilian wines and evening *aperitivi,* but what really sets it apart is the

OFF THE BEATEN TRACK

FAVARA

The mid-sized town of Favara, 10km east of Agrigento, makes for an interesting off-the-beaten-track day trip, thanks to the presence of its innovative artists' community, the Farm Cultural Park. The Farm's gallery of provocative modern art and its ongoing series of cultural events are the main points of interest for visitors. The adjacent town centre, focused on Piazza Cavour, has seen a recent influx of restaurants, bars and other new businesses, making it a pleasant place to while away an hour or two.

Back in 2010, married couple Andrea Bartoli and Favara-born Florinda Saieva bought several abandoned buildings in the dilapidated heart of Favara and set up **Farm Cultural Park** (www.farm-culturalpark.com; Cortile Bentivegna; gallery adult/reduced €4/2; 10am-10pm Tue-Thu, to midnight Fri-Sun), a unique neighbourhood devoted to art. In the intervening years, Farm has become a centre for exhibitions by international and local artists, housing a gallery of thought-provoking, often politically charged artwork, along with shops, a garden bar, cultural events, talks, screenings, workshops, and shows going on throughout the year.

The project has brought a whole new breath of life to Favara, previously known mostly for its general decrepitude and for having one of Italy's highest unemployment rates. Several elderly local women, who had clung to their homes in the semi-abandoned town centre, now live amongst the exhibition spaces, happy to have company and to once again reside in a neighbourhood that is safe and alive. Meanwhile, a growing number of local youth have come to volunteer at the project.

Building walls serve as giant canvases for paintings and sculptures, while courtyards are full of practical installations like plant-pot chairs and brick fountains. Farm also holds the world's biggest collection of Terry Richardson's provocative fashion photography. Everything is beautifully designed, with a pervasive sense of whimsy and innovative energy. Bartoli and Saieva have even managed to incorporate the local castle, the Castello dei Chiaramonte, a largely unused 13th-century building, into the Farm project, hosting occasional workshops there.

Favara is about 10km east of Agrigento via the SP80 or the SS122. Note that Farm Cultural Park is poorly signposted, and parking is nearly impossible on the narrow streets surrounding it. Your best bet is to look for parking along Via Umberto, the main street above Piazza Cavour, then ask directions and walk from there.

Cuffaro (p234) runs buses from Palermo to Favara (€9, two hours, six daily Monday through Friday, four on Saturday, two on Sunday).

adjacent 18th-century San Pietro church, accessed through a doorway just beyond the bar. Beautifully restored by the bar's owners over an eight-year period, the church now serves as a lively affiliated venue for concerts, films and other cultural events.

Caffè Concordia CAFE

(Piazza Pirandello 36; almond milk €2; 6am-9.30pm Tue-Sat) Since 1948, this simple cafe has been a local favourite for its delicious almond milk, made with fresh-ground local almonds, sugar, water and a hint of lemon peel.

Mojo Wine Bar WINE BAR

(339 3543211; www.mojo4music.it; Via San Francesco 15; 7.30pm-3am Wed-Mon) This trendy *enoteca* (wine bar) sits in a pretty piazza just off the main thoroughfare. Enjoy a cool *aperitivo* whilst munching on olives and listening to laid-back jazz.

Café Girasole BAR

(393 6288189; Via Atenea 68-70; 8am-late Mon-Sat) With outdoor seating in the thick of Via Atenea, this popular cafe morphs by evening into a trendy hangout for the 30-something *aperitivo* set, who stop by for cocktails, table snacks and occasional DJ sets.

☆ Entertainment

Teatro Pirandello THEATRE

(0922 59 02 20; www.teatroluigipirandello.it; Piazza Pirandello; tickets €18-23) This city-run theatre is Sicily's third largest, after Palermo's Teatro Massimo and Catania's Teatro Massimo Bellini. Works by local hero Luigi Pirandello figure prominently. The program runs from November to early May.

Information

Hospital (Ospedale San Giovanni di Dio; ☎0922 44 21 11; Contrada Consolida; ⏲24hr) North of the centre.

Police Station (☎0922 48 31 11; Piazza Vittorio Emanuele 2)

Post Office (Piazza Vittorio Emanuele I; ⏲8.30am-7pm Mon-Fri, to 12.30pm Sat)

Tourist Office (☎800 315555, 800 236837; www.provincia.agrigento.it; Piazzale Aldo Moro 1; ⏲8am-1.30pm & 2-7pm Mon-Fri, to 1.30pm Sat) In the provincial government building.

Train Station Tourist Information Booth (Train station, lower level; ⏲9am-1pm Mon-Fri)

Getting There & Away

BOAT

The industrial port of Porto Empedocle, 7km southwest of Agrigento, is the departure point for ferries and hydrofoils to Lampedusa (p236), the main beach destination in Sicily's Pelagic Islands.

BUS

From most destinations, the bus is the easiest way to get to Agrigento. The intercity bus station (Piazza Rosselli) and ticket booth are on Piazza Rosselli, just off Piazza Vittorio Emanuele.

Buses to Palermo (€9, two hours) are operated by **Cuffaro** (☎091 616 15 10; www.cuffaro.info), eight Monday through Friday, six on Saturday, three on Sunday, and **Camilleri** (☎0922 47 18 86; www.camilleriargentoelattuca.it), five Monday through Friday, four on Saturday, one on Sunday. **SAL** (Società Autolinee Licata; ☎0922 40 13 60; www.autolineesal.it) serves Palermo's Falcone-Borsellino airport (€12.60, 2¾ hours, three to four Monday through Saturday).

Lumia (☎0922 2 04 14; www.autolineelumia.it) runs to Trapani and its Birgi airport (€11.90, three to four hours, three daily Monday to Friday, two on Saturday, one on Sunday).

SAIS Trasporti (☎0922 2 93 24; www.saistrasporti.it) runs 10 to 14 buses daily to Catania and its Fontanarossa airport (€13.40, three hours) via Caltanissetta (€6.40, 1¼ hours).

CAR & MOTORCYCLE

Agrigento is easily accessible by road from all of Sicily's main towns. The SS189 and SS121 connect with Palermo, while the SS115 runs along the coast to Sciacca and Licata. For Enna or Catania, take the SS640 via Caltanissetta.

TRAIN

Trains run regularly to/from Palermo (€9, two hours, hourly). For Catania, the bus is a better option as there are no direct trains. The train station has left-luggage lockers (per 12 hours €2.50).

Valley of the Temples

Situated about 3km below the modern city of Agrigento, the Unesco-listed Valley of the Temples is one of the most mesmerising sites in the Mediterranean, boasting the best-preserved Doric temples outside Greece. On the travel radar since Goethe sang their praises in the 18th century, the temples now constitute Sicily's single biggest tourist site, with more than 600,000 visitors a year. As impressive as the temples are, what you see today are mere vestiges of the ancient city of Akragas, which was once the fourth-largest city in the known world.

★**Valley of the Temples** ARCHAEOLOGICAL SITE
(Valle dei Templi; www.parcovalledeitempli.it; adult/reduced €10/5, incl Museo Archeologico €13.50/7; ⏲8.30am-7pm year-round, plus 7.30-9.30pm Mon-Fri, 7.30-11.30pm Sat & Sun Jul–early Sep) Sicily's most enthralling archaeological site encompasses the ruined ancient city of Akragas, highlighted by the stunningly well-preserved Tempio della Concordia, one of several ridge-top temples that once served as beacons for homecoming sailors. The 1300-hectare park, 3km south of Agrigento, is split into eastern and western zones. Ticket offices with car parks are at the park's southwestern corner (the main Porta V entrance) and at the north-eastern corner near the Temple of Hera (Eastern Entrance).

Sights

The Valley of the Temples is well worth an entire day – in fact, nothing less does it justice. Start in the eastern zone, where you'll find the two most famous temples, the Tempio di Hera and the outstanding Tempio della Concordia, before crossing to the western zone and a picnic lunch in the Giardino della Kolymbetra (p236).

Eastern Zone

Tempio della Concordia RUINS
(Temple of Concordia) One of the best-preserved ancient Greek temples in existence, the Temple of Concordia has survived almost entirely intact since it was constructed in 430 BC. It was converted into a Christian basilica in the 6th century and the main structure reinforced, giving it a better chance of surviving earthquakes. In 1748 the temple was restored to its original form and given the name it is now known by.

Valley of the Temples

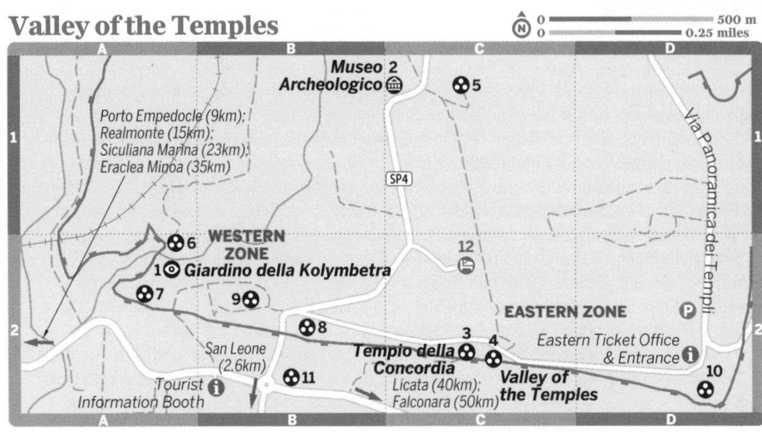

Another reason why it has survived while other temples have not, is that beneath the hard rock on which the temple stands is a layer of soft clay that acts as a kind of natural shock absorber, protecting it from earthquake tremors. Whether the Greek engineers knew this when they built the temple is the subject of debate, but modern scholars tend to think they did.

Tempio di Hera RUINS
(Temple of Hera, aka Juno) The 5th-century-BC Temple of Hera is also known as the Tempio di Giunone (Temple of Juno). Though partly destroyed by an earthquake in the Middle Ages, much of the colonnade remains intact, as does a long altar, originally used for sacrifices. The traces of red are the result of fire damage, most likely during the Carthaginian invasion of 406 BC.

Tempio di Ercole RUINS
(Temple of Hercules) The last of the temples in the eastern zone, the Tempio di Ercole is the oldest, dating from the end of 6 BC. Eight of its 38 columns have been raised and you can wander around the remains of the rest.

Tomba di Terone RUINS
(Tomb of Theron) A little temple set on a high base, the Tomb of Theron dates to 75 BC, about 500 years after the death of Theron, Agrigento's Greek tyrant.

Western Zone

Tempio di Giove RUINS
(Temple of Olympian Zeus) The main feature of the western zone is the crumbled ruin of the Tempio di Giove. Covering an area of 112m by 56m with columns 20m high, this would have been the largest Doric temple ever built had its construction not been interrupted by the Carthaginians sacking Akragas. The incomplete temple was later destroyed by an earthquake.

Lying flat on his back amid the rubble is an 8m-tall *telamon* (a sculpted figure of a man with arms raised), originally intended to support the temple's weight. It's actually a copy of the original, which is in the Museo Archeologico.

Valley of the Temples

Top Sights
1 Giardino della Kolymbetra A2
2 Museo Archeologico C1
3 Tempio della Concordia C2
4 Valley of the Temples C2

Sights
5 Quartiere Ellenistico-Romano C1
6 Santuario delle Divine Chtoniche A2
7 Tempio dei Dioscuri A2
8 Tempio di Ercole B2
9 Tempio di Giove B2
10 Tempio di Hera D2
11 Tomba di Terone B2

Sleeping
12 Villa Athena C2

Tempio dei Dioscuri RUINS
(Temple of Castor and Pollux) Four columns mark the Tempio dei Dioscuri, also known as the Temple of Castor and Pollux. Built towards the end of the 5th century, it was destroyed by the Carthaginians, later restored in Hellenistic style, and then destroyed

WORTH A TRIP

LAMPEDUSA

Lampedusa, the largest of the three Pelagic Islands (the other two are **Linosa** and **Lampione**), lies about 200km south of Sicily, closer to Tunisia than Italy. Surrounded by stunning aquamarine waters, it's a popular summer holiday destination whose year-round population of 6300 more than trebles in July and August. In winter transport connections are cut back and almost every hotel and restaurant shuts up shop.

The island's main attraction are its beaches, which are strung along the 11km south coast. The most famous, and one of the Mediterranean's most beautiful, is **Spiaggia dei Conigli** (aka Rabbit Beach) at Isola dei Conigli, a dreamy secluded bay lapped by shallow, turquoise waters. The beach is part of a nature reserve, one of the few places in Italy where *Caretta caretta* (loggerhead sea turtles) lay their eggs (between May and August). Other beaches include **Cala Francese**, **Cala Galera** and **Cala Greca**.

Società Navigazione Siciliana (Siremar; 090 36 46 01; www.siremar.it) and **Traghetti delle Isole** (www.traghettidelleisole.it) both run year-round ferries from Porto Empedocle to Lampedusa (€47, 8½ to 9¾ hours). Between late June and September, **Liberty Lines** (0923 87 3813; www.libertylines.it) also runs four to five weekly hydrofoils along this same route (€65, 4¼ hours).

Alitalia (www.alitalia.com) offers direct flights (one hour) from Palermo (twice daily) and Catania (once daily) to **Aeroporto di Lampedusa** (0922 97 07 31; www.aeroportodilampedusa.com). Lampedusa's airport is just 1km east of the main town and the ferry dock.

again by an earthquake. What you see today dates from 1832, when it was rebuilt using materials from other temples.

Santuario delle Divine Chtoniche ARCHAEOLOGICAL SITE

(Sanctuary of the Chthonic Deities) Just behind the Tempio dei Dioscuri is a complex of altars and small buildings believed to be part of the Santuario di Demetra e Kore. The Sanctuary of the Chthonic Deities, as it is known, dates from the early 6th century BC.

Giardino della Kolymbetra GARDENS

(335 1229042; www.visitfai.it/giardinodellakolymbethra; adult/reduced €5/2; 9.30am-7.30pm Jul-Sep, to 6.30pm Apr-Jun, to 5.30pm Mar & Oct, to 2.30pm Nov-Feb, closed Jan 7-31) In a natural cleft between walls of soft *tufo* (volcanic rock), the Giardino della Kolymbetra is a lush garden of olive and citrus trees interspersed with more than 300 labelled species of plants and some welcome picnic tables. Managed independently by the non-profit historical preservation organisation FAI, it's a peaceful, shady spot, perfect for escaping the heat of the valley and breaking for a picnic lunch. The climb down is steep (best avoided if you've got dicky knees).

Other Sites

★Museo Archeologico MUSEUM

(0922 40 15 65; Contrada San Nicola 12; adult/reduced €8/4, incl Valley of the Temples €13.50/7; 9am-7.30pm Tue-Sat, to 1.30pm Sun & Mon) North of the temples, this wheelchair-accessible museum is one of Sicily's finest, with a huge collection of clearly labelled artefacts from the excavated site. Noteworthy are the dazzling displays of Greek painted ceramics and the awe-inspiring reconstructed *telamon*, a colossal statue recovered from the nearby Tempio di Giove.

Quartiere Ellenistico-Romano ARCHAEOLOGICAL SITE

(Hellenistic-Roman Quarter; admission incl with Valley of the Temples ticket) To the east of the museum is the Hellenistic-Roman Quarter, featuring a well-preserved street layout which was part of urban Akragas (and later, under the Romans, Agrigentum). The regular grid is made up of main streets *(plateiai)* intersected at right angles by secondary streets *(stenopoi)*, all of which were laid out towards the end of the 4th century BC.

Eating

Kokalos PIZZA €

(0922 60 64 27; www.ristorante-kokalos.com; Via Cavaleri Magazzeni; pizzas €6-11, meals €20-30; 12.30-2.30pm & 7-11.30pm) This eatery, resembling a Wild West ranch, is the perfect place to enjoy wood-fired pizza on the summer terrace while gazing out over the temples. You will need a car to get here – it's up a dusty track 2km southeast of the Valley of the Temples site.

Accademia del Buon Gusto MODERN SICILIAN €€
(☎0922 51 10 61; www.accademiadelbuongusto.it; Contrada Maddalusa; meals €35-45; ⏰7pm-midnight Mon-Fri) The restaurant of the Foresteria Baglio della Luna is an elegant fine-dining establishment offering innovative Sicilian cuisine and views over the Valley of the Temples. Fresh local seafood appears in sophisticated creations such as sea bream with pecorino cheese and aubergine tartare, or grilled tuna with mint couscous and pepper sauce. Reservations required.

Leon d'Oro Vittorio SEAFOOD €€
(☎0922 41 32 56; www.leondorovittorio.it; Viale Emporium 102, San Leone; meals €25-40; ⏰12.30-3pm & 7.30-11pm Wed-Mon) A much-lauded local favourite along the road from the temples to San Leone, Leon d'Oro specialises in beautifully prepared fish dishes. The menu is in local dialect, in keeping with the rustic ambience. Dishes to look out for include fish of the day with pistachios and caramelised lemons, swordfish ravioli, or *calamari su agrumi* (cuttlefish served with local citrus fruits).

Information

Valley of the Temples Eastern Ticket Office & Entrance If your visit is focused on the eastern temples, this is the best place to enter the archaeological site.

Valley of the Temples Main (Porta V) Ticket Office & Entrance (Piazzale dei Templi; ⏰8.30am-7pm year-round, plus 7.30-9.30pm Mon-Fri, 7.30-11.30pm Sat & Sun Jul-early Sep) By the entrances to the two zones of the archaeological park is the car park and main ticket office where you can enquire about guided tours or pick up an audio guide (in English and Italian only, fee payable).

Valley of the Temples Tourist Information Booth (Piazzale Porta V; ⏰9am-1pm Mon-Fri) In a small wooden shack adjacent to the parking lot at the main (Porta V) entrance to the Valley of the Temples.

Getting There & Away

City bus 1, operated by **TUA** (Trasporti Urbani Agrigento; ☎0922 41 20 24; www.trasportiurbaniagrigento.it), runs half-hourly from Agrigento's bus and train stations to the archaeological museum (15 minutes) and the Porta V entrance to the temples (20 minutes). 'Bus 2/', as distinct from 'bus 2' (which has a different route – watch out for the hard-to-spot slash!) runs every hour or so to the temples' eastern entrance near the Tempio di Hera (10 to 15 minutes). Tickets cost €1.20 if purchased in advance from a tobacconist, or €1.70 on board the bus.

Beaches & Beauty Spots

With your own wheels, you'll find some stunning beaches and beauty spots west of Agrigento. From south to north, these include Scala dei Turchi, Siculiana Marina and Torre Salsa, all within an easy 30- to 45-minute drive of the city via the SS115.

Sights

★Scala dei Turchi BEACH
One of the most beautiful sights in the Agrigento area, this blindingly white rock outcropping, shaped like a giant staircase, juts into the sea near Realmonte, 15km west of Agrigento. It's a popular spot with local sunseekers who come to sunbathe on the milky-smooth rock and dive into the indigo sea. To escape the crowds, walk another few hundred metres north along the white rocky shelf, and descend to the long sandy beach below.

The beach was named after the Arab pirates who used to hide out from stormy weather here (known colloquially as Turchi, or 'Turks').

★Riserva Naturale Torre Salsa PARK
(www.wwftorresalsa.it) This stunning 761-hectare natural park, administered by the World Wildlife Fund, is signposted off the SS115. Exit at Siculiana Marina (a small coastal settlement with its own great sandy beach) or continue 10km north to the second Montallegro exit and follow the signs for 'WWF Riserva Naturale Torre Salsa'. There's plenty of scope for walkers here with well-marked trails and sweeping panoramic views of the surrounding mountains and coast.

The long, deserted Torre Salsa beach (reached from the northern entrance) is especially beautiful, although the access road is rough.

Getting There & Away

All beaches are signposted off the coastal SS115 highway. Coming from Agrigento, leave the SS115 for Scala dei Turchi at the signposted exit just north of Porto Empedocle (about 10km from Agrigento) and continue northwest along the coastal SP68, following the signs. The Siculiana Marina exit off SS115 is about 20km from Agrigento, while the turnoff for Torre Salsa is at Campobianco, 34km northwest of Agrigento.

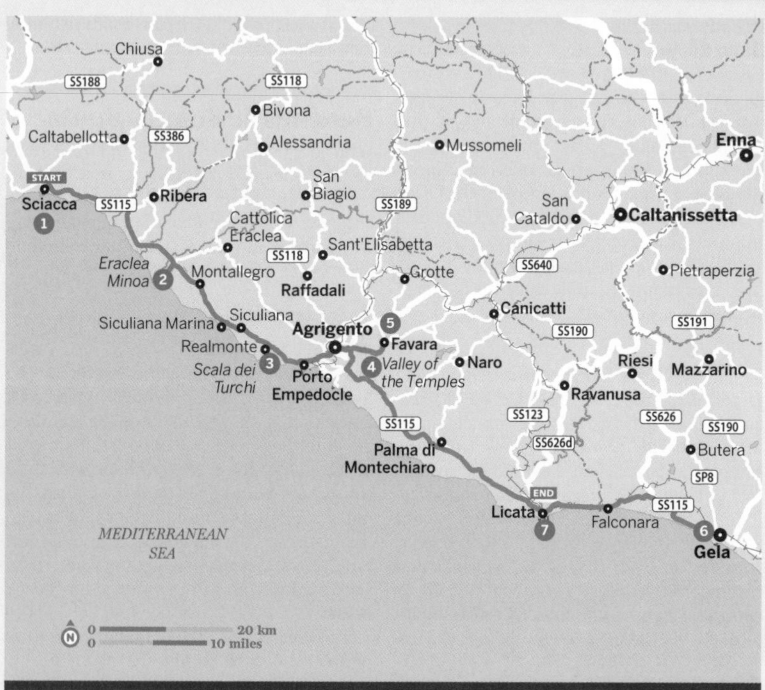

Driving Tour
Temples, Art & Beaches

START SCIACCA
END LICATA
LENGTH 150KM; THREE TO FOUR DAYS

Start in the lovely seaside town of 1 **Sciacca** (p239), where you can explore the historic centre's many elegant *palazzi* or spend the morning shopping for ceramics before descending to the picturesque working port for a lunch of fresh-caught fish. Afterwards, stroll around the nearby Castello Incantato, where you'll see eccentric local art in natural surroundings.

Next, hit the beaches east of Sciacca. Some 30km down the coast at 2 **Eraclea Minoa** (p239), dip your toes first into ancient history at the archaeological park and then into seawater on the sandy strand below. Follow the green-coloured people and smother yourself with rejuvenating clay scraped off the rock at the beach's far end before continuing down the coast to the spectacular 3 **Scala dei Turchi** (p237), a chalky-white rock formation in the shape of a giant staircase. It's a great place to linger over dinner while watching the sun set over the Mediterranean.

The peak of the tour is Agrigento's 4 **Valley of the Temples** (p234), Sicily's greatest archaeological site. Take an entire day to wander the expansive park and discover its magnificent Greek temples. At the end, dine at one of the restaurants overlooking the temples, lit by lights beaming over the valley. On your way out of town, be sure to stop in at the innovative 5 **Farm Cultural Park** (p233) at Favara, 10km east of Agrigento – this local art project has taken over an entire part of the historic centre of the dilapidated town and injected vibrancy into the local community.

Spend your final afternoon taking the slow road and exploring the beaches east of Agrigento, culminating in the wild and unspoilt expanses along the Gela Riviera. At the western edge of Gela, check out 6 **Capo Soprano** (p243), where you'll find the town's ancient Greek fortifications and the ruins of Sicily's only surviving Greek baths. Double back on the SS115 to end your tour at 7 **Licata** (p242), where the double Michelin-starred Ristorante La Madia awaits – considered one of Sicily's finest, it makes a great finale for the journey.

Eraclea Minoa

0922 / POP 3810

Nowadays a small summer resort – empty most of the year, packed in July and August – Eraclea Minoa was an important Greek settlement in ancient times. It was legendarily founded by the Cretan king Minos, who came to Sicily in pursuit of Daedalus after his escape from Crete. Historical evidence suggests the city was established by Greek colonists in the 6th century BC and went on to flourish in the 4th and 5th centuries. The ancient city's scant remains can be seen at the archaeological park above town.

Today Eraclea Minoa's greatest attraction is its **beach**, a photogenic strip of golden sand backed by willowy eucalyptus trees, cypress groves and chalk cliffs. At the beach's western end there's a natural mud rock, which you can scrape off and massage into your skin. Dry off in the sun, then rinse in the sea and you'll have removed 10 years in 10 minutes.

Sights

Area Archeologica Eraclea Minoa ARCHAEOLOGICAL SITE

(0922 84 60 05; adult/reduced €4/2; 9am-1hr before sunset) Set on a headland above the seaside village of Eraclea Minoa, the vestiges of this ancient Greek city are limited to the crumbling remains of a soft sandstone theatre, covered with protective plastic – but the surrounding coastal scenery is gorgeous.

Getting There & Away

Eraclea Minoa is 4km off the SS115, roughly halfway between Agrigento and Sciacca. Upon exiting the main highway, follow SP30 southwest to the beach.

Sciacca

0925 / POP 41,080

Famous for its historic spas and flamboyant carnival celebrations, Sciacca was founded in the 5th century BC as a thermal resort for nearby Selinunte. It later flourished under the Saracens, who arrived in the 9th century and named it Xacca (meaning 'water' in Arabic), and the Normans.

Until 2015, when financial woes forced the spa to shut down indefinitely, Sciacca's healing waters continued to be the big drawcard, attracting coachloads of Italian tourists who came to treat their ailments in the sulphurous vapours and mineral-rich mud.

Spas and thermal cures apart, Sciacca remains a laid-back town with an attractive medieval core and some excellent seafood restaurants. The city retains its original layout, with neighbourhoods built on strips of rock descending towards the sea. The historic centre revolves around its main thoroughfare, Corso Vittorio Emanuele, and the vast square Piazza Scandaliato, where views (and staircases) extend to the fishing harbour below.

Sights

Chiesa di Santa Margherita CHURCH

(Via Incisa; 8am-noon & 4-7pm) This 14th-century church features a superb Renaissance portal and a rather chipped baroque interior.

Porta San Salvatore CITY GATE

This 16th-century town gate is covered in Renaissance ornamentation.

Chiesa Madre CHURCH

(Piazza Duomo; 8am-noon & 4.30-7.30pm) Northeast of Piazza Scandaliato is Sciacca's cathedral, first erected in 1108 and rebuilt in 1656. Only the three apses survive from the original Norman structure. The unfinished baroque facade features a set of marble statues by Gagini.

SCIACCA'S CARNIVAL

Sciacca's carnival, **SciacCarnevale** (Carnevale di Sciacca; www.sciaccarnevale.it; Feb or Mar), is famous for its flamboyance and fabulous party atmosphere. Held between the last Thursday before Lent and Shrove Tuesday, it features an amazing parade of huge papier-mâché figures mounted on floats. The festival opens with carnival king Peppe Nappa receiving the city's keys. The technicolour floats are then released into the streets with their bizarre cast of grotesque caricatures.

The figures are handmade each year using traditional methods and are modelled on political and social personalities. The floats wind through the streets of the old town, while masked revellers dance to locally composed music and satirical poetry is read aloud.

Sciacca

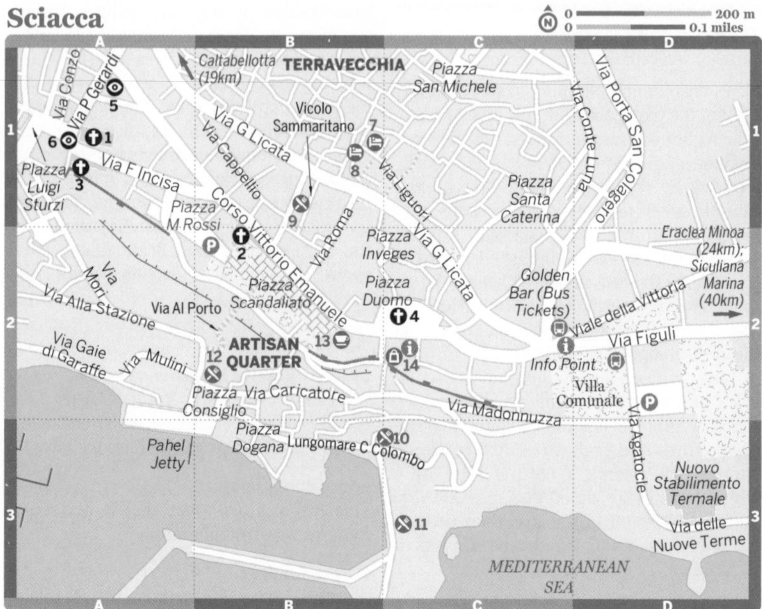

Sciacca

Sights

1 Chiesa del Carmine A1
2 Chiesa di San Domenico B2
3 Chiesa di Santa Margherita A1
4 Chiesa Madre C2
5 Palazzo Steripinto A1
6 Porta San Salvatore A1

Sleeping

7 Al Moro B1
8 B&B Da Lulo e Gagà B1

Eating

9 Hostaria Del Vicolo B1
10 La Lampara C3
11 Porto San Paolo C3
12 Trattoria Al Faro B2

Drinking & Nightlife

13 Gran Caffè Scandaglia B2

Shopping

14 Ceramiche Gaspare Patti C2

Palazzo Steripinto ARCHITECTURE

(Corso Vittorio Emanuele) This most imposing of Sciacca's *palazzi* is recognisable by its twin-mullioned windows and diamond-point rustication. It was built in the Catalan-Gothic style at the beginning of the 16th century.

To the *palazzo's* south, the Porta San Salvatore (p239), a 16th-century town gate, is covered in Renaissance ornamentation.

Castello Incantato PUBLIC ART

(Enchanted Castle; 339 2340174; www.castelloincantatosciacca.it; Via Filippo Bentivegna 16; €3.50; 9.30am-1pm & 3.30-8pm Apr-Oct, 9.30am-1pm & 3.30-5.30pm Nov-Mar) About 3km east of town, the Castello Incantato is actually a large park festooned with thousands of sculpted heads. The man behind this bizarre collection was Filippo Bentivegna (1888–1967), a local artist who used sculpture to exorcise the memories of an unhappy sojourn in the USA – each head is supposed to represent one of his memories.

His eccentricities were legion and still today people enjoy recalling them. Apparently, he regarded his work as a sexual act and demanded to be addressed as 'Eccellenza' (Your Excellency).

Chiesa di San Domenico CHURCH

(Piazza Scandaliato) This 18th-century reconstruction of a 16th-century church sits on the western end of Piazza Scandaliato.

Chiesa del Carmine CHURCH

(Via Incisa; 8am-noon & 4-7pm) This architectural mish-mash of a church has an odd-looking 13th-century rose window that predates the maiolica-tiled dome by some 600 years.

Eating

Osteria Il Grappolo OSTERIA €

(0925 8 52 94; www.osteriailgrappolo.it; Via Conzo 9a; meals €21-28; 12.30-3pm & 7.30-11pm Wed-Mon) The very essence of a friendly neighborhood *osteria* (casual tavern), Salvatore Ciaccio's 'Grappolo' embraces the Slow Food aesthetic: carefully chosen local ingredients incorporated into classic Sicilian dishes like *cozze al limone* (mussels with fresh lemon), *pasta con sarde e finocchietto* (pasta with sardines, wild fennel, pine nuts, raisins and breadcrumbs) or *maltagliati pesce spada e melanzane* (rough-cut pasta with swordfish and aubergine).

Trattoria Al Faro SEAFOOD €

(092 52 53 49; Via Al Porto 25; set menu €17.50-25; 12.30-3pm & 7-11pm Mon-Sat) If the idea of budget seafood usually sets alarm bells ringing, think again. This welcoming portside trattoria is one of the few places you can feast on delicious fresh fish and still get change from €20. What's served depends on what the boats have brought in.

Tasty staples to look out for include *pasta con le sarde* (with sardines, fennel, breadcrumbs and raisins) and grilled calamari.

Porto San Paolo PIZZERIA, SEAFOOD €€

(0925 2 79 82; www.ristoranteportosanpaolo.it; Largo San Paolo 1; pizzas €5.50-8, meals €25-40; noon-3pm & 7.30pm-midnight Thu-Tue) Yes, you can dine on seafood here – as with all of Sciacca's portside restaurants – but the budget-minded will also find it a prime spot to sip sunset *aperitivi* and nosh on wood-fired pizza. Either way, the big drawcard is the spectacular panoramic terrace, with divine views over Sciacca's fishing harbour.

La Lampara SEAFOOD €€

(0925 8 50 85; www.lalamparasciacca.com; Lungomare C Colombo 13; meals €30-45; noon-2pm & 7.30-11pm Mon-Sat) In contrast to the scruffy portside streets, La Lampara is a modish, contemporary restaurant serving a modern, creative fish menu. Highly recommended is the tuna steak, cooked in sesame seeds and served with balsamic vinegar, and the chocolate cake with pistachio ice cream.

Hostaria Del Vicolo MODERN SICILIAN €€€

(0925 2 30 71; www.hostariadelvicolo.it; Vicolo Sammaritano 10; meals €40-60; 12.30-2pm & 7.30-10.30pm Tue-Sun;) Tucked away in a tiny alley in the old town, this formal restaurant is a culinary tour de force, with heavy tablecloths, noiseless service and an ample wine list. A perennial Slow Food favourite, it serves a traditional Sicilian menu embellished with modern twists, including many gluten free and vegetarian offerings.

For a *primo* (first course) try the *taglioni al nero di seppia e ricotta salata* (flat strings of fresh pasta with cuttlefish ink and salted ricotta), followed by a *secondo* (main course) of *merluzzo ai fichi secchi* (cod with dried figs).

Drinking & Nightlife

Gran Caffè Scandaglia CAFE

(0925 2 10 82, 334 3265648; Piazza Scandaliato 5-6; 7.30am-10.30pm) This is the perfect place to enjoy breakfast in the shade, or a sunset drink, overlooking the harbour. Soft pastry, caffè latte in tall glasses and fresh orange juice are delicious, as are the *granite* (flavoured crushed ice) and gelati. You'll have the local seniors for company, who congregate here in the mornings to discuss politics and their physical ailments.

Shopping

Ceramiche Gaspare Patti CERAMICS

(092 599 32 98; Corso Vittorio Emanuele 95; 9am-1pm & 3.30-7pm) Sciacca has a long-standing tradition of ceramic production and there are numerous shops selling brightly coloured crockery. For something more original, look up this Aladdin's cave of a shop in front of the Chiesa Madre. Gaspare Patti prides himself on his idiosyncratic style and his shop is packed with strange and original creations, well worth a look even if you're not going to buy.

Information

Hospital (Ospedale Giovanni Paolo II; 0925 96 21 11; Via Pompei; 24hr)

Info Point (324 8720502; www.prolocosciaccaterme.com; Piazza Friscia; 10am-1pm & 4-7pm) Tourist information kiosk operated by Sciacca's Pro Loco.

Police Station (092 596 50 11; Via Jacopo Ruffini 12)

Tourist Office (0925 2 04 78; www.prolocosciaccaterme.com; Corso Vittorio Emanuele 87; 4-7pm Tue-Fri, 10am-1pm & 4-7pm Sat

& Sun) On the main strip, with helpful English-speaking staff.

Getting There & Away

BUS

Lumia (0925 2 11 35; www.autolineelumia.it) serves Agrigento (€6.50, 1½ hours, 11 daily Monday to Saturday, one Sunday) and Trapani (€9, 2¼ hours, three Monday to Saturday, one Sunday). All buses arrive at the bus stop by the Villa Comunale on Via Figuli and leave from Via Agatocle. Buy your tickets at **Golden Bar** (Piazza Friscia) on Piazza Friscia.

CAR & MOTORCYCLE

Sciacca is about 65km from Agrigento along the SS115. There's parking on Via Agatocle near the Nuovo Stabilimento Termale, and on Piazza M Rossi, adjacent to Piazza Scandaliato.

Caltabellotta

0925 / POP 3730 / ELEV 949M

It's quite a drive up to Caltabellotta: the road rises almost vertically as it winds 19km up to the hilltop village. But make it to the top and you're rewarded with some amazing panoramic views of 21 (apparently) surrounding villages. The highest vantage point is the ruined **Norman castle** at the top of the village, where a peace treaty was signed in 1302 ending the Sicilian Vespers. Viewed from here, the town's terracotta roofs and grey houses appear to cling to the cliffside like a perfect mosaic. The town was originally named Kal'at Bellut by the Arabs, meaning 'oak rock'.

On the edge of the village lies the derelict monastery of **San Pellegrino**, from where you can see caves that were used as tombs as far back as prehistoric times.

Sights

Chiesa Madre CHURCH

(10.30am-1pm & 3.30-7pm) Dating to the late 11th century, this lovely hilltop church with its broad stone facade retains an original Gothic portal and pointed arches.

Eating

★**M.A.T.E.S.** SICILIAN €€

(0925 95 23 27; www.matesonline.it/ristorante.html; Vicolo Storto 3; meals €30-35; noon-2pm & 7-10pm Mon-Sat, noon-2pm Sun, closed 2 weeks in Oct) For fabulous traditional Sicilian fare in cosy, rustic surroundings, head for this highly recommended Slow Food restaurant in Caltabellotta's historic centre. Try the tagliatelle with broad-bean puree and sausage, vegetable risottos, or juicy, falling-off-the-bone roast pork and lamb, and finish up with one of their fantastic *cannoli*.

Getting There & Away

From Sciacca, allow at least half an hour for the sinuous 20km drive up the SP37 to Caltabellotta. Upon arrival in the lower town, follow signs left up the hill and be prepared to brave some narrow streets en route to Piazzale Ruggero di Laurìa, where you can park between the castle and the Chiesa Madre.

If you're without a car, Lumia runs buses to Caltabellotta from Sciacca (€2.90, 40 minutes, five daily Monday to Friday, four on Saturday).

Licata

0922 / POP 38,000

The workaday port of Licata doesn't look like much as you approach, but hidden behind the dreary suburbs is a charming, if rather worn, historic centre. The centre of action is **Piazza Progresso**, which divides the two main streets, Corso Roma, flanked by elegant baroque *palazzi,* and Corso Vittorio Emanuele. At the top of town, a 16th-century **castle** affords views down to the harbour.

Some 22km west of Licata, the unexceptional town of **Palma di Montechiaro** is the ancestral seat of the princes of Lampedusa, made famous by Giuseppe Tomasi di Lampedusa, author of *Il Gattopardo* (The Leopard). The family's 17th-century ancestral palace has been unoccupied for some time, but the **Chiesa Matrice** still stands and can be visited.

Eating

★**Ristorante La Madia** MODERN SICILIAN €€€

(0922 77 14 43; www.ristorantelamadia.it; Via Filippo Re Capriata 22; meals €85-120; 1-2pm & 8-10pm Wed-Mon) One of Sicily's finest restaurants, double Michelin-starred La Madia is a labour of love for local-born chef Pino Cuttaia. It serves modern Sicilian dishes based on authentic Mediterranean ingredients, such as *merluzzo* (cod) smoked over pine cones or cuttlefish served with fennel cream. Items on the elaborate tasting menus are presented as works of art, with exquisite flavours to match.

Hostaria L'Oste e il Sacrestano SICILIAN €€€
(☎0922 77 47 36; www.losteeilsacrestano.it; Via Sant'Andrea 19; meals €45-65; ⏰12.30-2pm Tue-Sun, 7.30-10pm Tue-Sat) Feast on local meat and freshly caught seafood at this Slow Food favourite just off Corso Vittorio Emanuele. Choose from the *à la carte* menu of three appetisers, three *primi*, three *secondi* and three desserts – many with fanciful names including 'evolution of the octopus' and 'a stroll through Sicily' – or go all out with the seven-course tasting menu.

Getting There & Away

Licata is on the coastal SS115, 50km southeast of Agrigento and 32km west of Gela.

Hourly buses operated by SAL (p234) connect Licata with Agrigento (one hour) and Gela (45 minutes).

Falconara

☎0934 / POP 100

The tiny settlement of Falconara consists of a few hotels, campgrounds and holiday homes on Sicily's southern coast between Licata and Gela. The prime draw for travellers is the superb sandy beach overlooked by an impressive 14th-century castle, the **Castello di Falconara**. The castle is privately owned by an aristocratic family and closed to the public for visits, but you can stay there overnight.

The road from Falconara towards Gela passes several more wild and unspoilt beaches before arriving at the so-called Gela Riviera on the outskirts of Gela. This section of Sicily's southern coast was heavily defended against the threat of an Allied invasion during WWII, and abandoned pillbox defences still litter the area.

Getting There & Away

Falconara sits on the SS115 between Gela (21km to the east) and Licata (11km to the west).

Gela

☎0933 / POP 76,700

Despite a distinguished past as one of Sicily's great ancient cities, modern Gela is a disappointment – a chaotic industrial city with a reputation as a mafia hot spot. Little remains of its heyday as the economic engine room of the great Greek colony that eventually founded Akragas, Eraclea Minoa and Selinunte. The city was sacked by Carthage in 405 BC and then razed by forces from Agrigento in 282 BC. More recently it was the first Italian town to be liberated by the Allies in WWII (in July 1943), but not before it had been bombed to rubble in the build-up to the invasion. Postwar development saw the construction of the vast petrochemical refineries that still blight the city along with swathes of cheap housing blocks. Other than a fascinating archaeology museum and remains of the city's ancient fortifications, there are few reasons to stop by.

Sights

★**Museo Archeologico** MUSEUM
(☎0933 91 26 26; Corso Vittorio Emanuele; adult/reduced incl Acropoli & Capo Soprano €4/2; ⏰9am-6pm Mon-Sat, plus 1st Sun of month) This splendid archaeological museum offers insight into Gela's great artistic past. It contains artefacts from the city's ancient acropolis and is famed for its fine collection of red-and-black *kraters;* these terracotta vases, used to mix wine and water, were a local specialty between the 7th and 4th centuries BC, admired throughout the Greek world for their delicate designs and superb figurative work. Other treasures include a remarkable collection of 530 silver coins minted in Agrigento, Gela, Syracuse, Messina and Athens.

At one time the coin collection numbered over 1000 pieces, but it was stolen in 1976 and only about half of it was ever recovered. More recently, the museum has acquired a Greek ship dating to the 6th century BC (discovered in 1988 on the sandy sea bottom off Gela) and three unusual terracotta altars (discovered in 2003 in a 5th-century-BC warehouse that had been buried under 6m of sand).

Greek Baths RUINS
(☎0933 91 26 26; Via Europa; ⏰9am-2pm & 3-8pm) FREE Some 500m from the city walls, next to the hospital, are Sicily's only surviving Greek baths, which date from the 4th century BC.

Greek Fortifications of Capo Soprano RUINS
(Mura Timoleontee di Capo Soprano; adult/reduced incl Acropoli & Museo Archeologico €4/2; ⏰9.30am-1pm & 2-6pm Mon-Sat Apr-Oct, to

OFF THE BEATEN TRACK

BUTERA & MAZZARINO

For anyone travelling north from Gela or Licata to Piazza Armerina, the back roads through these picturesque hilltop villages offer a scenic detour.

Prosperous, self-sufficient and content from its years under the rule of the Branciforte family, Butera lacks the down-at-heel atmosphere of many rural interior towns. Its lovely town church, the **Chiesa Madre**, boasts some modest treasures (a Renaissance triptych and a Madonna by 16th-century Tuscan painter Filippo Paladini), but the star attraction here is the dizzying panorama that unfolds from the hilltop **Norman castle**.

Mazzarino, the historic seat of the Branciforte clan, is now just a small, sleepy town, but merits a quick look for its clutch of baroque churches, decorated with the ostentatious funerary monuments of the Branciforte princes and more artworks by Paladini. Many of the churches are closed to the public, but you can request access at the helpful **tourist office** (☎093 438 49 84; Corso Vittorio Emanuele 410; ⌚9am-1pm & 4-8pm summer, 9am-1pm & 3-7pm winter) on Mazzarino's main street.

From Gela, it's an easy 18km drive along the SP8 to Butera. Continue another 18km north on the SP8 and the SS191 to reach Mazzarino. From here, a 24km jaunt northeastward along the SP26, SP169 and SP15 will bring you to Piazza Armerina.

4.30pm Nov-Mar) Built along Gela's western coastline at Capo Soprano by the tyrant of Syracuse, Timoleon, in 333 BC, Gela's ancient Greek fortifications are remarkably well preserved, most likely the result of being covered by sand dunes for thousands of years before their discovery in 1948. The 8m-high walls were originally built to prevent huge amounts of sand being blown into the city by the blustery sea wind. Today authorities have planted trees to act as a buffer against the encroaching sand.

Planted with mimosa and eucalyptus trees, the site is perfect for a picnic. To get here from Gela's archaeological museum, follow the *lungomare* (waterfront road) 4km west.

Acropoli RUINS

(Acropolis; ⌚9am-1hr before sunset) Behind Gela's archaeological museum, you can see the scant remains of the city's ancient Greek acropolis. Adding little to the atmosphere are the belching chimneys of a nearby petrochemical plant.

Getting There & Away

BUS

From Piazza Stazione, in front of the train station, SAL (p234) runs buses to Licata (45 minutes) and Agrigento (1¾ to 2¼ hours). There are also buses to Syracuse and Caltanissetta.

CAR & MOTORCYCLE

Gela is well connected by road: the SS115 leads westwards to Agrigento and east to Ragusa and Modica, while the SS117bis connects with Caltagirone (via the SS417) and Piazza Armerina.

Arriving in town, follow the signs for the city centre and museum, which is at the eastern end of Corso Vittorio Emanuele, the town's principal east–west street.

Accommodation

Includes ➡

Best Places to Stay

- ➡ Hotel Ravesi (p252)
- ➡ Pensione Tranchina (p247)
- ➡ Palazzo Bianco (p256)
- ➡ Palazzu Stidda (p254)

Best Agriturismi

- ➡ Baglio San Pietro (p259)
- ➡ Azienda Agrituristica Bergi (p249)
- ➡ Casa Migliaca (p250)

Best B&Bs

- ➡ B&B Al Salvatore di Lipari (p251)
- ➡ Casa Turchetti (p254)
- ➡ B&B Crociferi (p255)
- ➡ Nòtia Rooms (p257)

Where to Stay

The best place to base yourself in Sicily will depend on your interests and travel style. Cities such as Palermo, Catania, Taormina and Syracuse have the most cosmopolitan mix of higher-end and boutique hotels. If you're happier in a rural setting, the *agriturismi* (farm stay accommodation) of Central Sicily and the Madonie and Nebrodi Mountains are some of the nicest on the island. Budget travellers also have plenty of options to choose from: hostels in Palermo and Catania, mountain chalets in the Madonie Mountains and Mt Etna region, or excellent low- to midrange B&Bs throughout the region, in places such as Syracuse, Agrigento, Lipari and Marsala. Syracuse, Catania and Palermo make convenient bases for anyone travelling by train or other public transport, while beach-lovers benefit from an appealing mix of accommodation in Cefalù and Taormina.

Pricing

The following price ranges refer to a double room with private bathroom (breakfast included) in high season. July, August and Christmas are generally considered high season. Low-season rates usually apply from October to Easter (with the exception of the Christmas holidays), while mid-season rates apply the remainder of the year.

CATEGORY	COST
€	less than €110
€€	€110–€200
€€€	more than €200

PALERMO

★Stanze al Genio Residenze B&B $

(Map p58; ☎340 0971561; www.facebook.com/stanzealgenio.residenze; Via Garibaldi 11; s €50-60, d €70-80; ❄📶) Speckled with Sicilian antiques, this recently opened B&B offers four gorgeous bedrooms, three with 19th-century ceiling frescoes. All four are spacious and thoughtfully appointed, with Murano lamps, old wooden wardrobes, the odd balcony railing turned bedhead, and top-quality, orthopedic beds. That the property features beautiful maiolica tiles is no coincidence; the B&B is affiliated with the wonderful Museo delle Maioliche (p57) downstairs.

Palazzo Pantaleo B&B $

(Map p62; ☎091 32 54 71; www.palazzopantaleo.it; Via Ruggero Settimo 74h; s/d/ste €80/100/140; P📶) Offering unbeatable comfort and a convenient location, Giuseppe Scaccianoce's elegant B&B occupies the top floor of an old *palazzo* (mansion) half a block from Piazza Politeama, hidden from the busy street in a quiet courtyard with free parking. Glowing with warm, earthy tones, five rooms and one spacious suite feature high ceilings, marble, tile or wooden floors, soundproof windows and modern bathrooms.

B&B Amélie B&B $

(Map p62; ☎091 33 59 20, 328 8654824; www.bb-amelie.it; Via Principe di Belmonte 94; s €40-60, d €60-90, tr €90-100; ❄@📶) On a car-free street a stone's throw from Teatro Politeama, the affable, multilingual Angela has converted her grandmother's spacious 6th-floor flat into a cheery B&B. Rooms are simple, comfy and spotless, and the corner triple has a sunny terrace. Angela, a native Palermitan, generously shares her local knowledge and serves a finger-licking breakfast that includes homemade cakes and jams.

A Casa di Amici Hostel HOSTEL $

(Map p62; ☎091 765 46 50; www.acasadiamici.com; Via Dante 57; dm €14-23, d €40-70; ❄📶) Vibrant, friendly and filled with artwork left by former guests, this funky hostel-cum-guesthouse is a great choice. Beds are in female-only or mixed dorms, or in several imaginatively decorated, music-themed rooms, complemented by a kitchen and yoga room. Multilingual owner Claudia provides helpful maps and advice, and also runs the **A Casa di Amici B&B** (Map p52; ☎091 58 48 84; www.acasadiamici.com; Via Volturno 6; s €20-40, d €40-60; ❄📶) behind Teatro Massimo.

★BB22 Palace B&B $$

(Map p58; ☎091 32 62 14; www.bb22.it; cnr Via Roma & Via Bandiera; d €120-170, whole apt €600-950) Occupying a flouncy *palazzo* in the heart of the city, BB22 Palace offers four chic, contemporary rooms, each with its own style. Top billing goes to the Stromboli room, complete with spa bath and a bedroom skylight offering a glimpse of its 15th-century neighbour. Peppered with artworks, coffee-table tomes and an honour bar, the communal lounge makes for an airy, chi-chi retreat.

Massimo Plaza Hotel HOTEL $$

(Map p52; ☎091 32 56 57; www.massimoplazahotel.com; Via Maqueda 437; r €100-250; P❄📶) The 15-room Massimo Plaza sits in a prime location along vibrant, newly pedestrianised Via Maqueda. Tieback curtains and wooden furniture give rooms a classic feel, seven of which offer a prime-time view of the iconic Teatro Massimo across the street. Breakfast (continental or American) is included in the price and can be delivered directly to your room at no extra charge.

Butera 28 APARTMENT $$

(Map p58; ☎333 3165432; www.butera28.it; Via Butera 28; apt per day €60-200, per week €400-1320; ❄📶) Delightful multilingual owner Nicoletta rents 11 comfortable apartments in the 18th-century Palazzo Lanzi Tomasi, the last home of Giuseppe Tomasi di Lampedusa, author of *The Leopard*. Units range from 30 to 180 sq metres, most sleeping a family of four or more. Four apartments face the sea, most have laundry facilities and all have well-equipped kitchens. Nicoletta also offers fabulous cooking classes.

Hotel Principe di Villafranca BOUTIQUE HOTEL $$$

(Map p62; ☎091 611 85 23; www.principedivillafranca.it; Via Turrisi Colonna 4; d €176-363; P❄📶) Furnished with fine linens and antiques, this sophisticated slumber pad is just west of Viale della Libertà in one of Palermo's most peaceful, exclusive neighbourhoods. Public spaces include a cosy sitting area with library, fireplace and displays of local designers' work; among the comfortable, high-ceilinged rooms, junior suite 105 stands out, decorated with artwork loaned by Palermo's modern art museum.

Grand Hotel Villa Igiea HOTEL $$$

(☎091 631 21 11; www.villa-igiea.com; Salita Belmonte 43; d €190-380; P❄@📶🏊) What can you say about an art nouveau villa that was designed by Ernesto Basile for the Florio family (of tuna and Marsala-wine fame)? This is Palermo's top hotel, located around 3km north of the city centre and with its own private beach, swimming pool, tennis court, spa centre, gym and restaurants. The rooms are expectantly elegant, with blissful beds and palatial bathrooms.

Prices drop significantly in the low season, when mere mortals get a taste of the high life. While the hotel is tricky to reach without a car/private chauffeur/taxi, it does offer a free shuttle bus service to central Palermo from late March to October.

Grand Hotel Piazza Borsa HOTEL **$$$**
(Map p58; 091 32 00 75; www.piazzaborsa.com; Via dei Cartari 18; s €126-200, d €169-225, ste €370-813; P) Grandly situated in Palermo's former stock exchange, this four-star show-off encompasses three separate buildings housing 127 rooms. Nicest of the lot are the high-ceilinged suites with spa baths and windows facing Piazza San Francesco. Parking costs €18 per 24-hour period.

Around Palermo

Ustica

Le Terrazze APARTMENT **$**
(091 844 93 99; www.leterrazzeustica.it; Via C Colombo 3; d apt €40-99, q apt €85-150;) The lovely Carmen presides over this family-run cluster of apartments, all with kitchens and – as the name would imply – terraces with harbour views. Rooms number 1 through 8 sleep two to three people, with sea views improving as the numbers increase. There's also a family unit (number 9), sleeping four, with its own private terrace.

Hotel Clelia HOTEL **$$**
(0918449039; www.hotelclelia.it; Via Sindaco I 29; s €55-128, d €60-160; @) Especially good value in the off-season, this centrally located three-star hotel with attached restaurant offers simple, comfortable rooms in bright, summery hues. The hotel also offers holiday houses sleeping two to four people, and staff can help organise scooter and boat hire, diving and snorkelling tours and guided walks.

Corleone

Antica Stazione Ferrovia di Ficuzza HOTEL **$**
(091 846 00 00; www.anticastazione.it; Via Vecchia Stazione, Ficuzza; per person €35, with half board €55;) Off the SS118, between Palermo and Corleone, this hotel and restaurant (meals €20 to €25) offers a truly unique accommodation option, occupying a decommissioned 19th-century train station in the middle of thick woods where Bourbon princes once hunted game. Rooms are simple but comfortable, and the food – focused on regional produce and recipes – is wonderful.

Staff can assist you with outdoor activities in the nearby national park, including horse-riding, hiking and mountain-bike riding, and the hotel hosts two annual live jazz and blues events: the Ficuzza J & B Summerfest in July/August and the Ficuzza J & B Winter Club in late February/early March.

WESTERN SICILY

Scopello

★**Pensione Tranchina** PENSION **$**
(0924 54 10 99; www.pensionetranchina.com; Via Diaz 7; B&B per person €36-48, half board per person €55-75;) Wonderful home-cooked meals, a prime location in the centre of Scopello, and the friendly welcome of hosts Marisin and Salvatore make this one of western Sicily's most beloved *pensioni* (guesthouse). Rooms are modern, with the best enjoying balconies with distant sea views. On chilly evenings, guests share stories over *aperitivi* (pre-dinner drinks) around the blazing fire downstairs.

Trapani

Ai Lumi B&B B&B **$**
(Map p92; 0923 54 09 22; www.ailumi.it; Corso Vittorio Emanuele 71; s €40-70, d €70-100, tr €90-125, q €100-150;) Housed in an 18th-century *palazzo*, this centrally located B&B offers 13 rooms of varying size. Best are the spacious apartments (numbers 32, 34 and 35), with kitchenettes and balconies overlooking Trapani's most elegant pedestrian street. Upstairs apartment 23 is also lovely, with a private balcony reached by a spiral staircase. Guests get discounts at the hotel's atmospheric restaurant next door.

Albergo Maccotta HOTEL **$**
(Map p92; 0923 2 84 18; www.albergomaccotta.it; Via degli Argentieri 4; s €30-40, d €55-75, breakfast per person €3; @) This unassuming hotel

smack in the centre of the old town offers clean and neat rooms. There's no atmosphere to speak of, but prices are reasonable, the location is quiet and there's satellite TV in every room.

La Gancia APARTMENT **$$**
(Map p92; ☎0923 43 80 60; www.lagancia.com; Piazza Mercato del Pesce; s €70-85, d €82-164, q €120-250; ❄📶) Well-positioned on the waterfront at the north end of Trapani's historic centre, this immaculate hotel offers 20 comfortable kitchenette-equipped rooms, ranging from lower-priced interior-facing units to a spacious 4th-floor junior suite with its own sea-view terrace. The breakfast room enjoys pretty views of the water, and the port is just a five-minute walk away.

Erice

Hotel San Domenico HOTEL **$$**
(Map p97; ☎0923 86 01 28; www.hotel-sandomenico.it; Via Tommaso Guarrasi 26; s €55, d €85-125, d with panoramic terrace €125-145; ❄📶) The most comfortable rooms in town are on offer at this immaculately kept, family-run hotel. The best of the bunch, room 301, has its own panoramic terrace, but all offer modern conveniences including minibars, LCD TVs and updated bathrooms. The delicious breakfast features fresh pastries.

Hotel Elimo HOTEL **$$**
(Map p97; ☎0923 86 93 77; www.hotelelimo.it; Via Vittorio Emanuele 75; s €80-110, d €90-130, ste €150-170; ❄📶) Communal spaces at this atmospheric historic house are filled with tiled beams, marble fireplaces, intriguing art, knick-knacks and antiques. The bedrooms are more mainstream, although many (along with the hotel terrace and restaurant) have breathtaking vistas south and west towards the Saline di Trapani, the Egadi Islands and the shimmering sea.

Egadi Islands

Favignana

Il Giardino delle Aloe AGRITURISMO **$**
(☎393 8017226; www.ilgiardinodellealoe.it; Contrada Grotta Perciata 68d; 2-person apt €55-125, 4-person apt €75-145, 6-person apt €110-195, half board per adult/child extra €30/15; ⏲Mar-Oct) Only 200m by footpath from Grotta Perciata beach, this family-friendly *agriturismo* is beautifully landscaped, with lush lawns, herb gardens and desert plants, including several aloe species. Each of the seven apartments (including one built into a tufa cave) comes with full kitchen. There's an onsite restaurant, and rental bikes (€5) are available for the easy 3km commute into Favignana town.

Albergo Egadi HOTEL **$$**
(☎0923 92 12 32; www.albergoegadi.it; Via Colombo 17, Favignana; r €65-125, d €100-220; ❄📶) The classiest of several in-town hotel options, Albergo Egadi is a real treat. The stylish rooms feature attractive colour schemes and excellent bathrooms; the two on the top floor share a panoramic terrace. The hotel also has a restaurant, which offers a seafood-dominated tasting menu that changes each night.

Cas'almare BOUTIQUE HOTEL **$$$**
(☎320 4766389; www.casalmarefavignana.com; Strada Comunale Frascia, Favignana; d €160-300, ste €200-320; ⏲Apr-Oct; P❄) This stylish resort right at the water's edge has only five rooms, all converted from an old fisherman's house, with lovely views of the sea and the striking rock formations just offshore, which shelter natural warm pools for guests to soak in. The nicest two rooms upstairs have splendid bathtubs and can be joined together into a family suite.

Marettimo

★ **Marettimo Residence** APARTMENT **$$**
(☎0923 92 32 02; www.marettimoresidence.it; Via Telegrafo 3; d with breakfast €80-170, weekly apt without breakfast d €360-1200, q €600-1800, plus cleaning charge of €40-60; @📶🏊) Lovingly landscaped with bougainvillea, palms and herbs, this hillside complex south of the port is ideal for families or anyone wishing to linger a while on Marettimo. Each of the 44 apartments comes with a kitchen and porch. It has a small swimming pool, a pair of spa baths, a kids playground, a cafe, a barbecue area and a multilingual library.

Marsala

★ **Il Profumo del Sale** B&B **$**
(Map p104; ☎0923 189 04 72; www.ilprofumodelsale.it; Via Vaccari 8; s/d €35/60; 📶) Perfectly positioned in Marsala's historic city centre, this lovely B&B offers three attractive rooms – including a palatial front unit with cathedral views from its small balcony – enhanced by welcoming touches like almond cookies, fine

soaps and ample breakfasts featuring homemade bread and jams. Sophisticated owner Celsa is full of helpful tips about Marsala and the surrounding area.

Hotel Carmine HOTEL **$$**
(Map p104; ☎0923 71 19 07; www.hotelcarmine.it; Piazza Carmine 16; s €75-100, d €105-125; P ❄ @ ☎) This lovely hotel in a converted 16th-century monastery has elegant rooms (especially numbers 7 and 30), with original blue-and-gold maiolica tiles, stone walls, antique furniture and lofty beamed ceilings. Enjoy your cornflakes in the baronial-style breakfast room with its historic frescoes and over-the-top chandelier, or sip your drink by the roaring fireplace in winter. Modern perks include a rooftop solarium.

Mazara del Vallo

★Melia Resort Dimore Storiche BOUTIQUE HOTEL **$$**
(☎335 1250100, 0923 90 64 97; www.meliaresort.it; Via Bagno 2; r/apt/ste from €70/110/120; ❄ ☎) Smack in the middle of La Casbah, this unique small hotel features two beautifully restored rooms and three grandiose suites in a historic *palazzo*, complemented by four apartments equipped with private terrace or kitchen. There are lovely period features throughout, and the best of the suites (€180) even comes with its own grand piano! A delicious Sicilian breakfast is included.

TYRRHENIAN COAST

Cefalù

Dolce Vita B&B **$**
(Map p116; ☎0921 92 31 51; www.dolcevitabb.it; Via Bordonaro 8; s €35-50, d €50-100) This popular B&B in a Liberty-style waterfront building has one of Cefalù's loveliest terraces, with deck chairs overlooking the sea and a barbecue for balmy evenings. The six main rooms – three facing the sea and three with double-glazed windows facing town – are airy and light. Even better are the three kitchen-equipped apartments, newly added in 2016.

La Plumeria HOTEL **$$**
(Map p116; ☎092 192 58 97; www.laplumeriahotel.it; Corso Ruggero 185; d €159-189; P ❄ ☎) Midway between the *duomo* (cathedral) and the waterfront, with free parking a few minutes away, this small hotel offers four-star service in a prime location. Rooms are mostly unexceptional but well-appointed; the sweetest of the lot is room 301, a cosy top-floor eyrie with checkerboard tile floors and a small terrace looking up to the *duomo*.

Hotel Kalura HOTEL **$$**
(☎0921 42 13 54; www.hotelkalura.com; Via Vincenzo Cavallaro 13; s €74-115, d €125-189, 4-person apt €189-239; P ❄ @ ≋) East of town on a rocky outcrop, this German-run, family-oriented hotel has its own pebbly beach, restaurant and fabulous pool. Most rooms have sea views, and the hotel staff can arrange loads of activities, including mountain biking, hiking, canoeing, pedalos, diving and dance nights. It's a 20-minute walk into town.

Parco Naturale Regionale delle Madonie

Villa Rainò AGRITURISMO **$**
(☎338 7798444, 0921 64 46 80; www.villaraino.it; Contrada Rainò, Gangi; s/d/tr/q €50/80/100/115, per person with half board/full board €60/75; ☎ ≋) Tucked into its own private valley at the foot of the medieval town of Gangi, this former baronial villa, now converted into a comfortable *agriturismo*, is an oasis of tranquillity. Among its 14 rooms, the most attractive are the high-ceilinged first-floor units with pretty tiled floors and tall windows opening up onto views of the surrounding greenery.

Castelbuono

★Azienda Agrituristica Bergi AGRITURISMO **$**
(☎0921 67 20 45; www.agriturismobergi.com; SS286, Km 17.6, Contrada Bergi; d €81-89, tr €95-106, q €110-122; ☎ ≋) Just south of Castelbuono on the winding SS286, this family-run *agriturismo* has a cluster of modern rooms – including several family-friendly quads – surrounded by olive groves and mountain vistas. Guests have access to a swimming pool and tasty meals featuring the family's home-grown produce, olive oil and award-winning honey.

Relais Santa Anastasia HOTEL **$$**
(☎0921 67 22 33; www.abbaziasantanastasia.com; Contrada Santa Anastasia; s €80-170, d €125-220, ste €175-270; ☎ ≋) Set amid the picturesque vineyards of a highly regarded wine estate, this converted 12th-century abbey boasts extremely comfortable rooms, a sensational

pool terrace with views of the Aeolian Islands and two restaurants serving food and wine from the estate. You'll find it 9km from Castelbuono in the direction of Cefalù.

Petralia Soprana

Hotel Residenza Petra INN $

(☎0921 68 13 21; www.residenzapetra.it; Via Errante 9; s/d/ste/tr/q €65/85/100/110/136; ⊙closed Nov) This sleek stone-walled inn in a former baronial *palazzo* has 15 well-appointed rooms clustered around a courtyard in the heart of town. Amenities include comfy beds, handsome wood furnishings, radiant floor heat, mini-fridges stocked with free drinks and TVs that double as computers. The lone suite has its own terrace and a later check-out time.

Petralia Sottana

★**Albergo Il Castello** HOTEL $

(☎0921 64 12 50; www.il-castello.net; Via Generale di Maria 27; s/d €50/70, ste €85-95; ❄📶) Tucked into a back street above Petralia Sottana's Duomo, this pretty-as-a-picture inn has immaculate rooms and three-star amenities. Its restaurant specialises in pizza (weekends only) and top-notch mountain cuisine featuring local mushrooms and truffles. In chilly weather, consider spending a bit extra for a suite with wood-burning fireplace. There's parking in the square half a block beyond the hotel entrance.

Piano Battaglia

Rifugio Piero Merlino HOSTEL $

(☎347 8511511, 0921 64 99 95; www.rifugiopieromerlino.it; r per person €35, with half board/full board €50/65) Run by the Club Alpino Siciliano, this simple chalet with wood-panelled rooms sleeping two or four is open year-round. There are eating and drinking areas, and staff can provide information on skiing, cycling and walking.

Parco Regionale dei Nebrodi

Agriturismo Pardo AGRITURISMO $

(☎0941 66 40 03, 388 8287240; www.agriturismopardo.it; Contrada Pardo, Ucria; r per person with breakfast/half board €35/55; P) Run by an octogenarian retired vascular surgeon, this *agriturismo* in Ucria (on the road to Floresta) offers high-ceilinged rooms with sweeping sea and valley views in an old stone building surrounded by hazelnut orchards. The fabulous dinners feature locally sourced seasonal treats such as battered and delicately fried sage leaves, wild asparagus risotto or pasta with hazelnuts, bacon and anchovies.

★**Casa Migliaca** AGRITURISMO $$

(☎0921 33 67 22; www.casamigliaca.com; SP176, Km 7, Pettineo; d with breakfast/half board €120/156, apt per week €600-900; 📶) Built around a 17th-century olive-oil mill and surrounded by olive and citrus groves, this serene *agriturismo* in the hills south of Castel di Tusa offers double and quad rooms in a beautiful old stone farmhouse, along with an apartment sleeping up to six people. Meals incorporating produce from the farm are served family-style around the historic olive press.

San Marco d'Alunzio

B&B La Tela di Penelope B&B $

(☎0941 79 77 34; Via Aluntina 48; s €35-45, d €50-70; ❄📶) Attached to a traditional weaving studio, this three-room B&B is perfectly placed in the heart of picturesque San Marco d'Alunzio. Rooms (two with private balconies) enjoy views of the historic centre or the distant Aeolian Islands, and all guests share a small kitchen. Owners can arrange tours of the weaving studio, the town and the nearby Parco Regionale dei Nebrodi.

Castel di Tusa

Atelier Sul Mare BOUTIQUE HOTEL $$

(☎0921 33 42 95; www.ateliersulmare.com; Via Battisti 4; s €63-100, d €100-160; P❄@📶🐾) Founded by Antonio Presti, the entrepreneur and art collector behind the town's Fiumara d'Arte project, this quirky hotel at the water's edge has 23 'art rooms' conceptualised and realised by Italian and international artists between 1990 and 2016. There are also 17 standard rooms, all with original artworks and many with sea views. Check the website for special offers.

The entire hotel is treated like an art project, with weekend tours offered (free for guests, €5 for non-guests). Guests who stay longer than one night are invited to change rooms as often as they like to get an intimate perspective on multiple artists' work.

Milazzo

Locanda del Bagatto DESIGN HOTEL $
(☎090 922 42 12; www.locandadelbagatto.com; Via Massimiliano Regis 7; s €70-80, d €90-110, q €140-160; ❄📶) High-end amenities and state-of-the-art fixtures make for a comfortable stay at this sleek new six-room hotel upstairs from the excellent Al Bagatto wine bar/restaurant. The modern Italian designer decor ranges from the artsy (black-and-white photos of Sicilians, easels used as towel racks in a whimsical painter-themed room) to the borderline tacky (two larger-than-life women puffing on cigars above one bed).

B&B L'Alberghetto B&B $
(☎393 9633705, 090 928 82 98; www.lalberghettobeb.it; Via Umberto I 208; d €50-100, 3-person apt €75-130, 4-person apt €90-150; ❄📶) Run by the super-friendly Stefano and Barbara, this B&B halfway between the port and the castle has been lovingly remodelled, retaining historical details while incorporating brand-new fixtures throughout. There are three rooms in the main house, but families will want to look across the street at the pair of comfortable apartments with clean white walls, exposed stone-and-brick arches and full kitchens.

Petit Hotel HOTEL $
(☎090 928 67 84; www.petithotel.it; Via dei Mille 38; s €40-60, d €75-95; ❄📶) Right opposite the hydrofoil dock, the Petit Hotel features spic-and-span rooms with lovely Caltagirone tile floors; front-facing units enjoy ferry-port views, as does the 2nd-floor terrace.

AEOLIAN ISLANDS

Lipari

★**Diana Brown** B&B $
(Map p132; ☎338 6407572, 090 981 25 84; www.dianabrown.it; Vico Himera 3; s €30-70, d €40-80, tr €50-100; ❄📶) Tucked down a narrow alley, South African Diana's delightful rooms sport tile floors, abundant hot water and welcome extras such as kettles, fridges, clothes-drying racks and satellite TV. Units downstairs are darker but have built-in kitchenettes. There's a sunny breakfast terrace and solarium with deck chairs, plus a book exchange and laundry service. Optional breakfast costs €5 extra per person.

Enzo Il Negro GUESTHOUSE $
(Map p132; ☎090 981 31 63; www.enzoilnegro.com; Via Garibaldi 29; s €40-50, d €60-90; ❄📶) Family run for decades, this down-to-earth guesthouse in a perfect location near picturesque Marina Corta offers spacious, tiled, pine-furnished rooms with fridges. Two panoramic terraces overlook the rooftops, the harbour and the castle walls.

★**B&B Al Salvatore di Lipari** B&B $$
(☎335 8343222; www.alsalvatore.it; Via San Salvatore, Contrada al Salvatore; d €80-150; ⏲Apr-Oct) It's a trek to reach this hillside oasis 3.5km south of town, but once here, you'll never want to leave. Artist Paola and physicist Marcello have transformed their Aeolian villa into a green B&B that works at all levels, from dependable wi-fi to a panoramic terrace where Sicily's best breakfast is served, featuring home-marinated tuna, omelettes, and marmalade made on-site.

Marcello and Paula offer free transfers from/to the hydrofoil dock upon arrival and departure, but if you plan to do any exploring, you may find it easier to rent your own wheels (bike, car or scooter) at the port; the only public transport option is to take the 'Linea Blanca' bus from Marina Lunga to Capistello (€1.30, 10 minutes, seven daily except Sunday) and walk 200m steeply uphill.

Vulcano

★**Casa delle Stelle** B&B $
(☎347 3626282, 334 9804104; Contrada Gelso; s €30-45, d €50-90; P) This lovely hideaway, high in the hills above the island's south shore, is run by former Gelso lighthouse keeper Sauro and his wife Maria. The two guest rooms share a living room, fully equipped kitchen and panoramic terrace with spectacular views of the Mediterranean and a distant Mt Etna. In summer, local buses will drop you at the gate.

Casa Arcada B&B, APARTMENT $
(☎347 6497633; www.casaarcada.it; Strada Provinciale 178; d €60-80, d apt per week €420-650; ❄📶) Conveniently located at the volcano's edge, 20m back from the main road between the port and the crater path, this sweet whitewashed complex offers bed and breakfast in five immaculate tile-floored rooms with air-con and mini-fridges, along with weekly rental apartments. The communal upstairs sun terrace affords lovely views up to the volcano and across the water to Lipari.

Salina

★Hotel Ravesi HOTEL $$

(☎090 984 43 85; www.hotelravesi.it; Via Roma 66, Malfa; d €90-240, ste €160-300; ⊙mid-Apr–mid-Oct; ❄📶🏊) Star attractions at this peach of a hotel in a converted family home beside Malfa's town square include the delightful grassy lounge and bar area, the chiming of church bells next door and the outdoor deck with infinity pool overlooking Panarea, Stromboli and the sea. Especially nice are the brand-new honeymoon suite with private terrace and corner room 12 upstairs.

Hotel Mamma Santina BOUTIQUE HOTEL $$

(☎090 984 30 54; www.mammasantina.it; Via Sanità 40, Santa Marina Salina; d €110-250; ⊙Apr-Oct; ❄@📶🏊) A labour of love for its architect owner, this boutique hotel has inviting rooms decorated with pretty tiles in traditional Aeolian designs. Many of the sea-view terraces come equipped with hammocks, and on warm evenings the attached restaurant (meals €35 to €40) has outdoor seating overlooking the glowing blue pool and landscaped garden.

A Cannata PENSION $$

(☎090 984 30 57; www.hotelacannata.it; Via Alfieri 9, Lingua; d €100-200, with half board €170-270; 📶) Remodelled in Aeolian style, with peach-coloured stucco, cheerful blue doors, and floors clad in reproductions of historic tiles, this family-run *pensione* offers 25 spacious units, many overlooking Lingua's picturesque salt lagoon. Half board is offered at the acclaimed Slow Food restaurant next door, with menus built around freshly caught seafood and home-grown veggies and herbs.

★Hotel Signum BOUTIQUE HOTEL $$$

(☎090 984 42 22; www.hotelsignum.it; Via Scalo 15, Malfa; d €150-600, ste €450-750; ❄📶🏊) Hidden in Malfa's hillside lanes is this alluring labyrinth of antique-clad rooms, peach-coloured stucco walls, tall blue windows and vine-covered terraces with full-on views of Stromboli. The attached wellness centre, a stunning pool and one of the island's best-regarded restaurants make this the perfect place to unwind for a few days in utter comfort.

Capofaro BOUTIQUE HOTEL $$$

(☎090 984 43 30; www.capofaro.it; Via Faro 3; d €220-530, ste €390-720; ⊙late Apr-early Oct; ❄@📶🏊) Immerse yourself in luxury at this five-star boutique resort halfway between Santa Marina and Malfa, surrounded by well-tended Malvasia vineyards and a picturesque lighthouse. The 20 rooms all have sharp white decor and terraces looking straight out to smoking Stromboli. Tennis courts, poolside massages, wine tasting and vineyard visits complete this perfect vision of island chic.

Panarea

Hotel Cincotta HOTEL $$

(☎090 98 30 14; www.hotelcincotta.it; d €130-290; 📶🏊) Perfectly perched just above the port, this whitewashed complex of hotel rooms has dreamy views out to sea and across to Stromboli. Numerous panoramic terraces, a swimming pool and a good restaurant onsite add to the appeal.

B&B Da Luca B&B $$

(☎333 6753547; www.bed-breakfast-panarea.it; Via Iditella; d €80-140; ❄📶) At the top of a dead-end street in Ditella (15 minutes north of the port), you'll find this whitewashed cluster of five Aeolian-style rooms with private terraces, including a four-person apartment with kitchen and multicoloured tile floors. Owner Luca does very little to advertise the place; ask someone to point the way once you arrive in Ditella.

Stromboli

★Casa del Sole GUESTHOUSE $

(Map p148; ☎090 98 63 00; www.casadelsolestromboli.it; Via Cincotta; dm €25-35, s €30-55, d €60-110) This cheerful Aeolian-style guesthouse is only 100m from a sweet black-sand beach in Piscità, the tranquil neighbourhood at the west end of town. Dorms, private doubles and a guest kitchen all surround a sunny patio, overhung with vines, fragrant with lemon blossoms, and decorated with the masks and stone carvings of sculptor-owner Tano Russo. It's a pleasant 25-minute walk or a €10 taxi ride from the port 2km away.

Pensione Aquilone GUESTHOUSE $

(Map p148; ☎090 98 60 80; www.aquiloneresidence.it; Via Vittorio Emanuele 29; d €50-110) A short distance west of Stromboli's hilltop church square, this cheerful place has a sunny central garden patio and views up to the volcano; three rooms come with cosy cooking nooks; otherwise, friendly owners Adriano and Francesco provide breakfast.

B&B Luna Rossa B&B $
(Map p148; ☎090 988 00 49; www.ginostra-stromboli.it/bed-breakfast.php; Via Piano 3, Ginostra; r per person from €20) In the sleepy village of Ginostra on Stromboli's west coast, Stromboli native Giovanna and her Sicilian partner Dione offer a variety of accommodation options: a three-room B&B, along with rental rooms and a pair of Aeolian houses.

La Sirenetta Park Hotel HOTEL $$
(Map p148; ☎090 98 60 25; www.lasirenetta.it; Via Marina 33; s €90-110, d €120-250; ⊙late Apr-late Oct; ❄📶🏊) A lovely terraced complex on the beach at Ficogrande, this was Stromboli's first-ever hotel – the current owner's father counted Ingrid Bergman as an early guest. It's a laid-back place with white, summery rooms, a large pool, a first-class restaurant and its own amphitheatre used to screen films and stage theatrical performances.

Filicudi

Casa Monti de Luca B&B $$
(☎328 2404807, 347 1868044; www.casamontideluca.it; Contrada Rocca di Ciaule 29; d €70-150) Run by Italian-Argentine couple Renzo and Miguel, this three-room B&B has all the charm of a small home, with ample outdoor lounging space and an upstairs salon for reading on rainy days. Decor ranges from family heirlooms to modern art from Renzo's years in the fashion industry. Two front rooms share a panoramic terrace, while the third (out the back) offers greater privacy.

It's about 2km uphill from the port.

Hotel La Canna HOTEL $$
(☎090 988 99 56; Via Rosa 43; d €70-140, with half board €140-220; ❄🏊) Perched like a private paradise high above the port, this long-established, family-run hotel features rooms with beams, terracotta tiles and panoramic terraces boasting a seagull's-eye view of the harbour sparkling below. Delicious traditional meals at the attached restaurant feature produce from the adjacent gardens.

Alicudi

Casa Mulino HOTEL $
(☎090 988 96 81, 368 3351265; www.alicudicasamulino.it; Via Regina Elena; d €70-100; ⊙mid-Apr–Oct; 📶) This peach-and-white honeycomb of rooms is the first thing you'll see when you get off the boat...meaning you don't have far to lug your bags. Rooms come in three categories, many with sea views: simple doubles, doubles with kitchen and terrace, or two-room suites with kitchen. Owner Carlo proudly displays his family tree, revealing roots in Alicudi since 1688.

Marcella & Isabella Taranto GUESTHOUSE $
(☎090 988 99 17; r per person €25-30) Sisters Marcella and Isabella preside over three simple but spic-and-span rooms with shared bathroom and communal balcony overlooking the port. It's less than five minutes' walk from the docks; bear left along the waterfront as you leave the pier and ask a local to point you in the right direction. Per-person rates drop from €30 to €25 for multinight stays.

IONIAN COAST

Messina

B&B del Duomo B&B $
(Map p158; ☎393 9934500, 090 641 32 93; www.bedandbreakfastdelduomo.it; Via I Settembre 156; s €45-60, d €60-80; ❄📶) Just off Piazza del Duomo is this cheerful B&B, run by the young, charming Guendalina (who also lives onsite). Rooms are simple, clean and functional, with modular furniture and decent, modern bathrooms. In-room TVs include international Sky channels and breakfast is served either in your room or at a neighbouring bar.

Taormina

Villa Nettuno PENSION $
(Map p162; ☎0942 2 37 97; www.hotelvillanettuno.it; Via Luigi Pirandello 33; s €38-44, d €60-78, breakfast €4; ❄📶) A throwback to another era, this conveniently located salmon-pink *pensione* has been run by the Sciglio family for seven decades. Its low prices reflect a lack of recent updates, but the inviting lounge, pretty gardens (complete with olive trees and potted geraniums) and the sea views from the breakfast terrace offer a measure of charm you won't find elsewhere at this price.

Hostel Taormina HOSTEL $
(Map p162; ☎0942 62 55 05; www.hosteltaormina.com; Via Circonvallazione 13; dm €17-23,

r €58-85;) Friendly and laid-back, this year-round hostel occupies a house with pretty tiled floors and a roof terrace commanding panoramic sea views. It's a snug, homey set-up with accommodation in three brightly coloured dorms and one private room. Facilities are basic but the owners are helpful and there's a small communal kitchen for DIY catering. Locks are also provided for the lockers.

Isoco Guest House GUESTHOUSE **$$**
(0942 2 36 79; www.isoco.it; Via Salita Branco 2; s €104-60, d €130-200; Mar-Nov; P) Each room at this welcoming, LGBT-friendly guesthouse is dedicated to an artist, from Botticelli to Keith Haring. While the older rooms are highly eclectic, the newer suites are chic and subdued, each with a modern kitchenette. Breakfast is served around a large table, while a pair of terraces offer stunning sea views and a hot tub. Multinight or prepaid stays earn the best rates.

Extra perks include optional multicourse Sicilian dinners (€30) and (if requested in advance) parking.

Hotel del Corso HOTEL **$$**
(Map p162; 0942 62 86 98; www.hoteldelcorsotaormina.com; Corso Umberto I 238; s €49-89, d €79-140; closed Jan;) Offering a prime position on the main drag, this welcoming hotel is one of the few located in the Borgo Medievale. It's a modest affair, with bright, unfussy rooms and a small breakfast terrace overlooking the crenellated Palazzo Duca di Santo Stefano.

★ **Casa Turchetti** B&B **$$$**
(Map p162; 0942 62 50 13; www.casaturchetti.com; Salita dei Gracchi 18/20; d €220-260, junior ste €360;) Every detail is perfect at this painstakingly restored former music school turned luxurious B&B, on a back alley near Piazza IX Aprile. Vintage furniture and fixtures (including a giant four-poster bed in the suite), handcrafted woodwork and fine homespun sheets exude a quiet elegance. Topping it off is a breathtaking rooftop terrace and the warmth of Sicilian hosts Pino and Francesca.

★ **Hotel Villa Belvedere** HOTEL **$$$**
(Map p162; 0942 2 37 91; www.villabelvedere.it; Via Bagnoli Croce 79; s €70-280, d €80-380, ste €120-450; Mar–late-Nov;) Built in 1902, distinguished Villa Belvedere was one of Taormina's original grand hotels. Well-positioned with fabulous views and luxuriant gardens, its highlights include a swimming pool complete with century-old palm. Rooms offer neutral hues and understated style. Parking is an extra €16 per day.

Casa Cuseni B&B **$$$**
(Map p162; 0942 2 82 22; www.casacuseni.com; Via Leonardo da Vinci 5; d €150-230, ste €190-280; P) Pre-booking is essential at this early-20th-century villa once frequented by Tennessee Williams, DH Lawrence, Greta Garbo and Bertrand Russell. Rooms are simple yet graceful, with parquetry floors, art, antique furniture and heavenly coastal views. More swooning awaits in the seven-tiered, panoramic garden. Best of all, the B&B and its blissful tranquillity is only a five-minute walk from the buzz of Corso Umberto.

Hotel Villa Schuler HOTEL **$$$**
(Map p162; 0942 2 34 81; www.hotelvillaschuler.com; Via Roma, Piazzetta Bastione; d €150-260; P) Surrounded by shady terraced gardens and with views of Mt Etna, the rose-pink Villa Schuler has been run by the same family for over a century (longer than any other Taormina hotel) and preserves a homely atmosphere. Rooms are a simple, pared back combo of wooden furniture, sconce lighting and tiled floors. The lovely hotel breakfast is served on a panoramic terrace.

Catania

★ **Palazzu Stidda** APARTMENT **$**
(Map p170; 338 6505133, 095 34 88 26; www.palazzu-stidda.com; Vicolo della Lanterna 5; d €80-100, q €120-140;) Creative, multilingual young hosts Giovanni and Patricia have poured their hearts into creating these three family-friendly apartments on a peaceful dead-end alley, with all the comforts of home plus a host of whimsical touches. Each has a flowery mini-balcony, and all are decorated with the owners' artwork, handmade furniture, family heirlooms and upcycled vintage finds.

Apartments L'Incanto and L'Odissea each come with a washing machine, kitchen and ample space for a family of four. Apartment L'Amuri is smaller and costs €10 to €20 less. Bikes, strollers and high chairs are available.

Check the website for seasonal variations in price.

★B&B Crociferi B&B $

(Map p170; 095 715 22 66; www.bbcrociferi.it; Via Crociferi 81; d €75-85, tr €100-110, apt €120-130;) Perfectly positioned on pedestrianised Via Crociferi, this B&B in a beautifully decorated family home affords easy access to Catania's historic centre. Three palatial rooms (each with private bathroom across the hall) feature high ceilings, antique tiles, frescoes and artistic accoutrements from the owners' travels. The B&B also houses two apartments, the largest (called Lilla) with a leafy panoramic terrace. Book ahead.

B&B Faro B&B $

(Map p170; 349 4578856; www.bebfaro.it; Via San Michele 26; s/d/tr €50/80/100, apt €130-150;) Polished-wood floors, double-glazed windows, modern bathroom fixtures and antique tiles set a stylish tone at this cosy, art-slung B&B, owned by artist couple Anna and Antonio. Suites can sometimes be booked for the price of a double during slower periods, free bikes are provided, and there's a studio downstairs at number 30 where visiting artists are invited to come and paint.

The property also houses two new, on-site apartments, sleeping four to five people respectively and each with its own kitchenette.

Ostello degli Elefanti HOSTEL $

(Map p170; 095 226 56 91; www.ostellodeglielefanti.it; Via Etnea 28; dm €19-25, s €40-45, d €60-70;) Housed in a 17th-century *palazzo* a stone's throw from the Duomo, this newish hostel offers incredible location and value. Three dorms and one private room have lofty frescoed ceilings and panoramic balconies, with reading lights, USB ports and curtains for every bed. The marble-floored former ballroom doubles as a restaurant-lounge, while the rooftop terrace-bar offers incomparable Etna vistas.

5 Balconi B&B B&B $

(095 723 45 34; www.5balconi.it; Via Plebiscito 133; s €35-45, d €50-60;) The warm and generous hospitality of British-Sicilian hosts Rob and Cristina more than compensates for the slightly out-of-centre location at this lovingly remodelled antique *palazzo* in a workaday neighbourhood near Castello Ursino. Three high-ceilinged rooms share a pair of bathrooms. Breakfast includes freshly baked croissants, organic bread, fruit and organic marmalades. Be advised that the street out front gets lots of traffic.

★B&B Habitat B&B $$

(Map p170; 095 826 67 55; www.bbhabitatcatania.it; Via Teatro Massimo 29; s €74-119, d €84-119;) Fit for the pages of *Domus* magazine, this 19th-century factory turned B&B is the work of two young architects. Smart, minimalist rooms feature high-quality mattresses and linen, coffee machine and custom-made furniture in wood and steel. Superior rooms add warmth with wooden floors. The seasonal breakfast buffet is served in a striking communal lounge, lined with floor-to-ceiling jars filled with Sicilian ingredients.

There's a svelte decked courtyard laced with Sicilian plants and herbs, and plans to transform the B&B into a 22-room boutique hotel.

Riviera dei Ciclopi

Acireale

Al Duomo B&B $

(Map p162; 347 9078323; www.alduomo.org; Via Calì 5; s/d/tr/q €60/80/110/140;) Just off Piazza Duomo, this four-room apartment occupies a restored 19th-century *palazzo.* Rooms are individually coloured and simply decorated, with vaulted ceilings and balcony views towards the town's baroque centre.

Aci Trezza

Epos B&B B&B $

(392 4848113; www.bbepos.it; Via Provinciale 262; s €35-60, d €50-70; closed Dec-Feb;) About five minutes' walk from the seafront, this charming, friendly B&B occupies an early-20th-century house. Its five rooms, each named after a character from Homer's *Odyssey,* are simple, homely affairs, painted in uplifting hues and speckled with antique-style furniture. Guests have use of a kitchen and access to a small, inviting terrace.

Mount Etna

Agriturismo San Marco AGRITURISMO $

(389 4237294; www.agriturismosanmarco.com; Rovittello; per person B&B/half board/full board €35/53/68;) Get back to basics at this delightful *agriturismo* near Rovittello, on Etna's northern flank. The bucolic setting, rustic rooms, swimming pool, kids play area

and superb country cooking make it a relaxed place to kick back for a couple of days. Call ahead for directions.

Hotel Alle Pendici HOTEL $
(☎095 791 43 10; www.hotelallependici.com; Viale della Regione 18, Nicolosi; s €50-70, d €65-90, tr €85-115; P ❄ 📶) In Nicolosi, just off the main route up to the cable-car station, this country-style hotel offers excellent value for money. Its rooms are tasteful, combining exposed brickwork with rustic wood furniture and the occasional hanging chandelier. Some have views up Etna's southern slopes.

B&B La Giara B&B $
(☎347 9025049, 095 791 90 22; www.giara.it; Viale della Regione 12a, Nicolosi; s €35-50, d €50-70; P ❄ 📶) The rooms here are washed in bright colours and sport wrought-iron beds, rattan furniture, colourful prints and large balconies. There's free wi-fi, and your friendly, English-speaking hostess Patrizia can help with excursions, bike rental and transfers from the Catania airport (€40).

Rifugio Sapienza CHALET $
(☎095 91 53 21; www.rifugiosapienza.com; Piazzale Funivia; s/d €46/92; P 📶) Offering comfortable accommodation with a good restaurant, this place adjacent to the cable car is the closest lodging to Etna's summit.

Shalai BOUTIQUE HOTEL $$
(☎095 64 31 28; www.shalai.it; Via Marconi 25, Linguaglossa; d €130-190, d with frescoed ceiling €220-280; ⏱restaurant 7.30-10.30pm daily, also 12.30-2.30pm Sat & Sun; P ❄ 📶) After a day tackling Etna, retreat to this luxe spa hotel. Softly lit and in muted shades, the hotel's 13 rooms are minimalist and contemporary, with crisp white linen, flowing drapes, designer lighting and (in rooms 101 and 102) original frescoed ceilings. Then there's the stucco-adorned 19th-century lounge, the candlelit spa (for that post-trek massage), bar and highly regarded, fine-dining restaurant. Bliss.

BOOK YOUR STAY ONLINE

For more accommodation reviews by Lonely Planet authors, check out http://lonelyplanet.com/italy/sicily/hotels. You'll find independent reviews, as well as recommendations on the best places to stay. Best of all, you can book online.

SYRACUSE & THE SOUTHEAST

Syracuse

B&B Aretusa Vacanze APARTMENT $
(Map p188; ☎0931 48 34 84; www.aretusavacanze.com; Vicolo Zuccalà 1; d €59-90, tr €70-120, q €105-147; P ❄ 📶) This great budget option, elbowed into a tiny pedestrian street in a 17th-century building, has large rooms and apartments with kitchenettes, wi-fi, satellite TV and small balconies from where you can shake hands with your neighbour across the way. Parking costs €7 per day.

B&B dei Viaggiatori, Viandanti e Sognatori B&B $
(Map p188; ☎0931 2 47 81; www.bedandbreakfastsicily.it; Via Roma 156; s €35-50, d €55-70, tr €75-85, q €80-100; ❄ 📶) Decorated with verve and boasting a prime Ortygia location, this relaxed B&B exudes an easy, boho vibe. It's a homely place, graced with books, antique furniture and imaginatively decorated rooms. The sunny roof terrace – complete with sweeping sea views – is a fine place for breakfast, whose offerings include biological bread and homemade marmalades.

★**Palazzo Bianco** APARTMENT $$
(Map p188; www.casedisicilia.com; Via Castello Maniace; small apt per night €140-170, min 3 nights, per week €935-1124, large apt per night €150-180, min 3 nights, per week €945-1134; ❄ 📶) Two exquisite apartments await in this *palazzo,* owned by a Milanese art-collector. The larger apartment is utterly decadent, with luxurious sofas, king-size bed, dining table, precious artworks and stone, vaulted ceiling. There's a sea-view terrace and bathroom with original stonework and hydro-massage shower. The smaller apartment wows with a floor-to-ceiling artwork and romantic four-poster bed. Both have kitchenettes and can accommodate up to four.

★**Hotel Gutkowski** HOTEL $$
(Map p188; ☎0931 46 58 61; www.guthotel.it; Lungomare Vittorini 26; s €60-80, d €75-140; ❄ @ 📶) Book well in advance for one of the sea-view rooms at this stylish, eclectic hotel on the Ortygia waterfront, at the edge of the Giudecca neighbourhood. Divided between two buildings, its rooms are simple yet chic, with pretty tiled floors, walls in teals, greys, blues and browns, and a sharply curated mix of vintage and industrial details.

Extra perks include a fetching sun terrace with sea views, and a cosy internet area fit for an *Architectural Digest* spread.

La Via della Giudecca B&B **$$**
(Map p188; ☎0931 6 84 46, 389 6429934; www.laviadellagiudecca.it; Vicolo III alla Giudecca 4; d €70-120; ❄@🛜) Founded in 2010, this charming, immaculate B&B rose phoenix-like from the ashes of a ruined older structure. Winning amenities include crisp white decor, wood floors, spacious rooms (three with sea-view balconies and several accommodating families), a prime location on a picturesque Giudecca piazza, and the warm reception of the Bellomo family (mother and daughters) who run the place.

Palazzo del Sale B&B **$$**
(Map p188; ☎0931 6 59 58; www.palazzodelsale.com; Via Santa Teresa 25; s €75-95, d €90-115, d with terrace €100-135; ❄🛜) Housed in a historic *palazzo,* the six rooms at this stylish, minimalist B&B are hot property in summer, so be sure to book ahead. All are well sized, with high ceilings, original touches, neutral hues and comfortable beds. Coffee and tea are always available in the communal lounge, a delightfully plush place to kick back with a book.

Henry's House HOTEL **$$$**
(Map p188; ☎0931 2 13 61; www.hotelhenryshouse.com; Via del Castello Maniace 68; s €160-200, d €190-230, ste €290-330; ❄🛜) Directly overlooking Ortygia's waterfront, with three communal sun terraces perfect for lounging and soaking up the views, this gorgeous 17th-century *palazzo* was lovingly restored by antique collector Signor Corsaro before opening as a hotel in 2014. If money isn't an issue, book one of the two upstairs suites (one with terrace, both with water views). Complimentary bikes are available to guests.

Noto

Ostello Il Castello HOSTEL **$**
(Map p198; ☎320 8388869; www.ostellodinoto.it; Via Fratelli Bandiera 1; dm €18, d €50-70; ❄🛜) Directly uphill from the centre, this hostel offers excellent value for money and is a great option for families or groups. There's one dorm (mixed with 18 beds), with all other rooms private and capable of accommodating up to six people. Some rooms come with a terrace, delivering commanding views over Noto's cathedral and rooftops. Wi-fi in communal areas only. Breakfast included.

★**Nòtia Rooms** B&B **$$**
(Map p198; ☎0931 83 88 91, 366 5007350; www.notiarooms.com; Vico Frumento 6; d €100-150, tr €120-170; 🛜) In Noto's historic workers' quarter, this sophisticated B&B is owned by the gracious Giorgio and Carla, who gave up the stress of northern Italian life to open this three-room beauty. Crisp white interiors are accented with original artworks, Modernist Italian lamps and upcycled vintage finds. Rooms seduce with sublimely comfortable beds and polished modern bathrooms. Gorgeous breakfasts maintain the high standards.

Melodia 3 B&B **$$**
(Map p198; ☎0931 196 71 23, 340 4659366; www.melodia3.com; Vico Giuseppe Melodia 4; d €80-130, tr €110-150, q €130-170; ❄🛜) Eclectic and subtly sophisticated, Melodia 3 revels in contrasting old and new: lofty vintage ceilings, sculptural lamps, antique drawers, Modernist armchairs, contemporary bathroom fixtures. Choose from three spacious suites (double, triple and quad) and a cosier double room, the latter with a curious, grotto-like shower. Breakfast focuses on the fresh and is served in the designer owners' bright, contemporary kitchen.

The Noto Coast

La Corte del Sole INN **$$**
(☎0931 82 02 10; www.lacortedelsole.it; Contrada Bucachemi, Eloro, Lido di Noto; s €61-147, d €122-230; P❄@🛜≋) Ease that stress at La Corte del Sole, an atmospheric hotel housed in a traditional Sicilian *masseria* (working farm). Overlooking the fields of Eloro, it's a delightful place to stay, with a swimming pool and range of activities including cooking lessons (p193) run by the hotel chef. Rooms are simple but tasteful, most with wrought-iron beds and classic wooden furniture.

Modica

★**Villa Quartarella** AGRITURISMO **$**
(☎360 654829; www.quartarella.com; Contrada Quartarella Passo Cane 1; s €40, d €75-80, tr €85-100, q €90-120; P❄🛜≋) Spacious rooms, welcoming hosts and ample breakfasts make this converted villa in the countryside

south of Modica an appealing choice for anyone travelling by car. Owners Francesco and Francesca are generous in sharing their love and encyclopedic knowledge of local history, flora and fauna and can suggest a multitude of driving itineraries in the surrounding area.

B&B Il Cavaliere B&B **$**
(☎0932 94 72 19; www.palazzoilcavaliere.it; Corso Umberto I 259, Modica Bassa; s €39-59, d €65-89, ste €85-130; ❄📶) Angle for the beautiful front suite with original tiled floors and frescoed ceilings at this nostalgic B&B in a 19th-century *palazzo,* just down from the bus stop on Modica's main strip. Equally charming are the large, high-ceilinged common rooms, including an elegant breakfast room with lovely views of the Chiesa di San Giorgio. Standard rooms are less inspiring.

Albergo I Tetti di Siciliando GUESTHOUSE **$**
(☎0932 94 28 43; www.siciliando.com; Via Cannata 24, Modica Bassa; s €26-40, d €50-70; ❄📶) Tucked at the end of a Lower Town back street, just above central Corso Umberto, this cyclist-friendly guesthouse features simple, spacious and airy rooms, many with views of Modica's steeply stacked houses. Free wi-fi is available in the common area and in some rooms and extras on offer include bike hire (per day/week €15/80).

★**Casa Gelsomino** APARTMENT **$$**
(www.casedisicilia.com; Via Raccomandata, Modica Bassa; per night €130-190, per week €820-1195; ❄📶) It's easy to pretend you're a holidaying celebrity in this stunning abode, its balconies and private terrace serving up commanding views over Modica. Incorporating an airy lounge, fully equipped kitchen, stone-walled bathroom, laundry room, sitting room and separate bedroom, its combination of vaulted ceilings, antique floor-tiles, original artworks and plush furnishings take self-catering to sophisticated highs. Start planning that swank, sunset soirée.

Casa Talía BOUTIQUE HOTEL **$$**
(☎0932 75 20 75; www.casatalia.it; Via Exaudinos 1/9, Modica Bassa; s €120, d from €150, house from €300; P❄📶) Run by two Milanese architects, this urbane oasis of ten rooms and two houses occupies a series of converted stone cottages, graced with lush gardens and town views. Rooms – each with a private terrace – are simple and detail-orientated, whether it's worn stone floors, vintage tiles, original bamboo ceilings or artisanal iron bed frames. Quality, seasonal breakfasts are served in a chic communal lounge.

The two houses can accommodate four and five people respectively.

Palazzo Failla HOTEL **$$**
(☎0932 94 10 59; www.palazzofailla.it; Via Blandini 5, Modica Alta; s €55-69, d €79-139; ❄@📶) Smack in the heart of Modica Alta, this four-star hotel in an exquisitely restored 18th-century palace has retained much of its historical splendour, with original frescoed ceilings, hand-painted Caltagirone floor-tiles and elegant drapes. Start the day with the generous breakfast buffet and end it at the well-regarded restaurant down the lane, run by the hotel's management.

Ragusa

L'Orto Sul Tetto B&B **$**
(Map p208; ☎0932 24 77 85; www.lortosultetto.it; Via Tenente di Stefano 56; s €45-60, d €70-110; ❄📶) This sweet little B&B behind Ragusa's Cattedrale di San Giorgio offers an intimate experience, with just three rooms and a lovely roof terrace where breakfast is served.

Risveglio Ibleo B&B **$**
(Map p208; ☎0932 24 78 11; www.risveglioibleo.com; Largo Camerina 3; d/tw/q €70/85/100; P❄📶) Housed in an 18th-century Liberty-style villa, this welcoming place has spacious, high-ceilinged rooms, walls hung with family portraits and a flower-flanked terrace overlooking the rooftops. The older couple who run the place go out of their way to share local culture, including their own homemade culinary delights.

Caelum Hyblae B&B **$$**
(Map p208; ☎334 3957631; www.bbcaelumhyblae.it; Salita Specula 11; d €100-120; 📶) With its exposed stonework and crisp white decor, this stylish, family-run B&B exudes quiet sophistication. Each of the seven rooms has views over the cathedral, and while they're not the biggest, they're immaculately turned out with unadorned walls, pristine beds and functional modern furniture.

CENTRAL SICILY

Enna

Baglio Pollicarini AGRITURISMO $

(0935 54 19 82; www.bagliopollicarini.it; Contrada Pollicarini; campsite per person/tent €7/9, s/d from €50/85, with half board €70/125, with full board €90/165; P ❄ ☎ ≋) This splendid *agriturismo* is housed in a 17th-century convent near the Lago di Pergusa. The monks' cells have long since been converted into comfortable guest rooms, but the thick stone walls, vaulted ceilings and fading frescoes leave a historical imprint. There's also a dedicated camping area and an in-house restaurant (meals from €25).

Nicosia

★ **Baglio San Pietro** AGRITURISMO $$

(0935 64 05 29; www.bagliosanpietro.com; Contrada San Pietro; r per person incl breakfast/half board/full board €45/62/75; P ☎ ≋) Near the entrance to Nicosia (on the SS117 to Leonforte), this is an *agriturismo* in the true sense of the word, a working farm boasting 10 comfortable, rustic-style rooms and a restaurant with authentic regional cuisine. Burn those extra restaurant-related calories on horseback (one hour/half-day €18/50) or simply kick back by the pool.

Piazza Armerina

Azienda Agrituristica Gigliotto AGRITURISMO $

(0933 97 08 98; www.gigliotto.com; Contrada Gigliotto, SS117; s €60-80, d €80-100; P ≋) An ancient *masseria* dating to the 14th century, Gigliotto is set in rolling Tuscan-style countryside 9km south of Piazza Armerina. The homestead has 25 rural-styled rooms and a farmhouse restaurant with a picturesque outdoor terrace. It produces its own wine; visits to the in-house winery and wine tastings can be arranged.

Suite d'Autore HOTEL $$

(Map p221; 0935 68 85 53; www.suitedautore.it; Via Monte 1; d €80-100; ❄ ☎) With lime-green polystyrene furniture, 19th-century frescoes and a giant circular bed floating in a floor of liquid tiles, this unique slumber number is one of Piazza Armerina's great sights. Each of its seven rooms is themed after a period in design, and everything you see – and that includes works of contemporary art – is for sale.

The owner, Ettore, is a great source of local information and a guide around the newly restored Villa Romana del Casale.

Caltagirone

★ **B&B Tre Metri Sopra Il Cielo** B&B $

(0933 193 51 06; www.bbtremetrisoprailcielo.it; Via Bongiovanni 72; d €60-80; ❄ ☎) Just off Caltagirone's famous staircase, this fantastic B&B is run by a friendly and enthusiastic young couple. The decor varies between the six rooms but is universally tasteful and there can be few finer places to breakfast than on the spectacular balcony overlooking Caltagirone's rooftops and the hills beyond.

Vecchia Masseria AGRITURISMO $$

(0935 68 40 03, 333 8735573; www.vecchiamasseria.com; SS117bis, Km 67.5, Contrada Cutuminello; d €85-140, 2-person apt €100-120, 4-person apt €110-160; P ❄ ≋) It takes some getting to, but once you've found this *agriturismo* 18km west of Caltagirone, you won't want to leave. With elegant, soothing rooms, a highly reputed restaurant, a pair of swimming pools and outdoor spa baths overlooking the olive groves, and a long list of services, it's ideally set up as a rural hideaway. Multicourse dinners cost €28 extra.

MEDITERRANEAN COAST

Agrigento

★ **PortAtenea** B&B $

(Map p231; 349 0937492; www.portatenea.com; Via Atenea, cnr Via C Battisti; s €35-50, d €50-75, tr €70-95; ❄ ☎) This five-room B&B wins plaudits for its panoramic roof terrace overlooking the Valley of the Temples, and its super-convenient location at the entrance to the old town, five minutes' walk from the train and bus stations. Best of all is the generous advice about Agrigento offered by hosts Sandra and Filippo (witness Filippo's amazing Google Earth tour of nearby beaches!).

Terrazze di Montelusa B&B $

(Map p231; 0922 59 56 90, 347 7404784; www.terrazzedimontelusa.it; Piazza Lena 6; s €50, d €65-75, ste €75-85; ❄ ☎) Occupying a beautifully preserved *palazzo* that's been in the same family since the 1820s, this charming B&B is filled with antique photos, original furniture and period details. As the name implies, it also boasts an inspiring collection of panoramic terraces, the most ample of which is reserved for the upstairs suite (well worth the extra €10).

Camere a Sud B&B $
(Map p231; ☎349 6384424; www.camereasud.it; Via Ficani 6; s €40, d €50-70, tr €75-90; ❄@📶) This lovely B&B in the medieval centre has three guest rooms decorated with style and taste – traditional decor and contemporary textiles are matched with bright colours and modern art. Breakfast is served on the terrace in the warmer months.

Valley of the Temples

★Fattoria Mosè AGRITURISMO $
(☎0922 60 61 15; www.fattoriamose.com; Via Mattia Pascal 4a; r per person €48, incl breakfast/half board €58/81, 2-/4-/6-person apt per week €500/800/1100; 🏊) If Agrigento's urban jungle has got you down, head for this authentic organic *agriturismo* 6km east of the Valley of the Temples. Four suites, six self-catering apartments and a pool offer ample space to relax. Guests can opt for reasonably priced dinners (including wine) built around the farm's organic produce, cook for themselves or even enjoy cooking courses on site.

★Villa Athena HISTORIC HOTEL $$$
(Map p235; ☎0922 59 62 88; www.hotelvillaathena.it; Via Passeggiata Archeologica 33; d €281-423, ste €417-891; P❄@📶🏊) With the Tempio della Concordia lit up in the near distance and palm trees lending an exotic *Arabian Nights* feel, this historic five-star hotel in an aristocratic 18th-century villa offers the ultimate luxury experience. The cavernous Villa Suite, floored in antique tiles with a free-standing spa bath and a vast terrace overlooking the temples, might well be Sicily's coolest hotel room.

Sciacca

★B&B Da Lulo e Gagà B&B $
(Map p240; ☎349 6140880; www.bedbreakfastlulogaga.com; Vicolo Muscarnera 9; d €60; ❄) Kooky, fun and original, this sweet B&B apartment has everything you could ask for: a double room, a sitting room with fold-out couch where kids can sleep and a kitchen with washing machine. Owner Lulo's artworks (owls made of multicoloured pebbles, mosaic-framed mirrors and painted ceramics) adorn the sunny living space, while cacti and Egyptian hieroglyphics brighten the pint-sized terrace.

Fazio Bed & Breakfast B&B $
(☎0925 8 59 72, 338 4186179; www.faziobb.com; Via Conzo 9; s €40-50, d €60-80; ❄📶) With all the amenities of a boutique hotel, this classy B&B on the western edge of Sciacca's historic centre is run by friendly father-son team Vincenzo and Aldo. Catering equally to business travellers and casual tourists, it offers spacious, comfortable rooms with good lighting, modern bathrooms, air-con and dependable wi-fi. Don't miss the pistachio cream-filled *cornetti* (croissants) at breakfast time!

Al Moro B&B $
(Map p240; ☎0925 8 67 56; www.almoro.com; Via Liguori 44; s €45-53, d €55-90, tr €75-105, q €90-120; ❄) Cool 21st-century decor combines with 13th-century architecture in Sciacca's historic centre. Al Moro is a slick, good-looking boutique B&B, with rooms revealing a clean, white colour scheme, exposed girders and jazzy mosaic-tiled bathrooms. The abundant breakfast is served downstairs in a vaulted stone hall just off a small courtyard.

Caltabellotta

★B&B Sotto Le Stelle B&B $
(☎0925 95 23 27, 338 2817862; www.bbsottolestelle.it; Via San Paolo 35; d €60-80, ste €100; ❄📶) Owned by the same family that runs Caltabellotta's renowned M.A.T.E.S. restaurant, this B&B is charmingly set in an historic *palazzo* with pretty views down the hillside to the distant sea. The five colourfully decorated rooms and one suite come with vaulted ceilings, antique furniture and gorgeous tile floors, and there's a lovely terrace where breakfast is served in warm weather.

Falconara

Castello di Falconara B&B $$
(☎091 32 90 82; www.castellodifalconara.it; SS115, Km245, Falconara; d €150; 🏊) For an unforgettable experience, spend the night in this gorgeous 14th-century castle, now converted to an atmospheric beachfront B&B. It sits atop a coastal promontory about 11km east of Licata.

Understand Sicily

Sicily Today

Desperate asylum seekers, unscrupulous *mafiosi* (Mafia), and soaring unemployment: Sicily is not short of challenges. The island is now the main stage for Europe's asylum-seeker crisis, its ports awash with mainly Africans seeking refuge. Lurking in the shadows is Sicily's Cosa Nostra, ready to exploit and profiteer. Meanwhile, job shortages continue to stifle the aspirations of many ordinary Sicilians. Thankfully, it's not all bad news, with innovative Sicilians transforming towns and vines into headline-worthy role models.

Best on Film

Nuovo Cinema Paradiso (Cinema Paradiso, 1988) Semi-autobiographical tale of small-town life from Sicilian director Giuseppe Tornatore.

Il Postino (The Postman, 1994) On the gorgeous island of Salina, Pablo Neruda philosophises with a humble Sicilian postman.

Stromboli, Terra di Dio (Stromboli, Land of God, 1950) Bergman and Rossellini's explosive tale of romance, with Stromboli's volcanic fireworks as a backdrop.

Best in Print

The Leopard (Giuseppe Tomasi di Lampedusa, 1958) Sicily's greatest novel, examining the Risorgimento's impact on Sicilian culture through the eyes of an ageing aristocrat.

Sicily: A Short History, from the Greeks to Cosa Nostra (John Julius Norwich, 2015) A deeply engaging journey through Sicilian history and culture through the eyes of one of Sicily's greatest fans.

Seeking Sicily (John Keahey, 2011) Engaging Sicilian travelogue, touching on many aspects of the island's culture and history, by a veteran American journalist.

Sea of Desperation

Ongoing political turmoil in Africa and the Middle East is driving a surge in the number of asylum seekers reaching Sicily from North Africa. According to the United Nations' refugee agency (UNHCR), more than 48,500 asylum seekers arrived in Italy by boat in the first half of 2016. Of these, almost 90% landed in Sicily. Thousands drown at sea each year, trapped on overcrowded boats.

People-smuggling is big business, with smugglers charging up to €5200 per person for the dangerous sea crossing. Among those cashing in is the Sicilian Mafia, which promises many asylum seekers support and onward travel north once in Italy. In reality, government funds set aside for the welfare of refugees are often pocketed and some refugees are ushered into prostitution and drug-dealing.

Italy's high unemployment provides challenges of its own for the refugees allowed to stay. The situation is frustrating a growing number of Sicilians, who argue that the refugees add further strain on Sicily's already inadequate job market, housing and infrastructure. The murder in August 2015 of two Sicilian pensioners by an 18-year-old Ivorian living in Sicily's Mineo refugee centre was quickly seized upon by right-wing political groups, one of which directly blamed the government and its 'lax' approach to immigration. The brutal crime also provoked a revenge attack, with two innocent refugees assaulted and robbed near Catania.

Economic Woes & Innovation

Sicilian unemployment for the first quarter of 2016 was around 24%, compared to 11.7% nationally. Among youth, the figure exceeded 70% in some parts of the island. GDP (Gross Domestic Product) figures paint an equally asymmetrical picture: €17,000 per capita in Sicily compared to Italy's €26,500. The phrase *Non ci sono fondi* (There are no funds) is a commonly uttered one, used to explain everything from the forlorn state of smaller museums and archaeological sites to the uncompetitive nature of universities. Lack-lustre scholarships and student services see almost one-third of students opt to study in central and northern Italy.

Sicily's long and steady exodus has forced one Sicilian hill town southeast of Palermo to take radical action. In 2014 sleepy Gangi started gifting many of its long-abandoned houses to Italian and foreign house hunters. In return, recipients are expected to restore the properties within a set number of years, in the hope of attracting tourism and diversifying the economy. According to the council, the scheme is working.

Further south, the village of Sutera has also taken an innovative approach to its dwindling population and stagnant economy, welcoming African refugees into its empty buildings. Supported by funding from the European Union, the town's new locals have boosted the population, classroom numbers and job opportunities. The scheme has also fostered greater cross-cultural understanding.

The New Tuscany?

Fresh thinking is also revolutionising Sicily's wine industry. Known for producing little more than bulk plonk and blending wines a few decades ago, the region's vineyards are now considered among the nation's most dynamic. At the helm is a new breed of local winemakers, working with smaller yields, using artisanal winemaking methods and showcasing local grapes. Among these reborn varietals are the white-wine producing Ansonica (Inzoli), Grillo, Catarratto Bianco and Carricante, as well as red-wine varietals Frappato and Nerello Mascalese.

The minimum-interventionist approach of many Sicilian winemakers has seen the island become a leader in the production of natural wines. Here, industrial production methods are commonly snubbed for a purer, more artisan approach. This might include a ban on vine grafting and engineered yeasts, or the low (or complete ban of) sulphur dioxide at both the vinifying and bottling stages of production. Some local winemakers are following the lead of the island's ancient Greeks, storing particular wines in terracotta amphorae, partially buried in volcanic soil.

Many new-school Sicilian wineries are biodynamic, and according to the major wine association Assovini Sicilia, three-quarters of its member wineries produce clean energy. Driving this enlightened approach to winemaking is a widespread desire to create wines that vividly and uncompromisingly reflect Sicily's unique terroirs. It's a method that seems to be working, with the region's ever-expanding cast of vibrant, intriguing creations punctuating fashionable wine lists from Modica to Manhattan.

POPULATION: **5.07 MILLION**

AREA: **25,832 SQ KM**

GDP: **€84.5 BILLION**

YOUTH UNEMPLOYMENT: **55.9%**

if Sicily were 100 people

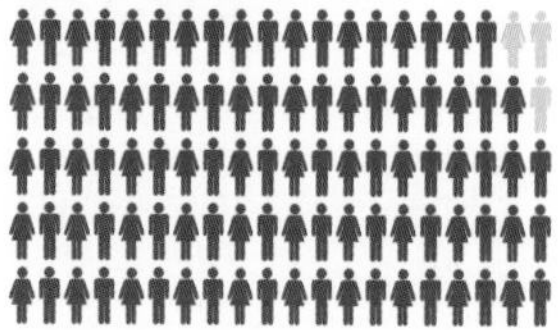

97 would be Italian
3 would be foreign citizens

Occupation

(% of population)

Tourism & commerce

Construction & manufacturing

Fishing & agriculture

10
Financial & professional services

6
Transport & communications

Other

population per sq km

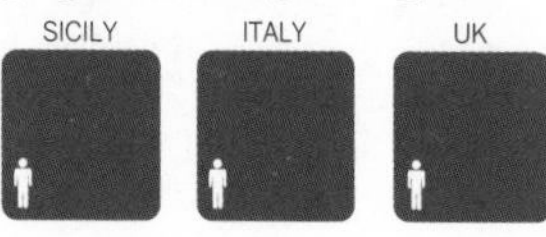

≈ 196 people

History

Over the millennia, Sicily's strategic position in the middle of the Mediterranean has lured culture after culture to its shores, resulting in one of Europe's richest and most remarkable histories. Disputed for centuries by a steady parade of ancient peoples including the Greeks, Carthaginians and Romans, the island saw subsequent rule by invading forces of Byzantines, Saracens, Normans, Germans, Angevins, Spanish and others before finally claiming its pivotal role within a unified Italy in the early 1860s.

Some of Sicily's earliest population centres grew up around Lipari, in the Aeolian Islands. Thanks to Lipari's volcanic origins, it was a prime source of obsidian, valued by Bronze Age peoples as an ideal material for making cutting tools. Obsidian mined in Lipari during the second millennium BC has been found throughout the Mediterranean.

Early Settlement

The first evidence of an organised settlement on Sicily belongs to the Stentillenians, who came from the Middle East and settled on the island's eastern shores sometime between 4000 and 3000 BC. But it was the settlers from the middle of the second millennium BC who radically defined the island's character and whose early presence helps us understand Sicily's complexities. Thucydides (c 460–404 BC) records three major tribes: the Sicanians, who originated either in Spain or North Africa and settled in the north and west (giving these areas their Eastern flavour); the Elymians from Greece, who settled in the south; and the Siculians (or Sikels), who came from the Calabrian peninsula and spread out along the Ionian Coast.

Greeks & Phoenicians

The acquisition of Sicily was an obvious step for the ever-expanding Greek city-states. Following the earlier lead of the Elymians, the Chalcidians landed on Sicily's Ionian Coast in 735 BC and founded a small settlement at Naxos. They were followed a year later by the Corinthians, who built their colony on the southeastern island of Ortygia, calling it Syracoussai (Syracuse). The Chalcidians went further south from their own fort and founded a second town called Katane (Catania) in 729 BC, and the two carried on stitching towns and settlements together until three-quarters of the island was in Hellenic hands.

The growing Greek power in the south and east created tensions with the Phoenicians, who had settled on the western side of the island

TIMELINE

1250–850 BC

Settlers found small colonies at Stentinello, Megara Hyblaea and Lipari. They begin the lucrative business of trading obsidian.

735–580 BC

Greek cities are founded at Naxos in 735 BC, Syracuse in 734 BC, Megara Hyblaea in 728 BC, Gela in 689 BC, and Selinunte and Messina in 628 BC. Agrigento is established in 581 BC.

480 BC

Commanding a vast army of mercenaries, the Carthaginian general Hamilcar seeks to wrest control of Himera from the Greeks, but is soundly defeated by the Greek tyrant Gelon.

around 850 BC; in turn, the Phoenicians' alliance with the powerful city-state of Carthage (in modern-day Tunisia) was of serious concern to the Greeks. By 480 BC the Carthaginians were mustering a huge invading force of some 300,000 mercenaries. Commanded by one of their great generals, Hamilcar, the force landed on Sicily and besieged Himera (near Termini Imerese), but the vast army was defeated by the crafty Greek tyrant Gelon, whose troops breached Hamilcar's lines by pretending to be Carthaginian reinforcements.

A much-needed period of peace followed in Sicily. The Greek colonies had lucrative trade deals thanks to the island's rich resources, and the remains of their cities testify to their wealth and sophistication.

With the advent of the Peloponnesian Wars, Syracuse decided to challenge the hegemony of mainland Greece. Athens, infuriated by the Sicilian 'upstart', decided to attack Syracuse in 415 BC, mounting the 'Great Expedition' – the largest fleet ever assembled. Despite the fleet's size and Athens' confidence, Syracuse fought back and the mainland Greek army suffered a humiliating defeat.

Though Syracuse was celebrating its victory, the rest of Sicily was in a constant state of civil war. This provided the perfect opportunity for Carthage to seek its revenge for Himera, and in 409 BC a new army led by Hamilcar's bitter but brilliant nephew Hannibal wreaked havoc in the Sicilian countryside, completely destroying Selinunte, Himera, Agrigento and Gela. The Syracusans were eventually forced to surrender everything except the city of Syracuse itself to Carthage.

Best Prehistoric Sites

Necropoli di Pantalica, near Syracuse

Capo Graziano, Filicudi, Aeolian Islands

Punta Milazzese, Panarea, Aeolian Islands

Roman Oppression & the Siege of Syracuse

The First Punic War (264–241 BC) saw Rome challenge Carthage for possession of Sicily, and at the end of the war the victorious Romans claimed the island as their first province outside the Italian mainland. Under the Romans, the majority of Sicilians lived in horrifyingly reduced circumstances; native inhabitants were refused the right to citizenship and forced into indentured slavery on *latifondi* – huge landed estates that were to cause so many of the island's woes in later years. Not surprisingly, Rome's less-than-enlightened rule led to two (unsuccessful) revolts by slaves in Sicily; the First Servile War (135–132 BC) and the Second Servile War (104–101 BC).

While the sweetness of victory extended to the First Punic War against the Carthaginians, the Romans would soon suffer a gatecrasher in the form of Hannibal. Breaking into Italy via the Alps, the mighty Carthaginian military commander would lead a number of victories against the Romans, including at the Battle of Cannae (216 BC) in modern-day Puglia. Hannibal's gains soon led many in Sicily to question whether their allegiance to Rome was sensible. Among these doubters was teen

415 BC

An emboldened Syracuse seeks to assert its independence from Greece, provoking a massive backlash from Athens. The Great Expedition, an Athenian fleet of unprecedented size, is defeated by Syracusan troops.

409 BC

Hannibal's army wreaks havoc on Selinunte, Agrigento, Himera and Gela, forcing the Syracusans to surrender their western Sicilian territories to Carthage and retreat to Syracuse.

241 BC

Sandwiched between the superpowers of Carthage and Rome, Sicily becomes the battleground for a war whose outcome is to place it firmly within the Roman Empire.

241 BC–AD 470

As Rome's first colony, Sicily suffers the worst of Roman rule: native inhabitants are refused the right of citizenship and forced into indentured slavery.

Sunken ships litter the seafloor around Sicily. Discoveries from these shipwrecks are displayed at museums throughout the region. Three of the most extraordinary are the remains of a Carthaginian warship in Marsala, the statue of a dancing satyr in Mazara del Vallo and the collection of ancient amphorae in Lipari.

tyrant Hieronymos (231–214 BC), who became king of Syracuse in 215 BC aged 15. While some Syracusans supported Hieronymos' courting of the Carthaginians, others did not, and the king's assassination in 214 BC sparked a civil war between the city's pro-Roman and pro-Carthaginian factions. Rome, determined to maintain control of the Mediterranean, was hardly impressed by the pro-Carthaginians' victory in Syracuse, dispatching esteemed Roman General Marcus Claudius Marcellus (268–208 BC) to gain control of the city. Little did they know what a long and arduous task it would be.

The source of their frustration was Greek Syracusan Archimedes (c 287–212/211 BC), considered the most brilliant mathematician and inventor in ancient Greece. Before Hieronymos' rise to power, his predecessor and grandfather Hiero II (died c 216/215 BC) had assigned Archimedes the task of developing weapons to defend Syracuse. Archimedes did not fail, creating a series of ingenious war machines. Among these were catapults capable of hurling objects weighing in excess of 300kg and the extraordinary Claw of Archimedes, a giant wooden crane attached to a grappling hook. Dangling over the city walls of Ortygia (Syracuse's historic centre), the crane would reach down and grab the Roman galleys by the prow, lifting them out of the water and causing them to capsize or sink. While many modern historians doubt it ever existed, legend persists that Archimedes even created a death ray. The invention reputedly used copper or bronze shields to reflect the sun's rays onto approaching Roman vessels, causing the wooden ships to catch fire.

Archimedes' clever contraptions managed to keep the Romans out of the city for two years, until lax defences during a festival in honour of Artemis allowed a small group of Roman soldiers to scale Ortygia's walls and enter the outer city in 212 BC and, eventually, take control of the town. Despite the humiliation Archimedes' war machines had inflicted on the Romans, Marcus Claudius Marcellus could not help but admire Archimedes and his technical brilliance, so much so that he ordered his men not to harm the mathematician. Alas, it was too honourable an order for one Roman soldier, whose sword cut short the mathematician's life.

Best Classical Sites

- *Valley of the Temples, Agrigento*
- *Selinunte*
- *Segesta*
- *Parco Archeologico della Neapolis, Syracuse*
- *Teatro Greco, Taormina*

Vandals, Byzantines & Saracens

After Rome fell to the Visigoths in AD 470, Sicily was occupied by Vandals from North Africa, but their tenure was relatively brief. In 535 the Byzantine general Belisarius landed an army and was welcomed by a population that, despite over 700 years of Roman occupation, was still largely Greek, both in language and custom. The Byzantines were eager to use Sicily as a launching pad for the retaking of lands owned by the

214–212 BC

Ingenious defensive weapons developed by Greek mathematician, philosopher and engineer Archimedes keep Syracuse safe from invading Roman forces for two years. Among these weapons is a boat-capsizing crane.

535

Keen to use the island as a launching pad for retaking Saracen lands, the Byzantines conquer Sicily; Syracuse temporarily becomes the empire's capital in 663.

827–965

The Saracens land at Mazara del Vallo in 827. Sicily is united under Arab rule and Palermo is the second-largest city in the world after Constantinople.

1059–72

The Norman conquistador Robert Guiscard vows to expel the Saracens from Sicily. With the help of his younger brother, Roger I, he seizes Palermo in 1072.

combined forces of Arabs, Berbers and Spanish Muslims (collectively known as the Saracens), but their dreams were not to be realised.

In 827 the Saracen army landed at Mazara del Vallo. Palermo fell in 831, followed by Syracuse in 878. Under the Arabs, churches were converted to mosques and Arabic was made the common language. At the same time, much-needed land reforms were introduced and trade, agriculture and mining were fostered. New crops were introduced, including citrus trees, date palms and sugar cane, and a system of water supply and irrigation was developed. Palermo became the capital of the new emirate and, over the next 200 years, it became one of the most splendid cities in the Arab world, a haven of culture and commerce rivalled only by Córdoba in Spain.

The Kingdom of the Sun

The Arabs called the Normans 'wolves' because of their barbarous ferocity and the terrifying speed with which they were mopping up territory on the mainland. By 1053, after six years of mercenary activity, Robert Guiscard (c 1015–85), the Norman conquistador, had comprehensively defeated the combined forces of the Calabrian Byzantines, the Lombards and the papal forces at the Battle of Civitate.

Having established his supremacy, Robert turned his attentions to expanding the territories under his control. To achieve this, he had to deal with the Vatican. In return for being invested with the titles of duke of Puglia and Calabria in 1059, Robert agreed to chase the Saracens out of Sicily and restore Christianity to the island. He delegated this task – and promised the island – to his younger brother Roger I (1031–1101), who landed his troops at Messina in 1061, capturing the port by surprise. In 1064 Roger tried to take Palermo but was repulsed by a well-organised Saracen army; it wasn't until Robert arrived in 1072 with substantial reinforcements that the city fell into Norman hands.

Impressed by the island's cultured Arab lifestyle, Roger shamelessly borrowed and improved on it, spending vast amounts of money on palaces and churches and encouraging a cosmopolitan atmosphere in his court. He also wisely opted for a policy of reconciliation with the indigenous people; Arabic and Greek continued to be spoken along with French, and Arab engineers, bureaucrats and architects continued to be employed by the court. He was succeeded by his widow, Adelasia (Adelaide), who ruled until 1130 when Roger II (1095–1154) was crowned king.

Roger II was a keen intellectual whose court was unrivalled for its exotic splendour and learning. His rule was remarkable for his patronage of the arts, and also for his achievement in building an efficient and multicultural civil service that was the envy of Europe. He also enlarged

Best Norman Sites

- *Cappella Palatina, Palermo*
- *Palazzo dei Normanni, Palermo*
- *Cattedrale di Palermo, Palermo*
- *Cattedrale di Monreale, Monreale*
- *Duomo di Cefalù, Cefalù*
- *Castello di Caccamo, Caccamo*

1072–1101

Sicily's brightest period in history ensues under Roger I, with a cosmopolitan and multicultural court. Many significant palaces and churches are built during this time.

1130–1154

Roger II builds one of the most efficient civil services in Europe. His court is responsible for the creation of the first written legal code in Sicilian history.

1145

El Idrisi's planisphere (a large, silver global map) – an important medieval geographical work that accurately maps Europe, North Africa and western Asia – is completed for Roger II.

1154-91

William I inherits the kingdom, triggering a power struggle between church and throne. Walter of the Mill is appointed Palermo's archbishop. The great cathedrals of Monreale and Palermo are built.

the kingdom to include Malta, most of southern Italy and even parts of North Africa.

The Setting Sun

Roger's son and successor, William I (1108–66), inherited the kingdom upon his father's death in 1154. Nicknamed 'William the Bad', he was a vain and corrupt ruler.

The appointment of Walter of the Mill (Gualtiero Offamiglia) as archbishop of Palermo at the connivance of the pope was to create a dangerous power struggle between church and throne for the next 20 years – a challenge that was taken up by William II (1152–89) when he ordered the creation of a second archbishopric at Monreale.

William II's premature death at the age of 36 led to a power tussle, and an assembly of barons elected Roger II's illegitimate grandson Tancred (c 1130–94) to the throne. His accession was immediately contested by the German (or Swabian) king Henry VI (1165–97), head of the House of Hohenstaufen, who laid claim to the throne by virtue of his marriage to Roger II's daughter, Constance.

Tancred died in 1194, and no sooner had his young son, William III, been installed as king than the Hohenstaufen fleet docked in Messina. On Christmas Day of that year Henry VI declared himself king and young William was imprisoned in the castle at Caltabellotta in southern Sicily, where he eventually died (in 1198).

Best Archaeological Museums

Museo Archeologico Regionale, Palermo

Museo Archeologico, Agrigento

Museo Archeologico Eoliano, Lipari

Museo Archeologico Paolo Orsi, Syracuse

Wonder of the World

Henry paid scant attention to his Sicilian kingdom, and died of malaria in 1197. He was succeeded by his young heir Frederick (1194–1250), known as both Frederick I of Sicily and Frederick II of Hohenstaufen.

Frederick was a keen intellectual with a penchant for political manoeuvring, but he was also a totalitarian despot who fortified the eastern seaboard from Messina to Syracuse and sacked rebellious Catania in 1232. Under his rule, Sicily became a centralised state playing a key commercial and cultural role in European affairs, and Palermo gained a reputation as the continent's most important city. In the latter years of his reign Frederick became known as Stupor Mundi, 'Wonder of the World', in recognition of his successful rule.

When Frederick died in 1250, he was succeeded by his son Conrad IV of Germany (1228–54), but the island was initially ruled by Frederick's younger and illegitimate son, Manfred (1232–66). Conrad arrived in Sicily in 1252 to take control but died of malaria after only two years. Manfred again took the reins, first as regent to Conrad's infant son Conradin and then, after forging an alliance with the Saracens, in his own right in 1258.

1198–1250

Under Frederick I, Palermo is considered Europe's most important city and Sicily is a key player in Europe. But Frederick imposes heavy taxes and restrictions on free trade.

1266–82

Charles of Anjou is crowned king in 1266, leading to a brief and unpopular period of French rule, characterised by high taxes and transfer of land ownership to the Angevin aristocracy.

1282

The Sicilian Vespers, a violent uprising in Palermo, sparks countrywide revolt against the Angevin troops. Peter of Aragon rushes in to fill the vacuum, initiating 500 years of Spanish rule.

1487

The end of religious tolerance is cemented by the expulsion of Jews from all Spanish territories. The Spanish Inquisition terrorises Sicily with nearly three centuries of imprisonment, torture and killings.

UNCONVENTIONAL HISTORY MUSEUMS

Mixed in with all of Sicily's fabulous archaeological museums and ancient sites are a couple of off-the-beaten-track treasures that shine a light on the island's more recent history.

Palermo's Museo dell'Inquisizione sheds light on the history and impact of the Inquisition on Sicily. Housed in the historic prisons of Palermo's Palazzo Chiaromonte Steri, its series of cells are pimped with the revealing graffiti and artwork of both prisoners and prison staff. Guided tours (in Italian and English) provide fascinating historical context.

CIDMA, south of Palermo in Corleone, brings you face-to-face with the sordid history of the Sicilian Mafia, as well as the powerful resistance movement that's sprung up on the island in recent years. Photos graphically document the Mafia's historical power over Sicilian society, while bilingual tour guides are actively engaged in the museum's anti-Mafia mission.

Southwest of Ragusa, the Castello di Donnafugata houses the Collezione Gabriele Arezzo di Trifiletti, a highly esteemed cache of Sicilian costumes and fashions from the 16th to 20th centuries. Focused mainly on the 1700s and 1800s, it offers a fascinating look at Sicilian style and society through the ages. Rare treasures include mid-18th-century liveries worn by the servants of aristocratic families.

Sicilian Vespers, Spanish Inquisition

In 1266 the Angevin army, led by Charles of Anjou, brother of the French King Louis IX, defeated and killed Manfred at Benevento on the Italian mainland. Two years later Manfred's 15-year-old nephew and heir, Conradin, was defeated at Tagliacozzo, captured by the Angevins and publicly beheaded in Naples.

After such a bloody start, the Angevins were hated and feared. Sicily was weighed down by onerous taxes, religious persecution was the order of the day and Norman fiefdoms were removed and awarded to French aristocrats.

On Easter Monday 1282 the city of Palermo exploded in rebellion. Incited by the alleged rape of a local girl by a gang of French troops, peasants lynched every French soldier they could get their hands on. The revolt spread to the countryside and was supported by the barons, who had formed an alliance with Peter of Aragon, who landed at Trapani with a large army and was proclaimed king. For the next 20 years the Aragonese and the Angevins were engaged in the War of the Sicilian Vespers – a war that was eventually won by the Spanish.

Alas, Sicily's prospects did not improve under Spanish rule. By the end of the 14th century the island had been thoroughly marginalised. The eastern Mediterranean was sealed off by the Ottoman Turks, while the

1669

The worst eruption in Etna's history levels Catania and the east-coast towns. It's preceded by a three-day earthquake. The eruption lasts four months, flooding the city with rivers of lava.

1693

A devastating earthquake and associated tsunami destroy dozens of communities in southeastern Sicily, leading to the eventual reconstruction of Noto, Ragusa, Modica and several other cities in baroque style.

1799–1815

Napoleon takes control of Naples, leading to a weakening of Bourbon powers and the drafting of an 1812 constitution that establishes a two-chamber parliament and abolishes feudal privileges.

1820–48

The first uprising against the Bourbons occurs in Palermo. It is followed by others in Syracuse in 1837 and again in Palermo in 1848.

Italian mainland was off-limits on account of Sicily's political ties with Spain. As a result the Renaissance passed the island by, reinforcing the oppressive effects of poverty and ignorance. Even Spain lost interest in its colony, choosing to rule through viceroys.

By the end of the 15th century, the viceroy's court was a den of corruption, and the most influential body on the island became the Catholic Church (whose archbishops and bishops were mostly Spaniards). The church exercised draconian powers through a network of Holy Office tribunals, otherwise known as the Inquisition.

The Wrath of Nature

Punishment of the geological kind hit the island in March 1669, when a fissure on Mt Etna's southern slopes erupted with unprecedented force. Lasting four months and releasing 800 million cu metres of lava, the eruption would go down as the volcano's most violent in recorded history. The lava submerged a dozen towns in the area, prompting 50 valiant Catanians to dig a trench to reroute the molten rock and save Catania. Reroute it they did, right in the direction of Paternò, a move that sparked clashes between the towns and saw the breach refilled.

Despite the renewed threat, few Catanians fled their hometown, putting their faith instead in the city's ancient defence walls. Alas, the lava proved too much in the end, with part of the wall collapsing and lava entering Catania from the west. Solidified lava is still visible at the Monastero degli Benedettini l'Arena. Thankfully, the hasty erection of walls across city streets managed to halt the flow of lava further into the city centre. By the time Etna had called it a day in mid-July, an estimated 15,000 to 20,000 people had lost their lives in the region and Catania's topography had been dramatically and permanently altered. A case in point is the landlocked Castello Ursino, which originally stood by the sea.

Mother Nature delivered an even crueller blow in January 1693 when two earthquakes shook the Val di Noto in Sicily's southeast. The first – striking on 9 January and measuring an estimated 6.2 on the Richter scale – a mere precursor to an estimated 7.4 quake two days later. Damaged buildings that had not collapsed in the first tremor toppled like sandcastles in the second. The quake also triggered a tsunami along Sicily's Ionian Coast. Over 60,000 people lost their lives, including two-thirds of Catania's population, and over 45 cities, towns and villages were damaged or completely destroyed.

Yet out of the tragedy came a unique opportunity for the day's great architects – among them Rosario Gagliardi and Francesco Gagliari – to rebuild the area in an exuberant style that would become the very pinnacle of Sicilian baroque. While Syracuse's historical core was rebuilt based on the existing town plan, Catania opted to superimpose a completely

1860–61

Garibaldi lands in Marsala and defeats the Bourbon army, taking Palermo two weeks later. King Victor Emmanuel II becomes the first king of a unified Italy on 17 March 1861.

1860–94

The emergence of the *mafiosi* (Mafia) fills the vacuum between the people and the state. The need for social reform strengthens the growing trade union, the *fasci*.

1908

A powerful earthquake measuring 7.1 on the Richter scale jolts Messina and southern Calabria on 28 December. The tremor and subsequent tsunami reduce Messina to rubble. Over 80,000 people lose their lives.

1922–43

Benito Mussolini brings fascism and almost succeeds in stamping out the Mafia. He drags Sicily into WWII by colonising Libya. Sicily suffers greatly from Allied bombing.

new plan as part of reconstruction. Other places, such as Noto, were rebuilt in a completely new location. All delivered an abundance of new architectural wonders, including the show-stopping Piazza del Duomo in both Catania and Syracuse, the Chiesa di San Giorgio in Modica, the Cattedrale di San Giorgio in Ragusa, not to mention the extraordinary cast of *palazzi* (mansions) and churches flanking Noto's main thoroughfare, Corso Vittorio Emanuele.

Exit Feudalism, Enter Risorgimento

Back on the political front, the weight of state oppression drove ordinary Sicilians to demand reform. But Spanish monarchs were preoccupied by the wars of the Spanish succession and Sicily was subsequently passed around from European power to European power like an unwanted Christmas present. Eventually the Spanish reclaimed the island in 1734, this time under the Bourbon king Charles I of Sicily (1734–59). Under the reign of Charles I's successor, Ferdinand IV, the landed gentry vetoed any attempts at liberalisation. Large exports of grain continued to enrich the aristocracy while normal Sicilians died of starvation.

Although Napoleon never occupied Sicily, his capture of Naples in 1799 forced Ferdinand to move to Sicily. The Bourbon king's ridiculous tax demands were soon met with open revolt by the peasantry and the more far-sighted nobles, who believed that the only way to maintain the status quo was to usher in limited reforms. After strong pressure, Ferdinand reluctantly agreed in 1812 to the drawing up of a constitution whereby a two-chamber parliament was formed and feudal privileges were abolished.

With the final defeat of Napoleon in 1815, Ferdinand once again united Naples and Sicily as the 'Kingdom of the Two Sicilies', taking the title Ferdinand I. For the next 12 years the island was divided between a minority who sought an independent Sicily, and a majority who believed that the island's survival could only be assured as part of a unified Italy, an ideal being promoted on the mainland as part of the political and social movement known as the Risorgimento (reunification period).

On 4 April 1860 the revolutionary committees of Palermo gave orders for a revolt against the tottering Bourbon state. The news reached Giuseppe Garibaldi, who decided this was the moment to begin his campaign for the unification of Italy. He landed in Marsala on 11 May 1860 with about 1000 soldiers – the famous *mille* – and defeated a Bourbon army of 15,000 at Calatafimi on 15 May, taking Palermo two weeks later.

Despite his revolutionary fervour, Garibaldi was not a reformer in the social sense, and his soldiers blocked every attempt at a land grab on the part of the ordinary worker. On 21 October a referendum was held that saw a staggering 99% of eligible Sicilian voters opt for unification with

Sicilian History in Print

- Sicily: A Short History, from the Greeks to Cosa Nostra *by John Julius Norwich*
- The Leopard *by Giuseppe Tomasi di Lampedusa*
- Seeking Sicily *by John Keahey*

1943–44
The Mafia collaborates with the Allied forces, assisting in the capture of the island. Sicily is taken in 39 days. Mafia Don Calogero Vizzini is appointed as the island's administrator.

1950
The *Cassa per il Mezzogiorno* is established to help fund public works and infrastructure in southern Italy. Poor management and corruption sees at least one-third of the money squandered.

1951–75
Sicily's petrochemical, citrus and fishing industries collapse, leading to widespread unemployment. One million Sicilians emigrate to northern Europe.

1969
Caravaggio's painting *The Nativity with St Francis and St Lawrence* is stolen from the Oratorio di San Lorenzo in Palermo. The theft remains one of the FBI's top 10 unsolved art crimes.

the Piedmontese House of Savoy, which controlled most of Northern and Central Italy. Its head, King Victor Emmanuel II, aspired to rule a united Italy and had supported Garibaldi's expedition to Sicily. He was to become the first king of a unified Italy on 17 March 1861.

Fascism, Conservatism & WWII

Sicily struggled to adapt to the Savoys. The old aristocracy by and large maintained their privileges, and hopes of social reform soon dwindled.

What the island really needed was a far-reaching policy of agrarian reform, including a redistribution of land. The partial break-up of large estates after the abolition of feudalism still only benefited the *gabellotti* (agricultural middlemen who policed the peasants on behalf of the aristocracy), who leased the land from the owners only to then charge prohibitive ground rents to the peasants who lived and worked on it.

When half a ton of explosives was detonated to kill anti-Mafia crusader Giovanni Falcone, the bombing registered on local earthquake monitors. The explosives were planted under a stretch of the A29 motorway between Palermo and the airport and ordered by Mafia kingpin Salvatore 'Totò' Riina, who reputedly celebrated the death with champagne.

To assist them with their rent collections the bailiffs enlisted the help of local gangs, who acted as intermediaries between the tenant and the owner, sorting out disputes and regulating affairs in the absence of an effective judicial system. These individuals were called *mafiosi* and were organised into small territorial gangs drawn up along family lines. They effectively filled the vacuum that existed between the people and the state, slotting into the role of local power brokers.

In 1922 Benito Mussolini took power in Rome. With the growing influence of the Mafia dons threatening his dominance in Sicily, Mussolini dispatched Cesare Mori to Palermo with orders to crush lawlessness and insurrection in Sicily. Mori did this by ordering the round-up of individuals suspected of involvement in 'illegal organisations'.

By the 1930s Mussolini had bigger fish to fry – his sights were set on the colonisation of Libya as Italy's Fourth Shore, ultimately dragging Sicily into WWII. Chosen as the springboard for the recapture of mainland Italy, Sicily suffered greatly from heavy Allied bombing. Ironically, the war presented the Mafia with the perfect opportunity to get back at Mussolini and it collaborated with the Allied forces, assisting in the capture of the island in 1943.

Postwar Woes & Mani Pulite

The most powerful force in Sicilian politics in the latter half of the 20th century was the Democrazia Cristiana (DC; Christian Democrats), a centre-right Catholic party that appealed to the island's traditional conservatism. Allied closely with the Church, the DC promised wide-ranging reforms while at the same time demanding vigilance against godless communism. It was greatly aided in its efforts by the Mafia, which ensured that the local DC mayor would always top the poll. The Mafia's

1988

Sicilian film director Giuseppe Tornatore releases Nuovo Cinema Paradiso. Shot in numerous Sicilian locations – including Bagheria and Cefalù – the film goes on to win Best Foreign Language Film at the 1989 Academy Awards.

1992

Sicilian anti-Mafia magistrates Giovanni Falcone and Paolo Borsellino are murdered within two months of each other. Their deaths provoke widespread outrage and strengthen popular resistance to the Mafia.

1995–99

Giulio Andreotti, the former Italian prime minister, is charged with Mafia association, and goes on trial. He is acquitted due to lack of evidence in 1999.

2006

The Sicilian Godfather, Bernardo Provenzano, is arrested after 40 years on the run. His arrest marks an important milestone in the fight against the Mafia.

reward was *clientelismo* (political patronage) that ensured it was granted favourable contracts.

This constant interference by the Mafia in the island's economy did much to nullify the efforts of Rome to reduce the gap between the prosperous north and the poor south. The well-intentioned Cassa del Mezzogiorno (Southern Italy Development Fund), set up in 1950, was aimed at kick-starting the pitiful economy of the south, and Sicily was one of its main beneficiaries, receiving state and European Communities (EC) money for all kinds of projects. However, the disappearance of large amounts of cash eventually led the central government to scrap the fund in 1992, leaving the island to fend for itself.

In the same year, the huge Tangentopoli (Bribesville) scandal (the institutionalisation of kickbacks and bribes, which had been the country's modus operandi since WWII) made headline news. Although it was largely focused on the industrial north of Italy, the repercussions of the widespread investigation into graft (known as *Mani pulite*, or Clean Hands) were inevitably felt in Sicily, a region where politics, business and the Mafia were long-time bedfellows. The scandal eventually brought about the demise of the DC party.

In the meantime, things were changing in regard to how the Sicilians viewed the Mafia, thanks to the investigating magistrates Paolo Borsellino and Giovanni Falcone. They contributed greatly to turning the climate of opinion against the Mafia on both sides of the Atlantic, and made it possible for ordinary Sicilians to speak about and against the Mafia more freely. When they were tragically murdered in the summer of 1992, it was a great loss for Italy and Sicily, but it was these deaths that finally broke the Mafia's code of *omertà* (silence), which had ruled the island for so long. A series of high-profile arrests have followed in the two decades since, including the apprehensions of legendary Mafia kingpins Salvatore 'Totò' Riina in 1993, Leoluca Bagarella in 1995, Bernardo 'the Tractor' Provenzano in 2006, Salvatore Lo Piccolo in 2007 and Domenico 'the Veterinarian' Raccuglia in 2009.

Italy's *Mani pulite* (Clean Hands) political scandal became the eponym for an artwork by Geneva-based artist Gianni Motti in 2005. The work, a simple bar of soap, was reputedly made with the body fat of then Italian prime minister Silvio Berlusconi. Motti purchased the fat from a liposuction clinic.

2012

Rosario Crocetta becomes the first openly gay governor of Sicily. Staunchly and vocally anti-Mafia, the centre-left politician has survived several attempts on his life by the Sicilian Mafia.

2013

Sicily continues to grapple economically, with early 2013 figures presenting a harsh reality: overall unemployment at 20.71% and youth unemployment at 52%.

2015

Italian Prime Minister Matteo Renzi revives talk about building a bridge across the Strait of Messina despite the area's high seismic risk and fears of Mafia involvement in the bridge's construction.

2016

The number of illegal migrants reaching Sicily by boat increases by a dramatic 90% in the first three months of the year. Of the 20,000 migrants who enter Italy in the same period, 90% land in Sicily.

Sicilian Table

Food plays such a central role in Sicilian culture that even the mobsters in *The Godfather* turned to it for comfort. Indeed, Sicily boasts one of the finest cuisines in Italy, standing out for its uniqueness and quality even in a nation where food is at the centre of existence and where there are so many delicious regional variations. A huge part of anyone's visit here will be taken up with eating and drinking. Prepare to have your taste buds pampered!

Land of Timeless Culinary Traditions

Sicily's kitchen is packed with fresh ingredients, unexpected flavours and delectable sweet and sour combinations. The island's rich pantry has evolved over a long period, shaped by successive waves of invaders but always finding its roots in Sicily's fertile volcanic soil and surrounding waters. Over the centuries, many traditional recipes have taken hold, surviving to the present day. Fish and shellfish from the Mediterranean form one of the lasting foundations of the island's cuisine. The abundance of fruit and vegetables has also been evident since the times of the ancient Greeks – Homer famously said of the island, 'Here luxuriant trees are always in their prime, pomegranates and pears, and apples glowing red, succulent figs and olives swelling sleek and dark', and wrote about wild fennel and caper bushes growing on the hills. But it wasn't until the Arabs came to the island that the cuisine really took shape. The Saracens brought the ever-present aubergine (eggplant), as well as citrus fruits, and they are believed to have introduced pasta to the island. They also spiced things up with saffron and sultanas, and contrasted the dishes' delicate flavours with the crunch of almonds and pistachios. Another Arab influence is the seafood couscous still present on every menu in western Sicily. On top of all this, the Saracens brought sugar cane to these shores, helping Sicily develop all those fantastic sweets.

Sicilian restaurants typically open for lunch between noon and 1pm, closing around 2.30pm or 3pm. Places reopen for dinner between 7pm and 8pm, but most Sicilians don't show up until 9pm or later, especially in summertime.

Another fascinating aspect of Sicilian cuisine is that so many of the region's amazing flavours evolved out of poverty and deprivation. The extravagant recipes of the *monsù* (chefs; from the French *monsieur le chef*) employed by the island's aristocrats were adapted to fit the budget and means of the less fortunate, with aubergines substituted for meat, or breadcrumbs taking the place of grated cheese. Ordinary Sicilians applied the aristocratic principles of preserving the freshness of the ingredients and, most importantly, never letting one taste overpower another. And that's the crunch of it, so to speak, the key to so many of Sicily's dishes: simplicity.

Almost all restaurants in Sicily charge €1 to €3 per person for *pane e coperto* (bread and cover charge). Theoretically this pays for the basket of bread that's brought out while you wait for the rest of your meal to arrive. If the waiter forgets, just ask!

Staples

Ubiquitous, locally grown staples that appear repeatedly in Sicilian cuisine include aubergines, wild fennel, citrus fruits, almonds, pistachios, capers, olives, fresh ricotta, swordfish, tuna, sardines and shellfish. You'll also find loads of traditional regional specialities to sample, many made with products showcased by the Fondazione Slow Food organisation (www.fondazioneslowfood.com).

Bread

Bread has always been a staple food for the Sicilian peasant. Made from durum wheat, Sicilian bread is coarse and golden, fashioned into myriad ritualistic and regional shapes, from braids to rings to flowers, and sometimes finished off with sesame seeds. Baked bread is treated with the greatest respect and in the past only the head of the family had the privilege of slicing the loaf.

In Palermo, it's not uncommon to compliment a woman by calling her *bella come una cassata* (lovely as a *cassata*).

Periods of dire poverty and starvation no doubt gave rise to the common use of breadcrumbs, which served to stretch meagre ingredients and fill up hungry stomachs. Such economy lives on in famous dishes such as *involtini,* in which slices of meat or fish are wrapped around a sometimes-spicy breadcrumb stuffing and then pan-fried or grilled. Breadcrumbs (rather than grated cheese) are also sprinkled on some pasta dishes, such as *pasta con le sarde* (pasta with sardines, pine nuts, raisins and wild fennel). Some other popular dishes made with a bread-dough base include *sfincione (*local form of pizza made with tomatoes, onions and sometimes anchovies), *impanata* (bread-dough snacks stuffed with meat, vegetables or cheese) and *scaccie* (pancake-like discs of bread dough spread with a filling and rolled up).

Antipasti

Sicilians' love of strong flavours and unusual combinations lend themselves well to the antipasto (literally 'before the meal', or appetiser) platter. Helping yourself to a selection of antipasti from the buffet is a great way to explore some of Sicily's wonderful flavours, ranging from marinated sardines and slivers of raw herring to fruity cheeses and a whole range of marinated, baked and fresh vegetables, including artichokes, peppers, sun-dried tomatoes, aubergine and the most famous of all – *caponata* (cooked vegetable salad made with tomatoes, aubergines,

SICILIAN IGP & DOP VARIETIES

A number of Sicilian food specialities have earned special recognition under Italy's national DOP (protected origin) program and the European Union's IGP (protected geographical indication) program. These designations help promote and safeguard the reputations of quality agricultural products throughout the island. Some of the most famous DOP and IGP products are listed here, each followed by the name of the region where it's cultivated.

Arance di Ribera DOP Oranges from the Ribera region (Mediterranean Coast).

Arance Rosse di Sicilia IGP Sicilian red oranges (Syracuse and the Southeast, Ionian Coast, Central Sicily).

Capperi di Pantelleria IGP Capers from the island of Pantelleria, off Sicily's southwestern coast.

Fichidindia dell'Etna DOP Prickly pear cactus fruit from Mt Etna (Ionian Coast).

Limoni di Siracusa IGP Lemons from Syracuse (Southeastern Sicily).

Nocellara del Belice DOP Olives from the Belice valley (Western Sicily).

Pecorino Siciliano DOP Sheep's milk cheese, available island-wide.

Pesche di Leonforte IGP Peaches from the Enna region (Central Sicily).

Pistacchi Verdi di Bronte DOP Green pistachios from Bronte, on Mt Etna's western slopes (Ionian Coast).

Pomodori di Pachino IGP Cherry tomatoes from Ragusa and Syracuse (Southeastern Sicily).

Ragusano DOP Cow's milk cheese from Ragusa (Southeastern Sicily).

celery, capers, olives and onions). In mountainous regions, the antipasto selection tends to shift more towards sausages, cheeses, mushrooms or hearty *arancine* or *arancinette*, fried balls of rice stuffed with meat and tomato sauce. If you're lucky, you'll also find rare treats such as delicately breaded and fried sage leaves or squash blossoms.

Classic Antipasti

Sarde a beccafico *Rolled, stuffed sardines.*

Arancine *Savoury, fried rice balls.*

Caponata *Sweet-and-sour mix of aubergines, capers and olives.*

Pasta

Pasta is possibly Italy's (and Sicily's) most famous export. While fresh pasta *(pasta fresca)* is now common on most Sicilian restaurant menus – with Trapani's hollow corkscrew-shaped *busiate* being one of the most distinctive varieties – it is dry pasta that has always been the staple of Sicily and southern Italy, mainly because dry pasta is more economical.

The most famous of all Sicilian pasta dishes is *pasta con le sarde*: pasta with sardines, wild mountain fennel (unique to Sicily), onions, pine nuts and raisins that combine to create a wonderfully exotic flavour. Other famous dishes include Catania's *pasta alla Norma,* with its rich combination of tomatoes, aubergines and salted ricotta, the Aeolian Islands' *pasta all'eoliana*, made with local olives, capers, cherry tomatoes, olive oil and basil, the ever-popular *spaghetti ai ricci* (with sea urchins) and *pasta al pesce spada e menta*, made with fresh swordfish and mint. In the interior you will often find sauces made from meat and game (including wild boar, rabbit and beef) as well as *pasta alle nocciole*, with a sauce based on the hazelnuts of the Nebrodi and Madonie Mountains. Baroque Modica is where the island's best lasagne *(lasagne cacate)* is made; in this version, two kinds of cheese – ricotta and pecorino – are added to minced beef and sausage, and spread between layers of homemade pasta squares.

Classic First Courses

Pasta alla Norma (Catania)

Pasta con le sarde (Palermo)

Couscous alla trapanese (Trapani)

Pasta all'eoliana (Aeolian Islands)

Seafood

The extensive development of fishing and – until recent years – the widespread presence of fish such as sardines, tuna and mackerel off the island's shores have ensured that fish is a staple food.

A Palermitan favourite is *sarde a beccafico alla Palermitana* (sardines stuffed with anchovies, pine nuts, currants and parsley), served either as an appetiser or a second course. However, the filet mignon of the marine world is the *pesce spada* (swordfish), served either grilled with lemon, olive oil and oregano, or as *involtini* (slices of swordfish rolled around a spicy filling of onions, currants, pine nuts and breadcrumbs).

The best swordfish is caught in Messina, where they serve the classic *agghiotta di pesce spada* (also called *pesce spada alla Messinese*), a mouth-watering dish flavoured with pine nuts, sultanas, garlic, basil and tomatoes. The Egadi Islands are home to two splendid fish dishes: *tonno 'nfurnatu* (oven-baked tuna with tomatoes, capers and green olives) and *alalunga di Favignana al ragù* (fried albacore served in a spicy sauce of tomatoes, red chilli peppers and garlic). It is not uncommon to see the latter sauce also appear as part of your pasta dish.

Shellfish are popular throughout the island, especially calamari or *totani* (squid) and *calamaretti* (baby squid), which are prepared in a variety of ways, including stuffed, fried, roasted or cooked in a tomato sauce. You'll also find plenty of *cozze* (mussels), *vongole* (clams) and *gamberi* (shrimp) – the most famous variety being *gamberi rossi di Mazara* (red shrimp from Mazara del Vallo). Another popular and ubiquitous treat is *frittura mista* (sometimes called *fritto misto*), a blend of lightly breaded and fried shrimp, squid and/or fish.

Classic Second Courses

Scaloppine al marsala *Veal cutlets with Marsala wine.*

Involtini di pesce spada *Swordfish roll-ups with raisins, pine nuts and bread crumbs.*

Frittura mista *Fried squid, shrimp and other seafood.*

Meat

Although you can find a limited number of meat dishes along the coast, you won't taste the best until you move further inland. The province of Ragusa is renowned for its imaginative and varied uses of meat, particu-

VEGETARIANS & VEGANS

Vegetarianism is not specifically catered to in Sicily but the abundance of excellent fruit and veg means that many *antipasti,* pastas and *contorni* (side dishes) feature veg in some form or other. Salads are common and tasty, though you'll need to watch out for the odd anchovy or slice of ham. Similarly, check that your tomato sauce has not been cooked with meat in it. Vegans will be in for a tough time, with many dishes featuring some sort of animal product (butter, eggs or animal stock), although the situation has improved in recent years. Restaurants catering specifically to vegetarians and/or vegans include Bioesserì (p65) in Palermo, Millefoglie (p173) and Ostello (p174) in Catania, Moon (p193) in Syracuse and Hostaria del Vicolo (p241) in Sciacca.

larly mutton, beef, pork and rabbit. Its most famous dish is *falsomagro,* a stuffed roll of minced beef, sausages, bacon, egg and *pecorino* cheese. Another local speciality is *coniglio all'agrodolce* (sweet-and-sour rabbit), which is marinated in a sauce of red wine flavoured with onions, olive oil, bay leaves and rosemary. The Nebrodi Mountains are famous for a variety of pork products derived from the indigenous *nero dei Nebrodi,* also known as *suino nero* (literally, black pig). In the neighbouring Madonie Mountains, the town of Castelbuono is the home of *capretto in umido* (stewed kid) and *agnello al forno alla Madonita* (Madonie-style roast lamb). Locally caught *cinghiale* (wild boar) is served in stews, sauces and sausages. Don't be put off if goat or kid dishes are described on the menu as *castrato* – it means the goat was castrated, giving the meat a tender quality.

Ever wonder where Sicily's two favourite desserts got their names? *Cassata* comes from the Arabic word *qas'ah,* referring to the terracotta bowl used to shape the cake; *cannolo* comes from *canna* (cane, as in sugar cane).

Sweets

Sicily's extraordinary pastries are rich in colour and elaborately designed. The queen of Sicilian desserts, the *cassata,* is made with ricotta, sugar, vanilla, diced chocolate and candied fruits. The equally famous *cannoli,* pastry tubes filled with sweetened ricotta and sometimes finished off with candied fruit, chocolate pieces or crumbled pistachios, are found pretty much everywhere. Another ubiquitous treat is *frutta martorana,* named after the church in Palermo that first began producing them. These marzipan confections, shaped to resemble fruits (or whatever takes the creator's fancy), are part of a Sicilian tradition that dates back to the Middle Ages. In late October they're sold in stalls around Palermo in anticipation of Ognissanti (All Souls' Day), but they're also commonly available year-round in painted souvenir boxes throughout Sicily.

Other Sicilian sweets worth sampling are *paste di mandorla* (almond cookies), *gelo di melone* (something like watermelon jelly), *biscotti regina* (sesame-coated biscuits that originated in Palermo but are now widely available throughout the island), *cassatelle* (pouches of dough stuffed with sweetened ricotta and chocolate, originally from Trapani province), *cuccia* (an Arab cake made with grain, honey and ricotta, sold in western Sicily) and *sfogli polizzani* (a speciality of Polizzi Generosa in the Madonie Mountains, made with chocolate, cinnamon and fresh sheep's milk cheese).

While it's perfectly normal to order 'a *biscotti*' or 'a *cannoli*' back home, note that these are actually plural forms in Italian; use the singular form *'un biscotto'* or *'un cannolo'* while in Sicily – unless of course you truly want a pile of them!

Plenty of seasonal treats are prepared in conjunction with religious festivals. These include the cute little *pecorelle di marzapane* (marzipan lambs) that start appearing in pastry shop windows around Easter Week, *pupe* (sugar dolls made to celebrate All Souls' Day on 1 November), *ucchiuzzi* (biscuits shaped like eyes, made for the Festa di Santa Lucia on 13 December) and *buccellati* (dough rings stuffed with minced figs, raisins, almonds, candied fruit and/or orange peel, especially popular around

Sweet tooths take note: in Sicily it's perfectly acceptable to eat ice cream first thing in the morning. Two of the island's most popular summertime breakfasts are *gelato e brioche* (a roll filled with ice cream) or *granita con panna* (flavoured crushed ice topped with whipped cream)!

As any Sicilian can tell you, *cannoli* are meant to be eaten with your fingers, even in a fancy restaurant. Leave the knife and fork behind, grasp that little sugary beauty between thumb and forefinger, and crunch away to your heart's content!

Cappuccino and *caffè* latte are served everywhere at breakfast time, but you'll stick out like a sore thumb if you ask for milk in your coffee after noon – at lunch and dinner time, Sicilians only drink it black.

Christmas, but also sometimes available out-of-season at the Monastero di Santo Spirito in Agrigento).

Looking for something a little more daring? A good place to start is the southeastern town of Modica, where you can try chocolate laced with spicy peppers (prepared from an Aztec recipe brought here directly from Mexico when Sicily was under Spanish rule) or *'mpanatigghi* (Modican pastries stuffed with minced meat, almonds, chocolate, cloves and cinnamon).

Any decent *pasticceria* (pastry shop) will have an enormous spread of freshly made cakes and pastries. It is very common for Sicilians to have their meal in a restaurant and then go to a pastry shop, where they have a coffee and cake while standing at the bar.

Gelati & Granite

Despite Etna's belly of fire, its peak is a natural freezer, and snow that falls on its slopes lasts well into the searing summer, insulated by a fine blanket of volcanic ash. The Romans and Greeks treasured the snow, using it to chill their wine, but it was the Arabs who first started the Sicilian mania for all things icy – *granita* (flavoured crushed ice), gelato (ice cream) and *semifreddo* (literally 'semi-frozen'; a cold, creamy dessert).

The origins of ice cream lie in the Arab *sarbat* (sherbet), a concoction of sweet fruit syrups chilled with iced water, which was then developed into *granita* (where crushed ice was mixed with fruit juice, coffee, almond milk and so on) and *cremolata* (fruit syrups chilled with iced milk), the forerunner to gelato.

Home-made gelato (gelato *artigianale)* is sold at cafes and bars across the island, and is truly delicious. You should try it like a Sicilian – first thing in the morning in a brioche!

Granite are sometimes topped with fresh whipped cream, and are often eaten with a brioche. Favourite flavours include coffee and almond, though lemon is great in summer. During July, August and September, try a *granita di gelsi* (mulberry), a delicious seasonal offering.

Wine

Sicily's vineyards cover nearly 120,000 hectares, making it the second-largest wine-producing region in Italy. But while grapes have always been grown here, Sicilian wine is for the most part not well known outside the island.

The most common varietal is Nero d'Avola, a robust red similar to syrah or shiraz. Vintages are produced by numerous Sicilian wineries, including Planeta (www.planeta.it), which has four estates around the island; Donnafugata (www.donnafugata.it) in Western Sicily; Azienda Agricola COS (www.cosvittoria.it) near Mount Etna; and Azienda Agricola G Milazzo (www.milazzovini.com) near Agrigento. Try Planeta's Plumbago and Santa Cecilia labels, Donnafugata's Mille e una Notte, COS' Nero di Lupo and Milazzo's Maria Costanza and Terre della Baronia Rosso.

Local cabernet sauvignons are less common but worth sampling; the version produced by Tasca d'Almerita (www.tascadalmerita.it) at its Regaleali estate in Caltanissetta province is particularly highly regarded (the estate also produces an excellent Nero d'Avola under its Rosso del Conte label).

The sangiovese-like Nerello Mascalese and Nerello Cappuccio are used in the popular Etna Rosso DOC; try the Contrada Porcaria and Contrada Sciaranuova vintages produced by the Passopisciaro estate (www.passopisciaro.com) or the Serra della Contessa, Rovittello and Pietramarina produced by Vinicola Benanti (www.vinicolabenanti.it).

Cerasuolo di Vittoria, a blend of Nero d'Avola and Frappato grapes, is Sicily's only DOCG *(denominazione d'origine controllata e garantita)* wine. The more restrictive DOCG classification indicates that Cerasuolo is routinely analysed and tasted by government inspectors before bottling, and sealed with an official label to prevent tampering. Look for Planeta's vintages, which are produced at its estate in Dorilli, and those by COS.

Though the local reds are good, the region is probably best known for its white wines, including those produced at Abbazia Santa Anastasia (www.abbaziasantanastasia.com) near Castelbuono, and Fazio (p95) near Erice, and by Tasca d'Almerita and Passopisciaro.

Common white varietals include Carricante, chardonnay, Grillo, Inzolia, Cataratto, Inzolia, Cataratto, Grecanico and Corinto. Look out for Tasca d'Almerita's Nozze d'Oro Inzolia blend, Fazio's Catarratto Chardonnay, Abbazia Santa Anastasia's chardonnay blends, and Passopisciaro's Guardiola chardonnay.

Most wines are fairly cheap, though (as for any wine) prices vary according to the vintage. In a restaurant a bottle of decent wine should cost you around €15 to €25, with a table wine *(vino da tavola)* at around €10.

Sicilian dessert wines are excellent, and are well worth buying to take home. Top of the list is Marsala's sweet wine; the best (and most widely known) labels are Florio (p104) and Pellegrino (www.carlopellegrino.it). Sweet Malvasia (from the Aeolian island of Salina) is a honey-sweet wine whose best producers include Carlo Hauner (p145), Capofaro (www.capofaro.it/en/malvasia) and Fenech (p145) – just look for one of these names on the bottle and you'll know you have a good drop. Italy's most famous Moscato (Muscat), made from *zibibbo* grapes, is the Passito di Pantelleria from the island of the same name; it has a deep-amber colour and an extraordinary taste of apricots and vanilla.

The Gambero Rosso Vini d'Italia wine guide (www.gamberorosso.it) is generally considered to be the bible of Italian wines and offers plenty of information about Sicilian wines and wineries.

In late afternoon, just before dinnertime, Sicilians go to local bars to socialise over *aperitivi* – glasses of wine and alcohol, often accompanied by free snacks. This ritual is a great way to mingle with Italians, and it can even serve as a light dinner if you're not particularly hungry.

FOOD GLOSSARY

For more food terms see page 308.

acciughe a•*choo*•geh – anchovies

aceto a•*che*•to – vinegar

acqua *a*•kwa – water

aglio *a*•lyo – garlic

agnello a•*nye*•lo – lamb

aragosta a•ra•*go*•sta – lobster

arancia a•*ran*•cha – orange

arrosto/a *a*•*ros*•*to/a* – roasted

asparagi as•*pa*•ra•jee – asparagus

bicchiere bee•*kye*•re – glass

birra *bee*•ra – beer

bistecca bi•*ste*•ka – steak

burro *boo*•*ro* – butter

caffè ka•*fe* – coffee

cameriere/a ka•mer•*ye*•re/a – waiter (m/f)

capretto kap•*re*•to – kid (goat)

carciofi kar•*chyo*•fee – artichokes

carota ka•*ro*•ta – carrot

carta dei vini *kar*•ta dey•*vee*•nee – wine list

cavolo *ka*•vo•lo – cabbage

cena *che*•na – dinner

ciliegia chee•*lye*•ja – cherry

cipolle chee•*po*•le – onions

coltello kol•*te*•lo – knife

coniglio ko•*nee*•lyo – rabbit

conto *kon*•to – bill/cheque

cozze *ko*•tse – mussels

cucchiaio koo•*kya*•yo – spoon

enoteca e•no•*te*•ka – wine bar

fagiolini fa•jo•*lee*•nee – green beans

fegato fe•*ga*•to – liver

fico *fee*•ko – fig

finocchio fee•*no*•kyo – fennel

forchetta for•*ke*•ta – fork

formaggio for•*ma*•jo – cheese

fragole *fra*•go•le – strawberries

friggitoria free•jee•to•*ree*•a – fried-food stand

frutti di mare *froo*•tee dee *ma*•re – seafood

funghi *foon*•gee – mushrooms

gamberoni gam•be•*ro*•nee – prawns

granchio *gran*•kyo – crab
insalata een•sa•*la*•ta – salad
lampone lam•*po*•ne – raspberry
latte *la*•te – milk
limone lee•*mo*•ne – lemon
manzo *man*•dzo – beef
mela *me*•la – apple
melanzane me•lan•*dza*•ne – aubergine
melone me•*lo*•ne – cantaloupe; rock melon
merluzzo mer•*loo*•tso – cod
miele *mye*•le – honey
olio *o*•lyo – oil
oliva o•*lee*•va – olive
osteria *os•te•ree•a* – informal restaurant
ostriche os•*tree*•ke – oysters
pane *pa*•ne – bread
panna *pa*•na – cream
pasticceria *pas•tee•che•ree•a* – pastry shop
patate pa•*ta*•te – potatoes
pepe *pe*•pe – pepper
peperoncino pe•pe•ron•*chee*•no – chilli
peperoni *pe•pe•ro•nee* – capsicum
pera *pe*•re – pear
pesca *pes*•ka – peach
pesce spada *pe*•she *spa*•da – swordfish
piselli pee•*se*•lee – peas
pollo *po*•lo – chicken
polpo *pol*•pee – octopus
pomodori po•mo•*do*•ree – tomatoes
pranzo *pran*•dzo – lunch
prima colazione *pree*•ma ko•la•*tsyo*•ne – breakfast
riso *ree*•so – rice
ristorante ree•sto•*ran*•te – restaurant
rucola *roo*•ko•la – rocket; arugula
sale *sa*•le – salt
salsiccia sal•*see*•cha – sausage
sarde *sar*•de – sardines
sgombro *sgom*•bro – mackerel
spinaci spee•*na*•chee – spinach
spuntino spoon•*tee*•no – snack
tartufo tar•*too*•fo – truffle
tè te – tea
tonno *to*•no – tuna
tovagliolo to•va•*lyo*•lo – napkin/serviette
trattoria tra•to•*ree*•a – informal restaurant
trippa *tree*•pa – tripe
uovo/uova *wo*•vo/*wo*•va – egg/eggs
uva *oo*•va – grapes
vegetaliano/a ve•je•ta•*lya*•no/a – vegan (m/f)
vegetariano/a ve•je•ta•*rya*•no/a – vegetarian (m/f)
vino bianco *vee*•no *byan*•ko – white wine
vino rosso *vee*•no *ro*•so – red wine
vitello vee•*te*•lo – veal
vongole *von*•go•le – clams
zucchero *tsoo*•ke•ro – sugar

Sicilian Way of Life

When asked to name their nationality, most locals will say 'Sicilian' rather than 'Italian', reinforcing a generally held Italian belief that the Sicilian culture and character are markedly different to those of the rest of the country. Though sharing many traits with fellow residents of the Mezzogiorno (the part of southern Italy comprising Sicily, Abruzzo, Basilica, Campania, Calabria, Apulia, Molise and Sardinia), Sicilians have a dialect and civil society that are as distinctive as they are fascinating.

Identity

The uniqueness of the Sicilian experience is perhaps summed up best by author Giuseppe Tomasi di Lampedusa in Sicily's most famous novel, *Il Gattopardo* (The Leopard). In one memorable passage, his protagonist the Prince of Salina tries to explain the Sicilian character to a Piedmontese representative of the new Kingdom of Italy as follows: 'This violence of landscape, this cruelty of climate, this continual tension in everything, and even these monuments of the past, magnificent yet incomprehensible because not built by us and yet standing round us like lovely mute ghosts...All these things have formed our character...'

In modern Sicily, the prevailing stereotype is that Palermo and Catania stand at opposite ends of the island's character. Palermitans are commonly viewed as being more traditional, while Catanians are considered more outward looking and better at business. Some ascribe the Palermitans' conservative character to their Arab predecessors, while the Greeks get all the credit for the Catanians' democratic outlook, their sense of commerce and their alleged cunning. Beyond this divide, Sicilians are generally thought of as conservative and suspicious (usually by mainland Italians), stoical and spiritual, confident and gregarious, and as the possessors of a rich and dark sense of humour.

Colonised for centuries, Sicilians have absorbed myriad traits – indeed, writer Gesualdo Bufalino wrote in *Cento Sicilie* (2008) that Sicilians suffered from an 'excess of identity', at the core of which was the islanders' conviction that Sicilian culture stands at the centre of the world. This can make the visitor feel terribly excluded, as there is still an awful lot of Sicily that is beyond the prying eyes of the tourist.

That said, it is difficult to make blanket assertions about Sicilian culture, if only because there are huge differences between the more modern-minded city dwellers and those from the traditionally conservative countryside. It is certain, however, that modern attitudes are changing conservative traditions. In the larger university cities such as

SICILIAN PROVERBS

Sicilian culture is big on proverbs. Even as Sicilians embrace many aspects of modern life, their everyday speech is laced with traditional sayings whose roots go back several centuries. Spoken in Sicilian (a language in its own right and quite distinct from Italian), these proverbs often require translation even for other Italians.

Ogni beni di la campagna veni. All good things come from the countryside.

Palermo, Catania, Syracuse and Messina, you will find a vibrant youth culture and a liberal lifestyle.

Public vs Private

Family is the bedrock of Sicilian life, and loyalty to family and friends is one of the most important qualities you can possess. As Luigi Barzini (1908–84), author of *The Italians*, noted, 'A happy private life helps tolerate an appalling public life'. This chasm between the private arena and public forum is a noticeable aspect of Sicilian life, and has evolved over years of intrusive foreign domination.

Maintaining a *bella figura* (beautiful image) is very important to the average Sicilian, and striving to appear better off than you really are (known as *spagnolismo*) is a regional pastime. Though not confined to Sicily, *spagnolismo* on the island has its roots in the excesses of the Spanish-ruled 18th century, when the race for status was so competitive that the king considered outlawing extravagance. In this climate, how you and your family appeared to the outside world was (and still is) a matter of honour, respectability and pride. In a social context, keeping up appearances extends to dressing well, behaving modestly, performing religious and social duties and fulfilling all essential family obligations; in the context of the extended family, where gossip is rife, a good image protects one's privacy.

Testa c'un parra si chiama cucuzza. A head that doesn't speak is called a pumpkin. (If something's on your mind, don't keep it to yourself!)

In this heavily patriarchal society, 'manliness' is a man's prime concern. The main role of the 'head of the family' is to take care of his family, oil the wheels of personal influence and facilitate the upward mobility of family members. Women, on the other hand, are traditionally the repository of the family's honour, and even though unmarried couples commonly live together nowadays, there are still young couples who undertake lengthy engagements for the appearance of respectability.

Traditionally, personal wealth is closely and jealously guarded. Family money can support many individuals, while emigrant remittances have vastly improved the lot of many villagers.

A megghiu parola e chidda ca unsi rici. The best word is the one that remains unspoken.

A Woman's Place

In Francis Ford Coppola's *The Godfather*, Fabrizio (played by Angelo Infanti) describes women as more dangerous than shotguns. Writer Giovanni Verga proclaimed 'A woman at the window is a woman to be shunned' in the 19th century, while a judge faced with a female Mafia suspect in the 1990s declared that women were too stupid to partake in the complexities of finance. As in many places in the Mediterranean, a woman's position in Sicily has always been a difficult one.

TIDES OF CHANGE

For all of its supposed conservatism, modern-day Sicily has been at the centre of some major cultural shifts. Two of these are the growing acceptance of gays in Italian society and the repudiation of Mafia control. Both of these threads converge in the story of Rosario Crocetta, elected governor of Sicily in 2012.

Back in 2003, Mr Crocetta became the first openly gay Italian politician to win a mayoral election, though he had to fight the Mafia to get there. The original vote tally showed him losing by a narrow margin, but after Crocetta discovered evidence of Mafia tampering, he managed to convince a court to overturn the results. Since then he's ridden a wave of public popularity all the way to the governor's office, ending over six decades of right-wing rule. Along the way, despite three Mafia attempts on his life, he has remained an outspoken critic of organised crime.

A Sicilian mother and wife commands the utmost respect within the home, and is expected to act as the moral and emotional compass for her family. Although, or perhaps because, male sexuality holds an almost mythical status, women's modesty – which includes being quiet and feminine, staying indoors and remaining a virgin until married – has had to be ferociously guarded. To this day the worst insult that can be directed to a Sicilian man is *cornuto,* meaning that his wife has been unfaithful.

Cu mancia fa muddica. He who eats leaves breadcrumbs. (If you do something wrong, people will find out.)

Improvements in educational opportunities and changing attitudes mean that the number of women with successful careers is growing – the 2015 Global Gender Gap Index published by the World Economic Forum ranked Italy at number 41 overall in 2015, up a dramatic 28 spots from 2014. This said, the country still sat near the bottom of the list of European nations in regard to political, professional and economic parity between the sexes.

Saints & Sinners

Religion remains a big deal in Sicily. With the exception of the small Muslim communities of Palermo and the larger Tunisian Muslim community in Mazara del Vallo, the overwhelming majority of Sicilians consider themselves practising Roman Catholics. Even before the 1929 Lateran Treaty between the Vatican and Italy, when Roman Catholicism became the official religion of the country, Sicily was incontrovertibly Catholic, mostly due to 500 years of Spanish domination. In 1985 the treaty was renegotiated, so that Catholicism was no longer the state religion and religious education was no longer compulsory, but this only reflected the reality of mainland Italy north of Rome; in Sicily, the Catholic Church remains strong and extremely popular.

Sparagna la farina mentre la coffa e' china; quannu lu furnu pari, servi a nenti lu sparagnari. Save flour while the bag is full; when you can see the bottom, there's nothing left to save.

In the small communities of the interior you will find that the mix of faith and superstition that for centuries dictated Sicilian behaviour is still strong. The younger, more cosmopolitan sections of society living in the cities tend to dismiss their elders' deepest expressions of religious devotion, but most people still maintain an air of respect.

Pilgrimages remain a central part of the religious ritual, with thousands of Sicilians travelling to places such as the Santuario della Madonna at Tindari or the Santuario di Gibilmanna in the Madonie Mountains. The depth of religious feeling associated with these sanctuaries is underscored by the large number of *ex votos* (votive offerings) brought to both places by worshippers seeking divine intervention or giving thanks for a miracle attributed to the Madonna.

Cu sparti avi a megghiu parti. The one who divides things up gets the better share.

Annual feast days of patron saints are also enthusiastically celebrated throughout the island, morphing into massive city-wide events in the larger urban areas. Palermo's mid-July Festa di Santa Rosalia spans three solid days, with the patroness paraded down Via Vittorio Emanuele from the cathedral to the waterfront in a grandiose *carro triunfale* (triumphal carriage), flanked by adoring crowds. In Catania, the Festa di Sant'Agata in early February also lasts for three days, with over a million devotees pouring into the streets to follow a silver reliquary bust of the saint. Syracuse's mid-December Festa di Santa Lucia, while smaller, is celebrated with similar fervour. All three festivals are accompanied by spectacular fireworks.

Cu si voli 'imbriacari, di vino bonu l'avi a fare. He who wants to get drunk should do it with good wine.

Easter celebrations mark the high point in Sicily's religious calendar. Settimana Santa (Holy Week) is traditionally a time for Sicilians to take time off from work, get together with their families and participate in religious observances. Many places around the island celebrate Holy Week with elaborate processions. The most famous of these is Trapani's I Misteri, a four-day event in which 20 life-sized statues representing different moments in Christ's Passion are carried through the streets by members of the city's traditional guilds. Other cities that have noteworthy Easter processions include Caltanissetta, Lipari and Enna.

SPEAKING SICILIAN

One of Sicily's cultural legacies is *sicilianu* (Sicilian). While both modern Italian and *sicilianu* have shared roots in Vulgar Latin (the common language of ancient Rome), Sicilian is considered by many as a distinct language, with 11 regionally based dialects. Indeed, UNESCO lists it as a 'minority language'.

Centuries of foreign occupation have helped shape its lexicon, with numerous words rooted in Greek, Arabic, French, Catalan, Spanish and Lombard. Take *cirasa* (cherry), from the Greek *kerási*, *bucceri/vucceri* (butcher) from the Old French *bouchier*, or *azzizzari* (to embellish), which hails from the Arabic *azīz*, meaning 'beautiful' or 'precious'. Arabic is also the root of numerous place names, among them Caltagirone (from *qal'at-al-jarar*, meaning 'castle of pottery jars'), Marsala (port of God) and La Kalsa (from *al Khalesa*, meaning 'the chosen'). The use of written Sicilian has been sporadic over the centuries. In the southeastern town of Scicli, the Chiesa di Santa Teresa is home to a 16th-century fresco with a rare inscription in Sicilianised Latin.

Today, *sicilianu* is mostly spoken in informal situations between friends and family, and more often by Sicily's working class. Decades of mass media has seen a steady influx of Italian words and, according to UNESCO, the language is now 'vulnerable'. Interestingly, the overwhelming majority of Sicilian speakers live abroad in countries including the US, Canada, Argentina and Australia, reflecting both the size of the Sicilian diaspora and the endurance of older traditions in many immigrant communities.

Immigration & Emigration

Immigration and emigration are among the most pressing contemporary issues, and Sicily is no stranger to the subject. Since the end of the 19th century the island has suffered an enormous drain of human resources through emigration. Between 1880 and 1910, over 1.5 million Sicilians left for the US, and in 1900 the island was the world's main area of emigration. In the 20th century, tens of thousands of Sicilians moved away in search of a better life in Northern Italy, North America, Australia and other countries. Today, huge numbers of young Sicilians – often the most educated – continue to leave the island. This brain-drain epidemic is largely the result of the grim unemployment rate and the entrenched system of patronage and nepotism, which makes it difficult for young people to get well-paid jobs without having the right connections.

Agneddu e sucu e finiu u vattiu. When the lamb's all gone, the baptism is over. (When the food's all gone, the party's over.)

Also, the fact that Sicily is one of the favoured ports of call for the thousands of *extracomunitari* (immigrants from outside the EU) who have flooded into Italy, some of them illegally, has led to extra strain being placed on housing and infrastructure as well as increased competition for jobs. It's a pressure that has fuelled a growing frustration among many Sicilians, despite a general hospitality towards these newcomers and an understanding of the difficulties faced by political and economic refugees from neighbouring countries, most notably Libya and Tunisia.

Sicily on Page & Screen

Writers and filmmakers have long been inspired by Sicily's harsh landscape, rich history and complex society. They have rarely seen the island through rose-tinted glasses – endemic poverty and corruption are hard to romanticise or whitewash – and their words, images and narratives offer an invaluable insight into the local culture and society.

Sicily in Print

Dogged by centuries of isolation, and divided into an illiterate peasantry and a decadent aristocracy, Sicily prior to the 19th century suffered from a complete absence of notable literature. And yet, the first official literature in Italian was written in Palermo in the 13th century at the School of Poetry, patronised by Frederick II. Alas, such high-minded works were irrelevant to the peasants, whose main pleasure was the celebration of religious festivals and, later, the popular *opera dei pupi* (Sicilian puppet theatre).

Top Reads

- I Malavoglia *by Giovanni Verga*
- Midnight in Sicily *by Peter Robb*
- On Persephone's Island *by Mary Taylor Simeti*
- The Day of the Owl *by Leonardo Sciascia*
- The Silent Duchess *by Dacia Maraini*

Local Voices

The political upheaval of the 19th and 20th centuries finally broke the silence of the Sicilian pen, and the literary colossus Giovanni Verga (1840–1922) emerged onto the scene. Living through some of the most intense historical vicissitudes of modern Italy – the unification of Italy, WWI and the rise of Fascism – his work was to have a major impact on Italian literature. His greatest novel, *I Malavoglia* (The Malavoglia Family; 1881), essentially a story about a family's struggle for survival through desperate times in Sicily, is still a permanent fixture on every Sicilian schoolchild's reading list.

Since then Sicilian writers have produced fiction to rival the best contemporary European works. Playwright and novelist Luigi Pirandello (1867–1936) was awarded the Nobel Prize for Literature in 1934 for a substantial body of work, which included the play *Sei personaggi in cerca d'autore* (Six Characters in Search of an Author; 1921). Poet Salvatore Quasimodo (1901–68) won the award in 1959 for his exquisite lyric verse, which included delightful translations of works by Shakespeare and Pablo Neruda. Elio Vittorini (1908–66) captured the essence of the Sicilian migration north in his masterpiece *Conversazione in Sicilia* (1941), the story of a man's return to the roots of his personal, historical and cultural identity.

Sicily's most famous novel was a one-off by an aristocrat whose intent was to chronicle the social upheaval caused by the end of the old regime and the unification of Italy. Giuseppe Tomasi di Lampedusa (1896–1957) published *Il Gattopardo* (The Leopard) in 1958 to immediate critical acclaim. Though a period novel, its enduring relevance lies in the minutely accurate observations of what it means to be Sicilian.

Much of Sicily's 20th-century literature is more political than literary. None is more so than the work of Danilo Dolci (1924–97), a social activist commonly known as the 'Sicilian Gandhi'. His *Report from Palermo*

A collection of short stories by acclaimed postwar Sicilian writer Leonardo Sciascia, entitled *The Wine-Dark Sea*, explores the complicated world of the island's mafia culture. Sciascia's candid and powerful writings on organised crime played a significant role in changing the way ordinary Italians perceived the mafia.

(1959) and subsequent *Sicilian Lives* (1981), both detailing the squalid living conditions of many of Sicily's poorest inhabitants, earned him the enduring animosity of the authorities and the Church. (Cardinal Ernesto Ruffini publicly denounced him for 'defaming' all Sicilians.) He, too, was nominated for the Nobel Prize and was awarded the Lenin Peace Prize in 1958.

The other great subject for modern Sicilian writers is, of course, the Mafia. For a masterful insight into the island's destructive relationship with organised crime, search out the work of Leonardo Sciascia (1921–89), whose novel *Il giorno della civetta* (The Day of the Owl; 1961) was the first Italian novel to take the Mafia as its subject. Throughout his career, Sciascia probed the topic, practically inventing a genre of his own. His protégé Gesualdo Bufalino (1920–96) won the prestigious Strega Prize in 1988 for his novel *Le menzogne della notte* (Night's Lies), the tale of four condemned men who spend the eve of their execution recounting the most memorable moments of their lives. Bufalino went on to become one of Italy's finest writers, mastering a style akin to literary baroque – intense, tortured and surreal. His haunting novel *Diceria dell'untore* (The Plague Sower; 1981), which won Italy's Campiello Prize, is the story of a tuberculosis patient at a Palermo sanatorium in the late 1940s. Guiding the reader through a landscape of doom, Bufalino invokes the horrors of wartime and the hopelessness of the patients who come to know each other 'before our lead-sealed freight car arrives at the depot of its destination'.

Well-known feminist novelist and playwright Dacia Maraini (b 1936) has written a number of novels set in Sicily, including the award-winning historical romance *La lunga vita di Marianna Ucrìa* (The Silent Duchess; 1990), which was made into the film *Marianna Ucrìa* by Italian director Roberto Faenze in 1997.

Through Foreign Eyes

A number of foreigners or expats have also written about Sicily. Enjoyable but lightweight titles include Peter Moore's humorous travelogue *Vroom by the Sea* (2007), which recounts his adventures exploring the island on a Vespa named Donatella (because it's the same shade of lurid orange as Donatella Versace); Brian P Johnston's *Sicilian Summer: A Story of Honour, Religion and the Perfect Cassata* (2007), which is full of village politics and eccentric personalities; and Marlena de Blasi's *That Summer in Sicily* (2008), a Mills and Boon–ish story about a Sicilian woman's relationship with a much-older member of the Sicilian aristocracy.

Mary Taylor Simeti's *On Persephone's Island* (1986) and Peter Robb's *Midnight in Sicily* (1996) and John Julius Norwich's *Sicily: An Island at the Crossroads of History* (2015) are much more substantial. Simeti, an American who has been living on the island since 1962, offers fascinating insights into its history, culture and cuisine; and both Robb's and Norwich's portraits of the island's history, culture and struggles are marked by impeccable research and compelling narrative. Norwich's other historical account is the eminently readable *The Normans in Sicily* (2004).

Historical novels of note include Barry Unsworth's *The Ruby in Her Navel* (2006) and Tariq Ali's *A Sultan in Palermo* (2005). Both are set against the backdrop of the Norman court of Roger II (known to his Arabic subjects as Sultan Rujeri).

Sicily on Film

The rich emotional, psychological and physical landscapes of Sicily have inspired some of the world's best filmmakers.

Visconti's two classics, *La terra trema* (The Earth Shook; 1948) and *Il Gattopardo* (The Leopard; 1963), illustrate the breadth of Sicilian tales –

the former a story of grinding poverty and misfortune in a benighted fishing family, while the latter oozes the kind of grand decadence that one imagines preceded the French Revolution.

Antonioni's enigmatic mystery *L'avventura* (The Adventure; 1960) focuses on the disappearance of one member of a group of bored and spoiled Roman socialites on a cruise around the Aeolian Islands, and though its existentialist plot has been described by many critics as impenetrable and pretentious, its stunning visuals are universally admired.

In Rossellini's *Stromboli: Terra di Dio* (Stromboli: Land of God; 1950), the explosive love affair between a Lithuanian refugee and a local fisherman is aptly viewed against the backdrop of the erupting volcano, while the hypnotic beauty of Michael Radford's *Il Postino* (The Postman; 1994) seduces viewers into a false sense of security, which is shattered by the film's tragic denouement.

It is, however, Francis Ford Coppola's modern masterpiece, *The Godfather* trilogy (Part I, 1972; Part II, 1974; Part III, 1990), that really succeeds in marrying the psychological landscape of the characters with their physical environment. The varying intensities of light and dark superbly mirror the constant undercurrent of quivering emotion and black betrayal.

Other directors who have worked here include the Taviani brothers, who filmed *Kaos* in 1984, seeking to reproduce the mad logic of Sicilian-born author Luigi Pirandello's universe. The aptly named film is a series of tales about loss, lust, love, emigration and death played out through fantastical story lines. The film's title comes from the village near Agrigento where Pirandello was born (although it is spelled with a 'C').

Sicilians enjoy a good guffaw, and Pietor Germi's *Divorzio all'italiana* (Divorce, Italian Style), set on the island, was a big hit here when it was released in 1961. More recent comedies include Roberto Benigni's *Il piccolo diavolo* (The Little Devil; 1988), *Johnny Stecchino* (Johnny Toothpick; 1991) and satirist Franco Maresco's *Belluscone: Una storia siciliana* (Belluscone: A Sicilian Story; 2014), a wry, quasi documentary about Berlusconi, his rumoured links to the Mafia and the latter's chokehold on Sicily society.

See a careful study of 21st-century Sicily in Emanuele Crialese's film *Terraferma*, dealing with illegal immigration.

Other films set in Sicily include Wim Wender's *Palermo Shooting* (2008), lambasted by most critics as pretentious and boring; and *Sicilia!* (1999), a film version of Elio Vittorini's acclaimed novel *Conversazione in Sicilia*, directed by Danièle Huillet and Jean-Marie Straub,

Sicily itself has produced few directors of note, with the best-known exception being Giuseppe Tornatore (b 1956). Tornatore followed up on the incredible success of his semi-autobiographical film *Nuovo Cinema Paradiso* (Cinema Paradiso; 1988) with films including *Malèna* (2000), starring Monica Bellucci in a coming-of-age story set in Sicily in the 1940s; *L'uomo delle stelle* (The Star Maker; 1995), also set in rural Sicily in the 1940s; and *Baarìa – La porta del vento* (Baarìa - Door of the Wind; 2009), the story of three generations of a local family between 1920 and 1980. Two versions of *Baarìa* were made: the first in the local Sicilian dialect of Baariotu and the second dubbed in Italian.

Like Tornatore, Roman-born Emanuele Crialese has made Sicily his muse. Two of his films, *Respiro* (2002) and *Nuovomondo* (The Golden Door; 2006), are set here. *Respiro* is about a woman whose unorthodox behaviour challenges her family and islander neighbours, while *Nuovomondo* is a dreamy record of a Sicilian family's emigration to New York at the turn of the 20th century. Crialese's 2011 film *Terraferma* deals with the very contemporary issue of illegal immigration on the island of Linosa through a story of a fisherman's family.

The Mafia

For many people, the word 'Mafia' is synonymous with Sicily, thanks to the country's infamous historical relationship with the organisation and the many films made about the Cosa Nostra – namely, and most famously, *The Godfather* trilogy. Starting life in the 18th century, the Mafia has shaped today's Sicily both through its criminal activities and, more recently, the brave and crucial anti-Mafia movement, which has involved a gradual resistance from all levels of Sicilian society.

The residents of Corleone once petitioned to change the town's name in order to get away from its criminal connotations.

Origins

The word 'Mafia' was in common usage for more than 110 years before it was officially acknowledged as referring to an actual organisation. Although formally recorded by the Palermitan prefecture in 1865, the term was not included in the Italian penal code until 1982.

The origins of the word have been much debated. The author Norman Lewis has suggested that it derives from the Arabic *mu'afah* or 'place of refuge'. Nineteenth-century etymologists proposed *mahjas,* the Arabic word for 'boasting'. Whatever the origin, the term *mafioso* existed long before the organisation known as the Mafia, and was used to describe a character who was elegant and proud, with an independent vitality and spirit.

The concept of the *mafioso* goes all the way back to the late 15th century when commercial opportunities were so restricted that even the overprivileged feudal nobles were forced to make changes in order to survive. They introduced a policy of resettlement that forced thousands of farmers off the land and into new towns; the idea was to streamline crop growth, but it also destroyed the lives of the peasants in the process. Many of the aristocrats moved to big cities such as Palermo and Messina, leaving their estates in the hands of *gabellotti* (bailiffs), who were charged with collecting ground rents. They, in turn, employed the early *mafiosi* – who were small gangs of armed peasants – to help them solve any 'problems' that came up on the way. The *mafiosi* were soon robbing large estates and generally causing mayhem, but the local authorities were inept at dealing with them as they would quickly disappear into the brush.

The bandits struck a mixture of fear and admiration into the peasantry, who were happy to support any efforts to destabilise the feudal system. They became willing accomplices in protecting the outlaws, and although it would be another 400 years before crime became 'organised', the 16th and 17th centuries witnessed a substantial increase in the activities of brigand bands. The bands were referred to as Mafia, while the peasants' loyalty to their own people resulted in the name Cosa Nostra (Our Thing). The early-day Mafia's way of protecting itself from prosecution was to become the modern Mafia's most important weapon: the code of silence, or *omertà.*

The 'New' Mafia

Up until WWII the Mafia had operated almost exclusively in the countryside, but with the end of the conflict Cosa Nostra began its expansion into the cities. It took over the construction industry, channelling funds into its bank accounts and creating a network of kickbacks that were factored into every project undertaken. In 1953 a one-off meeting between representatives of the US and Sicilian Mafias resulted in the creation of the first Sicilian Commission, which had representatives of the six main Mafia families (or *cosche,* literally meaning 'artichoke') to efficiently run its next expansion into the extremely lucrative world of narcotics. At the head of the commission was Luciano Liggio from Corleone, whose 'family' had played a vital role in developing US–Sicilian relations.

Throughout the 1960s and '70s the Mafia earned billions of dollars from the drug trade. Inevitably, the raised stakes made the different Mafia families greedy for a greater share and from the late 1960s onwards Sicily was awash with vicious feuds that left hundreds dead.

The most sensational assassination was that of the chief prefect of police, General Carlo Alberto Dalla Chiesa, whom the national government had sent to Sicily to direct anti-Mafia activities. Dalla Chiesa was ambushed in the heart of Palermo in 1982, and his brutal murder led to prosecutors and magistrates being granted wider powers of investigation.

The first real insight into the 'New Mafia' came with the arrest of *mafioso* Tommaso Buscetta, also in 1982. After nearly four years of interrogation, headed by the courageous Palermitan investigating magistrate Giovanni Falcone, Buscetta broke the code of silence. His revelations shocked and fascinated the Italian nation, as he revealed the innermost workings of La Società Onorata (the Honoured Society; the Mafia's chosen name for itself). Tragically, Falcone was assassinated in 1992, as was another courageous anti-Mafia magistrate, Paolo Borsellino.

In 1986, 500 top *mafiosi* were put on trial in the first *maxiprocesso* (maxi-trial) in a specially constructed bunker near Palermo's Ucciardone prison. The trial resulted in 347 convictions, of which 19 were life imprisonments and the others jail terms totalling a staggering 2665 years.

In January 1993 the authorities arrested the infamous *capo di tutti capi* (boss of bosses), Salvatore (Totò) Riina, the most wanted man in Europe. He was charged with a host of murders, including those of magistrates Falcone and Borsellino, and sentenced to life imprisonment.

The Anti-Mafia Movement

The anti-Mafia movement is alive and kicking in Sicily, tracing its roots back to the beginning of today's Mafia. According to historians, the movement first appeared in the late 19th century, and lasted in its first incarnation until the 1950s. The movement strove for agrarian reform, targeting the Mafia, conservative political elites and the *latifondisti* (big landowners), but its efforts were shattered when the lack of economic prospects in the postwar era drove thousands of young Sicilians to emigrate in search of work and a better life.

During the 1960s and 1970s, the anti-Mafia movement was headed by political radicals, mainly members of the left-wing groups disenchanted with the Socialist and Communist parties. Giuseppe 'Peppino' Impastato became famous during this period; the son of a *mafioso,* Impastato mocked individual *mafiosi* on his popular underground radio show. He was assassinated in 1978. Things were at their worst for the anti-Mafia movement in the 1980s, when the Mafia was particularly intolerant of anyone perceived as a potential threat. The assassination in 1982 of General Dalla Chiesa is now seen as one of the major elements in sparking a new wave in the anti-Mafia movement, with Sicilians from all sections of society – from educators and students to political activists and parish priests – becoming involved.

The reformist Christian Democrat Leoluca Orlando, who was elected mayor of Palermo during the 1980s, also helped to increase anti-Mafia

The anti-*pizzo* (protection money) movement was inspired by the defiance of a shopkeeper called Libero Grassi, whose anonymous letter to an extortionist was featured on the front page of a local newspaper in 1991. Grassi was murdered three weeks later.

THE MAFIA ON SCREEN

Il Capo dei Capi (The Boss of all Bosses) Italian TV miniseries (2007) about Salvatore Riina.

Dimenticare Palermo (To Forget Palermo) Italian political thriller (1989) directed by Francesco Rosi and co-written by Gore Vidal.

Excellent Cadavers Alexander Stille's 1995 book about Giovanni Falcone was made into a TV movie directed by Ricky Tognazzi in 1999 and a documentary directed by Marco Turco in 2005.

Il Giorno della Civetta (The Day of the Owl) Damiano Damiani's 1968 film was based on Leonardo Sciascia's novel.

The Godfather Trilogy Francis Ford Coppola's 1972–90 masterwork.

In Nome della Legge (In the Name of the Law) Pietro Germi's 1949 Italian neorealist film was co-written by Federico Fellini.

La Piovra (The Octopus) Hugely popular 1984–2001 Italian TV miniseries.

Salvatore Giuliano Francesco Rosi's 1962 neorealist film.

sentiment. He led an alliance of left-wing movements and parties to create Palermo Spring, which invalidated the public-sector contracts previously given to Mafia families, restored and reopened public buildings, and aided in the arrests of leading *mafiosi*. During the 1990s Orlando left the Christian Democrats and set up the anticorruption movement La Rete (the Network), bringing together a broad collection of anti-Mafia individuals and reform organisations. (The party was eventually absorbed by Romano Prodi's Democrat Party in 1999.)

Civilian efforts saw housewives hanging sheets daubed with anti-Mafia slogans from their windows, shopkeepers and small entrepreneurs forming associations to oppose extortion, and the formation of groups such as Libera (www.libera.it), cofounded in 1994 by Rita Borsellino, the sister of the murdered judge Paolo Borsellino. Libera managed to get the Italian parliament to permit its member organisations to legally acquire properties that had been seized from the Mafia by the government, establishing agricultural cooperatives, *agriturismi* and other legitimate enterprises on these lands (see www.liberaterra.it). Even the Catholic Church, long silent on the Mafia's crimes, finally began to have outspoken anti-Mafia members. The best known was Giuseppe Puglisi, who organised local residents to oppose the Mafia, and who was murdered in 1993.

The Mafia Today

Since Salvatore Riina's conviction, other top *mafiosi* have followed him behind bars, most notably his successor Leoluca Bagarella, arrested in 1995; the Sicilian 'Godfather', Bernardo Provenzano, caught in 2006 after 20 years on the run; Salvatore Lo Piccolo, Provenzano's successor, arrested in 2007; and Domenico Raccuglia (aka 'the Veterinarian'), number two in the organisation, arrested in 2009 after 15 years on the run.

The year 2013 was an eventful one for the anti-Mafia movement. April of that year saw the biggest ever seizure of Mafia-related assets, from businessman Vito Nicastri, who is alleged to have been a front man for the Cosa Nostra. In May more than 50,000 people attended the beatification of Don Giuseppe Puglisi, the Catholic priest shot by a Mafia hitman in 1993. Puglisi was the first Mafia victim to be officially declared a martyr by the Roman Catholic Church, a powerful statement for the anti-Mafia movement. The same month, Italy's former head politicians were on trial alongside Mafia bosses such as Salvatore Riina, for involvement with the Mafia in Sicily. Among the accused politicians was Nicola Mancino, the former interior minister.

No one would be so foolish to suggest that the power of the Mafia is a thing of the past, but these events have meant that the powerful core of the organisation is being weakened and that the silence, which for so many years has made progress difficult, is finally being broken.

Today's Mafia has infiltrated daily life, becoming intertwined with legal society: its collaborators and their children are now 'respectable' and influential citizens. Indeed, the Sicilian Mafia is considered the most bourgeois of Italy's four main crime syndicates, with associates holding significant roles in mainstream politics and business. In late 2015 a police investigation code-named Revenge 5 led to the arrest of 37 suspected clan members in Catania, among them the owners of a funeral home and a nonprofit NGO providing emergency medical care. While the funeral home served as a logistics base for drug trafficking, the NGO's ambulances were used for the transportation of illegal substances.

The arrest of Palermitan Teresa Marino in December 2015 revealed the growing role of women in Sicily's Cosa Nostra. The mother of five became a leading crime figure following the arrest of Marino's mafioso husband Tommaso Lo Presti in 2014, her duties included the management of cocaine shipments from South America.

Despite its involvement in drug trafficking, Cosa Nostra today is upstaged by Calabria's more powerful 'Ndrangheta at an international level. Instead, the Siclian Mafia mainly busies itself with local criminal activities, in particular the running of extortion rackets and the infiltration of public construction works. It's estimated that around 70% of businesses in Sicily pay *pizzo* (protection money) to the Mafia. In return, businesses receive immunity from theft or vandalism, as well as the help of local *mafiosi* to cut through bureaucratic red tape. In some cases, the *pizzo* is demanded in kind, whether through obligatory transactions with Mafia-run businesses, subcontracting to Mafia-owned companies, or the employment of Mafia-affiliated individuals. Those who refuse to yield are often intimidated with property damage or even physical assault. Critics call this 'the Invisible Mafia'.

Thankfully, not all Sicilians are willing to obey the Mafia's rules. The organisation Addiopizzo (www.addiopizzo.org), which campaigns against these iniquitous payments, urges consumers to support businesses that have said 'no' to paying *pizzo*. Its catchcry that a society subject to extortion is one without dignity seems to have struck a chord across the island and a number of tourism businesses – among others – are actively supporting the campaign, devising tours that support restaurants, shops and hotels that have said no to Mafia extortion (see www.addiopizzotravel.it).

Arts & Architecture

Millennia of foreign domination have left Sicily with a lavish artistic and architectural legacy. Ancient Greek temples litter the long southern coast, blazing mosaics adorn Roman villas and Byzantine churches, and forbidding Norman castles guard remote hilltop towns. Then there are Sicily's one-of-a-kind offerings, from East-meets-West Arab-Norman churches and palaces, to the lavish stuccowork, frescoes and stone-carved flourishes of its bombastic take on baroque.

Palermo's Galleria Regionale della Sicilia is home to the unnerving *Trionfo della Morte* (Triumph of Death), a 15th-century fresco believed to have influenced Pablo Picasso's iconic painting *Guernica*.

Prehistoric Art

Prehistoric art enthusiasts will find rock paintings and graffiti all over Sicily.

The Museo Archeologico Eoliano, in Lipari, showcases a fascinating collection of prehistoric and ancient finds from early Mediterranean times; highlights include attractive ceramics and terracotta produced by the first Neolithic indigenous cultures in the region.

The Upper Palaeolithic wall paintings and Neolithic incised drawings at the Grotta del Genovese were accidentally discovered in 1949 by the painter Francesca Minellono. Between 6000 and 10,000 years old, the images predominantly portray terrestrial animals, including deer and horses, though you can spot tuna too, a fish traditionally found in the waters off Sicily.

The Greeks & Romans

The Greeks settled in the 8th century BC and left the most enduring architectural legacy on the island. Sicily has some of the most impressive Doric temples in the Western world – the most enchanting are those at the Valley of the Temples in Agrigento. Other magnificent remains are at Selinunte, followed by those at the Parco Archaeologico della Neapolis at Syracuse. The remains of the city of Segesta form one of the world's most mesmerising ancient sites with a theatre high on the mountain and a never-completed Doric temple dating from around 430 BC. The Teatro Greco at Syracuse is a masterpiece of classical architecture that could seat 16,000 people, while Taormina's Teatro Greco, built in the 3rd century BC, is the most dramatically situated Greek theatre in the world. It's also the second largest in Sicily, after that of Syracuse.

Some of the most impressive Doric temples in the Western world are to be found in Sicily – the best are at Agrigento's Valley of the Temples (Valle dei Templi).

Sicily's most important Roman sight is the Villa Romana del Casale in Piazza Armerina, an ancient pleasure palace with an extraordinary array of vivid, large-scale floor mosaics dating from the 3rd century. Smaller in scale but nonetheless impressive are the themed floor mosaics at Villa Romana del Tellaro, south of Noto.

The Normans

The Normans collaborated with Byzantine and Arab architects and artisans, transforming Greek temples into basilicas and building innovative Moorish structures. Norman cathedrals remain some of Sicily's most impressive sights – the Cattedrale di Monreale, the Duomo in Cefalù, and the Cappella Palatina in Palermo are this period's glittering stars.

Indeed, the Cattedrale di Monreale is considered the finest example of Norman architecture in Sicily, completely smothered in show-stopping mosaics, and holding 200 slender columns incorporating Norman, Arab, Byzantine and classical elements. Cefalù's Duomo also holds its own, its elaborate Byzantine mosaics are Sicily's oldest and best preserved.

Palermo's Palazzo dei Normanni was originally constructed by the Arabs in the 9th century and extended by the Normans (namely Roger II) in 1130. At its centre is the Cappella Palatina, Palermo's prime attraction. Hypnotic mosaics aside, the chapel claims one of the finest examples of an Islamic ceiling in the Mediterranean, reputedly created by craftsmen shipped in from Cairo. Other splendid examples from this period are the churches of La Martorana and San Giovanni degli Eremiti, both in Palermo.

Alas, innovative Sicilian art slowly died out in the 13th century with the arrival of the Hohenstaufen rulers.

The southeastern Sicilian city of Ragusa is home to FestiWall, an annual street-art festival which sees Italian and foreign artists commissioned to create giant, permanent murals on the city's walls.

The Renaissance: Painting & Sculpture

Although no great architectural heritage remains in Sicily from the Renaissance era, painting and sculpture flourished. The era would also deliver Sicily's best-known painter, Antonello da Messina.

The Gagini family were sculptors and architects who founded Sicily's Gagini school, which flourished until the mid-1600s. Domenico Gagini (1420–92), the school's founder, often worked in conjunction with his son, Antonello Gagini (1478–1536). Antonello's most notable work is the decorated arch in the Capella della Madonna in Trapani's Santuario dell'Annunziata. He also produced ecclesiastical sculpture in Messina, and a large collection of his works can be seen at Palermo's Galleria Regionale della Sicilia – look out for his statue of the *Madonna del riposo* (1528).

Francesco Laurana (1430–1502), a Dalmatian-born sculptor considered both Italian and Croatian (the Croatian version of his name is Frane Vranjanin), worked in Sicily between 1466 and 1471. Among other works, he produced the tomb of Pietro Speciale in the Chiesa di San Francesco d'Assisi in Palermo, and his bust of Eleanor of Aragon, in the city's Galleria Regionale della Sicilia, is particularly sumptuous.

ANTONELLO DA MESSINA

The first – some would say only – great Sicilian painter was Antonello da Messina (1430–79). Originally from Messina, the artist is thought to have painted his first portraits in the late 1460s. They follow a Dutch model, the subject being shown bust-length, against a dark background, full face or in three-quarter view. Most Italian painters had adopted the semi-profile pose for individual portraits up to that point. In *The Portrait in the Renaissance* (1966) John Pope-Hennessy described him as 'the first Italian painter for whom the individual portrait was an art form in its own right'. In *The Lives of the Artists* (1550), Giorgio Vasari described da Messina as 'a man well skilled in his art' and claimed that he was the first Italian painter to use oil paint, a technique Vasari says he had learned in Flanders, though there is no evidence of da Messina having travelled outside Italy.

Sicily remains home to a small number of his luminous paintings. You'll find his graceful *Annunziata* (The Virgin Annunciate, 1474–77) in Palermo's Galleria Regionale della Sicilia and his splendid *Ritratto di un uomo ignoto* (Portrait of an Unknown Man, 1465) – considered to be one of the most distinctive portraits of the Italian Renaissance – in Cefalù's Museo Mandralisca. On the east coast, Syracuse's Galleria Regionale di Palazzo Bellomo claims *L'Annunciazione* (Annunciation, 1474), while Messina's Museo Regionale is home to his *San Gregorio* (St Gregory, 1473) polyptych.

TOP ART GALLERIES

Galleria Regionale della Sicilia (p56) Home to works dating from the Middle Ages to the 18th century.

Galleria d'Arte Moderna (p57) Sicilian paintings and sculptures from the 19th and 20th centuries.

Museo Regionale (p159) Paintings by Caravaggio and home-town boy Antonello da Messina.

Baroque Beauties

The Sicilian baroque period was a result of the 1693 earthquake that flattened cities such as Catania and left the space for the flourishing of this highly flamboyant architectural style. Sicily's brand of baroque combined the Spanish baroque with Sicily's own decorative and structural elements, among them the generous use of *putti* (cherubs) and masks as decorative motifs.

Two architects that dominated the scene were Rosario Gagliardi (1700–70), designer of the magnificent Cattedrale di San Giorgio in Ragusa, and Giovanni Battista Vaccarini (1702–69), who spent 30 years recreating Catania's historical core. Noto's baroque centre is one of Sicily's most powerful examples of this architectural style.

The most important artist from this period was Giacomo Serpotta, born in Palermo in 1656. Working mostly with plaster, Serpotta helped elevate stuccowork in Italy from a craft to a high art, creating a technique for polishing plaster that bestowed his creations with a stone-like lustre. His work adorns numerous churches and oratories in Palermo, among them the Oratorio di Santa Cita, home to his masterpiece, *Battle of Lepanto*.

Palermitan architect Ernesto Basile (1857–1932) was one of Italy's most prolific exponents of Liberty (Italian art nouveau) and modernism. His legacies include Palermo's Grand Hotel Villa Igiea, Teatro Massimo and Villino Florio. The term Liberty was inspired by London department store Liberty & Co, which famously sold art-nouveau arts and craft.

Liberty

Palermo flourished in the art-nouveau (or 'Liberty') period. The innovation of architects such as Giovan Battista Basile and his son Ernesto, and artists such as Salvatore Gregorietti and Ettore Maria de Begler, who painted the dining room of the Grand Hotel Villa Igiea, marked the epoch. Two kiosks in front of Palermo's Teatro Massimo and one opposite Teatro Politeama Garibaldi are fine examples of Sicilian art nouveau, while Villa Malfitano features some early Liberty elements. Unfortunately, much of the city's Liberty architecture was bulldozed in the Mafia-driven building boom of the mid-20th century.

Modern & Contemporary Art

Salvatore Fiume (1915–97) and Renato Guttuso (1911–87) remain two of the biggest names in modern Sicilian art. Guttuso's masterful 1974 painting of the Vucciria market is one of Sicily's most impressive recent art works. On display at Palermo's Museo dell'Inquisizione, its vibrant colours are the product of the artist's innovative approach – he used crumbled bricks to produce the reds, and burnt wood and candles for the black strokes.

Among the current crop of prolific creatives is Palermo-based multimedia artist Ignazio Mortellaro (b 1973) and Catanian illustrators Carlo and Fabio Ingrassia (b 1985). The latter, identical twins, work simultaneously on the same pieces, drawing from the outside of an image towards the centre to create harmonious, obsessively detailed works.

The best place for a shot of contemporary Sicilian art is Favara's Farm Cultural Park, where provocative art and social activism go hand in hand and serve art's great purpose – to try to make a real change.

Survival Guide

Directory A–Z

Customs Regulations

Goods bought and exported within the EU incur no additional taxes, provided duty has been paid somewhere within the EU and the goods are for personal use.

Travellers entering Italy from outside the EU are allowed to import the following duty free: 200 cigarettes, 1L of spirits, 4L of wine (or 2L of fortified wine), 60mL of perfume, and other goods up to the value of €300 (€430 if travelling by sea). Anything over this limit must be declared on arrival and the appropriate duty paid.

On leaving the EU, non-EU citizens can reclaim any *Imposta di Valore Aggiunto* (IVA) value-added tax on purchases equal to or over €155. The refund only applies to purchases made within the past three months in affiliated outlets that display a 'Tax Free for Tourists' or similar sign. You have to complete a form at the point of sale, then get it stamped by Italian customs as you leave.

Discount Cards

At many state museums and archaeological sites, EU citizens under 18 enter free, and those aged between 18 and 25 get a 50% discount. To claim these discounts you officially need a passport, driving licence or ID card as proof of age and nationality; non-EU citizens are technically ineligible for discounts, although some ticket-takers are more lenient than others in enforcing these rules.

The 'reduced' rate in our prices refers to the student discount. Since 2014, discounts for seniors have been significantly scaled back at state-run sites.

At private museums, children under 18 usually receive some kind of discount, with young children often entering free of charge.

Electricity

Italian plugs have two or three round pins; travellers from countries with a different plug type should bring an adapter.

The current is 230V, 50Hz.

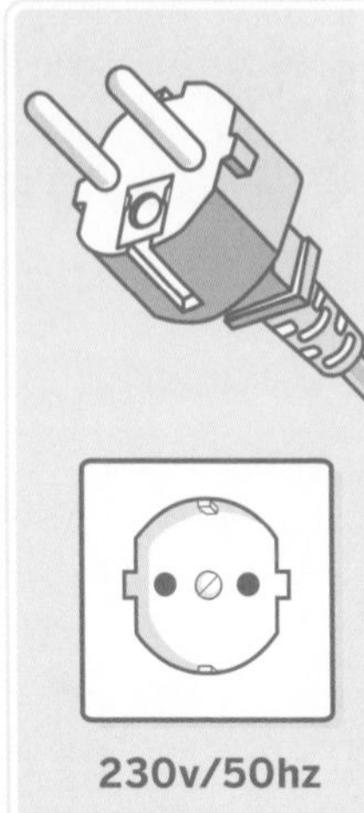

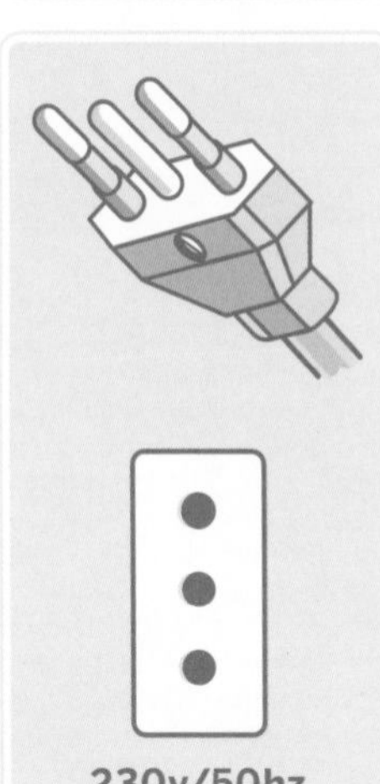

GLBTI Travellers

Homosexuality (over the age of 16) is legal in Sicily. The gay scene is centred on cities including Catania, Taormina and Palermo. In rural areas, attitudes remain largely conservative.

Large pride parades take place annually in Palermo (www.palermopride.it) and Catania (www.cataniapride.com) – in mid-June and early July, respectively.

EATING PRICE RANGES

Most restaurants have a *coperto* (cover charge) of €1 to €3 per person; some also include a *servizio* (service charge) of 10% to 15%.

The following price ranges refer to a meal consisting of two courses (antipasto or *primo*, plus *secondo*), glass of house wine and *coperto*.

€ less than €25

€€ €25–€45

€€€ more than €45

Online resources include the following (all in Italian):

Arcigay (www.arcigay.it) Italy's largest gay organisation, with branches in Catania (www.arcigaycatania.com), Palermo (www.arcigaypalermo.wordpress.com), Syracuse, Agrigento and Messina.

Coordinamento Lesbiche Italiano (CLR; www.clrbp.it) The national organisation for lesbians, holding regular conferences and literary meetings.

Gay.it (www.gay.it) Website featuring LGBT news, feature articles and gossip.

GuidaGay (www.guidagay.it) Details on gay-friendly bars, clubs, beaches and hotels.

Pride (www.prideonline.it) National monthly magazine of art, music, politics and gay culture.

Spartacus World (www.spartacusworld.com) Lists male-only venues all over Italy.

Health

Before You Go

HEALTH INSURANCE

If you're an EU citizen, an EHIC (European Health Insurance Card) covers you for free or reduced-cost public medical care but not for emergency repatriation. It is available from health centres in your home country. Citizens from countries outside the EU should find out if there is a reciprocal arrangement for free medical care between their country and Italy (Australia, for example, has such an agreement; carry your Medicare card with you).

US citizens should check whether their health-insurance plan offers coverage for hospital or medical costs abroad – many don't. The US Medicare service provides no coverage outside the US. If you do need health insurance, make sure you get a policy that covers you for the worst possible scenario, such as an accident requiring an emergency flight home. Find out in advance if your insurance plan will make payments directly to providers or reimburse you later for overseas health expenditures abroad.

VACCINATIONS

No vaccinations are required for travel to Italy.

In Sicily

AVAILABILITY & COST OF HEALTH CARE

Italy's public-health system is legally bound to provide urgent care to everyone. For emergency treatment go to the *pronto soccorso* (casualty) section of an *ospedale* (public hospital), where it's also possible to receive emergency dental treatment. For less serious ailments call the local *guardia medica* (duty doctor) – ask at your hotel or nearest tourist office for the number. Pharmacists will fill prescriptions and can provide basic medical advice.

TAP WATER

While tap water is reliable and safe throughout the region, most Sicilians prefer to drink *acqua minerale* (bottled mineral water). It will be either *frizzante* (sparkling) or *naturale* (still) and you will be asked in restaurants and bars which you prefer. If you want a glass of tap water, ask for *acqua dal rubinetto*.

Insurance

A travel-insurance policy to cover theft, loss and medical problems is highly recommended. It may also cover you for cancellation of and delays in your travel arrangements.

Paying for your ticket with a credit card can often provide limited travel accident insurance, and you may be able to reclaim the payment if the operator doesn't deliver.

Note that some policies specifically exclude 'dangerous activities', which can include scuba diving, motorcycling and even trekking.

Worldwide travel insurance is available at www.lonelyplanet.com/travel-insurance. You can buy, extend and claim online anytime – even if you're already on the road.

Internet Access

Public wi-fi hotspots are fairly common in cafes and bars, and most hotels and B&Bs now offer free wi-fi. In accommodation listings the internet icon is used to indicate that there is a computer available for guest use, while the wi-fi icon indicates there is wi-fi access. Wi-fi is specifically mentioned in reviews only when charges apply.

Legal Matters

The most likely reason for a brush with the law is if you have to report a theft. If you do have something stolen and you want to claim it on insurance, you must make a statement to the police; insurance companies won't pay up without proof of a crime.

The Italian police is divided into three main bodies: the black-clad *carabinieri;* the *polizia*, who wear navy blue jackets; and the *guardia di finanza*, who fight tax evasion and drug smuggling. If you run into trouble in Italy, you're likely to end up dealing with either the *polizia* or the *carabinieri*. If, however, you land a parking ticket, you'll need to speak to the *vigili urbani* (traffic wardens).

The legal blood-alcohol limit is 0.05% (0.5g/L), and random breath tests do occur. Penalties for driving under the influence of alcohol can be severe.

In general, your embassy should be able to provide a list of local lawyers, interpreters and translators.

Maps

Arbatus (www.arbatus.com) publishes excellent trekking maps (€5) for each of the seven Aeolian islands. For walking in the Mt Etna area, Selca's 1:25,000 *Mt Etna* map (€7), available from Stella Alpina (www.stella-alpina.com), is a good bet. Several trails in the Madonie Mountains are detailed on the Parco Regionale delle Madonie's 1:50,000 *Carta dei Sentieri e del Paesaggi* (€3), available from park offices in Cefalù and Petralia Sottana.

PRACTICALITIES

Weights & Measures Sicily uses the metric system.

Smoking Prohibited in all public spaces, as per EU law.

Money

ATMs

Credit and debit cards can be used in ATMs (which are widespread and known locally as *bancomat*). Most ATMs have multilingual screens, making life easy for English-speakers, but in a pinch, the Italian term for international cash withdrawal is *prelievo internazionale*. Visa and MasterCard are widely recognised, as are Cirrus and Maestro. Remember that every time you withdraw cash there will be fees. Typically you'll be charged a withdrawal fee as well as a conversion charge; if you're using a credit card, you'll also be hit by interest on the cash withdrawn.

If an ATM rejects your card, don't despair. Try a few more ATMs displaying your credit card's logo before assuming the problem lies with your card.

Credit & Debit Cards

Though widely accepted, credit cards are not as ubiquitous in Sicily as they are in the UK or the US, and it's always a good idea to have some cash on hand. Some small guesthouses, trattorias and shops don't take credit cards, and you can't always use them at petrol stations, parking meters or motorway ticket barriers.

Major cards such as Visa, MasterCard and Eurocard are accepted throughout Sicily. Amex is also recognised but it's less common.

Before leaving home, make sure to advise your credit-card holder of your travel plans. Otherwise, you risk having your card blocked – as a security measure, banks block cards when they notice out-of-the-ordinary transactions. Check also any charges you'll incur and what the procedure is if you experience problems or have your card stolen. Most card suppliers will give you an emergency number you can call free of charge for help and advice.

Currency

Italy's currency is the euro (€). The euro is divided into 100 cents. Coin denominations are one, two, five, 10, 20 and 50 cents, €1 and €2. The notes are €5, €10, €20, €50, €100, €200 and €500.

Opening Hours

Banks 8.30am to 1.30pm and 2.45pm to 3.45pm Monday to Friday.

Cafes 7am to 8pm (or later if offering bar service at night).

Museums Hours vary, but many close on Monday.

Restaurants Noon to 2.30pm and 7.30pm to 11pm; many close one day per week.

Shops 9.30am to 1.30pm and 4pm to 7.30pm Monday to Saturday.

Postal Services

Sicily's postal system, **Poste** (☎80 31 60; www.poste.it), is never going to win any awards for efficiency but sooner or later letters generally arrive. Delivery is guaranteed to Europe within three days and to the rest of the world within four to eight days.

Stamps *(francobolli)* are available at post offices and authorised tobacconists (look for the official *tabacchi* sign, a big 'T', often white on black), which you'll find in every town and village.

For more important items, use registered mail *(raccomandato)* or insured mail *(assicurato);* the cost depends on the value of the object being sent.

Public Holidays

Most Sicilians take their annual holiday in August, deserting the cities for the cooler seaside or mountains. This means that many businesses and shops close for at least part of the month, usually around the Feast of the Assumption (Ferragosto) on 15 August. Easter is another busy period, with many resort hotels opening for the season the week before Easter.

Italian schools close for three months in summer, from mid-June to mid-September, for two weeks at Christmas and for a week at Easter.

Individual towns have public holidays to celebrate the feasts of their patron saints. National public holidays in Sicily include the following:

Capodanno (New Year's Day) 1 January

Epifania (Epiphany) 6 January

Pasqua (Easter) March/April

Pasquetta (Easter Monday) March/April

Giorno della Liberazione (Liberation Day) 25 April

Festa del Lavoro (Labour Day) 1 May

Festa della Repubblica (Republic Day) 2 June

Ferragosto (Feast of the Assumption) 15 August

Festa di Ognissanti (All Saints' Day) 1 November

Festa della Immacolata Concezione (Feast of the Immaculate Conception) 8 December

Natale (Christmas Day) 25 December

Festa di Santo Stefano (Boxing Day) 26 December

Safe Travel

Despite Mafia notoriety, Sicily is not a dangerous place and the biggest threat you face is not from the local *capo* (Mafia boss) but from the odd petty thief.

Theft

Modern-day Sicily is generally a very safe place to travel, and the likelihood of your vacation being affected by crime is low, especially if you follow a few common sense precautions.

In urban centres such as Palermo and Catania, you should exercise the same basic caution as you would in any large European or North American city. When walking through crowded markets or riding on buses at rush hour, be aware of your surroundings and don't flaunt your valuables or carry large amounts of cash in unsecured pockets. Pickpockets and bag-snatchers exist, as in any metropolitan setting, but your attitude should be one of prevention rather than of paranoia. Don't carelessly leave purses, cameras or phones lying about in streetside cafes, and don't keep valuables in plain view in a parked vehicle. If you're driving a rental car and feel unsure about the security of your neighbourhood, use an enclosed car park.

In the relatively unlikely event that you are a victim of petty theft or other crime, always report it to the police within 24 hours, and ask for a statement; otherwise, your travel insurance company is unlikely to pay out.

Traffic

Sicilian traffic can be a daunting prospect, particularly in Palermo where the only rule seems to be survival of the fastest. However, outside the main urban areas, the situation calms down and the main concerns become curvy roads, potholes and iffy signposting. As a general rule, traffic is at its quietest around lunchtime, especially on Sunday, when few people are out and about.

Drivers are not keen to stop for pedestrians, even at pedestrian crossings. Sicilians simply step off the pavement and walk through the swerving traffic. In the major cities, roads that appear to be for one-way traffic often have special lanes for buses travelling in the opposite direction, so always look both ways before stepping out. On a positive note, pedestrian zones have expanded in recent years in the city centres of Palermo, Catania and other popular destinations.

Telephone

TIM/Telecom Italia (www.tim.it) is Italy's biggest telecommunications company, offering both landline and cellular service.

Mobile Phones

Italian mobile phones operate on the GSM 900/1800 network. If you have an unlocked GSM phone that supports these frequencies, you can purchase a *pre-pagato* (pre-paid) SIM card in Italy for as little as €10.

SIM CARDS

As a general rule, local SIM card rates are cheaper than the roaming rates incurred for using your home mobile phone in Italy.

TIM, Wind (www.wind.it), Vodafone (www.vodafone.it) and Tre (www.tre.it) all sell a variety of SIM cards offering voice, data and/or international calling, and all have plentiful retail outlets in Sicily. You'll need your passport to open an account. To recharge your card, simply pop into the nearest outlet or buy a ricarica (charge card) from a tobacconist.

Useful Numbers & Codes

Italian area codes all begin with '0' and consist of up to four digits. The area code is followed by a telephone number of anything from four to eight digits. Area codes are an integral part of all telephone numbers in Italy, even if you are calling within a single zone. For example, any number you ring in Palermo will start with ☎091, even if it's next door. When making domestic calls you must always dial the full number including the initial zero. Mobile-phone numbers begin with a three-digit prefix such as ☎333, ☎347 or ☎390.

To make an international call from Sicily, dial the international access code (☎00), then the relevant country and area codes followed by the telephone number.

To dial a Sicilian number from outside Italy, dial your international access code, followed by Italy's country code (☎39), the relevant city code (including the initial '0') and the number.

International access code (for international calls from Italy)	☎00
Italy's country code (for international calls to Italy)	☎39
International operator	☎170
Directory enquiries	☎1254

Time

Sicily is one hour ahead of GMT. Daylight-saving time starts on the last Sunday in March, when clocks are put forward one hour. Clocks go back an hour on the last Sunday in October. Italy operates on the 24-hour clock, so rather than 6.30pm, you'll see 18.30 on transport timetables.

Toilets

Public toilets are rare in Sicily except at major tourist sites and archaeological parks. Most people use the facilities in bars and cafes – although you might need to buy a coffee first. In many places public loos are pretty grim; try to go armed with some tissues.

Tourist Information

You'll find tourist offices located throughout Sicily. Some are more helpful than others but most are able to provide accommodation lists, rudimentary maps and information on local tourist attractions. Most will also respond to telephone and email requests for information, though responses to the latter can be maddeningly slow.

Opening hours vary but as a general rule are 9am to 1pm and from 3pm to 7pm Monday to Friday. Hours are usually extended in summer, when some offices also open on Saturday or Sunday. Some cities have subsidiary information booths at train stations, though these often keep shorter hours or operate only in summer.

Offices in popular destinations such as Palermo, Catania, Taormina, Syracuse and the Aeolian Islands are usually well stocked and staffed by employees with a working knowledge of at least one other language, usually English but also French or German.

Officially, Sicilian tourist offices are known as *Servizi Turistici Regionali* (Regional Tourist Services) but for the sake of simplicity we refer to them as 'tourist offices'.

Travellers with Disabilities

Sicily is not an easy island for travellers with disabilities. Narrow cobbled streets, hair-raising traffic, blocked pavements and tiny lifts make life very difficult for wheelchair users, and those with sight or hearing difficulties.

Under European law, airports are obliged to provide assistance to passengers with reduced mobility, so if you need help en route to Sicily, or on arrival/departure, tell your airline when you book your ticket and they should inform the airport. Facilities are available at both Palermo and Catania airports.

If travelling by rail, ring Trenitalia's national helpline (☎199 303060) to arrange assistance with wheelchairs, guides and getting on and off trains. Further information is available online at www.trenitalia.com/tcom-en; choose the 'Person with reduced mobility' link under Information and Contacts.

If you are driving, the UK blue badge is recognised in Italy, giving you the same parking rights that local drivers with disabilities have.

Download Lonely Planet's free Accessible Travel guide from http://lptravel.to/AccessibleTravel. Lonely Planet offers a number of other online resources, including its Travel for All community on Google+, the Travellers with Disabilities branch of the Thorn Tree forum (www.lonelyplanet.com/thorntree/forums/travellers-with-disabilities), and an Accessible Travel Pinterest page (www.pinterest.com/lonelyplanet/accessible-travel).

Other online resources:

Accessible Italy (www.accessibleitaly.com) A San Marino–based company that specialises in holiday services for people with disabilities, ranging from tours to the hiring of adapted transport.

Italian Tourism Official Website (www.italia.it/en/useful-info/accessibility.html) Italy-specific links for travellers with disabilities.

Sage Traveling (www.sagetraveling.com) A US-based agency offering advice and tailor-made tours to assist mobility-impaired travellers in Europe.

Tourism for All (www.tourismforall.org.uk) A British charity that can provide general travelling information – check out the website's useful FAQ section.

Visas

For up-to-date information on visa requirements, see www.esteri.it/visti.

EU citizens do not need a visa to enter Italy. Nationals of some other countries, including Australia, Canada, Israel, Japan, New Zealand and the USA, do not need visas for stays of up to 90 days in Italy.

Other people wishing to visit Italy have to apply for a Schengen visa, which allows unlimited travel in Italy and 24 other European countries for a 90-day period. You must apply for a Schengen visa in your country of residence and you can not apply for more than two in any 12-month period. They are not renewable inside Italy.

Technically, all foreign visitors to Italy are supposed to register with the local police within eight days of arrival. However, if you're staying in a hotel or hostel you don't need to bother as the hotel will do it for you – this is why they always take your passport details.

Women Travellers

Sicily in general is a welcoming and safe place for women travellers, including those travelling solo. Cultural stereotypes of Italian men harassing lone foreign women are largely outdated and exaggerated.

That said, eye-to-eye contact remains the norm in Italy's daily flirtatious interplay, and with some men this may segue into overt staring. Usually a simple show of disinterest is enough to nip unwanted attention in the bud. If ignoring them doesn't work, politely say that you're waiting for your *marito* (husband) or *fidanzato* (boyfriend) and, if necessary, walk away. If you are visibly in distress, people near you or passersby will generally step in to assist.

Transport

GETTING THERE & AWAY

Flights, cars and tours can be booked online at lonelyplanet.com/bookings.

Air

Fares to Sicily fluctuate throughout the year: tickets tend to be cheapest between November and March and most expensive between June and September. Holidays such as Christmas, New Year's and Easter see large price hikes. Flight schedules are also subject to seasonal variations, with the number of flights increasing considerably in summer.

Several low-cost airlines serve Sicily from European destinations, including Ryanair (www.ryanair.com), easyJet (www.easyjet.com), Vueling (www.vueling.com) and TUIFly (www.tuifly.com).

Airports & Airlines

Sicily's two main airports serve the island's two biggest cities: Palermo and Catania.

Named after two assassinated anti-Mafia judges, Palermo's **Falcone-Borsellino Airport** (☎800 541880, 091 702 02 73; www.gesap.it) is at Punto Raisi, 30km west of the city. Alitalia (www.alitalia.com), Meridiana (www.meridiana.it) and two dozen other airlines operate regular flights to/from major Italian and international destinations including Frankfurt, London, Madrid, Milan, Munich, New York City and Zürich; Ryanair, easyJet and Vueling are among the low-cost carriers serving other cities including Amsterdam, Barcelona, Bologna, Florence, Paris and Rome.

Just 7km outside Catania, **Fontanarossa Airport** (☎095 723 91 11; www.aeroporto.catania.it) is served by many national and international airlines, with connections to destinations across Europe including London, Paris, Zürich, Munich and Berlin.

Sicily's third-busiest airport, **Vincenzo Florio Airport** (Birgi Airport; TPS; ☎0923 61 01 11; www.airgest.it) is 16km south of Trapani. Ryanair serves two dozen destinations throughout Italy and Europe, including Bologna, Brussels, Frankfurt, Milan and Rome. Alitalia flies to the offshore island of Pantelleria.

The much smaller **Comiso Airport** (☎0932 96 14 67; www.aeroportodicomiso.eu), 27km northwest of Ragusa, is served year-round by Alitalia and Ryanair flights to destinations including Rome, Milan, Pisa, Brussels and London (Stansted).

Land

Bus

SAIS Trasporti (☎091 617 11 41; www.saistrasporti.it) operates long-distance buses between Sicily and

CLIMATE CHANGE & TRAVEL

Every form of transport that relies on carbon-based fuel generates CO_2, the main cause of human-induced climate change. Modern travel is dependent on aeroplanes, which might use less fuel per kilometre per person than most cars but travel much greater distances. The altitude at which aircraft emit gases (including CO_2) and particles also contributes to their climate change impact. Many websites offer 'carbon calculators' that allow people to estimate the carbon emissions generated by their journey and, for those who wish to do so, to offset the impact of the greenhouse gases emitted with contributions to portfolios of climate-friendly initiatives throughout the world. Lonely Planet offsets the carbon footprint of all staff and author travel.

Italian mainland destinations including Rome and Naples. While reservations are not generally necessary on Sicilian buses, they're highly recommended in the high season for long-haul, overnight journeys of this sort.

Car & Motorcycle

Driving to Sicily can be an arduous and expensive proposition. In terms of budget, you'll need to account for the cost of toll roads and the fact that Italian fuel prices are among the highest in Europe. Your journey time will also depend on where you catch the ferry.

The shortest ferry to Sicily is the 20-minute crossing from Villa San Giovanni (on the toe of the Italian mainland) to Messina. It's about a 13-hour drive from the French or Swiss border to Villa San Giovanni, but only if you keep to the motorways, go flat out (the speed limit is 130km/h) and avoid traffic, which is something of a vain hope in the summer holiday period (July and August).

A less-demanding option is to drive north to south to Genoa, Livorno, Civitavecchia, Naples or Salerno and take a ferry from there.

Once in Sicily, a car or motorbike is a major plus, but it is probably easier to hire one than to take your own.

Note that as of mid-2016, Italy's national rail company Trenitalia had discontinued its former service of transporting private cars by train.

BRINGING YOUR OWN VEHICLE

To bring your own vehicle to Sicily, you will need to have a valid driving licence, proof of vehicle ownership and evidence of third-party insurance. If your vehicle is registered and insured in an EU country, your home-country insurance is sufficient. Ask your insurer for a European Accident Statement (EAS) form, which can simplify matters in the event of an accident. The form can also be downloaded online at www.cartraveldocs.com/european-accident-statement.

If bringing a motorcycle to Sicily, be aware that a crash helmet and a motorcycle licence (for any vehicle over 125cc) are compulsory.

Every vehicle travelling across an international border should display a nationality plate of its country of registration. A warning triangle (to be used in the event of a breakdown) is compulsory throughout Europe.

Train

If you have the time, getting to Sicily by train is worth considering: it's more environmentally friendly than flying, it's more relaxed and, perhaps best of all, it gives you the option of breaking up your journey, since most north-to-south Italian rail itineraries involve a change of trains in Rome or Naples.

Italy's national rail company, **Trenitalia** (☎892021, 06 6847 5475; www.trenitalia.com), operates direct InterCity trains to Sicily from both Rome and Naples, along with direct night trains (InterCityNotte) from Milan, Rome and Naples; on the latter, you can often book a *cuccetta* (sleeping compartment) for little more than the cost of a normal seat on the day train. Upon arrival at the tip of Italy's boot, Intercity trains have traditionally been loaded onto ferries for the crossing of the Straits of Messina into Sicily. This service was still operating as of mid-2016, though Trenitalia has proposed discontinuing the direct loading of trains onto ferries and instituting a new system whereby passengers would disembark for the ferry crossing and board a different train on the far side of the Straits.

For detailed info on getting to Sicily from London, check out www.seat61.com. Another helpful resource is the *European Rail Timetable*, a Europe-wide compendium of train schedules, available online at www.europeanrailtimetable.co.uk.

Sea

Unless you're flying, arriving in Sicily involves a ferry crossing. Regular car/passenger ferries cross the Strait of Messina (the 3km stretch of water that separates Sicily from the Italian mainland) between Villa San Giovanni and Messina, or Reggio di Calabria and Messina. Ferries also sail to Sicily from Genoa, Livorno, Civitavecchia, Naples, Salerno, Cagliari (Sardinia), Malta and Tunisia.

Across the Strait of Messina

For detailed timetables, see www.trasportisullostretto.it.

Caronte & Tourist (☎090 36 46 01, 800 627414; www.carontetourist.it) Car ferries to Messina from Villa San Giovanni.

Liberty Lines (☎0923 87 38 13; www.libertylines.it) Hydrofoils to Messina from Reggio Calabria.

Meridiano Lines (☎0965 81 04 14, 335 8255909; www.meridianolines.it) Car ferries to Messina from Reggio Calabria.

From Italy, Tunisia & Malta

During the high season, all routes are busy and you'll need to book several weeks in advance. The helpful search engine **Traghetti Online** (☎89 341341; www.traghettionline.net) provides comprehensive route details and an online booking service.

For Palermo, high-season fares (for an adult and car) start at approximately €91 from Genoa, €119 from Civitavecchia, and €93 from Naples. From Naples to Catania, fares start at around €58. Crossing the Straits of Messina costs from €13 to

€37 depending on the vehicle, number of passengers and routing. Fares can increase sharply during peak periods.

Note that although you do not need to show your passport on internal routes, you should still keep photo ID handy.

Caronte & Tourist (☎090 36 46 01, 800 627414; www.carontetourist.it) Ferries to Messina from Salerno.

Grandi Navi Veloci (☎010 209 45 91; www.gnv.it) Ferries to Palermo from Civitavecchia, Genoa, Naples and Tunis.

Grimaldi (☎081 49 64 44; www.grimaldi-ferries.com) Ferries to Palermo from Livorno, Salerno and Tunis.

Liberty Lines (☎0923 87 38 13; www.libertylines.it) Runs summer-only hydrofoils to Trapani and Ustica from Naples

Società Navigazione Siciliana (Siremar; ☎090 36 46 01; www.siremar.it) Ferries to Milazzo and the Aeolian Islands from Naples.

Tirrenia (☎892123; www.tirrenia.it) Ferries to Palermo from Naples and Cagliari.

TTT Lines (☎095 34 85 86; www.tttlines.com) Ferries to Catania from Naples.

Virtu Ferries (☎095 703 12 11; www.virtuferries.com) Ferries to Pozzallo from Malta, with connecting bus service to Catania.

GETTING AROUND

Air

The only commercial flights within Sicily are those connecting the main island with smaller islands offshore. **Alitalia** (☎06 6 56 40; www.alitalia.com) flies daily from Palermo and Catania to Lampedusa, and from Palermo and Trapani to Pantelleria. **Air Panarea** (☎090 983 44 28; www.airpanarea.com) offers helicopter service from Palermo, Catania and Trapani to the Aeolian Islands.

Bicycle

There are no special road rules for cyclists, but you would be wise to carry a helmet and lights. If cycling during the summer, make sure you have plenty of water and sunblock as the heat can be exhausting.

Bike hire isn't widespread but it's usually available at coastal resorts and on smaller islands. Some small *pensioni* and *agriturismi* also offer the use of bikes to guests. Bank on €5 to €10 per day for bike hire.

Boat

Sicily's offshore islands are served by *traghetti* (ferries) and *aliscafi* (hydrofoils). To the Aeolian Islands, services run from Milazzo and Messina; to the Egadi Islands, from Trapani and Marsala; to Ustica, from Palermo and Trapani; and to the Pelagic Islands, from Porto Empedocle (near Agrigento).

Services run year-round, although they are pared back considerably in winter and can be affected by adverse sea conditions.

On overnight services (for example, to the Pelagic Islands or Pantelleria) travellers can choose between cabin accommodation or a *poltrona*, which is an airline-type armchair. Deck class is available only during the summer and only on some ferries, so ask when making your booking. All ferries carry vehicles.

Operators include the following:

Liberty Lines (☎0923 87 38 13; www.libertylines.it) Runs hydrofoils to Pantelleria and the Egadi Islands from Trapani; to the Aeolian Islands from Milazzo and Messina; to the Pelagic Islands from Porto Empedocle; and to Ustica from Palermo. Also offers summer-only service from Palermo to the Aeolians, from Trapani to Ustica, and from Marsala to the Egadi Islands.

NGI (Navigazione Generale Italiana; ☎800 250000; www.ngi-spa.it) Runs ferries from Milazzo to the Aeolian Islands.

Società Navigazione Siciliana (Siremar; ☎090 36 46 01; www.siremar.it) Operates ferries from Palermo to Ustica, from Milazzo to the Aeolian Islands, from Trapani to Pantelleria and the Egadi Islands, and from Porto Empedocle to the Pelagic Islands.

Traghetti delle Isole (☎0923 2 24 67; www.traghettidelleisole.it) Runs ferries from Trapani to Pantelleria and from Porto Empedocle to the Pelagic Islands.

Bus

Away from the main coastal train routes, buses are generally the best way of getting around Sicily. Buses offer faster, more direct service on certain intercity routes, such as Catania to Agrigento, Syracuse to Palermo or Palermo to Trapani, and they are the only form of public transport serving many interior towns. Note that in rural areas services are sometimes linked to school hours and market opening times, which can mean leaving incredibly early or finding yourself stranded after mid-afternoon. Also watch out for Sundays when services are cut to the bone.

In larger cities, the main intercity bus companies have ticket offices or operate through agencies. In smaller towns and villages, bus tickets are often sold in bars or on the bus.

Sicily's major bus companies – **AST** (☎091 620 81 11; www.aziendasicilianatrasporti.it), **Interbus** (☎091 616 79 19; www.interbus.it), **Lumia** (☎0922 2 04 14; www.autolineelumia.it), **SAIS Autolinee** (☎0935 52 41 11, 800 211020; www.saisautolinee.it), **SAIS Trasporti** (☎091 617 11 41; www.saistrasporti.it) and **Salemi** (☎0923 98 11 20; www.autoservizisalemi.it) – cover most destinations.

While it is not usually necessary to make reservations on buses, it's best to do so during peak travel periods or for time-senstive journeys – for example, if you're returning from Taormina to catch a plane at Catania's Fontanarossa airport.

Car & Motorcycle

There's no escaping the fact that a car makes getting around Sicily much easier. That said, driving on the island is not exactly stress-free, particularly in the big cities where traffic congestion, one-way systems and impossible parking can stretch nerves to the limit. But once on the open road, things calm down considerably and the going is generally pretty good.

Roads vary in quality. Some, like the main autostradas (motorways), are excellent, but small rural roads can be dodgy, especially after heavy rain, when axle-breaking potholes appear and landslides lead to road closures.

Sicily has a limited network of motorways, which you'll see prefixed by an A on maps and signs on the island. The most convenient east–west link is the A19, which runs from Catania to Palermo. The A18 runs along the Ionian Coast between Messina and Catania, while the A20 runs along the Tyrrhenian Coast from Palermo to Messina. Both the A18 and A20 are toll roads. The toll-free A29, along with its offshoot, the A29D, goes from Palermo to the west coast, linking the capital with Trapani, Marsala and Mazara del Vallo.

After autostradas, the best roads are the *strade statali* (state roads), represented on maps as 'SS'. *Strade provinciali* (provincial roads) are sometimes little more than country lanes, but provide access to small towns and villages and some beautiful scenery. They are represented as 'SP' on maps.

Automobile Associations

The Italian automobile association is called the **Automobile Club d'Italia** (ACI; ☎803116; www.aci.it). Members and nonmembers alike can call ACI for 24-hour roadside assistance, though nonmembers will be charged a fee for this service.

Driving Licences

When driving in Sicily, always carry your driving licence, the vehicle's registration papers and proof of third-party (liability) insurance. All EU member states' driving licences are recognised in Sicily, as are licences from the United States and most other major countries.

Fuel

Petrol stations are located on the main autostradas (motorways) and state roads, as well as in cities and towns. The bigger ones are often open 24 hours, but smaller stations generally open 7am to 7pm Monday to Saturday with a lunchtime break. Many stations also offer self-service. To use the self-service pumps, you'll need to insert a bill (in denominations of €5, €10, €20 or €50) or an approved credit or debit card into the machine and then press the number of the pump you're using.

The cost of fuel in Sicily is high – at the time of research €1.45 for a litre of unleaded petrol *(benzina senza piombo)* or €1.28 for diesel *(gasolio)*.

If you run into mechanical problems, the nearest petrol station should be able to suggest a local mechanic, although few have workshops on-site.

Hire

The major car-rental firms are all represented at Palermo, Catania and Trapani airports and in major cities. Agencies in seaside resorts also rent out scooters and motorcycles.

Avis (☎06 452 10 83 91; www.avisautonoleggio.it)

Europcar (☎199 307030; www.europcar.it)

Hertz (☎02 6943 0019; www.hertz.it)

Maggiore (☎199 151120; www.maggiore.it)

Sicily by Car (☎800 334440; www.sicilybycar.it)

Sixt (☎06 65 21 11; www.sixt.it)

Rates for advance online reservations made from overseas are often significantly better than those offered on-site. Similarly, airport agencies sometimes charge more than city-centre branches.

To hire a car, you'll need to be over 21 (over 23 for some companies) and have a credit card; for a scooter, the minimum age is generally 18. When hiring, always make sure you understand what's covered in the rental agreement (unlimited mileage, tax, insurance, collision-damage waiver and so on) and what your liabilities are. It is also a good idea to get fully comprehensive insurance to cover any untoward bumps or scrapes that are quite likely to happen.

Reputable car-hire companies will usually give you an emergency number to call in the case of breakdown.

Note that most hire cars have manual transmission.

Parking

Parking in Sicilian towns and cities can be difficult. Blue lines by the side of the road denote pay-and-display parking – buy tickets at the meters or from tobacconists – with rates ranging from €0.50 to €1 per hour. Typically, charges are applied Monday through Saturday between 8am and 1.30pm and then from 3.30pm to 8pm – outside these hours you can leave your car free. You'll also find

SPEED LIMITS

- **Autostrade** 130km/h
- **Main, nonurban highways** 110km/h
- **Secondary, nonurban roads** 90km/h
- **Built-up areas** 50km/h

enclosed car parks in the main cities and ports, charging daily rates of €7 and up. As a general rule, the easiest time to find street parking is the early afternoon between 2pm and 4pm.

Fines for parking violations are applied and your car-rental agency will use your credit card to settle any outstanding charges.

Road Rules

Contrary to appearances there are road rules in Sicily.

- Drive on the right and overtake on the left.
- Seat belt use (front and rear) is required. Violators are subject to an on-the-spot fine.
- Wear a helmet when riding all two-wheeled vehicles.
- Carry a warning triangle and fluorescent vest to be worn in the event of an emergency.
- Keep your blood-alcohol limit under 0.05% while driving.
- Keep your blood-alcohol limit at zero while driving if a new licence holder (those with a licence for less than three years).
- Do not use hand-held mobile phones while driving.
- Day or night, turn on your headlights while driving on roads outside municipalities.

Toll Roads

Sicily's toll roads are the Messina–Palermo A20 autostrada and the Messina–Catania A18. Messina to Palermo costs €10.10, Messina to Catania €3.70. The process is simple: pick up a ticket at the automatic machine as you get on the autostrada and pay a cashier as you exit. Make sure you get into the correct lane when you exit – follow the white signs illustrated with a black hand holding bank notes; lanes marked exclusively with the blue-on-yellow 'Telepass' logo are only open to Italian residents who participate in the Telepass prepaid toll program. Credit cards are not always accepted, so have cash on hand.

Taxi

Official taxis are white, metered and expensive. If you need a taxi, you can usually find one in taxi ranks at train and bus stations or by telephoning for one. If you book a taxi by phone, you will be charged for the trip the driver makes to reach you.

Rates vary from city to city, but as a rule the minimum charge is about €5. There's also an array of supplementary charges for night-time/Sunday rides, to/from the airport, extra luggage etc. Reckon on about €10 to €15 for most urban routes.

Train

Rail travel is reasonably priced and generally reliable, though routes are limited and trains are slow compared to their counterparts in mainland Italy. Services are all operated by **Trenitalia** (☎892021, 06 6847 5475; www.trenitalia.com), except for those that trundle around the base of Mt Etna, which are run by the private **Ferrovia Circumetnea** (☎095 54 11 11; www.circumetnea.it).

There are several types of train: Intercity (IC) or Intercity Night (ICN) trains are the fastest, stopping only at major stations; *espresso* trains stop at all but the most minor stations, while *regionale* trains are the slowest of all, halting at every stop on the line.

Note that all tickets must be validated before you board your train. Simply insert them in the yellow machines installed at the entrance to all train platforms. If you don't validate them, you risk a fine. This rule does not apply to tickets purchased outside Italy.

Classes & Costs

There are 1st- and 2nd-class seats on Intercity trains but not on the slower *espresso* and *regionale* trains. Travel on Intercity trains means paying a supplement, which is included in the ticket and determined by the distance you are travelling. If you have a *regionale* ticket and end up hopping on an Intercity train, you'll have to pay the difference on board.

Sample prices for one-way train fares are as follows (return fares are generally double):

FROM	TO	FARE
Catania	Messina	€7.60
Catania	Syracuse	€6.90
Palermo	Agrigento	€9
Palermo	Catania	€13.50
Palermo	Messina	€12.80

Reservations

There's no need to reserve tickets for travel within Sicily, but if you're heading up to the Italian mainland on weekends or during holiday periods, it's probably a good idea. A small booking fee for reserved seats generally applies. Tickets can be booked online, at station ticket booths, or at most travel agencies.

Language

Standard Italian is Sicily's official language and is spoken almost universally on the island, although most locals speak Sicilian among themselves. Sicilian is referred to as an Italian dialect, but is sufficiently different for some to consider it a language in its own right. Sicilians will readily revert to standard Italian when speaking to anyone from the mainland or abroad, though with the occasional Sicilian word thrown in.

The sounds used in spoken Italian can all be found in English. If you read our coloured pronunciation guides as if they were English, you'll be understood. The stressed syllables are indicated with italics. Note that ai is pronounced as in 'aisle', ay as in 'say', ow as in 'how', dz as the 'ds' in 'lids', and that r is a strong and rolled sound. Keep in mind that Italian consonants can have a stronger, emphatic pronunciation – if the consonant is written as a double letter, it should be pronounced a little stronger, eg *sonno* son·no (sleep) versus *sono* so·no (I am).

BASICS

In this chapter the polite/informal and masculine/feminine options are included where necessary, indicated with 'pol/inf' and 'm/f' respectively.

Hello.	*Buongiorno.*	bwon·*jor*·no
Goodbye.	*Arrivederci.*	a·ree·ve·*der*·chee
Yes./No.	*Sì./No.*	see/no

WANT MORE?

For in-depth language information and handy phrases, check out Lonely Planet's *Italian Phrasebook*. You'll find it at **shop.lonelyplanet.com**, or you can buy Lonely Planet's iPhone phrasebooks at the Apple App Store.

Excuse me.	*Mi scusi.* (pol) *Scusami.* (inf)	mee *skoo*·zee *skoo*·za·mee
Sorry.	*Mi dispiace.*	mee dees·*pya*·che
Please.	*Per favore.*	per fa·vo·re
Thank you.	*Grazie.*	*gra*·tsye
You're welcome.	*Prego.*	*pre*·go

How are you?
Come sta/stai? (pol/inf) — *ko*·me sta/stai

Fine. And you?
Bene. E Lei/tu? (pol/inf) — *be*·ne e lay/too

What's your name?
Come si chiama? pol — *ko*·me see *kya*·ma
Come ti chiami? inf — *ko*·me tee *kya*·mee

My name is ...
Mi chiamo ... — mee *kya*·mo ...

Do you speak English?
Parla/Parli inglese? (pol/inf) — *par*·la/*par*·lee een·*gle*·ze

I don't understand.
Non capisco. — non ka·*pee*·sko

ACCOMMODATION

Do you have a ... room?	*Avete una camera ...?*	a·*ve*·te *oo*·na *ka*·me·ra ...
double	*doppia con letto matrimoniale*	*do*·pya kon *le*·to ma·tree·mo·*nya*·le
single	*singola*	*seen*·go·la

How much is it per ...?	*Quanto costa per ...?*	*kwan*·to *kos*·ta per ...
night	*una notte*	*oo*·na *no*·te
person	*persona*	per·*so*·na

Is breakfast included?
La colazione è compresa? — la ko·la·*tsyo*·ne e kom·*pre*·sa

air-con	*aria condizionata*	a·rya kon·dee·tsyo·*na*·ta
bathroom	*bagno*	*ba*·nyo
campsite	*campeggio*	kam·*pe*·jo
guesthouse	*pensione*	pen·*syo*·ne
hotel	*albergo*	al·*ber*·go
youth hostel	*ostello della gioventù*	os·*te*·lo de·la jo·ven·*too*
window	*finestra*	fee·*nes*·tra

DIRECTIONS

Where's ...?
Dov'è ...? do·*ve* ...

What's the address?
Qual'è l'indirizzo? kwa·*le* leen·dee·*ree*·tso

Could you please write it down?
Può scriverlo, per favore? pwo *skree*·ver·lo per fa·*vo*·re

Can you show me (on the map)?
Può mostrarmi (sulla pianta)? pwo mos·*trar*·mee (soo·la *pyan*·ta)

at the corner	*all'angolo*	a·*lan*·go·lo
at the traffic lights	*al semaforo*	al se·*ma*·fo·ro
behind	*dietro*	*dye*·tro
far	*lontano*	lon·*ta*·no
in front of	*davanti a*	da·*van*·tee a
left	*a sinistra*	a see·*nee*·stra
near	*vicino*	vee·*chee*·no
opposite	*di fronte a*	dee *fron*·te a
right	*a destra*	a *de*·stra
straight ahead	*sempre diritto*	*sem*·pre dee·*ree*·to

EATING & DRINKING

What would you recommend?
Cosa mi consiglia? *ko*·za mee kon·*see*·lya

What's in that dish?
Quali ingredienti ci sono in questo piatto? *kwa*·li een·gre·*dyen*·tee chee *so*·no een *kwe*·sto *pya*·to

What's the local speciality?
Qual'è la specialità di questa regione? kwa·*le* la spe·cha·lee·*ta* dee *kwe*·sta re·*jo*·ne

That was delicious!
Era squisito! e·ra skwee·*zee*·to

Cheers!
Salute! sa·*loo*·te

Please bring the bill.
Mi porta il conto, per favore? mee *por*·ta eel *kon*·to per fa·*vo*·re

KEY PATTERNS

To get by in Italian, mix and match these simple patterns with words of your choice:

When's (the next flight)?
A che ora è (il prossimo volo)? a ke o·ra e (eel *pro*·see·mo *vo*·lo)

Where's (the station)?
Dov'è (la stazione)? do·ve (la sta·*tsyo*·ne)

I'm looking for (a hotel).
Sto cercando (un albergo). sto cher·*kan*·do (oon al·*ber*·go)

Do you have (a map)?
Ha (una pianta)? a (*oo*·na *pyan*·ta)

Is there (a toilet)?
C'è (un gabinetto)? che (oon ga·bee·*ne*·to)

I'd like (a coffee).
Vorrei (un caffè). vo·*ray* (oon ka·*fe*)

I'd like to (hire a car).
Vorrei (noleggiare una macchina). vo·*ray* (no·le·*ja*·re *oo*·na *ma*·kee·na)

Can I (enter)?
Posso (entrare)? *po*·so (en·*tra*·re)

Could you please (help me)?
Può (aiutarmi), per favore? pwo (a·yoo·*tar*·mee) per fa·*vo*·re

Do I have to (book a seat)?
Devo (prenotare un posto)? *de*·vo (pre·no·*ta*·re oon *po*·sto)

I'd like to reserve a table for ...	*Vorrei prenotare un tavolo per ...*	vo·*ray* pre·no·*ta*·re oon *ta*·vo·lo per ...
(eight) o'clock	*le (otto)*	le (*o*·to)
(two) people	*(due) persone*	(*doo*·e) per·*so*·ne

I don't eat ...	*Non mangio ...*	non *man*·jo ...
eggs	*uova*	*wo*·va
fish	*pesce*	*pe*·she
nuts	*noci*	*no*·chee
(red) meat	*carne (rossa)*	*kar*·ne (*ro*·sa)

Key Words

bar	*locale*	lo·*ka*·le
bottle	*bottiglia*	bo·*tee*·lya

breakfast	*prima colazione*	pree·ma ko·la·*tsyo*·ne
cafe	*bar*	bar
cold	*freddo*	*fre*·do
dinner	*cena*	*che*·na
drink list	*lista delle bevande*	*lee*·sta de·le be·*van*·de
fork	*forchetta*	for·*ke*·ta
glass	*bicchiere*	bee·*kye*·re
grocery store	*alimentari*	a·lee·men·*ta*·ree
hot	*caldo*	*kal*·do
knife	*coltello*	kol·*te*·lo
lunch	*pranzo*	*pran*·dzo
market	*mercato*	mer·*ka*·to
menu	*menù*	me·*noo*
plate	*piatto*	*pya*·to
restaurant	*ristorante*	ree·sto·*ran*·te
spicy	*piccante*	pee·*kan*·te
spoon	*cucchiaio*	koo·*kya*·yo
vegetarian (food)	*vegetariano*	ve·je·ta·*rya*·no
with	*con*	kon
without	*senza*	*sen*·tsa

Meat & Fish

beef	*manzo*	*man*·dzo
chicken	*pollo*	*po*·lo
duck	*anatra*	*a*·na·tra
fish	*pesce*	*pe*·she
herring	*aringa*	a·*reen*·ga
lamb	*agnello*	a·*nye*·lo
lobster	*aragosta*	a·ra·*gos*·ta
meat	*carne*	*kar*·ne
mussels	*cozze*	*ko*·tse
oysters	*ostriche*	*o*·stree·ke
pork	*maiale*	ma·*ya*·le
prawn	*gambero*	*gam*·be·ro
salmon	*salmone*	sal·*mo*·ne
scallops	*capasante*	ka·pa·*san*·te
seafood	*frutti di mare*	*froo*·tee dee *ma*·re
shrimp	*gambero*	*gam*·be·ro
squid	*calamari*	ka·la·*ma*·ree
trout	*trota*	*tro*·ta
tuna	*tonno*	*to*·no
turkey	*tacchino*	ta·*kee*·no
veal	*vitello*	vee·*te*·lo

Fruit & Vegetables

apple	*mela*	*me*·la
beans	*fagioli*	fa·*jo*·lee
cabbage	*cavolo*	*ka*·vo·lo
capsicum	*peperone*	pe·pe·*ro*·ne
carrot	*carota*	ka·*ro*·ta
cauliflower	*cavolfiore*	ka·vol·*fyo*·re
cucumber	*cetriolo*	che·tree·*o*·lo
fruit	*frutta*	*froo*·ta
grapes	*uva*	*oo*·va
lemon	*limone*	lee·*mo*·ne
lentils	*lenticchie*	len·*tee*·kye
mushroom	*funghi*	*foon*·gee
nuts	*noci*	*no*·chee
onions	*cipolle*	chee·*po*·le
orange	*arancia*	a·*ran*·cha
peach	*pesca*	*pe*·ska
peas	*piselli*	pee·*ze*·lee
pineapple	*ananas*	*a*·na·nas
plum	*prugna*	*proo*·nya
potatoes	*patate*	pa·*ta*·te
spinach	*spinaci*	spee·*na*·chee
tomatoes	*pomodori*	po·mo·*do*·ree
vegetables	*verdura*	ver·*doo*·ra

Other

bread	*pane*	*pa*·ne
butter	*burro*	*boo*·ro
cheese	*formaggio*	for·*ma*·jo
eggs	*uova*	*wo*·va
honey	*miele*	*mye*·le
ice	*ghiaccio*	*gya*·cho
jam	*marmellata*	mar·me·*la*·ta
noodles	*pasta*	*pas*·ta
oil	*olio*	*o*·lyo

SIGNS

Aperto	Open
Chiuso	Closed
Donne	Women
Entrata/Ingresso	Entrance
Gabinetti/Servizi	Toilets
Informazioni	Information
Proibito/Vietato	Prohibited
Uomini	Men
Uscita	Exit

pepper	*pepe*	pe·pe
rice	*riso*	ree·zo
salt	*sale*	sa·le
soup	*minestra*	mee·nes·tra
soy sauce	*salsa di soia*	sal·sa dee so·ya
sugar	*zucchero*	tsoo·ke·ro
vinegar	*aceto*	a·che·to

Drinks

beer	*birra*	bee·ra
coffee	*caffè*	ka·fe
(orange) juice	*succo (d'arancia)*	soo·ko (da·ran·cha)
milk	*latte*	la·te
red wine	*vino rosso*	vee·no ro·so
soft drink	*bibita*	bee·bee·ta
tea	*tè*	te
(mineral) water	*acqua (minerale)*	a·kwa (mee·ne·ra·le)
white wine	*vino bianco*	vee·no byan·ko

EMERGENCIES

Help!
Aiuto! — a·yoo·to

Leave me alone!
Lasciami in pace! — la·sha·mee een pa·che

I'm lost.
Mi sono perso/a. (m/f) — mee so·no per·so/a

Call the police!
Chiami la polizia! — kya·mee la po·lee·tsee·a

Call a doctor!
Chiami un medico! — kya·mee oon me·dee·ko

Where are the toilets?
Dove sono i gabinetti? — do·ve so·no ee ga·bee·ne·tee

I'm sick.
Mi sento male. — mee sen·to ma·le

It hurts here.
Mi fa male qui. — mee fa ma·le kwee

I'm allergic to ...
Sono allergico/a a ... (m/f) — so·no a·ler·jee·ko/a a ...

QUESTION WORDS

How?	*Come?*	ko·me
What?	*Che cosa?*	ke ko·za
When?	*Quando?*	kwan·do
Where?	*Dove?*	do·ve
Who?	*Chi?*	kee
Why?	*Perché?*	per·ke

SHOPPING & SERVICES

I'd like to buy ...
Vorrei comprare ... — vo·ray kom·pra·re ...

I'm just looking.
Sto solo guardando. — sto so·lo gwar·dan·do

Can I look at it?
Posso dare un'occhiata? — po·so da·re oo·no·kya·ta

How much is this?
Quanto costa questo? — kwan·to kos·ta kwe·sto

It's too expensive.
È troppo caro. — e tro·po ka·ro

Can you lower the price?
Può farmi lo sconto? — pwo far·mee lo skon·to

There's a mistake in the bill.
C'è un errore nel conto. — che oo·ne·ro·re nel kon·to

ATM	*Bancomat*	ban·ko·mat
credit card	*carta di credito*	kar·ta dee kre·dee·to
post office	*ufficio postale*	oo·fee·cho pos·ta·le
tourist office	*ufficio del turismo*	oo·fee·cho del too·reez·mo

TIME & DATES

What time is it?
Che ora è? — ke o·ra e

It's one o'clock.
È l'una. — e loo·na

It's (two) o'clock.
Sono le (due). — so·no le (doo·e)

Half past (one).
(L'una) e mezza. — (loo·na) e me·dza

in the morning	*di mattina*	dee ma·tee·na
in the afternoon	*di pomeriggio*	dee po·me·ree·jo
in the evening	*di sera*	dee se·ra

yesterday	*ieri*	ye·ree
today	*oggi*	o·jee
tomorrow	*domani*	do·ma·nee

Monday	*lunedì*	loo·ne·dee
Tuesday	*martedì*	mar·te·dee
Wednesday	*mercoledì*	mer·ko·le·dee
Thursday	*giovedì*	jo·ve·dee
Friday	*venerdì*	ve·ner·dee
Saturday	*sabato*	sa·ba·to
Sunday	*domenica*	do·me·nee·ka

NUMBERS

1	*uno*	oo·no
2	*due*	doo·e
3	*tre*	tre
4	*quattro*	kwa·tro
5	*cinque*	cheen·kwe
6	*sei*	say
7	*sette*	se·te
8	*otto*	o·to
9	*nove*	no·ve
10	*dieci*	dye·chee
20	*venti*	ven·tee
30	*trenta*	tren·ta
40	*quaranta*	kwa·ran·ta
50	*cinquanta*	cheen·kwan·ta
60	*sessanta*	se·san·ta
70	*settanta*	se·tan·ta
80	*ottanta*	o·tan·ta
90	*novanta*	no·van·ta
100	*cento*	chen·to
1000	*mille*	mee·lel

January	*gennaio*	je·na·yo
February	*febbraio*	fe·bra·yo
March	*marzo*	mar·tso
April	*aprile*	a·pree·le
May	*maggio*	ma·jo
June	*giugno*	joo·nyo
July	*luglio*	loo·lyo
August	*agosto*	a·gos·to
September	*settembre*	se·tem·bre
October	*ottobre*	o·to·bre
November	*novembre*	no·vem·bre
December	*dicembre*	dee·chem·bre

TRANSPORT

Public Transport

At what time does the ... leave/arrive?	*A che ora parte/ arriva ...?*	a ke o·ra par·te/ a·ree·va ...
boat	*la nave*	la na·ve
bus	*l'autobus*	low·to·boos
ferry	*il traghetto*	eel tra·ge·to
plane	*l'aereo*	la·e·re·o
train	*il treno*	eel tre·no

... ticket	*un biglietto ...*	oon bee·lye·to
one-way	*di sola andata*	dee so·la an·da·ta
return	*di andata e ritorno*	dee an·da·ta e ree·tor·no

bus stop	*fermata dell'autobus*	fer·ma·ta del ow·to·boos
platform	*binario*	bee·na·ryo
ticket office	*biglietteria*	bee·lye·te·ree·a
timetable	*orario*	o·ra·ryo
train station	*stazione ferroviaria*	sta·tsyo·ne fe·ro·vyar·ya

Does it stop at ...?
Si ferma a ...? see fer·ma a ...

Please tell me when we get to ...
Mi dica per favore quando arriviamo a ... mee dee·ka per fa·vo·re kwan·do a·ree·vya·mo a ...

I want to get off here.
Voglio scendere qui. vo·lyo shen·de·re kwee

Driving & Cycling

I'd like to hire a/an ...	*Vorrei noleggiare un/una ...* (m/f)	vo·ray no·le·ja·re oon/oo·na ...
4WD	*fuoristrada* (m)	fwo·ree·stra·da
bicycle	*bicicletta* (f)	bee·chee·kle·ta
car	*macchina* (f)	ma·kee·na
motorbike	*moto* (f)	mo·to

bicycle pump	*pompa della bicicletta*	pom·pa de·la bee·chee·kle·ta
child seat	*seggiolino*	se·jo·lee·no
helmet	*casco*	kas·ko
mechanic	*meccanico*	me·ka·nee·ko
petrol/gas	*benzina*	ben·dzee·na
service station	*stazione di servizio*	sta·tsyo·ne dee ser·vee·tsyo

Is this the road to ...?
Questa strada porta a ...? kwe·sta stra·da por·ta a ...

(How long) Can I park here?
(Per quanto tempo) Posso parcheggiare qui? (per kwan·to tem·po) po·so par·ke·ja·re kwee

The car/motorbike has broken down (at ...).
La macchina/moto si è guastata (a ...). la ma·kee·na/mo·to see e gwas·ta·ta (a ...)

I have a flat tyre.
Ho una gomma bucata. o oo·na go·ma boo·ka·ta

I've run out of petrol.
Ho esaurito la benzina. o e·zow·ree·to la ben·dzee·na

GLOSSARY

abbazia – abbey
affi ttacamere – rooms for rent
agora – marketplace, meeting place
agriturismo – farm stay
albergo – hotel
alimentari – grocery shop, delicatessen
anfi teatro – amphitheatre
ara – altar
arco – arch
autostrada – motorway, freeway

badia – abbey
baglio – manor house
bancomat – ATM
belvedere – panoramic viewpoint
benzina – petrol
borgo – ancient town or village; sometimes it's used to mean the equivalent of via

cambio – money exchange
campanile – bell tower
campo – field
cappella – chapel
carabinieri – police with military and civil duties
Carnevale – carnival period between Epiphany and Lent
casa – house
cava – quarry
centro – centre
chiesa – church
città – town, city
clientelismo – system of political patronage
comune – equivalent to municipality or county; town or city council
contrada – district
corso – main street, avenue
cortile – courtyard
Cosa Nostra – Our Thing; alternative name for the Mafia

diretto – direct; slow train
duomo – cathedral

enoteca – wine bar, wine shop

fangho – mud bath
faraglione – rock tower
ferrovia – train station
festa – festival
fiume – river
fontana – fountain
fossa – pit, hole
funivia – cable car

gola – gorge
golfo – gulf
grotta – cave
guardia medica – emergency doctor service

IC – Intercity; fast train
interregionale – long-distance train that stops frequently
isola – island

lago – lake
largo – small square
latomia – small quarry
lido – beach
locale – slow local train; also called *regionale*
locanda – inn, small hotel
lungomare – seafront road, promenade

mare – sea
mercato – market
molo – wharf
monte – mountain
municipio – town hall, municipal offices
museo – museum

Natale – Christmas

oratorio – oratory
ospedale – hospital
osteria – inn

palazzo – palace, mansion
parco – park
Pasqua – Easter
passeggiata – evening stroll
pensione – small hotel
piazza – square
piazzale – large open square
ponte – bridge
porta – gate, door

questura – police station

reale – royal
regionale – slow local train; also called *locale*
rifugio – mountain hut
riserva naturale – nature reserve
rocca – fortress; rock

sagra – festival, generally dedicated to one food item or theme
sala – room
santuario – sanctuary
scalinata – staircase, steps
spiaggia – beach
stazione – station
strada – street, road

teatro – theatre
tempio – temple
tonnara – tuna-processing plant
torre – tower
traghetto – ferry, boat
treno – train

via – street, road
viale – avenue
vicolo – alley, alleyway

Behind the Scenes

SEND US YOUR FEEDBACK

We love to hear from travellers – your comments keep us on our toes and help make our books better. Our well-travelled team reads every word on what you loved or loathed about this book. Although we cannot reply individually to your submissions, we always guarantee that your feedback goes straight to the appropriate authors, in time for the next edition. Each person who sends us information is thanked in the next edition – the most useful submissions are rewarded with a selection of digital PDF chapters.

Visit **lonelyplanet.com/contact** to submit your updates and suggestions or to ask for help. Our award-winning website also features inspirational travel stories, news and discussions.

Note: We may edit, reproduce and incorporate your comments in Lonely Planet products such as guidebooks, websites and digital products, so let us know if you don't want your comments reproduced or your name acknowledged. For a copy of our privacy policy visit lonelyplanet.com/privacy.

OUR READERS

Many thanks to the travellers who used the last edition and wrote to us with helpful hints, useful advice and interesting anecdotes: Adam Davis, Adele Batchelder, Alexander & Caroline Wrigley, Anamaria Tejos, Andy Miller, Beatrix Schostok, Benoît Mars, Brigitte Bocoleu, Cameron Girgenti, Carol Drew, Costy Blumellow, Dawn Girardi, Deniz Yüzüak, Donald Cannon, Dorothea Loefler, Fábio Di Silvestri, Gareth Jones, Ineke van Kessel, Jerry Tane, Joan Conti, John Jepson, John Tanzawa, Jonathan Ward, Marlies van Ginkel, Martina de Buhr, Mary Chayka-Crawford, Patrick Mulvihill, Patty Housburgen, Peter Coldwell, Peter Jones, Peter Voerman, Petrr Coldwell, Sue Yearley, Sylvia Lubberts, Tony Theil, Trevor Coultas

WRITER THANKS

Gregor Clark

Grazie mille to the many people who shared their knowledge of Sicily with me, especially Filippo and Sandro in Agrigento, Patrizia and Diego in Petralia Soprana and Carmelina in Cefalù. Back in Vermont, hugs to Gaen, Meigan and Chloe, who always make coming home the best part of the trip.

Cristian Bonetto

Grazie mille to the wonderful friends and strangers who shared their insights and secrets. Extra special thanks and love to Cristina Delli Fiori, William J Brockschmidt and Richard Dragisic, Rosario Fillari and Massimo Musso, Giorgio Puglisi, Cesare Setmani, Pierfrancesco Palazzotto, Vincenzo Cascone, Giorgio Ferravioli and Carla Bellavista, Norma Gritti, Mary-Ann Gardner and Lambros Hajisava, Joe Brizzi, Ty Holliman, Angelo Enrico Santangelo, Cecilia Grappone, Jerry Maggi and Mehall Griffey, Isabella Spadaro and Sam Ashby.

ACKNOWLEDGEMENTS

Climate map data adapted from Peel MC, Finlayson BL & McMahon TA (2007) 'Updated World Map of the Köppen-Geiger Climate Classification', Hydrology and Earth System Sciences, 11, pp1633–44.

Cover photograph: Cefalù, Palermo district, Antonino Bartuccio/4Corners ©

THIS BOOK

This 7th edition of Lonely Planet's *Sicily* guidebook was researched and written by Gregor Clark and Cristian Bonetto. The previous edition was written by Gregor Clark and Vesna Maric. This guidebook was produced by the following:

Destination Editor Anna Tyler

Product Editors Kate Chapman, Grace Dobell, Kathryn Rowan

Senior Cartographer Anthony Phelan

Book Designer Clara Monitto

Assisting Editors Carolyn Boicos, Katie Connolly, Andrea Dobbin, Victoria Harrison, Rosie Nicholson, Saralinda Turner

Cartographer Gabriel Lindquist

Cover Researcher Naomi Parker

Thanks to Cheree Broughton, Neill Coen, Daniel Corbett, Matthew Hardy, Lauren Keith, Karyn Noble, Claire Naylor, Kirsten Rawlings, Ellie Simpson, Angela Tinson, Tony Wheeler

Index

Map Pages **000**
Photo Pages **000**

Map Pages **000**
Photo Pages 000

S

T

U

V

W

Map Legend

Sights

- Beach
- Bird Sanctuary
- Buddhist
- Castle/Palace
- Christian
- Confucian
- Hindu
- Islamic
- Jain
- Jewish
- Monument
- Museum/Gallery/Historic Building
- Ruin
- Shinto
- Sikh
- Taoist
- Winery/Vineyard
- Zoo/Wildlife Sanctuary
- Other Sight

Activities, Courses & Tours

- Bodysurfing
- Diving
- Canoeing/Kayaking
- Course/Tour
- Sento Hot Baths/Onsen
- Skiing
- Snorkelling
- Surfing
- Swimming/Pool
- Walking
- Windsurfing
- Other Activity

Sleeping

- Sleeping
- Camping

Eating

- Eating

Drinking & Nightlife

- Drinking & Nightlife
- Cafe

Entertainment

- Entertainment

Shopping

- Shopping

Information

- Bank
- Embassy/Consulate
- Hospital/Medical
- Internet
- Police
- Post Office
- Telephone
- Toilet
- Tourist Information
- Other Information

Geographic

- Beach
- Gate
- Hut/Shelter
- Lighthouse
- Lookout
- Mountain/Volcano
- Oasis
- Park
- Pass
- Picnic Area
- Waterfall

Population

- Capital (National)
- Capital (State/Province)
- City/Large Town
- Town/Village

Transport

- Airport
- Border crossing
- Bus
- Cable car/Funicular
- Cycling
- Ferry
- Metro station
- Monorail
- Parking
- Petrol station
- S-Bahn/Subway station
- Taxi
- T-bane/Tunnelbana station
- Train station/Railway
- Tram
- Tube station
- U-Bahn/Underground station
- Other Transport

Note: Not all symbols displayed above appear on the maps in this book

Routes

- Tollway
- Freeway
- Primary
- Secondary
- Tertiary
- Lane
- Unsealed road
- Road under construction
- Plaza/Mall
- Steps
- Tunnel
- Pedestrian overpass
- Walking Tour
- Walking Tour detour
- Path/Walking Trail

Boundaries

- International
- State/Province
- Disputed
- Regional/Suburb
- Marine Park
- Cliff
- Wall

Hydrography

- River, Creek
- Intermittent River
- Canal
- Water
- Dry/Salt/Intermittent Lake
- Reef

Areas

- Airport/Runway
- Beach/Desert
- Cemetery (Christian)
- Cemetery (Other)
- Glacier
- Mudflat
- Park/Forest
- Sight (Building)
- Sportsground
- Swamp/Mangrove

OUR STORY

A beat-up old car, a few dollars in the pocket and a sense of adventure: In 1972 that's all Tony and Maureen Wheeler needed for the trip of a lifetime – across Europe and Asia overland to Australia. It took several months, and at the end – broke but inspired – they sat at their kitchen table writing and stapling together their first travel guide, *Across Asia on the Cheap*. Within a week they'd sold 1500 copies. Lonely Planet was born.

Today, Lonely Planet has offices in Franklin, London, Melbourne, Oakland, Dublin, Beijing and Delhi, with more than 600 staff and writers. We share Tony's belief that 'a great guidebook should do three things: inform, educate and amuse'.

OUR WRITERS

Gregor Clark

Aeolian Islands, Mediterranean Coast, Tyrrhenian Coast, Western Sicily Gregor caught the Sicily bug at age 14 when his professor dad took him to discover the mosaics of Cefalù, Monreale and Palermo's Cappella Palatina. Since then he's explored every corner of Sicily and its offshore islands, from Syracuse to Stromboli and Erice to Agrigento, falling head over heels for Sicily's cultural treasures, landscapes and cuisine. A lifelong polyglot with a Romance Languages degree, Gregor has written for Lonely Planet since 2000, with an emphasis on Mediterranean Europe and Latin America. Gregor also wrote the Planning section of this book.

Read more about Gregor at:
https://auth.lonelyplanet.com/profiles/gregorclark

Cristian Bonetto

Palermo, Ionian Coast, Syracuse & the Southeast, Central Sicily Sicily first hooked Cristian in his backpacking days. The lust has never faded. The Italo-Australian is especially drawn to the island's complexities, history and coasts. He's also a self-confessed slave to fresh cannoli and a glass or three of Occhipinti SP68. Cristian has been writing about Italy for Lonely Planet for over a decade, his titles to date including *Italy*, *Naples & the Amalfi Coast* and *Venice & the Veneto*. Follow his global adventures on Twitter (@CristianBonetto) and Instagram (@rexcat75). Cristian also wrote the Understand section of this book.

Read more about Cristian at:
https://auth.lonelyplanet.com/profiles/cristianbonetto

Published by Lonely Planet Global Limited
CRN 554153
7th edition – January 2017
ISBN 978 1 78657 224 0

10 9 8 7 6 5 4 3 2 1
Printed in China